CEDU쎄듀는 A **C**omprehensive **E**nglish e**DU**cation(종합적 영어교육)의 약자입니다.

펴낸이 김기훈 I 김진희
펴낸곳 (주)쎄듀 I 서울특별시 강남구 논현로 305 (역삼동)
발행일 2020년 10월 12일 초판 1쇄
내용문의 www.cedubook.com
구입문의 콘텐츠 마케팅 사업본부
Tel. 02-6241-2007
Fax. 02-2058-0209
등록번호 제 22-2472호
ISBN 978-89-6806-204-9

절대평가 수능대비
수능 영어
정복의 첫걸음

독해실전편

모의고사 12회

저자
김기훈
現 ㈜쎄듀 대표이사
現 메가스터디 영어영역 대표강사
前 서울특별시 교육청 외국어 교육정책자문위원회 위원
저서 천일문 / 천일문 Training Book / 천일문 GRAMMAR
첫단추 BASIC / 쎄듀 본영어 / 어휘끝 / 어법끝 / 문법의 골든룰 101
절대평가 PLAN A / 리딩 플랫폼 / ALL씀 서술형
Reading Relay / The 리딩플레이어 / 빈칸백서 / 오답백서
첫단추 / 파워업 / 수능영어 절대유형 / 수능실감 등

쎄듀 영어교육연구센터
쎄듀 영어교육센터는 영어 콘텐츠에 대한 전문지식과 경험을 바탕으로
최고의 교육 콘텐츠를 만들고자 최선의 노력을 다하는 전문가 집단입니다.
장정문 선임연구원

Project Managing | **박순정**
개발에 도움을 주신 분 | **조원웅** 선생님(클라비스 학원) · **최대호** 선생님(전북과학고)

마케팅 콘텐츠 마케팅 사업본부
제작 정승호
영업 문병구
인디자인 편집 한서기획
디자인 윤혜영
영문교열 Adam Miller · Janna Christie

Preface

본 교재는 2014년 발간된 <Sense Up! 쎄듀 독해 모의고사>를 토대로 한 것으로, 실전 모의고사 10회와 고난도 모의고사 2회로 구성된 <첫단추 독해유형편>의 후속 교재이다. 고1~고2 학력평가 수준의 난이도이므로 반드시 <첫단추 독해유형편>이 아니더라도 유형별 전략을 익혔다면 실전에서 적용해볼 수 있는 데 최적의 교재가 되리라 생각한다. 유형별로 어떤 포인트를 잡아 어떤 부분에 주목하고 어떻게 풀이를 해야 하는지를 빠짐없이 신속하게 적용할 수 있도록 하자.

이와 함께 실전 모의고사 교재는 본인의 예상되는 현재 등급을 알려주고 실력을 한층 업그레이드할 수 있는 좋은 학습서의 기능도 겸한다. 수능을 바로 코앞에 두지 않은 이상, 아래와 같은 실질적인 학력 증진을 함께 도모하기에 좋다. 좀 더 자세하게는 How to Use This Book(p.6)을 참고하기 바란다.

1 버려야 할 습관은 찾아내 버리고 **익혀야 할 좋은 습관을 체화**한다.
특히, 실수는 습관이 되기 쉬우므로 똑같은 실수를 반복하지 않도록 해야 한다.

2 본인의 **강약점을 파악하여 약점을 해결**한다.
유독 자주 틀리는 유형이 있다면 유형별 해결전략을 다시 점검해 보도록 한다. 만약 어휘에서 자주 막힌다면 어휘 복습에 중점을 두고 본인의 전반적인 어휘 학습을 좀 더 강화해서 이를 보강할 수 있을 것이다.

3 풀이 속도를 향상시켜 **제한 시간을 넘기지 않도록** 한다.
풀이 속도는 전반적인 실력 향상과 함께 자연히 해결될 수도 있지만 제한 시간을 습관적으로 넘긴다면 이를 해결하기 위해 시간을 효율적으로 사용할 수 있는 전략을 강구해서 차츰차츰 풀이 시간을 줄여나가도록 해야 한다.

우리 모두의 바람은 목표 등급에 도달하고 이를 잘 유지하여 수능에서도 이루는 것이다. 학년이 올라갈수록 난이도는 예상을 뛰어넘게 높아지므로 목표 등급 달성이나 점수 유지는 절대로 녹록지 않다. 독해 실력의 기본이 되어주는 어휘, 구문의 학습도 중요하고 실전에서의 능력을 확인하면서 적용 능력을 기르는 것도 중요하다. 항상 목표 등급을 마음에 새기면서 품질 좋은 실전 모의고사로 꾸준히 그리고 전략적으로 학습하라. 모든 독자 여러분의 선전과 건승을 진심으로 기원한다.

저자

이 책의 구성과 특징

Before & After Testing

시험 전후로 학습을 계획하고 복습하는 데
도움을 주는 가이드를 제공합니다.

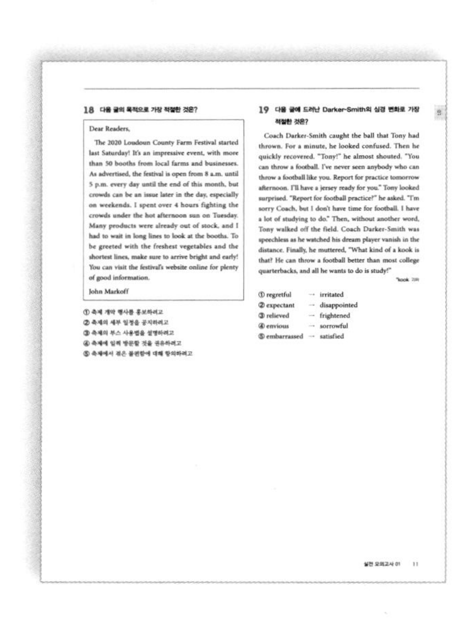

독해 모의고사

최신 수능 출제 경향을 100% 반영한
고품질 모의고사 12회분으로
수능시험에 완벽하게 대비합니다.

정답 및 해설

혼자서 학습하는 데에도 어려움이 없도록
글의 소재와 주제문, 친절한 해설과 구문풀이,
어휘를 수록하였습니다.

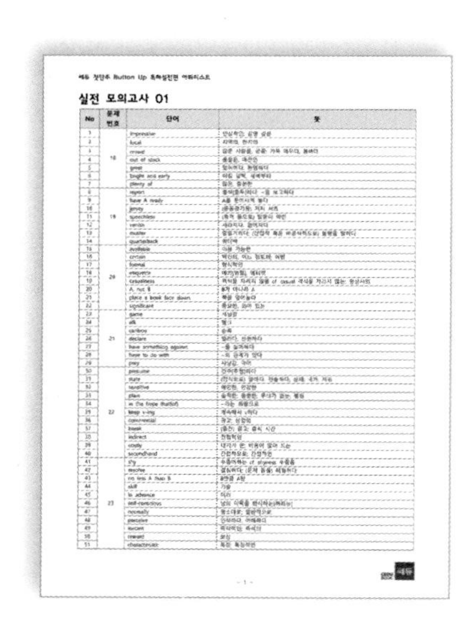

어휘리스트·어휘테스트·어휘출제프로그램

교재에 나온 중요 어휘를 모두 정리한 어휘리스트로
단어를 암기하고, 어휘테스트로 확인해보세요.
(무료 다운로드 www.cedubook.com)

Contents

How to Use This Book

1 Before Testing

1 제한 시간을 답안지 OMR 마킹시간을 포함하여 45분으로 설정한다.
만약 문제를 다 풀고 채점 및 해설 확인 시간이 충분치 못하거나 버겁게 느껴진다면 문제를 14문제씩 절반으로 나눠서 학습할 것을 권한다.

2 어휘는 예습하지 않고 문맥을 통해 최대한 추론한 뒤에 나중에 해설지로 확인하는 것이 좋다. 그러나 어휘 때문에 막히는 경우가 너무나 많아서 유형별 전략 적용 훈련을 제대로 할 수 없다면, 예습을 하고 문제 풀이를 할 것을 권한다.

2 During Testing

1 문제를 풀며 실전과 동일하게 OMR 답안지(p. 181)에 정답을 마킹한다.

2 제한 시간 내에 문제를 다 풀었더라도 애매한 문제를 다시 검토하는 등 주어진 시간을 모두 활용하도록 한다. 제한 시간을 넘어가면 총 몇 문제를 못 풀었는지 체크하고, 추가시간이 얼마나 필요했는지를 기록하여 초과한 시간은 문제 풀이에 적응하면서 차차 줄여나가도록 한다. 시간이 모자라더라도 대충 풀지 말고 추가시간을 들여서라도 반드시 문제를 다 풀어야 한다.

3 정답의 근거라고 생각되는 부분에 표시하여 해설지의 정오답 해설과 맞춰본다. 정답을 맞혔다고 해도 간혹 본인이 생각하는 정답의 근거와 해설지의 정답 근거가 틀릴 경우가 있으므로 이를 확인하고 수정하는 과정이 필요하다.

4 모르거나 헷갈리는 문제의 번호에 따로 표시를 해두어 추후에 해설지를 참고할 수 있도록 한다. 정답을 맞혔더라도 실력 향상을 위해 꼭 필요하다.

5 이해가 잘 안 되는 어휘나 문장(선택지 포함)에 표시하여 해설지를 참고할 수 있도록 한다.

<예시>

→ 자신 없는 문제에 ✓표시

34 **다음 빈칸에 들어갈 말로 가장 적절한 것을 고르시오.** [모의]

Interestingly, in nature, ______________________________. The distinction between predator and prey offers a clarifying example of this. The key feature that distinguishes predator species from prey species isn't the presence of claws or any other feature related to biological weaponry. The key feature is *the position of their eyes*. Predators evolved with eyes facing forward — 〈which allows for binocular vision that offers accurate depth perception when pursuing prey〉. Prey, on the other hand, often have eyes facing outward, maximizing peripheral vision, which allows the hunted to detect danger that may be approaching from any angle. Consistent with our place at the top of the food chain, humans have eyes that face forward. We have the ability to gauge depth and pursue our goals, but we can also miss important action on our periphery.

→ 정답 근거에 밑줄

→ 잘 모르는 부분에 < > 표시

→ 정답 근거에 밑줄

*depth perception: 거리 감각 ** periphery: 주변

① eyes facing outward are linked with the success of hunting
✓② the more powerful species have a narrower field of vision
③ humans' eyes facing forward enable them to detect danger
④ eyesight is closely related to the extinction of weak species
⑤ animals use their eyesight to identify members of their species

위와 같이 본인이 표시한 모든 부분은 바로 본인의 약점을 고스란히 알려주는 바로미터가 된다. 이를 잘 활용할 줄 알아야 실질적인 학습 능력의 향상을 꾀할 수 있으므로 일일이 표시하는 이 과정이 다소 번거롭더라도 반드시 실천하기를 권한다.

3 After Testing

1 채점을 진행하여 등급을 확인한 후, 어떤 유형의 문제를 틀렸는지 살펴보고 전략 적용에 문제가 있다면 유형별 전략을 복습하고 다른 어려움이 있다면 해설지를 통해 해결한다.

2 틀린 문제들만을 확인하고 학습을 마칠 것이 아니라 전체 문제에서 정확히 알지 못하는 모든 부분에 대한 학습을 가능한 세세하게 진행할 것을 권한다. 시험을 보면서 표시한 정답 근거나 잘 모르는 부분을 해설지에서 참고하여 암기할 것은 암기하고 다음 회차 문제를 풀 때 유념할 것을 확실히 알아둔다.

3 점수에 일희일비하지 않는다. 모의고사 결과를 지금까지 해온 학습에 대한 피드백이라 생각하고 부족한 점을 보완할 기회로 삼도록 한다.

Reading & Vocabulary

1 모든 단어를 알아야 한다고 생각하지 마라.

알다시피 수능 독해는 한 문장 한 문장을 빠짐없이 정확한 번역을 해야 하는 시험이 아니라 주어진 문제에 답하는 형태이다. 즉, 지문 내의 모든 단어를 알아야만 정답을 낼 수 있는 것이 아니다. 정답의 근거는 보통 주제문과 주요 세부사항에 있기 때문에 그 이외의 사소한 정보는 무시해도 대개는 정답 도출에 지장을 받지 않는다.

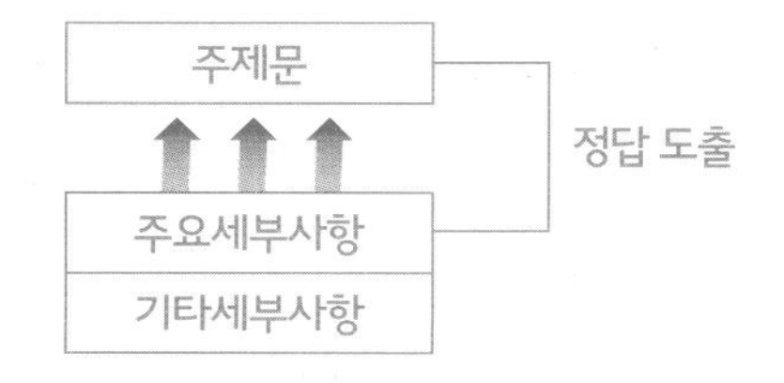

물론 한 지문의 사소한 정보에 해당하는 단어가 다른 지문의 주제문에 포함될 수도 있기 때문에 학습을 할 때는 출제 예상 단어를 가급적 많이 암기해야 하지만, 독해문제를 풀 때는 몰라도 지장이 없는 단어가 있다는 것을 명심하고 과감히 무시할 수 있는 용기를 가져라.

2 독해 지문을 어휘 암기용으로 적극 활용하라.

대개 전문 어휘서로 학습할 때는 단어와 한두 가지 뜻에만 집중하는 경제적인 학습을 하게 된다. 그러나 독해에서는 그 단어의 중요한 제2, 3의 뜻이 사용되는 경우가 적지 않다. 알고 있는 단어인데 문맥상 잘 들어맞지 않는 경우 대부분 제2, 3의 뜻으로 사용된 것이다. 어휘서에서 그냥 넘어갔던 중요한 뜻을 독해를 통해 접하게 되면 암기 효과가 크다. 분명 외웠는데 잘 생각이 안 나는 단어들, 어렴풋하게 알고 있던 단어들도 독해로 접하면 마찬가지로 학습효과가 배가된다.

3 문맥을 이용하는 어휘 의미 추론의 범위를 넓혀라.

문제 해결의 관건이 되는 어휘의 의미를 모를 때 문맥의 도움을 받아 최대한 의미를 추론하게 되는데, 사실 그 어휘의 아주 정확한 의미를 추론하는 데 충분한 문맥이 제공되는 경우는 많지 않다. 우리가 어렸을 때 했던 스무고개를 예로 들어보자. 정답이 되는 단어를 맞추기까지 몇 단계의 과정을 거치게 되는데, 그러한 과정들이 모두 문맥으로 주어지는 독해지문은 거의 없다.

Quiz I am not alive, but I grow.
I don't have lungs, but I need air.
I don't have a mouth, but water kills me.
What am I?

Answer Fire

그러므로 문맥으로 완벽하게 해결할 수 있다는 기대보다는 그 어휘의 대강의 의미 파악에 목표를 두는 것이 현실적이다. 예를 들어 성격을 말하는 것, 직업을 말하는 것, 질병을 말하는 것 등이나 긍정적인 것인지 부정적인 것인지에 대해서만이라도 감을 잡을 수 있으면 충분하다.

When I tried to pay in pounds sterling, the clerk explained that the store accepted only American dollars.

· pounds sterling의 뜻은?
· American dollars는 허용된다는 문맥을 통해, pounds sterling은 화폐 종류일 것으로 추론 가능
· 실제로 pounds sterling은 '영국의 파운드화'를 의미한다.

How to Tackle Unfamiliar Vocabulary: Using Context Clues (출처: 어휘끝 수능편 p. 24)

1 유사 의미 표현을 활용하라.

단서 어구 as / also / like / likewise / similar to / the same as 등
'signal words'가 명시적으로 드러나지 않는 경우도 있으나, 이때도 문맥과 약간의 논리력을 발휘하여 판단이 가능할 수 있다.

> The number of people who need medical help for breathing problems [like] asthma tends to increase during very windy weather.
> (breathing problems ≒ asthma)

· asthma의 뜻은?
· breathing problem(호흡 장애) 증상을 보이는 어떤 질병의 이름일 것으로 추론 가능
· asthma → 천식

2 상반되는 의미의 표현을 활용하라.

단서 어구 but / whereas / however / although / on the contrary / by contrast / in contrast to / on the other hand 등

> I tried reading his notes but I found them illegible. [However], yours were easy to read.
> (illegible ↔ easy to read)

· illegible의 뜻은?
· illegible ↔ easy to read(읽기 쉬운)
· illegible → 읽기 어려운

> The economy faltered badly last year [but] has now started to improve.
> (faltered ↔ improve)

· falter의 뜻은?
· 경기가 나아지는 것과 상반되는 개념으로 추론 가능
· falter → 불안정해지다, 흔들리다

3 정의하거나 부연 설명을 해주는 표현을 찾아라.

단서 어구 be동사 / 대시(—) / 콜론(:) / 세미콜론(;) / 동격을 나타내는 콤마(,)나 of / that is / refer to / mean 등
'A=B'라고 직접적으로 정의되거나 뒤에 부연 설명이 이어진다.

> Temporocentrism [is] the belief that your times are the best of all possible times. All other times are thus inferior. [수능]
> (Temporocentrism = the belief that your times are the best of all possible times)

· temporocentrism의 뜻은?
· temporocentrism → 자기 시대 중심주의

4 이어지는 예시나 설명을 활용하라.

단서 어구 such as / for example / for instance / including 등

> Recently, sales of major home appliances such as refrigerators and ranges have risen. [수능]
> (home appliances = refrigerators and ranges)

· home appliance의 뜻은?

· home appliance = refrigerator, range와 같은 것 → 가전제품

5 원인과 결과 구조를 활용하라.

단서 어구 because / since / therefore / consequently / as a result / when 등

> Sunny became incensed when I refused to give her my biology notes, and she hasn't spoken to me since.
> (incensed ← I refused to give her my biology notes, and she hasn't spoken to me since)

· incensed의 뜻은?

· 내가 Sunny에게 생물학 노트를 보여주지 않자, 그녀가 incensed되었고 그 이후로 내게 말을 하지 않았으므로 Sunny가 화가 났다는 의미일 것으로 추론 가능

· incensed → 몹시 화난

실전 모의고사 01

BEFORE TESTING

시작 시 분

1 **제한시간** (OMR 마킹시간 포함) ☐ 40분 ☐ 45분
2 **어휘예습** ☐ 해당 없음 ☐ 완료
3 **문제풀이순서** ☐ 순서대로 ☐ 2점 → 3점 ☐ 기타 ....
4 **기타 목표** ....

Check Point

1 **정답 근거** *e.g.* 밑줄 긋기
2 **잘 모르는 부분** *e.g.* 〈 〉 또는 ? 표시
3 **자신 없는 문제** *e.g.* 문제 번호에 ✓표시

18 다음 글의 목적으로 가장 적절한 것은?

Dear Readers,

The 2020 Loudoun County Farm Festival started last Saturday! It's an impressive event, with more than 50 booths from local farms and businesses. As advertised, the festival is open from 8 a.m. to 5 p.m. every day until the end of this month, but crowds can be an issue later in the day, especially on weekends. I spent over 4 hours fighting the crowds under the hot afternoon sun on Tuesday. Many products were already out of stock, and I had to wait in long lines to look at the booths. To be greeted with the freshest vegetables and the shortest lines, make sure to arrive bright and early! You can visit the festival's website online for plenty of good information.

John Markoff

① 축제 개막 행사를 홍보하려고
② 축제의 세부 일정을 공지하려고
③ 축제의 부스 사용법을 설명하려고
④ 축제에 일찍 방문할 것을 권유하려고
⑤ 축제에서 겪은 불편함에 대해 항의하려고

19 다음 글에 드러난 Darker-Smith의 심경 변화로 가장 적절한 것은?

Coach Darker-Smith caught the ball that Tony had thrown. For a minute, he looked confused. Then he quickly recovered. "Tony!" he almost shouted. "You can throw a football. I've never seen anybody who can throw a football like you. Report for practice tomorrow afternoon. I'll have a jersey ready for you." Tony looked surprised. "Report for football practice?" he asked. "I'm sorry Coach, but I don't have time for football. I have a lot of studying to do." Then, without another word, Tony walked off the field. Coach Darker-Smith was speechless as he watched his dream player vanish in the distance. Finally, he muttered, "What kind of a kook is that? He can throw a football better than most college quarterbacks, and all he wants to do is study!"

*kook: 괴짜

① regretful → irritated
② expectant → disappointed
③ relieved → frightened
④ envious → sorrowful
⑤ embarrassed → satisfied

20 다음 글에서 필자가 주장하는 바로 가장 적절한 것은?

The habit of reading is one of the greatest resources available to us; we enjoy reading books that are ours much more than books we borrow. While borrowed books are like guests and must be treated with a certain formal etiquette, our own books are like family, and we usually treat them with friendly casualness. Books are for use, not for show; you should own no book that you are afraid to write notes in or to place face down and wide open on a table. A good reason for marking passages in your books is that it helps you to remember those significant parts and to find them more quickly when you need to.

① 책을 함부로 보관해서는 안 된다.
② 어려서부터 책을 읽는 습관을 길러야 한다.
③ 다른 사용자를 위해 책을 깨끗이 이용해야 한다.
④ 자원을 보존하기 위해 책 바꿔 읽기를 실천해야 한다.
⑤ 책은 빌리기보다는 개인적으로 구매하여 소장해야 한다.

21 밑줄 친 the hunters did가 다음 글에서 의미하는 바로 가장 적절한 것은?

Tim was a guide for hunters searching for big game, such as elk and caribou, in Canada. One day, he declared to his boss that he would give up his job as a hunter's guide and become a guide for anglers. His boss asked Tim the reason for this change. "Why? Do you have something against hunters?" the boss asked. "No. I like them," Tim answered. "Do anglers pay more?" asked the boss. "No, anglers give me less money than hunters," he replied. "Then why anglers?" asked his boss. "It has much to do with my life," said Tim. "So far, none of the anglers have mistaken me for their prey. But sometimes the hunters did."

*angler: 낚시꾼

① The hunters didn't pay me on time.
② The hunters sometimes became lost.
③ The hunters used to shoot me by mistake.
④ The hunters were less polite than the anglers.
⑤ The hunters ignored me when I needed them.

22 다음 글의 요지로 가장 적절한 것은?

Part of healthy communication is actually saying what needs to be said. You should not just presume that everybody knows what's on your mind. However, many people are afraid to state their sensitive feelings in plain words. Instead, they drop hints in the hope that you will get the hint. There's a woman who kept turning the volume down during TV commercials. She wanted her husband to talk to her more during the breaks. But he didn't get the hint, and just picked up the sports pages, and she got even more upset. Strategies like hers are ineffective. Being indirect can be emotionally costly. Hints are far too hard to be understood. In any case, even if the message is well understood, nobody likes to hear about your feelings secondhand.

① 자신의 감정을 전달할 적절한 때를 알아야 한다.
② 간접적인 의사소통 방식은 완전히 이해하기 어렵다.
③ 언어 외에 다양한 의사소통 방식을 활용하는 것이 좋다.
④ 감정을 표현하는 방식은 개인마다 다름을 이해해야 한다.
⑤ 민감한 주제의 대화일수록 간접적인 표현을 사용해야 한다.

23 다음 글의 주제로 가장 적절한 것은?

Nearly everyone is at least partly shy, but if shyness is a big problem for you, it may be time to do something about it. To start, resolve to be heard. What you have to say is no less important than what anyone else says. So, make a list of the ideas, experiences, and skills that you would like others to know you have. Think about what you want to say in advance, and then just say it. If you start to feel self-conscious, just breathe normally and focus your attention on other people. Remember, everyone else is worrying about how he or she is being perceived, too. Just making an effort to control shyness can bring instant rewards. Among good reasons for fighting shyness, perhaps the best is giving others a chance to know how special you are.

① tips for parents on coping with a shy child
② common characteristics seen in shy people
③ advice on being a good leader for shy people
④ methods for people to deal with their shyness
⑤ ways for shy people to make speeches in public

24 다음 글의 제목으로 가장 적절한 것은?

Rather than an unbiased snapshot of a region, maps are human creations developed by individuals and organizations that hold various aims and beliefs. They are never completely neutral or objective, and it is not accidental that map makers tend to emphasize territory and boundaries rather than mountains or plains. Maps are redrawn for political reasons; witness the changes brought about by the Versailles Conference just after World War I. New states were created in the Middle East, and Austria-Hungary was broken into fragments. Maps may also influence events, not just reflect them. This became apparent in regard to strategies applied during World War II and the Cold War when the type of map used was closely connected with policymaking.

① Maps: A Trusted Form of Communication
② Understanding and Interpreting a Map
③ Maps: A Dialogue with World Politics
④ How to Influence Events with Maps
⑤ The Strategic Use of Maps in War

25 다음 도표의 내용과 일치하지 않는 것은?

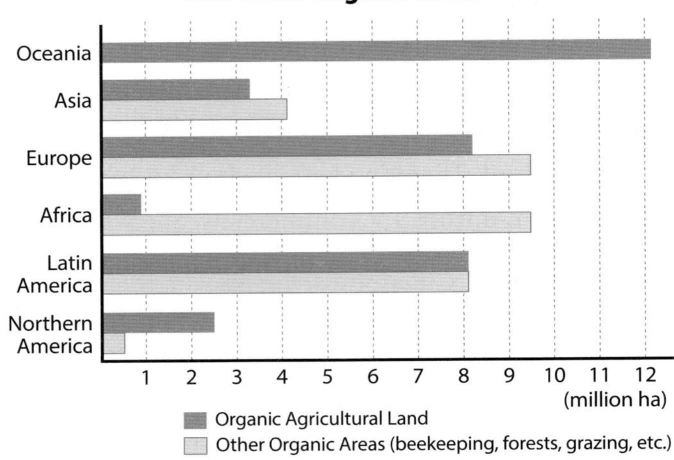

This graph compares global proportions of organic agricultural land and other areas of land that produce organic food but are not farmland. It shows us in particular that: ① Oceania has the greatest amount of land devoted to organic farming, 12.1 million hectares. ② Asia has a greater number of hectares of other organic areas than it has of organic agricultural land. ③ Both Europe and Africa have 9.5 million hectares of other organic areas, but Europe has over 7 million more hectares of organic agricultural land than Africa. ④ Latin America has equal parts, 8.1 million hectares each, of organic farmland and other organic areas. ⑤ Northern America has only half a million hectares of other organic areas, the least among the continents.

26 David Hume에 관한 다음 글의 내용과 일치하지 않는 것은?

David Hume was a philosopher and historian from the town of Edinburgh, Scotland. After working for some months in a merchant's office in 1734, he headed to France, where he spent 4 years writing. Then, he applied for a philosophy position at the University of Edinburgh in 1744 but was turned down because he was considered to be an atheist. Later, during the Jacobite Rebellion of 1745, Hume tutored a noble, named George Bempde, though the arrangement ended badly after only one year. Thereafter, Hume began work on *The History of England*. The work took 15 years to complete and was published in six volumes, between 1754 and 1762. Hume's later years were spent in Edinburgh, where he acted as a mentor to the young Adam Smith, and he was just able to read the first part of Smith's *The Wealth of Nations* before his death.

*atheist: 무신론자

① 프랑스에서 4년 동안 집필 활동을 했다.
② Edinburgh 대학에 일자리를 지원했으나 거절당했다.
③ 일 년 동안 한 귀족의 가정교사로 일했다.
④ 15년에 걸쳐 쓴 저서를 총 여섯 권으로 출판했다.
⑤ Adam Smith의 *The Wealth of Nations*를 전혀 읽어보지 못한 채 사망했다.

27 Digital Services Analyst 모집에 관한 다음 안내문의 내용과 일치하지 않는 것은?

Digital Services Analyst

Our university is committed to hiring and developing staff who desire to work in a high-performing culture that encourages the outstanding work of our faculty and students.

Location: Main Campus
Full/Part Time: Full-time (temporary position)
Department: Library
Application Review Date: November 28, 2020

Responsibilities
- Organizing and maintaining the library's primary website and related websites
- Conducting studies on the effectiveness of the library's online services

Required Qualifications
- Basic knowledge of at least one programming language
- A minimum of 1 year of relevant work experience

For details about the salary and compensation offered by the university visit: http://atyourservice.ucop.edu.

How to Apply
Please submit your cover letter and résumé as a single attachment when applying through http://jobs.berkeley.edu.

① 전일제로 근무하는 임시직이다.
② 대학 도서관 소속으로 일하게 된다.
③ 웹사이트를 관리하는 업무를 맡는다.
④ 최소 1년의 관련 업무 경력이 있어야 한다.
⑤ 지원 서류는 우편과 온라인으로 제출 가능하다.

28 The Green Fitness Aquatics에 관한 다음 안내문의 내용과 일치하는 것은?

The Green Fitness Aquatics

The Green Fitness Aquatics are among the best in Lake County. A full range of swim lessons for children and adults are available.

Adult Swim Only

Open pool hours for adults are reserved from 2:00 to 3:00 p.m., Monday through Friday each week.

All Ages Supervised Swim

Tuesdays	3:30 to 5:30 p.m.
Fridays	6:00 to 8:00 p.m.
Saturdays	12:00 to 2:00 p.m.
Sundays	12:00 to 2:00 p.m.

All ages are welcome to enjoy swimming during Supervised Swim. A certified lifeguard will be on duty. A parent must be in the pool with children under the age of 10. Children ages 11 to 15 do not need adult supervision; however, a parent must remain inside the building at all times. Use of the Therapy Pool is reserved for adults ages 18 and older.

**For more information, please call us at (810) 535-7600.*

① 수영 강습은 어린이만을 대상으로 한다.
② 성인 자유 수영은 평일과 주말에 모두 가능하다.
③ 매일 2시간씩 안전요원의 감독하에 수영을 할 수 있다.
④ 15세 미만의 어린이는 부모가 수영장 내에 함께 있어야 한다.
⑤ 치료용 수영장은 18세 이상의 성인들만 이용이 가능하다.

29 다음 글의 밑줄 친 부분 중, 어법상 틀린 것은? [3점]

Most people are neither complete optimists nor total pessimists, but rather tend to be optimistic some of the time and pessimistic at ① other times. What's interesting is that events often turn out according to your beliefs about ② them. If a person believes that an outcome will be good or ③ feel generally optimistic about it, the result tends to meet the person's expectations. Unfortunately, the same is true for the reverse. When you believe that something will go ④ badly, it very often does. Why does this happen? A famous quotation of Henry Ford's about believing in yourself is "If you think you can, or you think you can't, you are right!" It means that ⑤ what we think about, whether it be success or failure, tends to happen.

30 다음 글의 밑줄 친 부분 중, 문맥상 낱말의 쓰임이 적절하지 않은 것은? [3점]

Most of us have experienced nerves before an ① upcoming speech, or a dry mouth when asked to answer questions in front of a camera. There's nothing wrong with butterflies, because they give you the energy you need to perform ② well. But if you are totally ③ overcome by panic and terror, then it isn't just pre-performance nerves, it's full-on performance anxiety — otherwise known as stage fright. Stage fright is a type of fear, and like any other variety of fear, it causes ④ physical symptoms. These include sweaty palms, a dry mouth, nausea, dizziness, muscle tension, and a strong urge to escape. It can also ⑤ reduce temporary mental problems, such as memory loss, difficulty speaking, and an inability to focus.

[31~34] 다음 빈칸에 들어갈 말로 가장 적절한 것을 고르시오.

31 Once we make a choice or commit to a decision, we start to encounter pressure to behave according to that commitment. This is why salespeople ask questions like "Would you buy it if the price was right?" The aim is to get you to admit very quickly that you have a position on an issue; this is because once you admit it, you will feel obliged to honor it. When salespeople get you to make a statement about yourself and how you think you would behave in a certain situation, they know that later you will want to behave in a way that goes along with what you have said. They know that ________________ is valued by society, even though it can make people behave in ways that aren't in their best interests. [3점]

① speech ② experience
③ humility ④ consistency
⑤ publicity

32 Supermarket checkouts provide a striking example of the power of ________________________.
As anyone who has been to a grocery store knows, checkout clerks differ wildly in their speed and competence. In one major chain, clerks with differing abilities are more or less randomly shuffled across shifts, which enabled two economists to look at the impact of productive peers. It turns out that the productivity of average clerks rises substantially when there is a star clerk working on their shift, and those same average clerks get worse when their shift is filled with below-average clerks. Modern statistical evidence also finds that young professionals today work longer hours if they live in a metropolitan area with plenty of competitors in their own occupational field.

*shuffle: 뒤섞다

① social status ② mutual interest
③ first impression ④ physical nearness
⑤ individual preferences

33 The Netherlands was once the world's trading superpower. The Dutch East India Company, one of the first joint stock companies, was a government-business alliance that controlled most of the world's trade in spices, silk, porcelain, coffee, tea, and precious metals and stones. It also dominated shipbuilding, shipping, finance, resource development, and mining. It's no surprise that Amsterdam became the home of one of the world's first stock exchanges. In fact, considering its history, the Netherlands might be summed up as "________________________________." It rose to power with a population of just 1.5 million thanks to the people's adventurous spirit, seafaring expertise, and pursuit of innovation. The ships they built loaded more cargo, and their joint stock company system reduced risk. Innovative technology and financial systems were behind the accumulation of great wealth. [3점]

*joint stock company: 합자 회사 **seafaring: 항해의

① a geographically low-lying country
② a minor player in the world markets
③ one of the smallest countries in Europe
④ a very crowded country with few resources
⑤ a small country that accomplished great success

34 When you ask passionate readers how much time they spend reading every day, most can't tell you a concrete number of minutes or hours. They don't know. Passionate readers don't keep reading logs. Nevertheless, 78 percent of our Passionate Reader Survey respondents reported reading more than four hours a week, and many shared that they read as much as twenty hours a week. During weekends, holiday breaks, and vacations, passionate readers read upwards of forty hours a week. Passionate readers don't have more hours in a day than other people, so how do they find the time? It turns out that they read during short breaks, grabbing a few minutes of reading time between appointments, while waiting for their children during dance practice, or before falling asleep at night. Life ______________________. [3점]

① is a series of natural and spontaneous changes
② is full of wasted moments between our daily duties
③ isn't about finding yourself; it is about creating yourself
④ isn't really complicated, but we insist on making it complicated
⑤ is ten percent what happens and ninety percent how you respond to it

35 다음 글에서 전체 흐름과 관계 없는 문장은?

In July and August across many parts of the United States, the weather becomes extremely hot and humid. This period is commonly called the "dog days" of summer. ① The name is derived from Sirius, which is also known as "the Dog Star" because its home is the constellation Canis Major ("Greater Dog"). ② Sirius is the night sky's brightest star, but during the hottest part of summer it rises at dawn with the Sun. ③ As the summer heat arrives just after the star rises with the Sun, in the days of ancient Greece, people believed Sirius was the reason things got so hot. ④ Many ancient civilizations worshipped the Sun as a divine being. ⑤ They believed that Sirius added its heat to the heat of the Sun and that the combined effect was the unbearably hot weather they called the "dog days."

*constellation: 별자리

[36~37] 주어진 글 다음에 이어질 글의 순서로 가장 적절한 것을 고르시오.

36

When artists draw the human body, one of the challenges they face is seeing the whole as a shape in itself.

(A) For example, you might have a model who is rather large and short — someone whose basic form appears to be more like a square than like anything else. In such a case, you would start by drawing the square.

(B) Once you have done this, you continue to draw by filling in the parts inside the square. In this way, your drawing will be in proportion and well balanced.

(C) This is a challenge because it's our experience to see the human body as a collection of many separate parts. So, before you start your drawing, look for your subject's overall shape.

① (A) — (C) — (B)
② (B) — (A) — (C)
③ (B) — (C) — (A)
④ (C) — (A) — (B)
⑤ (C) — (B) — (A)

37

Concerns about air and water pollution, the spread of pesticides and toxic chemicals, and the alarming loss of species have led many governments to take aggressive action for the environment.

(A) For instance, strict controls over new sources of air pollution can prolong the use of older, dirtier sources and thus increase pollution, at least in the short term. Also, where countries have introduced strict environmental protection laws, certain corporations have simply moved their factories to the third world.

(B) Much of their work has done a lot of good; stricter air pollution laws have saved lives and reduced the incidence of many illnesses. However, some regulations can make problems worse.

(C) Doing this not only robs the home nation of jobs and income but also makes the global environmental crisis more severe.

① (A) — (C) — (B)
② (B) — (A) — (C)
③ (B) — (C) — (A)
④ (C) — (A) — (B)
⑤ (C) — (B) — (A)

[38~39] 글의 흐름으로 보아, 주어진 문장이 들어가기에 가장 적절한 곳을 고르시오.

38

> Perhaps a disease results in the near extinction of one species, leaving another species with no natural predator.

The members of a living community exist together in a particular balanced relationship. (①) One animal species eats another animal species which in turn eats another. (②) Over years, a balance is worked out among the plants and animals in a community, and it remains basically stable. (③) However, at times this balance in nature is disturbed, resulting in a number of possibly unforeseen effects. (④) The result can be a significant increase in that one species' population. (⑤) This could further result in the destruction of a shared food supply, which could in turn affect another species.

39

> As long as it's fit for human consumption, it's actually quite legal to sell food past its date.

In these days of pre-packed and preserved food, there are no obvious clues to lack of freshness. (①) Instead, food products sold in a supermarket are usually marked with "best before," "sell by," and "display until" dates. (②) Shoppers often assume that these are all the same, but they are in fact very different. (③) "Sell by" and "display until" dates are not for consumers, but for supermarket employees, who use the dates to manage stock levels and price reductions. (④) "Best before" dates are only guidelines to indicate when a product is at its highest quality and guaranteed to be free of any health risk. (⑤) Once they have expired, you can still consume the product; you just shouldn't expect it to be as good as a fresher product. [3점]

40 다음 글의 내용을 한 문장으로 요약하고자 한다. 빈칸 (A), (B)에 들어갈 말로 가장 적절한 것은?

> The losing animal in a fight may try to end the fight and save itself by showing an "I give up!" sign. For instance, it may show to the winning animal a very vulnerable part of its body such as the top of its head, or its stomach. The winner's brain recognizes the "meaning" of the presentation, which usually switches off the instinct to kill. Typical of this natural pattern is the behavior of wolves in combat. As soon as one feels that it cannot win, it shows the front of its neck to the stronger wolf. Instead of ripping open the neck, as he had seemed so intent on doing just moments before, the stronger wolf stops fighting, understanding that he has won.

↓

> To save itself from being killed, an animal losing a fight may ____(A)____ by showing a ____(B)____ part of its body to its opponent.

(A)		(B)
① compromise	……	painful
② cheat	……	damaged
③ understand	……	precious
④ overcome	……	vital
⑤ surrender	……	weak

[41~42] 다음 글을 읽고, 물음에 답하시오.

Playing games is usually strongly (a) encouraged in schools. This is partly because it strengthens the muscles and uses up surplus physical energy. Yet team games are also believed to improve social skills. The essence of a team game is to balance selfishness, the desire to shine and triumph, and the desire to help one's team win. When to keep the ball and when to pass it to another is an art that stretches into many of our activities. The balance between cooperation and (b) self-interest is well taught within the structured environment of the rules of a game. While the game is on, we follow certain rules. Then the whistle blows and we no longer have to. Learning how to handle defeat and feel relaxed with someone who has outplayed you is another important art. You need to (c) control your emotions no matter how things turn out. Likewise, the subtle art of playing within the rules, but using as much scope and skill within them as possible, is one that is (d) meaningless in almost every branch of life. You have to learn the rules of your trade or occupation, but if you just stick to them without creative thought then you will end up as nothing special. If you break them and are caught, the result is even worse. How can you follow the rules and still (e) excel? Skill, personal tricks, long training and perceptive observation of others are among what's needed.

41 윗글의 제목으로 가장 적절한 것은?

① How Do Games Build Sportsmanship?
② Playing Games Teaches Social Life Skills
③ Promoting Emotional Learning with Games
④ What Is the Psychological Value of Games?
⑤ Using Games as an Educational Tool at School

42 밑줄 친 (a)~(e) 중에서 문맥상 낱말의 쓰임이 적절하지 않은 것은? [3점]

① (a) ② (b) ③ (c) ④ (d) ⑤ (e)

[43~45] 다음 글을 읽고, 물음에 답하시오.

(A)

A long time ago, during the age of the Qajar Dynasty in Persia, there lived a good man who worked hard as the army's chief blacksmith. One morning, he was summoned to the palace by the Minister of War, who ordered him to produce two hundred thousand horseshoes by the following day, when the minister was set to declare war. The poor man could not believe his ears. (a) He began to explain that it would be impossible to produce so many even within a week.

(B)

He returned home and informed his wife, who did her best to comfort (b) him. "Darling, you must not worry," she said. "You must drink wine and eat bread and be cheerful, for we can never be certain what the dawn may bring." "Ah. There is one thing I do know," he replied. "The dawn will not bring two hundred thousand horseshoes, and it will cost me my head."

(C)

At sunrise the following morning, there was a tremendous knocking at the smith's door. Trembling with fear, believing these few moments to be his last, (c) he went and opened it. It was the Minister's guards. "Haste, smith!" they shouted. "Give us some nails, for the Minister of War has died suddenly in the night!" The blacksmith could hardly believe his luck. He gave the men a bag of his very best nails and, filled with joy, said, "Nail the coffin well, my friends! Shut (d) him tight! If the dawn had not brought this news, I would be the one in a coffin tonight!"

(D)

His words, however, were swiftly cut short. "It is the order of his Majesty, the Aga Khan!" the Minister shouted at (e) him. "If the horseshoes are not ready by tomorrow, then I shall present his Majesty with your head!" "Minister, please!" begged the smith, "With such a threat hanging over my head, I shall be too nervous to make even ten shoes!" But the cold-hearted Minister was unmoved, and the poor man was dismissed from the palace.

43 주어진 글 (A)에 이어질 내용을 순서에 맞게 배열한 것으로 가장 적절한 것은?

① (B) — (C) — (D)
② (B) — (D) — (C)
③ (C) — (B) — (D)
④ (D) — (B) — (C)
⑤ (D) — (C) — (B)

44 밑줄 친 (a)~(e) 중에서 가리키는 대상이 나머지 넷과 다른 것은?

① (a) ② (b) ③ (c) ④ (d) ⑤ (e)

45 윗글에 관한 내용으로 적절하지 않은 것은?

① 국방대신이 대장장이를 궁으로 불러들였다.
② 대장장이의 아내는 남편에게 포도주와 빵을 권했다.
③ 왕의 신하가 새벽에 대장장이의 집을 찾아왔다.
④ 대장장이는 경비대에게 가장 좋은 못을 주었다.
⑤ 국방대신은 대장장이의 간청을 들어주지 않았다.

AFTER TESTING

◷ 종료	시	분
⌛ 소요시간		분

1 채점하기 | 정답 및 해설 p.2

(주의) 틀린 문제를 다시 풀 수 있도록 정답을 본문에 표기하지 마세요.

2 등급 확인

3 틀린 유형 확인 후 전략 적용 복습 및 해설지 확인

How to Review

1 틀린 문제와 ✓ 표시한 문제는 다시 풀고 해설 확인하기

2 내가 표시한 정답 근거가 해설과 일치하는지 확인하기

3 잘 모르는 부분으로 표시한 내용은 해설을 통해 완전히 이해하기

4 어휘 외우기 (어휘 목록 다운로드 www.cedubook.com)

5 다음 회에 개선할 점 정리하기 (시간 엄수, 취약 유형 보완 등)

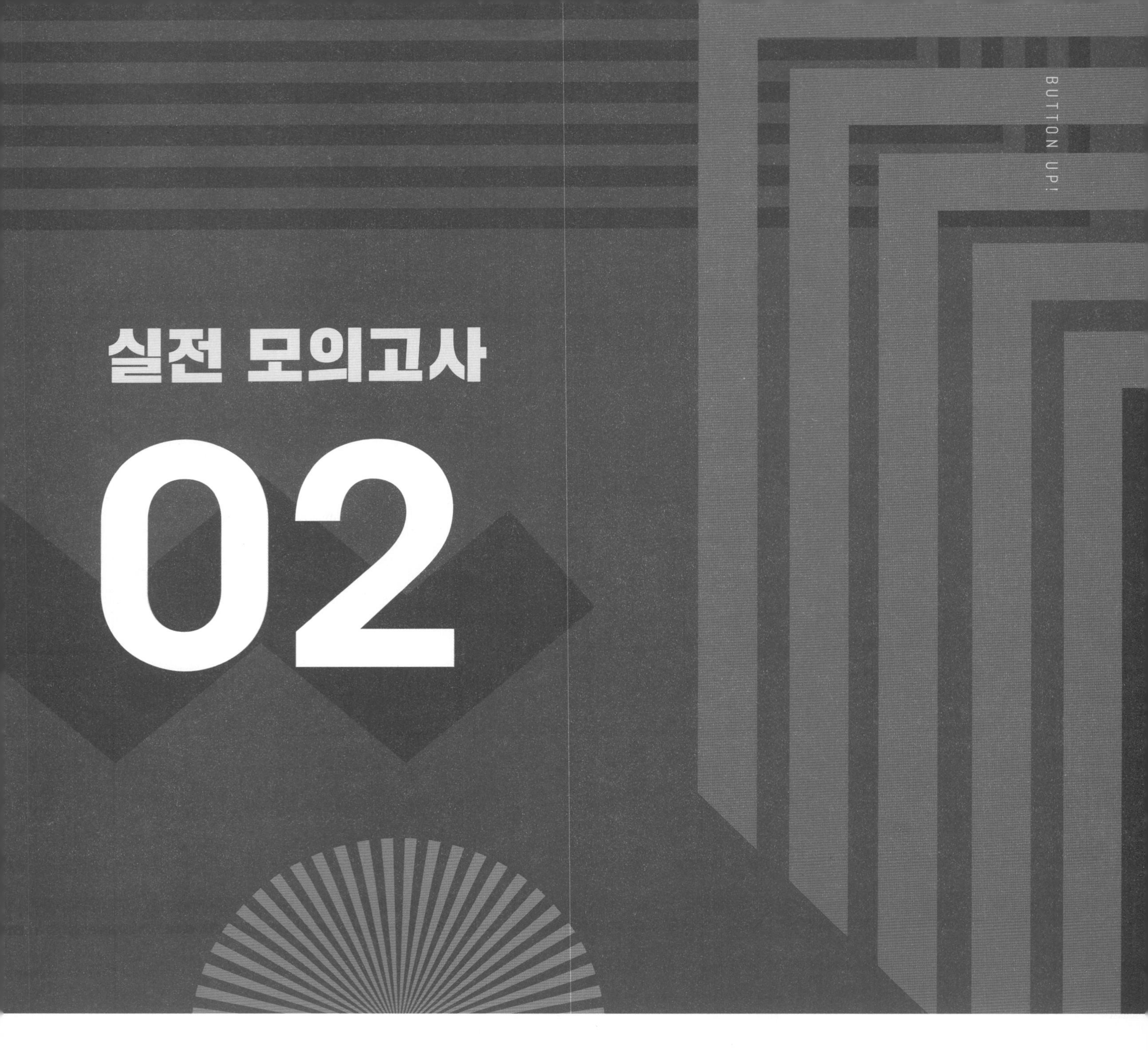

BEFORE TESTING

시작 시 분

1 **제한시간** (OMR 마킹시간 포함) ☐ 40분 ☐ 45분
2 **어휘예습** ☐ 해당 없음 ☐ 완료
3 **문제풀이순서** ☐ 순서대로 ☐ 2점 → 3점 ☐ 기타
4 **기타 목표**

Check Point

1 **정답 근거** *e.g.* 밑줄 긋기
2 **잘 모르는 부분** *e.g.* 〈 〉 또는 ? 표시
3 **자신 없는 문제** *e.g.* 문제 번호에 ✓표시

18 다음 글의 목적으로 가장 적절한 것은?

Dear Ms. Jones,

We are very sorry to hear that your LaserBrite Skin Care System is unsatisfactory. Each LaserBrite product is inspected with great care before it leaves our factory. Unfortunately, small problems can sometimes be overlooked, and damage can occur during shipping. Please return your LaserBrite to the address below; the address on our catalogue is only for placing orders. If possible, please pack the product in its original container and enclose a letter describing the problem in detail. The more information you can provide, the faster we can fix the problem. Thousands of satisfied customers are experiencing the power of the LaserBrite every day. We do hope that you can be one of them very soon.

Customer Service Team

① 불량품 반송 방법을 안내하려고
② 제품 발송 지연에 대해 사과하려고
③ 제품 품질 개선 제안에 감사하려고
④ 제품 사용법 문의에 대해 답변하려고
⑤ 신제품 출시 관련 정보를 소개하려고

19 다음 글에 드러난 'I'의 심경으로 가장 적절한 것은?

If I had to do it over again, I certainly wouldn't have gone to that corporation. At that company I never believed in myself. I never really believed that I was better than the people I was working with. And you can't do that in a company that is so based on intense competition. I would not take initiative — stand up for what I wanted. I would never do that, you know. I would allow myself to be somewhat intimidated. I would say to young people entering the workforce, "Stand up and shout." But, I didn't do that. I was much too timid. I think you have to be not so hard on yourself, and I was really hard on myself.

① angry
② jealous
③ astonished
④ regretful
⑤ scared

20 다음 글에서 필자가 주장하는 바로 가장 적절한 것은?

To my mind, the ideal teacher should be pleasantly lively, somewhat attractive, good-humored, and really smart. I don't mean to say that teachers who are plain or even ugly are out of the question, because many such people have plenty of other charms. But it does rule out anyone who is angry, boring, or mean-spirited, and anyone with a dull or purely negative personality. The list of desirable qualities is long, but it is absolutely essential for my ideal teacher to have a deep capacity for empathy — literally, a great natural talent for tuning in to the needs and feelings of others; in particular, since most teachers are schoolteachers, they must have a special ability to empathize with kids.

① 교사는 훌륭한 성품을 갖춰야 한다.
② 교사는 타인과의 공감 능력이 있어야 한다.
③ 교사는 각자의 개성에 따라 학생을 지도해야 한다.
④ 획일화된 교사 양성 체계를 변화시켜야 한다.
⑤ 더욱 체계적인 교사 연수가 필요하다.

21 밑줄 친 the machine won't ask me about my knee pain이 다음 글에서 의미하는 바로 가장 적절한 것은?

The technology of our age has enabled us to make connections with one another in ways we never imagined just a few years ago. But we know very well that in spite of all our wired connections, we are having trouble staying meaningfully connected to each other. We understand something about what Mamie Adams was talking about. Mamie Adams always went to a branch post office in her town because the postal employees there were friendly. She went there to buy stamps just before Christmas one year, and the lines were particularly long. Someone pointed out that there was no need to wait in line because there was a stamp machine in the lobby. "I know," said Mamie, "but the machine won't ask me about my knee pain."

① I'd like to chat with the post office staff
② I don't want to be examined by a machine
③ my knee hurts, and I can't get to the machine
④ there is a record of my knee pain in the machine
⑤ it's cheaper to buy stamps from the post office staff

22 다음 글의 요지로 가장 적절한 것은?

Parents choose different toys for their children based on their gender, with toys for girls and boys fostering different skills. Girls are given more dolls and household items, which encourage passivity and reinforce women's domestic and caring role in society. Conversely, boys are given more tools, trucks, cars, and sport-related toys, which encourage creation, aggression, and competition, and emphasize men's dominant role in society. Studies on gender stereotyping and toys show that toys for boys and girls of all ages are stereotyped according to gender, though this is somewhat less true among toys for infants and toddlers. Regardless, when parents and other family members give girls and boys different types of toys to play with, they are also giving them messages about appropriate gender play.

① 장난감이 성별에 따른 역할을 강화시킬 수 있다.
② 어린이의 발달 단계에 맞는 장난감을 주어야 한다.
③ 어린이들은 성별에 따라 선호하는 장난감이 다르다.
④ 어린이들이 스스로 장난감을 선택할 수 있게 해야 한다.
⑤ 다양한 종류의 장난감을 갖고 놀수록 창의성이 신장된다.

23 다음 글의 주제로 가장 적절한 것은?

People say, "If it tastes good, it must be bad for you." So, when the zero-calorie artificial sweetener called saccharin first appeared on the market, many thought it too good to be true. But saccharin is indigestible and therefore, unlike sugar, can't be absorbed by the body and converted into fat. Likewise, it cannot cause tooth decay, since the bacteria that cause the decay cannot digest it. One study showed that saccharin causes bladder cancer in rats, which led to widespread fear. But the study was disproved when it was revealed that the rats had received doses of saccharin equal to humans drinking 100 cans of diet soda every day for their entire lives.

*bladder: 방광

① process used to develop artificial sweeteners
② harmful effects of saccharin on people's health
③ misconceptions and knowledge about saccharin
④ difference between the use of saccharin and sugar
⑤ recent expansion of variety in artificial sweeteners

24 다음 글의 제목으로 가장 적절한 것은?

When on their own in coffee bars and other public places, many people now use their mobiles as "barrier signals" as an alternative to the traditional use of a newspaper or a magazine to signal unavailability and mark personal "territory." Even when not in use, the mobile placed on the table acts as an effective symbolic bodyguard, a protector against unwanted social contact: people will touch the phone or pick it up when a potential "intruder" approaches. The idea of one's social support network of friends and family being somehow "inside" the mobile phone means that even just touching or holding the phone gives a sense of being protected — and sends a signal to others that one is not alone and vulnerable.

① The Dark Side of Modern Technology
② We Always Want to Stay Connected
③ Mobile Phones: The Modern Fence
④ Emerging Rules Regarding Phone Use
⑤ Competition in Teenage Mobile Phone Use

25 다음 도표의 내용과 일치하지 않는 것은?

Numbers of Threatened Animal Species in Africa

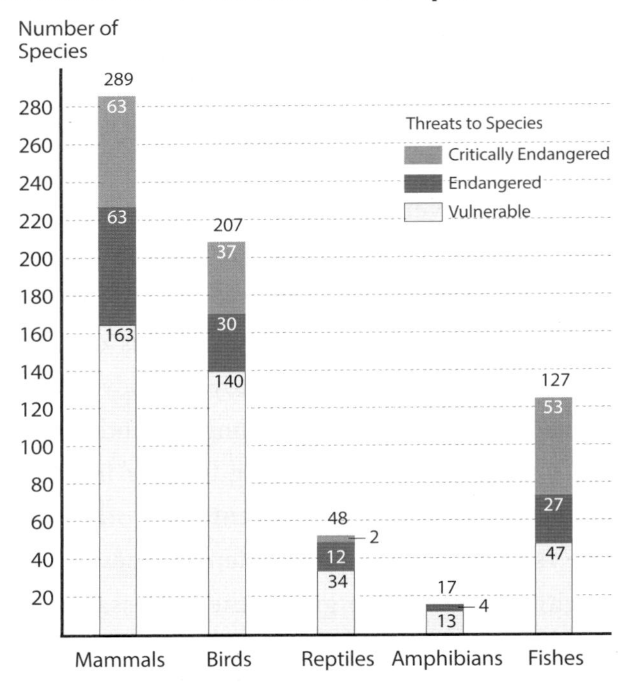

The IUCN (International Union for Conservation of Nature and Natural Resources) created the standard for sorting animal species threatened with extinction into three categories of severity: 'vulnerable,' 'endangered,' and 'critically endangered.' The above graph shows the number of species in each class in Africa. ① Out of 289 threatened mammals in Africa, equal numbers are listed as endangered and critically endangered, 63 species for each. ② Birds make up the second largest class in this graph with 37 of the 207 total threatened bird species listed as critically endangered. ③ The third largest out of all five classes consists of 48 threatened African reptiles, 2 of which are critically endangered. ④ The number of threatened amphibians is less than half the number of threatened reptiles, and none of them are critically endangered. ⑤ In the class of fish, critically endangered species make up a larger portion than endangered species or vulnerable species.

26 Martin Handford에 관한 다음 글의 내용과 일치하지 않는 것은?

Martin Handford, who was born in London in 1956, is an English children's book author and illustrator. He began drawing when he was around 4 years old and later got his inspiration from the toy soldiers he played with during his childhood. After graduating from university, Martin worked as a freelance illustrator, specializing in drawing crowd scenes for numerous clients. In 1986, Handford was asked by his art director to come up with a unique character to place in his pictures. After much thinking, he invented a character named "Wally," a backpacking tourist who would appear in each location and always dresses in red and white, and published a book. He went on to publish seven more *Where's Wally?* books, and Wally is licensed in at least 17 countries. His *Where's Wally?* series was a huge success, so he became famous all over the world in the mid-1980s.

① 런던 출신의 동화 작가이자 삽화가이다.
② 어린 시절의 장난감 병정에서 그림에 대한 영감을 얻었다.
③ 대학 졸업 후, 군중 장면을 전문으로 그리는 프리랜서로 일했다.
④ 총 일곱 권의 *Where's Wally?* 시리즈를 출판했다.
⑤ 1980년대 중반에 전 세계적인 유명세를 얻었다.

27 Homecoming Festival에 관한 다음 안내문의 내용과 일치하지 않는 것은?

Homecoming Festival

The Alumni Association would like to extend a special invitation to all alumni, the community, students, faculty and staff to attend this year's Homecoming Festival from 3 to 6 p.m., Saturday, Oct. 7 at the Alumni Center.

The Homecoming Festival will include:

- An outdoor BBQ
- Live music and entertainment
- Kids Zone with face painting, a bounce house, games and more
- Alumni Village featuring booths representing various colleges, departments, and campus programs

There's more...

The first 200 people to attend will receive a new logo gift for free.

Reunion year?

If you're an alumnus of the classes of 1976, 1991, 1996 or 2006, you're eligible for a reunion package which includes a special gift and complimentary food tickets for two.

① 졸업생들뿐만 아니라 지역 주민들도 참가할 수 있다.
② 아이들을 위한 행사도 준비되어 있다.
③ 각 학부를 상징하는 부스가 세워질 예정이다.
④ 선착순 200명에게 새로운 로고가 무료로 제공된다.
⑤ 모든 졸업생은 무료 식사권을 받을 수 있다.

28 Behind-the-Scenes Tour에 관한 다음 안내문의 내용과 일치하는 것은?

Behind-the-Scenes Tour

Don't miss your chance to get close to the aquarium's sharks. Explore behind-the-scenes shark areas with an expert and discover the truth about these incredible ocean predators.

Activities

- Walk on the feeding bridge, where sharks swim silently just inches beneath you
- Learn how aquarium staff cares for sharks
- Visit the food prep area to learn how diets are planned and monitored

Price

Adult $50
Senior (65+) $47
Child (8-11) $41

- Children ages 8 and up are welcome with an accompanying adult.
- Price includes aquarium admission, a guided tour with access to behind-the-scenes areas, and an aquarium souvenir.

For questions or to make a reservation, contact Central Reservations Monday through Friday, between 9 a.m.–4:30 p.m. at 410-573-3344.

① 상어에게 직접 먹이를 줄 수 있다.
② 먹이 준비하는 곳을 방문할 수 있다.
③ 8세 미만의 어린이는 어른과 동반해야 한다.
④ 수족관 기념품은 개별적으로 구매해야 한다.
⑤ 전화 문의와 예약은 평일 오후에만 가능하다.

29 다음 글의 밑줄 친 부분 중, 어법상 틀린 것은? [3점]

As keeping fit has become a way of life, a large number of people now regularly ① work out at fitness centers — doing weight training, running on the treadmills, riding the bikes, or using the cross-training machines. And long-distance marathons have become ② so popular that organizers often have to limit the number of people who can participate. In the States, the Boston and New York marathons are the most famous, but there are plenty of others held in other cities and even in small towns, ③ drawn many thousands of participants. ④ Few of the runners in marathons expect to win; most just aim to finish. Most marathons are open to anyone who wants to race, young and old ⑤ alike, and even people in wheelchairs.

30 다음 글의 밑줄 친 부분 중, 문맥상 낱말의 쓰임이 적절하지 않은 것은? [3점]

Considering its relatively small size, England has a ① huge number of important historical sites, including 28 UNESCO World Heritage Sites. What about the many sites that don't have World Heritage protection? Construction companies planning any major work in England have to ② follow the "polluter pays" principle, whose purpose is to protect any sites that archaeologists have not yet had the chance to study. The principle views any company that plans to build in ③ developed areas as a polluter. It says that construction companies must pay an archaeologist to examine a site ④ prior to development. It aims to ensure that nothing of historical importance will be ⑤ destroyed by new buildings and constructions.

[31~34] 다음 빈칸에 들어갈 말로 가장 적절한 것을 고르시오.

31 The pioneering psychologist Jean Piaget spent much of his career with children: listening to them, watching them, writing about them, and studying the work of international psychologists who were doing the same. He observed that children don't think like adults at all. For example, very young children often believe that the moon follows them and that dreams come in through windows at night. Their sense of justice, observed Piaget, is also rather ______________ since it takes into account only the damage caused, and not the intention of the one who caused it. This is why a girl who breaks three teacups while helping her mother would think she deserves more punishment than if she were to break just one teacup in anger. [3점]

① complex
② primitive
③ unconditional
④ prominent
⑤ sufficient

32 One of the great masters of ____________________ was the graphic artist M. C. Escher, who apparently practiced this skill daily. According to his son, George Escher, "The wall in the small downstairs washroom was decorated with irregular swirls of green, yellow, red and brown. Father would take a pencil and emphasize a line here, a shade there, and find a face 'laughing, sad, or serious.' Over the course of many months the wall 'came alive with faces.' He also enjoyed identifying animal shapes in seemingly random forms like clouds or wood grain!" When we look at his interlocking animals, we realize that no matter how complicated the figures, there is always a simple, repeating symmetrical form underneath. Escher's genius was to see in a regular, repeating polygon the possibility of fish, birds, lizards, angels, devils, and other unexpected surprises — and to teach us how to see these things, too. [3점]

*interlock: 서로 맞물리다 **polygon: 다변형, 다각형

① fantasy arts
② instant insight
③ selective attention
④ pattern recognition
⑤ mathematical accuracy

33 Bathing was rare in seventeenth-century Europe. Even the very wealthy took a bath just a few times a year. Unwashed hair stinks and attracts lice and bugs, so people cut it short and covered it with cloth or a wig. The wealthy bought fashionable wigs made of wool and silk, and the fashion was for ever-bigger, increasingly costly wigs. The more important you were — or considered yourself — the bigger your wig. Some wigs were so big they looked like small cows sitting on people's heads. This is where we got the word "bigwig," which is an expression that makes fun of ______________________________. Don't say "you're a bigwig" to a person you think is a bigwig. Only say it to friends, behind the bigwig's back. [3점]

*lice: 이, 머릿니

① those who have more than you
② someone who wears an ugly wig
③ someone who has little or no hair
④ people who think they're important
⑤ people who say bad things about you

34 Scientists have estimated that there is a 1 in 38 chance that an asteroid will collide with Earth in 2029. This is obviously some cause for concern. Luckily, scientists have developed a strategy for avoiding a crash. Rather than destroy the asteroid and risk its pieces falling down on Earth, the strategy aims ______________________. Using a nuclear-powered engine that consumes very little fuel, a spacecraft would travel beside the asteroid for several years. Because of the force of gravity, the spacecraft's mass would pull on the asteroid. The force would be weak, but since there is no resistance in space, the asteroid would be safely moved off its course over many years. [3점]

*mass: 질량

① to burn it up in the atmosphere
② to gradually change the asteroid's direction
③ to alter its orbit by exploding nuclear bombs
④ to block its path by colliding a spacecraft with the asteroid
⑤ to change its speed so that it doesn't collide with the Earth

35 다음 글에서 전체 흐름과 관계 없는 문장은?

Movies can deepen your knowledge of history. How else can you fully comprehend, say, a lecture about the Black Death in Europe in the 1300s, unless you have some lifelike images of it in your head? ① Your textbook may have maps and illustrations to help you understand the disease. ② Your lecturer may be a great storyteller who manages to convey a feeling of what it was like to be alive back then. ③ But if you were to see *The Seventh Seal*, a classic film by the Swedish director Ingmar Bergman, you would have a much more powerful sense of the historical period. ④ Watching movies can be a great way to balance study with leisure. ⑤ With all of the great historical movies that have been made, it would be difficult to get more vivid representations of the past anywhere else.

*the Black Death: 흑사병

[36~37] 주어진 글 다음에 이어질 글의 순서로 가장 적절한 것을 고르시오.

36

It is easy to say "I should be saving more" (or studying more, exercising more, spending more time with family and friends, etc.) — but our actions say more about us than our words do.

(A) Furthermore, when people say, "I should be doing [A, B, C...] more," it's generally understood to mean, "I'm open to suggestions, advice, strategies, or anything that will motivate me to get started."

(B) However, it can be a meaningful way to be a better person to make such "should" statements. Lots of people make New Year's Resolutions to eat better and exercise more, but few say they hope to start smoking or to watch more TV.

(C) And it's probably true that few people who say they should be saving more money or whatever actually make any changes in their habits.

① (A) — (C) — (B)
② (B) — (A) — (C)
③ (B) — (C) — (A)
④ (C) — (A) — (B)
⑤ (C) — (B) — (A)

37

The gestures birds make when they put dust on their feathers and then shake themselves and arrange their feathers with their beaks look like the movements they make when bathing in water.

(A) A bird bathing in dust is much like you rubbing your hands with sand to get dust and dirt off. The rough dust helps the birds to get rid of the bugs.

(B) Other than that, there's a theory that birds may do it for another reason: to keep their feathers fluffy by removing excess oil and water. But there's no convincing evidence to support that theory yet.

(C) But the purpose isn't quite the same. Birds take dust baths to rid themselves of parasites that crawl in their feathers. Lice and mites are common problems for birds and there can be very many of them in feathers.

*mite: 진드기

① (A) — (C) — (B)
② (B) — (A) — (C)
③ (B) — (C) — (A)
④ (C) — (A) — (B)
⑤ (C) — (B) — (A)

[38~39] 글의 흐름으로 보아, 주어진 문장이 들어가기에 가장 적절한 곳을 고르시오.

38

It was in such high demand that whenever a fresh shipment of it arrived from Cyrene, people would line up and pay huge prices.

The ancient Libyan city of Cyrene was famed for *silphium*, a plant highly prized by the ancient Greeks and Romans alike. (①) The ancients ate silphium fresh, like lettuce, and added it to soups and stews for its strong and spicy flavor. (②) The plant was also highly demanded for treating a wide range of problems, from stomach pain to bad breath. (③) It also had a very pleasant smell, which made it an essential component of various perfumes. (④) Unfortunately, the great profits that could be made tempted the Cyrenians to harvest silphium before it could seed. (⑤) That's the reason why this amazing plant was extinct by 100 A.D.

39

For example, after marinating raw meat in a dish, don't put the meat back in the same dish after cooking it.

Meat, poultry, and fish demand special handling because they often have high levels of bacteria. (①) Additionally, they provide a moist, nutritious environment — ideal for microbial growth. (②) Wash anything that has been in contact with such foods to prevent cross-contamination. (③) Wash it in hot, soapy water before reusing it; otherwise, the bacteria inevitably remaining in the dish from the raw meat can contaminate and grow in the cooked product or other food — a classic example of cross-contamination. (④) Likewise, wash a cutting board (and your hands) after, say, skinning chicken on it. (⑤) If you don't, and you use the contaminated board to cut up raw vegetables for a salad, the vegetables can be contaminated by bacteria from the poultry.

*marinate: (고기를) 양념장에 재우다 **microbial: 세균의

40 다음 글의 내용을 한 문장으로 요약하고자 한다. 빈칸 (A), (B)에 들어갈 말로 가장 적절한 것은?

Norman Triplett of Indiana University conducted dozens of experiments in the field of social psychology. In the experiments, he pushed cyclists to ride as fast as they could on stationary bikes, occasionally leaving them alone in the lab and free from distraction, at other times pacing them against a motor-driven cycle, and sometimes asking them to ride in the presence of other cyclists. Across his observations, Triplett noticed that one cyclist rode a mile in 2 minutes 49 seconds when alone, but managed to ride the same mile in 2 minutes 37 seconds when he was riding with four pacing cyclists; similarly, he rode ten miles in 33 minutes 17 seconds while riding alone, but rode the same distance two minutes faster when riding with several pacers.

↓

According to the experiments, cyclists tend to exert ___(A)___ effort when they're in the ___(B)___ of others.

	(A)		(B)
①	less	……	care
②	less	……	company
③	unexpected	……	absence
④	more	……	company
⑤	more	……	care

[41~42] 다음 글을 읽고, 물음에 답하시오.

When you let somebody down, or when things don't go the way you wanted them to go, it's very tempting to "point the finger" at someone or something else. When you're late for an appointment, for instance, it's easy to say, "It wasn't my fault; the traffic was a nightmare!" But once you get into the habit of blaming other people or situations for things that go wrong, you lose your power over your own outcomes.

You can take charge of your circumstances and what happens in your life when you stop searching for targets to blame and start focusing on ____________________. This is how winners think. If you are often late because of traffic, then maybe you should try more efficient ways of getting around. Or you might consider leaving much earlier for appointments, allowing time for unexpected delays. This is what being a winner is all about: putting your mind and talents to work to make you more successful no matter what happens. Winners don't have fewer problems in life; they deal with as many difficulties as anybody else. They are just better at using problems as challenges and as opportunities to learn and act smarter next time. So stop looking around to find fault. Step up and say, "I can solve this problem; this problem is mine!" — and then use it as a stepping-stone to success.

41 윗글의 제목으로 가장 적절한 것은?

① Take Control to Create Your Own Success
② Think Like a Winner: Gain Power over Others
③ Why Blaming Others Cannot Fix Your Problems
④ Don't Be Hard on Yourself, Start Loving Yourself
⑤ How to Succeed in Life: Win More and Lose Less

42 윗글의 빈칸에 들어갈 말로 가장 적절한 것은? [3점]

① who looks like a winner
② what you really want now
③ what others expect of you
④ how you can remedy the problem
⑤ how you can use evidence for support

[43~45] 다음 글을 읽고, 물음에 답하시오.

(A)

A man was driving his car when he saw an old lady, stranded on the side of the road in the countryside. So he stopped his car and got out. He could tell she was frightened, so he tried to calm her, "I'm here to help you, don't worry. My name is Bryan Anderson." Her tire was flat, so he had to crawl under the car. When the job was finished, she asked how much she owed him for his help. Smiling, Bryan said, "If you really want to pay me back, the next time you see someone in need, give that person the needed assistance."

*stranded: 오도 가도 못하는

(B)

The lady had finished her meal and paid with a hundred dollar bill. The waitress left to get change and when she came back, the lady was gone. The waitress wondered where (a) she could be. Then she noticed something written on the napkin. It said, "You don't owe me anything. Somebody once helped me, just like now I'm helping you." The waitress discovered four more $100 bills under the napkin.

(C)

That night the waitress came home early. She was thinking about the lady and the money (b) she left. How could the lady have known how badly she and her husband needed it? With the baby due next month, money was going to be tight. (c) She knew that her husband worried about that, so she was glad to tell him the good news. Then she kissed him and whispered, "I love you, Bryan Anderson."

(D)

A few miles down the road the lady spotted a small cafe. She went in to grab a bite to eat. The cafe was dingy. Then (d) she saw a waitress, nearly eight months pregnant. The waitress had a sweet, friendly smile, even though she had spent the entire day on her feet. The old lady wondered how someone who had so little could be so caring toward a stranger. Then (e) she remembered Bryan.

*dingy: (장소가) 초라한

43 주어진 글 (A)에 이어질 내용을 순서에 맞게 배열한 것으로 가장 적절한 것은?

① (B) — (D) — (C)
② (C) — (B) — (D)
③ (C) — (D) — (B)
④ (D) — (B) — (C)
⑤ (D) — (C) — (B)

44 밑줄 친 (a)~(e) 중에서 가리키는 대상이 나머지 넷과 다른 것은?

① (a) ② (b) ③ (c) ④ (d) ⑤ (e)

45 윗글에 관한 내용으로 적절하지 않은 것은?

① 남자는 노부인을 안심시키려고 자기 이름을 알려주었다.
② 노부인이 수고비를 주려고 했지만 남자는 받지 않았다.
③ 노부인은 종업원과 인사를 나누고 카페를 떠났다.
④ 카페 종업원의 남편이 노부인의 차를 고쳐주었다.
⑤ 노부인은 카페 종업원의 친절에 감동했다.

AFTER TESTING

종료 시 분
소요시간 분

1 채점하기 | 정답 및 해설 p.10
주의 틀린 문제를 다시 풀 수 있도록 정답을 본문에 표기하지 마세요.
2 등급 확인
3 틀린 유형 확인 후 전략 적용 복습 및 해설지 확인

How to Review

1 틀린 문제와 ✓ 표시한 문제는 다시 풀고 해설 확인하기
2 내가 표시한 정답 근거가 해설과 일치하는지 확인하기
3 잘 모르는 부분으로 표시한 내용은 해설을 통해 완전히 이해하기
4 어휘 외우기 (어휘 목록 다운로드 www.cedubook.com)
5 다음 회에 개선할 점 정리하기 (시간 엄수, 취약 유형 보완 등)

BUTTON UP!

실전 모의고사

03

BEFORE TESTING

시작 시 분

1 **제한시간** (OMR 마킹시간 포함) ☐ 40분 ☐ 45분

2 **어휘예습** ☐ 해당 없음 ☐ 완료

3 **문제풀이순서** ☐ 순서대로 ☐ 2점 → 3점 ☐ 기타 ______

4 **기타 목표** ______

Check Point

1 **정답 근거** *e.g.* 밑줄 긋기

2 **잘 모르는 부분** *e.g.* 〈 〉 또는 ? 표시

3 **자신 없는 문제** *e.g.* 문제 번호에 ✓표시

18 다음 글의 목적으로 가장 적절한 것은?

Dear Jeremy,

How have you been? I hope your senior thesis is coming along nicely. I'm sure you're quite busy with everything you have to do, but I'm confident you can handle it. You were always an excellent student with an amazing gift for writing. In fact, your name was the first to come to mind when considering candidates for the writing center. As you may already know, the student writing center offers assistance to students working on papers and other writing-related assignments. As a tutor, you would work alongside students and advise them on how to improve their writing. In return, tutors not only receive valuable teaching experience but also a decent hourly wage. If this sounds like something you might be interested in, please let me know.

Susan Kim

① 글쓰기의 중요성을 강조하려고
② 논문 작성에 필요한 자료를 요청하려고
③ 글쓰기 센터의 설립 목표를 설명하려고
④ 글쓰기 센터에서 자원 봉사할 것을 부탁하려고
⑤ 글쓰기를 지도하는 개인 교사 자리를 제안하려고

19 다음 글에 드러난 'I'의 심경 변화로 가장 적절한 것은?

I had completely forgotten he was coming until I heard the housekeepers call: "The guest has arrived!" His room was in an awful state. Hurry up! Hurry up! In a panic, I brushed the dust from my hair, my beard, and my clothes, and went to receive my guest. I tried to look as calm as if I had been resting comfortably all afternoon as I went through the shaking of hands. We dined and conversed until finally I had to show him to his room. When I saw it, I breathed a sigh of relief. The housekeepers had made it tidy enough, and if the cockroaches are quiet during the night, my guest may get a good night's rest.

① depressed → angry
② nervous → relieved
③ joyful → grateful
④ peaceful → irritated
⑤ expectant → disappointed

20 다음 글에서 필자가 주장하는 바로 가장 적절한 것은?

The word "natural" appears in large letters across many cans and boxes of food. But this word sometimes gives shoppers false ideas about the food inside. Even though laws require that all food labels give truthful information, this does not always happen. The word "natural" has not been defined by the FDA, the agency in charge of food labels. So any food maker can use the word on a package. Even the worst junk food is certain to have something natural in it. So the makers of these foods can use "natural" on their packages. The FDA needs to modify its current policy on food labeling and make a law requiring that the information on the package reflect the actual contents.

① 식품업자와 FDA의 불법적인 관계를 끊어야 한다.
② FDA의 업무를 줄이기 위해 조직 개편을 해야 한다.
③ 올바른 식품 성분 표시를 위해 제도를 정비해야 한다.
④ 비양심적인 식품업자들의 처벌을 더욱 강화해야 한다.
⑤ 시중에서 판매되는 건강식품의 가격을 규제해야 한다.

21 밑줄 친 an unusual talent가 다음 글에서 의미하는 바로 가장 적절한 것은?

When he was 29 years old, William Wrigley started a business of his own. Besides unlimited enthusiasm and energy, he possessed an unusual talent. He started out selling soap. As an incentive to merchants to carry Wrigley's soap, he offered them free baking powder. When baking powder proved to be more popular than soap, he quickly switched to the baking powder business. Then Wrigley got the idea to offer merchants free chewing gum with each can of baking powder. Again, the offer was a big success. Now he decided it was time to change the company's direction. Without hesitation, he began marketing the chewing gum under his own name. Soon his product became very popular.

① the capacity to cooperate with other businesses
② the confidence to start a business with little capital
③ the ability to capture business opportunities quickly
④ the power to set lower prices that appeal to customers
⑤ the determination to overcome the fears of business failure

22 다음 글의 요지로 가장 적절한 것은?

Is there a proper way to make new friends? Yes. Act as if you already have all the friends you need. This may seem like strange advice. But, for some reason, teens are turned off by people who seem desperate to be friends. Maybe they figure that if you want to be friends with them, there must be something wrong with you. So the trick is to have the right attitude. Totally at ease and confident. Relaxed, yet respectful. Cool, but not with rock-star arrogance. Curious, but not like a little puppy dog. Polite, but not distant. And smile enough to show that you feel good, but not so much as to suggest you're crazy. With your attitude well tuned, new friends will come easily.

① 친구를 사귈 때는 솔직한 모습을 보일 필요가 있다.
② 친구를 만들기 위해 애쓰는 사람은 피하는 것이 좋다.
③ 친구가 없는 사람에게 먼저 다가가는 것이 바람직하다.
④ 좋은 친구를 사귀려면 자신부터 좋은 사람이 되어야 한다.
⑤ 편안하고 자신감 있는 태도가 친구를 사귀는 데 도움이 된다.

23 다음 글의 주제로 가장 적절한 것은?

We know that praise from adults can help children, but psychologists tell us inappropriate praise can also hurt them. Suppose a Little League baseball player who usually swings and misses hits a foul ball. "Good try" is sincere and appropriate praise. But a comment like "That's terrific!" sends the message that you don't think the child is capable of playing well. Too much praise for good grades can make grades seem more important than what is learned. And remember that praise for specific tasks, such as "You did a good job of putting together that puzzle," will mean more than a comment like "You're a smart girl." Encourage children by praising their efforts, but be sure your praise is sincere and constructive.

① pros and cons of praising children
② ways to develop a child's confidence
③ hidden messages conveyed by praise
④ effective methods of praising children
⑤ dangers of praising children too much

24 다음 글의 제목으로 가장 적절한 것은?

In this modern age of technologically driven business, it can be easy to push aside actual physical human interaction for communication via electronic devices. We email, we use social media, we text, we talk on the phone, but we often forget that all of these are missing one common component — real, face-to-face human interaction. Developing a real conversation with someone is far more difficult if you never get to speak to them face to face. When it comes to your team, you are likely going to need to develop at least a decent amount of trust for each other, so why give up face-to-face interaction when it could serve to better strengthen the bonds of trust between two people who are going to be relying on each other and working together? Avoiding in-person interaction may definitely hinder this natural process from running its course.

① How to Use Conversations to Build Trust
② Face-to-Face Communication Creates a Bond
③ Pros and Cons of Face-to-Face Communication
④ Online Communication vs. Face-to-Face Communication
⑤ Face-to-Face Communication: Breaking Down the Barriers

25 다음 도표의 내용과 일치하지 않는 것은?

A Comparison of Social Media Use Between Universities and Corporations

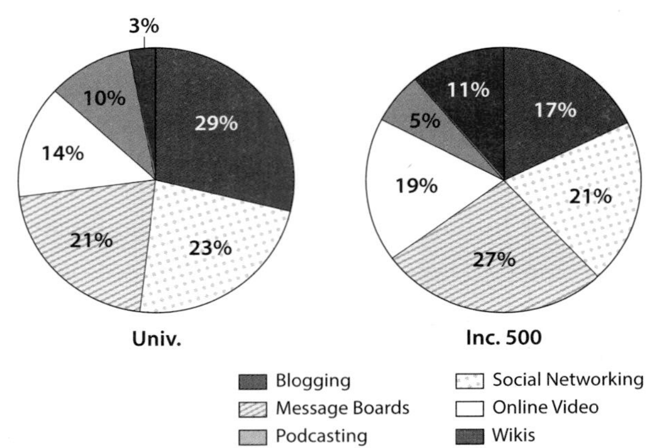

The above graph compares the proportion of various types of social media used by university admissions departments and the Inc. 500, which are the 500 fastest-growing corporations in the U.S. ① 29% of the universities used blogging, making it the most popular choice for universities, followed by social networking, 23%, and then message boards at 21%. ② On the other hand, only 17% of the Inc. 500 used blogging, while a 10%p greater amount used their most popular choice, message boards. ③ The Inc. 500 used 5%p more online video than the universities, making it their 4th most used form of social media. ④ Podcasting was the least used form of social media used by the Inc. 500, with only 5% of them using it. ⑤ Meanwhile, 10% of the universities used podcasting, while only 3% used wikis.

26 Chuck wagon에 관한 다음 글의 내용과 일치하지 않는 것은?

"Chuck wagon" was the name given to the wagon that carried food and cooking supplies for settlers traveling in wagon trains across the great plains of North America. Chuck wagons also travelled to feed cowboys or loggers in remote areas. The wagon cook had to carry enough food to last for two months through the heat of the western summer, with no refrigeration. Therefore, fresh vegetables and eggs were never carried; only dried foods could last in such conditions. A good chuck wagon cook kept his cowboys well-fed with one-pot stews based on high-calorie foods such as beans, potatoes, bread, and rice. In modern times, chuck wagons are used in certain cooking competitions, events and even in a type of horse race known as "chuck wagon racing."

① 대평원을 횡단하는 마차 행렬에 붙여진 이름이다.
② 외진 지역에 사는 카우보이들도 이용할 수 있었다.
③ 신선한 식재료를 보관할 수 없었다.
④ 요리사들은 고칼로리 음식을 제공했다.
⑤ 현대에는 경마에 사용되기도 한다.

27 Video Contest about Korea에 관한 다음 안내문의 내용과 일치하지 않는 것은?

Video Contest about Korea

If you think you can make an interesting video of a Korean friend or Korean food, you may want to join this video contest.

Requirements:
- A video should not be longer than 3 minutes.
- A video in English or Korean is preferred. (Videos in other languages should have a detailed description written in Korean or English.)

How to apply:
- Upload the video to YouTube or any other legal video-sharing website
- Download the application form on the Ministry of Foreign Affairs homepage, www.mofa.go.kr, and submit it by August 9, 2020 no later than 17:00

The winning entries will be announced on September 30, 2020. Winners will be notified individually.

① 주제는 한국인 친구나 한국 음식이어야 한다.
② 영상은 3분을 초과하면 안 된다.
③ 한국어나 영어로 녹화된 영상만 출품이 가능하다.
④ 합법적 영상 공유 사이트에 업로드해야 한다.
⑤ 수상자는 개별 통지된다.

28 MIC Mathematics Tournament에 관한 다음 안내문의 내용과 일치하는 것은?

MIC Mathematics Tournament

The MIC Mathematics Tournament is an event for high school students. Organized by MIC undergraduate students, it has been held annually at MIC University since 1981. The MIC Mathematics Tournament hopes to offer a challenging and exciting day for all participants.

Contest categories:
Algebra, Geometry and Calculus
(All tests present challenging problems that involve high levels of critical thinking.)

Online Registration:
- Registration deadline ($6.00/student): February 1, 2021
- Late registration deadline ($10.00/student): February 8, 2021

Your registration will not be considered complete until the appropriate fees have been paid.

If you have any questions or comments, please email the tournament directors at mic.eure@email.com.

*algebra: 대수학 **geometry: 기하학 ***calculus: 미적분학

① 1981년부터 격년으로 개최되었다.
② 경시대회는 모두 4개 분야이다.
③ 일부 과목에서 비판적 사고를 요하는 문제가 출제된다.
④ 추가 등록은 2월 1일까지 해야 한다.
⑤ 등록비를 납부해야 등록이 완료된다.

29 다음 글의 밑줄 친 부분 중, 어법상 틀린 것은? [3점]

Controlling for emotional bias is a skill the best scientists learn, in order to lessen the influence, as ① much as possible, of their own feelings upon their study. The idea of men in white coats ② investigating the natural world in a lab, using only the tools of pure reason, is a false belief. The best scientists aren't emotionless beings; they're exactly the opposite. The best scientists are as filled with passion for their subject ③ than artists are enthusiastic about their artwork. They're not satisfied with cold facts; they want to see the universe in all ④ its beauty. These people, though they use science, don't have minds that have been separated from their hearts and souls, but are whole people looking to understand ⑤ themselves and the world they inhabit.

30 (A), (B), (C)의 각 네모 안에서 문맥에 맞는 낱말로 가장 적절한 것은? [3점]

Dreams don't follow the laws of logic that govern our waking reality. For example, the category of time is (A) [altered / fixed]. People we know who have died, we see alive; we become involved in events that actually occurred many years ago. We dream of two or more events occurring (B) [simultaneously / spontaneously] when in reality they could not possibly occur at the same time. And dreams also pay little attention to the laws of space. It's simple for us to move to a (C) [nearby / distant] place in an instant, to be in two places at once, or to fuse two persons into one. Indeed, in our dreams, we create a new world where logic has no power.

	(A)		(B)		(C)
①	altered	……	simultaneously	……	nearby
②	altered	……	simultaneously	……	distant
③	altered	……	spontaneously	……	distant
④	fixed	……	spontaneously	……	distant
⑤	fixed	……	simultaneously	……	nearby

[31~34] 다음 빈칸에 들어갈 말로 가장 적절한 것을 고르시오.

31 One way that automobiles are produced in the States is by building them in factories in Detroit. Another is by growing them in Iowa. How does that work? It's quite simple: first, a farmer in Iowa grows corn, then the corn is loaded onto a ship and shipped overseas, and soon enough the ship comes back loaded up with new foreign-made automobiles. That's why, according to economist David Freedman, auto workers in Detroit and farmers in Iowa are actually in ________________ with one another. If Detroit factories receive increased government protection through tariffs and trade barriers, and it leads to decreased sales of imported cars, Iowa farmers will suffer. That's why more government assistance for car manufacturers is not necessarily in everybody's interest. [3점]

① harmony
② business
③ partnership
④ agreement
⑤ competition

32 If you see two babies sitting together and smiling at each other, what is the first thing that you think about? Parents often think that they are watching an exchange of body language which would be considered a friendly greeting in older children and adults. But at this very early stage, the behavior of babies who seem to be engaged in play with one another is likely to be nothing more than imitation. That is, it is not ________________________. Play activities at the earliest stages of life are usually done individually, with other babies treated largely as "toys." A smile may be an independent reaction, reflecting the amusement a baby feels at the sight of an interesting object. If a baby starts to cry, her companion will often become upset, but this is more likely to be discomfort caused by the unpleasant sound rather than genuine sympathy. [3점]

① just role playing
② individual action
③ true social interaction
④ intellectual development
⑤ honest emotional expression

33 In a neurology experiment, male responses to stress were found to be the opposite of female responses, in one particular respect. The participants were first deliberately made to feel very stressed; then they were asked to judge the emotions shown by faces in pictures. There was a striking difference between the way stress affected their ability to ________________ ____________. Women became more accurate and men became worse. Activity in the "face-assessing" part of the brain slowed down in the men, indicating that stress reduces their ability to correctly assess other people's feelings. But being stressed caused the women's brains to light up in that "face-reading" region. This indicates that it's an evolutionary survival impulse in women to bond with others in times of great stress. [3점]

*neurology: 신경학

① interpret emotions correctly
② predict the future accurately
③ get away from a conflict safely
④ quickly reduce their stress levels
⑤ influence other's feelings directly

34 As a result of the modernization of agriculture, the farm of today looks a lot like a factory. Food production and similar agricultural businesses have the potential to feed a nation. But not everyone is happy with the changes that have taken place on the farm. Some people say that the eggs that come from farm-factory chickens lack the flavor of the old-fashioned kind. Fruits and vegetables are no longer grown for flavor but for their ability to stand mechanical harvesting. The choice between old-fashioned flavor and modern abundance is not an easy one to make. Many people would rather keep to the old fashion, while others prefer the new ways. What is clear is that you cannot have both old-fashioned flavor and modern abundance. As a proverb goes, "________________________________"

① Necessity is mother of invention.
② One good turn deserves another.
③ You can't have your cake and eat it, too.
④ The grass is greener on the other side of the fence.
⑤ Better the devil you know than the devil you don't know.

35 **다음 글에서 전체 흐름과 관계 없는 문장은?**

Why do smaller earthquakes sometimes cause more damage than larger ones? On February 27, 2010, Chile was struck by one of the world's biggest-ever earthquakes. ① It registered 8.8 on the Richter scale, which NASA claims is strong enough to push Earth off its axis. ② Considering this, it's astonishing that the death toll for this disaster was only 800, while Haiti's far weaker earthquake claimed 200,000 lives just weeks earlier. ③ Overpopulation may be an even bigger threat to life than natural disasters. ④ The reason for this huge difference is simple: Chile is a well-functioning modern democracy whose wealth and laws guarantee that buildings are constructed to withstand disasters. ⑤ Haiti, on the other hand, has long been desperately poor, its government corrupt, and its buildings substandard.

*the Richter scale: (지진 규모를 나타내는) 리히터 척도

[36~37] 주어진 글 다음에 이어질 글의 순서로 가장 적절한 것을 고르시오.

36

Researchers who were training monkeys to do simple visual tasks found that success had a strong effect on the monkeys' brains.

(A) In other words, it was handicapped by its mistake. The head researcher says that success gave monkeys a surge of pleasure, thanks to a sudden increase of dopamine in the brain.

(B) For monkeys, as well as humans, this pleasure-giving chemical acts not only as a reward but also as a stimulating force that leads to further success.

(C) When a monkey did a task correctly, the neural processes in its brain became faster and the monkey's performance soared on its next task. But when a monkey made a mistake, it would perform poorly on its next task — even after mastering the previous one.

*dopamine: 도파민(신경전달물질)

① (A) — (C) — (B)
② (B) — (A) — (C)
③ (B) — (C) — (A)
④ (C) — (A) — (B)
⑤ (C) — (B) — (A)

37

After the 1988 wildfires that destroyed 739,000 acres of forest in Yellowstone National Park, researchers began studying the ecosystem to see how it recovered and changed.

(A) This phenomenon is critical to recovery, because untouched or lightly burned patches of forest re-seed destroyed areas. This is what happened after the 1988 fires.

(B) They found that, while the effects of fire vary in different ecosystems, some general principles apply. Depending on wind and available fuel, a wildfire burns in a mosaic, destroying some areas while leaving others untouched.

(C) Grasses that burned right to the ground regenerated from underground roots; fields were soon filled with the brilliant red bloom of fireweed; and certain rare and tiny plants also thrived.

*fireweed: 불탄 자리에 나는 잡초

① (A) — (C) — (B)
② (B) — (A) — (C)
③ (B) — (C) — (A)
④ (C) — (A) — (B)
⑤ (C) — (B) — (A)

[38~39] 글의 흐름으로 보아, 주어진 문장이 들어가기에 가장 적절한 곳을 고르시오.

38

It will be able to do such jobs as fetching household items and answering the front door.

Several kinds of voice-operated robots may soon be available to help disabled people. (①) One such robot, already developed, is a desktop machine. (②) It can do various chores that can be done by a human standing still, including brushing a person's teeth and opening a can of soup. (③) Also, a robot that can move freely from room to room inside a house is being developed for people with disabilities. (④) Another type of robot will be useful in the offices of disabled people. (⑤) This type of robot will do such office work as opening file cabinets and plugging USBs in a computer.

39

It is typical of these conversations that few of the remarks made on these subjects are informative.

When we are at a tea or dinner party, we all have to talk — about anything: the weather, the performance of the Chicago White Sox, Thomas Mann's latest book, or Myrna Loy's last picture. (①) Nevertheless, it is regarded as "rude" to remain silent. (②) Indeed, in such matters as greetings and farewells — "Good morning," "Lovely day," "Do look us up the next time you're in town" — it is regarded as a social error not to say these things. (③) There are numberless daily situations in which we talk simply because it would be impolite not to. (④) Every social group has its own form of this kind of talking. (⑤) From these social practices it is possible to infer that the prevention of silence is itself an important function of speech, and that it is completely impossible for us in society to talk only when we "have something to say." [3점]

40

다음 글의 내용을 한 문장으로 요약하고자 한다. 빈칸 (A), (B)에 들어갈 말로 가장 적절한 것은?

Alia Crum from Stanford University and her colleagues analyzed surveys from more than 60,000 American adults dating back over 20 years. The study focused on some questions: "Would you say that you are walking or biking to work more often, cleaning the house more, or taking stairs faster than other persons your age?" Using statistical models to control for factors like physical activity, age, body mass index and chronic illnesses, they then looked at the death records in 2020, which was 25 years after the first study took place. The researchers found that people who thought they performed fewer body activities than their peers were 71 percent more likely to die in that period than those who thought they did more — even when both groups had similar activity levels.

↓

Thinking that you're not as ___(A)___ as the people around you can actually ___(B)___ your life span.

	(A)		(B)
①	healthy	……	shorten
②	healthy	……	increase
③	positive	……	predict
④	active	……	shorten
⑤	active	……	increase

[41~42] 다음 글을 읽고, 물음에 답하시오.

When packing for trips, professional travelers take several steps over and over until they become habits. First, they make a list of everything that they will need for the upcoming trip. They do not trust their (a) memory. They write it all down. Second, they lay out everything they are going to take with them, in advance, before packing. (b) Preparation is the mark of a professional. Third, they pack completely so that they are ready to leave for the airport well in advance of the scheduled time. Professional travelers know that if you pack in a panic because you have not allowed enough time, you will forget things that can lead to unnecessary inconveniences later on your journey. One of the techniques that you can use to travel well and increase the likelihood that you will arrive at your destination is to prepare for an (c) unexpected situation. To do this, ask yourself, "What is the worst possible thing that could happen on this trip?" For me, as a professional speaker and seminar leader, the worst thing that could happen would be for my luggage to be lost and for me to arrive without the clothes and seminar materials that I need for my speaking engagement. To guard against this situation, I put all my (d) essentials into a smaller case and carry it on board with me, never out of my sight. The larger case can be checked, but if it gets lost in transit, the loss is just a (e) disaster. Because of this habit of advance planning, I have never had an insurmountable problem because of baggage delays or losses.

*insurmountable: 대처[극복]할 수 없는

41 윗글의 제목으로 가장 적절한 것은?

① Learn How to Enjoy Your Trip
② What You Get from Traveling Abroad
③ Life Is Like a Journey: Plan in Advance
④ Prepare in Every Detail for Your Journey
⑤ Develop a Plan B in Case Your First Plan Fails

42 밑줄 친 (a)~(e) 중에서 문맥상 낱말의 쓰임이 적절하지 않은 것은? [3점]

① (a) ② (b) ③ (c) ④ (d) ⑤ (e)

[43~45] 다음 글을 읽고, 물음에 답하시오.

(A)

Lisa loved to read. Every time her mom took her to the bookstore, she would buy two books. By the time she went to bed, Lisa had already read one of them. Mom said to Lisa the next day, "I think we need to get you your own library card. "Wow," cried Lisa. "I've always wanted a library card." The next day after school, Mom took Lisa to the library to get (a) <u>her</u> a card. The lady at the desk asked Mom to fill out a paper and then asked Lisa to print her name. She then told Lisa how many books she could borrow on her card. Lisa was so excited!

(B)

When Lisa got home, Mom told Lisa that a girl came to the house with (b) <u>her</u> library card, and she said she had found it on the sidewalk near the library. "It must have dropped out of one of the books I was carrying," said Lisa. "You were lucky that girl found your card," said Mom. "You need to be very careful. Having a library card is a big responsibility." Lisa said, "I think I will keep it in my wallet."

(C)

Mom said, "Let's go back to the library and get those books you wanted." "Sounds great," said Lisa. When they got to the library, Mom decided to get some books, too. While they were in the library, Mom told Lisa the girl that found (c) <u>her</u> card was sitting at the round table. Lisa went over to her and said, "Thank you for finding my card." She told Lisa (d) <u>she</u> was glad to help, and they both looked for some mystery books together. Lisa had her books, her card, and a new friend, too.

(D)

Lisa's favorite books were mysteries. Lisa had three books to return the next day. However, when Lisa got to the library desk, she didn't have her card. "Oh no!" Lisa said to the lady at the desk. "I can't find my library card." "I'm sorry," said the lady. "I can't let you take any books without your card." (e) <u>She</u> left the library feeling very sad.

43 주어진 글 (A)에 이어질 내용을 순서에 맞게 배열한 것으로 가장 적절한 것은?

① (B) — (D) — (C)
② (C) — (B) — (D)
③ (C) — (D) — (B)
④ (D) — (B) — (C)
⑤ (D) — (C) — (B)

44 밑줄 친 (a)~(e) 중에서 가리키는 대상이 나머지 넷과 <u>다른</u> 것은?

① (a) ② (b) ③ (c) ④ (d) ⑤ (e)

45 윗글에 관한 내용으로 적절하지 <u>않은</u> 것은?

① Lisa는 방과 후에 도서관 카드를 만들러 갔다.
② 엄마는 Lisa에게 도서관 카드 관리에 유의할 것을 당부했다.
③ 도서관 카드를 찾은 후에 Lisa는 혼자 도서관에 갔다.
④ Lisa는 도서관 카드를 찾아준 소녀를 도서관에서 만났다.
⑤ Lisa는 도서관 카드를 분실해서 책을 빌릴 수 없었다.

AFTER TESTING

종료	시	분
소요시간		분

1 채점하기 | 정답 및 해설 p.18
주의 틀린 문제를 다시 풀 수 있도록 정답을 본문에 표기하지 마세요.
2 등급 확인
3 틀린 유형 확인 후 전략 적용 복습 및 해설지 확인

How to Review

1 틀린 문제와 ✓ 표시한 문제는 다시 풀고 해설 확인하기
2 내가 표시한 정답 근거가 해설과 일치하는지 확인하기
3 잘 모르는 부분으로 표시한 내용은 해설을 통해 완전히 이해하기
4 어휘 외우기 (어휘 목록 다운로드 www.cedubook.com)
5 다음 회에 개선할 점 정리하기 (시간 엄수, 취약 유형 보완 등)

BUTTON UP!

실전 모의고사

04

BEFORE TESTING

시작 시 분

1 **제한시간** (OMR 마킹시간 포함) ☐ 40분 ☐ 45분
2 **어휘예습** ☐ 해당 없음 ☐ 완료
3 **문제풀이순서** ☐ 순서대로 ☐ 2점 → 3점 ☐ 기타 ....
4 **기타 목표** ....

Check Point

1 **정답 근거** *e.g.* 밑줄 긋기
2 **잘 모르는 부분** *e.g.* 〈 〉 또는 ? 표시
3 **자신 없는 문제** *e.g.* 문제 번호에 ✓표시

18 다음 글의 목적으로 가장 적절한 것은?

Attention Runners,

It's almost time once again for the Trout Community Fun Run! This entertaining and fun charity run is a yearly event sponsored by local businesses and attended by thousands from the community. It will be happening Saturday, June 17, at 11 a.m. However, its success relies on the generosity and support of people like you. We need staff to sign people up, manage snack booths, and collect donations. We also want people to help manage the crowds, as there are expected to be even more participants this year. If you've enjoyed this event in the past, why not get involved and make it fun for everyone else? I hope to see you there!

Jake Thompson, Organizer

① 자선 행사 개최를 홍보하려고
② 자선 행사 날짜 변경을 공지하려고
③ 자선 행사의 참가 자격을 알려주려고
④ 자선 행사의 자원봉사자를 모집하려고
⑤ 자선 행사에 후원해준 것을 감사하려고

19 다음 글에 드러난 Willie의 심경 변화로 가장 적절한 것은?

At the thought of being left alone at camp without his father, Willie began to cry. Matthew, an eighteen-year-old college student who was to be Willie's cabin counselor, noticed and walked over to him. He put his arm around Willie's shoulders and said, "Willie, why don't you sit by me? I'll tell you something about our camp." Matthew told Willie about the games they play, the campfires they have every evening, the swimming, and the delicious meals they eat. By then, the tears had stopped flowing. The boy listened to him with his eyes shining. That was probably because whenever Willie was being told stories of adventures, he was all ears instead of all tears.

① relieved → worried
② pleased → irritated
③ frightened → curious
④ grateful → embarrassed
⑤ hopeful → disappointed

20 다음 글에서 필자가 주장하는 바로 가장 적절한 것은?

Valuing differences — the mental, the emotional, the psychological differences between people — is the essence of synergy. And the key to valuing those differences is to realize that all people see the world not as it is, but as they are. If you think you see the world as it is, why would you want to value differences? You believe that everyone else is buried by the unimportant details, while you see the larger picture. If that's your belief, then you will never be effectively interdependent, or even effectively independent. If you want to be truly effective, you should have the humility and reverence to recognize your own perceptual limitations and to appreciate the rich resources available through interaction with the hearts and minds of other human beings. Value the differences, because those differences add to your knowledge and understanding of reality.

*reverence: 경외[존경]하는 마음

① 옳다고 생각하는 가치에 대해서는 신념을 굽히지 마라.
② 상대방이 잘못된 의견을 가졌을 때 과감하게 반박하라.
③ 자신의 한계를 인정하고 타인과의 교류를 통해 발전하라.
④ 세부적인 것에 집착하지 말고 큰 그림을 보도록 노력하라.
⑤ 자신과 의견이 다른 타인을 겸손과 존중의 자세로 설득하라.

21 밑줄 친 The barometer's needle had been right가 다음 글에서 의미하는 바로 가장 적절한 것은?

A man who lived on Long Island was one day able to satisfy a lifelong ambition by purchasing for himself a very fine barometer. When the instrument arrived at his home, he was extremely disappointed to find that the indicating needle appeared to be stuck, pointing to the sector marked 'HURRICANE.' After shaking the barometer vigorously several times, its new owner sat down and wrote a letter of complaint to the store from which he had purchased the instrument. The following morning on the way to his office in New York, he mailed the letter. That evening he returned to Long Island to find not only the barometer missing but also his house. The barometer's needle had been right.

① The barometer had just been found.
② The barometer began to work again.
③ The barometer's needle was missing.
④ There really had been a hurricane there.
⑤ The course of the hurricane suddenly shifted.

22 다음 글의 요지로 가장 적절한 것은?

Conventional wisdom suggests counting to ten before expressing our anger. Delay is an excellent strategy. However, the point is not simply to count during this delay but instead to define why we are angry. This method enables us to give a response that is more congruent with the problem. Identifying the reason of our anger enables us to respond to the right person instead of lashing out at others when we really feel angry at ourselves. Taking time to discern the reason for our anger will enable us to avoid responding in the wrong way to the wrong person. Then our response can be directed at the true source of our anger and can address the true reason for our anger.

*congruent: 일치하는, 적합한

① 분노의 감정은 표출할수록 더욱 커진다.
② 분노의 감정은 정신적인 힘을 소진시킨다.
③ 분노는 시간이 지나면 수그러들게 마련이다.
④ 분노를 적절하게 표현하는 것이 건강에 좋다.
⑤ 분노의 이유를 알아야 분노를 다스릴 수 있다.

23 다음 글의 주제로 가장 적절한 것은?

Sometimes we're not aware of our true thoughts and feelings until we capture them with the written word. Writing is a way of learning about yourself and the world around you. It forces you to focus your thoughts, providing the opportunity to solve problems. The next time you find yourself confronted with a problem, try writing about it. A journal provides a place to record what is known about the problem as well as to brainstorm potential solutions. Expressing ideas in written form requires a different thought process than does thinking. We must think in new ways in order to write, which may allow us to see problems differently and come to solutions more quickly. Journal-writing will quickly reveal a variety of techniques and exercises that may help to inspire new ways of thinking and expressing yourself.

① some ways to improve writing skills
② psychological benefits of writing every day
③ usefulness of writing as a method for learning
④ writing as an effective tool for problem solving
⑤ importance of understanding the elements of writing

24 다음 글의 제목으로 가장 적절한 것은?

If you want to live your dream after retirement, you should plan ahead as far in advance as possible — at least five years before your final day at work. First of all, it is strongly recommended that you invest your money in a range of different schemes, such as company shares, real estate, government bonds, and high-interest bank accounts, to give you as much financial strength as possible. Start spending less and saving more, and stop buying anything that's unnecessary. Avoid taking out bank loans, and make sure you pay off the balance on your credit cards on time to avoid paying their high interest fees. And update your life insurance and medical insurance policies to ensure that you are properly covered for later life.

① Is Retiring Early Too Risky?
② How to Retire Five Years Early
③ Financial Planning Before Retirement
④ After Retirement, Retired but Working
⑤ The Right Way to Save for a Rainy Day

25 다음 도표의 내용과 일치하지 않는 것은?

Reasons Given by Scientists and Engineers for First Coming to the United States

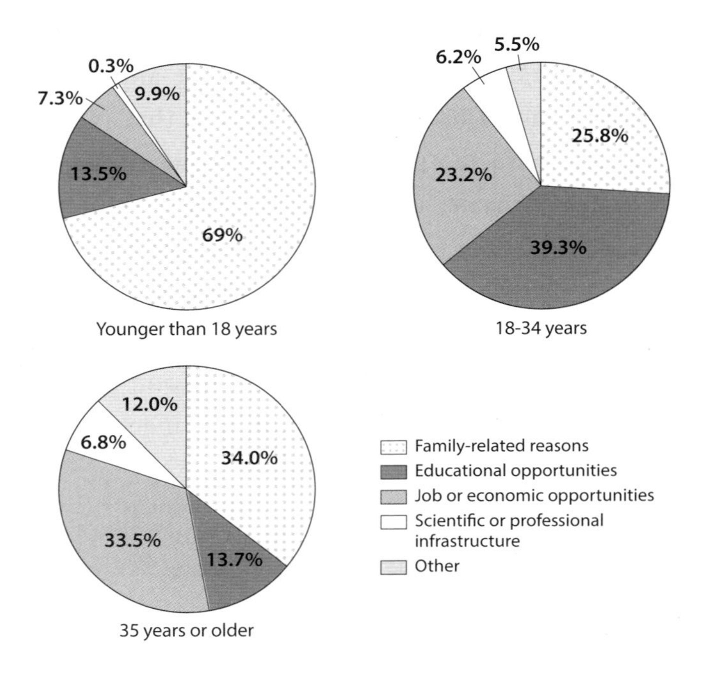

The above chart shows the age of first entry of immigrant scientists and engineers and the most important reasons they gave for coming to the United States at that time. ① For those that entered the US before the age of 18, nearly 70% came for family-related reasons, but this number was significantly lower for those who entered at an older age. ② For scientists and engineers who entered between the ages of 18 and 34, educational opportunities were the most important, followed by family-related reasons and then job or economic opportunities. ③ Those who came when they were 35 or older came mainly for family-related reasons and job or economic opportunities. ④ Scientific or professional infrastructure was the least chosen of the five categories in all three groups. ⑤ Finally, between 5.5 and 12% of those surveyed in each age group had other reasons for coming to the United States.

26 Clara Barton에 관한 다음 글의 내용과 일치하지 않는 것은?

Born in Massachusetts on Christmas Day, 1821, Clara Barton was the founder of the American Red Cross. She was only eleven when she started teaching herself medicine and nursing after her brother was seriously injured in a fall from a barn roof. Thirty years later, with the Civil War raging, she established a medical supplies agency and nursed the wounded at the front line, which earned her the nickname the "Angel of the Battlefield." When the war was over, Abraham Lincoln appointed Barton head of a mission to find missing soldiers. Later, in 1870, she sailed to Europe to work for the Red Cross during the Franco-Prussian War. Upon returning home, she founded the American Red Cross and was its president until 1904, when she retired at the age of eighty-three.

① 열한 살 때부터 의학 기술을 독학하기 시작했다.
② 남북전쟁 당시 의약품을 보급하는 단체를 설립했다.
③ 부상병을 돕는 간호사 대표로 임명되었다.
④ 1870년에 유럽으로 건너가 적십자사에서 일했다.
⑤ 미국 적십자사를 세우고 초대 회장을 맡았다.

27 Free Fun Fitness Week에 관한 다음 안내문의 내용과 일치하지 않는 것은?

Free Fun Fitness Week

You and one lucky friend are invited to the Free Fun Fitness Week!

Win a prize! 

Over $3,000 worth of personal training packages for 9 lucky people!

You can get one of the following:

– 1 month of FREE personal training valued at $400
– 2 months of FREE online personal training valued at $320
– 3 months of FREE group classes valued at $280

Our training programs will help you strengthen all the problem areas you wish to focus on by using personalized meal plans and fitness plans.

Simply participate in our one-week FREE trial program to enter into the drawing!
There are limited places, so hurry as they will disappear extremely fast.

① 총 아홉 명에게 상품이 주어진다.
② 온라인상으로도 프로그램이 진행된다.
③ 단체 수업의 정상가는 3개월에 280달러이다.
④ 개인별 식단과 운동 계획이 제공된다.
⑤ 유료 프로그램에 등록하면 응모 기회가 생긴다.

28 The Wilson Museum에 관한 다음 안내문의 내용과 일치하는 것은?

The Wilson Museum

We invite you to explore invention, ideas, and innovation. The Wilson Museum features some of the latest research, the history of artificial intelligence, and special galleries for holography.

Opening Hours

- Daily 10 a.m. to 5 p.m. except major holidays
- **July and August only:** Thursdays 10 a.m. to 7 p.m.

Admission

- Adults: $10.00
  Youth under 18, Students, Seniors 65 and over: $5.00
  Children under 5: free
- Free admission on the last Sunday of each month
- Evening programs, featuring a guest speaker from the IT community, are free with museum admission.

Educational Visits

Educational Programs are available for groups of 8 or more people. Advance reservations are required for all groups.

① 인류 문명의 역사에 관한 박물관이다.
② 7, 8월에는 목요일 관람 시간이 2시간 더 짧다.
③ 5세 미만 어린이의 입장료는 성인의 50%이다.
④ 매달 마지막 주 일요일에는 무료로 입장할 수 있다.
⑤ 단체를 위한 교육 프로그램은 현장에서 신청할 수 있다.

29 다음 글의 밑줄 친 부분 중, 어법상 틀린 것은? [3점]

Sleeping well is very important for our health and well-being, and experts say that we need to get between seven and nine hours of sleep a day. It helps prevent sickness and depression by ① strengthening the immune system. But too many of us are getting less than the ② recommended amount. In fact, Koreans are the "most awake" people in the OECD, getting ③ much less sleep in general than what other people get. Only recently ④ have health professionals begun to take our lack of sleep seriously. We are ⑤ depriving of sleep because of pressure to compete at school and at work. But when we keep working rather than getting rest, we not only lose productivity, but we also become more unhappy.

30 다음 글의 밑줄 친 부분 중, 문맥상 낱말의 쓰임이 적절하지 않은 것은? [3점]

We are taught as children that the best gifts are homemade. What comes with a handmade gift is not only the gift itself but, more importantly, the ① invaluable time the other person put into it. In this respect, letters fit the priceless bill ② perfectly not only because of the time but also the raw emotion and thought they require. If we take it to an extreme, a relationship where nothing but diamond necklaces and gold rings are exchanged would ③ pale in comparison to a relationship where nothing but letters are exchanged. Since the people who love us the most tend to be the people we take for granted the ④ least, it never hurts to send an unexpected reminder that you think the world of them. It will be more cherished than a ⑤ luxurious gift. I promise.

[31~34] 다음 빈칸에 들어갈 말로 가장 적절한 것을 고르시오.

31 Many people in the workplace have personal goals but no commitment to the mission of the corporation. They want to be a superstar at the office or go after the promotion, but they don't support the team concept and inevitably fail to understand that they were hired to enhance the team and not compete with the team. Ultimately, I'm afraid it all comes down to selfishness, and as harsh as that word sounds, we'd better identify it or we won't be able to correct it. If you don't believe in the power of a team, then start a sole proprietorship and work on your dream solely and exclusively. If you don't believe in the team, don't join one, because if you do, you have to give up on some of the "me" of it all for the "we" of it all! You have to realize that the true nature of teamwork is really ______________. [3점]

*sole proprietorship: 개인 사업

① sacrifice
② vision
③ trust
④ patience
⑤ flexibility

32 Food plays an integral role in Puerto Rican life. Unlike in some other countries, one way in which a good mother and wife expresses her love for her husband and children is by presenting them with large helpings of food and showing concern over amounts of food eaten. A more unusual part of Puerto Rican life is ______________________, which is an expected part of a woman's social life, especially upon marriage. It is a sign, particularly to her family, that she is adequately provided for. Women who lose weight get negative reactions. One woman whose weight declined from 170 to 140 pounds when she divorced her husband reported: "When I lost weight, people said: 'You're so skinny! What happened to you?' So many people told me that fat didn't look bad and I looked better when I had curves."

*helping: 한 번 담는 분량, 한 그릇

① food supply
② weight gain
③ special recipes
④ flavor sensitivity
⑤ unfailing patience

33 Reading fiction provides ____________________. In her article published in the Sunday Review of the *New York Times*, Annie Murphy Hall discusses how reading works of fiction affects our brains. Murphy says, "The brain, it seems, does not make much of a distinction between reading about an experience and encountering it in real life." Indeed, reading produces a vivid simulation of reality, one that "runs on minds of readers just as computer simulations run on computers." Our children are transported to a different world as they read. Reading fiction helps children take a break from daily worries and gives them the chance to unplug and relax. While constantly living in a fantasy world may be harmful, an hour or two of suspended reality might be just what the doctor ordered! [3점]

① a life lesson
② reading skills
③ a healthy escape
④ a lively imagination
⑤ inspiration for children

34 A simple word association test can ____________________. Since this test works on a non-thinking, automatic level, it actually reveals your deepest and most persistent feelings for another person. In the test, words are flashed one at a time on a monitor, and you have to identify very quickly whether or not the word relates to your partner. The words were in three categories: "good words," such as *love* and *water*; "bad words," such as *hurt* and *scream*; and "partner words," such as pet names and personal traits. The inventors of the test say the results are consistent and clear: the higher the number of "bad words" you associate with your partner, the higher the likelihood that you'll break up within a year. [3점]

① reveal a person's unspoken intentions
② provide solid evidence of cheating and lying
③ indicate whether a relationship is going to last
④ confirm your beliefs about long-term relationships
⑤ teach us the importance of thinking quickly and clearly

35 다음 글에서 전체 흐름과 관계 없는 문장은?

What makes you happy at school? Your favorite teacher? A particular class? Scoring 100% on a test? What about your friendships? ① When kids are asked to say what they like about school, one thing stands out far above the rest — and that's friendship. ② In a survey of 3,457 schoolchildren in Yorkshire, 62.8% said that when they felt happy at school it was because of their friendships. ③ "Friendships" were defined as not only close attachments to best buddies, but also friendly connections with classmates and teachers. ④ Among many friendships, those formed in high school are the most lasting and strong. ⑤ In addition to friendships, feeling safe and being liked by others were cited by many kids as reasons for being happy at school.

[36~37] 주어진 글 다음에 이어질 글의 순서로 가장 적절한 것을 고르시오.

36

An American scientist has found that certain tiny, colorful, poisonous frogs of South America do not actually produce their poison themselves.

(A) In fact, the poison is so deadly that a single frog can kill a hundred mice or disable a man. As part of her research, the scientist examined the contents of hundreds of these frogs' stomachs.

(B) She is confident that it's the ants the frogs eat that produce the poison. She found that the frogs are harmless when born, and that only the skin of mature frogs is coated in the deadly poison.

(C) The stomachs revealed 135 species of ants, including many that produce highly toxic substances. These ants, she discovered, make up 70 percent of the diet of the deadliest frogs.

① (A) — (C) — (B)　② (B) — (A) — (C)
③ (B) — (C) — (A)　④ (C) — (A) — (B)
⑤ (C) — (B) — (A)

37

Speed is contagious. Slower media, such as magazines and newspapers, imitate the fastest media, such as the Internet and television.

(A) What gets lost in this hectic information environment is context and understanding. Time pressure forces consumers of information to scan multiple channels, taking in and filtering large amounts of data in search of what is interesting or important.

(B) Articles become shorter and shorter with clearer messages and less analysis. Super-brief news items are constantly being updated. Everyone has 10 seconds to spare, but who has a few minutes to spare? Fears over simplifying and speeding up information give the edge to the fastest and most compact media.

(C) But they do not necessarily remember much of what they scanned; the last piece of data pushes out from consciousness the piece of data previous to it.

[3점]

*hectic: 정신없이 바쁜

① (A) — (C) — (B)　② (B) — (A) — (C)
③ (B) — (C) — (A)　④ (C) — (A) — (B)
⑤ (C) — (B) — (A)

[38~39] 글의 흐름으로 보아, 주어진 문장이 들어가기에 가장 적절한 곳을 고르시오.

38

For this reason, the terms "possession" and "ownership" can sometimes be confused.

"Possession is nine-tenths of the law" is a saying that suggests that just having a thing in your possession is almost the same as legally owning it. (①) Thus, it gives people the idea that if they just hold onto a thing, it will be hard for the real owner to get it back, which will make the thing theirs. (②) Just imagine how hard it would be to get your piano back from somebody who has been looking after it for you for ten years. (③) He might think he owns it. (④) Yet, they are definitely not the same things in legal terms. (⑤) For instance, you lend your car to a friend and now your friend *possesses* the car, but you still legally *own* it.

39

However, there are often subtle cultural differences in body language which can lead us to make the wrong assumptions about a person.

Observations of people's behavior, both at work and in everyday life, suggest that most individuals possess both favorable and unfavorable characteristics. (①) Strong impressions of a person's character are often made by observing body language. (②) In many instances this can be helpful. (③) For example, in some cultures, individuals will not look an interviewer in the eye to show respect. (④) Unfortunately, this, in other cultures, is often misread by interviewers as evidence that the interviewee is "hiding something," or as evidence that they are a "shifty character who couldn't look me in the eye." (⑤) Improving the level of knowledge of cultural differences in body language can aid in building international competencies.

40 다음 글의 내용을 한 문장으로 요약하고자 한다. 빈칸 (A), (B)에 들어갈 말로 가장 적절한 것은?

Eating is essential for survival. So it's not surprising that our body will "extend" the sense of "taste" by linking it to the sense of "smell." It sounds reasonable — after all, good food usually smells good. But there is another factor which influences how we feel about food. The University of Oxford ran a study in which their subjects wore noise-canceling headphones and sat in front of a microphone while eating chips. The only way the volunteers could hear the crunch was via the loudspeakers inside the headphones — which the psychologists controlled. If the crunching noise was played back at a normal level, the chip eaters thought the chips were normally crisp. If the noise was made louder, or the high frequencies increased, they rated them crispier. And when the crunch or the high frequencies were lowered, the chips seemed less crisp.

↓

Not only the smell but also the ____(A)____ affects how we ____(B)____ what we eat.

	(A)		(B)
①	appearance	……	perceive
②	appearance	……	identify
③	texture	……	control
④	sound	……	perceive
⑤	sound	……	identify

[41~42] 다음 글을 읽고, 물음에 답하시오.

On his long journey home after the Trojan War, the hero Odysseus faced sea nymphs, the Sirens. They sang so beautifully that sailors were compelled to approach and crashed their ships on the surrounding rocks. Odysseus tied himself to his ship's pole, packed the ears of his crew with wax, and gave them strict instructions to ignore his facial expressions. There the (a) cunning hero stood as they sailed into dangerous waters; the Sirens called to him, and he heard their song. He begged his men to set him free, but his men couldn't hear his pleas. It was precisely his planned (b) powerfulness that saved him from destruction. He became the first person to hear the beauty of the Sirens' singing without dying. Odysseus anticipated his (c) weakness and took steps to prevent his predictable passions from coming to destructive ends. The drama of the Sirens is about a (d) self-control battle. Every day is like such a battle. If you eat candy bars from vending machines at work, you can choose not to have any coins in your purse. This small change can make a big improvement in your diet. Our temptations are powerful and constant, but we are not destined to (e) surrender. Because we can predict their influence, self-knowledge plus discipline can provide a winning strategy in the battle to lead satisfying and moral lives.

41 윗글의 제목으로 가장 적절한 것은?

① Don't Avoid Your Temptation, Face It
② What Strengthens Us to Resist Temptation?
③ Temptation: Harder to Resist Than You Think
④ Passion: Why We Give in to Our Temptations
⑤ Overcome Temptation by Preventing It in Advance

42 밑줄 친 (a)~(e) 중에서 문맥상 낱말의 쓰임이 적절하지 않은 것은? [3점]

① (a) ② (b) ③ (c) ④ (d) ⑤ (e)

[43~45] 다음 글을 읽고, 물음에 답하시오.

(A)

One day, a little rabbit was drinking from a clear spring and saw herself reflected in the water. She was so pleased with (a) what she saw that she stayed for quite some time, putting her ears up and down, and shaking her tail left and right.

(B)

She frowned as she looked them up and down. "If only the rest of me could be as cute as my tail and my ears! (b) They are the very ones that satisfy me the most! But these legs, *eugh*! They make me ashamed to run fast and jump high. I don't even care if you say (c) they are the right shape for my body! To me, they're just unshapely and ugly-looking things; I wish I didn't have them at all!" And there she stayed, beside the spring, admiring herself and wondering what on earth to do about her legs. At that moment, suddenly came the sound of hunters and barking dogs.

(C)

They had picked up her scent. She jumped and bounded strongly across the hills, much faster than the dogs could run. After running a mile or more, she found a thorny bush and crawled into it to rest, but her fluffy white tail stayed just outside of the bush, like a bright white sign. The dogs came again. She tried to jump out the other side, but her soft ears were caught in the thorns and the dogs had her by her tail! It was (d) they that caused her to be caught in this terrible trap.

(D)

"Ohh, Rabbit-pie!" She said to herself (for that was her nickname,) "What a pretty pair of soft white ears you have! How cute they look when you style them like that! How they highlight your delicate little face and lovely eyes! And your fluffy white tail, how perfect it is! Such a tail must be the envy of every sister rabbit in the wood!" And so she went on, admiring and praising (e) her assets, until she stretched and caught sight of her back legs.

43 주어진 글 (A)에 이어질 내용을 순서에 맞게 배열한 것으로 가장 적절한 것은?

① (B) — (D) — (C)
② (C) — (B) — (D)
③ (C) — (D) — (B)
④ (D) — (B) — (C)
⑤ (D) — (C) — (B)

44 밑줄 친 (a)~(e) 중에서 가리키는 대상이 나머지 넷과 다른 것은?

① (a) ② (b) ③ (c) ④ (d) ⑤ (e)

45 윗글의 토끼에 관한 내용으로 적절하지 않은 것은?

① 자신의 뒷다리가 마음에 들지 않았다.
② 샘물가에 있다가 개 짖는 소리를 들었다.
③ 개를 피해 가시덤불로 기어 들어갔다.
④ 뒷다리 때문에 사냥개에게 잡혔다.
⑤ 자신을 Rabbit-pie라고 불렀다.

AFTER TESTING

⏱ 종료 시 분

⌛ 소요시간 분

1 채점하기 | 정답 및 해설 p.26

주의 틀린 문제를 다시 풀 수 있도록 정답을 본문에 표기하지 마세요.

2 등급 확인

3 틀린 유형 확인 후 전략 적용 복습 및 해설지 확인

How to Review

1 틀린 문제와 ✓ 표시한 문제는 다시 풀고 해설 확인하기

2 내가 표시한 정답 근거가 해설과 일치하는지 확인하기

3 잘 모르는 부분으로 표시한 내용은 해설을 통해 완전히 이해하기

4 어휘 외우기 (어휘 목록 다운로드 www.cedubook.com)

5 다음 회에 개선할 점 정리하기 (시간 엄수, 취약 유형 보완 등)

BUTTON UP!

실전 모의고사

05

BEFORE TESTING

시작 시 분

1 **제한시간** (OMR 마킹시간 포함) ☐ 40분 ☐ 45분
2 **어휘예습** ☐ 해당 없음 ☐ 완료
3 **문제풀이순서** ☐ 순서대로 ☐ 2점 → 3점 ☐ 기타 ....
4 **기타 목표** ....

Check Point

1 **정답 근거** *e.g.* 밑줄 긋기
2 **잘 모르는 부분** *e.g.* 〈 〉 또는 ? 표시
3 **자신 없는 문제** *e.g.* 문제 번호에 ✓표시

18 다음 글의 목적으로 가장 적절한 것은?

Dear Mr. Hall,

About a year ago I read your booklet, *How to Write Letters for All Occasions,* and I want to tell you how much it helped me recently. You see, my aunt's beloved cat died a while ago after a long illness, and I felt I had to say something — but what? I didn't know the cat, who was called Allie, very well, but I did know how much Aunty Peggy loved her. Then I remembered what your booklet said about writing condolence letters, and I wrote Aunty Peggy a little story I remembered about Allie. Aunty Peggy wrote back later to thank me for "making her smile again." She said my letter helped her remember many other happy memories of life with Allie.

Sincerely,
Martin Garrix

① 편지를 쓰는 데 조언을 구하려고
② 도움을 받은 책을 소개하려고
③ 슬퍼하는 고모를 위로하려고
④ 작가에게 감사의 말을 전하려고
⑤ 효과적인 위로 방법을 설명하려고

19 다음 글의 상황에 나타난 분위기로 가장 적절한 것은?

The students were sitting very straight at their desks. Ms. Morgan's face had turned pure white and her mouth was opening and shutting like a fish out of water as she drew in noisy breaths of air. The piece of chalk stopped writing on the blackboard, danced for a moment in mid-air, then suddenly dropped to the floor and broke in two. Then came a great big "THUMP!" and someone in the front row yelled, "Ms. Morgan has fallen down! Ms. Morgan is on the floor!" This was the most sensational news of all. The entire class jumped up at once and ran forward to get a good look. And there indeed she was: Ms. Morgan flat on her back on the floor, unconscious.

① lively and festive
② serious and solemn
③ discouraging and hopeless
④ boring and monotonous
⑤ shocking and urgent

20 다음 글에서 필자가 주장하는 바로 가장 적절한 것은?

Kids do annoying things — not maliciously, but because they don't think like adults. You are likely to have a miserable day if you let every kid-created mess bother you. As you enter the kitchen, you see your two-year-old at the sink splashing water all over the floor. You could sink into a "poor me" mindset. But here's a healthier choice. Instead of first considering your own inconvenience, immediately click into your child's viewpoint: "This is fun. Look at all the different things you can do with dishes and water." In this way, you'll remember that what she is doing is developmentally appropriate. If you wait a few minutes, she'll go on to something else. Getting out of yourself and into your child saves mental strain. You don't have to clean up the mess in your mind along with the water on the floor.

① 자녀가 예의바르게 행동하도록 가르쳐야 한다.
② 자녀의 불만을 먼저 이해하도록 노력해야 한다.
③ 아이의 행동을 아이의 관점에서 바라보아야 한다.
④ 자녀가 스스로 정리정돈 할 수 있게 유도해야 한다.
⑤ 발달 단계에 따라 아이에 대해 어느 정도 무관심이 필요하다.

21 다음 글의 요지로 가장 적절한 것은?

If you want to make learning English as a foreign language more fun for students, you could start by leaving aside the grammar. Memorizing vocabulary and complete sentences is the most important thing. If you have a good vocabulary then you can get by — even if the sentences you make aren't perfect. On the other hand, if you have a good grasp of grammar but a poor vocabulary, you'll struggle to understand and to be understood. The more vocabulary a student understands, the more encouraged they'll be to speak. The best way to get better at a language is to learn more and more words, and to think with them and speak them aloud.

① 영어 학습에서 가장 중요한 것은 흥미이다.
② 조기 영어 교육은 모국어 습득에 방해가 된다.
③ 체계화된 문법 학습은 영어 학습에 필수적이다.
④ 어휘 학습을 통해 영어 말하기 능력을 길러야 한다.
⑤ 영어 학습의 최종 목표는 쓰기 능력을 갖추는 것이다.

22 다음 글의 주제로 가장 적절한 것은?

Part of being an effective manager or employer involves knowing how to be a good bearer of bad news. First of all, you have to break the news yourself, face to face with the person who receives it. You can't write memos to tell staff that they will not get raises this year, that they have made an error, or that they are not performing as well as expected. You have to show them how you feel about the matter and that you are personally sorry and that you sympathize with them. If you indicate that you are ready to listen to their reactions to your bad news, you will undoubtedly save yourself from their anger. Give people time to digest your news and to control the emotion they will probably feel.

① ways to convey bad news to employees
② how to express sympathy for colleagues
③ a list of reasons for having to break bad news
④ inevitable bad news employees have to deal with
⑤ effective ways for employees to cope with bad news

23 다음 글의 제목으로 가장 적절한 것은?

NASA's primary goal is to explore and better understand the cosmos. But much of the technology NASA developed in reaching for the stars has inspired the masses, leading to innovations such as more nutritious infant formula, sunglasses that block harmful ultraviolet light, and many more. One third of all cellphone cameras use technology originally developed for NASA spacecraft. And in the 1960s, NASA scientists who wanted to enhance pictures of the moon invented digital image processing. The technology later found many other applications — particularly in the medical field, where it helped enable body imaging techniques such as magnetic resonance imaging (MRI).

*infant formula: 유아용 분유

① What Benefits Space Exploration
② Space Technology Brought to Earth
③ Is Space Exploration Worth the Cost?
④ NASA Inventions Originated from Daily Goods
⑤ NASA Opened up a New Era in Space Exploration

24 다음 도표의 내용과 일치하지 않는 것은?

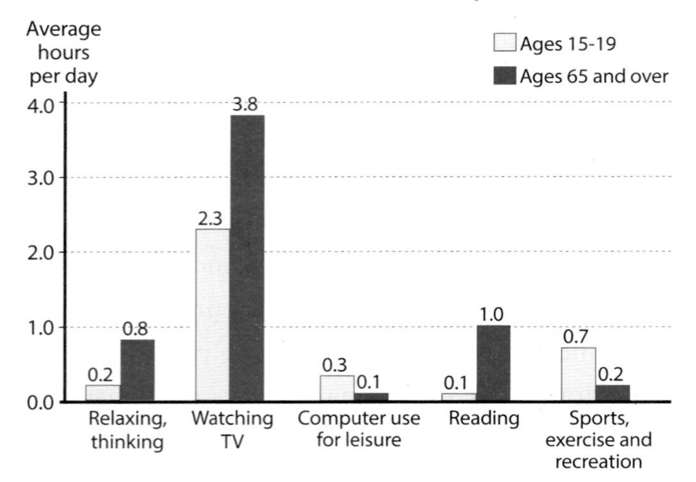

The above graph shows the average number of hours per day spent in various leisure activities by those aged 15 to 19 and those 65 and over in America, in 2018. ① Both groups spent the largest portion of their leisure time watching TV, 3.8 hours per day for those 65 and over, and 2.3 hours per day for those between 15 and 19. ② The older group spent the second largest portion of its time, an hour a day, reading. ③ The younger group averaged only 0.1 hours per day reading, equal to the time they spent using a computer for leisure. ④ The older group spent 0.2 hours on sports, exercise and recreation, which is less than the amount of time the younger group spent on the same activities. ⑤ However, the older group spent four times as much time relaxing and thinking as the younger group.

25 Doomsday Plane에 관한 다음 글의 내용과 일치하지 않는 것은?

Known as the "Doomsday Plane," one special Boeing 747 can serve as a floating Pentagon, the Department of Defense headquarters, in the event of a devastating attack upon the United States. The plane can carry enough food, water, and fuel to stay airborne for almost 36 hours. It operates with a crew of between 48 and 112, the biggest crew for any aircraft in Air Force history. It was built in the 1970s and designed to keep flying even in the middle of a nuclear war, which is why it can be refueled in midair. On occasion, the fuel hose from the floating fuel tanker has smashed the pilot's windshield like an angry giant snake, but has caused no serious damage.

① 비상시 미국 국방부의 역할을 한다.
② 하루 이상 비행이 가능한 연료를 실을 수 있다.
③ 미 공군 비행기 중 수용 인원이 가장 많다.
④ 핵전쟁 중에도 비행이 가능하도록 설계되었다.
⑤ 급유 탱크 문제로 심각하게 파손된 적이 있다.

26 National Orchid Garden Guided Tour에 관한 다음 안내문의 내용과 일치하지 않는 것은?

17 May (Sat):
National Orchid Garden Guided Tour

Explore the beauty and diversity of orchids in the National Orchid Garden at Singapore Botanic Gardens. Over 1,000 species and 2,000 hybrids are now part of the Garden's collection, with over 600 species and hybrids on display.

This walk is conducted by volunteers and is held every third Saturday of the month.

- Time: 9 a.m., 10 a.m., 11 a.m. (English) and 4 p.m. (Mandarin)
- Tour Duration: One hour
- Registration: Register at the Visitor Center 15 minutes prior to the tour on a first-come-first-served basis
- Cost: While the tour is free, admission charges to the Orchid Garden apply: $5/adult, $1/student, senior citizens (above 60 years) and children under 12 get in free
- Contact: Visitor Services 6471–7361

*orchid: 난초

① 전시 중인 난초는 600여 종에 달한다.
② 자원봉사자들에 의해 시행되는 도보 투어이다.
③ 영어 가이드 투어는 오전에 제공된다.
④ 등록은 투어 15분 전에 선착순으로 이뤄진다.
⑤ 입장료는 무료이지만 가이드 투어는 유료이다.

27 교내 버스 이용에 관한 다음 안내문의 내용과 일치하는 것은?

Bus Service

The University of Nebraska-Lincoln operates its bus routes Monday through Friday during the fall and spring semesters.

Transit Tips

- Print a route map and time schedule from our website.
- Bus does not stop at all stops — must be waiting at stop — must let driver know you need to get off.

Bus Pass

Both students and faculty/staff will need both the following to use transit services:
1. StarTran Pass
2. NCard

Students are issued a pass paid through student fees. This bus pass and all future transit improvements are supported by the student body.
Faculty/staff are issued a pass upon request for no charge (for holders of annual, nine-month, or semester parking permits).

① 가을과 봄 학기에는 주말에도 운행한다.
② 버스는 승객의 요청 없이도 모든 정류장에 정차한다.
③ NCard만 있으면 노선버스를 이용할 수 있다.
④ 학생들은 승차권을 별도로 구매해야 한다.
⑤ 한 학기 주차권이 있는 교직원은 무료로 승차권을 받을 수 있다.

28 (A), (B), (C)의 각 네모 안에서 어법에 맞는 표현으로 가장 적절한 것은? [3점]

I've tried many unsuccessful treatments for my snoring, so when my wife heard about Dr. Bronner's cure for snoring and suggested that I (A) [call / called] him for an appointment, I immediately did. At Dr. Bronner's clinic, I not only learned that a famous sleep clinic referred patients to him, (B) [but / and] many who had tried his invention had experienced dramatic results. He fitted me with the oral appliance, and the results were truly amazing! My snoring has been cured, and my wife is overjoyed that she sleeps all night now without ever being woken by the awful noise I used to make. After years of restless nights, we both sleep easily! Both of us wish I (C) [had / had had] this appliance fitted years ago.

	(A)		(B)		(C)
①	call	……	but	……	had
②	call	……	but	……	had had
③	call	……	and	……	had
④	called	……	but	……	had had
⑤	called	……	and	……	had

29 다음 글의 밑줄 친 부분 중, 문맥상 낱말의 쓰임이 적절하지 <u>않은</u> 것은? [3점]

In a traditional economic system, the questions of what and how to produce and whom to produce for are answered by tradition. The Kalahari Bushmen live in one of the world's harshest environments, where even the most basic resources are in ① <u>limited</u> supply. In order to survive and have enough food, the Bushmen have developed a division of labor based on ② <u>gender</u>. Women perform the food gathering and men perform the hunting. The food is then shared with the whole tribe. In this type of system, stability and continuity are ③ <u>favored</u> over innovation and change. In this system, the old, young, weak, and disabled are cared for by the group. The group shares the few possessions they have, and private property is an ④ <u>alien</u> concept. For the most part, everyone in this system understands his or her relationship to the community, and as a result, life goes on in a fairly ⑤ <u>unpredictable</u> way.

30 밑줄 친 him[he]이 가리키는 대상이 나머지 넷과 다른 것은?

The pounding was driving Edward crazy. A new neighbor, who had moved into the apartment below ① him, was playing music loud enough to shake the walls and windows. So ② he went downstairs and asked the new tenant to please turn it down. He looked surprised and embarrassed and said, "Sorry, I didn't realize it was so loud." After that, Edward went back to his apartment feeling proud of himself because ③ he had taken a firm stand and let the newcomer know that loud music was not going to be tolerated. It was quiet for the rest of that night and the following day, and ④ he continued to be pleased with himself. But that night, he was awakened by the same thumping from downstairs: it was ⑤ him again.

[31~34] 다음 빈칸에 들어갈 말로 가장 적절한 것을 고르시오.

31 *Art* literally means "a production or something specially made." *Artful, artisan,* and *artistic* are related and also contain the idea of something that was planned. Dictionary definitions of art usually include words like *effort* and *arrangement*. They all support the idea that there's a difference between a rock you happen to sit on in a forest, and a rock that you carry out of the forest and arrange in your garden with other rocks to create a circle of seats. The latter is art because you have deliberately assembled things in a way that's satisfying to you as the *artist* or *producer*. It's clear that art has as much to do with the producer's ________________ as with the product itself. [3점]

① style　② skills
③ feelings　④ creativity
⑤ intentions

32 Imagine walking on the surface of Mars. You follow channels where water once may have flowed, and hike across flat plains covered with rocks of all sizes. Seem impossible? Virtual reality (VR) is a technology that allows you to look at, listen to, and move around inside a computer world every bit as fantastic as the wildest reality. Unlike a video game or computer art, virtual reality eliminates the computer screen and lets you step into a three-dimensional artificial world. All you have to do is put on special video goggles and a wired glove, and ______________________________. You can climb mountains or fly above them, explore distant planets or play with molecules, paint in three dimensions or design a house as you're walking through it. [3점]

*molecule: (화학) 분자

① you can feel your past life
② it's the Earth in full miniature
③ the impossible becomes possible
④ you will measure things accurately
⑤ it is the real world, not a virtual one

33 Let's say that you've been angry at an ex-girlfriend for ages, and you happen to see her one day. You stop and chat and then suddenly you say it: "I am so angry at you." There. Guess what you've done. You've changed the anger. It's no longer that big ugly thing that exists in your head. Now, out in the open, it's something else: something you both can look at and maybe even laugh about. Stating a fear changes the size of it: it can shrink or grow, depending on how you say it. It's like how telling somebody "I'm lost" is a big step toward finding your way back home again. And ______________________________ because it connects us to others and gives us greater perspective. [3점]

① being together promotes closeness
② asking for help is helping ourselves
③ speaking about emotions transforms them
④ managing our moods can benefit our health
⑤ the right information can lead to understanding

34 Here's a trick researchers teach chimps. In one hand, the researchers hold something the chimps want. They will only give the item to the chimp, however, if it points to the researcher's other hand. Chimps quickly learn this little game and point to the researcher's left hand to get their prize from the right hand, or vice versa. This ability to learn disappears, however, if the desired item is food. When the chimps see food (a juicy banana, for example), they go straight for it, forgetting the game completely. Even after dozens of failures they keep pointing, with growing frustration, at the hand with the food they desire and don't get. Chimps simply cannot ______________________________.

① have the time to make a choice
② make an action plan and take action
③ develop a set criteria to judge all options by
④ gather information to make the right decision
⑤ use their intelligence to overcome their passion

35 다음 글에서 전체 흐름과 관계 없는 문장은?

Books are storehouses of lives gone by. For example, there's the story of the Kolkata Jews. ① Originally traders from Baghdad, they settled in Kolkata, India, in the late 1700s and established a vibrant community with its own unique customs, cuisine, and way of life. ② Today only a handful of elderly Kolkata Jews remain and they too will soon be gone with their synagogues, bakeries, and stores. ③ All that will be left of them will be their books: memoirs and cookbooks that they published, and other books that they collected. ④ Reading a wide variety of books is a way of becoming familiar with different customs. ⑤ Without these, we would lose the memory of the Jews of Kolkata.

*synagogue: 유대교 회당 **memoir: 회고록

[36~37] 주어진 글 다음에 이어질 글의 순서로 가장 적절한 것을 고르시오.

36

While wind turbines are highly beneficial to the environment, they are very dangerous for birds, bats, and other creatures who spend time in the air.

(A) But the study says that white turbines attract bugs, which often leads the birds and bats that eat them to their death. While white, light gray and yellow were most attractive, purple was the opposite.

(B) While this doesn't mean that all turbines should now be painted purple, it does indicate that something as simple as a change in color could prevent birds and bats from flying into wind turbines.

(C) A new study concludes that this danger could be solved by changing the color of turbines. It may seem unlikely to you that white, the current trend for turbine color, could be the problem.

① (A) — (C) — (B)
② (B) — (A) — (C)
③ (B) — (C) — (A)
④ (C) — (A) — (B)
⑤ (C) — (B) — (A)

37

It's not normal to feel extremely sleepy after eating. But there's no need to worry about being really tired after a meal once in a while.

(A) To avoid this problem, choose lighter foods that are low in sugar and fat and high in complex carbohydrates, especially fruit, vegetables, nuts, and wholegrain cereals. These are easy to digest and help your body to generate a lot of energy, no matter how much you work!

(B) If it's happening every day, however, you may need to change your diet. Tiredness is a useful feeling that can indicate there is a problem with your body.

(C) When you eat foods that are high in sugar, and you don't exercise enough to burn the energy, your blood sugar levels go up like a rocket. And then, not long afterward, the levels come crashing down again, and this crazy seesawing of sugar levels leaves you feeling very worn out.

*complex carbohydrates: 복합 탄수화물

① (A) — (C) — (B)
② (B) — (A) — (C)
③ (B) — (C) — (A)
④ (C) — (A) — (B)
⑤ (C) — (B) — (A)

[38~39] 글의 흐름으로 보아, 주어진 문장이 들어가기에 가장 적절한 곳을 고르시오.

38

The logs often rolled under the weight of coaches and caused horses to slip and stumble.

Modern roads are vastly different from what they used to be — the average 19th-century road or street was a dirt path six to eight feet wide. (①) In spring, with the rain, these roads became muddy and full of puddles. (②) The roads dried up completely in hot summers and huge clouds of dust flew up whenever anyone traveled on them. (③) Roads began to be improved during this period by laying round logs of wood side by side across the dirt. (④) These log-covered roads had fewer problems with dust and puddles but had other problems. (⑤) Sometimes, their feet got trapped in the gaps between the logs, which caused heavy falls and broken bones.

39

Over the past year, what portion of what you ate did you get directly from nature, by picking it from plants or hunting and killing animals?

Many animals spend the majority of their waking hours looking for food and eating it. They search their environment for things to eat. (①) Some animals search alone, and others search together, but in general they get their food directly from nature. (②) Human food also originates in nature, but most people now get their food from other people. (③) Probably most, if not all, of what you ate came either from supermarkets, where food is prepared and sold by others, or in restaurants and cafeterias, where food grown by some people is cooked and served by others. (④) If all those institutions were to suddenly vanish and people had to get their food directly from nature, most of us would not know how to go about it. (⑤) Many people would starve.

40 다음 글의 내용을 한 문장으로 요약하고자 한다. 빈칸 (A), (B)에 들어갈 말로 가장 적절한 것은? [3점]

In an experiment, psychologist Karl Duncker sat participants down at a table positioned against a wall. He gave each one a candle, a box of tacks, and matches and asked them to attach the candle to the wall. Some participants tried pinning the candle directly to the wall using the tacks. Others attempted to stick the candle to the wall using melted wax, but the tacks were too short, and melted wax didn't bind to the wall. Only a handful of participants thought to use the tack box. These few creative thinkers tacked the box onto the wall, effectively transforming it into a candleholder. Duncker realized that participants were so focused on the tack box's traditional function that they couldn't think of it as a possible solution to the problem.

*tack: 압정; 압정으로 고정하다

↓

In the experiment, participants had a difficult time completing the task because their ____(A)____ with the intended use of the box ____(B)____ their ability to imagine a new use.

	(A)		(B)
①	contact	……	increased
②	contact	……	blocked
③	experience	……	determined
④	familiarity	……	increased
⑤	familiarity	……	blocked

[41~42] 다음 글을 읽고, 물음에 답하시오.

We have more wealth and opportunities in our society than any other in history. But the truth is also that we are among the most __________ people on record. It's not that having a lot of things is harmful in itself. It's the unceasing desire for *more* and *more* that's hurting us. As soon as we get something, we immediately start wanting something better. This eats into our ability to appreciate our many blessings. I know a couple, for example, who bought a beautiful house in a nice area. They loved it until they settled in. Then they started thinking they should have bought a bigger house in a better area, and this way of thinking stopped them from truly enjoying their home.

The trick to overcoming this tendency is to convince ourselves that more *isn't* better. The problem doesn't lie in what we don't have, but in the longing to have it. An excellent measure of happiness is how much difference there is between what you have and what you want. You can spend your lifetime thinking that you'll *really* be happy when you have more — or you can make a conscious decision to want less. This latter strategy is infinitely easier and more fulfilling.

41 윗글의 제목으로 가장 적절한 것은?

① Spending Less, Having More
② Longing for More Is Life Itself
③ A Losing Idea: "More Is Better"
④ Modern Society, Modern Needs
⑤ Modern Desires and Social Conflict

42 윗글의 빈칸에 들어갈 말로 가장 적절한 것은? [3점]

① unhealthy
② intelligent
③ advanced
④ dissatisfied
⑤ lazy

[43~45] 다음 글을 읽고, 물음에 답하시오.

(A)

Paul received an automobile from his brother as a Christmas present. On Christmas Eve when Paul came out of his office, a boy was walking around the shiny new car, admiring it. "Is this your car, Mister?" he asked. Paul nodded. "My brother gave it to me for Christmas." The boy was astounded. "You mean your brother gave it to you and it didn't cost you anything? Boy, I wish..." (a) He hesitated. Of course Paul knew what he was going to wish for. He was going to wish he had a brother like that.

(B)

Paul smiled a little. He thought he knew what the boy wanted. (b) He wanted to show his neighbors that he could ride home in a big automobile. But Paul was wrong again. "Will you stop where those two steps are?" the boy asked. He ran up the steps. Then in a little while Paul heard him coming back, but he was not coming fast. (c) He was carrying his handicapped little brother. He sat him down on the bottom step, then pointed to the car.

(C)

But what the boy said surprised Paul. "I wish," the boy went on, "that I could be a brother like that." Paul looked at the boy in astonishment, then impulsively he added, "Would you like to take a ride in my automobile?" "Oh yes, I'd love that," (d) he said. After a short ride, the boy turned and with his eyes glowing, said, "Mister, would you mind driving in front of my house?"

(D)

"There (e) he is, Buddy, just like I told you upstairs. His brother gave it to him for Christmas and it didn't cost him a cent. And someday I'm going to give you one just like it... then you can see for yourself all the pretty things in the Christmas windows I've told you about." Paul got out and lifted the handicapped boy into the front seat of his car. The shining-eyed older brother climbed in beside him and the three of them began a memorable holiday ride. That Christmas Eve, Paul learned the true meaning of "holiday spirit."

43 주어진 글 (A)에 이어질 내용을 순서에 맞게 배열한 것으로 가장 적절한 것은?

① (B) — (D) — (C)
② (C) — (B) — (D)
③ (C) — (D) — (B)
④ (D) — (B) — (C)
⑤ (D) — (C) — (B)

44 밑줄 친 (a)~(e) 중에서 가리키는 대상이 나머지 넷과 다른 것은?

① (a) ② (b) ③ (c) ④ (d) ⑤ (e)

45 윗글에 관한 내용으로 적절하지 않은 것은?

① Paul은 형에게서 크리스마스 선물로 자동차를 받았다.
② 소년은 동생을 데리고 Paul에게 빨리 오지 못했다.
③ 소년은 동생에게 Paul의 형과 같은 사람이 되길 바랐다.
④ 소년은 Paul에게 차를 태워줄 수 있는지 물었다.
⑤ Paul은 소년의 동생을 차의 앞좌석에 태웠다.

AFTER TESTING

⏲ 종료	시	분
⌛ 소요시간		분

1 채점하기 | 정답 및 해설 p.34
주의 틀린 문제를 다시 풀 수 있도록 정답을 본문에 표기하지 마세요.
2 등급 확인
3 틀린 유형 확인 후 전략 적용 복습 및 해설지 확인

How to Review

1 틀린 문제와 ✓ 표시한 문제는 다시 풀고 해설 확인하기
2 내가 표시한 정답 근거가 해설과 일치하는지 확인하기
3 잘 모르는 부분으로 표시한 내용은 해설을 통해 완전히 이해하기
4 어휘 외우기 (어휘 목록 다운로드 www.cedubook.com)
5 다음 회에 개선할 점 정리하기 (시간 엄수, 취약 유형 보완 등)

BUTTON UP!

실전 모의고사

06

BEFORE TESTING

시작 시 분

학습 목표

1 **제한시간** (OMR 마킹시간 포함) ▢ 40분 ▢ 45분
2 **어휘예습** ▢ 해당 없음 ▢ 완료
3 **문제풀이순서** ▢ 순서대로 ▢ 2점 → 3점 ▢ 기타
4 **기타 목표**

Check Point

1 **정답 근거** *e.g.* 밑줄 긋기
2 **잘 모르는 부분** *e.g.* 〈 〉 또는 ? 표시
3 **자신 없는 문제** *e.g.* 문제 번호에 ✓표시

18 다음 글의 목적으로 가장 적절한 것은?

Dear Linda,

I was very pleased to receive your last letter, and I'm glad you're doing well. Since you mentioned possibly registering your son for Maple Middle School's basketball camp, I want to share my own son's experience. Despite low expectations, my son Dan was quite satisfied with the camp. We paid $200 for a one-week session, and I have no regrets. Dan and the other boys had plenty of time to play on the court each day, and he made several friends who have common interests. Moreover, he said the one-on-one instruction time really improved his game, and he can't stop talking about it. In other words, you won't be disappointed with this camp.

Talk to you soon,
Samantha

① 농구 캠프 참가를 권유하려고
② 전문 농구 코치를 모집하려고
③ 농구 캠프 등록비 환불을 요구하려고
④ 농구 캠프의 문제점에 관해 조언하려고
⑤ 농구 캠프의 만족스런 운영을 칭찬하려고

19 다음 글에 드러난 Brian의 심경 변화로 가장 적절한 것은?

Watching his daughter perform on stage was never easy for Brian. As the head theater teacher at the school, he was both the parent and the director in these situations. Even worse, his daughter had caught a bad cold recently, so he was concerned she wouldn't do as well as she usually did. He began to sweat a little because he thought he wouldn't be able to give her the part. But then he listened more closely to her audition. She wasn't making any mistakes, and her singing was pleasing and confident. As a matter of fact, she was giving her best performance ever. He breathed out slowly and sat back in his chair with a slight smile. He would be able to remain fair and still make her happy. This time, she deserved the lead role, and everyone knew it.

① confident → afraid
② worried → relieved
③ determined → confused
④ outraged → delighted
⑤ nervous → indifferent

20 다음 글에서 필자가 주장하는 바로 가장 적절한 것은?

The government and the press have conflicting purposes. Their perceptions differ; they see things in different ways. But this is not a bad thing. The differences should not be resolved. The government should continue on its course and the media on theirs, as imperfect and unsatisfactory as these courses often are. Certainly there could be improvements. But the basic conflicts should not be removed. The government and the press should function at arm's length. If they do not stay apart, if their purposes are formed into an artificial and unnatural agreement, the nation is harmed.

① 정부와 언론은 자연스러운 갈등 관계를 유지해야 한다.
② 국가의 발전을 위해서는 언론의 자유를 보장해야 한다.
③ 언론을 바라보는 관점은 시대에 따라 바뀌어야 한다.
④ 언론은 국가 정책을 국민에게 정확하게 전달해야 한다.
⑤ 언론은 정부 입장과 여론을 적절하게 조율해야 한다.

21 밑줄 친 flight simulators가 다음 글에서 의미하는 바로 가장 적절한 것은?

When asked how he could succeed, a champion golfer describes how he uses flight simulators in his life. The golfer says, "What you think while playing golf is probably the most important single part of your game." He stresses practicing it on a regular basis. "One secret of a good shot is seeing the ball going where you want it to go before you hit it." Champions must confidently keep the image of a perfect shot in mind, imagining the ball going exactly where it is supposed to go. This principle also works in life. You must know precisely what you want to do in life. You need to set a goal and determine exactly how you will achieve it. Then, you should visualize it at all times. Only then will you be able to accomplish your objective.

① seeing the big picture in life
② using mental images to achieve goals
③ setting a realistic goal and focusing on it
④ imagining success and failure in advance
⑤ understanding the power of positive thinking

22 다음 글의 요지로 가장 적절한 것은?

For many years, literary studies were absorbed in the historical settings of literature. Analysis and criticism of the works themselves were trivial in comparison to the enormous effort expended on the study of the circumstances in which these works were produced. This over-emphasis on the social and political realities of the period in which a work was produced may have prevented real enjoyment of the work itself. In fact, the natural and logical starting point for literary scholarship is the interpretation of the work of literature itself. Only the poems, novels, plays, essays, etc. themselves justify our interest in the lives of authors and the social, political, and historical circumstances in which they worked.

① 풍부한 배경지식으로 작품에 대한 이해를 높일 수 있다.
② 작가를 이해해야 문학 작품을 온전히 이해할 수 있다.
③ 역사를 통한 문학 작품 연구의 한계를 인정해야 한다.
④ 문학을 이해하려면 작품 자체를 깊이 연구해야 한다.
⑤ 시대적 배경과 작품은 밀접한 관계를 맺고 있다.

23 다음 글의 주제로 가장 적절한 것은?

Where do you get information from? You may say the best place to start looking for information is the Internet. Before the invention of the Internet, we acquired information from books. Information from books was typically refined and polished. These days, however, you are able to download all sorts of information that has not been filtered by authorities. The Internet has made it very easy for people to anonymously post their personal ideas and other pieces of writings. As a result, there is a lot of information that is inaccurate and unreliable. There are problems with research based on unfounded sources and biased analyses. The misleading information on the Internet can cause prejudice. You may have heard that knowledge is power. But you should know only reliable information is power.

① problems with information on the Internet
② impact of creating false information online
③ ethics of using information on the Internet
④ tips for searching for information on the Internet
⑤ advantages and disadvantages of Internet information

24 다음 글의 제목으로 가장 적절한 것은?

We human beings love collecting things. We collect toys, coins, seashells — in short, anything that is interesting or curious. There may be many causes for our strong desire to collect things, but one theory says that this desire stems from a feeling that something in one's past is unfinished. Collecting can make us feel as though we are completing something that's missing in our lives. While we are collecting, we are engaged in a kind of worship, experiencing the kind of feeling that people usually associate with meditation or prayer or romantic love. It's almost as if having your own collection of special things is a kind of psychological protection against uncertainty and loss.

① What Items Should You Collect?
② Great Collection Items for Beginners
③ Tips and Tricks to Become a Collector
④ How to Obtain Collectibles with Ease
⑤ Why Do People Collect Things?

25 다음 도표의 내용과 일치하지 않는 것은?

Used Tire Circuit

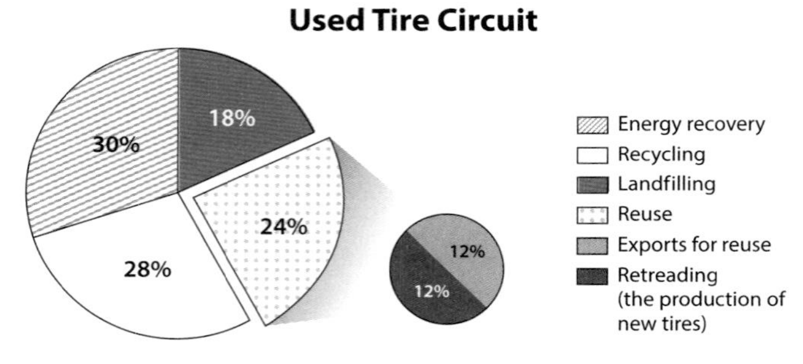

A decade ago, used tires ended up mostly in landfills. Today, old tires can take other routes and return to the economic cycle. ① Around 30% of these tires are used for energy recovery — either in power plants that convert them to electricity or in the market for tire-derived fuel (TDF). ② Just under 30% are recycled into such things as asphalt paving for new roads. ③ The percentage of tires that go to either recycling or energy recovery is over 50%. ④ Landfills unfortunately still account for 18% of used tires. ⑤ Over a fourth of used tires are exported for reuse or go into retreading.

*tire-derived fuel (TDF): 폐타이어를 사용해 만든 연료

26 Hans von Bulow에 관한 다음 글의 내용과 일치하지 않는 것은?

Hans von Bulow was born in 1830 in Dresden. In his youth, Bulow studied piano under Friedrich Wieck, and then with Franz Liszt at Weimer. Later, in Berlin, he was the principal piano teacher at the Stern and Marx school of music and championed the works of the "New German School" of Liszt and Wagner. Beginning in the 1850s, he toured Europe, England, and the United States as an expert pianist; he is said to have known virtually every major work of his day. He became director of music at the Munich court in 1864, where he conducted the first performances of two of Wagner's works. He conducted at Hannover from 1878 to 1880 and at Meiningen from 1880 to 1885, where his orchestra became one of the finest in Europe. His interpretations were widely respected for their integrity and emotional power.

① Friedrich Wieck 문하에서 피아노를 배웠다.
② Stern and Marx 음악 학교의 피아노 교사가 되었다.
③ 1850년대에 유럽, 잉글랜드, 미국 순회공연을 했다.
④ Munich에서 Liszt의 두 작품의 초연 지휘를 맡았다.
⑤ 1880년대 전반기에 Meiningen에서 지휘자로 활동했다.

27 Book Dating Club에 관한 다음 안내문의 내용과 일치하지 않는 것은?

Book Dating Club

A new way to share the books you love, and maybe find new love

- Takes place on the 3rd Sunday of the month, from 6:00-7:30 p.m.
- Registration is available online until 24 hours before the program, and over the phone (702-338-4565) up until the start of the program.

Frequently Asked Questions:

How does it work?
Grab a couple of books you'd like to share: Any genre of book is welcome.

Who attends?
We've hosted guests ranging in age from their early 20s to early 60s. In January, we had 39 attendees!

And then?
Each book date will be timed at 4 minutes, allowing all participants an opportunity to meet and chat about their reading.

① 매월 세 번째 일요일 오후에 열린다.
② 등록은 사전에 전화와 방문으로 가능하다.
③ 가져오는 책의 장르에 특별한 제한은 없다.
④ 20대부터 60대에 이르는 연령층이 참여한다.
⑤ 한 책에 대해 4분간 공유할 시간이 주어진다.

28 *The Story* Writing Contest에 관한 다음 안내문의 내용과 일치하는 것은?

***The Story* Writing Contest is now open.**
Submit today!

If you love to write, we're looking for one great story. *The Story* will consider original, unpublished fiction written by teens. We are interested in great fiction of any genre including literary, fantasy, sci-fi, romance, and horror.

Prizes
- $500 and 25 copies of the magazine featuring the prize-winning pieces
- An opportunity to edit his/her story for publication with an editor at *The Story*

Guidelines
- Short stories should be between 1,800 and 4,000 words and be the writer's own original, unpublished work.
- No entry form or fee is required.
- *The Story* reserves the right to publish the story in the form we choose.

Deadline
June 30

① 공상 과학 소설은 심사에서 제외된다.
② 당선되면 상금과 잡지 구독권을 받는다.
③ 당선작은 별도의 편집 과정 없이 출판된다.
④ 제출 작품의 최대 길이는 4,000 단어이다.
⑤ 저자는 자신이 정한 양식대로 출판할 권리를 가진다.

29 다음 글의 밑줄 친 부분 중, 어법상 틀린 것은? [3점]

The traditional idea about teaching English to ESL (English as a Second Language) students ① is that the students must become proficient in English before they can start studying science or math through English. But recent international conferences and studies involving education experts and experienced teachers have promoted the alternative view ② that the integration of science, math, and language studies can strengthen a student's overall progress and performance. In fact, many of the teachers concerned insist that integrating English-language instruction with science and math definitely ③ work for the students in their classrooms. The teachers have made their work ④ available online. This action encourages other schools and teachers ⑤ to adopt similar strategies for integrating science, math, and English-language acquisition.

30 (A), (B), (C)의 각 네모 안에서 문맥에 맞는 낱말로 가장 적절한 것은? [3점]

Suppose you get a bike for a Christmas present this year. If you're smart you will enjoy riding it for years before it (A) [wears out / works out]. But if you're not so smart, it won't be long before it's rusty, broken, useless, and forgotten. The same goes for your body. After all, it's not only a machine, but the best and most useful one in the world. (B) [With / Without] care, it should last at least 80 years, but it will soon fail you badly if you neglect and abuse it. The main difference between bodies and bikes is that you can always buy another two-wheeler. But when your body is ruined by neglect, a little money will not be enough to (C) [damage / restore] it.

	(A)		(B)		(C)
①	wears out	……	With	……	damage
②	wears out	……	With	……	restore
③	wears out	……	Without	……	damage
④	works out	……	With	……	damage
⑤	works out	……	Without	……	restore

[31~34] 다음 빈칸에 들어갈 말로 가장 적절한 것을 고르시오.

31

Former U.S. President Barack Obama is renowned as a great public speaker. During his campaign for health care reform, he often spoke of his mother's death from cancer, and the story was enough to move people to cry. "She should have been devoting everything to fighting the cancer," he said. "Instead, she had to fight her insurance company, who tried to get out of paying for her hospital bills." Painting a vivid picture of his mother's dying struggle helped Obama to win much support, and he eventually turned his health care reform bill into law. We have long understood the power of __________ in guiding people. As Barack Obama has shown, it can also help to bring about great social change. [3점]

① fear
② intuition
③ will
④ simplicity
⑤ storytelling

32 Have you ever noticed that there are lessons to be learned from the things that ______________________? It seems as if you have fallen in love with the same person several times in different bodies with different names. You may keep running into the same type of boss, or keep having the same conflicts with co-workers, no matter where you work. Eventually you may realize that these are opportunities to learn valuable lessons; for example, to treat your loved ones better, or how to get along with colleagues. In the 1993 movie *Groundhog Day*, Bill Murray plays the role of a selfish and bored TV weatherman, who wakes up on the same day over and over again. The same events replay, and the same things keep happening to him. At last he learns that to break the cycle and be free and happy, he himself must change. [3점]

① usually come from failure
② make you wiser and stronger
③ are presented at the right time
④ are likely to be learned too late
⑤ repeat themselves in everyday life

33 In 1968, a NASA scientist gave a creativity test to 1,600 five-year-olds and 98% passed it. Five years later the children were tested again. Incredibly, only 30% of the ten-year-old children passed the test. Twenty-eight thousand adults were given the same test; not more than 2% passed it. The results led the scientist to conclude that non-creative thinking is acquired. But how? Why do we become less creative? It's probably because creativity has been ______________________ ______________. "Modern" schools were born in the Industrial Revolution, more than 200 years ago, and were designed for the purpose of producing obedient factory workers. In fact, the modern education system was once called the "factory model," because it was based on making children behave like well-regulated machines. [3점]

① studied from a regulated perspective
② discouraged by incompetent teachers
③ taken more seriously by governments
④ ignored across the school curriculum
⑤ regarded as an aspect of personality

34 You are driving down a dark, winding road in a rainstorm. It is a chilling fall rain that soaks through to the bone. You round a corner and hit a patch of leaves that unfortunately have covered a pile of glass. Within moments, your tire blows out and you find yourself stranded on the road. You reach for your cell phone and realize that the battery is dead. You should have charged it before you left the office. Before heading out in the rain, you reach for your umbrella and realize it is broken from the last windy storm. You should have replaced it. You get out in the rain, open your trunk and realize your jacket is missing because you let a neighbor borrow it and it was never returned. What will you do now? Remember that Boy Scout motto from when you were a kid? ______________________________.

① Don't seek hot water in a well
② Dig a well before you are thirsty
③ It's the thirsty man who digs a well
④ Keep digging a well until you find water
⑤ It is impossible to dig a well with a shovel

35 **다음 글에서 전체 흐름과 관계 없는 문장은?**

In certain parts of the world, visitors from English-speaking countries may find themselves in trouble if they aren't aware that it's not polite to give "no" as an answer. ① One such part of the world is Indonesia, where the native language, Bahasa Indonesia, has twelve words to say "yes" but actually mean "no." ② Unless you are fluent in Bahasa, you will not convey the correct message of disagreement. ③ Even with a proper translation, you may not convey quite the right tone of "no" and your listener may misunderstand you. ④ However, most Indonesians, aside from speaking Bahasa, are often fluent in another regional language which is commonly used within the local community. ⑤ Since it isn't polite for Indonesians to say "no," visitors shouldn't think that their positive answer means "yes."

[36~37] 주어진 글 다음에 이어질 글의 순서로 가장 적절한 것을 고르시오.

36

When it comes to emotions, we often pay attention to cultural differences. European attitudes about the people of Asia are a good example. For a long time in England and other parts of Europe, people from Asia were commonly described as being mysterious.

(A) The Japanese do, in fact, try harder to hide their emotions than do people in Europe and North America. In Europe and North America, people encourage vivid facial expressions that show emotions; a poker face is generally regarded as dull or dishonest.

(B) In Japan, on the other hand, excessive emotional displays are often perceived as rude, and Japanese people consequently make an effort to minimize their emotional expressions.

(C) This stereotype was from the fact that European travellers found it hard to read the locals' emotions. They wondered, for example, whether the poker face of the Japanese might hide emotions that were very different from their own. [3점]

*poker face: 무표정한 얼굴

① (A) — (C) — (B)
② (B) — (A) — (C)
③ (B) — (C) — (A)
④ (C) — (A) — (B)
⑤ (C) — (B) — (A)

37

If you lend your friend the money in your wallet, your opportunity cost is the sacrifice of its immediate use. When your friend eventually pays you back, the money will have lost purchasing power due to inflation.

(A) When you deposit money in your savings account, you expect to earn interest for the same reason. Otherwise you would just stuff the money under your mattress.

(B) There is also the risk that your friend will move to Costa Rica and "forget" to pay you back. As a result, when people lend money, they often ask to be rewarded with an additional payment — interest — to offset the opportunity cost and inflation.

(C) For example, the chair that cost $50 when you loaned the money might cost $55 two years later when your friend pays you back, meaning not only were you unable to buy the chair when you first needed it, but it will cost you more to buy it now.

① (A) — (C) — (B)
② (B) — (A) — (C)
③ (B) — (C) — (A)
④ (C) — (A) — (B)
⑤ (C) — (B) — (A)

[38~39] 글의 흐름으로 보아, 주어진 문장이 들어가기에 가장 적절한 곳을 고르시오.

38

> It's hardly surprising that men are tempted to eat if the cupboards are suddenly filled with ready-to-eat foods.

It's not just women who gain weight during pregnancy. (①) A survey found that 25 percent of fathers-to-be also gained weight during their partner's pregnancy. (②) One of the reasons they gave for gaining weight was "eating out of sympathy for my partner." (③) In other words, they eat more to make their partner feel better about her weight gain by gaining weight themselves. (④) Besides, pregnant women tend to crave snacks and thus keep more of them in the house. (⑤) This new abundance of snacking opportunities, rather than "sympathy" eating, is the more likely cause of weight gain in fathers-to-be.

39

> By contrast, baseball, football, and basketball players really do what spectators see them do.

Actors give scripted performances, which are designed by others and in which all cooperate to achieve a planned outcome. (①) The tension in movies, and all forms of drama, affects the audience but usually not the participants. (②) But players in games give unscripted performances in which two sides compete, with each trying to produce a different — indeed the opposite — outcome. (③) Actors who appear to do dangerous, difficult things on the screen almost never actually do them. (④) Their doubles take the real hazards, and the acts are usually made to appear more dangerous than they actually are. (⑤) What they do is real and the outcome of their efforts is unknown in advance to both audience and participants.

*double: 대역배우

40 다음 글의 내용을 한 문장으로 요약하고자 한다. 빈칸 (A), (B)에 들어갈 말로 가장 적절한 것은?

> Are you feeling down? Why not take the advice of two famous psychologists? Psychologist Carl Menninger once was answering questions from the audience at one of his lectures. Someone asked, "What would you advise a person to do if that person felt depressed?" Most people thought he would say, "Go and see a doctor immediately," but he didn't. To their surprise, Dr. Menninger replied, "Lock up your house, go across the railroad tracks, find somebody in trouble, and help that person. Don't focus on yourself; instead, get involved in the lives of other people." Once, psychologist Alfred Adler gave similar advice to his clients. He claimed that he could cure anyone of depression in just fourteen days. Adler used to tell his clients: "If you do something for another person every day for two weeks, your depression will be gone."

↓

> According to two psychologists above, the effective way to overcome depression is not to be ____(A)____ but to be ____(B)____ to others.

	(A)		(B)
①	self-absorbed	......	indifferent
②	self-confident	......	compassionate
③	self-willed	......	polite
④	self-absorbed	......	compassionate
⑤	self-confident	......	indifferent

[41~42] 다음 글을 읽고, 물음에 답하시오.

The essence of friendship is equality. True friendship is not just the power and gifts. It must also be based on (a) common interests and feelings and thoughts. What is certain is that pretended friendship, where there is nothing to share, does not work. Friendship is not a (b) variable thing. It is like a river, meaningful only if it is heading in some direction. It must always be developing, expanding, and absorbing new experiences. As someone once put it, "The English do not have friends; they have friends about things." A (c) shared activity or need is behind friendship. There are so many people in the world. Why spend time with just this one? Because one enjoys their company, they are "good fun," amusing, supportive, and kind. As we shall see, this often finds its strongest expression in playing games with them. Friends must not be (d) calculating. True friends show you who they really are. Friendship follows a central rule of ethics — namely that "We should treat people as ends in themselves and not as a means to an end." If you feel a friend is "using you," then the friendship ends. Just as true love and beauty cannot be bought or sold, so friendship cannot be purchased. You cannot go to an agency and buy or hire a friend, while you certainly can hire a person's mind or body for a particular task. So friendship is about the long-term liking of two equal people for each other. We have to work at friendship; it neither comes naturally nor remains without constant (e) attention. Friends can be compared to an orchard: they have to be carefully planted, pruned and protected.

*prune: 가지치기하다

41 윗글의 제목으로 가장 적절한 것은?

① How Do Friends Communicate?
② Good Friends Are Hard to Find
③ How Friendships Change over Time
④ Friendship: Conditions and Meanings
⑤ Importance of Developing a Healthy Friendship

42 밑줄 친 (a)~(e) 중에서 문맥상 낱말의 쓰임이 적절하지 않은 것은? [3점]

① (a) ② (b) ③ (c) ④ (d) ⑤ (e)

[43~45] 다음 글을 읽고, 물음에 답하시오.

(A)

If you worry about where you're at in life, and you think you're not getting any closer to that dream of yours, then ask yourself this: "What am I doing with what I have right now?" If the answer is, "Not much, because what I have is not enough to do much with," then the only problem is you. Because the world rewards effort, not excuses.

(B)

Well, (a) he got the job. A month later, the prep cook quit, and Tony was on his way to becoming the best chef that the restaurant's owner had ever had. That restaurant owner is Bernard, and Tony is the old friend. Regarding Tony's journey, the lesson you can learn from (b) him, in short, is to start wherever you can. Put your best into whatever is there in front of you, and opportunities will start knocking on your door. It's putting the "one thing leads to another" principle into action.

(C)

Think, for instance, of those people you admire for their amazing jobs or wonderful achievements. Well, one thing for sure is that they all made an effort to start somewhere, and that's what led to the next opportunity and the next. When I hear people say "There aren't any jobs out there!" I think of a story that my friend Bernard, a very successful owner of restaurants, once told me. He told me how an old friend of (c) his, named Tony, got his first job in New York.

(D)

He had just arrived from Italy, had no money, spoke no English, and went to an Italian restaurant to apply for work as a dishwasher. After being told to wait, (d) he went to the bathroom, found a brush, and scrubbed the tiles and toilets until they were spotless. By the time he was interviewed, everyone in the restaurant was asking what had happened to the bathroom. They soon found out that it was Tony's way of saying, "(e) I'm a hard worker and serious about cleaning."

43 주어진 글 (A)에 이어질 내용을 순서에 맞게 배열한 것으로 가장 적절한 것은?

① (B) — (C) — (D)　② (B) — (D) — (C)
③ (C) — (B) — (D)　④ (C) — (D) — (B)
⑤ (D) — (C) — (B)

44 밑줄 친 (a)~(e) 중에서 가리키는 대상이 나머지 넷과 다른 것은?

① (a)　② (b)　③ (c)　④ (d)　⑤ (e)

45 윗글의 Tony에 관한 내용으로 적절하지 않은 것은?

① 식당의 최고 요리사가 되었다.
② Bernard의 식당에서 일한다.
③ 미국에 온 후 뉴욕에서 처음 일자리를 구했다.
④ 식당을 청소하는 일에 지원했다.
⑤ 면접을 기다리는 동안 식당 화장실을 청소했다.

AFTER TESTING

⏱ 종료 시 분

⧗ 소요시간 분

1 채점하기 | 정답 및 해설 p.41

주의 틀린 문제를 다시 풀 수 있도록 정답을 본문에 표기하지 마세요.

2 등급 확인

3 틀린 유형 확인 후 전략 적용 복습 및 해설지 확인

How to Review

1 틀린 문제와 ✓ 표시한 문제는 다시 풀고 해설 확인하기

2 내가 표시한 정답 근거가 해설과 일치하는지 확인하기

3 잘 모르는 부분으로 표시한 내용은 해설을 통해 완전히 이해하기

4 어휘 외우기 (어휘 목록 다운로드 www.cedubook.com)

5 다음 회에 개선할 점 정리하기 (시간 엄수, 취약 유형 보완 등)

BUTTON UP!

실전 모의고사

07

BEFORE TESTING

시작 시 분

1 **제한시간** (OMR 마킹시간 포함) ☐ 40분 ☐ 45분
2 **어휘예습** ☐ 해당 없음 ☐ 완료
3 **문제풀이순서** ☐ 순서대로 ☐ 2점 → 3점 ☐ 기타
4 **기타 목표**

Check Point

1 **정답 근거** *e.g.* 밑줄 긋기
2 **잘 모르는 부분** *e.g.* 〈 〉 또는 ? 표시
3 **자신 없는 문제** *e.g.* 문제 번호에 ✓표시

18 다음 글의 목적으로 가장 적절한 것은?

To Whom It May Concern,

My family and I recently participated in one of your "Treetop Adventure" courses for families, and while it was certainly fun and exciting, there was a small problem. Now, let me be clear, the fault here is entirely mine. Our guide was clear that no jewelry should be worn when attempting the zip line or the rope swing, but it seems my daughter didn't listen carefully. Upon arriving home, she realized she had lost her gold necklace. As this was a gift from her grandmother, she is understandably upset. So, if anyone should happen to find a necklace in the woods beneath the zip line, please contact me. I would greatly appreciate your help, and I'm also willing to offer a small reward for your trouble. Thank you in advance for your help, and keep up the good work in running such a wonderful program!

Sincerely,
Chaerin Lee

*zip line: 집라인(강이나 계곡을 건너는 운송수단으로 이용되는 밧줄 기구)

① 취득한 습득물에 대해 문의하려고
② 딸의 잘못된 행동에 대해 사과하려고
③ 분실물 회수에 대한 도움을 요청하려고
④ 모험 프로그램의 진행에 대해 항의하려고
⑤ 프로그램 안내원의 친절한 행동을 알리려고

19 다음 글에 드러난 'I'의 심경 변화로 가장 적절한 것은?

I'm waiting by the pool. In a few minutes, I'll start my first race. My heart beats fast, my knees begin to tremble. I want to do well, but I'm going to finish last. I know it. I'm not a very strong swimmer. All I can do is to do my best. Finally they call all 50-meter freestyle race participants. I feel sick, but I stand up. I am in group two, but it doesn't help my feelings. The first group goes, and the second group prepares to dive in. The whistle blows. Wheeeeet! We are off! Splash! Splish, splosh, splish, splosh. I grab the wall and look around. I am not the last. In fact, almost everyone is behind me. Someone hands me a blue stick for second place. Wow, I am not last! I am almost first. I did it.

① sad → happy
② nervous → excited
③ satisfied → disappointed
④ bored → delighted
⑤ fearful → angry

20 다음 글에서 필자가 주장하는 바로 가장 적절한 것은?

It has become trendy to argue that aid isn't the solution to Africa's troubles; this argument has its weaknesses and strengths. The weaknesses lie in the fact that aid directly saves lives — especially when it targets such diseases as HIV and malaria. On the other hand, the strengths of this argument lie in the fact that aid *alone* won't reverse Africa's poverty or underdevelopment. I am incredibly proud of the progress that has been achieved by those countries working with the Africa Governance Initiative, which supports reconstruction programs in Rwanda and Sierra Leone. The leaders of the member nations are serious about ending corruption and protecting investors. They believe, as I do, that good governance, a strong economy, and non-reliance on aid are the keys to recovery and prosperity for Africa.

① 아프리카 원조 기금은 질병 치료에 우선 쓰여야 한다.
② 아프리카가 가난한 이유는 정권의 부정부패 때문이다.
③ 선진국은 아프리카 국가들을 원조해야 할 책임이 있다.
④ 아프리카 국가들은 자립을 통해 문제를 해결해야 한다.
⑤ 아프리카의 빈곤 문제가 대물림되지 않도록 해야 한다.

21 밑줄 친 The wind always won이 다음 글에서 의미하는 바로 가장 적절한 것은?

A log cabin is a small log house, with a less finished structure. Log cabins have an ancient history in Europe and in America are often associated with first-generation home building by settlers. Living rooms, dining rooms, and bedrooms did not exist in most 19th-century log cabins in the United States. There was just one room without inside walls. The floor was made of mud. These cabins were very cold with no protection from the cold and no way to keep the damp from coming up through the earthen floor. What is more, the wind blew through gaps in the log walls. To prevent this, settlers made a cement out of mud and straw, but rarely could they fill every gap. The wind always won.

① The wind came through the walls
② It was always windy near log houses
③ The cracks in the wall became wider
④ The house was surrounded by a light wind
⑤ The wind dried up the humidity in the house

22 다음 글의 요지로 가장 적절한 것은?

Imagine a situation in which a parent provides his/her child with feedback: "Mary, I like the way you handled the disappointment of not being able to go to the movies. I know that you were a little upset. You handled your feelings well. You told me you were mad, and then you went into the other room and found a craft project to do." The parent here pointed out to the child exactly what she did. This kind of feedback is instructive to the child; it reinforces good problem-solving skills and good communication skills. Parents can help their children succeed by providing productive feedback. This is an evaluation we make of another person's performance and behavior that is direct, specific, objective, and accurate. It is rational, and it is provided for positive as well as for negative behavior.

① 진심이 담긴 피드백이 자녀의 마음을 움직인다.
② 간결하고 핵심적인 피드백이 자녀 지도에 효과적이다.
③ 의사소통 능력이 뛰어난 아이가 부모의 피드백에 수용적이다.
④ 부정적인 행동에는 중재자를 통해 피드백을 제시하는 것이 좋다.
⑤ 구체적이고 객관적인 피드백이 자녀의 성공에 도움이 된다.

23 다음 글의 주제로 가장 적절한 것은?

Farmers in China's Sichuan Province can no longer rely on honeybees to pollinate their fruit trees. Instead, workers have been doing the job by hand. The Chinese farmers' experience is only one of many troubling signs of an environmental and agricultural disaster in the making. All over the world, colonies of bees have been dying mysteriously, which has caused crops to fail. Thirty-five percent of U.S. bee colonies collapsed last winter, after 30 percent collapsed the year before. Losses have been equally devastating in countries as widespread as Australia, Brazil, India, and South Africa, as well as throughout Europe. The British Beekeepers Association has warned that honeybees could disappear entirely from the U.K. within 10 years, along with all of the apples, pears, almonds, and every other crop that needs them.

① merits of bee pollination and organic farming
② disappearance of bees and its possible impacts
③ recent developments in beekeeping techniques
④ worldwide comparison of crop pollination methods
⑤ strategies for dealing with impending agricultural crisis

24 다음 글의 제목으로 가장 적절한 것은?

Most people have a list of "someday whens" — things they will do someday when.... Someday when they have more time, they will take the family on that grand vacation. Someday when they have more money, they will start contributing to the causes that mean something to them. And the list goes on and on. And all of these "someday whens" become a burden. The quickest way to throw off that yoke is to make "someday whens" today. You can't make footprints in the sands of time while sitting on your butt. You know people who are currently making butt prints in the sands of time. They have lots of dreams and ambitions, but unfortunately none of them are accompanied by any real action.

*yoke: 멍에, 굴레

① Set a Realistic Goal to Pursue
② Become a Doer, Not a Dreamer
③ Divide Your Tasks and Conquer
④ Always Focus on Your Strengths
⑤ Try to Do Important Things First

25 다음 도표의 내용과 일치하지 않는 것은?

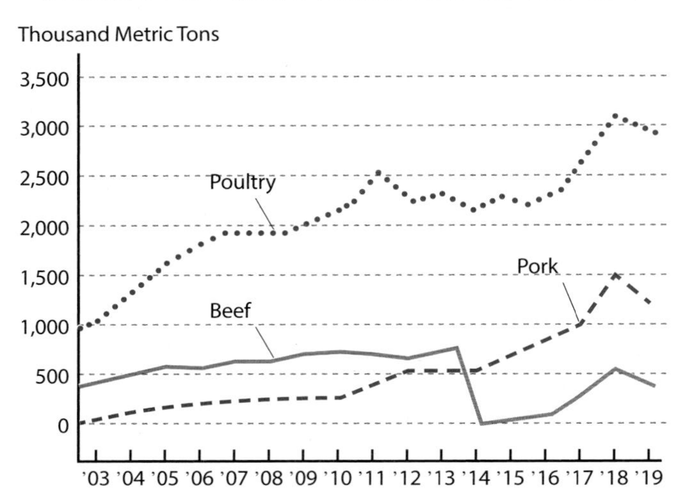

This chart illustrates U.S. exports of meat, measured in units of thousand metric tons, in three animal groups: beef (cows), pork (pigs), and poultry (chickens, turkeys), from 2003 to 2019. ① Poultry exports over the entire period were greater than exports of both beef and pork. ② There was a very sharp drop in beef exports beginning in 2013 and ending in 2014. ③ The gap between beef exports and pork exports narrowed after 2014. ④ Exports of pork showed steady growth until 2017, and a sudden upward movement was shown between 2017 and 2018. ⑤ The year 2018 saw a decline in all three export categories, and none regained growth.

*metric ton: 미터톤(1,000kg에 해당하는 단위)

26 Komodo dragon에 관한 다음 글의 내용과 일치하지 않는 것은?

The Komodo dragon is a species of lizard native to the Indonesian islands of Komodo, Rinca, Flores, and Gili Motang. It's the largest lizard species in existence, averaging between two and three meters in length and around 70 kilograms in weight as an adult. Despite its big ear holes, it has a limited hearing range and is unable to detect both very low-pitched and very high-pitched sounds. It sees in color, and its range of vision extends to 300 meters, but it can't see well at night or detect non-moving objects very easily. Like many other reptiles, the Komodo dragon has a highly sensitive tongue and uses it to detect movements, smells, temperature changes, and other important signals in its environment.

*reptile: 파충류

① 인도네시아의 4개 섬에 서식한다.
② 평균적으로 2~3미터까지 자란다.
③ 귓구멍의 크기에 비해 청각은 좋지 않다.
④ 야간에도 300미터 전방까지 볼 수 있다.
⑤ 잘 발달한 혀로 온도 변화를 감지한다.

27 SFA Student Design Contest에 관한 다음 안내문의 내용과 일치하지 않는 것은?

Scholarship: SFA Student Design Contest

Have you ever imagined what it'd be like to design your own lab? This is what Scientific Furniture Association (SFA) is looking to do. Innovative designs for any piece of laboratory equipment or furniture are accepted.

How to Apply:

- All required information must be provided and your entry/abstract received on or before April 1. Your abstract summarizing your design must be less than 250 words.
- There is no fee to enter this competition.

Award Amount: $6,000
Number of Awards Available: 3
Requirements: Must be a senior in high school. Students can work individually or as part of a team with teams consisting of a maximum of 3 participants.

① 연구실 관련 디자인 경연 대회이다.
② 4월 1일까지 응모할 수 있다.
③ 대회 참가비는 무료이다.
④ 고등학교 3학년만 참가 가능하다.
⑤ 3명 이상이면 팀으로 참가할 수 있다.

28 The National Museum of the American Indian에 관한 다음 안내문의 내용과 일치하는 것은?

The National Museum of the American Indian

The museum's permanent and temporary exhibitions — as well as many public programs, including music and dance performances — explore the diversity of the native people of America.

Hours & Admission

The museum is open 10 A.M. – 5 P.M. daily, Thursdays 10 A.M. – 8 P.M. Admission is free.

Getting Here

The museum is located on the National Mall between the Smithsonian's National Air & Space Museum and the U.S. Capitol Building.

- **Metro**
  L'Enfant Plaza (Blue/Orange lines), exit Maryland Avenue/Smithsonian Museums
- **Bus**
  Lines 30, 32, 34 — Southern Avenue
- **Parking**
  Parking is not available but there are several parking garages located nearby.

Security

Check the Smithsonian website for the latest on security procedures at Smithsonian museums.

① 전시물들은 모두 영구적으로 전시되는 것들이다.
② 목요일은 다른 날보다 개관 시간이 짧다.
③ National Mall과 Smithsonian 박물관 사이에 있다.
④ 박물관에는 주차할 수 없지만 근처에 주차장이 있다.
⑤ 보안 절차는 따로 마련되어 있지 않다.

29 다음 글의 밑줄 친 부분 중, 어법상 틀린 것은? [3점]

Questions surrounding language and its relationship to the way we think ① have been food for thought to philosophers and linguists for centuries. For instance, do people who speak different languages think and behave ② differently because of their language? According to the Sapir-Whorf hypothesis, the answer is yes. The hypothesis ③ was named after the American anthropologists Edward Sapir and Benjamin Whorf, who argued strongly that human thought is shaped by language. People at the time found ④ them hard to agree with a hypothesis that says we are all controlled by language and cannot think independently. But Sapir and Whorf's studies of the Hopi Indian language do suggest ⑤ that language does at least partially determine thought.

*hypothesis: 가설

30 다음 글의 밑줄 친 부분 중, 문맥상 낱말의 쓰임이 적절하지 않은 것은?

It seems that it never snows on the very coldest of winter days. Can the weather get too ① cold to snow? Well, the colder the air is, the less evaporated water it can hold, and any temperature lower than 40 degrees below zero makes it very ② hard to produce snow. There's essentially no moisture in the air at very low temperatures. This is because most of it has already condensed at ③ higher temperatures and fallen back to earth in the form of rain or snow. As temperatures rise, the amount of moisture in the air ④ rises. That's why Antarctica is not only the coldest place on earth but also the ⑤ wettest continent.

[31~34] 다음 빈칸에 들어갈 말로 가장 적절한 것을 고르시오.

31 Creative geniuses develop special abilities that make their thoughts ______________. These abilities give them the flexibility to display information in different ways. The explosion of creativity in the Renaissance was intimately tied to the development of graphic illustration by Leonardo da Vinci. Galileo Galilei showed his ideas through graphs while his contemporaries used more conventional means. Similarly, Albert Einstein thought in terms of spatial forms rather than along purely mathematical or verbal lines. Oftentimes he would draw just to illustrate how he saw the problem in his head. In fact, he believed that words and numbers, as they are written or spoken, did not play a significant role in his thinking process.

① logical
② visible
③ simple
④ interesting
⑤ conceptual

32 Believe it or not, it seems that taking a shower might not always be good for you. Researchers at the University of Colorado found that harmful bacteria grow very well in shower heads. The researchers also said that, in showers that have the bacteria, the first sprays of water coming out of the shower are the most likely to harm you. The shower acts like an aerosol, spraying the bacteria into the air, which means that our daily shower may not be the clean-and-healthy necessity that we like to think it is. Fifty different types of showers were tested in hundreds of homes across the States. A third of these had very high levels of bacteria that can cause lung damage. Head researcher Leonie Baum gave the following advice: "To avoid getting a lot of the bacteria into your body, don't stand under the shower ______________________________." [3점]

① if it is too old to use
② when it first starts running
③ before the water gets warm
④ after finishing your bath
⑤ while washing your hair

33 Once leaders start getting employees to collaborate, they face a different problem: overdoing it. Collaboration becomes something that slows things down instead of something that aids productivity. Effective collaborative leaders ______________________________. Team members need the freedom to be creative, but there must also be someone in charge who can make final decisions and end discussions. When teams meet, people should propose ideas and challenge one another. They may debate loudly and even furiously until the best idea wins. But if no obvious agreement is reached in time, the person leading the meeting must make a decision that the rest of the group will accept. [3점]

① take a strong role in directing teams
② listen to the opinions of every participant
③ distribute tasks evenly among team members
④ allow members to work at their own pace
⑤ use a variety of management techniques

34 Scientists at Oregon Health & Science University in the United States carried out tests on 47 female monkeys. Their study was originally designed to find out more about the relationship between female hormones and weight gain. However, unexpectedly, the researchers found no link between when the animals ate and how much weight they put on. "We've been told that eating late at night should be avoided because it will cause weight gain. However, it may in fact be somewhat of an urban myth," said Dr. Cameron. "I think it dates back to when people started taking an interest in diets. People are more likely to eat fatty snacks at night when they are watching television. In order to try to avoid that, they put restrictions on when they should eat," he added. So if you feel the urge to creep into the kitchen late at night, don't worry. ______________________. [3점]

*urban myth: 도시 괴담

① There are simple ways to beat an eating disorder
② You can easily fix the hormones that make you obese
③ Your body doesn't really recognize what time of day it is
④ How much weight you gain doesn't depend on what you eat
⑤ Weight measurement alone cannot determine body fat status

35 **다음 글에서 전체 흐름과 관계 없는 문장은?** [3점]

Different people are motivated by different things. Politicians chase after power, bankers chase after big profits. Others may be motivated by moral ideals. ① The main thing is that everyone is motivated by something, and a lack of motivation causes boredom, frustration, unhappiness, and idleness. ② To stay productive at work, how you are compensated for your work should be closely tied to what motivates you. ③ Respecting workers' skills and learning styles is the key to encouraging happiness and productivity. ④ For example, if you are motivated by security, it would be a bad idea for you to work in a high-risk job. ⑤ Likewise, it's a mistake to make someone work longer hours if they are motivated by having leisure time, because their productivity will slide even if you increase their pay.

[36~37] 주어진 글 다음에 이어질 글의 순서로 가장 적절한 것을 고르시오.

36

Cross-cultural difficulties can happen when there are conflicting ideas about what friends are supposed to do.

(A) And even in the case of close friends, people can still feel uncomfortable when asked or asking such favors. It's easy to see how misunderstandings can arise in situations where expectations of friendship do not match.

(B) But, in most of North America, much depends on the individual friendship itself rather than on broader social customs. Generally, it isn't acceptable to ask big favors of anyone except very close friends you've known for a long time.

(C) What one culture considers to be a routine favor that any friend can ask may be considered terribly rude elsewhere. For instance, it's fine in Mexico to ask a friend to get you a job or loan you money.

① (A) — (C) — (B)
② (B) — (A) — (C)
③ (B) — (C) — (A)
④ (C) — (A) — (B)
⑤ (C) — (B) — (A)

37

When an animal is injured, the first thing it will do, if it is able, is get back on its feet.

(A) Just labeling this as denial misses the deeper truth. The organism, animal or human, is trying not only to *look* fine in order to avoid attack, but trying to *be* fine.

(B) Despite the fact that this action will probably cause further pain, the instinct to get up drives the animal because the alternative, taking no action to get up, invites predators who will kill and eat the defenseless one.

(C) Emotionally, we do the same thing. Often a person who has just suffered an injury or a great shock or loss will respond, "Fine" when asked, "How are you doing?"

*get back on one's feet: 재빨리 일어나다

① (A) — (C) — (B)
② (B) — (A) — (C)
③ (B) — (C) — (A)
④ (C) — (A) — (B)
⑤ (C) — (B) — (A)

[38~39] 글의 흐름으로 보아, 주어진 문장이 들어가기에 가장 적절한 곳을 고르시오.

38

> While it changes as we age and can be altered by makeup or cosmetic surgery, it's the essence of what we look like.

Many cultures have original proverbs expressing the belief that one's face is a reflection of one's soul. (①) The very popularity of these proverbs tells us of the human fascination with faces. (②) One thing that's especially fascinating is that we are really talking about *three* faces. (③) The first is what we might call our "foundation" face, the one we're born with. (④) Another is the face we are able to change at will, for instance when we decide to smile, frown, look surprised, and so on. (⑤) Finally, there's the one that changes according to the situations we may be in, or the messages we're receiving.

39

> More specifically, they were "shark finning" — cutting off a shark's fins and throwing the shark back into the water to die a terrible death.

Costa Rican biologist Randall Arauz won the Goldman Prize — the "Nobel of ecological activism" — for bringing international attention to a cruel and environmentally disastrous industry. (①) He was investigating fishing practices associated with the deaths of turtles when he discovered an even greater problem. (②) He found that Chinese fishing boats were hunting for sharks in Costa Rica's waters. (③) It's cheaper to throw the sharks back like this, because the fins alone are worth a fortune. (④) In fact, they sell for as much as $100 per kilogram in China, where the appetite for shark fin soup is huge. (⑤) Arauz managed to end shark finning in Costa Rica, which is now the global leader in the protection of sharks.

*fin: 지느러미

40

다음 글의 내용을 한 문장으로 요약하고자 한다. 빈칸 (A), (B)에 들어갈 말로 가장 적절한 것은? [3점]

> Imagine that you are out walking with a friend and you find two lottery tickets. You decide to take one ticket each. Your friend kindly says that you can decide which of the two tickets you want to keep. One ticket has the numbers 1, 2, 3, 4, 5, 6. The other ticket has the numbers 5, 18, 19, 31, 35, 45. Which ticket would you choose to keep? Statistically, both tickets have an equal probability of winning. So it doesn't matter which ticket you choose because they both have the same chance of winning. However, many people would choose the second ticket over the first. Why is this? We view the second ticket to be more representative of a winning lottery ticket. That is, you ignore the fact that they both have an equal chance and instead make the decision based on how similar you think it is to a winning ticket.

↓

> People have the tendency to judge the ___(A)___ of an event on the basis of how much it ___(B)___ something they are already familiar with.

	(A)		(B)
①	probability	……	resembles
②	probability	……	influences
③	frequency	……	benefits
④	frequency	……	influences
⑤	quality	……	resembles

[41~42] 다음 글을 읽고, 물음에 답하시오.

Domesticated animals are the earliest and most effective "machines" available to humans. They take the strain off the human back and arms. Animals can (a) raise human living standards very considerably both as a food source (protein in meat and milk) and by carrying things, lifting water, and grinding grains. Since they are so obviously of great benefit, we might expect to find that over the centuries humans would increase the number and quality of the animals they kept. Surprisingly, this has not usually been the case. In Japan, domesticated animals were quite (b) widely used in the period up to about 1600. There were large numbers of horses and oxen. After that, as the population grew, the animals were gradually replaced by human labor. By the later nineteenth century there were practically no large domestic animals in the intensive rice-growing areas of central Japan. All the land was being used to grow crops, so there was nowhere for the animals to be kept. In any case, human labor was (c) more expensive. It was not only in Asia that this was happening. It is possible to see the (d) same pattern over many parts of Western Europe. For instance in France, the animal energy available per head in terms of oxen, horses, sheep and goats was higher in the thirteenth than the eighteenth century. People could no longer "afford" to keep them. It seems a law of nature that animals are replaced by humans. Animals are in many ways a (e) luxury. Only the relatively well off can afford them. Poverty gradually drives them out. A son will replace a donkey or ox, carry goods on his back or dig with a shovel rather than plough with an animal.

*plough: 쟁기로 갈다

41 윗글의 제목으로 가장 적절한 것은? [3점]

① Human Labor Has Been Increased by Animals
② Why Do Humans Often Give up Using Animals?
③ Where Did the Domestication of Animals Begin?
④ How Domesticated Animals Transformed Early Farming
⑤ Relationships Between Domesticated Animals and Humans

42 밑줄 친 (a)~(e) 중에서 문맥상 낱말의 쓰임이 적절하지 않은 것은?

① (a) ② (b) ③ (c) ④ (d) ⑤ (e)

[43~45] 다음 글을 읽고, 물음에 답하시오.

(A)

Once upon a time there was a young student whose only dream was to be like his hero Pi, a philosopher who was renowned throughout the land for (a) his great wisdom and kindness. The boy decided to visit the great old man to seek his counsel. When they met, he asked Pi how he too might acquire the gift of great wisdom. The philosopher replied, "I shall not tell you the answer now, but if you come with me you will see it."

(B)

Of course, there was a terrible struggle as the one held the other's head under water. But before death could take hold, the boy was released. Gasping for air, he immediately determined to seek his revenge. He looked around for the old man and couldn't believe what he saw. There was Pi, already back on the beach, calmly watching. When the boy stumbled onto the beach beside (b) him, he shouted tearfully: "You tried to kill me! Why?" The old man's reply was another question: "When you were underwater, and you thought that you were about to die, what did you desire more than anything in the world?"

*gasp for air: 거칠게 숨을 쉬다

(C)

Thinking the question could be another trick, he hesitated a few moments before admitting the truth. Softly (c) he said, "I wanted to breathe." Pi now gave the young student a beautiful smile and spoke in a comforting voice. "My dear boy, do you see? When you want the gift of wisdom as badly as you wanted to breathe, then you shall have your gift."

(D)

He took the boy by the hand and walked with him to the seashore. There, still fully clothed, Pi walked straight out into the waves and called to the student to come too. (d) He often did surprising things like this when he was trying to prove a point to one of his followers. Obediently, the boy walked into the sea and joined Pi where he stood in water that reached up to their chins. Without another word, Pi placed his hands firmly on the other's shoulders and, smiling kindly, (e) he pushed down with all his might.

43 주어진 글 (A)에 이어질 내용을 순서에 맞게 배열한 것으로 가장 적절한 것은?

① (B) — (D) — (C)
② (C) — (B) — (D)
③ (C) — (D) — (B)
④ (D) — (B) — (C)
⑤ (D) — (C) — (B)

44 밑줄 친 (a)~(e) 중에서 가리키는 대상이 나머지 넷과 다른 것은?

① (a) ② (b) ③ (c) ④ (d) ⑤ (e)

45 윗글에 관한 내용으로 적절하지 않은 것은?

① 바닷속에서 소년은 숨 쉬기 위해 발버둥쳤다.
② 소년은 Pi에게 복수하기로 마음먹었다.
③ 소년은 마침내 갈구하던 지혜를 얻게 되었다.
④ Pi는 소년을 바닷가로 데리고 갔다.
⑤ Pi는 옷을 입은 채로 바다로 걸어 들어갔다.

AFTER TESTING

종료 시 분

소요시간 분

1 채점하기 | 정답 및 해설 p.49

주의 틀린 문제를 다시 풀 수 있도록 정답을 본문에 표기하지 마세요.

2 등급 확인

3 틀린 유형 확인 후 전략 적용 복습 및 해설지 확인

How to Review

1 틀린 문제와 ✓ 표시한 문제는 다시 풀고 해설 확인하기

2 내가 표시한 정답 근거가 해설과 일치하는지 확인하기

3 잘 모르는 부분으로 표시한 내용은 해설을 통해 완전히 이해하기

4 어휘 외우기 (어휘 목록 다운로드 www.cedubook.com)

5 다음 회에 개선할 점 정리하기 (시간 엄수, 취약 유형 보완 등)

BEFORE TESTING

시작 시 분

1 **제한시간** (OMR 마킹시간 포함) ☐ 40분 ☐ 45분
2 **어휘예습** ☐ 해당 없음 ☐ 완료
3 **문제풀이순서** ☐ 순서대로 ☐ 2점 → 3점 ☐ 기타
4 **기타 목표**

Check Point

1 **정답 근거** *e.g.* 밑줄 긋기
2 **잘 모르는 부분** *e.g.* 〈 〉 또는 ? 표시
3 **자신 없는 문제** *e.g.* 문제 번호에 ✓표시

18 다음 글의 목적으로 가장 적절한 것은?

Customer Support:

I'm writing in regard to the Raven X7 drone on your company's website. According to the advertisement, the Raven X7 is able to fly while carrying up to 3 kilograms. However, my experience with other drones makes me question this. I will need to equip the Raven X7 with some simple camera equipment weighing just over a kilogram. Will this affect the drone's range of flight? Also, I'm unable to find a maximum flying height for the drone online. I'd like to be able to fly at least 50 meters above the ground. If you could provide me with this information, I'd really appreciate it.

Sincerely,
Mark Spencer

① 제품 사용법에 관하여 안내하려고
② 새로운 제품으로 교환을 요청하려고
③ 구매한 제품의 모델명을 확인하려고
④ 제품의 품질 개선 방향을 제안하려고
⑤ 구매할 제품의 정확한 성능을 문의하려고

19 다음 글에 드러난 'I'의 심경으로 가장 적절한 것은?

Every day at 5 p.m., instead of playing with our fourth- and fifth-grade friends or sneaking out to the empty lot to hunt ghosts and animal bones, my brother and I had to go to Chinese school. No amount of kicking, screaming, or pleading could convince my mother, who was strongly determined to have us learn the language of our heritage, otherwise. With her mind made up, she walked us the seven long, hilly blocks from our home to school, dropping our miserable, tearful faces before the stern principal. My only memory of him is that he constantly rocked back and forth while keeping his hands hidden behind his back. To me, he was a horrifying monster, and I knew that if we ever saw his hands we'd be in big trouble.

① jealous and upset
② bored and uninterested
③ satisfied and determined
④ frustrated and terrified
⑤ sympathetic and sad

20 다음 글에서 필자가 주장하는 바로 가장 적절한 것은?

It's a mistake to make your success or failure depend on the opinions of others. Competing to impress your parents, teachers, peers, co-workers, or anybody else will be ultimately unrewarding. You can't conform to their every hope and ideal, and you will probably feel disappointed and frustrated when you find that your accomplishments don't win their approval. If you start with a strong belief in what you can do that depends on no one else's mind, you will have a much easier time tolerating those for whom nothing is enough. Moreover, having a firm sense of self-esteem actually increases your share of good health, high motivation, and great achievement in life.

① 자기 자신에 대한 존중심을 가져야 한다.
② 가까운 사람들로부터 인정받도록 해야 한다.
③ 비판을 현명하게 극복하는 법을 배워야 한다.
④ 다른 사람의 의견을 존중할 줄 알아야 한다.
⑤ 정신과 신체 모두 건강을 유지해야 한다.

21 다음 글의 요지로 가장 적절한 것은?

More and more people are becoming concerned about the food they eat. It is often impossible to find out who grew it, what pesticides were used on it, or which route it travelled from farm to store. For those who want more control over what they put into their mouths, locally grown food makes a lot of sense. And buying locally is better for the local economy. Farmers on average receive only 20 cents of each food dollar spent, with the rest going to transportation, processing, packaging, refrigeration, and marketing. Farmers who sell food directly to shoppers receive the full retail value of their produce: 100 cents for each food dollar spent.

① 친환경 농산물의 인기가 높아지고 있다.
② 소비자는 식품 생산 정보를 알 권리가 있다.
③ 생산자와 소비자를 이어주는 플랫폼 구축이 필요하다.
④ 복잡한 식품 유통 과정이 소비자의 가격 부담을 높인다.
⑤ 지역 식품을 구매하는 것이 소비자와 지역 경제에 이롭다.

22 다음 글의 주제로 가장 적절한 것은?

In a study conducted by researchers — David Just, Ph.D., Ozge Sigirci, and Brian Wansink, Ph.D., author of the book *Slim by Design: Mindless Eating Solutions for Everyday Life* — 139 diners in an Italian all-you-can-eat buffet restaurant were either charged $4 or $8 for the lunch buffet. The buffet offered pizza, salad, breadsticks, pasta, and soup. After finishing their meal, the diners were asked to rate how much they enjoyed the dining experience on a 9-point scale. The diners who paid the higher price for the buffet rated the food as being 11% tastier. Based on this finding, the researchers recommend that buffet owners think twice before setting a low buffet cost; even though cheap all-you-can-eat buffets are popular, people tend to stick to the "you get what you pay for" mentality and will rate the food lower in quality.

① scientific principle applied to buffet prices
② strategies for keeping the price low for a buffet
③ necessity of an objective assessment of food taste
④ impact of the price in evaluating food satisfaction
⑤ concerns about the quality of food with low prices

23 다음 글의 제목으로 가장 적절한 것은?

For the past three decades, birthday celebrations in elementary schools have ballooned into giant competitions centered around providing sugary treats stacked upon cupcakes for the whole class. Recognizing the negative impact of sugar on kids, many school districts have tried to shift the focus of celebrations. If your school hasn't changed its practices yet on birthday celebrations, a few ideas that other schools have adopted include a "celebrate me" book or card where each kid writes one thing that is special about that child; a special school birthday crown that is worn all day; being the teacher assistant for the day, the line leader, or the activity chooser. Taking the focus off sugary foods results in a healthier classroom and children who can celebrate all day long. Teachers are often supportive of these ideas because they keep kids focused and ready to learn.

① Sweet, Sweet Projects for Children
② Problems with Sugary Treats as Rewards
③ Healthy Gifts to Move Your Child's Heart
④ Celebrations for Kids: A Valuable Tradition
⑤ Changing the Focus in Celebrations for Children

24 다음 도표의 내용과 일치하지 않는 것은?

National Population Growth Rates Compared to Fastest-growing City: 2010-2020

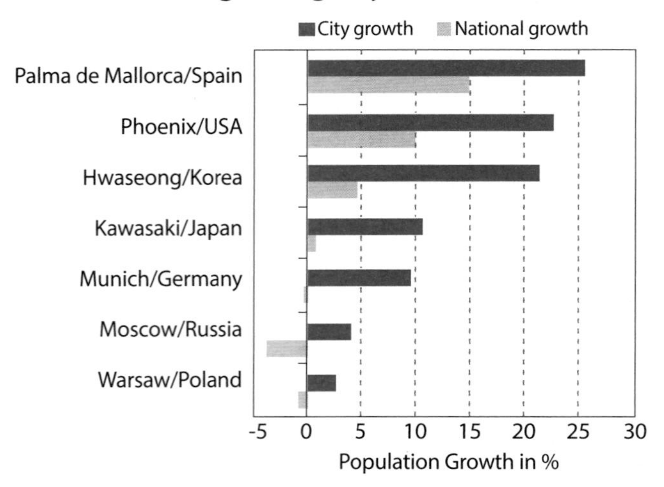

The graph above shows the population growth rates of seven countries alongside that of their fastest-growing cities from 2010 to 2020. ① Out of the seven countries, all but three showed population increases between 2010 and 2020. ② During the same period, Spain showed the highest rate of population growth out of the seven countries, as did Palma de Mallorca, of the seven cities. ③ The populations of Palma de Mallorca, Phoenix, and Hwaseong each increased by more than twenty percent during the period. ④ The growth rates of Kawasaki and Munich were both around ten percent, while their countries, Japan and Germany, showed almost no changes in population. ⑤ Of the cities, Moscow registered the lowest growth rate during the period, and Warsaw the second lowest.

25 Albrecht Dürer에 관한 다음 글의 내용과 일치하지 않는 것은?

Albrecht Dürer was a German painter and printmaker of the German Renaissance. He was born in Nuremberg in May of 1471 as the second son of his parents. Historians now believe he had at least thirteen and possibly as many as seventeen siblings. His father was a successful goldsmith who taught Dürer the basics of working with gold and drawing at a young age. By his twenties, Dürer was already becoming famous for his high-quality woodcuts. During his lifetime, he associated with many of the great artists of the era, including Raphael, Giovanni Bellini, and Leonardo da Vinci. After 1512, his work was sponsored by emperor Maximilian I. Dürer's works include carvings, portraits and self-portraits, and watercolors. Moreover, his introduction of classical themes into Northern European art has made him one of the most important figures of the Northern Renaissance.

① 독일의 화가이자 판화 제작자였다.
② 어린 나이에 아버지에게 그림을 배웠다.
③ 20대에 목판화로 유명해지고 있었다.
④ 1512년 이후에는 황제의 후원을 받지 못했다.
⑤ 고전적인 테마를 북유럽 예술에 도입했다.

26 Parker High School Drama Club에 관한 다음 안내문의 내용과 일치하지 않는 것은?

Parker High School Drama Club

The purpose of the club is to support the drama program and actors here at our school, to share information about various drama-related events, and to have a place for theater enthusiasts here to meet and share!

JOIN THE DRAMA CLUB!

You do not have to be a member of the Acting Club or be enrolled in a drama class to join the Drama Club.

Dues: Annual dues are $5.00.

Benefits:

- Members get discount tickets to shows.
- Receive a copy of the drama newsletter *Actors in Action*.

Activities & Events:

- Meetings on the second Tuesday of each month during the school year (begins at 3:20 p.m.)
- Service projects to benefit the school & community
- Holiday parties

① 학교의 배우들을 지원하는 동아리이다.
② 연극단원이 아니어도 가입할 수 있다.
③ 회원은 뉴스레터를 직접 제작한다.
④ 학기 중 매월 둘째 주 화요일에 모임이 있다.
⑤ 학교와 지역 사회를 위한 봉사활동을 한다.

27 Field Trip에 관한 다음 안내문의 내용과 일치하는 것은?

Field Trip

We will go on a field trip to Central Zoo on Wednesday, May 10. Thank you to the Parents' Club for providing the cost of admission for each student.

What you need to know:

- Siblings and parents are more than welcome but will need to pay admission.
- You will need to pack a sack lunch for your child the day of the trip.
- Send your child dressed for the outdoors.

To join us:

- There will only be enough room for the students and teachers on the bus, so you will need to drive separately.

Departure time: 9:15 a.m.
Return time: 3:15 p.m.

① 학생들의 동물원 입장료는 학부모 단체에서 제공했다.
② 학생의 형제자매는 무료로 입장할 수 있다.
③ 학생들에게 점심 도시락이 제공된다.
④ 학부모를 위한 교통편이 따로 마련된다.
⑤ 동물원 도착 시간은 오전 9시 15분이다.

28 다음 글의 밑줄 친 부분 중, 어법상 틀린 것은? [3점]

No matter how old you are, you need to get a good night's sleep every night ① to keep your body and mind functioning at their best. Catching up on lost sleep with short naps or weekend lie-ins ② don't help much, because it's regular, deep, extended sleep that you need. Experts at the Mayo Clinic say that insufficient sleep causes memory problems, dull reaction time, and ③ decreased alertness. Furthermore, say the experts, long-term sleep deprivation harms your physical and mental health. A good night's sleep boosts your immune system ④ so that you are better protected against viruses and bacteria. In addition, they say that sleep-deprived drivers and workers are more prone to cause serious accidents after falling asleep at the wheel or ⑤ when operating machinery.

*sleep deprivation: 수면 부족

29 다음 글의 밑줄 친 부분 중, 문맥상 낱말의 쓰임이 적절하지 않은 것은? [3점]

When people think of aging, most tend to think first of the changes in physical health. Many associate aging with numerous medications, disease, ① inability to function on one's own, and a body waiting to die. However, this is a ② misconception, especially in today's society in which people are living longer, healthier, and more productive lives. There are three stages of adulthood: young adulthood (twenties and thirties), middle adulthood (forties and fifties), and later adulthood (sixty and older). People in any of these stages are not subjected to ③ suffering due to problems associated with aging. There are physical changes that take place with aging, but even these do not necessarily lead to a ④ healthy lifestyle in later years. A major factor in how ⑤ well your body functions in later years is how well you treat it in the younger years.

30 밑줄 친 them[they]이 가리키는 대상이 나머지 넷과 다른 것은?

Only one hundred years ago, there were at least 100,000 tigers in the wild in Asia. Now the number of ① them has fallen to fewer than 3,000, says the World Wildlife Fund. The organization warns that ② they will be extinct in the wild by 2030 unless immediate action is taken to save these extremely endangered animals. In the 1950s and '60s, in the name of progress, China engaged in extermination campaigns against ③ them. Later, under international pressure, China introduced laws protecting tigers, but they were not consistently enforced. Now, China promises better protection of ④ them and greater efforts to stop illegal trade in tiger parts. One animal rights activist remains skeptical: "China already has adequate protection laws. What we need now is for ⑤ them to be strictly enforced."

*extermination: 몰살

[31~34] 다음 빈칸에 들어갈 말로 가장 적절한 것을 고르시오.

31 In one study, we asked people to engage in disliked activities. Those who hated watching football were to watch football; those who disliked classical or rap music were to listen to it; those who didn't like art were to spend time looking at paintings. In each case, we formed four groups: one group just did the activity, one group was told to notice one new thing about it, one group was told to notice three new things, and the final group was told to notice six new things. The more they noticed, the more they liked the activity. This study shows us that almost any activity can be interesting and pleasurable if it is undertaken ______________.

① mindfully ② repeatedly
③ collectively ④ immediately
⑤ unpredictably

32 A recent study by the International Panel for Sustainable Resource Management acknowledges that biofuels are an effective means of cutting greenhouse gas emissions. However, the study also noted that some biofuels are ______________________________. Depending on the natural resource used to manufacture the biofuel, the biofuel can either reduce emissions or worsen the problem. For example, the study notes that emissions reductions of up to 100% have been achieved in Brazil and other countries that use sugarcane to produce ethanol fuel. But in Southeast Asian countries such as Indonesia and Malaysia, the production of bio-diesel from palm oil has led to major increases in emissions. The main problem is that rainforests are cleared to grow the palm trees for the oil, which greatly adds to carbon in the atmosphere. [3점]

① different from country to country
② more cost-efficient than fossil fuels
③ less climate-friendly than they seem
④ too dependent upon geographical areas
⑤ obtained from various natural resources

33 Something every sports fan knows is that the game is rarely over, even when the majority think it is. Kicker Adam Vinatieri, for example, kept struggling to bring victory for the New England Patriots football team over the Miami Dolphins in December 2002. The Dolphins were completely defeating the Patriots, and many fans thought it was over and were already leaving the stadium when Vinatieri kicked a crucial field goal in the final seconds. Their belief in his ability to keep fighting led to the saying, "It's not over until Vinatieri kicks." Then, incredibly, in the 2004 Super Bowl, Vinatieri again kicked the game-winning points for the Patriots in the final few seconds. Vinatieri's example shows that winning is often the result of ______________________________________. [3점]

① not making a single mistake
② training harder than one's rivals
③ not giving up when all appears to be lost
④ not placing oneself above one's teammates
⑤ continuously competing with stronger opponents

34 The idea of a "natural happening" is not as familiar or acceptable for Americans as it is for the Chinese and many other non-Westerners. Events do not just occur or happen naturally; they require a cause or an agent that can be held responsible. Americans are not satisfied with statements of occurrence until they have determined who is responsible — who did it or who caused it to be done. "Where there's smoke, there's fire" means that each effect or event is caused by a factor. The English language reflects this quality of American (and English) thinking. For example, in English one ______________________________. Unlike Romance languages that allow the statement, "Is raining," the English speaker must invent a dummy subject to say, "It is raining." The *it* in this English statement fills the subject position, normally associated with the agent of a verb. [3점]

① doesn't place an object after a passive verb
② doesn't need a subject when there's no action
③ can reverse the subject and the object in a sentence
④ cannot refer to a natural occurrence without a subject
⑤ can communicate ideas without the aid of a single word

35 다음 글에서 전체 흐름과 관계 없는 문장은?

A strange natural phenomenon that has disappeared was the occasional mass emigration of the gray squirrel. ① Caused by an excessive build-up of their populations that led to extreme hunger, these movements involved millions of the squirrels. ② A half-billion were estimated to have migrated across southern Wisconsin in 1843. ③ And the first gray squirrels were brought to Britain to amuse the rich, probably in the early 19th century. ④ Moving in huge numbers, they devoured crops on the way, and even managed to swim across mighty rivers. ⑤ Currently, the squirrel population, although far smaller, is on the increase; emigrations still occur but they are not as noticeable as they were in the past.

[36~37] 주어진 글 다음에 이어질 글의 순서로 가장 적절한 것을 고르시오.

36

For many frustrating years before he invented the sewing machine, Elias Howe simply could not find a way to make his idea work.

(A) As he lay there, still frightened by the dream, he recalled those spears with the oddly placed holes and suddenly realized: my machine needs a needle like those! And so it was a dream that turned Howe's idea into one of the world's most successful inventions.

(B) So the savages surrounded Howe and raised their spears and, as they did, Howe saw that the spears had strange eye-shaped holes in their tips. Then he awoke.

(C) Then one night he dreamed that savages captured him and said they would murder him unless he made them a sewing machine. He worked desperately but could not produce the machine.

① (A) — (C) — (B)
② (B) — (A) — (C)
③ (B) — (C) — (A)
④ (C) — (A) — (B)
⑤ (C) — (B) — (A)

37

It's well known that good verbal communication is the foundation of any successful relationship. It's important to recognize, though, that it's our nonverbal cues that speak the loudest when we communicate.

(A) These messages don't stop when you stop speaking either. Even when you're silent, you're still communicating nonverbally. Oftentimes, what comes out of our mouths and what we communicate through our body language are two totally different things.

(B) When we interact with others, we continuously give and receive such wordless signals. All of our nonverbal behaviors — the gestures we make, the way we sit, how close we stand — send strong messages.

(C) When faced with these mixed signals, a listener has to choose whether to believe your verbal or nonverbal message, and, in most cases, the listener is going to choose the nonverbal because it's a natural, unconscious language that broadcasts our true feelings and intentions in any given moment. [3점]

① (A) — (C) — (B)
② (B) — (A) — (C)
③ (B) — (C) — (A)
④ (C) — (A) — (B)
⑤ (C) — (B) — (A)

[38~39] 글의 흐름으로 보아, 주어진 문장이 들어가기에 가장 적절한 곳을 고르시오.

38

Many people find themselves overeating and drinking to cope with their feelings.

What are some of the problems associated with major holiday periods? (①) One common problem is that these periods see a sharp increase in people seeking help for depression. (②) This is related to the fact that holidays intensify feelings of loneliness and isolation for the elderly, singles, and those without family. (③) Events that are known to cause stress also increase during these holidays: there are presents to buy, dishes to prepare, long lines in stores, and traffic chaos everywhere. (④) Surrounded by all this, people can't help but feel under pressure. (⑤) It's easy to do when there's all that holiday food to eat and all those holiday drinks to drink.

39

This growth in trade led to the emergence of the influential merchant class.

For as long as there have been people, there has been trade. At first, trade was a simple matter. (①) For example, people in a family exchanged food with their neighbors. (②) Over time, trade expanded as people were exposed to new goods from faraway places and developed a taste for them. (③) As tribes became kingdoms and kingdoms became empires, trade grew in importance. (④) These new economic agents braved hardships in search of profit, and their activities helped to form the modern world. (⑤) Although the scale of trade has grown incredibly throughout history, what has not changed is that trade always occurs between individuals.

40 다음 글의 내용을 한 문장으로 요약하고자 한다. 빈칸 (A), (B)에 들어갈 말로 가장 적절한 것은?

Do happier students get better grades? Is one crowned player the happiest? Consider the bronze and silver medalists at an Olympic competition; who do you suppose is happier? In such competitions, there is a qualitative difference between the gold medalist and everyone else; only the gold medalist has won the competition, attained glory, and can expect highly profitable sponsorships. The silver medalist in such a competition has come closer to winning gold than has the bronze medalist and so is more likely to be tormented by thoughts of what might have happened. In contrast, the bronze medalist has come dangerously close to winning nothing at all and may therefore be especially pleased at having avoided this misfortune. If the silver medalist is upset because "I could have won gold" whereas the bronze medalist is gratified because "At least I won a medal," the silver medalist may feel less happy than the bronze medalist.

↓

People who are objectively better off than others can feel ____(A)____ if they can imagine an even more ____(B)____ outcome.

	(A)		(B)
①	better	……	negative
②	better	……	positive
③	down	……	negative
④	worse	……	positive
⑤	worse	……	unexpected

[41~42] 다음 글을 읽고, 물음에 답하시오.

Fear of failing is a very common fear. The major cause of this fear is that we worry very much about what people might say if we fail. The idea that people will laugh at you and reject you can be even scarier than the thought of failure itself.

Imagine if the great tragic characters of art and literature were treated so badly! Take Shakespeare's *Hamlet*, for instance. For hundreds of years, readers and audiences have viewed Hamlet with understanding, because the play represents him as a complex human being. He has weaknesses and sometimes acts badly, yet we remain on his side, feeling for him. Were he alive today, however, it's unlikely he would get as much respect. In particular, bloggers and other "netizens" would likely say horrible things about him online and blame only him for his tragedy.

In real life, it seems that people who fail get treated very badly. So, what gives Hamlet and other tragic characters of literature respect and understanding? Perhaps it's that we have been taught to see them as noble by their creators and our teachers. We are encouraged to give them a level of ____________ that ordinary people also deserve but rarely get. Great tragic stories make us sense how easy it is for disasters to happen to us, how hard it is to lead a good life, and why we shouldn't judge others too quickly or too harshly for their problems and mistakes.

41 윗글의 제목으로 가장 적절한 것은?

① Why Do We Judge Ourselves So Harshly?
② View the Failures of Others with Patience
③ Essential for Success: Embracing Your Failures
④ What We Have in Common with Stories: Tragedy
⑤ Learn About Respect from Great Tragic Characters

42 윗글의 빈칸에 들어갈 말로 가장 적절한 것은? [3점]

① sympathy
② self-esteem
③ happiness
④ enthusiasm
⑤ opportunity

[43~45] 다음 글을 읽고, 물음에 답하시오.

(A)

It was early summer, and the weather was really hot. Tyler and his mom were on the beach. Mom found a good spot on the sand that was close to the water. They put the blankets down and set up some chairs. Sitting close by them was (a) a boy about Tyler's age. He came over and said his name was Gary and asked Tyler if he wanted to build a sand castle with (b) him. "Sure," said Tyler. His mom began talking to Tyler's mom about school, work, and things moms usually talk about.

(B)

Gary's mom was so scared, but she realized if it hadn't been for Tyler's quick action, Gary might have drowned. Gary and his mom thanked Tyler for his fast thinking and great swimming skills. That night Gary's mom invited Tyler and his mom to go to dinner with them. "It's my thank-you treat," said Gary's mom. Not only did the boys become friends, but their moms did as well!

(C)

The boys built a great sand castle. They decided to head for the water. "Be careful," shouted Gary's mother. "We will," Gary shouted back. The boys were running in and out of the water and jumping through the waves laughing. They were having a great time. Suddenly, they ran to jump in a big wave, but Tyler couldn't find Gary. Tyler looked around and finally saw (c) him waving his hands and yelling for help.

(D)

Tyler sprang into action and remembered the lifesaving skills he had learned during (d) his swimming class at the local pool. I've got to get to Gary, thought Tyler. Tyler swam to where Gary was and put his arm around (e) him and told him to hold on tight. Just then the lifeguard spotted them. He rushed into the water and took over. He was able to get Gary from Tyler and bring him safely back to shore.

43 주어진 글 (A)에 이어질 내용을 순서에 맞게 배열한 것으로 가장 적절한 것은?

① (B) — (D) — (C)
② (C) — (B) — (D)
③ (C) — (D) — (B)
④ (D) — (B) — (C)
⑤ (D) — (C) — (B)

44 밑줄 친 (a)~(e) 중에서 가리키는 대상이 나머지 넷과 다른 것은?

① (a) ② (b) ③ (c) ④ (d) ⑤ (e)

45 윗글에 관한 내용으로 적절하지 않은 것은?

① Tyler는 어머니와 함께 해변에 놀러왔다.
② Gary는 Tyler에게 모래성을 만들자고 제안했다.
③ Gary의 어머니는 Tyler와 그의 어머니를 초대했다.
④ Tyler는 물에 빠진 Gary를 향해 헤엄쳐 갔다.
⑤ Tyler는 Gary를 무사히 해변으로 데려왔다.

AFTER TESTING

종료 시 분
소요시간 분

1 채점하기 | 정답 및 해설 p.57
주의 틀린 문제를 다시 풀 수 있도록 정답을 본문에 표기하지 마세요.
2 등급 확인
3 틀린 유형 확인 후 전략 적용 복습 및 해설지 확인

How to Review

1 틀린 문제와 ✓ 표시한 문제는 다시 풀고 해설 확인하기
2 내가 표시한 정답 근거가 해설과 일치하는지 확인하기
3 잘 모르는 부분으로 표시한 내용은 해설을 통해 완전히 이해하기
4 어휘 외우기 (어휘 목록 다운로드 www.cedubook.com)
5 다음 회에 개선할 점 정리하기 (시간 엄수, 취약 유형 보완 등)

BUTTON UP!

실전 모의고사

09

BEFORE TESTING

시작 시 분

학습 목표

1 제한시간 (OMR 마킹시간 포함) ☐ 40분 ☐ 45분
2 어휘예습 ☐ 해당 없음 ☐ 완료
3 문제풀이순서 ☐ 순서대로 ☐ 2점 → 3점 ☐ 기타
4 기타 목표

Check Point

1 정답 근거 *e.g.* 밑줄 긋기
2 잘 모르는 부분 *e.g.* 〈 〉 또는 ? 표시
3 자신 없는 문제 *e.g.* 문제 번호에 ✓표시

18 다음 글의 목적으로 가장 적절한 것은?

Dear Mayor Green,

Thank you for taking the time to read my letter. I learned from my teacher in school that you love cats and dogs just like I do. In fact, I have two dogs, both of which I adopted from Ravenwood Animal Shelter. My mom says animal shelters save as many dogs as they can. But still, there are hundreds of unwanted homeless dogs and cats on our city streets. I think that people want to help with this issue, but they don't know how. Our city needs more shelters to solve this problem. Perhaps you would consider establishing a new animal shelter in our area since you are the mayor of our city. Animals do so much for us, but they also depend on us for shelter. We have to do the right thing.

Sincerely,
Cindy Park

① 유기 동물 입양을 권장하려고
② 동물 보호법의 개정을 제안하려고
③ 동물 보호소의 문제점을 지적하려고
④ 새로운 동물 보호소 설립을 요청하려고
⑤ 동물 보호소의 보조금 지원을 촉구하려고

19 다음 글에 드러난 Mary의 심경 변화로 가장 적절한 것은?

Mary looked at the result of her efforts and smiled. It had taken many hours of hard work, but her vegetable garden now looked wonderful. The fresh smells from the herbs lifted her spirits as she thought about all the great recipes she could cook. And the sunlight hitting the tomato plants looked like something from a magazine. As Mary prepared to take a photo of her accomplishment, her neighbor's dog suddenly jumped over the garden fence. Mary stood frozen in place with her mouth wide open as the dog rushed into the garden, kicking up dirt and knocking over plants. She let out a tiny scream at the helplessness of her situation. When it was over, Mary could hardly believe it. All her hard work was ruined.

① amused → envious
② pleased → shocked
③ nervous → frustrated
④ astonished → ashamed
⑤ satisfied → indifferent

20 다음 글에서 필자가 주장하는 바로 가장 적절한 것은?

Many adults are distressed and confused by anger in children. This is because our own feelings of rage and frustration can so easily get stirred up when faced with an angry child. We should bear in mind that most of us were never taught anger-management skills when we were kids ourselves. Most likely, you were led to believe that when you got angry you were not good. You got the message that only bad kids get angry, and that showing anger is very bad. We have to free ourselves from this self-damaging view. To properly handle children who have angry feelings, one must first accept anger as a natural part of being human. We must acknowledge a child's anger without judgment and help him or her to direct it to a positive outcome.

① 어릴 때 분노를 통제하는 법을 가르쳐야 한다.
② 교육상 아이들에게 화를 내지 않도록 해야 한다.
③ 아이의 분노는 어른의 분노와 다르게 다루어야 한다.
④ 아이들이 화를 낼 때 부정적인 시선으로만 봐서는 안 된다.
⑤ 아이들의 정서 안정을 위해 부모는 일관된 양육 태도를 가져야 한다.

21 밑줄 친 get rid of it이 다음 글에서 의미하는 바로 가장 적절한 것은?

A Swiss jet bound for the Mexican resort of Cancun over the weekend was grounded for a day in Zurich. Crews searched for a mouse that made an appearance during the aircraft's incoming flight. About 200 passengers couldn't board the plane overnight until the mouse, which posed a safety risk if it chewed on cables, was found. This story is a good analogy of your relationship with others. The smallest thing can damage your relationship with your child, partners, or clients. In a relationship, thinking small is important. Thinking small means taking care of something you often ignore when you deal with people. Remember that your little gestures or actions can leave lasting impressions. Is there a mouse in your relationships? You should get rid of it.

① be polite to other people
② learn from your mistakes
③ pay attention to the details
④ prepare for unexpected events
⑤ look at things with an open mind

22 다음 글의 요지로 가장 적절한 것은?

There is an old proverb that says, "If you love something, set it free. If it comes back, it is yours. If not, it never was." Remember this saying the next time you're tempted to hold onto someone's friendship. You can put your dog on a leash and lock your bike in the garage, but your friends must have freedom to live their own lives. If the two of you can share your experiences and respect each other's individuality, that's great. If not, you may be good acquaintances, but you are not really good friends. Trying to hold onto a friendship that has already died can only be a cause of heartache. Accept the pain, try to understand why it happened, and move on. There are other people out there, and once they see an opportunity for friendship with you, they'll come in and fill up any emptiness you may feel.

① 지나친 집착은 친구 관계를 깨뜨린다.
② 소수의 친구를 깊이 사귀는 것이 좋다.
③ 서로의 마음이 통할 때 우정이 형성된다.
④ 상대방에 대한 신뢰가 우정을 깊게 만든다.
⑤ 우정도 변할 수 있다는 것을 받아들여야 한다.

23 다음 글의 주제로 가장 적절한 것은?

Stored correctly, fine wine can last for many years and continue to improve in character and complexity. Very old wine has been found in excellent drinking condition in many shipwrecks, thanks to the near-perfect storage conditions at the bottom of the sea. Darkness, stillness, humidity, and the right temperature are vital for keeping good wine in good shape. The right temperature, a cool 13-15 degrees Celsius, is a particularly important factor in storage, because the complex organic reactions that give wine its character occur in this range of temperatures. Also important is humidity, which must be kept at around 70%. Low humidity causes corks to dry and shrink, which allows oxygen and bacteria into the bottle, where they quickly spoil the wine.

① factors affecting the life span of wine
② role of temperature in preserving wine
③ importance of production year for wine
④ impact of bacteria on the character of a wine
⑤ benefits of chemical reactions in developing a wine's flavor

24 다음 글의 제목으로 가장 적절한 것은?

Wetlands are, not surprisingly, naturally very wet areas of land. Throughout the 20th century, they were mostly considered a waste of good land and were developed into golf courses, shopping centers, and other "more profitable" areas. That view was a serious mistake. In 2006, in a single day, 13.3 inches of rain fell in Newburyport, Massachusetts. Only 10 inches fell in nearby Haverhill, but Haverhill suffered terrible flooding and destruction, and Newburyport did not. Both cities are on the Merrimac River; why the huge difference? It was because Haverhill had covered and developed its wetlands, while Newburyport had allowed its wetlands to remain untouched. Wetlands act like giant sponges: quickly absorbing huge amounts of water from overflowing rivers and allowing the water to spread safely.

① Conflicting Views on Wetlands
② Measuring the Value of Wetlands
③ How to Restore Disappearing Wetlands
④ Link Between Wetlands and Biodiversity
⑤ Wetlands: Effective Prevention of Floods

25 다음 도표의 내용과 일치하지 않는 것은?

Donating or Volunteering?

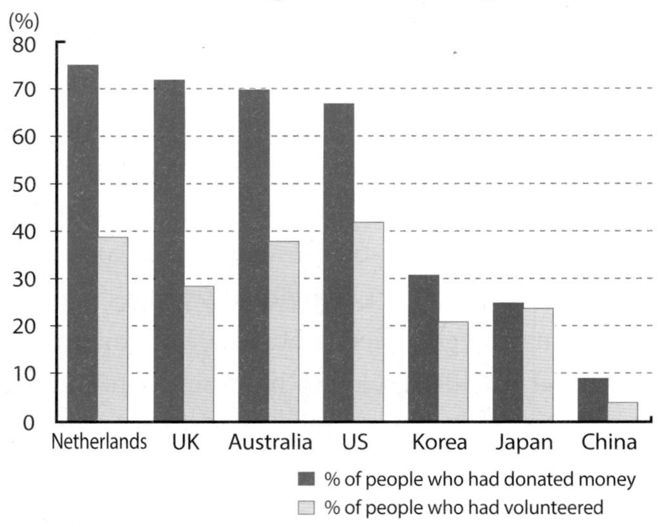

This graph compares the results from various nations of a survey that asked people if they had donated money or volunteered in the previous month. ① The top three countries for donations were the Netherlands, the UK, and Australia, where at least 70% of people had donated money. ② The results from all nations indicate a general preference for donating money rather than volunteering. ③ Although the US didn't make the top three for money donors, it recorded the highest rate of volunteering. ④ Among the Asian nations, Korea recorded the highest levels of charitable giving both in terms of time and money. ⑤ The least generous country was China, with by far the lowest levels of both volunteering and donating.

26 Carl Ludwig Luz Long에 관한 다음 글의 내용과 일치하지 않는 것은?

Carl Ludwig Luz Long was a German Olympic long jumper born on April 27, 1913. He was quite successful at his sport, winning the German long jump championship six times, in 1933, 1934, 1936, 1937, 1938, and 1939. He is also remembered for winning a silver medal at the 1936 Summer Olympics in Berlin. During the event, he became friends with American long jumper Jesse Owens, and the two remained in contact for years afterward. Jesse Owens himself was even present at Long's son's wedding. When not competing, Long studied law at the University of Leipzig, and he practiced as a lawyer in Hamburg after graduating. Sadly, Long's life was cut short when he was injured during World War II and died just three days later from the wounds. However, his legacy lives on. After his death, he was honored for his great display of sportsmanship at the Berlin Olympics with a medal.

① 독일의 멀리뛰기 선수였다.
② 올림픽 멀리뛰기 종목에서 은메달을 땄다.
③ 미국 선수 Jesse Owens와 친구로 지냈다.
④ Hamburg에서 변호사로 활동했다.
⑤ 원인 불명으로 갑작스럽게 사망했다.

27 Alumni Games에 관한 다음 안내문의 내용과 일치하지 않는 것은?

Alumni Games

Each year, Steven alumni athletes gather for our Alumni Games, reviving athletic skills from the days when they proudly wore the Steven green and white.

Schedule

Alumni will gather on Saturday, December 10, 2020, for our 30th annual Alumni Games.

10:30 a.m.	Lacrosse Game (Women)
11:30 a.m.	Lacrosse Game (Men)
12:30 p.m.	BBQ at the Pirate Pool
1:30 p.m.	Basketball Game (Men)
2:30 p.m.	Basketball Game (Women)

Campus Store Special Hours

The Campus Store will be open during the Alumni Games from 10:00 a.m. to 2:00 p.m. Stop by and buy the latest in Steven logo sportswear for yourself and your friends.

① 참가자에게 녹색과 흰색의 운동복이 제공된다.
② 체육대회는 이번에 30주년을 맞는다.
③ 오전에는 남녀 라크로스 경기가 열린다.
④ 점심에는 수영장에서 바비큐 파티를 즐긴다.
⑤ 체육대회 당일에 매점은 4시간 동안 연다.

28 Belleville Flea Market에 관한 다음 안내문의 내용과 일치하는 것은?

Belleville Flea Market

July 5, 2020 | 9 a.m.–5 p.m.

(Vendors Arrive: 6:30–8:00 a.m.)

Address: 120 Park Ave. Belleville, NJ 07201

Our monthly Flea Market will feature new merchandise such as jewelry, sports collectibles, hats, handbags, and gift items to name a few. We have a large garage sale section where you can find something that you've been searching for. This event will be held outdoors but indoors if it rains.

Eligible Vendors:

- Retail vendors (selling new items)
- Arts, crafts & photography exhibitors
- Secondhand vendors, garage sale (selling used items)

This is an outdoor flea market: no application is required for outside spaces.

① 판매자는 오전 9시까지 도착하면 된다.
② 매주 열리는 행사이다.
③ 비가 오면 취소될 예정이다.
④ 신상품과 중고품 판매가 모두 가능하다.
⑤ 판매를 위해서는 신청서를 제출해야 한다.

29 다음 글의 밑줄 친 부분 중, 어법상 <u>틀린</u> 것은? [3점]

As a child, astronomer Carl Sagan was already thinking of the heavens. "I remember ① <u>to ask</u> my friends what the stars were," he says. "They said they were lights in the sky." ② <u>Unsatisfied</u> with this answer, Sagan found a book that told him that the stars were greatly distant suns. "Until then, my universe ③ <u>had been</u> my neighborhood," he says, "Now I got a sense of the incredible size of space, and fell in love with the stars and planets." His love grew when he read Edgar Rice Burroughs' stories about a man who could travel to Mars simply by looking at it and ④ <u>wishing</u> to be there. The young Sagan looked up and wished with all his heart to go there, too. It was a dream ⑤ <u>which</u> he never surrendered.

30 (A), (B), (C)의 각 네모 안에서 문맥에 맞는 낱말로 가장 적절한 것은? [3점]

Why is the name "John Doe" used to (A) [refer / appeal] to an unidentified male person? Anyone who has read a detective novel or seen a cops-and-robbers movie has heard the name John Doe used to describe an unidentified or unidentifiable male victim or suspect. As early as the mid-17th century, the name was used in British courts to (B) [release / represent] imaginary tenants being evicted from land whose ownership was ambiguous or disputed. John Doe (and Jane Doe, in the case of unnamed females) is widely used in North American courts whenever a person is unknown, or to (C) [invade / protect] the privacy of a person who cannot be named in public.

*evict: (법적 수단을 이용해) 쫓아내다

	(A)		(B)		(C)
①	refer	……	release	……	invade
②	refer	……	represent	……	protect
③	refer	……	represent	……	invade
④	appeal	……	release	……	invade
⑤	appeal	……	represent	……	protect

[31~34] 다음 빈칸에 들어갈 말로 가장 적절한 것을 고르시오.

31 All living creatures manage some form of ____________. The dance patterns of bees in their hive help to point the way to distant flower fields or announce successful gathering of pollen and nectar. Male stickleback fish regularly swim upside-down during a courtship. Male deer mark territorial ownership by rubbing their own body secretions on boundary stones or trees. Observers over the centuries have noted that crows use specific sounds under specific circumstances. Alarm calls, assembly calls, distress calls, and many others have been noted. Everyone has seen a frightened dog put his tail between his legs and run in panic. We, too, use gestures, expressions, postures, and movement to give our words point.

*stickleback: 큰가시고기(등에 가시가 있는 민물고기)

① threat
② conflict
③ interest
④ companionship
⑤ communication

32 A lack of sleep can do more than simply put you in a bad mood. It can actually ____________________. According to recent studies, when we don't get enough sleep, our metabolism slows down to save energy. That causes the release of the hormone cortisol, which increases appetite. In a vicious cycle, sleep loss also causes our bodies to release more ghrelin (another hormone that signals hunger) and less leptin (the hormone that tells your stomach that it's full). With your hormones out of balance, your body is set to overeat. Not to mention that being awake more hours gives you more time to eat snacks. And there is another reason that lack of sleep causes people to gain extra pounds. The majority of the calories that the body burns while sleeping are burned during REM sleep, a period of deep rest. And less sleep means less time in REM. [3점]

*metabolism: 신진대사

① keep you up until dawn
② affect your heart rate
③ ruin your waistline
④ make you dog-tired
⑤ put your mind in a fog

33 Children love nonsense rhymes and language games. They especially love *ludlings* — language games that have a secret "key" or rule for ________________ ________________. One ludling widely familiar in the English-speaking world is the "secret" language called "pig latin." The key is simply to move the first sound of a word to the end of the word and add "*-ay*." Thus, *finger* becomes disguised as *inger-fay*, *dog* becomes disguised as *og-day*, and so on. When you speak in pig latin, you distort the original English in such a way that people can't understand you unless they also know the key to the game. This is why ludlings are so popular with kids: kids love sharing a secret with friends while keeping it well hidden from "outsiders." [3점]

① communicating with friendly animals
② making new words from existing ones
③ talking to kids who can't speak English
④ inventing secrets about yourself and others
⑤ finding out what other people say about you

34 If someone is good at math, or solving problems with people, or writing, they do not possess just a single ability, but rather several that work in concert. Sometimes, it's easy to see a loaf of bread but miss the ingredients. If you think about it, there are few things you can do with a loaf of bread: make sandwiches and French toast, and feed the birds. But there are limitless possibilities when you combine the basic ingredients: flour, yeast, water, oil, and salt. In supermarkets everywhere, there are hundreds of items that are made from these few ingredients. Similarly, the correct way to evaluate your innate abilities in a way that helps you find your ideal career is to get down to the deepest level, ______________________________. [3점]

① the mastery of all underlying skills
② the development of efficient multitasking
③ the basic abilities that combine to make up your talents
④ an understanding of the process of combining ingredients
⑤ advanced preparation using as much information as possible

35 **다음 글에서 전체 흐름과 관계 없는 문장은?**

Many people think that memory loss is unavoidable with aging, but this is actually not true. We can prevent a decrease in our memories through regular physical activity. ① Studies have shown that the increased blood supply to the brain which occurs during vigorous activity improves our memories as well as our level of fitness. ② The one thing to avoid at any cost, however, is stress. ③ Stress makes our bodies produce a hormone called cortisol, which is harmful to brain cells and thus to memory. ④ Acute stress, which is the kind you feel before doing a bungee jump, actually boosts your immune system. ⑤ Reducing stress through meditation, exercise, or a relaxing hobby can help, then, to preserve our memory capacity.

[36~37] 주어진 글 다음에 이어질 글의 순서로 가장 적절한 것을 고르시오.

36

Birds will often migrate to warmer climates, and bears will hibernate in advance of winter famines. People tend to think that these and other animal behaviors are merely "dumb" instinctive reactions to nature's changing signs.

(A) After studying the bird's behavior, Raby and her colleagues are convinced that the behavior is more than just an instinct that says: "Bury food when cold."

(B) Despite this general assumption that animals aren't smart and don't think like we do, a recent study suggests that human beings may not be the only animals that plan for the future.

(C) In fact, Cambridge University researcher Caroline Raby believes that a mere bird — the Western scrub jay — does just that. The jay stores food in hiding places that become handy when food is scarce.

*the Western scrub jay: 《조류》 캘리포니아덤불어치

① (A) — (C) — (B)
② (B) — (A) — (C)
③ (B) — (C) — (A)
④ (C) — (A) — (B)
⑤ (C) — (B) — (A)

37

Installing a solar energy system on the roof of your home is a great leap forward in achieving independence from fossil fuels and reducing your domestic greenhouse gas emissions. Forward-thinking nations understand how important this is and are, therefore, supporting the switch to solar energy.

(A) States will do this through their Energy Buyback Scheme, which pays homeowners for any surplus electricity produced by their solar power system.

(B) The federal government's Solar Credits Scheme will subsidize the cost of installing your new system, and your state government will help your system to quickly pay for itself.

(C) In America, for example, the federal government and state governments are now offering substantial incentives to homeowners to install a solar power system.

*subsidize: 보조금을 주다

① (A) — (C) — (B)
② (B) — (A) — (C)
③ (B) — (C) — (A)
④ (C) — (A) — (B)
⑤ (C) — (B) — (A)

[38~39] 글의 흐름으로 보아, 주어진 문장이 들어가기에 가장 적절한 곳을 고르시오.

38

At the same time, myths were entertaining stories which have a beginning and middle and end, so people wanted to hear them.

A myth's explanatory element is important to its structure. (①) Like any other religion, classical mythology sought to provide definitive answers to seemingly unanswerable questions. (②) Because the ancients were not constrained by scientific and technical knowledge, they were free to develop some tales to explain these phenomena. (③) The oral tradition of the ancients thrived in part because of this dramatic element in these stories. (④) People listened to myths, retold them, remembered them after they'd been told, and eventually wrote them down. (⑤) That's why they are still in existence today. [3점]

39

Alternatively, you can manage all your boxes with just one master list.

When you move house, set up a system for keeping track of what's in what box. (①) With a thick magic marker, label each box on all four sides with the room it goes in, and this will save you the trouble of checking where it goes. (②) Then on top of the box you can write what's inside; for instance, "cups, plates, knives, cookbooks," but remember that trying to list *everything* can be very annoying. (③) Assign each room a code — *K* for kitchen, *BTH* for bathroom — and write the code plus a number for each box on your list. (④) Then, you can note on it as many items of the box's contents as you like. (⑤) So, if you have three boxes of bathroom things, your list might read, "BTH1: towels; BTH2: hair-care products; BTH3: electrical items."

40 다음 글의 내용을 한 문장으로 요약하고자 한다. 빈칸 (A), (B)에 들어갈 말로 가장 적절한 것은?

Your beliefs, attitudes, behavior, and prejudices are learned from the group with which you identify most. Living within your own culture is like sailing with the wind: the wind carries you along, and you hardly notice it's there. However, you feel its force whenever you have to sail against it. This is what happens when we come face to face with a different culture. The winds of the other culture blow in our face. North Americans who visit Europe may find the tiny cars and narrow streets odd. Visiting North America, people from Asia may find themselves fighting their instinct to remove their dirty street shoes before entering someone's house. They might also wonder why so many people find it pleasant to walk barefoot on the grass in parks.

↓

While we could hardly ____(A)____ the effect of our own culture, the power of a different culture can be so overwhelming that we may ____(B)____ what we are not accustomed to.

	(A)		(B)
①	accept	……	analyze
②	realize	……	resist
③	deny	……	absorb
④	admit	……	disregard
⑤	doubt	……	introduce

[41~42] 다음 글을 읽고, 물음에 답하시오.

Let's say you feel sick. You are experiencing fatigue, muscle soreness, nausea, and have a headache. What is your first course of action: call your doctor or turn to the Internet? If your answer was the latter, you aren't (a) alone. One Internet study found that three-quarters of respondents say they use websites to diagnose their symptoms before seeing a physician. It's easy to see why self-diagnosing on the Internet has become so incredibly (b) popular. We feel powerful, almost in control of our health care. With the click of a mouse, we can have access to an (c) unlimited supply of medical knowledge, saving us the time, money, and energy scheduling a doctor's visit requires. It seems like the perfect answer. But self-diagnosis online is inaccurate, panic inducing, and unreliable. In the same study, 90% of those who followed up with their doctors found their self-diagnosis to be (d) wrong. And more than half of the respondents said the Internet diagnosis caused them to panic. They will obsessively research symptoms and diagnose themselves with serious diseases. This can (e) reduce health anxiety. While Internet self-diagnosis seems like a practical solution to life's medical questions, it's always best to consult your doctor. After all, can an hour of Internet research really compete with years in medical school? When it comes to your or your child's health, you can never be too careful.

41 윗글의 제목으로 가장 적절한 것은?

① Is the Internet a Trigger for Health Anxiety?
② Online Search Behaviors and Their Influences
③ Worrying About Your Health Can Make You Sick
④ What Are the Problems with Online Self-Diagnosis?
⑤ Why Do We Look Up Our Symptoms on the Internet?

42 밑줄 친 (a)~(e) 중에서 문맥상 낱말의 쓰임이 적절하지 않은 것은? [3점]

① (a) ② (b) ③ (c) ④ (d) ⑤ (e)

[43~45] 다음 글을 읽고, 물음에 답하시오.

(A)

Monty Roberts was the son of a traveling horse trainer. When he was a senior in high school, his teacher asked him to write an essay about what he hoped to be and do when he grew up. He wrote about his dream in great detail and he even drew a diagram of a large farm. Then he drew a detailed floor plan for a 4,000-square-foot house that would sit on the 200-acre dream farm.

(B)

Then the scene changes, and Monty turns to the assembled group and says, "I tell you this story because you are here at my horse farm. I still have that school paper." He adds, "The best part is that two summers ago that same schoolteacher brought 30 kids to my ranch. When (a) he was leaving, he said, "I stole a lot of kids' dreams. Fortunately, you had the strength not to give up on yours."

(C)

He put a great deal of his heart into the assignment before handing it in to his teacher. When it was returned, there was a large red F with a note that read, "See me after class." The boy with the dream went to see the teacher and asked (b) him, "Why did I receive an F?" (c) He said, "This is an unrealistic dream for you. Owning a horse farm requires a lot of money. You'll never have this."

(D)

Then the teacher added, "If you rewrite this, I will reconsider your grade." The boy went home and asked his father for some advice. He said, "Look, son, don't take (d) him seriously. However, this is a very important decision." Eventually, the boy handed in the same paper, making no changes at all. (e) He stated, "You can keep the F and I'll keep my dream."

43 주어진 글 (A)에 이어질 내용을 순서에 맞게 배열한 것으로 가장 적절한 것은?

① (B) — (D) — (C)
② (C) — (B) — (D)
③ (C) — (D) — (B)
④ (D) — (B) — (C)
⑤ (D) — (C) — (B)

44 밑줄 친 (a)~(e) 중에서 가리키는 대상이 나머지 넷과 다른 것은?

① (a) ② (b) ③ (c) ④ (d) ⑤ (e)

45 윗글의 Monty Roberts에 관한 내용으로 적절하지 않은 것은?

① 말 조련사의 아들이었다.
② 자신의 꿈에 관한 글에 그림까지 첨부했다.
③ 목장을 소유한 후에도 고등학교 시절의 과제를 간직했다.
④ 선생님에게서 꿈이 비현실적이라는 지적을 받았다.
⑤ 아버지의 충고를 듣고 난 뒤 과제를 수정해서 제출했다.

AFTER TESTING

종료 시 분
소요시간 분

학습 마무리

1 채점하기 | 정답 및 해설 p.65
주의 틀린 문제를 다시 풀 수 있도록 정답을 본문에 표기하지 마세요.
2 등급 확인
3 틀린 유형 확인 후 전략 적용 복습 및 해설지 확인

How to Review

1 틀린 문제와 ✓ 표시한 문제는 다시 풀고 해설 확인하기
2 내가 표시한 정답 근거가 해설과 일치하는지 확인하기
3 잘 모르는 부분으로 표시한 내용은 해설을 통해 완전히 이해하기
4 어휘 외우기 (어휘 목록 다운로드 www.cedubook.com)
5 다음 회에 개선할 점 정리하기 (시간 엄수, 취약 유형 보완 등)

BEFORE TESTING

시작 시 분

1 **제한시간** (OMR 마킹시간 포함) ☐ 40분 ☐ 45분
2 **어휘예습** ☐ 해당 없음 ☐ 완료
3 **문제풀이순서** ☐ 순서대로 ☐ 2점 → 3점 ☐ 기타
4 **기타 목표**

Check Point

1 **정답 근거** *e.g.* 밑줄 긋기
2 **잘 모르는 부분** *e.g.* 〈 〉 또는 ? 표시
3 **자신 없는 문제** *e.g.* 문제 번호에 ✓표시

18 다음 글의 목적으로 가장 적절한 것은?

Dear Prospective Tutors,

For over 15 years, Sunshine Tutoring has provided elementary and middle school students with the tools they need to succeed. Our award-winning system of computer-based reading, writing, and math programs is the best anywhere. Of course, the real magic comes from our brilliant and dedicated tutors. This is where you come in! Sunshine Tutoring now has openings for tutors. If you'd like the opportunity to teach one-on-one with young learners, this is your chance. All materials and training are provided, and students are matched with tutors after careful testing. Become a part of the greatest tutoring academy around! For more information, visit www.sunshineacademy.com today.

Thank you.

① 일대일 수업의 장점을 알리려고
② 변경된 시험 기준을 공지하려고
③ 새로운 개인 지도 교사를 모집하려고
④ 컴퓨터 기반 학습 프로그램을 홍보하려고
⑤ 개인 지도 교사의 헌신에 감사를 표하려고

19 다음 글의 상황에 나타난 분위기로 가장 적절한 것은?

A full-faced sun confronted visitors as they began to arrive from remote villages and lonely uplands. Every workman in Casterbridge was dressed in his cleanest shirt. Suddenly the taller members of the crowd turned their heads, and the shorter stood on tip-toe. A whisper began to pass along the rows: the royal parade is approaching! The railway did not yet reach as far as Casterbridge, so the remainder of the journey from London had to be traveled by road. Thus, amid the ringing of bells and the chattering of tongues, everybody waited and watched the far-stretching London highway, hardly believing that the king would ever come.

① calm and peaceful
② wishful and magical
③ exciting and expectant
④ glorious and triumphant
⑤ disappointing and boring

20 다음 글에서 필자가 주장하는 바로 가장 적절한 것은?

All over the country people are swimming, jogging, doing yoga, taking belly-dance classes — anything to keep fit. Newspapers, magazines, and websites claim we are in the middle of a health revolution. In direct opposition to this positive trend, our college continues to refuse to provide financial support or land for fitness facilities and sporting programs. So far this year, the administrators have denied a request for a running track around the football field, rejected a donor's offer to build a swimming pool on unused college land, and even refused to begin a dance program for students. Students thus have nowhere to exercise except in their own rooms! It's time college administrators did something positive about this problem.

① 대학 스포츠 팀에 대한 지원을 늘려야 한다.
② 비인기 종목에 대한 지속적인 관심이 필요하다.
③ 대학 행정 업무 처리 과정을 학생들이 감시해야 한다.
④ 대학은 학생들을 위해 운동 시설 및 프로그램을 갖추어야 한다.
⑤ 대학 건물 증축을 위한 기금 모금에 학생들의 참여가 필요하다.

21 다음 글의 요지로 가장 적절한 것은?

Have you ever thought someone was telling you a lie? Your intuition was probably right — on average people tell two to three lies in a ten-minute conversation. Even more frightening, 91% of people lie regularly at home and work. But we can detect these lies only about half of the time — no better than a coin toss. Learning how to decode and interpret nonverbal behavior such as facial expressions, gestures, physical movements and vocal tone is an integral part of communication. As much as 93% of interpersonal communication is nonverbal, yet we often base all of our interactions on verbal content alone. By paying attention to such nonverbal cues, you will no longer wonder helplessly if the person you are with is trying to deceive you.

① 거짓말을 자주 하면 남의 말도 거짓이라고 믿게 된다.
② 말보다는 비언어적 행동이 보다 많은 정보를 담고 있다.
③ 비언어적인 행동을 통해 거짓말 여부를 알아낼 수 있다.
④ 남의 이익을 위한 선의의 거짓말은 비난 대상이 아니다.
⑤ 가까운 사이일수록 진실과 거짓말을 구별하기가 힘들다.

22 다음 글의 주제로 가장 적절한 것은?

In heritage tourism, supply usually precedes demand; in most other industries, including some types of tourism, demand typically precedes supply. Heritage supply includes material objects, most notably historic buildings, vehicles, cities and towns, rural cultural landscapes, historic sites, museums and portable artifacts. It also encompasses intangible elements of culture and history that are passed down from previous generations and appreciated, used or consumed in some form in the present day. Some of the best examples of intangible heritage include music and dance, cultural traditions, social customs, language, social networks, foodways and cuisine, worldviews, immigration and cultural diversity, lifestyles, poetry and art and literature. These intangible and tangible features of the past combine to make one of the most prominent attraction bases for tourism, and indeed embody much of the tourism product.

*artifact: (인공) 유물 **intangible: 무형(無形)의

① reasons for why heritage tourism is preferred
② necessity for the development of tourism products
③ prospect of heritage tourism for future generations
④ overview of the unique features of heritage tourism
⑤ importance of conserving and promoting cultural heritage

23 다음 글의 제목으로 가장 적절한 것은?

Dehydration is a medical condition defined by an extreme loss of body fluid. Children are more likely to suffer from dehydration than adults. Some of the common symptoms of dehydration in children are weakness, increased sweating, too much going to the toilet, too much vomiting, or a combination of these problems. The most common causes of dehydration in children are infections caused by viruses such as the flu or by bacteria. Because they tend to touch things that are dirty and not wash their hands very well, children get these infections more often. Dehydration is especially bad for children because they are weaker than adults and cannot take care of themselves very well.

① First Aid for Dehydration in Children
② Ways to Prevent Fluid Loss in Advance
③ The Danger of Dehydration in Old People
④ Drinking Water: The Best Cure for Dehydration
⑤ Dehydration in Children: Causes and Symptoms

24 다음 도표의 내용과 일치하지 않는 것은?

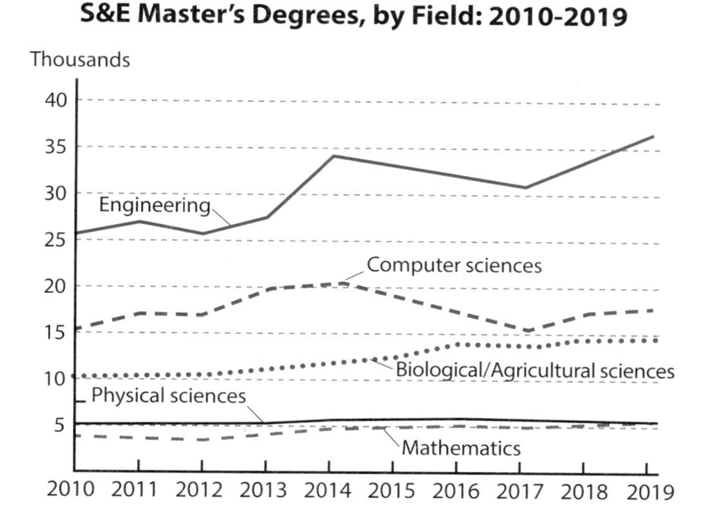

The above graph shows the number of master's degrees handed out in science and engineering (S&E) fields from 2010 to 2019. ① During this time, there were more master's degrees awarded in engineering than in any of the other fields, and the number peaked in 2019. ② Master's degrees awarded in computer sciences took the second place and remained above 15,000 throughout the given period. ③ At the same time, the number of master's degrees in biological and agricultural sciences gradually increased from just over 10,000 in 2010 to almost 15,000 in 2019. ④ Master's degrees in physical sciences were a bit more common than those in mathematics in 2010, but by 2019 they were tied at slightly over 5,000. ⑤ Throughout the period, the fewest master's degrees were awarded in mathematics, and it showed the lowest rate of increase from 2010 to 2019.

25 Jane Austen에 관한 다음 글의 내용과 일치하지 않는 것은?

Jane Austen was the first female novelist in England who lived from 1775 to 1817. Jane grew up in a large family. She had six brothers and one sister, Cassandra, who was a helpful assistant to Jane's novel ideas. The two would discuss the characters, their roles, their lives, and in turn make them seem 'real' to them. Jane's only educational background came from a relative and a brief attendance at the Reading Ladies Boarding School. When she was a girl, she wrote stories. Remaining unwed, she created novels that mirrored women's position in society at the time. Her works were printed only after much revision. Only four of her novels were printed while she was alive. Jane passed away at the early age of 41, but her novels remain an important part of any academic study program of English literature.

① 8남매의 대가족 속에서 성장했다.
② Cassandra와 소설에 대해 논의했다.
③ 당대 여성의 지위를 보여주는 소설을 썼다.
④ 4편의 소설은 사후에 출판되었다.
⑤ 영문학에서 학문적 연구 대상이 된 소설을 남겼다.

26 Lost Pet Safety Information에 관한 다음 안내문의 내용과 일치하지 않는 것은?

Lost Pet Safety Information

Pets can break loose and become separated from their families. If you find a lost pet, look up your local shelter on www.petsafety.org and call immediately for advice.

What to Do If You Find a Lost Cat:
- Offer the cat food and water.
- Never force the cat into your car.
- Never touch an injured cat without the help of professionals.
- Arrange for the cat to go to a shelter so it can be scanned for a microchip and included in the shelter's lost pet listings.
- Keep the cat away from other pets to avoid potential fights or the spread of diseases.
- Seek medical attention immediately if you are bitten or scratched, even if the wound seems minor.

① 길 잃은 고양이를 발견하면 음식물과 물을 주어야 한다.
② 길 잃은 고양이를 강제로 차에 태우려고 해서는 안 된다.
③ 길 잃은 고양이는 보호소의 목록에 올리도록 조치한다.
④ 길 잃은 고양이를 다른 반려동물과 같이 두어선 안 된다.
⑤ 길 잃은 고양이가 상처를 입었으면 즉시 치료해야 한다.

27 Youth Speech Contest에 관한 다음 안내문의 내용과 일치하는 것은?

Youth Speech Contest

Each year the Farm Bureau sponsors a Youth Speech Contest starting at the county level. The topic for 2020 is: Food security is an important issue to the people of the United States. How can Florida agriculture continue to provide quality solutions for the future?

Rules

- Competitors must be at least 14 years of age and not over 18 years of age on or before September 19, 2020.
- The competitor must prepare and present the speech personally. No form of video conferencing or visual aids will be permitted.
- Speeches must be 5 minutes in length +/− 30 seconds, and speeches that are too short or too long will result in subtracted points.

① 농업국에서 주관하며 2년에 한 번 열린다.
② 주제는 농산물 품질 향상에 관한 것이다.
③ 14세 이상의 청소년은 누구나 참가할 수 있다.
④ 연설 시 시각 자료를 활용할 수 있다.
⑤ 연설이 5분 30초를 넘어가면 감점을 받는다.

28 (A), (B), (C)의 각 네모 안에서 어법에 맞는 표현으로 가장 적절한 것은? [3점]

Why have horoscopes and palm readings been so popular for such a long time? One explanation is the "Barnum Effect." It is the tendency for people to accept very general or vague characterizations of (A) [them / themselves] to be accurate. It is named after P. T. Barnum, who believed that a good circus "has a little something, which makes everybody (B) [attracted / attracting] to those elements." Horoscopes and palm readings often sound something like this: "You have a great deal of unused ability. At times, you are shy." People are often amazed by how "accurate" such reports are. The trick is (C) [what / that] such a general statement is likely to sound accurate to just about anyone.

*horoscope: 별점, 점성술

	(A)		(B)		(C)
①	them	……	attracted	……	what
②	themselves	……	attracting	……	that
③	themselves	……	attracting	……	what
④	themselves	……	attracted	……	that
⑤	them	……	attracting	……	what

29 다음 글의 밑줄 친 부분 중, 문맥상 낱말의 쓰임이 적절하지 않은 것은? [3점]

The presentation of televised sports involves a highly structured and controlled production. Because of the ①complexity involved with producing a sports event, it is important to control as many variables as possible. The production staff generally includes a hierarchical ②division of labor, typically between the producer, the director, commentators, camera operators, visual and sound mixers, and technicians. Each individual has clearly defined responsibilities, which they are expected to ③fulfill despite any deficiencies in equipment. Each is employed in a particular role according to skills and previous experience, although flexibility is also a desired quality. The pressures involved come not just from time limitations but also from ④certainty, as producers have to react to unpredictable occurrences both within the event and external to it. Thus, the game itself may be ⑤unscripted, but the production of the sporting event is as organized as possible.

*commentator: 실황 방송 아나운서

30 밑줄 친 him[he]이 가리키는 대상이 나머지 넷과 다른 것은?

Some names can be hard to pronounce. But many people don't even make an effort to learn how to say someone's name properly. My uncle, Sid Levy, a grocery store supplier, had a customer named Theodoros Andriopoulos. Most people just called ① him Theo. Uncle Sid, however, made a special effort to learn the right way to say the name before ② he made a visit. When Sid walked into Theo's Grocery Store and said, in a perfect Greek accent, "Good afternoon Mr. Theodoros Andriopoulos," ③ he was shocked. For a while, there was no reply from ④ him at all. Finally, ⑤ he said with tears in his eyes, "My friend, in the 20 years since I left my country, this is the only time I've heard my name spoken just like my family used to say it."

[31~34] 다음 빈칸에 들어갈 말로 가장 적절한 것을 고르시오.

31 There are many creative ways to add your own special touch to an apology, and using songs is one of the best. For example, Chicago's "Hard to Say I'm Sorry" has some beautiful lyrics about promising to be a better partner. You can make your apology more effective by including the song in a letter. Secondly, think about a favorite song that you share and how you can bring it into your apology or offer it as a gift, but remember to relate the song to the situation. Perhaps it's a song you were dancing with your partner to on your first date. Or both of you might have listened to it on a memorable vacation. If it's suitable in some important way to your relationship or the situation, then adding music or lyrics will likely improve your apology. __________ is a key to success when choosing a song to say, "sorry." [3점]

① Honesty
② Tolerance
③ Relevance
④ Promptness
⑤ Bravery

32 Observation is the solid foundation of the sciences, and many scientists believe that the secret to it lies in ____________________. Karl von Frisch, who studied the dance language of bees, wrote that his ability to observe came from simply lying down: "Watching living things I could see on and between the slimy green stones just below the surface of the water, I discovered that wonderful worlds may reveal themselves to a long-suffering observer where the casual passer-by sees nothing at all." Konrad Lorenz, whose studies of geese, fish, and other animals revealed their hidden worlds, also commented on the need to focus one's love of looking: "To really understand animals and their behavior, you must look at them long enough to see something." Other scientists, such as geologist Nathaniel Shaler, at Harvard, were given exercises that forced them to look at a specimen over and over until some facts, for example, that in some fish the scale pattern differs on the two sides, became obvious.

① time and patience
② vision and passion
③ harmony and balance
④ honesty and diligence
⑤ analysis and comparison

33 Some psychologists link a slack posture and a slow walking pace to a bad attitude about life. Look around and you'll see that ____________________. Very depressed people walk very slowly and hardly lift their feet at all. They have zero self-confidence. Average people have an "average" walk. They're neither up nor down. Then there's a third group, the super-confident. These people's faster-than-average walking pace and excellent posture declare: "I'm *really* going somewhere. And I will succeed at whatever I have to do when I get there." If you just copy the way they walk, you will build self-confidence. Try it: throw those shoulders back, speed up that pace, and see how much different you feel. [3점]

*slack: 맥 빠진

① the pace that fits you is the best
② confidence matters in success
③ slow and steady wins the race
④ we have different walking styles
⑤ the way you move can change you

34 Scientists at Kingston University in England are promoting the idea that ______________________ may be better for your health. These scientists are experts in dust mites, those microscopic animals that like to live in our beds, pillows, sofas, cushions, or anywhere they can find some human sweat to drink. We can easily inhale dust mite poo when we're asleep, and this can cause severe allergies and asthma. But, as the scientists point out, dust mites can survive only in moist and sweaty places. If sheets and blankets are left in a mess in the morning, air circulates through them and the mattress and dries your sweat. This kills the dust mites by robbing them of what they need to survive. [3점]

① not making your bed after you get up
② washing your sheets as often as possible
③ sleeping on the floor rather than in a bed
④ not messing up your room with your clothes
⑤ keeping your bedroom windows closed at night

35 **다음 글에서 전체 흐름과 관계 없는 문장은?**

If you download free files and software from the Net — especially games, music, and movies from the highly popular file-sharing sites — chances are you've also gotten more than you originally expected. ① Freeloading programs can quietly come into your PC during the download process and then do things secretly once they get there. ② The software can track your surfing habits, record the sites you visit, use your Net connection to report to a remote base and deliver targeted ads to you. ③ At one time, advertising online was expensive, but today, promoting your business online is fast and affordable. ④ For example, if you search for your favorite band, the software may deliver to you an ad for the band's upcoming concert. ⑤ It can also collect private information stored on your computer and allow your computer to be used remotely.

[36~37] 주어진 글 다음에 이어질 글의 순서로 가장 적절한 것을 고르시오.

36

> In December of 1988, a severe earthquake struck Armenia. A boy named Armand was at school when the quake struck. Armand's father rushed to the son's school to rescue him, only to find the school destroyed.

(A) Every time people would try to stop him and tell him it's useless, he'd reply: "Join me or leave me alone!" After digging by hand for thirty-eight hours, he heard a soft voice: "Daddy, is that you?"

(B) His son and fourteen of his classmates were alive under collapsed walls. He lifted them all out from the darkness they had endured into the light of day. Armand turned to his friends and said, "See, I told you my father wouldn't forget us."

(C) He knew that his son's classroom was at a back corner of the school, and he climbed over the pile and began digging by hand to try to uncover where the classroom had been.

① (A) — (C) — (B)
② (B) — (A) — (C)
③ (B) — (C) — (A)
④ (C) — (A) — (B)
⑤ (C) — (B) — (A)

37

The "Chinese Room Argument" was formulated in 1980 by John Searle, an influential professor of philosophy. He created it to demonstrate that a program cannot provide a computer with intelligence.

(A) So it is with a computer; given bits of information and simple instructions, it can follow the instructions, but it cannot "understand" the information.

(B) The argument goes like this: Imagine that you're locked in a room. Pieces of Chinese writing, none of which you can read, come into the room. Then come instructions, written in your language, for relating one piece of Chinese to another.

(C) The result is that you seem able to respond in Chinese to instructions given in Chinese, when in fact you cannot understand a single word of it.

① (A) — (C) — (B)
② (B) — (A) — (C)
③ (B) — (C) — (A)
④ (C) — (A) — (B)
⑤ (C) — (B) — (A)

[38~39] 글의 흐름으로 보아, 주어진 문장이 들어가기에 가장 적절한 곳을 고르시오.

38

Aside from this, there are no rules on how to conduct "correctly," which is why so many different conducting styles exist.

Singers in choirs and musicians in orchestras all rely on the art of conducting. (①) Basically, conducting is how conductors communicate their instructions to the performers in "real time" during a performance. (②) Therefore, the only rule of conducting is that it must be precise and meaningful. (③) There is a particular distinction between orchestral conducting and choral conducting. (④) Orchestra conductors typically use a baton to indicate the beat and to convey how softly or strongly the musicians should play. (⑤) Choir conductors, on the other hand, rarely use a baton to conduct but instead use their face and hands expressively to focus on emotional tone and musical shape.

39

> Similarly, the use of euphemistic expressions in politics is a must, since it helps calm down tense situations, especially during peace negotiations.

Euphemism is a literary term that represents a word or a phrase that is said to avoid saying something that might sound offensive. (①) It is a polite way of saying something that would normally sound unpleasant. (②) For example, in an effort to hide what some consider to be an unpleasant occupation, the neighborhood garbage collector has been called a "sanitary engineer." (③) Nothing is wrong with this, but the term sanitary engineer may confuse anyone who still thinks of an engineer as a highly skilled, technically oriented professional. (④) If you say that one side has killed 10,000 soldiers of the opposing side, it is likely to make the situation tense and won't help the negotiations, but if you say that one side has 10,000 casualties, it is somewhat less probable to create discomfort or rage. (⑤) Thus the euphemism acts the same way as the sugar coating on a bitter pill.

*euphemism: 완곡어법

40 다음 글의 내용을 한 문장으로 요약하고자 한다. 빈칸 (A), (B)에 들어갈 말로 가장 적절한 것은? [3점]

> Have you ever noticed that when you are in a really bad mood, doing a crossword puzzle, solving a sudoku puzzle, or memorizing a poem can make you completely forget your feelings for a while? And as soon as you finish the little task that you set yourself, the bad feelings start to come right back again. This happens because negative emotions take up a lot of mental energy: bad feelings are a big drain on your brain. When you focus your mind on something challenging, mental resources are pulled away from the "bad feelings factory" and put to work to solve the puzzle or to memorize the poem. This is why you seem to temporarily escape from your troubled emotional state.

↓

> One way to ___(A)___ the effects of a negative emotion is to take your brain's resources away from the emotional work and apply them to a mentally ___(B)___ task.

	(A)		(B)
①	eliminate	……	simple
②	investigate	……	trivial
③	correct	……	stressful
④	evaluate	……	continuous
⑤	lessen	……	demanding

[41~42] 다음 글을 읽고, 물음에 답하시오.

Modern civilization has blessed us with riches unimaginable by our ancestors. Thus, it's strange that so many people feel that what they have and who they are is not enough. However, it may not seem so strange if we consider the psychology behind the way we judge "enough." We don't judge what we have in isolation. We do it by comparing it with that of the people whom we consider ________________.

We feel fortunate only if we have as much as, or more than, the people we grow up with, go to school with, or work with. It's the achievements of these people that bother us the most. If you are short and live among short people, you won't be overly bothered by your size. But if the people in your group suddenly grow taller, you will probably start to feel annoyed and envious, even though you yourself haven't lost a millimeter in height.

Given the great inequalities we see everywhere, it's remarkable that we don't have terrible feelings of envy about *everyone* who is richer or more successful than we are. A Saudi Arabian prince's enormous wealth and privileges, for instance, don't make us feel like losers. However, we can feel sick with envy if a classmate has a really cool cell phone or a bag that our parents won't buy for us. The members of our reference group are the mirrors we measure ourselves against. That's why the hardest successes to endure are those of the people we're close to.

41 윗글의 제목으로 가장 적절한 것은?

① How to Be Satisfied with Your Life
② Do Achievements Exist in Isolation?
③ Success Comes from Others' Regard
④ Why We Envy Our Neighbors' Success
⑤ The Danger of Comparing Yourself with Others

42 윗글의 빈칸에 들어갈 말로 가장 적절한 것은? [3점]

① to help us grow
② to be our equals
③ as our role models
④ the most successful
⑤ experts in their fields

[43~45] 다음 글을 읽고, 물음에 답하시오.

(A)

Last summer, Jessica found herself in a deep depression. Nothing interested her, and her daily routines felt empty. People told her that she was suffering from summertime blues. One day, when a friend saw her in this condition, she recommended that Jessica try volunteer work. Jessica was reluctant at first but later decided to give it a try. As a result, Jessica learned an unforgettable lesson in life.

(B)

As they worked together, learning how to read built Marie's self-confidence. She began to make rapid progress and was even able to take the bus to the supermarket by (a) herself. After this successful trip, she described how self-confident she felt. At the end of the program, (b) she began helping her youngest son, Tony, with his reading. She sat with him before he went to sleep and together they would read bedtime stories.

(C)

Jessica signed up through a local program and became a literacy volunteer. Her first student, Marie, was a 44-year-old single mother of three. In the first lesson, Jessica discovered that she walked 5 kilometers to the nearest supermarket because (c) she didn't know which bus to take. She told Jessica that she also had trouble once she got to the supermarket because she could not make a shopping list.

(D)

When his eyes grew wide with excitement as (d) she read, pride was written all over her face, and she began to see how her own hard work paid off. As she talked about this experience, Jessica was proud of herself as well. She found that helping Marie was truly rewarding. Her depression vanished and (e) she felt a new zeal for life. Helping others was, in fact, helping herself.

43 주어진 글 (A)에 이어질 내용을 순서에 맞게 배열한 것으로 가장 적절한 것은?

① (B) — (D) — (C)
② (C) — (B) — (D)
③ (C) — (D) — (B)
④ (D) — (B) — (C)
⑤ (D) — (C) — (B)

44 밑줄 친 (a)~(e) 중에서 가리키는 대상이 나머지 넷과 다른 것은?

① (a) ② (b) ③ (c) ④ (d) ⑤ (e)

45 윗글의 Marie에 관한 내용으로 적절하지 않은 것은?

① Jessica와 함께 공부하며 실력이 빠르게 향상하였다.
② Jessica에게 Tony의 선생님이 되어 달라고 부탁했다.
③ 남편 없이 혼자 세 아이를 키우는 어머니이다.
④ 슈퍼마켓에서 장을 보는 데 어려움을 겪었다.
⑤ Jessica의 우울증 극복에 많은 도움이 되었다.

AFTER TESTING

종료 시 분

소요시간 분

1 채점하기 | 정답 및 해설 p.73

주의 틀린 문제를 다시 풀 수 있도록 정답을 본문에 표기하지 마세요.

2 등급 확인

3 틀린 유형 확인 후 전략 적용 복습 및 해설지 확인

How to Review

1 틀린 문제와 ✓ 표시한 문제는 다시 풀고 해설 확인하기

2 내가 표시한 정답 근거가 해설과 일치하는지 확인하기

3 잘 모르는 부분으로 표시한 내용은 해설을 통해 완전히 이해하기

4 어휘 외우기 (어휘 목록 다운로드 www.cedubook.com)

5 다음 회에 개선할 점 정리하기 (시간 엄수, 취약 유형 보완 등)

BUTTON UP!

고난도 모의고사

11

BEFORE TESTING

시작 시 분

1 **제한시간** (OMR 마킹시간 포함) ☐ 40분 ☐ 45분
2 **어휘예습** ☐ 해당 없음 ☐ 완료
3 **문제풀이순서** ☐ 순서대로 ☐ 2점 → 3점 ☐ 기타
4 **기타 목표**

Check Point

1 **정답 근거** *e.g.* 밑줄 긋기
2 **잘 모르는 부분** *e.g.* 〈 〉 또는 ? 표시
3 **자신 없는 문제** *e.g.* 문제 번호에 ✓표시

18 다음 글의 목적으로 가장 적절한 것은?

Dear Parents,

May is Environmental Awareness Month at Maple School. It's a month of in-class activities, assignments, and day trips aimed at educating the youth on the importance of environmental practices. Responsible water usage necessarily makes up a large part of this. To emphasize this, a trip to the Yellow Garden's one-day educational nature program is planned for May 25. Please fill out the attached permission slip and have your child bring it to class before the 25th, so he or she can participate. The day will include a wetland walk and introduce many concepts related to improving water quality and creating a sustainable water future. If you have any questions or worries, please call me or visit the Yellow Garden's website at yellowgarden.org.

Sincerely,
Patricia Wilkins

① 자연 교육 프로그램을 광고하려고
② 환경 인식의 달에 대해 설명하려고
③ 학부모 참여 교육 활동을 제안하려고
④ 물 절약 교육의 중요성을 강조하려고
⑤ 학부모에게 견학 허가서를 요청하려고

19 다음 글에 드러난 'I'의 심경 변화로 가장 적절한 것은?

I was ten years old and walking down Brooklyn's Fifty-second Street with my aunt. As we approached a railway station, I saw scattered before us on the sidewalk at least a hundred Batman trading cards. Overwhelmed by my good fortune — I loved Batman cards — I greedily began scooping them up. But almost immediately there was a gentle tug on my arm. "I know how much you want those cards," my aunt said, "but somebody might have dropped them by accident, and that person would be sad to find them gone, just like you would be if you were that person." Normally I would have been indignant, argued, complained, and raged against the ridiculous injustice of it all. Instead, I let go of the cards, gave my head a shake, and said to my aunt, "Yeah, you're right." I couldn't even lift my face up to look her in the eyes.

① happy → angry
② indifferent → curious
③ excited → ashamed
④ pleased → gloomy
⑤ perplexed → disappointed

20 다음 글에서 필자가 주장하는 바로 가장 적절한 것은?

Whether it is our children, our spouse, or a friend, when others share a story with us, we should be empathetic rather than authoritative while listening. We oftentimes miss the humor or joy of a situation when we feel we must give feedback for each situation or offer advice. It is actually a form of pride when we determine that we have to interrupt others in every situation. It suggests that we know better than they do. Unwanted advice can cause frustration, hurt and even anger. Not everything needs to be a teachable moment. We can lose an opportunity of shared friendship and the deepening of trust when we choose to talk over the other person. Whether it is a time to rejoice or mourn, we would do well to provide our undivided attention and simply listen.

① 충고를 하려면 완곡한 방법으로 하라.
② 상황에 맞는 유머를 사용하여 충고하라.
③ 상대방이 원하지 않을 때 충고하지 마라.
④ 먼저 상대방의 입장에서 생각한 뒤 충고하라.
⑤ 타인의 충고를 받아들여 발전의 기회로 삼아라.

21 밑줄 친 <u>a double-edged sword</u>가 다음 글에서 의미하는 바로 가장 적절한 것은?

Capsaicin, the ingredient in spicy foods, is a sticky poison — it adheres to mucous membranes, which is why your eyes burn if you ever rub them after handling peppers. In large quantities, capsaicin can be very harmful. Scientists are still debating the connection, but people in places like Sri Lanka — where hot peppers are almost a staple — tend to have much higher rates of stomach diseases. However, capsaicin, the "hot" in hot peppers, also stimulates the release of endorphins, which induce feelings of pleasure and reduce feelings of stress. Even more, there is a growing body of evidence that capsaicin may be helpful in reducing the chronic pain caused by conditions such as arthritis and diabetes. In light of the complex and seemingly conflicting actions, capsaicin has been referred to as <u>a double-edged sword</u>.

*mucous membranes: (콧속 · 입안 등의) 점막

① increasing the appetite but causing chronic illness
② triggering pain in the body but curing mental illness
③ difficult to eat, but after eating, good for your health
④ poison in a small quantity and medicine in a large quantity
⑤ causing pain and disease but reducing mental and physical pain

22 다음 글의 요지로 가장 적절한 것은?

At first glance, it appears that increasing media coverage of a problem means that the problem is getting worse. But is that really what is happening? In recent years, for example, we have seen more and more articles published and news stories produced about domestic violence and child abuse. These are serious issues, and the media plays a key role in raising public awareness of the issues, but this does not necessarily mean that more women and children are being assaulted and abused now. It more likely indicates a higher rate of reporting of the incidents to police, which in turn leads to even more extensive media coverage. We are merely hearing more about the incidents, not seeing an increase in their numbers.

① 소외 계층에 대한 심층적인 취재가 필요하다.
② 언론 보도가 중대 범죄의 증가를 막지는 못한다.
③ 언론 매체의 공정한 보도가 민주주의의 전제 조건이다.
④ 사회 문제에 대한 각 계층의 광범위한 토론이 필요하다.
⑤ 언론 보도가 증가했다고 사회 문제가 증가한 것은 아니다.

23 다음 글의 주제로 가장 적절한 것은?

Motivation to start exercising is powerful in the beginning and provides what's necessary to take the first steps toward healthier living. However, this positive enthusiasm often turns negative because the individual forgets another key component of success: moderation. When an exerciser starts eagerly and takes on workouts that are far too frequent or far too intense, then inevitably they burn out and quit altogether. As with most things in life, moderation in exercise is very important. A moderate exercise program varies by individual and fitness level, but in general you should start slow and build from there. An effective workout plan will slowly increase your exercise intensity each week in a safe manner.

① effective ways to avoid exercise burnout
② different motives for starting to exercise
③ effects of regular exercise on mental health
④ difficulties in determining exercise intensity
⑤ merits and demerits of moderate-level exercise

24 다음 글의 제목으로 가장 적절한 것은?

I am always amazed when people write or phone me and try to sell me their new idea. I ask them, "What is it?" They say that they can't tell me the idea until I have paid them for it. I try to explain to them that their ideas are of no value by themselves. They are often shocked. They think that their idea has value just because they thought of it. The fact is that 99 out of 100 ideas don't work, at least not in their original form. This is why you have to generate a lot of ideas if you are going to come up with the one that makes a difference. And the one idea that does work only has value when it is combined and re-combined with a variety of other ideas and information to achieve some worthy end.

① Action Creates New Ideas
② Ideas: Quantity Breeds Quality
③ Good Ideas Come from Creativity
④ All New Ideas Are Made from Old Ideas
⑤ Curiosity Fuels Imagination for New Ideas

25 다음 도표의 내용과 일치하지 않는 것은?

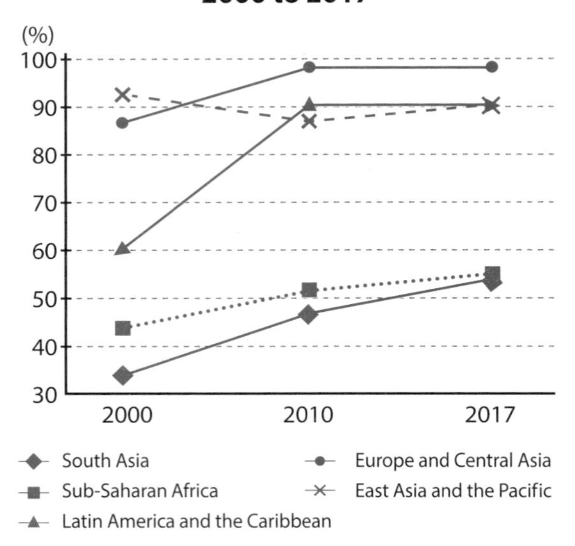

The graph above shows literacy rates among adult females from 2000 to 2017 by region. ① The rate in East Asia and the Pacific declined from 2000 until 2010, but showed a slight increase between 2010 and 2017. ② On the other hand, the rate in Europe and Central Asia as well as that in Latin America and the Caribbean increased during the 2000s and was followed by little or no progress. ③ Nevertheless, the adult female literacy rate in Europe and Central Asia ranked first in 2017, while Latin America and the Caribbean tied with East Asia and the Pacific for second place. ④ Meanwhile, the rates of South Asia and Sub-Saharan Africa showed steady improvement during the study period. ⑤ However, those areas remained far enough behind the others that over half of their women were illiterate in 2017.

26 Glennie에 관한 다음 글의 내용과 일치하지 않는 것은?

Glennie, born in Aberdeen, Scotland, in 1965, is referred to as the "First Lady" of solo percussion. She lost her hearing at the age of 12 and began to study percussion instruments at that time. Glennie made her professional debut in 1985, and it did not take long for her musical adventurousness to show itself. A composer herself, Glennie has written music for film and television. Glennie does not mention her deafness in press materials, and she has been known to react with annoyance when asked about it to the exclusion of musical matters. She is profoundly deaf, but she can feel some sound. She says she feels low sounds in her legs and feet, and high ones on her face, neck, and chest. Glennie contends that hearing is a form of touch, and that everyone, whether "deaf" or not, processes sound in an individual way.

*percussion: 타악기

① 타악기 독주 분야에서 최고로 여겨진다.
② 청각을 잃고 나서 타악기를 공부하기 시작했다.
③ 영화와 TV를 위한 음악을 작곡했다.
④ 청각장애인으로 언급되는 것을 개의치 않는다.
⑤ 촉각을 통해서 소리를 느낄 수 있다고 주장한다.

27 Smith Nature Tour Bike Ride에 관한 다음 안내문의 내용과 일치하지 않는 것은?

Smith Nature Tour Bike Ride

The Smith Nature Tour Bike Ride is a fun opportunity to learn about the Smith Wetlands while getting some exercise.

Friday, September 17
1:00 p.m.–5:00 p.m.

The ride: This is a 20-kilometer ride over flat ground, and we will be stopping frequently to appreciate natural attractions.

Guide: Jim Hendricks is a park naturalist with 17 years of experience. He's also an experienced bicyclist.

What to prepare: Bring your bicycle, a helmet, plenty of water, and appropriate clothing. Bicycles can also be rented from a stand near the park entrance for $5.

Meet at the south entrance to the Smith Wetlands next to the visitors center by 12:45 p.m.

① 자전거 타기는 4시간 동안 진행된다.
② 20km를 달리며 자연 명소들을 감상한다.
③ 가이드는 17년 경력의 동식물 연구가이다.
④ 참가비 5달러에 자전거 대여비가 포함된다.
⑤ 참가자들은 방문자 센터 옆 남쪽 입구에서 만난다.

28 Greentree Suspension Bridge Park에 관한 다음 안내문의 내용과 일치하는 것은?

Greentree Suspension Bridge Park

Established in 1914 to commemorate construction of the Greentree Suspension Bridge, this historic location receives over 75,000 visitors each year.

ATTENTION
OBSERVE ALL SAFETY SIGNS.
Unsafe behaviors may result in removal from the park or serious or fatal injury.

WHILE AT THE PARK:
Stay on the designated trails and walkways.
Walkways may be slippery when wet.
Parents/Guardians must supervise those under their care.

ON THE BRIDGE:
Do not retrieve dropped items.
Notify park staff.
Hold small children by the hand.
No running, jumping or intentionally shaking the bridges.
Babies should be carried below the level of the railing or in a purpose-designed child-carrying device.

① 1914년 건설된 이래 약 7만 5천 명이 방문했다.
② 위험한 행동을 하면 벌금이 부과된다.
③ 공원 내에서는 보도로만 다녀야 한다.
④ 다리에서 떨어뜨린 물품은 본인이 수거해야 한다.
⑤ 아기는 다리 난간보다 낮은 높이로만 데리고 다닐 수 있다.

29 다음 글의 밑줄 친 부분 중, 어법상 틀린 것은? [3점]

The possibility of life on the planets of distant stars ① has long been a favorite topic of science fiction writers and movie makers. Now this issue has drawn the serious interest of respected scientists. ② Using specially designed telescopes that are able to pick up very weak radio waves, they are scanning the sky above us every minute of each day and night. These radio telescopes can monitor over a million channels simultaneously as they search for any clue of a distant, advanced civilization ③ sends messages into space. No one can predict ④ if we'll ever receive a signal sent by intelligent beings from elsewhere in the universe. But one thing is sure. If we do receive such a message, we'll be hearing thoughts from the past. This is ⑤ because it takes radio waves a long time to travel the incredible distances that separate Earth from other planets that may contain life.

30 다음 글의 밑줄 친 부분 중, 문맥상 낱말의 쓰임이 적절하지 않은 것은? [3점]

A propagandist appeals to human ① emotions. He uses fear, hope, anger, frustration, or sympathy to direct audiences toward the desired goal. The bandwagon is another device that may be used by the propagandist. "Everyone is doing it. Therefore, you should be doing it, too." Of course, the statement is an ② oversimplification. Everyone is not doing it. The bandwagon is an appeal to our need for the sense of ③ independence. "So, hop on the bandwagon. Join the crowd and be happy and secure." The propagandist also gives the impression of ④ knowing what he is talking about. His voice is strong; his facial expressions are bold; his bodily gestures are decisive. The theory here is something like this: If this person is so ⑤ confident, he must be right. People prefer to support a winner, and such a manner makes a person look like a winner.

*propagandist: 선동가

[31~34] 다음 빈칸에 들어갈 말로 가장 적절한 것을 고르시오.

31 Writing a business letter need not be difficult as long as you remember that you are communicating with another business person that may be in a different field. The language of your letter should be adapted to the recipient. This means that you write in a matter-of-fact tone. Use specific examples the reader can relate to. Don't assume that your reader understands the technical terms of your trade. Remember, most letters may be read by people other than the recipient of the letter. These people may be unfamiliar with the technical language you use. You should also present your ideas in a logical order for the reader to understand precisely what you are saying. Your letter should not be a collection of random ideas. It should be single-minded in its purpose. In short, your business letter should be ______________.

① brief
② clear
③ accurate
④ professional
⑤ conversational

32 Learning to think should make your life easier. During my first university years, I crammed far too much for exams, trying to be on top of all the topics not given much of importance in my texts. As you expected, I didn't get good grades. It would have been much better to focus on questions my teachers were certain to ask, which I could have discerned if I had paid attention to their main take-home lessons. To get the best insight into what would be on the test, I looked to the instructors who designed it: my teachers or professors. Some made it easy by giving me a study guide for the exam. But even if they didn't, I tried to take cues from their lessons to figure out what would show up. Trying to put myself into my instructor's head became much easier when I began to concentrate on subjects of personal interest, and I could achieve success in examinations during my university years. My secret to getting good grades was ______________________.

① to think like my teachers
② to track down past exams
③ to identify my weaknesses
④ to upgrade my test-taking skills
⑤ to study with top-performing students

33 All experiences are neutral. They have no meaning. If you are a priest, you see evidence of God everywhere. If you are an atheist, you see the absence of God everywhere. IBM, an American multinational technology company, observed that no one in the world had a personal computer. IBM took this to mean there was no market. College dropouts Bill Gates and Steve Jobs looked at the same absence of personal computers and saw a massive opportunity. Once, Thomas Edison was approached by an assistant while working on the filament for the light bulb. The assistant asked Edison why he didn't give up. "After all," he said, "you have failed 5,000 times." Edison looked at him and told him that he didn't understand what the assistant meant by "failure." Edison said, "I have discovered 5,000 things that don't work." You construct your own reality by ______________________. [3점]

① seeing the best at the worst of times
② focusing on developing your strengths
③ dedicating time and energy to yourself
④ choosing to interpret your experiences
⑤ anticipating problems and preparing for them

11

34 To a high degree, what a man is capable of accomplishing in life depends on ________________________________. For example, medical progress has been held back by religious rules against cutting apart the human body. For this reason, Indian and Chinese physicians, who had developed sophisticated medical knowledge more than two thousand years ago, never had a chance to study the internal structure and function of organs. Without this direct access to the body, they were prevented from making many important discoveries. Western medicine was similarly slowed by the prohibition against examining dead bodies until well into the fourteenth century, but afterward it became increasingly permissible to analyze the body's internal workings. Thus, Western physicians caught up with and then surpassed their counterparts in Asia. [3점]

① the technological standard of his society
② whether he has the pioneer spirit or not
③ the values and beliefs shared by his culture
④ his ability to communicate his ideas to others
⑤ whether he believes all will be well in the end

35 **다음 글에서 전체 흐름과 관계 없는 문장은?**

If wealthy nations continue to live in peace and prosperity, their newborn babies can now expect to live over a hundred years. ①Since the 20th century, populations in developed countries have been living about thirty years longer than in the past. ②Surprisingly, this longevity trend shows no sign of slowing down. ③Improvements in health care continue to slow rates of aging, challenging the belief that there is a fixed ceiling on life expectancy. ④While problems such as heart disease, cancer, and diabetes are rising in the elderly, advances in medical treatment are also making it possible for them to remain alive and active for longer. ⑤The obesity epidemic, however, may complicate matters: being overweight leads to major health problems, especially for children raised on a typical Western, "wealthy nations" diet.

[36~37] 주어진 글 다음에 이어질 글의 순서로 가장 적절한 것을 고르시오.

36

One of the most common techniques that advertisers use to promote their products is association. Appealing to human psychology, this method uses images to create a whole chain of ideas behind a product.

(A) In this manner, advertisers try to make a customer believe that he will be more attractive if he uses the lotion. What is being produced is not product, but you, the customer.

(B) Let's say that the product being sold is men's lotion. The commercial that advertises it may tell you very little about the lotion.

(C) Instead, it shows attractive women who are chasing after the lucky man wearing the lotion. The effect of this method is dependent on connection of the object (the lotion) and the idea (attractiveness).

① (A) — (C) — (B)
② (B) — (A) — (C)
③ (B) — (C) — (A)
④ (C) — (A) — (B)
⑤ (C) — (B) — (A)

37

Pricing can be a strange thing. It has a huge influence on how you feel about the value of what you do.

(A) Therefore, it is essential to find the right balance both for you and for your customers. You need to feel satisfied with the price you charge your customers, and your customers must feel satisfied with the value they perceive themselves to be receiving.

(B) Over-charging comes with a different set of problems. You may set a price no one will pay, or find yourself under such intense pressure to appear as valuable as the high price you demand that your work suffers.

(C) If you charge too little, you may end up working very hard for very little. You may be perceived as cheap and therefore not so valuable. You may end up with a lot of work but no time to develop and grow your business or your skills.

① (A) — (C) — (B)　② (B) — (A) — (C)
③ (B) — (C) — (A)　④ (C) — (A) — (B)
⑤ (C) — (B) — (A)

[38~39] 글의 흐름으로 보아, 주어진 문장이 들어가기에 가장 적절한 곳을 고르시오.

38

Soon the press did not limit itself to religious texts, and works of poetry and philosophy made their way throughout Europe, which sparked a notable increase in literacy rates.

Around 1440, a German blacksmith and goldsmith named Johannes Gutenberg introduced his revolutionary version of the printing press. (①) The machine used the concept of "moveable type" to place individual molds of letters — which could be rearranged depending on the piece being printed — onto plates. (②) While not the first printing press in existence, Gutenberg's version was far more efficient and could produce more than 3,000 pages of text a day. (③) The impact on the literary world was both profound and immediate. (④) Gutenberg's press began mass-producing copies of the Bible for the first time in history, giving access to a text formerly reserved to members of religion and nobility. (⑤) The ability to quickly and efficiently communicate new thoughts and ideas to the masses also fueled the Protestant Reformation and helped break down the divide between upper- and lower-class citizens in Europe. [3점]

39

> Within a few months, however, you may be perplexed by a new reaction from your baby.

Pointing allows babies to exchange information with those around them. It is a social and communicative behavior. Babies never point when they are alone. Indeed, they will first actively attract your attention before they point, to ensure that their action will be noticed. At around six months, babies begin pointing to objects out of their reach in order to convey specific desires. (①) This form of pointing is called "instrumental pointing" and represents a very specific and intentional means-to-an-end action. (②) The resulting response from the parent — to pick up the toy and hand it to the baby — is predicted and confirmed. (③) When you hand him the toy he was pointing at, he may look displeased or push it away. (④) Your frustrated little one is feeling annoyed because this time you didn't understand his behavior. (⑤) In this case, he was sharing an experience by showing the toy to you, not asking for something to be given to him.

40 다음 글의 내용을 한 문장으로 요약하고자 한다. 빈칸 (A), (B)에 들어갈 말로 가장 적절한 것은? [3점]

> There are two large jars placed in front of you. You cannot see the contents in the jars. The jar on the left contains ten black marbles and ten white ones. The jar on the right contains twenty marbles, but you do not know the proportion of black to white. Now, the game is to draw a black marble from one of the jars. Let's play again. Now, the game is to draw a white marble. Most people when confronted with these choices choose the jar on the left. And therein lies the paradox. If you choose the left-hand jar when trying to pull a black marble, that means you think your chances are better for that jar. But because there are only two colors in both jars, the odds of pulling a white must be complementary to the odds of pulling a black. Logically, if you thought the left-hand jar was the better choice for a black marble, the right-hand jar should be the better choice for a white marble.

↓

> According to the passage, decision makers prefer options with ____(A)____ probabilities to options with ____(B)____ probabilities.

	(A)		(B)
①	objective	……	unknown
②	objective	……	precise
③	positive	……	predictable
④	subjective	……	precise
⑤	subjective	……	unknown

[41~42] 다음 글을 읽고, 물음에 답하시오.

According to the logic of democracy, the government should obey the will of the majority. This majority is likely to change frequently and have prejudiced views. The majority pursues (a) exclusively its own interests at the expense of those in the minority. It is known as the tyranny of the majority. An equal danger lies in politicians doing what they feel is best for the country, even if most of the people who elected them do not agree with them. Another difficulty lies in (b) reducing the complexity of life to a single decision between opposing political parties. At national elections, the parties put forward their ideas in their election promises. Many people agree with bits from each of the opposing party programs. But you can vote only for one side. When they come to power, the politicians may refer to their election promises (which most have not read) and then pursue policies that those who elected them did not anticipate. People consequently feel (c) cheated. Furthermore, the party in power often brings in new ideas, after a year or two, with which people who voted for the party totally disagree. They fight a war, or bring in new taxes or criminal laws that are (d) unacceptable to even their strongest supporters. People can write to their Member of Parliament, but they feel this has little effect. As the British Labor Prime Minister Clement Attlee candidly admitted, "Democracy means government by discussion but it is only effective if you can (e) keep people talking."

41 윗글의 제목으로 가장 적절한 것은?

① What Are the Deeper Roots of Democracy?
② Democracy Doesn't Guarantee Equality and Wealth
③ The Triumph of Democracy Is Not Assured Forever
④ Is Democracy the Best Political System for All of Us?
⑤ How Democracy Changed Its Meaning and Lost Its Purpose

42 밑줄 친 (a)~(e) 중에서 문맥상 낱말의 쓰임이 적절하지 않은 것은? [3점]

① (a) ② (b) ③ (c) ④ (d) ⑤ (e)

[43~45] 다음 글을 읽고, 물음에 답하시오.

(A)

Once there was a little girl named Elsa. She lived in a very small house that stood on a hill. Each day the sun shined brightly in the garden. But the sun never came to the grandmother's room since its windows were on the north side of the house. One day Elsa said to her mother, "Why doesn't Grandma come out to the garden? I know (a) she would like to have sunlight." "She is too old to walk to the garden," said her mother.

(B)

When she was in the garden one morning she felt the sun's warm rays in her golden hair. Then she sat down and she saw them in her lap. "I will take them in my dress," she thought, "and carry them to Grandma's room." So she jumped up and ran into the house. "Look, Grandma, look! I have some sunshine for you," she cried. And (b) she opened her dress, but there was not a ray to be seen.

(C)

After that Elsa tried and tried to think of how she could carry the sunshine to her grandmother. When she played in the garden, she saw the grass and the flowers nodding their heads. The birds sang sweetly as they flew from tree to tree. Everything seemed to say, "We love the sun. We love the bright, warm sun." "Grandma would love it, too," thought the child. "I must take some to (c) her."

(D)

"It peeps out of your eyes, my child," said her grandmother with a big smile, "and it shines in your sunny, golden hair. I do not need the sun when I have you with (d) me." Elsa did not understand how the sun could peep out of her eyes. But she was glad to make her dear grandmother happy. Every morning she played in the garden near grandma's room to carry the sunlight to (e) her quickly. Then she ran to her grandmother's room with the sunshine in her eyes and hair.

43 주어진 글 (A)에 이어질 내용을 순서에 맞게 배열한 것으로 가장 적절한 것은?

① (B) — (D) — (C)
② (C) — (B) — (D)
③ (C) — (D) — (B)
④ (D) — (B) — (C)
⑤ (D) — (C) — (B)

44 밑줄 친 (a)~(e) 중에서 가리키는 대상이 나머지 넷과 다른 것은?

① (a) ② (b) ③ (c) ④ (d) ⑤ (e)

45 윗글에 관한 내용으로 적절하지 않은 것은?

① 할머니 방은 북쪽으로 창문이 나 있었다.
② 할머니는 연로해서 정원에 나올 수 없었다.
③ Elsa는 할머니 방에 햇빛이 들게 하는 데 성공했다.
④ Elsa는 할머니에게 햇빛을 가져갈 방법을 궁리했다.
⑤ Elsa는 매일 아침 정원에서 놀다가 할머니 방에 갔다.

AFTER TESTING

종료 시 분
소요시간 분

학습 마무리

1 채점하기 | 정답 및 해설 p.81
주의 틀린 문제를 다시 풀 수 있도록 정답을 본문에 표기하지 마세요.
2 등급 확인
3 틀린 유형 확인 후 전략 적용 복습 및 해설지 확인

How to Review

1 틀린 문제와 ✓ 표시한 문제는 다시 풀고 해설 확인하기
2 내가 표시한 정답 근거가 해설과 일치하는지 확인하기
3 잘 모르는 부분으로 표시한 내용은 해설을 통해 완전히 이해하기
4 어휘 외우기 (어휘 목록 다운로드 www.cedubook.com)
5 다음 회에 개선할 점 정리하기 (시간 엄수, 취약 유형 보완 등)

BUTTON UP!

고난도 모의고사

12

BEFORE TESTING

시작 시 분

학습 목표

1 제한시간 (OMR 마킹시간 포함) ☐ 40분 ☐ 45분
2 어휘예습 ☐ 해당 없음 ☐ 완료
3 문제풀이순서 ☐ 순서대로 ☐ 2점 → 3점 ☐ 기타
4 기타 목표

Check Point

1 정답 근거 *e.g.* 밑줄 긋기
2 잘 모르는 부분 *e.g.* 〈 〉 또는 ? 표시
3 자신 없는 문제 *e.g.* 문제 번호에 ✓표시

18 다음 글의 목적으로 가장 적절한 것은?

Attention Students,

This year, 2020, marks the 35th anniversary of Sullivan's Art & Design School. As part of the celebration, a design exhibition will be held in the school's south gallery at the end of the month. It will feature the best entries from past design competitions. These works were selected out of hundreds of applications and awarded the highest honor. Everything from sculptures to paintings and posters will be on display. It's a great opportunity to see the works of now-famous artists when they were still students, like you are now. Everyone is welcome to come, including parents and the public. Donations will be accepted at the door, but they are by no means required. We look forward to seeing everyone there.

Yuna Lee, Vice Principal

① 예정된 학교 행사를 안내하려고
② 디자인 대회의 규칙을 설명하려고
③ 전시회를 위한 기부금을 요청하려고
④ 학교의 오랜 전통과 역사를 홍보하려고
⑤ 디자인 대회의 과거 우승자들을 기리려고

19 다음 글에 드러난 'I'의 심경 변화로 가장 적절한 것은?

I jacked the front end of the car up and cleared away the snow from under it. In the meantime, Daniel built a fire about two feet in front of the radiator to keep the car warm and us from freezing to death, and to furnish enough light for the operation. The wheel correction was surprisingly easy; we were ready to leave again in a few minutes. Then we discovered that it would be more difficult to get out of the lane than it had been to get in. Because of the density of the trees, there was no way of turning around without serious risk of getting stuck. And the whirling snow made the visibility extremely poor. There was nothing more we could do.

*jack up: (차 등을) 잭으로 들어 올리다

① affectionate → moved
② worried → pleased
③ relieved → frustrated
④ angry → sympathetic
⑤ mournful → embarrassed

20 다음 글에서 필자가 주장하는 바로 가장 적절한 것은?

We don't live in a bubble. We live in multifaceted, dynamic environments; each day, it seems like there are a thousand voices telling us what we should believe, say, do, and wear. They tell us what life should be like and what we ought to be doing with our time. It is easy to give in to these voices, listening to them and allowing them to take root inside our heads. It is easy to "be squeezed into shape" by whatever is popular today. But we have the power to say "no." We have the power to say, "This is not who I am. This is not who I want to be." By observing and monitoring what we think about and the choices we make, we can say no to "the present age." We have the power to determine the direction of our lives.

*multifaceted: 다양한 측면을 가진

① 목표 달성을 위해 철저하게 준비하라.
② 발전하기 위해서 능동적으로 변화하라.
③ 원대하고 구체적인 목표를 추구하며 살아라.
④ 주변에 휩쓸리지 말고 자기주도적인 삶을 살아라.
⑤ 환경 변화에 대처하기 위해 자기성찰의 시간을 가져라.

21 밑줄 친 stands on the shoulders of giants가 다음 글에서 의미하는 바로 가장 적절한 것은?

Approximately 250,000 years ago, a few thousand Homo sapiens migrated out of Africa, aided by a brain that was sophisticated enough to adapt to new environments but also one that had evolved the capacity for the transmission of knowledge from one generation to the next. We were born to learn. Long before writing and the Internet were invented, humans had the capacity to communicate with each other in ways that no other animal could. With communication came an explosion in technology and skills. This was not information in our genes but rather knowledge learned from others. Our parents, their parents and their parent's parents before them had thousands of years of knowledge passed down from each generation. That's why scientists say every newborn baby stands on the shoulders of giants.

① is willing to make intellectual progress
② spends so much time learning to survive
③ gains help from others when it is needed
④ pays attention to others in order to learn
⑤ uses intelligence gained by their ancestors

22 다음 글의 요지로 가장 적절한 것은?

It could be argued that art should exist in a vacuum and be appreciated for its beauty and the emotions that it induces from its viewer. However, some art cannot be properly understood without understanding where it came from. What is socially acceptable, socially forbidden, and socially comical can be seen through the eyes of the artist in a way that portrays society during the artist's time. What is funny to one society may be the opposite in another. It is through the art that we can see the way times were or the way times are. Art is a reflection of the society that served as a muse for the artist in many circumstances. Without societal recognition, its message may be lost in translation.

*muse: 뮤즈(작가 · 화가 등에게 영감을 주는 신)

① 예술의 기원은 종교에서 찾을 수 있다.
② 예술은 작품이 만들어진 시대를 반영한다.
③ 예술에 대한 평가는 주관적일 수밖에 없다.
④ 예술 작품의 가치는 시대에 따라 달라진다.
⑤ 예술 작품 감상을 통해 감정을 순화할 수 있다.

23 다음 글의 주제로 가장 적절한 것은?

Weeds can tell you a lot about your garden. If your weeds multiply rapidly, it is likely that your soil is extremely fertile and that you do not need fertilizer. If the amount of weeds is diverse, it is likely that you can grow a wide range of plants in your garden. If not, it will be worthwhile to determine the soil type. Weeds can provide important clues to the quality of your soil, such as low pH (acid soils), high pH (alkaline soils), and poor drainage. For example, very acidic soil will produce dandelion, while corn marigold is found on light acid soils. Learning about weeds and the types of soil they prefer can help you choose a better spot for your garden or use the knowledge as guides when trying to determine the state of your soil.

*dandelion: 민들레 **corn marigold: 공작국화

① ecological adaptability of weeds
② types of weeds growing in the garden
③ weeds as indicators of soil conditions
④ ways of controlling weeds in the garden
⑤ effects of weed competition on crop growth

24 다음 글의 제목으로 가장 적절한 것은?

Even if a language goes extinct, there's a chance to save it, provided there's enough documentation on the language. Even languages that have died in the past several decades have seen revitalization efforts that brought the language back to life dramatically. Hebrew and Cornish are two such examples. These languages were extinct until revitalization efforts reintroduced them into mainstream use. The key to bringing them back was that in both cases there were enough resources to teach the language to eager learners and strong community interest in saving them. Motivation is important when learning any language. Understanding what language means to both a person and a culture is key to inspiring people to want to step in and save the language. If the motivation is there and the language learners have a safe, supportive environment, the chances of saving the language increases.

① How Can We Save Extinct Languages?
② Extinct Languages: Causes and Results
③ Why Extinct Languages Are Important
④ When Do Languages Become Endangered?
⑤ Endangered Languages That Could Soon Disappear

25 다음 도표의 내용과 일치하지 않는 것은?

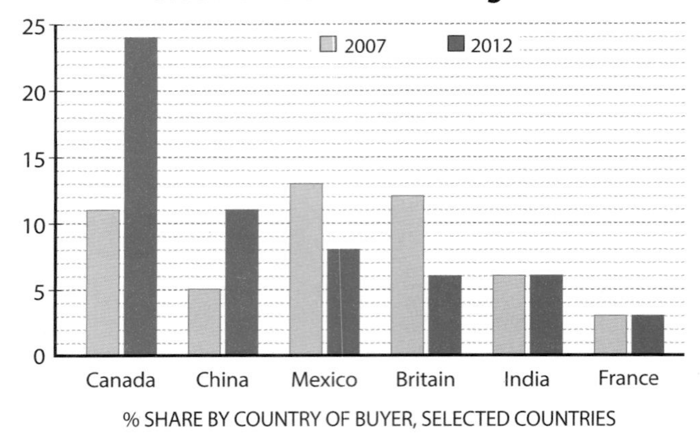

The graph above shows U.S. home sales to foreigners in 2007 and 2012 by percentage of buyers from six selected countries, including Canada, China, Mexico, Britain, India, and France. ① The percentages of buyers from both Canada and China were larger in 2012 relative to 2007, with the largest growth being seen in Canada. ② The largest buyer in 2012, Canada, accounted for more than twice the purchases of China, and this relationship was seen in 2007 as well. ③ On the other hand, Mexico dropped from the largest buyer in 2007 to the third largest in 2012, showing the largest decline among the six countries. ④ Britain and India were equal in 2012, with 6% of purchases each, which was double that of France. ⑤ India and France showed no change in their proportion of purchases, with the former remaining steady at 6% and the latter at 3%.

26 Herbert Spencer에 관한 다음 글의 내용과 일치하지 않는 것은?

Herbert Spencer was born in 1820 in England. Spencer initially pursued the scientific interests encouraged by his father and studied engineering. For a few years, until 1841, he was employed as a civil engineer working for the London and Birmingham Railway. His interest in evolution is said to have arisen from the examination of fossils discovered during the construction of railroads. Spencer later left the railroad industry to take up a literary career and to pursue some of his scientific interests. He began by contributing to *The Non-Conformist*, writing a series of letters called *The Proper Sphere of Government*. This was his first major work and contained his basic concepts of individualism and laissez-faire, which were to be later developed more fully in his *Social Statics* (1850) and other works. Especially stressed were the right of the individual and the ideal of noninterference on the part of the state.

*laissez-faire: 자유방임주의

① 아버지의 영향을 받아 공학을 공부했다.
② 1841년부터 수년 간 철도 회사에서 일했다.
③ 화석을 보고 진화에 대해 관심을 갖게 되었다.
④ *The Non-Conformist*에 글을 기고했다.
⑤ 개인의 권리와 국가의 불간섭을 강조했다.

27 Freshman Orientation Volunteer Opportunity에 관한 다음 안내문의 내용과 일치하지 않는 것은?

Freshman Orientation
Volunteer Opportunity

Join the Freshman Orientation Volunteer Team in welcoming our new freshman class and transfer students in their first days as new Stanford University students.

When: Monday, September 8–Friday, September 12, 2020 (Entrance ceremony begins on the last day of orientation at 10 a.m.)

Play a critical role
in welcoming new students by
- Greeting new students
- Moving students into their residences
- Setting up tables and chairs for events
- Directing students to workshops and answering general questions

Requirements:
- Attend mandatory training September 3–4
- Available September 8–12 (no schedule conflicts)

All volunteers are able to move into student housing two weeks early.

① 봉사 활동 기간은 5일이다.
② 봉사자들은 행사 준비를 돕고 길을 안내한다.
③ 봉사 활동에 앞서 의무 교육이 3일 간 진행된다.
④ 봉사자는 봉사 기간 내내 참여 가능해야 한다.
⑤ 봉사자들은 2주 일찍 기숙사로 들어갈 수 있다.

28 Adventure Days에 관한 다음 안내문의 내용과 일치하는 것은?

Adventure Days
Activities for Adults and Teens with Disabilities

Join us for fun crafts, exercise, and other activities, followed by a fun and social barbecue!
We meet every other Saturday. Activities begin at 10 a.m., and the barbecue will start at 12:30 p.m.

- Pre-registration and payment are required for participation.
- All activities are wheelchair accessible.
- Participants who need assistance should bring a helper. No fee is charged for the helper at any activity or barbecue.
- Guests of the barbecue are welcome to bring a side dish, but it's not required.
- Monthly Fee: $35/person for adults, and $30/person for teens.

All activities are held at the Bennett Senior Center, 704 Bennett Road, Rosemont.

For more information, contact Robin Sykes at 774-9345-6285 or email sykestobeyou@angelmail.com.

① 매주 토요일 오전 10시에 시작된다.
② 사전 등록하고 수강료는 당일에 지불한다.
③ 수강생의 도우미는 바비큐 비용만 내면 된다.
④ 바비큐 파티 때 함께 먹을 음식을 가져와야 한다.
⑤ 십 대 수강료는 성인 수강료보다 5달러 더 저렴하다.

29 다음 글의 밑줄 친 부분 중, 어법상 틀린 것은? [3점]

In 1347, when the Black Plague was raging through Europe, the citizens of Lubeck, Germany, ① to avoid the anger of God, descended on the churches with enormous amounts of money and riches. The monks and priests inside these churches, fearful of contamination, locked ② their gates and would not allow the citizens to enter. The crowd threw valuables, coins, gold, and jewels over the walls; the ③ frightened monks threw all of them back. The back-and-forth tossing continued for hours, until the monks finally gave up tossing back and ④ permitting the riches to remain. Within hours, piles 3 and 4 feet high arose, and the money remained ⑤ untouched for months following the incident.

30 다음 글의 밑줄 친 부분 중, 문맥상 낱말의 쓰임이 적절하지 않은 것은?

Until recently, Sweden was an agriculturally based society. About 90% of families lived on farms until the Industrial Revolution in the early 1900s brought workers to the cities. Sweden has changed ① quickly into an industrialized, city-based country. Thus, many Swedes remember life on the farm. ② Ties to the farm remain very strong. Although they enjoy city life, most Swedes are still peasants at heart who could easily return to the ways of their ancestors, because the past is not too ③ distant. Back-to-the-farm and back-to-nature romanticism constitutes a major part of Swedish culture. Swedes long for an ④ escape to the country where they can remind themselves of a simpler time. This is also true of younger Swedes who seem to devote a significant amount of time to their smartphones. Still, in the countryside, these younger Swedes behave in a fashion ⑤ opposite to their parents.

[31~34] 다음 빈칸에 들어갈 말로 가장 적절한 것을 고르시오.

31 During my graduate school year I faced usual oral exams to test whether I had sufficient background knowledge in my field. Knowing which professors were on the committee allowed me to predict which questions might be asked. Even so, oral exams are one of the occasions in graduate school when they can control, dominate, or hold power over you. The examiners, if so inclined, could ask just about anything they like. You do your best by answering them as you would to a police officer who has pulled you over for speeding. If you are prone to discourtesy, it is better to pretend to be nervous. Even mild confidence may inspire some examiners to make you realize that you are less talented than you think you are. The gestures you make, your posture, or your tone of voice can force you to retake part of the exam some months later. Thus, ______________ pays off during oral exams.

① positivity
② honesty
③ humility
④ endurance
⑤ passion

32 As the English poet Edward Young observed, "Procrastination is the thief of time." With all the choices available and other temptations that present themselves, we put off what we should do now until it is too late. All this work on decision-making should clearly tell you that our self is at the mercy of the choices with which we are presented. Our capacity for decision-making is dependent on the context. If there are too many choices, then the alternatives cancel each other out, and we are left with hesitation. Even when we do make a decision, we are less happy because we dwell on whether we made the right choice. If we have no choice, then there is no problem and the world is to blame. But then we get depressed. However, if we choose something that does not turn out to be ideal, then it is our fault for not choosing wisely. It's often ______________________. [3점]

*procrastination: 미루는 버릇

① a no-win situation
② a true-false question
③ a fight-or-flight approach
④ a value-free judgment
⑤ a carefree process

33 Ernest Hemingway was a keen student of human nature, and he set his goals to increase his performance. Like many writers, Hemingway found that the toughest part of writing was getting started each day. So he developed his own writing practice. When asked during an interview, "How much should you write in a day?" Hemingway advised that "The best way is always to stop when you are going good and when you know what will happen next. If you do that every day when you are writing a novel, you will never be stuck." He developed a practice of stopping each day with a chapter almost, but not quite, complete. The next morning he could ______________________ and eagerly sit down to finish the chapter. Once immersed in work and feeling good, he could continue writing until the next chapter was nearly complete. [3점]

① do a lot of work in a short time
② gain vitality from the rest at night
③ use the divide-and-conquer method
④ wait for inspiration to strike overnight
⑤ take advantage of his thirst for progress

34 There's an important difference between the sciences and art history. A scientist may, in the end, find a drug that is an effective cancer treatment, and her work then is done, or at least a phase of it reaches closure. But the interpretation of history, art, and culture is different: they express such a wide range of human ideas and experiences that there is no one result for the art historian to seek. Each person, each generation, and each culture reinterprets artworks, finding in them new significance. Certainly, some arguments are more persuasive than others and some arguments do a better job of accounting for a wider range of evidence. But when we're talking about interpreting the past, or interpreting cultural practice, ______________________. [3점]

① it must always be connected with our goals for the future
② we need to accept that science too has a complicated history
③ it's not a question of right and wrong but of looking for insight
④ it's not the facts of the past that matter, but the events of the present
⑤ we should gather all the evidence and accept the most persuasive parts

35 다음 글에서 전체 흐름과 관계 없는 문장은?

If you are continually spending more and more time at work, you are either doing too much or not doing it right. And wait a minute — was it really your job from the start? ① Whether you have chosen to do the work yourself or received it from your boss, set limits in your work life. ② This means setting a time to arrive and a time to go home, and taking all the breaks that your body needs in between. ③ And it also means scheduling time for building relationships and doing other important things that need to be done. ④ When a colleague asks for your help, you should respond willingly and politely to the request. ⑤ Finally, remember that it is not your job to handle everything and you can't be the most important player in every game.

[36~37] 주어진 글 다음에 이어질 글의 순서로 가장 적절한 것을 고르시오.

36

> Many people believe that they are very good at detecting deception. They may even cite examples where they were correct in spotting a lie when others around them were not so sensitive.

(A) The problem with such unproved evidence is that it's difficult to know when one is wrong in believing a lie. Unless there was independent evidence later that someone was lying, how would you discover your incorrect judgment?

(B) Specifically, with 50% as a baseline for chance accuracy, the average detection accuracy is approximately 55%. Furthermore, there is little or no relationship between confidence in judgments and accuracy.

(C) By definition, successful lies go undetected, and there is no way of keeping track of them. In fact, across scores of experiments, average detection accuracy is only slightly better than chance. [3점]

① (A) — (C) — (B)　　② (B) — (A) — (C)
③ (B) — (C) — (A)　　④ (C) — (A) — (B)
⑤ (C) — (B) — (A)

37

As the universe continued expanding and cooling, stars and galaxies began to form, and the chemical makeup of the universe changed.

(A) In this way, the composition of the universe is gradually enhanced by heavier elements. Throughout their life cycle, stars undergo many nuclear reactions in which lighter elements are converted into heavier elements by nuclear fusion.

(B) When a star dies, often explosively, the heavier elements that were formed in its core are returned to interstellar space and are available for inclusion in new stars.

(C) Initially, the universe was 100% hydrogen and helium, whereas today it is 98% hydrogen and helium and 2% all other elements by weight. How did such a change in the universe's composition occur?

① (A) — (C) — (B)
② (B) — (A) — (C)
③ (B) — (C) — (A)
④ (C) — (A) — (B)
⑤ (C) — (B) — (A)

[38~39] 글의 흐름으로 보아, 주어진 문장이 들어가기에 가장 적절한 곳을 고르시오.

38

But when the car makes its way to a dealership and is sold, the profit realized isn't sent back to the factory to be divided among the workers.

Goods are items you buy, such as food, clothing, and toothpaste, while services mean actions such as haircuts, medical check-ups, and car repair. (①) Under capitalism, goods and services are produced socially, but they and the wealth they generate are owned privately. (②) For example, if you were to visit a car factory, you wouldn't see each worker constructing only one car, building it from scratch, from engine to nuts. (③) Rather, you'd see the workers laboring together, each one performing a different task, or series of tasks, to help create the final product: a car. (④) It goes to whoever owns the factory — in this case, the shareholders, people who bought stock in the company. (⑤) The largest shareholders realize the greatest amount of profit.

39

Making them free maximizes these societal benefits.

There should be a sizable increase in public goods such as public transportation, public parks, and public museums and libraries in America. And they should be free of charge to users. (①) Such public goods improve the quality of life of those who cannot afford the equivalent private goods — their own cars, neatly cut gardens, art collections, and books, for example. (②) In this way, public goods somewhat offset the effect of stagnant or declining wages. (③) Public goods typically have less of an impact on scarce resources and the environment than their private equivalents, and they create jobs and add to overall demand in the economy. (④) For instance, an expanded system of free public transportation, including high-speed rail, would significantly decrease traffic congestion — estimated to cost Americans more than $85 billion a year in wasted hours and gas — and reduce carbon emissions. (⑤) The benefits far outweigh the costs. [3점]

*stagnant: 정체된

40 다음 글의 내용을 한 문장으로 요약하고자 한다. 빈칸 (A), (B)에 들어갈 말로 가장 적절한 것은?

Psychologists Kahneman and Tversky created a scenario describing the events leading to a car accident in which Mr. Jones was injured on his way home from work. In one version, Mr. Jones left work at the regular time but took an unusual route home to enjoy the view along the shore. In another version, he left work unusually early to do some chores but took his regular route home. Participants were asked how they thought Mr. Jones's family would complete "If only ..." sentences. Participants were more likely to say, "If only he had left at his regular time," or "If only he had taken his normal route" than say, "If only he had left earlier that day." Another scenario study showed that people also felt that someone involved in a car accident while taking an unusual route home would be more upset than someone involved in a similar accident while taking the normal route home.

People tend to be more upset by negative outcomes when these result from ____(A)____ behavior than they are when the identical outcomes result from ____(B)____ behavior.

	(A)		(B)
①	observed	······	routine
②	observed	······	self-directed
③	desired	······	prospective
④	exceptional	······	routine
⑤	exceptional	······	self-directed

[41~42] 다음 글을 읽고, 물음에 답하시오.

We all experience some anxiety at different periods in time. It's the brain's way of getting us ready to face or escape danger, or deal with stressful situations. It is (a) normal to feel anxious before an important business meeting or final exam, or when you are awaiting the results of a medical test. However, at times, the anxiety can be quite (b) severe or exaggerated in relation to the actual situation. This can lead to intense physical sensations, anxious thoughts, worries and avoidant behaviors that impact one's life. Unfortunately, many people tend to view emotional disorders such as depression or anxiety as a sign of personal weakness; however, medical research has shown this assessment to be completely (c) false. While the precise causes of anxiety and other emotional disorders are not yet fully understood, it is clear that (d) environmental stressors play a tremendous role. We know that extreme or long-lasting stress can cause changes in brain chemistry which controls mood and behavior; in addition, certain structures in the brain tend to show abnormalities in people with anxiety disorders. On the other hand, some scientists now believe chronic worry may be (e) learned. Last year, for example, a team at Massachusetts General Hospital found a gene variation associated with chronic worry and overthinking. Some professionals believe that anxiety attacks, chronic worry, and other symptoms indicate a biological disease, while various learning theories argue that anxiety is a learned behavior from childhood.

41 윗글의 제목으로 가장 적절한 것은?

① When Does Anxiety Become Chronic?
② Treating and Preventing an Anxiety Disorder
③ Signs and Symptoms of an Anxiety Disorder
④ Anxiety: Recognition, Assessment and Treatment
⑤ Anxiety: Is It Triggered from Inside or Outside of Us?

42 밑줄 친 (a)~(e) 중에서 문맥상 낱말의 쓰임이 적절하지 않은 것은? [3점]

① (a) ② (b) ③ (c) ④ (d) ⑤ (e)

[43~45] 다음 글을 읽고, 물음에 답하시오.

(A)

Once upon a time, in a region of the Roman Empire, a large association of citizens began refusing to pay their taxes. They demonstrated in the streets and attacked every tax collector who attempted to pass through. Unable to collect the money necessary for running the state, and fearing the unrest would spread, the Senate sent an official named Menenius Agrippa to prevent the crisis. When Menenius Agrippa arrived in the town, he addressed the angry crowd:

*the Senate: (고대 로마의) 원로원

(B)

"Each of you," said (a) he, "must surely understand that everything you send to me I immediately convert to your needs, and distribute throughout our Body for the good of us all." But he could not change their minds. From then on, the parts stopped giving him assistance, so (b) he soon starved, and the Body became thinner and thinner, until it was all bones. At last, Teeth, Tongue, Hands, and Feet realized they had made a terrible mistake, and tried desperately to return to work. But it was already too late, and they all perished together.

(C)

Citizens of Rome! Have you heard the tale of the Belly? It happened one time that some parts of the Human Body became offended by the Belly's behavior, and resolved to refuse (c) him his necessary supplies. First, the Tongue made an anti-Belly speech that stirred up deep resentment in the other parts. (d) He highly praised the diligent Hands and Feet and condemned the "fat, lazy, useless Belly." He claimed how unfair it was that the products of their labor went to the Belly "who never does a thing to help himself."

(D)

This speech was received with great applause, and immediately, the Hands declared that they would work no more, the Feet that they were finished carrying the Belly everywhere, and the Teeth that they would never again chew so much as a piece of bread for (e) him to digest. Amid all their shouting and complaining, the Belly begged them to calm down and stop being so crazy and senseless.

43 주어진 글 (A)에 이어질 내용을 순서에 맞게 배열한 것으로 가장 적절한 것은?

① (B) — (C) — (D)
② (B) — (D) — (C)
③ (C) — (B) — (D)
④ (C) — (D) — (B)
⑤ (D) — (C) — (B)

44 밑줄 친 (a)~(e) 중에서 가리키는 대상이 나머지 넷과 다른 것은?

① (a) ② (b) ③ (c) ④ (d) ⑤ (e)

45 윗글에 관한 내용으로 적절하지 않은 것은?

① 배는 받은 것을 다른 신체 부분들에 분배하는 일을 했다.
② 실수를 깨닫고도 치아, 혀, 손과 발은 아무 노력도 하지 않았다.
③ 신체의 다른 부분들은 배의 행동에 기분이 상했다.
④ 혀가 가장 먼저 배를 비난하는 연설을 했다.
⑤ 배는 다른 신체 부분들의 화를 진정시키려 했다.

AFTER TESTING

종료 시 분
소요시간 분

학습 마무리

1 채점하기 | 정답 및 해설 p.89
주의 틀린 문제를 다시 풀 수 있도록 정답을 본문에 표기하지 마세요.
2 등급 확인
3 틀린 유형 확인 후 전략 적용 복습 및 해설지 확인

How to Review

1 틀린 문제와 ✓ 표시한 문제는 다시 풀고 해설 확인하기
2 내가 표시한 정답 근거가 해설과 일치하는지 확인하기
3 잘 모르는 부분으로 표시한 내용은 해설을 통해 완전히 이해하기
4 어휘 외우기 (어휘 목록 다운로드 www.cedubook.com)
5 다음 회에 개선할 점 정리하기 (시간 엄수, 취약 유형 보완 등)

ANSWERS

01

18 ④ 19 ② 20 ⑤ 21 ③ 22 ② 23 ④ 24 ③ 25 ⑤ 26 ⑤ 27 ⑤ 28 ⑤ 29 ③ 30 ⑤ 31 ④
32 ④ 33 ⑤ 34 ② 35 ④ 36 ④ 37 ② 38 ④ 39 ⑤ 40 ⑤ 41 ② 42 ④ 43 ④ 44 ④ 45 ③

02

18 ① 19 ④ 20 ② 21 ① 22 ① 23 ③ 24 ③ 25 ③ 26 ④ 27 ⑤ 28 ② 29 ③ 30 ③ 31 ②
32 ④ 33 ④ 34 ② 35 ④ 36 ⑤ 37 ④ 38 ④ 39 ③ 40 ④ 41 ① 42 ④ 43 ④ 44 ③ 45 ③

03

18 ⑤ 19 ② 20 ③ 21 ③ 22 ⑤ 23 ④ 24 ② 25 ③ 26 ① 27 ③ 28 ⑤ 29 ③ 30 ② 31 ⑤
32 ③ 33 ① 34 ③ 35 ③ 36 ④ 37 ② 38 ④ 39 ① 40 ④ 41 ④ 42 ⑤ 43 ④ 44 ④ 45 ③

04

18 ④ 19 ③ 20 ③ 21 ④ 22 ⑤ 23 ④ 24 ③ 25 ④ 26 ③ 27 ⑤ 28 ④ 29 ⑤ 30 ④ 31 ①
32 ② 33 ③ 34 ③ 35 ④ 36 ② 37 ② 38 ④ 39 ③ 40 ④ 41 ⑤ 42 ② 43 ④ 44 ③ 45 ④

05

18 ④ 19 ⑤ 20 ③ 21 ④ 22 ① 23 ② 24 ③ 25 ⑤ 26 ⑤ 27 ⑤ 28 ② 29 ⑤ 30 ⑤ 31 ⑤
32 ③ 33 ③ 34 ⑤ 35 ④ 36 ④ 37 ③ 38 ⑤ 39 ③ 40 ⑤ 41 ③ 42 ④ 43 ② 44 ⑤ 45 ④

06

18 ① 19 ② 20 ① 21 ② 22 ④ 23 ① 24 ⑤ 25 ⑤ 26 ④ 27 ② 28 ④ 29 ③ 30 ② 31 ⑤
32 ⑤ 33 ④ 34 ② 35 ④ 36 ④ 37 ⑤ 38 ⑤ 39 ⑤ 40 ④ 41 ④ 42 ② 43 ④ 44 ③ 45 ④

07

18 ③ 19 ② 20 ④ 21 ① 22 ⑤ 23 ② 24 ② 25 ③ 26 ④ 27 ⑤ 28 ④ 29 ④ 30 ⑤ 31 ②
32 ② 33 ① 34 ③ 35 ③ 36 ⑤ 37 ③ 38 ④ 39 ③ 40 ① 41 ② 42 ③ 43 ④ 44 ③ 45 ③

08

18 ⑤ 19 ④ 20 ① 21 ⑤ 22 ④ 23 ⑤ 24 ⑤ 25 ④ 26 ③ 27 ① 28 ② 29 ④ 30 ⑤ 31 ①
32 ③ 33 ③ 34 ④ 35 ③ 36 ⑤ 37 ② 38 ⑤ 39 ④ 40 ④ 41 ② 42 ① 43 ③ 44 ④ 45 ⑤

09

18 ④ 19 ② 20 ④ 21 ③ 22 ⑤ 23 ① 24 ⑤ 25 ④ 26 ⑤ 27 ① 28 ④ 29 ① 30 ② 31 ⑤
32 ③ 33 ② 34 ③ 35 ④ 36 ③ 37 ⑤ 38 ③ 39 ③ 40 ② 41 ④ 42 ⑤ 43 ③ 44 ⑤ 45 ⑤

10

18 ③ 19 ③ 20 ④ 21 ③ 22 ④ 23 ⑤ 24 ⑤ 25 ④ 26 ⑤ 27 ⑤ 28 ④ 29 ④ 30 ② 31 ③
32 ① 33 ⑤ 34 ① 35 ③ 36 ④ 37 ③ 38 ③ 39 ④ 40 ⑤ 41 ④ 42 ② 43 ② 44 ⑤ 45 ②

11

18 ⑤ 19 ③ 20 ③ 21 ⑤ 22 ⑤ 23 ① 24 ② 25 ⑤ 26 ④ 27 ④ 28 ⑤ 29 ③ 30 ③ 31 ②
32 ① 33 ④ 34 ③ 35 ⑤ 36 ③ 37 ⑤ 38 ⑤ 39 ③ 40 ① 41 ④ 42 ⑤ 43 ② 44 ② 45 ③

12

18 ① 19 ③ 20 ④ 21 ⑤ 22 ② 23 ③ 24 ① 25 ③ 26 ② 27 ③ 28 ⑤ 29 ④ 30 ⑤ 31 ③
32 ① 33 ⑤ 34 ③ 35 ④ 36 ① 37 ⑤ 38 ④ 39 ④ 40 ④ 41 ⑤ 42 ⑤ 43 ④ 44 ④ 45 ②

첫단추 독해실전편 모의고사 12회 답안지

※ 답안지 작성(표기)은 반드시 컴퓨터용 사인펜만을 사용하고, 연필 또는 샤프펜을 절대 사용하지 마십시오.
※ 뒷면의 〈수험생이 지켜야 할 일〉을 꼭 읽어 보십시오.

③ 교시 영어 영역

※ 결시자 확인 (수험생은 표기하지 말것.)

컴퓨터용 사인펜을 사용하여 수험번호란과 옆란을 표기	0

※ 아래 '필적확인란'에 "○○○○○○○○○○○○○"를 정자로 반드시 기재하여야 합니다.

필 적 확인란	

성 명								
수 험 번 호								
				–				
	0	0	0		0	0	0	0
1	1	1	1		1	1	1	1
2	2	2	2		2	2	2	2
3	3	3	3		3	3	3	3
4	4	4	4		4	4		4
5	5	5	5		5	5		5
6	6		6		6	6		6
7	7		7		7	7		7
8	8		8		8	8		8
	9		9		9	9		9

문 형
홀수형 0
짝수형 0

※ 문제의 문형을 확인후 표기

※ 감독관 확인 (수험생은 표기하지 말것.)

본인여부, 수험번호 및 문형의 표기가 정확한지 확인, 옆란에 서명 또는 날인	(서 명 또는 날 인)

문번	답 란	문번	답 란	문번	답 란
1	① ② ③ ④ ⑤	21	① ② ③ ④ ⑤	41	① ② ③ ④ ⑤
2	① ② ③ ④ ⑤	22	① ② ③ ④ ⑤	42	① ② ③ ④ ⑤
3	① ② ③ ④ ⑤	23	① ② ③ ④ ⑤	43	① ② ③ ④ ⑤
4	① ② ③ ④ ⑤	24	① ② ③ ④ ⑤	44	① ② ③ ④ ⑤
5	① ② ③ ④ ⑤	25	① ② ③ ④ ⑤	45	① ② ③ ④ ⑤
6	① ② ③ ④ ⑤	26	① ② ③ ④ ⑤		
7	① ② ③ ④ ⑤	27	① ② ③ ④ ⑤		
8	① ② ③ ④ ⑤	28	① ② ③ ④ ⑤		
9	① ② ③ ④ ⑤	29	① ② ③ ④ ⑤		
10	① ② ③ ④ ⑤	30	① ② ③ ④ ⑤		
11	① ② ③ ④ ⑤	31	① ② ③ ④ ⑤		
12	① ② ③ ④ ⑤	32	① ② ③ ④ ⑤		
13	① ② ③ ④ ⑤	33	① ② ③ ④ ⑤		
14	① ② ③ ④ ⑤	34	① ② ③ ④ ⑤		
15	① ② ③ ④ ⑤	35	① ② ③ ④ ⑤		
16	① ② ③ ④ ⑤	36	① ② ③ ④ ⑤		
17	① ② ③ ④ ⑤	37	① ② ③ ④ ⑤		
18	① ② ③ ④ ⑤	38	① ② ③ ④ ⑤		
19	① ② ③ ④ ⑤	39	① ② ③ ④ ⑤		
20	① ② ③ ④ ⑤	40	① ② ③ ④ ⑤		

〈수험생이 지켜야 할 일〉

> 답안지 작성(표기)은 반드시 컴퓨터용 사인펜만을 사용하여야 합니다.
> (연필, 샤프펜 사용 시 불이익을 받을 수 있습니다.)

1. 성명란에는 수험생의 성명을 바르게 기재하여야 합니다.
2. 수험번호란에는 아라비아 숫자로 기재하고 해당란에 "⬮"와 같이 완전하게 표기하여야 합니다.
3. 문형란에는 배부받은 시험 문제지의 문형을 정확히 확인하고 해당란에 "⬮"와 같이 표기하여야 합니다.
   - 답안지의 '문형'란에 표기가 되어있지 않거나 이중으로 표기된 경우 불이익을 받을 수 있습니다.
   - 시험특별관리대상자의 문제지 문형은 홀수형 입니다.
4. 답란은 "⬮"와 같이 완전하게 표기하여야 하며, 바르지 못한 표기(⊘ ⦶ ⊙ ◐ ▨ 등)를 하였을 경우는 불이익을 받을 수 있습니다.
5. 답란 수정을 원할 경우에는 수정테이프만을 사용하여 완전하게 수정하여야 합니다. 불완전한 수정처리로 인해 발생하는 불이익은 수험생에게 있습니다.
   - 수정테이프는 감독관이 소지하고 있습니다.
   - 수정액이나 스티커 등은 절대로 사용할 수 없습니다.
   - 답란 수정 후 수정테이프가 떨어지지 않게 손으로 눌러 주십시오.
   - 답안지 교체를 원할 경우 교체 가능합니다.
6. 답안지에 낙서를 하거나 불필요한 표기를 하였을 경우 불이익을 받을 수 있으므로 답안지를 최대한 깨끗한 상태로 제출하여야 합니다.

첫단추 독해실전편 모의고사 12회 답안지

※ 답안지 작성(표기)은 반드시 컴퓨터용 사인펜만을 사용하고, 연필 또는 샤프펜을 절대 사용하지 마십시오.
※ 뒷면의 〈수험생이 지켜야 할 일〉을 꼭 읽어 보십시오.

③ 교시 영어 영역

※ 결시자 확인 (수험생은 표기하지 말것.)

컴퓨터용 사인펜을 사용하여 수험번호란과 옆란을 표기 ○

※ 아래 '필적확인란'에 "○○○○○○○○○○○○○"를 정자로 반드시 기재하여야 합니다.

필 적 확인란	

성 명								
수 험 번 호								
				–				
	⓪	⓪	⓪		⓪	⓪	⓪	⓪
①	①	①	①		①	①	①	①
②	②	②	②		②	②	②	②
③	③	③	③		③	③	③	③
④	④	④	④		④	④		④
⑤	⑤	⑤	⑤		⑤	⑤		⑤
⑥	⑥		⑥		⑥	⑥		⑥
⑦	⑦		⑦		⑦	⑦		⑦
⑧	⑧		⑧		⑧	⑧		⑧
	⑨		⑨		⑨	⑨		⑨

문 형
홀수형 ○
짝수형 ○

※ 문제의 문형을 확인후 표기

※ 감독관 확인 (수험생은 표기하지 말것.)

본인여부, 수험번호 및 문형의 표기가 정확한지 확인, 옆란에 서명 또는 날인	(서 명 또는 날 인)

문번	답 란	문번	답 란	문번	답 란
1	① ② ③ ④ ⑤	21	① ② ③ ④ ⑤	41	① ② ③ ④ ⑤
2	① ② ③ ④ ⑤	22	① ② ③ ④ ⑤	42	① ② ③ ④ ⑤
3	① ② ③ ④ ⑤	23	① ② ③ ④ ⑤	43	① ② ③ ④ ⑤
4	① ② ③ ④ ⑤	24	① ② ③ ④ ⑤	44	① ② ③ ④ ⑤
5	① ② ③ ④ ⑤	25	① ② ③ ④ ⑤	45	① ② ③ ④ ⑤
6	① ② ③ ④ ⑤	26	① ② ③ ④ ⑤		
7	① ② ③ ④ ⑤	27	① ② ③ ④ ⑤		
8	① ② ③ ④ ⑤	28	① ② ③ ④ ⑤		
9	① ② ③ ④ ⑤	29	① ② ③ ④ ⑤		
10	① ② ③ ④ ⑤	30	① ② ③ ④ ⑤		
11	① ② ③ ④ ⑤	31	① ② ③ ④ ⑤		
12	① ② ③ ④ ⑤	32	① ② ③ ④ ⑤		
13	① ② ③ ④ ⑤	33	① ② ③ ④ ⑤		
14	① ② ③ ④ ⑤	34	① ② ③ ④ ⑤		
15	① ② ③ ④ ⑤	35	① ② ③ ④ ⑤		
16	① ② ③ ④ ⑤	36	① ② ③ ④ ⑤		
17	① ② ③ ④ ⑤	37	① ② ③ ④ ⑤		
18	① ② ③ ④ ⑤	38	① ② ③ ④ ⑤		
19	① ② ③ ④ ⑤	39	① ② ③ ④ ⑤		
20	① ② ③ ④ ⑤	40	① ② ③ ④ ⑤		

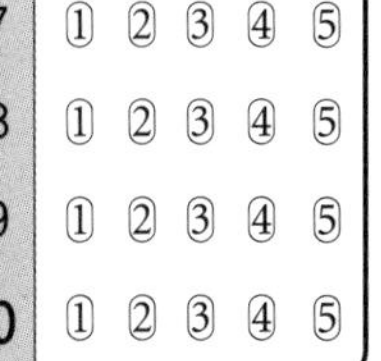
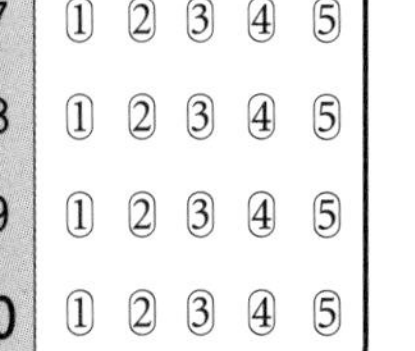
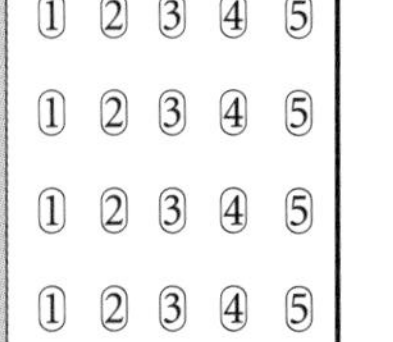
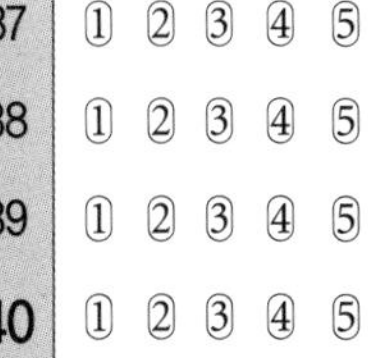

〈수험생이 지켜야 할 일〉

답안지 작성(표기)은 반드시 컴퓨터용 사인펜만을 사용하여야 합니다. (연필, 샤프펜 사용 시 불이익을 받을 수 있습니다.)

1. 성명란에는 수험생의 성명을 바르게 기재하여야 합니다.
2. 수험번호란에는 아라비아 숫자로 기재하고 해당란에 "●"와 같이 완전하게 표기하여야 합니다.
3. 문형란에는 배부받은 시험 문제지의 문형을 정확히 확인하고 해당란에 "●"와 같이 표기하여야 합니다.
   - 답안지의 '문형'란에 표기가 되어있지 않거나 이중으로 표기된 경우 불이익을 받을 수 있습니다.
   - 시험특별관리대상자의 문제지 문형은 홀수형 입니다.
4. 답란은 "●"와 같이 완전하게 표기하여야 하며, 바르지 못한 표기(✓ ◯ ⊙ ◐ ▨ 등)를 하였을 경우는 불이익을 받을 수 있습니다.
5. 답란 수정을 원할 경우에는 수정테이프만을 사용하여 완전하게 수정하여야 합니다. 불완전한 수정처리로 인해 발생하는 불이익은 수험생에게 있습니다.
   - 수정테이프는 감독관이 소지하고 있습니다.
   - 수정액이나 스티커 등은 절대로 사용할 수 없습니다.
   - 답란 수정 후 수정테이프가 떨어지지 않게 손으로 눌러 주십시오.
   - 답안지 교체를 원할 경우 교체 가능합니다.
6. 답안지에 낙서를 하거나 불필요한 표기를 하였을 경우 불이익을 받을 수 있으므로 답안지를 최대한 깨끗한 상태로 제출하여야 합니다.

첫단추 독해실전편 모의고사 12회 답안지

③ 교시 영어 영역

※ 결시자 확인 (수험생은 표기하지 말것.)

컴퓨터용 사인펜을 사용하여 수험번호란과 옆란을 표기	○

※ 아래 '필적확인란'에 "○○○○○○○○○○○○○"를 정자로 반드시 기재하여야 합니다.

필 적 확인란	

성 명								
수 험 번 호								
				–				
	0	0	0		0	0	0	0
1	1	1	1		1	1	1	1
2	2	2	2		2	2	2	2
3	3	3	3		3	3	3	3
4	4	4	4		4	4		4
5	5	5	5		5	5		5
6	6		6		6	6		6
7	7		7		7	7		7
8	8		8		8	8		8
	9		9		9	9		9

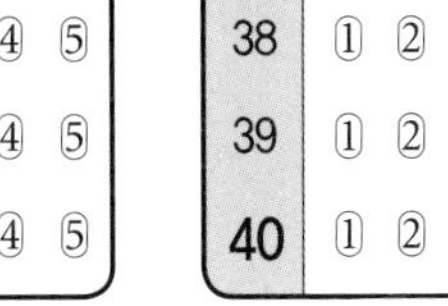

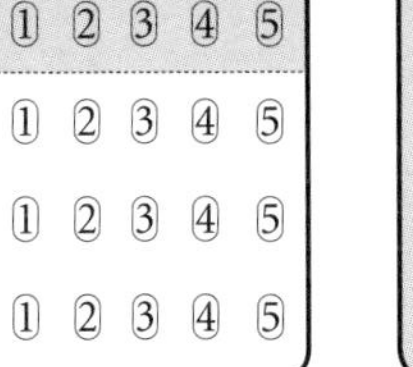

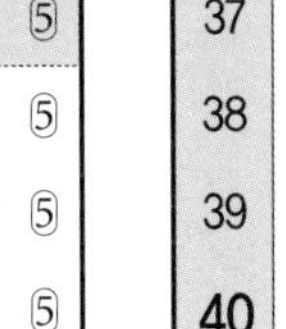

문 형
홀수형 ○
짝수형 ○

※ 문제의 문형을 확인 후 표기

※ 감독관 확인 (수험생은 표기하지 말것.)

본인여부, 수험번호 및 문형의 표기가 정확한지 확인, 옆란에 서명 또는 날인	(서 명 또는 날 인)

※ 답안지 작성(표기)은 반드시 컴퓨터용 사인펜만을 사용하고, 연필 또는 샤프펜을 절대 사용하지 마십시오.
※ 뒷면의 〈수험생이 지켜야 할 일〉을 꼭 읽어 보십시오.

문번	답 란
1	① ② ③ ④ ⑤
2	① ② ③ ④ ⑤
3	① ② ③ ④ ⑤
4	① ② ③ ④ ⑤
5	① ② ③ ④ ⑤
6	① ② ③ ④ ⑤
7	① ② ③ ④ ⑤
8	① ② ③ ④ ⑤
9	① ② ③ ④ ⑤
10	① ② ③ ④ ⑤
11	① ② ③ ④ ⑤
12	① ② ③ ④ ⑤
13	① ② ③ ④ ⑤
14	① ② ③ ④ ⑤
15	① ② ③ ④ ⑤
16	① ② ③ ④ ⑤
17	① ② ③ ④ ⑤
18	① ② ③ ④ ⑤
19	① ② ③ ④ ⑤
20	① ② ③ ④ ⑤

문번	답 란
21	① ② ③ ④ ⑤
22	① ② ③ ④ ⑤
23	① ② ③ ④ ⑤
24	① ② ③ ④ ⑤
25	① ② ③ ④ ⑤
26	① ② ③ ④ ⑤
27	① ② ③ ④ ⑤
28	① ② ③ ④ ⑤
29	① ② ③ ④ ⑤
30	① ② ③ ④ ⑤
31	① ② ③ ④ ⑤
32	① ② ③ ④ ⑤
33	① ② ③ ④ ⑤
34	① ② ③ ④ ⑤
35	① ② ③ ④ ⑤
36	① ② ③ ④ ⑤
37	① ② ③ ④ ⑤
38	① ② ③ ④ ⑤
39	① ② ③ ④ ⑤
40	① ② ③ ④ ⑤

문번	답 란
41	① ② ③ ④ ⑤
42	① ② ③ ④ ⑤
43	① ② ③ ④ ⑤
44	① ② ③ ④ ⑤
45	① ② ③ ④ ⑤

〈수험생이 지켜야 할 일〉

> 답안지 작성(표기)은 반드시 컴퓨터용 사인펜만을 사용하여야 합니다.
> (연필, 샤프펜 사용 시 불이익을 받을 수 있습니다.)

1. 성명란에는 수험생의 성명을 바르게 기재하여야 합니다.
2. 수험번호란에는 아라비아 숫자로 기재하고 해당란에 "⬮"와 같이 완전하게 표기하여야 합니다.
3. 문형란에는 배부받은 시험 문제지의 문형을 정확히 확인하고 해당란에 "⬮"와 같이 표기하여야 합니다.
   - 답안지의 '문형'란에 표기가 되어있지 않거나 이중으로 표기된 경우 불이익을 받을 수 있습니다.
   - 시험특별관리대상자의 문제지 문형은 홀수형 입니다.
4. 답란은 "⬮"와 같이 완전하게 표기하여야 하며, 바르지 못한 표기(⊘ ⦶ ⊙ ◐ ▨ 등)를 하였을 경우는 불이익을 받을 수 있습니다.
5. 답란 수정을 원할 경우에는 수정테이프만을 사용하여 완전하게 수정하여야 합니다. 불완전한 수정처리로 인해 발생하는 불이익은 수험생에게 있습니다.
   - 수정테이프는 감독관이 소지하고 있습니다.
   - 수정액이나 스티커 등은 절대로 사용할 수 없습니다.
   - 답란 수정 후 수정테이프가 떨어지지 않게 손으로 눌러 주십시오.
   - 답안지 교체를 원할 경우 교체 가능합니다.
6. 답안지에 낙서를 하거나 불필요한 표기를 하였을 경우 불이익을 받을 수 있으므로 답안지를 최대한 깨끗한 상태로 제출하여야 합니다.

첫단추 독해실전편 모의고사 12회 답안지

③ 교시 영어 영역

※ 결시자 확인 (수험생은 표기하지 말것.)

컴퓨터용 사인펜을 사용하여 수험번호란과 옆란을 표기	0

※ 아래 '필적확인란'에 "○○○○○○○○○○○○○"를 정자로 반드시 기재하여야 합니다.

필 적 확인란	

성 명								
수 험 번 호								
				—				
	0	0	0		0	0	0	0
1	1	1	1		1	1	1	1
2	2	2	2		2	2	2	2
3	3	3	3		3	3	3	3
4	4	4	4		4	4		4
5	5	5	5		5	5		5
6	6		6		6	6		6
7	7		7		7	7		7
8	8		8		8	8		8
	9		9		9	9		9

문 형
홀수형 0
짝수형 0

※ 문제의 문형을 확인후 표기

※ 감독관 확인 (수험생은 표기하지 말것.)

본인여부, 수험번호 및 문형의 표기가 정확한지 확인, 옆란에 서명 또는 날인	서 명 또는 날 인

※ 답안지 작성(표기)은 반드시 컴퓨터용 사인펜만을 사용하고, 연필 또는 샤프펜을 절대 사용하지 마십시오.
※ 뒷면의 〈수험생이 지켜야 할 일〉을 꼭 읽어 보십시오.

문번	답 란	문번	답 란	문번	답 란
1	① ② ③ ④ ⑤	21	① ② ③ ④ ⑤	41	① ② ③ ④ ⑤
2	① ② ③ ④ ⑤	22	① ② ③ ④ ⑤	42	① ② ③ ④ ⑤
3	① ② ③ ④ ⑤	23	① ② ③ ④ ⑤	43	① ② ③ ④ ⑤
4	① ② ③ ④ ⑤	24	① ② ③ ④ ⑤	44	① ② ③ ④ ⑤
5	① ② ③ ④ ⑤	25	① ② ③ ④ ⑤	45	① ② ③ ④ ⑤
6	① ② ③ ④ ⑤	26	① ② ③ ④ ⑤		
7	① ② ③ ④ ⑤	27	① ② ③ ④ ⑤		
8	① ② ③ ④ ⑤	28	① ② ③ ④ ⑤		
9	① ② ③ ④ ⑤	29	① ② ③ ④ ⑤		
10	① ② ③ ④ ⑤	30	① ② ③ ④ ⑤		
11	① ② ③ ④ ⑤	31	① ② ③ ④ ⑤		
12	① ② ③ ④ ⑤	32	① ② ③ ④ ⑤		
13	① ② ③ ④ ⑤	33	① ② ③ ④ ⑤		
14	① ② ③ ④ ⑤	34	① ② ③ ④ ⑤		
15	① ② ③ ④ ⑤	35	① ② ③ ④ ⑤		
16	① ② ③ ④ ⑤	36	① ② ③ ④ ⑤		
17	① ② ③ ④ ⑤	37	① ② ③ ④ ⑤		
18	① ② ③ ④ ⑤	38	① ② ③ ④ ⑤		
19	① ② ③ ④ ⑤	39	① ② ③ ④ ⑤		
20	① ② ③ ④ ⑤	40	① ② ③ ④ ⑤		

〈수험생이 지켜야 할 일〉

답안지 작성(표기)은 반드시 컴퓨터용 사인펜만을 사용하여야 합니다.
(연필, 샤프펜 사용 시 불이익을 받을 수 있습니다.)

1. 성명란에는 수험생의 성명을 바르게 기재하여야 합니다.
2. 수험번호란에는 아라비아 숫자로 기재하고 해당란에 "●"와 같이 완전하게 표기하여야 합니다.
3. 문형란에는 배부받은 시험 문제지의 문형을 정확히 확인하고 해당란에 "●"와 같이 표기하여야 합니다.
   - 답안지의 '문형'란에 표기가 되어있지 않거나 이중으로 표기된 경우 불이익을 받을 수 있습니다.
   - 시험특별관리대상자의 문제지 문형은 홀수형 입니다.
4. 답란은 "●"와 같이 완전하게 표기하여야 하며, 바르지 못한 표기(✓ ⦶ ⊙ ◐ ▨ 등)를 하였을 경우는 불이익을 받을 수 있습니다.
5. 답란 수정을 원할 경우에는 수정테이프만을 사용하여 완전하게 수정하여야 합니다. 불완전한 수정처리로 인해 발생하는 불이익은 수험생에게 있습니다.
   - 수정테이프는 감독관이 소지하고 있습니다.
   - 수정액이나 스티커 등은 절대로 사용할 수 없습니다.
   - 답란 수정 후 수정테이프가 떨어지지 않게 손으로 눌러 주십시오.
   - 답안지 교체를 원할 경우 교체 가능합니다.
6. 답안지에 낙서를 하거나 불필요한 표기를 하였을 경우 불이익을 받을 수 있으므로 답안지를 최대한 깨끗한 상태로 제출하여야 합니다.

첫단추 독해실전편 모의고사 12회 답안지

※ 답안지 작성(표기)은 반드시 컴퓨터용 사인펜만을 사용하고, 연필 또는 샤프펜을 절대 사용하지 마십시오.
※ 뒷면의 〈수험생이 지켜야 할 일〉을 꼭 읽어 보십시오.

③ 교시 영어 영역

※ 결시자 확인 (수험생은 표기하지 말것.)

컴퓨터용 사인펜을 사용하여 수험번호란과 옆란을 표기	▯

※ 아래 '필적확인란'에 "○○○○○○○○○○○○○"를 정자로 반드시 기재하여야 합니다.

필 적 확인란	

성 명								
수 험 번 호								
				–				
	⓪	⓪	⓪		⓪	⓪	⓪	⓪
①	①	①	①		①	①	①	①
②	②	②	②		②	②	②	②
③	③	③	③		③	③	③	③
④	④	④	④		④	④		④
⑤	⑤	⑤	⑤		⑤	⑤		⑤
⑥	⑥		⑥		⑥	⑥		⑥
⑦	⑦		⑦		⑦	⑦		⑦
⑧	⑧		⑧		⑧	⑧		⑧
	⑨		⑨		⑨	⑨		⑨

문 형	
홀수형	▯
짝수형	▯

※ 문제의 문형을 확인 후 표기

※ 감독관 확인 (수험생은 표기하지 말것.)

본인여부, 수험번호 및 문형의 표기가 정확한지 확인, 옆란에 서명 또는 날인	(서 명 또는 날 인)

문번	답 란
1	① ② ③ ④ ⑤
2	① ② ③ ④ ⑤
3	① ② ③ ④ ⑤
4	① ② ③ ④ ⑤
5	① ② ③ ④ ⑤
6	① ② ③ ④ ⑤
7	① ② ③ ④ ⑤
8	① ② ③ ④ ⑤
9	① ② ③ ④ ⑤
10	① ② ③ ④ ⑤
11	① ② ③ ④ ⑤
12	① ② ③ ④ ⑤
13	① ② ③ ④ ⑤
14	① ② ③ ④ ⑤
15	① ② ③ ④ ⑤
16	① ② ③ ④ ⑤
17	① ② ③ ④ ⑤
18	① ② ③ ④ ⑤
19	① ② ③ ④ ⑤
20	① ② ③ ④ ⑤

문번	답 란
21	① ② ③ ④ ⑤
22	① ② ③ ④ ⑤
23	① ② ③ ④ ⑤
24	① ② ③ ④ ⑤
25	① ② ③ ④ ⑤
26	① ② ③ ④ ⑤
27	① ② ③ ④ ⑤
28	① ② ③ ④ ⑤
29	① ② ③ ④ ⑤
30	① ② ③ ④ ⑤
31	① ② ③ ④ ⑤
32	① ② ③ ④ ⑤
33	① ② ③ ④ ⑤
34	① ② ③ ④ ⑤
35	① ② ③ ④ ⑤
36	① ② ③ ④ ⑤
37	① ② ③ ④ ⑤
38	① ② ③ ④ ⑤
39	① ② ③ ④ ⑤
40	① ② ③ ④ ⑤

문번	답 란
41	① ② ③ ④ ⑤
42	① ② ③ ④ ⑤
43	① ② ③ ④ ⑤
44	① ② ③ ④ ⑤
45	① ② ③ ④ ⑤

〈수험생이 지켜야 할 일〉

> 답안지 작성(표기)은 반드시 컴퓨터용 사인펜만을 사용하여야 합니다.
> (연필, 샤프펜 사용 시 불이익을 받을 수 있습니다.)

1. 성명란에는 수험생의 성명을 바르게 기재하여야 합니다.
2. 수험번호란에는 아라비아 숫자로 기재하고 해당란에 "●"와 같이 완전하게 표기하여야 합니다.
3. 문형란에는 배부받은 시험 문제지의 문형을 정확히 확인하고 해당란에 "●"와 같이 표기하여야 합니다.
   - 답안지의 '문형'란에 표기가 되어있지 않거나 이중으로 표기된 경우 불이익을 받을 수 있습니다.
   - 시험특별관리대상자의 문제지 문형은 홀수형 입니다.
4. 답란은 "●"와 같이 완전하게 표기하여야 하며, 바르지 못한 표기(⊗ ⦶ ⊙ ◐ ▨ 등)를 하였을 경우는 불이익을 받을 수 있습니다.
5. 답란 수정을 원할 경우에는 수정테이프만을 사용하여 완전하게 수정하여야 합니다. 불완전한 수정처리로 인해 발생하는 불이익은 수험생에게 있습니다.
   - 수정테이프는 감독관이 소지하고 있습니다.
   - 수정액이나 스티커 등은 절대로 사용할 수 없습니다.
   - 답란 수정 후 수정테이프가 떨어지지 않게 손으로 눌러 주십시오.
   - 답안지 교체를 원할 경우 교체 가능합니다.
6. 답안지에 낙서를 하거나 불필요한 표기를 하였을 경우 불이익을 받을 수 있으므로 답안지를 최대한 깨끗한 상태로 제출하여야 합니다.

첫단추 독해실전편 모의고사 12회 답안지

③ 교시 영어 영역

※ 결시자 확인 (수험생은 표기하지 말것.)

컴퓨터용 사인펜을 사용하여 수험번호란과 옆란을 표기 ⓪

※ 아래 '필적확인란'에 "○○○○○○○○○○○○○"를 정자로 반드시 기재하여야 합니다.

필 적 확인란	

성 명								
수험번호								
				–				
	⓪	⓪	⓪		⓪	⓪	⓪	⓪
①	①	①	①		①	①	①	①
②	②	②	②		②	②	②	②
③	③	③	③		③	③	③	③
④	④	④	④		④	④		④
⑤	⑤	⑤	⑤		⑤	⑤		⑤
⑥	⑥		⑥		⑥	⑥		⑥
⑦	⑦		⑦		⑦	⑦		⑦
⑧	⑧		⑧		⑧	⑧		⑧
	⑨		⑨		⑨	⑨		⑨

문 형

홀수형 ⓪

짝수형 ⓪

※ 문제의 문형을 확인후 표기

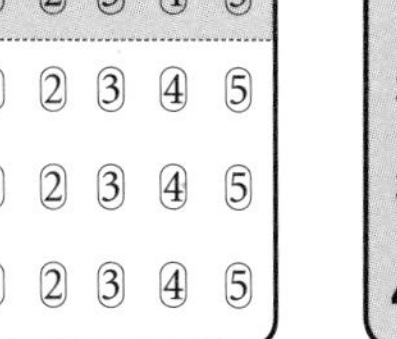
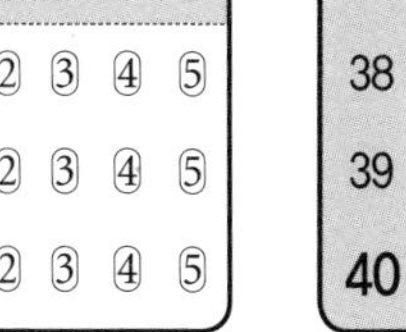
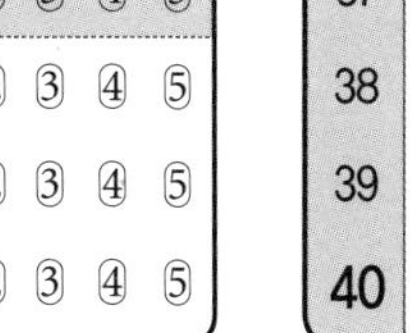

※ 감독관 확인 (수험생은 표기하지 말것.)

본인여부, 수험번호 및 문형의 표기가 정확한지 확인, 옆란에 서명 또는 날인 (서 명 또는 날 인)

※ 답안지 작성(표기)은 반드시 컴퓨터용 사인펜만을 사용하고, 연필 또는 샤프펜을 절대 사용하지 마십시오.

※ 뒷면의 〈수험생이 지켜야 할 일〉을 꼭 읽어 보십시오.

문번	답 란
1	① ② ③ ④ ⑤
2	① ② ③ ④ ⑤
3	① ② ③ ④ ⑤
4	① ② ③ ④ ⑤
5	① ② ③ ④ ⑤
6	① ② ③ ④ ⑤
7	① ② ③ ④ ⑤
8	① ② ③ ④ ⑤
9	① ② ③ ④ ⑤
10	① ② ③ ④ ⑤
11	① ② ③ ④ ⑤
12	① ② ③ ④ ⑤
13	① ② ③ ④ ⑤
14	① ② ③ ④ ⑤
15	① ② ③ ④ ⑤
16	① ② ③ ④ ⑤
17	① ② ③ ④ ⑤
18	① ② ③ ④ ⑤
19	① ② ③ ④ ⑤
20	① ② ③ ④ ⑤

문번	답 란
21	① ② ③ ④ ⑤
22	① ② ③ ④ ⑤
23	① ② ③ ④ ⑤
24	① ② ③ ④ ⑤
25	① ② ③ ④ ⑤
26	① ② ③ ④ ⑤
27	① ② ③ ④ ⑤
28	① ② ③ ④ ⑤
29	① ② ③ ④ ⑤
30	① ② ③ ④ ⑤
31	① ② ③ ④ ⑤
32	① ② ③ ④ ⑤
33	① ② ③ ④ ⑤
34	① ② ③ ④ ⑤
35	① ② ③ ④ ⑤
36	① ② ③ ④ ⑤
37	① ② ③ ④ ⑤
38	① ② ③ ④ ⑤
39	① ② ③ ④ ⑤
40	① ② ③ ④ ⑤

문번	답 란
41	① ② ③ ④ ⑤
42	① ② ③ ④ ⑤
43	① ② ③ ④ ⑤
44	① ② ③ ④ ⑤
45	① ② ③ ④ ⑤

〈수험생이 지켜야 할 일〉

> 답안지 작성(표기)은 반드시 컴퓨터용 사인펜만을 사용하여야 합니다.
> (연필, 샤프펜 사용 시 불이익을 받을 수 있습니다.)

1. 성명란에는 수험생의 성명을 바르게 기재하여야 합니다.
2. 수험번호란에는 아라비아 숫자로 기재하고 해당란에 “●”와 같이 완전하게 표기하여야 합니다.
3. 문형란에는 배부받은 시험 문제지의 문형을 정확히 확인하고 해당란에 “●”와 같이 표기하여야 합니다.
   - 답안지의 ‘문형’란에 표기가 되어있지 않거나 이중으로 표기된 경우 불이익을 받을 수 있습니다.
   - 시험특별관리대상자의 문제지 문형은 홀수형 입니다.
4. 답란은 “●”와 같이 완전하게 표기하여야 하며, 바르지 못한 표기(✓ ⦶ ⊙ ◑ ▨ 등)를 하였을 경우는 불이익을 받을 수 있습니다.
5. 답란 수정을 원할 경우에는 수정테이프만을 사용하여 완전하게 수정하여야 합니다. 불완전한 수정처리로 인해 발생하는 불이익은 수험생에게 있습니다.
   - 수정테이프는 감독관이 소지하고 있습니다.
   - 수정액이나 스티커 등은 절대로 사용할 수 없습니다.
   - 답란 수정 후 수정테이프가 떨어지지 않게 손으로 눌러 주십시오.
   - 답안지 교체를 원할 경우 교체 가능합니다.
6. 답안지에 낙서를 하거나 불필요한 표기를 하였을 경우 불이익을 받을 수 있으므로 답안지를 최대한 깨끗한 상태로 제출하여야 합니다.

첫단추 독해실전편 모의고사 12회 답안지

③ 교시 영어 영역

※ 결시자 확인 (수험생은 표기하지 말것.)

컴퓨터용 사인펜을 사용하여 수험번호란과 옆란을 표기	⓪

※ 아래 '필적확인란'에 "○○○○○○○○○○○○○"를 정자로 반드시 기재하여야 합니다.

필 적 확인란	

성 명								
수 험 번 호								
				—				
	⓪	⓪	⓪		⓪	⓪	⓪	⓪
①	①	①	①		①	①	①	①
②	②	②	②		②	②	②	②
③	③	③	③		③	③	③	③
④	④	④	④		④	④		④
⑤	⑤	⑤	⑤		⑤	⑤		⑤
⑥	⑥		⑥		⑥	⑥		⑥
⑦	⑦		⑦		⑦	⑦		⑦
⑧	⑧		⑧		⑧	⑧		⑧
	⑨		⑨		⑨	⑨		⑨

문 형
홀수형 ⓪
짝수형 ⓪

※ 문제의 문형을 확인 후 표기

※ 감독관 확인 (수험생은 표기하지 말것.)

본인여부, 수험번호 및 문형의 표기가 정확한지 확인, 옆란에 서명 또는 날인	(서 명 또는 날 인)

※ 답안지 작성(표기)은 반드시 컴퓨터용 사인펜만을 사용하고, 연필 또는 샤프펜을 절대 사용하지 마십시오.
※ 뒷면의 〈수험생이 지켜야 할 일〉을 꼭 읽어 보십시오.

문번	답 란	문번	답 란	문번	답 란
1	① ② ③ ④ ⑤	21	① ② ③ ④ ⑤	41	① ② ③ ④ ⑤
2	① ② ③ ④ ⑤	22	① ② ③ ④ ⑤	42	① ② ③ ④ ⑤
3	① ② ③ ④ ⑤	23	① ② ③ ④ ⑤	43	① ② ③ ④ ⑤
4	① ② ③ ④ ⑤	24	① ② ③ ④ ⑤	44	① ② ③ ④ ⑤
5	① ② ③ ④ ⑤	25	① ② ③ ④ ⑤	45	① ② ③ ④ ⑤
6	① ② ③ ④ ⑤	26	① ② ③ ④ ⑤		
7	① ② ③ ④ ⑤	27	① ② ③ ④ ⑤		
8	① ② ③ ④ ⑤	28	① ② ③ ④ ⑤		
9	① ② ③ ④ ⑤	29	① ② ③ ④ ⑤		
10	① ② ③ ④ ⑤	30	① ② ③ ④ ⑤		
11	① ② ③ ④ ⑤	31	① ② ③ ④ ⑤		
12	① ② ③ ④ ⑤	32	① ② ③ ④ ⑤		
13	① ② ③ ④ ⑤	33	① ② ③ ④ ⑤		
14	① ② ③ ④ ⑤	34	① ② ③ ④ ⑤		
15	① ② ③ ④ ⑤	35	① ② ③ ④ ⑤		
16	① ② ③ ④ ⑤	36	① ② ③ ④ ⑤		
17	① ② ③ ④ ⑤	37	① ② ③ ④ ⑤		
18	① ② ③ ④ ⑤	38	① ② ③ ④ ⑤		
19	① ② ③ ④ ⑤	39	① ② ③ ④ ⑤		
20	① ② ③ ④ ⑤	40	① ② ③ ④ ⑤		

〈수험생이 지켜야 할 일〉

> 답안지 작성(표기)은 반드시 컴퓨터용 사인펜만을 사용하여야 합니다.
> (연필, 샤프펜 사용 시 불이익을 받을 수 있습니다.)

1. 성명란에는 수험생의 성명을 바르게 기재하여야 합니다.
2. 수험번호란에는 아라비아 숫자로 기재하고 해당란에 "●"와 같이 완전하게 표기하여야 합니다.
3. 문형란에는 배부받은 시험 문제지의 문형을 정확히 확인하고 해당란에 "●"와 같이 표기하여야 합니다.
   - 답안지의 '문형'란에 표기가 되어있지 않거나 이중으로 표기된 경우 불이익을 받을 수 있습니다.
   - 시험특별관리대상자의 문제지 문형은 홀수형 입니다.
4. 답란은 "●"와 같이 완전하게 표기하여야 하며, 바르지 못한 표기(✓ ○ ⊙ ◐ ▨ 등)를 하였을 경우는 불이익을 받을 수 있습니다.
5. 답란 수정을 원할 경우에는 수정테이프만을 사용하여 완전하게 수정하여야 합니다. 불완전한 수정처리로 인해 발생하는 불이익은 수험생에게 있습니다.
   - 수정테이프는 감독관이 소지하고 있습니다.
   - 수정액이나 스티커 등은 절대로 사용할 수 없습니다.
   - 답란 수정 후 수정테이프가 떨어지지 않게 손으로 눌러 주십시오.
   - 답안지 교체를 원할 경우 교체 가능합니다.
6. 답안지에 낙서를 하거나 불필요한 표기를 하였을 경우 불이익을 받을 수 있으므로 답안지를 최대한 깨끗한 상태로 제출하여야 합니다.

첫단추 독해실전편 모의고사 12회 답안지

※ 답안지 작성(표기)은 반드시 컴퓨터용 사인펜만을 사용하고, 연필 또는 샤프펜을 절대 사용하지 마십시오.
※ 뒷면의 〈수험생이 지켜야 할 일〉을 꼭 읽어 보십시오.

③ 교시 **영어 영역**

※ 결시자 확인 (수험생은 표기하지 말것.)

컴퓨터용 사인펜을 사용하여 수험번호란과 옆란을 표기	○

※ 아래 '필적확인란'에 "○○○○○○○○○○○○○"를 정자로 반드시 기재하여야 합니다.

필 적 확인란	

성 명								
수 험 번 호								
				—				
	0	0	0		0	0	0	0
1	1	1	1		1	1	1	1
2	2	2	2		2	2	2	2
3	3	3	3		3	3	3	3
4	4	4	4		4	4		4
5	5	5	5		5	5		5
6	6		6		6	6		6
7	7		7		7	7		7
8	8		8		8	8		8
	9		9		9	9		9

문 형
홀수형 ○
짝수형 ○

※ 문제의 문형을 확인 후 표기

※ 감독관 확인 (수험생은 표기하지 말것.)

본인여부, 수험번호 및 문형의 표기가 정확한지 확인, 옆란에 서명 또는 날인	(서 명 또는 날 인)

문번	답 란
1	① ② ③ ④ ⑤
2	① ② ③ ④ ⑤
3	① ② ③ ④ ⑤
4	① ② ③ ④ ⑤
5	① ② ③ ④ ⑤
6	① ② ③ ④ ⑤
7	① ② ③ ④ ⑤
8	① ② ③ ④ ⑤
9	① ② ③ ④ ⑤
10	① ② ③ ④ ⑤
11	① ② ③ ④ ⑤
12	① ② ③ ④ ⑤
13	① ② ③ ④ ⑤
14	① ② ③ ④ ⑤
15	① ② ③ ④ ⑤
16	① ② ③ ④ ⑤
17	① ② ③ ④ ⑤
18	① ② ③ ④ ⑤
19	① ② ③ ④ ⑤
20	① ② ③ ④ ⑤

문번	답 란
21	① ② ③ ④ ⑤
22	① ② ③ ④ ⑤
23	① ② ③ ④ ⑤
24	① ② ③ ④ ⑤
25	① ② ③ ④ ⑤
26	① ② ③ ④ ⑤
27	① ② ③ ④ ⑤
28	① ② ③ ④ ⑤
29	① ② ③ ④ ⑤
30	① ② ③ ④ ⑤
31	① ② ③ ④ ⑤
32	① ② ③ ④ ⑤
33	① ② ③ ④ ⑤
34	① ② ③ ④ ⑤
35	① ② ③ ④ ⑤
36	① ② ③ ④ ⑤
37	① ② ③ ④ ⑤
38	① ② ③ ④ ⑤
39	① ② ③ ④ ⑤
40	① ② ③ ④ ⑤

문번	답 란
41	① ② ③ ④ ⑤
42	① ② ③ ④ ⑤
43	① ② ③ ④ ⑤
44	① ② ③ ④ ⑤
45	① ② ③ ④ ⑤

〈수험생이 지켜야 할 일〉

답안지 작성(표기)은 반드시 컴퓨터용 사인펜만을 사용하여야 합니다.
(연필, 샤프펜 사용 시 불이익을 받을 수 있습니다.)

1. 성명란에는 수험생의 성명을 바르게 기재하여야 합니다.
2. 수험번호란에는 아라비아 숫자로 기재하고 해당란에 "●"와 같이 완전하게 표기하여야 합니다.
3. 문형란에는 배부받은 시험 문제지의 문형을 정확히 확인하고 해당란에 "●"와 같이 표기하여야 합니다.
   - 답안지의 '문형'란에 표기가 되어있지 않거나 이중으로 표기된 경우 불이익을 받을 수 있습니다.
   - 시험특별관리대상자의 문제지 문형은 홀수형 입니다.
4. 답란은 "●"와 같이 완전하게 표기하여야 하며, 바르지 못한 표기(✓ ⃝ ⊙ ◑ ▨ 등)를 하였을 경우는 불이익을 받을 수 있습니다.
5. 답란 수정을 원할 경우에는 수정테이프만을 사용하여 완전하게 수정하여야 합니다. 불완전한 수정처리로 인해 발생하는 불이익은 수험생에게 있습니다.
   - 수정테이프는 감독관이 소지하고 있습니다.
   - 수정액이나 스티커 등은 절대로 사용할 수 없습니다.
   - 답란 수정 후 수정테이프가 떨어지지 않게 손으로 눌러 주십시오.
   - 답안지 교체를 원할 경우 교체 가능합니다.
6. 답안지에 낙서를 하거나 불필요한 표기를 하였을 경우 불이익을 받을 수 있으므로 답안지를 최대한 깨끗한 상태로 제출하여야 합니다.

첫단추 독해실전편 모의고사 12회 답안지

※ 답안지 작성(표기)은 반드시 컴퓨터용 사인펜만을 사용하고, 연필 또는 샤프펜을 절대 사용하지 마십시오.
※ 뒷면의 〈수험생이 지켜야 할 일〉을 꼭 읽어 보십시오.

③ 교시 영어 영역

※ 결시자 확인 (수험생은 표기하지 말것.)	
컴퓨터용 사인펜을 사용하여 수험번호란과 옆란을 표기	⓪

※ 아래 '필적확인란'에 "○○○○○○○○○○○○○"를 정자로 반드시 기재하여야 합니다.

필 적 확인란	

성 명								
수 험 번 호								
				–				
	⓪	⓪	⓪		⓪	⓪	⓪	⓪
①	①	①	①		①	①	①	①
②	②	②	②		②	②	②	②
③	③	③	③		③	③	③	③
④	④	④	④		④	④		④
⑤	⑤	⑤	⑤		⑤	⑤		⑤
⑥	⑥		⑥		⑥	⑥		⑥
⑦	⑦		⑦		⑦	⑦		⑦
⑧	⑧		⑧		⑧	⑧		⑧
	⑨		⑨		⑨	⑨		⑨

문 형
홀수형 ⓪
짝수형 ⓪

※ 문제의 문형을 확인 후 표기

※ 감독관 확인 (수험생은 표기하지 말것.)	
본인여부, 수험번호 및 문형의 표기가 정확한지 확인, 옆란에 서명 또는 날인	(서 명 또는 날 인)

문번	답 란	문번	답 란	문번	답 란
1	① ② ③ ④ ⑤	21	① ② ③ ④ ⑤	41	① ② ③ ④ ⑤
2	① ② ③ ④ ⑤	22	① ② ③ ④ ⑤	42	① ② ③ ④ ⑤
3	① ② ③ ④ ⑤	23	① ② ③ ④ ⑤	43	① ② ③ ④ ⑤
4	① ② ③ ④ ⑤	24	① ② ③ ④ ⑤	44	① ② ③ ④ ⑤
5	① ② ③ ④ ⑤	25	① ② ③ ④ ⑤	45	① ② ③ ④ ⑤
6	① ② ③ ④ ⑤	26	① ② ③ ④ ⑤		
7	① ② ③ ④ ⑤	27	① ② ③ ④ ⑤		
8	① ② ③ ④ ⑤	28	① ② ③ ④ ⑤		
9	① ② ③ ④ ⑤	29	① ② ③ ④ ⑤		
10	① ② ③ ④ ⑤	30	① ② ③ ④ ⑤		
11	① ② ③ ④ ⑤	31	① ② ③ ④ ⑤		
12	① ② ③ ④ ⑤	32	① ② ③ ④ ⑤		
13	① ② ③ ④ ⑤	33	① ② ③ ④ ⑤		
14	① ② ③ ④ ⑤	34	① ② ③ ④ ⑤		
15	① ② ③ ④ ⑤	35	① ② ③ ④ ⑤		
16	① ② ③ ④ ⑤	36	① ② ③ ④ ⑤		
17	① ② ③ ④ ⑤	37	① ② ③ ④ ⑤		
18	① ② ③ ④ ⑤	38	① ② ③ ④ ⑤		
19	① ② ③ ④ ⑤	39	① ② ③ ④ ⑤		
20	① ② ③ ④ ⑤	40	① ② ③ ④ ⑤		

〈수험생이 지켜야 할 일〉

> 답안지 작성(표기)은 반드시 컴퓨터용 사인펜만을 사용하여야 합니다.
> (연필, 샤프펜 사용 시 불이익을 받을 수 있습니다.)

1. 성명란에는 수험생의 성명을 바르게 기재하여야 합니다.
2. 수험번호란에는 아라비아 숫자로 기재하고 해당란에 "●"와 같이 완전하게 표기하여야 합니다.
3. 문형란에는 배부받은 시험 문제지의 문형을 정확히 확인하고 해당란에 "●"와 같이 표기하여야 합니다.
   - 답안지의 '문형'란에 표기가 되어있지 않거나 이중으로 표기된 경우 불이익을 받을 수 있습니다.
   - 시험특별관리대상자의 문제지 문형은 홀수형 입니다.
4. 답란은 "●"와 같이 완전하게 표기하여야 하며, 바르지 못한 표기(✓ ⦶ ⊙ ◐ ▨ 등)를 하였을 경우는 불이익을 받을 수 있습니다.
5. 답란 수정을 원할 경우에는 수정테이프만을 사용하여 완전하게 수정하여야 합니다. 불완전한 수정처리로 인해 발생하는 불이익은 수험생에게 있습니다.
   - 수정테이프는 감독관이 소지하고 있습니다.
   - 수정액이나 스티커 등은 절대로 사용할 수 없습니다.
   - 답란 수정 후 수정테이프가 떨어지지 않게 손으로 눌러 주십시오.
   - 답안지 교체를 원할 경우 교체 가능합니다.
6. 답안지에 낙서를 하거나 불필요한 표기를 하였을 경우 불이익을 받을 수 있으므로 답안지를 최대한 깨끗한 상태로 제출하여야 합니다.

첫단추 독해실전편 모의고사 12회 답안지

③ 교시 영어 영역

※ 결시자 확인 (수험생은 표기하지 말것.)

컴퓨터용 사인펜을 사용하여 수험번호란과 옆란을 표기 ⓪

※ 아래 '필적확인란'에 "○○○○○○○○○○ ○○○"를 정자로 반드시 기재하여야 합니다.

필 적 확인란	

성 명								
수 험 번 호								
				—				
	⓪	⓪	⓪		⓪	⓪	⓪	⓪
①	①	①	①		①	①	①	①
②	②	②	②		②	②	②	②
③	③	③	③		③	③	③	③
④	④	④	④		④	④		④
⑤	⑤	⑤	⑤		⑤	⑤		⑤
⑥	⑥		⑥		⑥	⑥		⑥
⑦	⑦		⑦		⑦	⑦		⑦
⑧	⑧		⑧		⑧	⑧		⑧
	⑨		⑨		⑨	⑨		⑨

문 형
홀수형 ⓪
짝수형 ⓪

※ 문제의 문형을 확인 후 표기

※ 감독관 확인 (수험생은 표기하지 말것.)

본인여부, 수험번호 및 문형의 표기가 정확한지 확인, 옆란에 서명 또는 날인 (서 명 또는 날 인)

※ 답안지 작성(표기)은 반드시 컴퓨터용 사인펜만을 사용하고, 연필 또는 샤프펜을 절대 사용하지 마십시오.
※ 뒷면의 〈수험생이 지켜야 할 일〉을 꼭 읽어 보십시오.

문번	답 란	문번	답 란	문번	답 란
1	① ② ③ ④ ⑤	21	① ② ③ ④ ⑤	41	① ② ③ ④ ⑤
2	① ② ③ ④ ⑤	22	① ② ③ ④ ⑤	42	① ② ③ ④ ⑤
3	① ② ③ ④ ⑤	23	① ② ③ ④ ⑤	43	① ② ③ ④ ⑤
4	① ② ③ ④ ⑤	24	① ② ③ ④ ⑤	44	① ② ③ ④ ⑤
5	① ② ③ ④ ⑤	25	① ② ③ ④ ⑤	45	① ② ③ ④ ⑤
6	① ② ③ ④ ⑤	26	① ② ③ ④ ⑤		
7	① ② ③ ④ ⑤	27	① ② ③ ④ ⑤		
8	① ② ③ ④ ⑤	28	① ② ③ ④ ⑤		
9	① ② ③ ④ ⑤	29	① ② ③ ④ ⑤		
10	① ② ③ ④ ⑤	30	① ② ③ ④ ⑤		
11	① ② ③ ④ ⑤	31	① ② ③ ④ ⑤		
12	① ② ③ ④ ⑤	32	① ② ③ ④ ⑤		
13	① ② ③ ④ ⑤	33	① ② ③ ④ ⑤		
14	① ② ③ ④ ⑤	34	① ② ③ ④ ⑤		
15	① ② ③ ④ ⑤	35	① ② ③ ④ ⑤		
16	① ② ③ ④ ⑤	36	① ② ③ ④ ⑤		
17	① ② ③ ④ ⑤	37	① ② ③ ④ ⑤		
18	① ② ③ ④ ⑤	38	① ② ③ ④ ⑤		
19	① ② ③ ④ ⑤	39	① ② ③ ④ ⑤		
20	① ② ③ ④ ⑤	40	① ② ③ ④ ⑤		

〈수험생이 지켜야 할 일〉

> 답안지 작성(표기)은 반드시 컴퓨터용 사인펜만을 사용하여야 합니다.
> (연필, 샤프펜 사용 시 불이익을 받을 수 있습니다.)

1. 성명란에는 수험생의 성명을 바르게 기재하여야 합니다.
2. 수험번호란에는 아라비아 숫자로 기재하고 해당란에 "●"와 같이 완전하게 표기하여야 합니다.
3. 문형란에는 배부받은 시험 문제지의 문형을 정확히 확인하고 해당란에 "●"와 같이 표기하여야 합니다.
   – 답안지의 '문형'란에 표기가 되어있지 않거나 이중으로 표기된 경우 불이익을 받을 수 있습니다.
   – 시험특별관리대상자의 문제지 문형은 홀수형 입니다.
4. 답란은 "●"와 같이 완전하게 표기하여야 하며, 바르지 못한 표기(⊗ ⦶ ⊙ ◑ ▨ 등)를 하였을 경우는 불이익을 받을 수 있습니다.
5. 답란 수정을 원할 경우에는 수정테이프만을 사용하여 완전하게 수정하여야 합니다. 불완전한 수정처리로 인해 발생하는 불이익은 수험생에게 있습니다.
   – 수정테이프는 감독관이 소지하고 있습니다.
   – 수정액이나 스티커 등은 절대로 사용할 수 없습니다.
   – 답란 수정 후 수정테이프가 떨어지지 않게 손으로 눌러 주십시오.
   – 답안지 교체를 원할 경우 교체 가능합니다.
6. 답안지에 낙서를 하거나 불필요한 표기를 하였을 경우 불이익을 받을 수 있으므로 답안지를 최대한 깨끗한 상태로 제출하여야 합니다.

첫단추 독해실전편 모의고사 12회 답안지

※ 답안지 작성(표기)은 반드시 컴퓨터용 사인펜만을 사용하고, 연필 또는 샤프펜을 절대 사용하지 마십시오.
※ 뒷면의 〈수험생이 지켜야 할 일〉을 꼭 읽어 보십시오.

③ 교시 영어 영역

※ 결시자 확인 (수험생은 표기하지 말것.)

컴퓨터용 사인펜을 사용하여 수험번호란과 옆란을 표기	0

※ 아래 '필적확인란'에 "○○○○○○○○○○○○○"를 정자로 반드시 기재하여야 합니다.

필 적 확인란	

성 명								
수 험 번 호								
				–				
	0	0	0		0	0	0	0
1	1	1	1		1	1	1	1
2	2	2	2		2	2	2	2
3	3	3	3		3	3	3	3
4	4	4	4		4	4		4
5	5	5	5		5	5		5
6	6		6		6	6		6
7	7		7		7	7		7
8	8		8		8	8		8
	9		9		9	9		9

문 형
홀수형 0
짝수형 0

※ 문제의 문형을 확인 후 표기

※ 감독관 확인 (수험생은 표기하지 말것.)

본인여부, 수험번호 및 문형의 표기가 정확한지 확인, 옆란에 서명 또는 날인	서 명 또는 날 인

문번	답 란	문번	답 란	문번	답 란
1	① ② ③ ④ ⑤	21	① ② ③ ④ ⑤	41	① ② ③ ④ ⑤
2	① ② ③ ④ ⑤	22	① ② ③ ④ ⑤	42	① ② ③ ④ ⑤
3	① ② ③ ④ ⑤	23	① ② ③ ④ ⑤	43	① ② ③ ④ ⑤
4	① ② ③ ④ ⑤	24	① ② ③ ④ ⑤	44	① ② ③ ④ ⑤
5	① ② ③ ④ ⑤	25	① ② ③ ④ ⑤	45	① ② ③ ④ ⑤
6	① ② ③ ④ ⑤	26	① ② ③ ④ ⑤		
7	① ② ③ ④ ⑤	27	① ② ③ ④ ⑤		
8	① ② ③ ④ ⑤	28	① ② ③ ④ ⑤		
9	① ② ③ ④ ⑤	29	① ② ③ ④ ⑤		
10	① ② ③ ④ ⑤	30	① ② ③ ④ ⑤		
11	① ② ③ ④ ⑤	31	① ② ③ ④ ⑤		
12	① ② ③ ④ ⑤	32	① ② ③ ④ ⑤		
13	① ② ③ ④ ⑤	33	① ② ③ ④ ⑤		
14	① ② ③ ④ ⑤	34	① ② ③ ④ ⑤		
15	① ② ③ ④ ⑤	35	① ② ③ ④ ⑤		
16	① ② ③ ④ ⑤	36	① ② ③ ④ ⑤		
17	① ② ③ ④ ⑤	37	① ② ③ ④ ⑤		
18	① ② ③ ④ ⑤	38	① ② ③ ④ ⑤		
19	① ② ③ ④ ⑤	39	① ② ③ ④ ⑤		
20	① ② ③ ④ ⑤	40	① ② ③ ④ ⑤		

〈수험생이 지켜야 할 일〉

> 답안지 작성(표기)은 반드시 컴퓨터용 사인펜만을 사용하여야 합니다.
> (연필, 샤프펜 사용 시 불이익을 받을 수 있습니다.)

1. 성명란에는 수험생의 성명을 바르게 기재하여야 합니다.
2. 수험번호란에는 아라비아 숫자로 기재하고 해당란에 "●"와 같이 완전하게 표기하여야 합니다.
3. 문형란에는 배부받은 시험 문제지의 문형을 정확히 확인하고 해당란에 "●"와 같이 표기하여야 합니다.
   - 답안지의 '문형'란에 표기가 되어있지 않거나 이중으로 표기된 경우 불이익을 받을 수 있습니다.
   - 시험특별관리대상자의 문제지 문형은 홀수형 입니다.
4. 답란은 "●"와 같이 완전하게 표기하여야 하며, 바르지 못한 표기(... 등)를 하였을 경우는 불이익을 받을 수 있습니다.
5. 답란 수정을 원할 경우에는 수정테이프만을 사용하여 완전하게 수정하여야 합니다. 불완전한 수정처리로 인해 발생하는 불이익은 수험생에게 있습니다.
   - 수정테이프는 감독관이 소지하고 있습니다.
   - 수정액이나 스티커 등은 절대로 사용할 수 없습니다.
   - 답란 수정 후 수정테이프가 떨어지지 않게 손으로 눌러 주십시오.
   - 답안지 교체를 원할 경우 교체 가능합니다.
6. 답안지에 낙서를 하거나 불필요한 표기를 하였을 경우 불이익을 받을 수 있으므로 답안지를 최대한 깨끗한 상태로 제출하여야 합니다.

첫단추 독해실전편 모의고사 12회 답안지

③ 교시 영어 영역

※ 답안지 작성(표기)은 반드시 컴퓨터용 사인펜만을 사용하고, 연필 또는 샤프펜을 절대 사용하지 마십시오.
※ 뒷면의 〈수험생이 지켜야 할 일〉을 꼭 읽어 보십시오.

※ 결시자 확인 (수험생은 표기하지 말것.)	
컴퓨터용 사인펜을 사용하여 수험번호란과 옆란을 표기	⓪

※ 아래 '필적확인란'에 "○○○○○○○○○○○○○"를 정자로 반드시 기재하여야 합니다.

필 적 확인란	

성 명								
수 험 번 호								
				–				
	⓪	⓪	⓪		⓪	⓪	⓪	⓪
①	①	①	①		①	①	①	①
②	②	②	②		②	②	②	②
③	③	③	③		③	③	③	③
④	④	④	④		④	④		④
⑤	⑤	⑤	⑤		⑤	⑤		⑤
⑥	⑥		⑥		⑥	⑥		⑥
⑦	⑦		⑦		⑦	⑦		⑦
⑧	⑧		⑧		⑧	⑧		⑧
	⑨		⑨		⑨	⑨		⑨

문 형
홀수형 ⓪
짝수형 ⓪

※ 문제의 문형을 확인 후 표기

※ 감독관 확인 (수험생은 표기하지 말것.)	
본인여부, 수험번호 및 문형의 표기가 정확한지 확인, 옆란에 서명 또는 날인	서 명 또는 날 인

문번	답 란
1	① ② ③ ④ ⑤
2	① ② ③ ④ ⑤
3	① ② ③ ④ ⑤
4	① ② ③ ④ ⑤
5	① ② ③ ④ ⑤
6	① ② ③ ④ ⑤
7	① ② ③ ④ ⑤
8	① ② ③ ④ ⑤
9	① ② ③ ④ ⑤
10	① ② ③ ④ ⑤
11	① ② ③ ④ ⑤
12	① ② ③ ④ ⑤
13	① ② ③ ④ ⑤
14	① ② ③ ④ ⑤
15	① ② ③ ④ ⑤
16	① ② ③ ④ ⑤
17	① ② ③ ④ ⑤
18	① ② ③ ④ ⑤
19	① ② ③ ④ ⑤
20	① ② ③ ④ ⑤

문번	답 란
21	① ② ③ ④ ⑤
22	① ② ③ ④ ⑤
23	① ② ③ ④ ⑤
24	① ② ③ ④ ⑤
25	① ② ③ ④ ⑤
26	① ② ③ ④ ⑤
27	① ② ③ ④ ⑤
28	① ② ③ ④ ⑤
29	① ② ③ ④ ⑤
30	① ② ③ ④ ⑤
31	① ② ③ ④ ⑤
32	① ② ③ ④ ⑤
33	① ② ③ ④ ⑤
34	① ② ③ ④ ⑤
35	① ② ③ ④ ⑤
36	① ② ③ ④ ⑤
37	① ② ③ ④ ⑤
38	① ② ③ ④ ⑤
39	① ② ③ ④ ⑤
40	① ② ③ ④ ⑤

문번	답 란
41	① ② ③ ④ ⑤
42	① ② ③ ④ ⑤
43	① ② ③ ④ ⑤
44	① ② ③ ④ ⑤
45	① ② ③ ④ ⑤

〈수험생이 지켜야 할 일〉

> 답안지 작성(표기)은 반드시 컴퓨터용 사인펜만을 사용하여야 합니다.
> (연필, 샤프펜 사용 시 불이익을 받을 수 있습니다.)

1. 성명란에는 수험생의 성명을 바르게 기재하여야 합니다.
2. 수험번호란에는 아라비아 숫자로 기재하고 해당란에 “●”와 같이 완전하게 표기하여야 합니다.
3. 문형란에는 배부받은 시험 문제지의 문형을 정확히 확인하고 해당란에 “●”와 같이 표기하여야 합니다.
   - 답안지의 ‘문형’란에 표기가 되어있지 않거나 이중으로 표기된 경우 불이익을 받을 수 있습니다.
   - 시험특별관리대상자의 문제지 문형은 홀수형 입니다.
4. 답란은 “●”와 같이 완전하게 표기하여야 하며, 바르지 못한 표기(✓ ⦶ ⊙ ◐ ▨ 등)를 하였을 경우는 불이익을 받을 수 있습니다.
5. 답란 수정을 원할 경우에는 수정테이프만을 사용하여 완전하게 수정하여야 합니다. 불완전한 수정처리로 인해 발생하는 불이익은 수험생에게 있습니다.
   - 수정테이프는 감독관이 소지하고 있습니다.
   - 수정액이나 스티커 등은 절대로 사용할 수 없습니다.
   - 답란 수정 후 수정테이프가 떨어지지 않게 손으로 눌러 주십시오.
   - 답안지 교체를 원할 경우 교체 가능합니다.
6. 답안지에 낙서를 하거나 불필요한 표기를 하였을 경우 불이익을 받을 수 있으므로 답안지를 최대한 깨끗한 상태로 제출하여야 합니다.

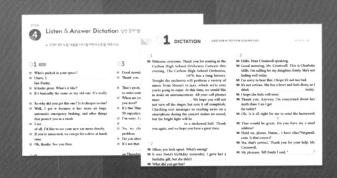

천일문·어법끝 온라인 복습테스트를 찾는다면?

쎄듀런 홈페이지 상단의 상품소개 → 쎄듀캠퍼스에서 똑똑한 온라인 영어학습을 시작해보세요!

절대평가 수능대비
수능 영어
정복의 첫걸음

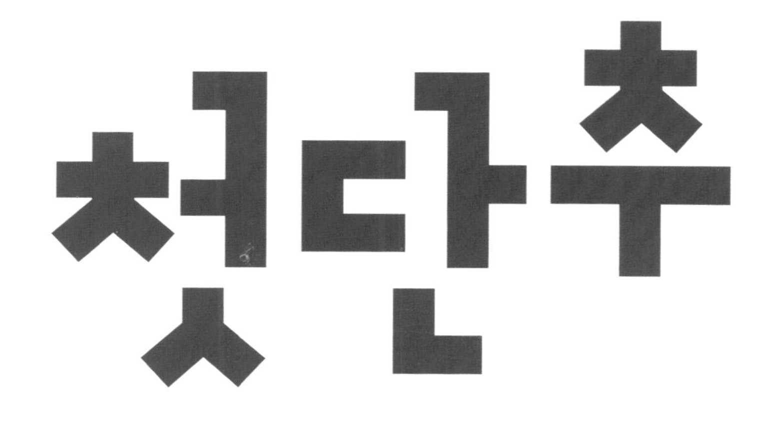

첫단추 독해실전편

모의고사 12회

BUTTON

정답 및 해설

쎄듀

절대평가 수능대비
수능 영어
정복의 첫걸음

첫단추

독해실전편

모의고사 12회

정답 및 해설

실전 모의고사 01

본문 p.13

18 ④	19 ②	20 ⑤	21 ③	22 ②	23 ④	24 ③	25 ⑤	26 ⑤	27 ⑤
28 ⑤	29 ③	30 ⑤	31 ④	32 ④	33 ⑤	34 ②	35 ④	36 ④	37 ②
38 ④	39 ⑤	40 ⑤	41 ②	42 ④	43 ④	44 ④	45 ③		

18 글의 목적 ④

소재 이른 시간대 축제 방문 권장

해설 글을 끝까지 읽고 글쓴이의 진짜 의도를 파악해야 한다. 앞부분에서 축제의 일정과 특징을 간략히 설명한 뒤, 중반부터는 오후에 축제에 온 많은 인파로 인해 불편했던 자신의 경험을 예로 들며 아침 일찍 방문할 것을 권유하는 것으로 글을 마무리하고 있다. 따라서 글의 목적으로 가장 적절한 것은 ④이다.

해석 독자 여러분께,
2020 Loudoun County 농장 축제가 지난 토요일에 개막했습니다! 이는 인상적인 행사로, 지역 농장과 기업에서 온 50개 이상의 부스가 있습니다. 광고된 대로, 축제는 이 달 말까지 매일 오전 8시부터 오후 5시까지 열리지만, 오후 늦게, 특히 주말에는 많은 사람들이 문제가 될 수 있습니다. 저는 화요일에 뜨거운 오후의 태양 아래서 많은 사람들과 씨름하는 데 4시간이 넘는 시간을 소비했습니다. 많은 상품들은 이미 품절되었고, 저는 부스를 구경하기 위해 긴 줄을 서서 기다려야 했습니다. 주제문 가장 신선한 채소들과 가장 짧은 줄을 맞이하기 위해, 꼭 아침 일찍 도착하세요! 많은 좋은 정보를 위해 축제의 온라인 웹사이트를 방문하실 수 있습니다.
John Markoff

구문 [5행~6행] **As advertised**, / the festival is open from 8 a.m. to 5 p.m. every day / until the end of this month, ~.
As advertised는 As the festival has been advertised를 분사구문으로 바꾼 것이며, 의미를 명확히 하기 위해 분사구문 앞에 접속사(As)를 두었다.

어휘 **impressive** 인상적인; 감명 깊은 **local** 지역의, 현지의 **crowd** 많은 사람들, 군중; 가득 메우다, 붐비다 **out of stock** 품절된, 매진인 **greet** 맞이하다, 환영하다 **bright and early** 아침 일찍, 새벽부터 **plenty of** 많은, 충분한

19 심경 변화 ②

소재 미식축구팀 선수 영입 실패

해설 Darker-Smith 코치는 Tony가 던진 공을 받아보고 쿼터백에 적격이라고 생각해서 연습에 나올 것을 제안하지만 Tony는 이를 거절한다. 코치는 꿈에 그리던 선수를 영입할 수 있다는 기대에 찼다가 실망하게 되므로 심경 변화는 ② '기대하는 → 실망한'이 가장 적절하다.

해석 Darker-Smith 코치는 Tony가 던진 공을 잡았다. 잠시 그는 어리둥절해하는 모습이었다. 그 뒤 그는 곧 정신을 차렸다. "Tony!" 그가 외치듯이 말했다. "너 미식축구공을 던질 줄 아는구나. 너처럼 미식축구공을 던질 수 있는 사람은 그 누구도 보지 못했어. 내일 오후 연습에 출석해라. 네 저지 셔츠를 준비해 놓으마." Tony는 매우 놀란 것처럼 보였다. "미식축구 연습에 나오라고요?" Tony가 물었다. "죄송하지만, 코치님, 전 미식축구를 할 시간이 없어요. 공부해야 할 게 많아서요." 그러고는 다른 말없이 Tony는 운동장에서 걸어 나갔다. 주제문 Darker-Smith 코치는 그가 꿈에 그리던 선수가 멀리 사라지는 것을 보고 말문이 막혀버렸다. 마침내 그는 "무슨 저런 괴짜가 다 있지? 대부분의 대학 쿼터백 선수보다 미식축구공을 더 잘 던질 수 있으면서 하고 싶은 게 공부뿐이라니!"라며 중얼거렸다.

① 후회하는 → 짜증이 난 ③ 안심한 → 겁이 난
④ 부러워하는 → 슬퍼하는 ⑤ 당혹한 → 만족한

어휘 **report** 출석[출두]하다; ~을 보고하다 **have A ready** A를 준비시켜 놓다 **jersey** (운동경기용) 저지 셔츠 **speechless** (충격 등으로) 말문이 막힌 **vanish** 사라지다, 없어지다 **mutter** 중얼거리다; (간접적 혹은 비공식적으로) 불평을 말하다 **quarterback** 쿼터백(미식축구에서 같은 팀원에게 길고 정확하게 공을 패스해 주는 역할을 하는 선수)

20 필자 주장 ⑤

소재 책을 소장해야 하는 이유

해설 빌린 책 말고 자신이 소장한 책을 읽는 것이 더 편하고 즐거우며, 책은 보여주기 위한 것이 아니라 사용하기 위한 것이라는 내용의 글이다. 조동사 should를 포함한 문장(Books are ~ on a table.)에서 책을 소장해야 하는 이유를 설명하고 있으므로, 필자의 주장으로 가장 적절한 것은 ⑤이다.

해석 독서 습관은 우리가 이용할 수 있는 가장 위대한 자원들 중 하나다. 주제문 그리고 우리는 빌려 온 책보다 우리가 소장한 책을 읽는 것을 훨씬 더 좋아한다. 빌려 온 책은 손님과 같아서 약간의 형식적 예의를 가지고 다루어져야 하지만, 우리 자신의 책은 가족과 같아서, 우리는 대개 친근하게 격식을 차리지 않고 그것들을 다룬다. 주제문 책은 사용하기 위한 것이지 보여주기 위한 것이 아니다. 메모를 하거나 테이블 위에 엎어놓거나 펼쳐 놓기가 두려운 책을 가지고 있어서는 안 된다. 책 속 구절에 표시하는 것이 좋은 이유는 당신이 그러한 중요한 부분을 기억하고, 필요할 때 더 빨리 찾을 수 있도록 도와주기 때문이다.

구문 [1행~3행] The habit of reading is / **one of *the greatest resources*** (available to us); we enjoy reading *books* [that are ours] **much** *more* / than *books* [(which[that]) we borrow].
「one of + the 최상급 + 복수명사」는 '가장 ~한 것들 중의 하나'라는 뜻이다. available to us는 the greatest resources를 수식하는 형용사구이다. 첫 번째 [ ] 부분은 주격 관계대명사 that이 이끄는 관계사절로 선행사 books를 수식하며, 두 번째 [ ] 부분은 목적격 관계대명사 which 또는 that이 생략된 관계사절로 선행사 books를 수식한다. much는 비교급 more를 수식하는 부사이며 다른 표현으로는 far, even, still, a lot 등이 있다.

[9행~12행] ***A good reason*** (for marking passages in your books) **is** // that it helps you to remember those significant parts and to find them more quickly // when you need **to** (find them).
(A good reason: S, is: V, it: S', helps: V', you: O', to remember those significant parts: C'1, to find them more quickly: C'2)

주어의 핵심어구인 A good reason에 수를 맞추어 단수동사 is가 쓰였다. for ~ books는 A good reason을 수식하는 전명구이다. that 이하는 동사 is의 보어로 쓰인 명사절로 that절 안에는 「help+O+C(to-v)」 구조의 to부정사구 2개가 and로 병렬 연결되어 있다. 마지막 to는 바로 앞의 to find them을 대신한다.

어휘 **available** 이용 가능한 **certain** 약간의, 어느 정도의; 어떤 **formal** 형식적인 **etiquette** 예의[범절], 에티켓 **casualness** 격식을 차리지 않음 *cf.* **casual** 격식을 차리지 않는; 평상시의 **A, not B** B가 아니라 A **place a book face down** 책을 엎어놓다 **significant** 중요한, 의미 있는

21 밑줄 함의 ③

소재 사냥꾼 안내원을 그만두는 이유

해설 낚시꾼은 Tim을 물고기로 여기지 않았지만 사냥꾼은 그랬다는 것은 사냥꾼이 자신을 사냥감으로 오해했다는 뜻이다. 따라서 밑줄 친 부분의 의미로 가장 적절한 것은 ③ '사냥꾼들은 실수로 나를 쏘곤 했다.'이다.

해석 Tim은 캐나다에서 엘크와 순록 같은 큰 사냥감을 찾는 사냥꾼들을 위한 안내원이었다. 어느 날, 그는 사장에게 사냥꾼의 안내원 일을 그만두고 낚시꾼들의 안내원이 되겠다고 선언했다. 그의 사장은 Tim에게 이렇게 바꾸려는 이유를 물었다. "왜죠? 사냥꾼들에게 거슬리는 뭔가가 있나요?" "아니요, 전 그들을 좋아해요."라고 Tim이 대답했다. "낚시꾼들이 돈을 더 많이 주나요?"라고 사장이 물었다. "아니요, 낚시꾼들은 사냥꾼보다 돈을 더 적게 줘요."라고 그가 답했다. "그러면 왜 낚시꾼이란 말이요?"라고 그의 사장이 물었다. "그것은 제 목숨과 큰 관련이 있어요."라고 Tim이 말했다. "지금까지 낚시꾼 중에서는 아무도 저를 사냥감으로 오해하지 않았어요. 하지만 가끔 사냥꾼들은 그래요."

① 사냥꾼들이 내게 제때 돈을 주지 않았다.
② 사냥꾼들은 때때로 길을 잃었다.
④ 사냥꾼들은 낚시꾼들보다 덜 공손했다.
⑤ 사냥꾼들은 내가 그들을 필요로 할 때 나를 무시했다.

구문 [2행~4행] One day, he declared to his boss // that he would give up his job as a hunter's guide [and] become a guide for anglers.
that절은 동사 declared의 목적어절이며 동사 give up과 become이 병렬구조를 이루고 있다.

어휘 **game** 사냥감 **elk** 엘크(사슴의 일종) **caribou** 순록 **declare** 알리다, 선언하다 **have something against** ~을 싫어하다 **have to do with** ~와 관계가 있다 **prey** 사냥감, 먹이

22 글의 요지 ②

소재 간접적 의사소통의 비효율성

해설 첫 문장(Part of ~ be said.)에서 원하는 것을 실제로 말해야 건강한 의사소통을 할 수 있다는 주제문을 제시한 후, 간접적 의사소통 방식이 감정 소모적이고 상대방이 이해하기 어렵다는 문제점을 설명하고 있다. 따라서 이 글의 요지로 가장 적절한 것은 ②이다.

해석 주제문 건강한 의사소통의 일부는 사실, 말할 필요가 있는 것을 말하는 것이다. 모든 사람이 당신 마음속에 있는 것을 안다고 그저 간주해서는 안 된다. 그러나 많은 사람들이 자신의 예민한 감정을 솔직하게 말하는 것을 두려워한다. 대신 그들은 당신이 알아주리라는 희망에 힌트를 던진다. 텔레비전 광고를 하는 동안 계속해서 (텔레비전) 볼륨을 줄인 한 여성이 있었다. 그녀는 남편이 광고 동안에 자신과 더 얘기하기를 원했다. 그러나 남편이 눈치를 채지 못했고, 그냥 스포츠 신문을 집어 들자 아내는 훨씬 더 화가 났다. 그녀가 한 것과 같은 전략은 효과적이지 못하다. 간접적이 되는 것은 감정적으로 소모가 클 수 있다. 힌트는 이해되기가 매우 어렵다. 어떤 경우에도, 심지어 그 메시지가 잘 이해된다 하더라도, 당신의 감정에 대해 간접적으로 듣고 싶어 하는 사람은 아무도 없다.

어휘 **presume** 간주[추정]하다 **state** (정식으로) 말하다, 진술하다; 상태; 국가; 지위 **sensitive** 예민한, 민감한 **plain** 솔직한; 평범한; 무늬가 없는; 평원 **in the hope that[of]** ~라는 희망으로 **keep v-ing** 계속해서 v하다 **commercial** 광고; 상업의 **break** (중간) 광고; 휴식 시간 **indirect** 간접적인 **costly** 대가가 큰; 비용이 많이 드는 **secondhand** 간접적으로; 간접적인

23 글의 주제 ④

소재 수줍음 극복 방법

해설 수줍음을 타는 것이 개인적으로 큰 문제가 된다면 조치를 취하라고 한 다음 수줍음을 극복하는 방법을 구체적으로 나열하고 있으므로, 이 글의 주제로는 ④ '사람들이 자신의 수줍음을 다루는 방법'이 가장 적절하다.

해석 주제문 거의 모든 사람이 적어도 조금은 수줍음을 타지만, 수줍음이 당신에게 큰 문제라면, 어떤 조치를 취해야 할 때인지도 모른다. 우선, 남이 듣게 하겠다고 결심하라. 당신이 말해야 하는 것은 다른 누가 말하는 것만큼이나 중요하다. 따라서 당신이 가지고 있다는 걸 다른 사람들이 알아줬으면 하는 생각과 경험, 그리고 기술들의 목록을 작성하라. 무엇을 말하고 싶은지 미리 생각해둔 다음, 그냥 말하라. 자신이 남에게 어떻게 보일지 신경 쓰이기 시작한다면, 그저 평소처럼 호흡하고 자신의 관심을 다른 사람에게 집중하라. 다른 사람도 모두 자신이 (남들에게) 어떻게 인식되고 있는지 걱정하고 있다는 걸 기억하라. 단지 수줍음을 조절하려고 노력하는 것만으로도 즉각적인 보상을 얻을 수 있다. 수줍음을 극복하려는 여러 좋은 이유 중 아마도 가장 최고는 다른 사람에게 당신이 얼마나 특별한지 알 기회를 주는 것일 것이다.

① 수줍음 타는 아이를 대하는 부모를 위한 비법
② 수줍음 타는 사람들에게서 보이는 공통적인 특징
③ 수줍음 타는 사람들을 위한 훌륭한 지도자가 되는 것에 대한 조언
⑤ 수줍음 타는 사람들이 대중 앞에서 연설하는 법

구문 [5행~6행] So, make a list of *the ideas*, *experiences*, *and skills* [**that** you would like others to know (that) you have ●].
that은 to know의 목적어 역할을 하는 절(you have)의 목적어를 대신하는 관계대명사이고, the ideas, experiences, and skills를 선행사로 받는다. to know의 목적어 역할을 하는 명사절 you have 앞에는 접속사 that이 생략되었다.

[12행~14행] Among good reasons for fighting shyness, / perhaps the best is giving others *a chance* (to know / how special you are).
C V S

「보어(the best) + 동사(is) + 주어(giving ~ you are)」의 구조인 문장으로 주어가 수식을 받아 길어질 때는 주어와 보어의 위치를 바꾸는 것이 일반적이다.

어휘 **shy** 수줍어하는 *cf.* **shyness** 수줍음 **resolve** 결심하다; (문제 등을) 해결하다 **no less A than B** B만큼 A한 **skill** 기술 **in advance** 미리 **self-conscious** 남의 이목을 의식하는[꺼리는] **normally** 평소대로; 일반적으로 **perceive** 인식하다; 이해하다 **instant** 즉각적인; 즉석의 **reward** 보상 [선택지 어휘] **characteristic** 특징; 특징적인 **deal with** 다루다, 취급하다; 거래하다 **in public** 대중 앞에서; 공공연하게

24 글의 제목 ③

소재 주관성이 개입된 지도

해설 지도와 정치의 연계성을 설명하는 글로, 지도는 객관적으로 지리적 지형만을 담아내는 것이 아니라 정치적 영향을 반영하고 정치적 목적으로도 이용된다는 내용이다. 따라서 제목으로 가장 적절한 것은 ③ '지도: 세계 정치와의 담화'이다.

해석 주제문 지도는 지역에 대한 편향 없는 스냅 사진이라기보다는 다양한 목적과 신념을 갖고 있는 개인과 조직에 의해 개발된 인간의 창조물이다. 그것은 결코 완전히 중립적이거나 객관적이지 않으며, 지도 제작자들이 산이나 평원보다 영토와 경계선을 강조하는 경향이 있다는 것은 우연이 아니다. 지도는 정치적 이유로 다시 그려진다. 제1차 세계대전 직후의 베르사유 회담으로 초래된 변화를 보라. 중동에 새로운 국가들이 만들어졌고, 오스트리아-헝가리 제국은 조각으로 분해되었다. 지도는 사건을 반영할 뿐만 아니라 사건에 영향을 줄 수도 있다. 이는 사용된 지도의 유형이 정책 결정과 밀접하게 연결되었던 제2차 세계대전과 냉전 동안 적용된 전략에 대하여 분명해졌다.

① 지도: 신뢰받는 의사소통의 한 형태
② 지도를 이해하고 해석하기
④ 지도로 사건에 영향을 주는 방법
⑤ 전쟁에서의 지도의 전략적 사용

구문 [4행~6행] ~ **it** is not accidental **that** map makers tend to emphasize territory and boundaries [rather than] mountains or plains.
A B

it은 가주어이고 that 이하가 진주어이다. 「A rather than B」는 'B라기보다는 오히려 A'라는 뜻이다.

어휘 **unbiased** 편향[선입견] 없는(↔ **biased** 편향된) **snapshot** 스냅 사진 **region** 지역 **neutral** 중립의 **objective** 객관적인 **accidental** 우연한 **emphasize** 강조하다 **territory** 영토, 영역 **boundary** 경계[한계](선)

political 정치의 **witness** 보다, 목격하다; 증언하다; 목격자 **bring about** 초래하다 **fragment** 조각, 파편 **influence** 영향을 미치다; 영향 **reflect** 반영하다; 반사하다 **apparent** 명백한 **in regard to** ~에 관해서 **strategy** 전략 *cf.* **strategic** 전략적인 **apply** 사용하다; 적용하다 **policymaking** 정책 결정 *cf.* **policy** 정책 [선택지 어휘] **interpret** 해석하다

25 도표 이해 ⑤

소재 전 세계 유기 농경지와 기타 유기 지역의 면적

해설 북미 지역의 기타 유기 지역이 50만 헥타르인 것은 맞지만 대륙들 가운데 가장 적지는 않다. 가장 적은 곳은 기타 유기 지역이 아예 없는 오세아니아이므로 정답은 ⑤이다.

해석 **〈전 세계 유기 농경지와 기타 유기 지역〉**

주제문 이 도표는 유기 농경지와 유기농 식품을 생산하지만 농경지는 아닌 기타 (유기) 지역의 전 세계적인 비율을 비교한다. 이것은 우리에게 특히 다음과 같은 사실을 보여준다. ① 오세아니아에는 유기 농업에 쓰이는 땅의 양이 1,210만 헥타르로 가장 많다. ② 아시아는 유기 농경지보다 기타 유기 지역의 면적이 더 넓다. ③ 유럽과 아프리카 모두 950만 헥타르의 기타 유기 지역을 가지고 있지만, 유기 농경지는 유럽이 아프리카보다 7백만 헥타르 이상 더 많다. ④ 남미는 유기 농경지와 기타 유기 지역이 각각 810만 헥타르로 동일하다. ⑤ 북미 지역은 기타 유기 지역이 50만 헥타르뿐으로, 대륙들 가운데 가장 적다.

어휘 **organic** 유기농의; 유기체의 **agricultural** 농업의 **beekeeping** 양봉 **grazing** 방목지, 목초지 **global** 세계적인; 전반적인 **proportion** 비율; 비례 **in particular** 특히, 특별히 **devote A to B** A를 B에 사용하다[바치다] **hectare** 헥타르(땅 면적의 단위) **continent** 대륙

26 내용 불일치 ⑤

소재 철학자이자 역사가인 David Hume의 삶

해설 마지막 문장에서 Hume이 죽기 전에 Adam Smith가 쓴 〈국부론〉의 첫 부분만 읽을 수 있었다고 했으므로 ⑤가 글의 내용과 일치하지 않는다.

해석 David Hume은 스코틀랜드의 에든버러 마을 출신의 철학자이자 역사가였다. 1734년에 몇 개월 동안 상사(商社)에서 근무한 뒤 ① 그는 프랑스로 향했고, 그곳에서 글을 쓰며 4년을 보냈다. 그러고 나서, 그는 1744년에 ② Edinburgh 대학의 철학 관련 직책에 지원했으나 무신론자로 간주되어 거절당했다. 그 후, 1745년 Jacobite의 반란 동안 ③ Hume은 George Bempde라는 이름의 귀족을 개인 교습으로 가르쳤지만, 일 년 만에 그 협정은 좋지 않게 끝났다. 그 후에 Hume은 〈영국사〉 작업에 착수했다. ④ 그 작업은 완료하는 데 15년이 걸렸고 1754년부터 1762년 사이에 여섯 권으로 출판되었다. Hume은 에든버러에서 말년을 보냈는데, 그곳에서 그는 젊은 Adam Smith의 조언자로서의 역할을 했고, ⑤ 죽기 전에 Smith가 쓴 〈국부론〉의 첫 부분만을 읽을 수 있었다.

어휘 **philosopher** 철학자 *cf.* **philosophy** 철학 **merchant** 무역상; 상인 **apply for** ~에 지원하다 **rebellion** 반란; (조직 · 정당 등의 내부의) 반대[저항] *cf.* **rebel** 반란을 일으키다; 반항[저항]하다; 반역자 **tutor** 개인 교습을 하다; 개인 지도 교수, 가정교사 **arrangement** 협정, 합의; 배열 **complete** 완료하다; 완성하다; 완전한 **mentor** 조언자, 멘토(경험 없는 사람에게 오랜 기간에 걸쳐 조언과 도움을 주는 유경험자나 선배)

27 안내문 불일치 ⑤

소재 디지털 서비스 분석가 채용 공고

해설 자기소개서와 이력서는 하나의 첨부 파일로 만들어 웹사이트를 통해 지원하라고 했으므로 우편 제출은 불가능하다. 따라서 ⑤는 안내문의 내용과 일치하지 않는다.

해석

디지털 서비스 분석가

저희 대학은 교직원과 학생들의 뛰어난 업무 처리를 장려하는, 성취도가 높은 문화에서 일하고자 하는 직원들의 고용과 계발에 헌신하고 있습니다.

장소: 본교

① **전일/시간제:** 전일제 (임시직)

② **부서:** 도서관

지원서 검토 일자: 2020년 11월 28일

직무

- ③ 도서관의 주 웹사이트와 관련 웹사이트들의 조직과 관리
- 도서관 온라인 서비스의 효율성에 대한 연구 수행

지원 자격

- 적어도 한 가지 프로그램 언어에 대한 기본 지식
- ④ 관련 업무 최소 1년 경력

대학 측에서 제공하는 급여와 보상에 대한 세부 내용을 확인하시려면 http://atyourservice.ucop.edu를 방문하세요.

지원 방법

⑤ http://jobs.berkeley.edu를 통해 지원하실 때 자기소개서와 이력서를 하나의 첨부 파일로 제출하세요.

어휘 **be committed to v-ing** v하는 것에 헌신[전념]하다; v할 것을 (엄숙히) 약속하다 **outstanding** 뛰어난; 두드러진 **faculty** 교수진, 교직원; 능력 **temporary** 일시적인, 임시의 **department** 부(서) **conduct** 수행하다; 행동하다 **relevant** 관련 있는; 적절한 **compensation** 보상(금) **submit** 제출하다; 항복하다 **cover letter** 자기소개서 **résumé** 이력서 **attachment** 첨부 파일; 애착

28 안내문 일치 ⑤

소재 수영장 이용 안내

해설 치료용 수영장(Therapy Pool)의 이용은 18세 이상 성인들을 위해 마련되어 있다고 했으므로 ⑤가 안내문의 내용과 일치한다.

해석

The Green Fitness Aquatics

The Green Fitness Aquatics는 Lake 카운티에 있는 것 중에 최고입니다.

① 어린이와 어른을 위한 폭넓은 수영 강습이 있습니다.

성인 전용 수영 시간

② 어른들을 위한 수영장 개장 시간은 매주 월요일에서 금요일 오후 2시부터 3시까지로 마련되어 있습니다.

③ 감독보호하에 모든 연령이 즐기는 수영 시간

화요일	오후 3:30~5:30
금요일	오후 6~8시
토요일	오후 12~2시
일요일	오후 12~2시

모든 연령대가 (안전 요원의) 감독 보호하의 수영 시간 동안 자유로이 수영을 즐길 수 있습니다. 공인 인명 구조원이 근무합니다. ④ 10세 미만의 어린이에 한해서는 부모 중 한 분이 반드시 수영장 내에 함께 계셔야 합니다. 11~15세의 어린이들은 성인의 감독이 필요 없지만, 부모 중 한 분이 항상 건물 내에 계셔야 합니다. ⑤ 치료용 수영장 이용은 18세 이상의 어른들을 위해 마련되어 있습니다.

**더 많은 정보를 원하시면 (810) 535-7600로 저희에게 전화 주시기 바랍니다.*

어휘 **aquatic** 수생의, 물속의 **among** ~ 중에 **a full range of** 폭넓은 **reserve** 마련해 두다, (자리 등을) 따로 남겨두다; 예약하다 **supervise** 감독하다, 지도하다 **certified** 공인의; 보증된 **lifeguard** 인명 구조원 **on duty** 근무 중인 **therapy** 치료, 요법

29 밑줄 어법 ③

소재 일은 믿음에 따라 일어난다.

해설 ③ 문맥상 앞의 동사 believes와 or로 연결된 병렬구조로 봐야 한다. 따라서 주어(a person)에 맞게 feel은 단수동사 feels가 되어야 한다.

오답 분석 ① 앞에 나온 some of the time에 호응하는 at other times가 적절히 쓰였다. ② 앞에 나온 events를 받는 복수형 대명사 them을 쓴 것은 적절하다. ④ 동사 go를 수식하므로 부사 형태가 적절하다. go bad는 '(음식이) 상하다'란 뜻이므로 문맥상 적절하지 않다. ⑤ what이 이끄는 명사절이 that절 내 주어 역할을 하므로 어법상 적절하다.

해석 대부분 사람들은 완전한 낙관론자도 아니고 완전한 비관론자도 아니며, 오히려 어떤 때는 낙관적인 경향을 보이고 다른 때는 비관적인 경향을 보인다. 주제문 **재미있는 것은, 종종 사건에 대한 당신의 믿음에 따라 사건이 펼쳐진다는 것이다.** 만약 어떤 사람이 결과가 좋을 거라고 믿거나 대개 그것(= 결과)에 관해 낙관적으로 느끼면, 그 결과는 그 사람의 기대를 충족시키는 경향이 있다. 불행히도 그 반대의 경우도 사실이다. 당신이 어떤 일이 잘못되리라고 믿으면, 그 일은 매우 흔히 그렇게 된다. 왜 이런 일이 일어나는 걸까? 자기 자신을 믿는 것에 관한 Henry Ford의 유명한 인용구는 "당신이 할 수 있다고 생각하든, 아니면 할 수 없다고 생각하든, 당신은 모두 옳다!"는 것이다. 이는 우리가 생각하는 것이, 그것이 성공이든 실패이든, 일어나는 경향이 있다는 것을 의미한다.

어휘 **neither A nor B** A도 B도 아닌 **optimist** 낙관론자 *cf.* **optimistic** 낙관적인 **pessimist** 비관론자 *cf.* **pessimistic** 비관적인 **tend to-v** v하는 경향이 있다 **turn out** 모습을 드러내다[나타내다]; (~임이) 판명되다 **outcome** 결과 **expectation** 기대; 예상 **reverse** 반대; 반대로 하다 **quotation** 인용구[문] **whether it be A or B** A이든 B이든

30 밑줄 어휘 ⑤

소재 무대 공포증이 야기할 수 있는 증상과 문제

해설 무대 공포증에 관한 글로 글 후반부에서 무대 공포증이 야기하는 증상과 문제에 대해 설명하고 있다. 문맥상 무대 공포증이 기억 상실과 같은 정신적 문제를 '줄이는' 것이 아니라 '일으키는' 것이 적절하므로 ⑤는 induce 등으로 바꾸어야 한다.

해석 우리 대부분은 ① 다가올 연설 전에 긴장하거나 카메라 앞에서 질문에 답할 것을 요구받을 때 입이 마르는 것을 경험해 본 적이 있다. 긴장감에 잘못된 것은 없는데, 왜냐하면 이러한 긴장감은 당신이 ② 잘 수행하기 위해 필요한 에너지를 주기 때문이다. 그러나 만약 당신이 공포나 두려움에 완전히 ③ 압도당한다면 그것은 단지 수행 전에 느끼는 긴장감이 아니라 극도의 수행 불안으로, 다른 말로는 무대 공포증으로 알려져 있다. 무대 공포증은 일종의 두려움으로, 다른 여러 가지 두려움과 마찬가지로 ④ 신체 증상을 야기한다. 이것들(= 신체 증상들)은 땀으로 축축한 손바닥, 입이 마름, 메스꺼움, 어지러움, 근육 긴장, 그리고 도망치려는 강한 충동을 포함한다. 그것(= 무대 공포증)은 또한 기억 상실, 말하는 것의 어려움, 집중 불능과 같은 일시적인 정신적 문제도 ⑤ 줄일(→ 일으킬) 수 있다.

구문 [3행~5행] There's nothing wrong with butterflies, // because they give(V′) you(IO′) *the energy*(DO′) [(which[that]) you need ● **to perform** well].

[ ] 부분은 the energy를 수식하는 관계대명사절로, you need the energy to perform well에서 목적어인 the energy를 대신하는 목적격 관계대명사가 생략되었다. to perform well은 '목적(~하기 위해서)'을 나타내는 to부정사의 부사적 용법으로 쓰였다.

어휘 **nerve** (복수형) 긴장, 신경과민; 신경 **upcoming** 다가올, 곧 있을 **butterfly** (복수형) 긴장감, 불안한 마음 *cf.* **have butterflies in one's stomach** (걱정으로) 조마조마하다 **overcome** (수동태로) 압도당하다; 극복하다 **full-on** 극도의, 최대의 **anxiety** 불안, 염려 **stage fright** 무대 공포증 **physical** 신체의 **symptom** 증상 **sweaty** 땀이 나서 축축한 **nausea** 메스꺼움 **dizziness** 현기증, 어지럼증 **tension** 긴장 **urge to-v** v하려는 욕구[충동] **mental** 정신의; 심적인 **inability** 불능, ~할 수 없음

31 빈칸 추론 ④

소재 결정에 있어 일관성의 함정

해설 우리는 자신이 내린 결정이나 내뱉은 말에 따라 행동하려는 경향이 있다는 내용의 글이다. 첫 문장(Once we ~ that commitment.)과 중반부의 예시(When salespeople ~ you have said.)를 단서로, 사회에서 가치 있는 것으로 여겨지는 것은 ④ '일관성'임을 추론할 수 있다.

해석 주제문 **일단 우리가 어떤 선택을 내리거나 어떤 결정을 하기로 약속하면, 우리는 그 약속에 따라 행동해야 한다는 압박감에 마주하게 된다.** 이것이 영업사원들이 "가격이 맞으면 그걸 사시겠습니까?"와 같은 질문을 하는 이유다. 그 (질문의) 목적은 당신이 어떤 사안에 대한 입장을 가지고 있다는 걸 아주 빨리 인정하게 만드는 것이다. 이것은 당신이 일단 그것을 인정하면 당신은 그것을 지켜야 할 의무감을 느끼게 되기 때문이다. 영업사원이 당신으로 하여금 당신 자신에 대해서 그리고 당신이 생각하기에 특정 상황에서 어떻게 행동할지에 대해 진술하게 할 때, 그들은 나중에 당신이 말했던 것에 따르는 방식으로 행동하고 싶어 할 것임을 알고 있다. 그들은 일관성이 사회에서 가치 있는 것으로 여겨진다는 것을 알고 있다. 비록 그것(= 일관성)이 사람들을 자신에게 가장 이익이 되지 않는 방식으로 행동하게 만든다 할지라도 말이다.

① 말 ② 경험 ③ 겸손 ⑤ 홍보

구문 [7행~11행] When salespeople(S′) **get**(V′) you(O′) **to make** *a statement*(C′) (about yourself [and] (about) how you think // (that) you would behave in a certain situation), // they(S) know(V) // **that** later you will want to behave in *a way* [**that** goes along with / what you have said](O).

「get+O+C(to-v)」는 'O가 v하게 하다'라는 뜻이다. 전치사 about의 목적어 역할을 하는 yourself와 how ~ situation이 and로 연결되어 있다. 주절의 첫 번째 that은 know의 목적어 역할을 하는 명사절을 이끌고, 두 번째 that은 주격 관계대명사를 이끌어 a way를 수식한다.

어휘 **commit** 약속하다 *cf.* **commitment** 약속 **encounter** 마주치다, 맞닥뜨리다 **salesperson** 영업사원, 판매원 **admit** 인정[시인]하다 **position** (특정 주제에 대한) 입장, 태도; 위치 **issue** (걱정거리가 되는) 문제; (논의·논쟁의 중요한) 주제, 사안 **feel obliged to-v** v해야 한다는 의무감을 느끼다 **honor** (약속 등을) 지키다; 존경하다 **make a statement** 진술을 하다, 성명을 발표하다 **go along with** ~을 따르다, ~에 동의하다 **value** 가치 있게 생각하다; 가치 **be in one's best interest(s)** 가장 이익이 되다 *cf.* **interest** 이익; 이자; 흥미

32 빈칸 추론 ④

소재 물리적 근접에 따른 능력 변화

해설 계산대 점원들이 생산성이 높은 동료와 같이 일할 때 자신의 생산성도 높아지고 생산성이 낮은 동료와 일할 때 자신의 생산성도 낮아졌다는 결과는 ④ '물리적 근접'의 위력을 시사하는 것이라 할 수 있다.

해석 주제문 **슈퍼마켓 계산대는 물리적 근접의 위력에 대한 인상적인 예를 제시한다.** 식료품 가게에 가본 적 있는 누구라도 알고 있다시피, 계산대의 점원들은 속도와 능력에 있어서 극도로 다르다. 한 주요 체인에서 다른 능력을 가진 점원들이 전체 교대근무에서 다소 임의적으로 뒤섞였는데, 이로 인해 두 경제학자들이 생산적인 동료의 영향을 관찰할 수 있었다. 일반 점원들의 생산성은 그들의 교대 시간에 근무하는 스타 점원이 있을 때 상당히 상승하며, 그 동일한 일반 점원들이 교대 시간에 평균 미만의 점원들로 가득하면 더 안 좋아진다는 것이 드러났다. 현대의 통계적 증거 또한 오늘날의 젊은 전문직 종사자들이 자신의 직업 분야의 경쟁자들이 많은 대도시 지역에서 거주하면 더 오랜 시간 일한다는 것을 밝혀내고 있다.

① 사회적 지위
② 상호 간의 관심
③ 첫인상
⑤ 개인적 선호

구문 [8행~10행] It turns out that the productivity of average clerks rises substantially // when there is *a star clerk* (working on their shift), and ~.
가주어 / 진주어

It은 가주어이고 that 이하가 진주어이다. ( )는 능동의 의미로 앞의 a star clerk을 수식한다.

어휘 **checkout** 계산대 **striking** 두드러진, 인상적인 **grocery** 식료품 **differ** 다르다 **wildly** 극도로 **competence** 능력, 능숙함 **more or less** 다소 **shift** 교대 근무 (시간) **economist** 경제학자 **productive** 생산적인 *cf.* **productivity** 생산성 **peer** 또래, 동료 **substantially** 상당히 **statistical** 통계의 **metropolitan** 대도시의 **plenty of** 충분한, 많은 **occupational** 직업의 [선택지 어휘] **mutual** 상호 간의; 공동의 **preference** 선호

33 빈칸 추론 ⑤

소재 네덜란드가 강대국이 될 수 있었던 배경

해설 네덜란드가 한때 무역 초강대국이었고 여러 산업 분야에서 선두였다는 내용의 글이다. 빈칸 바로 다음 문장(It rose to power ~ of innovation.)의 내용, 즉 적은 인구로 강대국이 되었고 거대한 부를 축적했다는 것을 단서로 네덜란드의 특징을 요약하면, 빈칸에는 ⑤ '커다란 성공을 거둔 작은 국가'가 가장 적절하다.

해석 네덜란드는 한때 세계의 무역 초강대국이었다. 최초의 합자 회사 중 하나인 네덜란드 동인도 회사는 향신료, 비단, 자기, 커피, 차, 그리고 귀금속과 보석의 세계 교역 대부분을 통제하는 정부-사업체 연합이었다. 그것(=네덜란드 동인도 회사)은 조선, 해운, 금융, 자원 개발과 광업도 지배했다. 암스테르담(네덜란드의 수도)이 세계 최초 주식 거래소의 발상지가 된 것이 그리 놀랄 일은 아니다. 주제문 사실 그 역사를 고려해볼 때, 네덜란드는 '커다란 성공을 거둔 작은 국가'로 요약될 수 있다. 네덜란드는 국민의 모험 정신, 항해 기술, 혁신의 추구 덕분에 단 150만 명의 인구로 강대국의 지위에 올랐다. 네덜란드 사람들이 만든 배는 더 많은 화물을 선적했으며, 그들의 합자 회사 시스템은 리스크(=위험)를 줄여 주었다. 그 거대한 부의 축적 이면에는 혁신적인 기술과 금융 시스템이 있었다.
① 지리적으로 저지대 국가
② 세계 시장에서의 비중요 국가
③ 유럽에서 가장 작은 국가 중 하나
④ 자원이 적고 인구밀도가 높은 국가

구문 [14행~16행] *The ships* [(which[that]) they built] loaded more cargo, // and their joint stock company system reduced risk.
S1 / V1 / S2 / V2

The ships는 목적격 관계사가 생략된 관계대명사절의 수식을 받는다. 접속사 and로 두 개의 절이 병렬 연결되어 있다.

어휘 **trading** 무역, 교역 **superpower** 초강대국 **alliance** 연합, 동맹 **porcelain** 자기, 사기 그릇 **precious metal** 귀금속 *cf.* **precious** 귀중한 **dominate** 지배[군림]하다 **shipbuilding** 조선(배를 만드는 일) **mining** 광업; 채굴 **stock exchange** 증권 거래소 **considering** ~을 고려하면 **sum up** 요약하다 **rise to power** 권력을 얻다 **expertise** 전문 기술[지식] **innovation** 혁신 *cf.* **innovative** 혁신적인 **cargo** 화물 **accumulation** 축적, 누적 [선택지 어휘] **geographically** 지리적으로 **low-lying** (땅이 평평하게) 낮은 **accomplish** 성취하다, 완수하다

34 빈칸 추론 ②

소재 자투리 시간에 책을 읽는 열렬한 독서가

해설 열렬한 독서가들은 다른 사람들과 동일한 24시간을 쓰지만 훨씬 더 많은 독서 시간을 확보하는데, 이는 자투리 시간에 틈틈이 책을 읽기 때문이다(It turns out ~ at night). 이렇게 자투리 시간이 모여 막대한 독서 시간을 만들어내는 것은 우리 삶에 활용할 수 있지만 버려지는 시간이 많다는 의미이기도 하다. 따라서 '삶은' 이후에 ② '우리의 일상적 임무 사이에서 낭비되는 짧은 순간들로 가득하다'가 오는 것이 적절하다.

해석 여러분이 열렬한 독서가들에게 매일 얼마나 많은 시간 책을 읽으며 보내는지 물어본다면 대부분은 구체적인 분(分)이나 시간의 수치를 여러분에게 말해줄 수 없을 것이다. 그들은 모른다. 열렬한 독서가들은 독서 일지를 기록하지 않는다. 그럼에도 불구하고 우리의 '열렬한 독서가' 설문 조사 응답자 중 78퍼센트가 일주일에 4시간이 넘게 책을 읽는다고 답했으며 많은 이들이 자신이 일주일에 20시간이나 책을 읽는다고 말했다. 주말과 휴일, 휴가 중에 열렬한 독서가들은 일주일에 40시간 이상 책을 읽는다. 열렬한 독서가들이 다른 사람들보다 하루에 시간이 더 많이 있는 것은 아닌데, 그렇다면 어떻게 그들이 그 시간을 찾는 것일까? 주제문 그들은 짧은 휴식 시간 동안에 책을 읽는데, 즉 약속과 약속 사이 시간에, 자녀의 춤 연습 중 기다리는 동안에, 혹은 밤에 잠들기 전에 몇 분의 책을 읽는 시간을 잡아내는 것으로 밝혀진다. 삶은 우리의 일상적 임무 사이에서 낭비되는 짧은 순간들로 가득하다.
① 자연적이고 자발적인 일련의 변화이다
③ 자신을 발견하는 것에 관한 것이 아니라, 자신을 창조하는 것에 관한 것이다
④ 정말로 복잡한 건 아니지만 우리는 그것을 복잡하게 만들기를 고집한다
⑤ 10%는 일어난 사건이고 90%는 그것에 대한 당신의 대응 방식이다

구문 [12행~15행] **It turns out** // **that** they read during short breaks, / **grabbing** *a few minutes of reading time* / between appointments, / while (they are) waiting for their children during dance practice, / or before falling asleep at night.

It turns out (that)은 '~인 것으로 드러나다, ~로 밝혀지다'를 의미한다. grabbing은 부대상황의 분사구문을 이끌며, while 다음에는 they are가 생략된 것으로 볼 수 있다. 분사구문 내에서 밑줄 친 부분은 or로 연결된 병렬구조이며 모두 a few minutes of reading time을 수식한다.

어휘 **passionate** 열정적인 **concrete** 구체적인 **log** 일지 **respondent** 응답자 **share** (생각 등을) 공유하다 **upwards of** ~ 이상 **grab** 움켜쥐다 **appointment** 약속 [선택지 어휘] **spontaneous** 자발적인 **daily** 일상의, 매일의 **complicated** 복잡한

35 무관한 문장 ④

소재 '개의 날'이라는 명칭의 유래

해설 여름 중 가장 더운 시기를 뜻하는 말인 'dog days'의 유래를 설명하는 글로 고대 사람들은 큰개자리에 속해 'the Dog Star'로도 알려진 별인 시리우스가 태양에 열기를 보태는 까닭에 무더워진다고 믿었다는 내용이다. 반면, ④는 태양을 신성한 것으로 숭배했다는 내용으로 'dog days'의 유래와는 무관하다.

해석 7, 8월에 미국의 많은 지역에서는 날씨가 매우 덥고 습해진다. 이 기간은 흔히 여름의 '개의 날'이라고 불린다. 이 이름은 시리우스에서 유래되었는데, 시리우스는 '큰개자리'에 속해 있기 때문에 '견성(犬星)'으로도 알려져 있다. 시리우스는 밤하늘에서 가장 밝은 별이지만, 여름 중 가장 더운 기간 동안 새벽에 태양과 함께 뜬다. 이 별이 태양과 함께 떠오르는 직후부터 여름의 열기가 나타나기 때문에, 고대에 그리스인들은 시리우스가 날이 그토록 무더워지는 원인이라고 생각했다. 많은 고대 문명들은 태양을 신성한 존재로 여겨 숭배했다. 주제문 그들은 시리우스가 태양의 열기에 그것의 열기를 더한다고 믿었고 그것들이 결합한 결과가 그들이 '개의 날'이라고 부르는 견딜 수 없이 더운 날씨라고 믿었다.

구문 [13행~15행] They believed // **that** Sirius added its heat to the heat of the Sun and **that** the combined effect was *the unbearably hot weather* [(which) they called ● the "dog days."]

believed의 목적어 역할을 하는 명사절 두 개가 and로 연결된 병렬구조이다. the unbearably hot weather는 목적격 관계대명사절의 수식을 받고 있다. 원래 they called it(=the unbearably hot weather) the "dog days"에서 목적어 it을 대신하는 관계대명사가 생략되었다.

어휘 **extremely** 대단히; 극도로 **humid** 습한, 습기 찬 **commonly** 흔히, 일반적으로 **be derived from** ~에서 나오다[유래하다] **Canis Major** 큰개자리 **dawn** 새벽, 동틀 녘 **ancient** 고대의, 옛날의 **civilization** 문명 **worship** 숭배하다, 예배하다 **divine** 신성한; 신의 **being** 존재, 실재 **combine** 결합시키다 **unbearably** 견딜 수 없게, 참을 수 없게

36 글의 순서 ④

소재 신체를 그릴 때의 어려운 점과 해결 방법

해설 주어진 글은 신체를 그릴 때의 어려운 점을 말하고 있고, (C)는 그것이 어려운 이유와 해결 방법을 말하고 있으며, (A)와 (B)는 예시를 통해 (C)의 해결 방법을 부연 설명하고 있다. 지칭어구 등의 추론의 단서를 살펴보자. (C)의 this는 내용상 주어진 문장의 seeing the whole as a shape in itself를 가리키며, (A)의 drawing the square가 (B)의 filling ~ the square보다 앞에 나와야 한다. 따라서 글의 순서는 ④ '(C)-(A)-(B)'가 적절하다.

해석 주제문 화가가 인간의 신체를 그릴 때 직면하는 어려움 중 하나는 전체를 어떤 형상 그 자체로 보는 것이다.

(C) 이것이 어려운 이유는, 인간의 신체를 여러 개별 부분이 모인 하나의 집합체로 보는 우리의 경험 때문이다. 그러므로 그림 그리기를 시작하기 전에 대상의 전체적 형상을 찾아라.

(A) 예를 들어, 당신은 다소 덩치가 크고 키가 작은 모델을 그릴지 모른다. 즉, 그는 기본적인 형상이 다른 무엇보다 더 정사각형처럼 보이는 사람이다. 그런 경우, 당신은 정사각형을 그려서 시작할 것이다.

(B) 일단 이렇게 한 다음, 당신은 정사각형 안에 부분들을 채워 넣음으로써 계속 그림을 그린다. 이런 방식으로, 당신의 그림은 비율이 잘 맞고 균형이 잘 잡혀질 것이다.

구문 [1행~3행] When artists draw the human body, // **one** of *the challenges* [(that) they face] **is** seeing the whole as a shape in itself.
(S: one of the challenges [(that) they face], V: is, C: seeing the whole as a shape in itself)

「one of+복수명사+단수동사」이므로 문장의 동사로 is가 쓰였다. seeing이 이끄는 동명사구는 문장의 보어이다.

[4행~7행] For example, you might have *a model* [**who** is rather large and short] — *someone* [**whose** basic form appears to be more like a square / than like anything else].

대시(—) 앞뒤의 a model과 someone은 동격이다. 각각 주격 관계대명사 who, 소유격 관계대명사 whose가 이끄는 절의 수식을 받는다.

어휘 **challenge** 어려움; 도전(하다) **face** 직면하다; 마주보다 **see A as B** A를 B로 보다[여기다] **in[of] itself** 그 자체로 **form** 형상, 모양 **appear** ~인 것 같이 보이다; 나타나다 **in proportion** 비율이 맞는 **balanced** 균형 잡힌, 안정된 **collection** 집합; 수집품 **separate** 개별적인, 별개의; 분리하다 **subject** 대상, 소재; 주제; 과목 **overall** 전체적인, 전반적인

37 글의 순서 ②

소재 정부 환경 규제의 명과 암

해설 정부의 환경 규제 활동이 큰 효과가 있었지만 반대로 문제를 더 악화시킬 수도 있다고 주장하는 글이다. 주어진 문장에서는 정부의 환경 보호 조치에 대해 언급하고 (B)에서 이 활동의 효과와 함께 문제 악화의 가능성을 언급했다. 이어서 (A)에서 문제 악화의 구체적인 예와 환경 보호법 때문에 기업이 제3세계로 공장을 옮긴다는 내용을 제시하고, 그 결과를 (C)에서 자국의 일자리가 줄고 세계 환경 위기가 악화될 수 있다고 설명하고 있다. 따라서 글의 순서는 ② '(B)-(A)-(C)'가 자연스럽다.

해석 대기 및 수질 오염과 살충제 및 독성 화학물질의 확산, 무서울 정도로 감소하는 생물 종(種)에 대한 우려는 많은 정부가 환경을 위해 적극적인 조치를 취하도록 이끌었다.

(B) 그들(=정부)의 활동 중 상당 부분은 큰 효과가 있었다. 더 엄격한 대기 오염 법으로 생명을 구하고 수많은 질병 발병률을 줄여 온 것이다. 주제문 그러나 어떤 규제는 문제를 더 악화시킬 수도 있다.

(A) 예를 들어, 새로운 대기 오염원에 대한 엄격한 통제는 더 오래되고 더 더러운 오염원의 사용을 연장해 적어도 단기적으로는 오염을 증가시킬 수 있다. 또한, 엄격한 환경 보호법을 도입한 나라들에서 특정 기업들은 단순히 공장을 제3세계로 옮겨 버린다.

(C) 이렇게 하는 것은 자국의 일자리와 수입을 빼앗을 뿐만 아니라 세계 환경 위기 또한 더욱 심각하게 만든다.

구문 [1행~4행] *Concerns* (about air and water pollution, the spread of pesticides and toxic chemicals, and the alarming loss of species) / **have led** many governments **to take** aggressive action for the environment.
(S: Concerns, O'1: air and water pollution, O'2: the spread of pesticides and toxic chemicals, O'3: the alarming loss of species, V: have led, O: many governments, C: to take aggressive action for the environment)

주어 Concerns가 뒤에 오는 전명구의 수식을 받아 길어졌다. 전명구를 이끄는 about 뒤에 세 개의 목적어가 콤마와 and로 연결된 구조이다. 「lead+O+C(to-v)」는 'O가 v하게 하다[이끌다]'의 의미이다.

[16행~18행] Doing this / **not only** robs the home nation of jobs and income / **but also** makes the global environmental crisis more severe.
(A: robs the home nation of jobs and income, B: makes the global environmental crisis more severe)

「not only A but also B」는 'A뿐만 아니라 B도'의 의미로 B를 강조한다.

어휘 **concern** 우려, 걱정; 염려하다 **pollution** 오염 **pesticide** 살충제, 농약 **toxic** 독성의, 유독한 **chemical** 화학물질; 화학의 **alarming** 걱정스러운, 두려운 **loss** 감소; 손실 **species** (생물) 종(種) **take action** 조치를 취하다 **aggressive** 적극적인, 공격적인 **prolong** 연장하다 **in the short[long] term** 단기[장기]적으로 **introduce** 도입[채택]하다; 소개하다 **corporation** 기업, 회사 **do good** 효과가 있다, 성과가 있다 **incidence** 발생 (정도) **regulation** 규제, 법규 **rob A of B** A에게서 B를 빼앗다 **crisis** 위기, 고비 **severe** 심각한, 극심한

38 문장 넣기 ④

소재 생태계 불균형의 악영향

해설 ④ 앞의 '자연의 균형이 흐트러진다'와 ④ 뒤의 '종의 개체수가 증가한다'는 내용 사이에 논리적 연결고리가 없는데, '질병으로 인해 어떤 종이 멸종 위기에 처하면 다른 종의 포식자가 없어지게 된다'는 주어진 문장이 ④에 들어가면 종의 개체수가 증가하게 되는 원인이 드러나 글의 흐름이 자연스러워진다.

해석 살아있는 공동체의 구성원들은 균형 잡힌 특정 관계 속에서 함께 존재한다. 한 동물 종(種)이 다른 동물 종을 먹고 그것은 차례로 다른 종을 먹는다. 세월이 흐르면 공동체 안의 식물과 동물 간에 균형이 이뤄지고, 그것은 기본적으로 안정적인 상태로 남는다. 그러나 때때로 자연의 이러한 균형이 흩뜨려져서 아마 예견하지 못했을 많은 결과를 일으킨다. 아마 어떤 질병으로 인해 한 종이 거의 멸종 직전에 이르러서, 다른 종에게 자연의 포식자가 남아있지 않을 수 있다. 결과는 그 한 종의 개체수의 상당한 증가로 나타날 수 있다. 이것은 더 나아가 공유되는 먹이 공급의 파괴를 일으킬 수 있고, 이는 차례로 다른 종에게 영향을 미칠 수 있다.

어휘 **extinction** 멸종, 소멸 **predator** 포식자 **in turn** 차례로; 결국 **work out** 초래하다; 만들어내다 **stable** 안정적인 **at times** 때때로 **disturb** 방해하다, 흩뜨리다 **result in** (결과를) 야기하다 **possibly** 아마 **unforeseen** 예측하지 못한 **significant** 상당한 **further** 더 나아가 **destruction** 파괴

39 문장 넣기 ⑤

소재 식품 유통기한의 의미

해설 주어진 문장은 식용에 적합하다면 날짜가 지난 식품을 판매하는 것이 합법적이라는 내용으로, 'best before' 날짜에 대한 설명인 '그 날짜는 제품의 상태가 가장 좋은 때와 먹어도 위험하지 않은 때를 나타내는 지침일 뿐이다'라는 내용과 '(판매가 합법적이기 때문에) 날짜가 지났더라도 먹을 수 있다'는 내용 사이에 오는 것이 가장 적절하다. 따라서 정답은 ⑤이다.

해석 포장식품과 보존식품의 시대가 된 오늘날, 신선함의 부족에 대한 확실한 단서는 없다. 대신, 슈퍼마켓에서 판매되는 식품들에는 보통 'best before(~이전이 최상)', 'sell by(~까지 판매)' 그리고 'display until(~까지 진열)' 등의 날짜가 표시되어 있다.

주제문 구매자들은 종종 이런 표현들이 모두 똑같다고 생각하지만 사실 그것들은 매우 다르다. 'sell by'와 'display until' 날짜는 소비자들이 아닌 슈퍼마켓 직원들을 위한 것으로, 직원들은 그 날짜를 재고 수준과 가격 할인을 관리하는 데 사용한다. 'best before' 날짜는 제품이 최상의 상태인 때와 (제품이) 어떠한 건강상의 위험도 없다고 보장되는 때를 나타내는 지침일 뿐이다. 식용으로 적합하기만 하다면, 그 날짜가 지난 식품을 판매하는 것은 실제로 완전히 합법적이다. 날짜가 지났더라도 당신은 여전히 그 제품을 먹을 수 있다. 다만, 당신은 그것이 더 신선한 제품만큼 좋을 것이라고 기대해서는 안 된다.

어휘 **fit for human consumption** 식용으로 적합한 *cf.* **consumption** 섭취; 소비 *cf.* **consume** 먹다, 마시다; 소비하다 **legal** 합법적인; 법률과 관련된 **pre-packed** (식품이 상점에 보내지기 전에) 사전 포장된 **obvious** 확실한, 명백한 **lack** 부족, 결핍 **mark A with B** A에 B를 표시하다 **assume** 생각하다, 추정하다 **stock** 재고, 저장품; 주식 **reduction** 할인, 인하; 축소, 감소 **indicate** 나타내다; 시사하다 **high quality** 양질, 고품질 **guarantee** 보장[보증]하다, 확신하다 **be free of** ~이 없다 **risk** 위험 (요소) **expire** 기한이 만료되다

40 요약문 완성 ⑤

소재 싸움에서 동물이 항복하는 방법

해설 요약문을 먼저 읽고 싸움에서 지고 있는 동물이 살아남으려고 신체의 '어떤' 부분을 보여줌으로써 '무엇을 하려' 하는지 찾으며 지문을 읽는다. 주제문인 첫 번째 문장에서 지는 동물은 '항복한다는(give up)' 신호를 보여줌으로써 목숨을 구하려 한다고 언급한 후, 이어지는 문장에서 머리 정수리나 배와 같은 '취약한(vulnerable)' 부분을 보여줄 것이라고 예를 들고 있다. 따라서 요약문의 (A), (B)에는 각각 give up, vulnerable과 각각 의미가 통하는 surrender, weak가 들어가는 것이 적절하다.

해석 주제문 싸움에서 지는 동물은 "나는 항복한다!"라는 신호를 보여줌으로써 싸움을 끝내고 자신의 목숨을 구하려고 노력할 것이다. 예를 들어, 그것(= 지는 동물)은 이기는 동물에게 자신의 머리 정수리나 배와 같이 자기 몸의 아주 취약한 부분을 보여줄 것이다. 이기는 동물의 뇌는 그러한 제시의 '의미'를 인지하게 되는데, 이는 (상대 동물을) 죽이고자 하는 본능을 대개 없애준다. 이러한 자연적 패턴의 대표적인 것은 싸움하는 늑대들의 행동이다. 한쪽이 이길 수 없다고 느끼는 순간, 그것(= 지는 늑대)은 더 강한 늑대에게 자신의 목의 전면부를 보여준다. 바로 조금 전까지 상대 늑대의 목을 물어뜯는 데 그렇게 전념했던 더 강한 늑대도 그 목을 물어뜯는 대신, 자신이 이겼다는 사실을 알고서 싸우는 것을 멈춘다.

⬇

죽임을 당하는 것에서 자신을 구하기 위해 싸움에서 지는 동물은 자기 몸의 (B) 약한 부분을 상대에게 보여줌으로써 (A) 항복할 것이다.

구문 [7행~8행] Typical of this natural pattern (C) is (V) the behavior of wolves in combat (S).

보어가 문장 앞으로 나가 주어와 동사가 도치되었다.

[10행~13행] Instead of ripping open the neck, / as he had seemed so intent on **doing** / just moments before, // the stronger wolf (S) stops (V) fighting (O), / **understanding** that he has won.

doing은 앞에 나오는 ripping open the neck을 대신하며, understanding 이하는 동시상황을 나타내는 분사구문이다.

어휘 **vulnerable** 취약한, 상처받기 쉬운 **recognize** 인지하다, 알아보다 **presentation** 제시; 발표 **switch off** 끄다; 없애다 **instinct** 본능 **typical** 대표적인, 전형적인 **combat** 싸움, 전투 **rip A open** A를 뜯어[찢어]내다 **intent on** ~에 전념하는 **opponent** 상대, 적수 [선택지 어휘] **compromise** 타협하다; 손상시키다 **cheat** 속이다; (시험에서) 부정행위를 하다 **vital** 필수적인 **surrender** 항복하다

41~42 장문 41 ② 42 ④

소재 팀 경기를 통한 사회성 함양

해설 41. 팀 경기를 하면서 이기적인 욕망을 제어하고, 규칙을 준수하면서도 창의성을 발휘하는 것과 같은 삶의 교훈을 배울 수 있다는 내용이므로, 제목으로 가장 적절한 것은 ② '경기를 하는 것은 사회생활 기술을 가르쳐준다'이다.

① 경기가 어떻게 스포츠 정신을 만들어주는가?
③ 경기로 정서학습 증진시키기
④ 경기의 심리적 가치는 무엇인가?
⑤ 학교에서 경기를 교육적 도구로 사용하기

42. 규칙 안에서 플레이하되 그 안에서 가능한 한 넓은 범위와 기술을 사용하는 절묘한 기술은 인생의 거의 모든 갈래에서 무의미한 것이 아니라 유의미한 것이다. 따라서 (d)의 meaningless를 meaningful로 바꿔 써야 한다.

해석 경기를 하는 것은 학교에서 보통 강력하게 (a) 장려된다. 이것은 부분적으로는 그것이 근육을 강화시키고 신체의 과잉 에너지를 소진시키기 때문이다. 주제문 그러나 팀 경기는 또한 사회적 기술도 향상시켜준다고 여겨진다. 팀 경기의 본질은 이기주의, 빛나고 싶고 승리하고 싶은 욕구, 그리고 자신의 팀이 이기도록 돕고자 하는 욕망의 균형을 잡는 것이다. 언제 공을 가지고 있고 언제 그것을 다른 사람에게 패스할 것인지는 우리의 많은 활동으로 뻗어나가는 기술이다. 협동과 (b) 사리사욕 간의 균형을 잡는 것은 경기의 규칙이라는 구조화된 환경 안에서 잘 교육된다. 경기가 진행되는 동안 우리는 특정한 규칙들을 따른다. 그러다 호루라기가 울리면 우리는 더 이상 그렇게 할(= 규칙들을 따를) 필요가 없다. 패배를 다루고 당신보다 더 뛰어난 플레이를 펼친 사람과도 편안한 마음을 가질 수 있는 방법을 배우는 것은 또 다른 중요한 기술이다. 당신은 일이 어떻게 펼쳐지더라도 당신의 감정을 (c) 제어할 필요가 있다. 마찬가지로 규칙 안에서 플레이하되 그 안에서 가능한 한 넓은 범위와 기술을 사용하는 절묘한 기술이 인생의 거의 모든 갈래에서 (d) 무의미한(→ 유의미한) 것이다. 당신은 사업이나 직업의 규칙을 학습해야 하지만, 창의적인 사고 없이 그저 거기에만 집착하면 결국 특별할 것 없는 하찮은 존재가 될 것이다. 그것들을 어기다가 잡히면, 결과는 훨씬 더 나쁘다. 어떻게 하면 규칙을 따르면서도 (e) 탁월할 수 있을까? 기술, 개인적인 비책, 오랜 훈련과 타인에 대한 통찰력 있는 관찰이 요건에 속한다.

구문 [7행~9행] **When to keep** the ball [and] **when to pass** it to another (S) / **is** (V) *an art* [that stretches into many of our activities].

and로 연결된 두 개의 명사구가 주어인데, 둘을 의미상 하나의 개념으로 보아 동사는 단수형인 is를 사용했다. 「when + to-v」는 '언제 v할지'의 의미이다.

[17행~20행] Likewise / *the subtle art* (of playing within the rules, [but] using **as** much scope and skill within them **as possible**) (S), / is (V) *one* [that is meaningful in almost every branch of life].

playing ~ rules와 using ~ possible은 but으로 연결되어 병렬구조를 이루며 둘 다 전치사 of의 목적어이다. 「as ~ as possible」은 '가능한 한 ~하게[한]'의 뜻이다.

어휘 **partly** 부분적으로 **strengthen** 강화하다 **surplus** 과잉의, 잉여의 **essence** 본질, 정수 **selfishness** 이기주의 **triumph** 승리를 거두다 **cooperation** 협동 **self-interest** 사리사욕 **defeat** 패배 **outplay** (경기에서) ~보다 훨씬 더 잘하다 **no matter how** 어떻게 ~하더라도 **likewise** 마찬가지로 **subtle** 미묘한, 절묘한 **scope** 범위 **occupation** 직업; 거주; 점령 **stick to A** A를 고수하다 **end up as** 결국 ~이 되다 **excel** 뛰어나다, 탁월하다 **trick** 비결, 묘책 **perceptive** 통찰력[직관력] 있는; 지각[인지]의 [선택지 어휘] **promote** 증진[촉진]시키다; 승진시키다; 홍보하다 **psychological** 심리적인

43~45 장문 43 ④ 44 ④ 45 ③

소재 국방대신의 무리한 명을 받은 대장장이

해설 43. (A)는 한 대장장이가 전쟁을 준비하는 국방대신으로부터 하루 만에 말편자 20만 개를 만들라는 명령을 받았다는 내용이다. 대장장이는 그 일이 불가능하다고 설명했지만, (D)에서 그의 말이 곧 무시되었다고 나온다. 이후 (B)에서 대장장이가 집에 돌아와

아내와 함께 이 일을 걱정했으나, 다음날 대신이 죽었다는 소식에 기뻐했다는 (C)가 이어지는 것이 적절하다. 따라서 정답은 ④ '(D)-(B)-(C)'이다.

44. (d)는 갑작스럽게 죽어 관 속에 있는 국방대신(the Minister of War)을 가리키지만 나머지는 모두 대장장이를 가리킨다.

45. (C)에서 대장장이의 집을 찾아온 것은 왕의 신하가 아니라 국방대신의 경비대였으므로 ③이 글의 내용과 일치하지 않는다.

해석 (A) 옛날에, 페르시아의 카자르 왕조 시대 동안에 군대 대장장이의 장(長)으로서 열심히 일하는, 마음씨 좋은 한 사람이 살았다. ① 어느 날 아침 국방대신이 그를 궁으로 불러들였고, 그에게 다음날까지 20만 개의 말편자를 만들라는 명령을 내렸는데, 그 날은 그 대신(大臣)이 전쟁을 선포하도록 되어 있었다. 그 가엾은 남자는 자신의 귀를 믿을 수 없었다. (a) 그(=대장장이)는 그렇게 많은 말편자라면 일주일 안에 만들기도 불가능할 것이라고 설명하기 시작했다.
(D) 그러나 그의 말은 곧장 무시되었다. "Aga Khan 폐하의 명령이시다!" 대신은 (e) 그(=대장장이)를 향해 소리쳤다. "만약 내일까지 말편자가 준비되지 않으면 폐하께 네 머리를 올리겠다!" "대신이여, 부디!" 대장장이는 간청했다. "그러한 위협이 제 머릿속에 맴도는 채로는, 너무 불안해서 말편자 10개도 만들 수 없습니다!" ⑤ 그러나 비정한 대신은 꿈쩍도 하지 않았고 그 가엾은 남자는 궁에서 물러 나와야 했다.
(B) 그는 집으로 돌아와 아내에게 자초지종을 이야기했고, 아내는 (b) 그(=대장장이)를 위로하기 위해 최선을 다했다. "여보, 걱정하지 마세요." 아내는 말했다. "② 포도주를 마시고 빵도 좀 드시고 기운 내요. 새벽이 되면 어떤 일이 일어날지 확신할 수 없잖아요." "아, 내가 한 가지 정말로 아는 것이 있소." 남편이 대답했다. "새벽이 온다고 20만 개의 말편자가 생기지는 않을 것이고 그 때문에 나는 머리가 날아갈 거란 거요."
(C) 다음날 아침 동이 틀 무렵, 대장장이의 집 문을 엄청 세게 두드리는 소리가 났다. 공포에 떨며, 이제 살아 있는 시간도 얼마 남지 않았다고 생각하면서 (c) 그(=대장장이)는 다가가 문을 열었다. ③ 대신의 경비대였다. "서두르시오, 대장장이!" 그들이 소리쳤다. "못을 좀 주시오. 국방대신께서 지난밤 갑자기 돌아가셨소!" 대장장이는 자신의 행운을 믿기 어려웠다. ④ 그는 경비대에게 가장 좋은 못을 한 자루 주며, 기쁨에 가득 차서 이렇게 말했다. "관에 못질을 단단히 하시오, 여러분! (d) 그(=국방대신)를 아주 단단히 가두시오! 새벽과 함께 이 소식이 들려오지 않았다면, 오늘 밤 관에 들어갈 사람은 바로 나였을 거요!"

구문 [(C) 2행~4행] **Trembling** with fear, / **believing** these few moments to be his last, // he went and opened it.
앞에 나온 두 개의 분사구문의 의미상 주어는 주절의 he이다. 문맥상 동시에 일어난 일을 나타내므로 '~하면서'라고 해석하면 된다.

[(C) 10행~12행] "~ **If** the dawn **had** not **brought** this news, // I **would be** the one in a coffin tonight!"
「If+S′+과거완료(had p.p.) ~, S+조동사의 과거형+동사원형 ...」인 혼합가정문의 형태이다. If절과 주절의 시제가 서로 다른 가정법 구문으로 '(과거에) 만약 ~했다면, (지금) …할 텐데'란 뜻이며, 과거 사실이 현재에까지 영향을 미칠 때 사용한다.

[(D) 6행~8행] "**With** *such a threat* **hanging** over my head, // I shall be **too** nervous **to** make even ten shoes!"
「With+명사(구)+분사, S+V」 구문은 문장의 동사와 동시에 일어나는 상황을 나타내며 '~을 …한 채로, …하면서'란 뜻이다. such a threat과 hang의 관계가 능동이므로 현재분사가 쓰였다. 「too ~ to-v」는 '너무 ~해서 v할 수 없다'란 뜻이다.

어휘 (A) **dynasty** 왕조 **blacksmith** 대장장이(=smith) **summon A to B** A를 B로 불러들이다[소환하다] **minister** 장관, 각료 **set A to-v** A가 v하도록 정하다 **declare war** 전쟁을 선포하다 (B) **comfort** 위로[위안]하다; 안락, 평안 **cheerful** 기운찬, 쾌활한 **cost A B** A가 B를 잃게 하다, A에게 B를 희생시키다 (C) **tremendous** 엄청난, 굉장한 **tremble with** ~로 떨다 **haste** 서두름, 급함 **nail** 못; 못을 박다; 손톱 **coffin** 관 **shut[close] A tight** A를 단단히 막다[닫다] (D) **swiftly** 곧장, 재빨리, 신속히 **cut A short** A의 말을 가로막다 **his[her, your] Majesty** 폐하 **threat** 위협, 협박 **hang over one's head** (걱정거리가) 머리에서 떠나지 않다, 머릿속을 맴돌다 **cold-hearted** 비정한, 냉정한 **unmoved** (마음이) 흔들리지 않는, 냉정한 **dismiss** 물러가게 하다; 해고하다; (의견 등을) 묵살하다

실전 모의고사 02

본문 p.27

18 ①	19 ④	20 ②	21 ①	22 ①	23 ③	24 ③	25 ③	26 ④	27 ⑤
28 ②	29 ③	30 ③	31 ②	32 ④	33 ④	34 ②	35 ④	36 ⑤	37 ④
38 ④	39 ③	40 ④	41 ①	42 ④	43 ④	44 ③	45 ③		

18 글의 목적 ①

소재 불량품 반송 방법 안내

해설 제품에 불만족을 느낀 고객에게 사과의 말과 함께 제품 반송 방법을 자세히 안내해주고 있으므로 글의 목적으로 가장 적절한 것은 ①이다.

해석 Jones 씨께,
고객님께서 레이저브라이트 스킨케어 시스템이 만족스럽지 않다고 하시니 대단히 죄송합니다. 각각의 레이저브라이트 제품은 저희 공장에서 출고되기 전 매우 세심하게 검사됩니다. 유감스럽게도 사소한 문제점들이 때로는 간과되거나 배송 도중 손상이 발생할 수 있습니다. 주제문 고객님의 레이저브라이트를 아래 주소로 반송해 주십시오. 저희 상품목록에 적혀 있는 주소는 오직 주문을 위한 주소입니다. 가능하면 제품을 원래의 용기에 담아 주시고 문제점을 자세히 기술한 편지를 동봉해 주시기 바랍니다. 고객님께서 더 많은 정보를 제공해 주실수록 저희가 그 문제를 더 빨리 해결해 드릴 수 있습니다. (제품에) 만족해하시는 수천 분의 고객님께서 매일 레이저브라이트의 위력을 경험하고 계십니다. 고객님께서도 곧 그러한 고객님들 중 한 분이 되시길 진심으로 희망합니다.
고객 서비스 팀 드림

구문 [11행~13행] **The more** information you can provide, **the faster** we can fix the problem.
「the 비교급 ~, the 비교급 ...」 구문으로 '~할수록 더 …하다'란 의미이다.

어휘 **unsatisfactory** 만족스럽지 못한 **inspect** 검사하다 **overlook** 간과하다 **shipping** 배송, (해상) 운송 **catalogue** 상품목록, 카탈로그 **place an order** 주문하다 **original** 원래의, 본래의 **container** 용기, 그릇; (화물 수송용) 컨테이너 **enclose** 동봉하다 **in detail** 자세히, 상세하게

19 심경 추론 ④

소재 소극적이었던 직장 생활에 대한 후회

해설 자신이 회사 생활을 너무 소극적으로 했던 것을 후회하면서 젊은이들에게 자신감을 가지고 주도적으로 회사 생활을 할 것을 당부하는 글이다. 따라서 'I'의 심경으로 적절한 것은 ④ '후회하는'이다.

해석 만약 내가 그 일을 다시 해야 한다면, 나는 확실히 그 회사에는 들어가지 않았을 것이다. 그 회사에서 나는 전혀 나 자신을 믿지 않았다. 나는 실제로 내가 함께 일하고 있는 사람들보다 낫다고 믿어본 적이 한 번도 없었다. 여러분은 너무나도 극심한 경쟁에 기반한 회사에서 그렇게 해서는 안 된다. 나는 내가 원했던 것을 옹호하는 주도권을 가지려 하지도 않았다. 절대로 그렇게 하려 하지 않았다는 것이다. 나는 어느 정도 나 자신이 겁먹도록 내버려 두곤 했었다. 주제문 나는 취업하는 젊은이들에게 "일어나서 외쳐라."라고 말하고 싶다. 하지만 나는 그렇게 하지 못했다. 나는 너무 자신감이 없었다. 주제문 나는 여러분이 스스로에게 지나치게 가혹해서는 안 된다고 생각한다. 나는 나 자신에게 정말로 가혹했다.
① 화난 ② 질투하는 ③ 깜짝 놀란 ⑤ 무서워하는

구문 [6행~7행] I **would** not take initiative — stand up for **what** I wanted.
would는 과거의 습관을 나타내는 조동사로 '~하곤 했다'의 의미를 나타낸다. what은 선행사를 포함한 관계대명사로 '~한 것'의 의미를 나타낸다.

어휘 **corporation** 회사, 기업 **intense** 심한, 강렬한 **competition** 경쟁 **take initiative** 주도권을 잡다; 솔선해서 하다 **stand up for** ~을 옹호하다[지지하다] **intimidated** 겁을 내는, 무서워하는 **enter the workforce** 취업하다 **timid** 자신감이 없는, 소심한

20 필자 주장 ②

소재 이상적인 교사의 자질

해설 글의 도입부에서 이상적인 교사의 자질을 나열한 후, 그중에서도 학생들과 공감하는 능력이 가장 중요하다고 글의 중반부(it is absolutely essential ~ capacity for empathy)에서 언급하였다. 또한 조동사 must가 포함된 마지막 문장(they must ~ empathize with kids)에 필자의 주장이 명시적으로 드러난다. 따라서 정답은 ②이다.

해석 내가 생각하기에 이상적인 교사는 기분 좋게 활기차고 어느 정도 매력 있으며 상냥하고 정말로 똑똑해야 한다. 나는 평범하거나 심지어는 못생긴 교사가 교사로서 가능성이 없다는 뜻으로 말하는 것이 아니다. 왜냐하면 그러한 많은 교사들도 다른 풍부한 매력을 가지고 있기 때문이다. 그러나 화를 내거나 재미없거나 인색하거나 무디거나 완전히 부정적인 성격을 가진 교사는 누구든 제외해야 한다. 주제문 (교사로서) 바람직한 자질의 항목은 많지만, 나의 이상적인 교사는 깊은 공감 능력을 갖추는 것이 절대적으로 필요한데, 이것은 말 그대로 타인의 필요와 감정에 자신을 맞출 줄 아는 굉장한 타고난 재능이다. 특히, 대부분의 교사가 학교 교사이므로 그들은 아이들과 공감하는 특별한 능력을 갖춰야 한다.

어휘 **to my mind** 내 생각[의견]에는 **somewhat** 어느 정도, 다소 **good-humored** 상냥한 **plain** 평범한; 분명한 **out of the question** 불가능한, 의논해 봐야 소용없는 **charm** 매력 **rule out** ~을 제외[배제]하다 **mean-spirited** 인색한, 옹졸한 **desirable** 바람직한, 가치 있는 **quality** 자질; 특성 **essential** 필수적인; 근본적인 **capacity (for)** (~할 수 있는) 능력 **empathy** 공감, 감정이입 *cf.* **empathize (with)** (~와) 공감하다 **tune in to** ~에 맞추다; 열심히 듣다 **need** (주로 복수형) 요구; 필요성

21 밑줄 함의 ①

소재 의미 있는 관계를 어렵게 하는 기계

해설 기계가 자신의 무류 통증에 관해 묻지 않을 것이라는 말은 Mamie Adams가 단순히 우표만 사러 우체국에 온 것이 아니고 친절한 우체국 직원과 의미 있는 대화를 나누고 싶다는 의미이다. 따라서 밑줄 친 부분의 의미로 가장 적절한 것은 ① '우체국 직원과 대화를 나누고 싶다'이다.

해석 우리 시대의 과학 기술은 우리로 하여금 단지 몇 년 전에는 결코 상상하지 못했던 방법으로 서로를 연결하는 것을 가능하게 했다. 주제문 그러나 우리의 유선으로 이루어진 모든 연결에도 불구하고, 우리는 서로에게 의미 있게 연결되어 있는 데 어려움을 겪고 있음을 매우 잘 알고 있다. 우리는 Mamie Adams가 말하고자 했던 것을 이해한다. Mamie Adams는 우체국 직원이 친절했기 때문에 언제나 그녀가 사는 도시의 우체국 지점에 갔다. 어느 해 그녀는 크리스마스 바로 전에 우표를 사러 거기 갔고, 줄이 특별히 길었다. 누군가가 로비에 우표 파는 기계가 있기 때문에 줄 서서 기다릴 필요가 없다고 언급했다. "나도 알고 있어요. 하지만 그 기계는 내 무릎 통증에 관해서 나한테 묻지 않을 거예요."라고 Mamie가 말했다.

② 기계로 진료를 받고 싶지 않다
③ 무릎이 아파서 그 기계로 갈 수가 없다
④ 기계에 내 무릎 통증의 기록이 있다
⑤ 우체국 직원에게 우표를 사는 것이 더 싸다

구문 [3행~6행] But we know very well // that **in spite of** all our wired connections, / we are having trouble staying meaningfully **connected** to each other.
that 이하는 동사 know의 목적어절이다. in spite of ~ connections는 양보를 나타내는 전명구이고, connected는 staying의 보어로 쓰였다.

어휘 **connection** 결합, 연결, 관계 **in spite of** ~에도 불구하고 **wired** 유선의 **postal** 우편의 **particularly** 특히 **point out** 언급하다, 지적하다

22 글의 요지 ①

소재 장난감의 성별 사회화 강화

해설 부모나 가족이 주는 장난감에 의해 남자아이들과 여자아이들에게 사회에서 각기 규정되는 역할이 강화된다는 내용의 글이므로, 요지로는 장난감이 성별 사회화를 강화시킨다는 내용인 ①이 적절하다.

해석 부모들은 여자아이와 남자아이를 위한 각기 다른 능력을 함양시켜주는 장난감으로, 자녀의 성별에 근거하여 자녀를 위해 다른 장난감을 골라준다. 여자아이들은 인형과 가정용품을 더 많이 받는데, 이는 수동성을 장려하고 사회에서 여성이 갖는 가정의 역할과 돌보는 역할을 강화시킨다. 반대로 남자아이들은 공구, 트럭, 자동차, 그리고 스포츠와 관련된 장난감을 더 많이 받는데, 이는 창작, 적극성, 그리고 경쟁을 장려하며 사회에서 남성이 갖는 지배적인 역할을 강조한다. 주제문 **성 고정관념과 장난감에 관한 연구는 비록 유아와 걸음마 단계 어린이를 위한 장난감에서는 다소 그렇지 않지만, 모든 연령대의 남자아이용 장난감과 여자아이용 장난감이 성별에 따라 정형화되어 있다는 것을 보여준다.** 여하튼, 부모들과 다른 가족 구성원들이 여자아이와 남자아이에게 다른 유형의 갖고 놀 장난감을 줄 때, 그들은 또한 그들(=아이들)에게 적절한 성별 놀이에 관한 메시지를 전달하고 있는 것이다.

구문 [1행~3행] Parents choose different toys for their children based on their gender, **with** *toys* (for girls and boys) **fostering** different skills.
「with + 목적어(명사(구)) + 분사」 구조의 분사구문으로 부대상황을 나타낸다. 목적어와 분사의 관계가 능동이므로 현재분사(fostering)를 썼다.

어휘 **gender** 성(별); 성 구분 **foster** 육성하다, 발전시키다 **household items** 가정용품, 살림살이 **passivity** 수동성, 소극성 **reinforce** (생각 등을) 강화하다; 보강하다 **domestic** 가정(용)의; 국내의 **conversely** 정반대로, 역으로 **aggression** 공격(성), 적극성 **emphasize** 강조하다 **dominant** 우세한, 지배적인 **gender stereotype** 성 고정관념 *cf.* **stereotype** 고정관념(을 형성하다) **regardless** 그것과는 관계없이, 여하튼; 개의치 않고

23 글의 주제 ③

소재 사카린의 특성

해설 사카린의 긍정적 특성을 설명한 뒤, 사람들에게 사카린이 암을 일으킬 수도 있다는 오해를 불러일으킨 연구 결과는 잘못된 것이었음을 밝히는 내용이므로, 이 글의 주제로 가장 적절한 것은 ③ '사카린에 대한 오해와 이해'이다.

해석 사람들은 "맛이 좋으면 몸에 나쁜 게 분명하다"라고 말한다. 그래서 사카린이라 불리는 0칼로리의 인공 감미료가 처음 시장에 나왔을 때, 많은 사람은 그것이 너무 괜찮아서 사실일 수 없다고 생각했다. 그러나 사카린은 소화되지 않아서, 설탕과는 달리 몸에 흡수될 수 없고 지방으로 전환될 수도 없다. 마찬가지로, 그것은 충치를 일으킬 수도 없는데, 이는 충치를 일으키는 박테리아가 그것(=사카린)을 소화시킬 수 없기 때문이다. 한 연구에서 사카린이 쥐에게 방광암을 일으켰다고 밝혔는데, 이는 (사카린에 대한) 만연한 공포를 야기했다. 하지만 쥐가 섭취한 사카린의 양이 인간이 전 생애 동안 매일 다이어트 탄산음료를 100캔씩 마시는 것과 같다는 것이 드러났을 때 그 연구는 잘못된 것임이 증명되었다.
① 인공 감미료 개발에 사용된 과정
② 사카린이 사람들의 건강에 끼치는 해로운 영향
④ 사카린과 설탕 사용의 차이점
⑤ 최근 늘어난 인공 감미료의 다양성

구문 [10행~13행] But the study was disproved // when **it** was revealed **that** the rats had received *doses of saccharin* (**equal to** humans drinking 100 cans of diet soda every day for their entire lives).
when이 이끄는 부사절에서 it은 가주어, that절이 진주어이다. equal to ~ entire lives는 doses of saccharin을 후치 수식하는 형용사구이다. equal to는 '(수량 · 가치 등이) ~와 같은'이란 뜻으로, 이때 to는 전치사이므로 뒤에 동명사 drinking이 왔다. humans는 동명사 drinking의 의미상 주어이다.

어휘 **artificial** 인공적인 **sweetener** 감미료 **appear** 나오다; ~인 것 같다 **too good to be true** 너무 좋아서 믿을 수 없는 **indigestible** 소화되지 않는 *cf.* **digest** 소화하다 **absorb** 흡수하다 **convert** 전환시키다 **likewise** 마찬가지로 **tooth decay** 충치 *cf.* **decay** 충치; 부패, 부식; 쇠퇴 **cancer** 암 **widespread** 널리 퍼진, 만연한 **disprove** ~의 반증을 들다, 그릇됨을 증명하다 **dose** 1회분(량), 복용량 **entire** 전체의 [선택지 어휘] **misconception** 오해 **expansion** 확장

24 글의 제목 ③

소재 사회적 장벽의 기능을 하는 휴대전화

해설 주제를 드러내는 첫 번째 문장의 many people now use their mobiles as "barrier signals"에서 알 수 있듯이 오늘날 사람들이 휴대전화를 다른 사람들이 접근하지 못하게 하고 자신의 영역을 표시하는 수단으로 사용한다는 내용이므로, 글의 제목으로는 ③ '휴대전화: 현대적 울타리'가 가장 적절하다.

해석 주제문 **많은 사람들은 이제 홀로 커피숍이나 다른 공공장소에 있을 때, 접근 불가를 나타내거나 개인적인 '영역'을 표시하기 위해서 전통적으로 신문이나 잡지를 사용하는 것에 대한 대안으로, 그들의 휴대전화를 '장벽의 신호'로 사용한다.** 심지어 사용을 하지 않을 때도 테이블 위에 놓인 휴대전화는 효과적인 상징적 경호원, 즉 원하지 않는 사회적 접촉으로부터 보호해주는 것으로서 작용을 하는데, 사람들은 잠재적인 '침입자'가 접근해 올 때 전화기를 만지거나 집어 들 것이다. 친구나 가족 같은 개인의 사회적 지지 네트워크가 어쨌거나 휴대전화 '안에' 있다는 생각은 단지 전화기를 만지거나 잡는 것만으로도 보호받는다는 느낌을 주며, 다른 사람들에게 자신은 혼자가 아니며 연약하지 않다는 신호를 보낸다는 것을 의미한다.
① 현대 기술의 어두운 면
② 우리는 항상 연결되기를 원한다
④ 전화 사용과 관련해서 생겨나는 규칙들
⑤ 십 대들의 휴대전화 사용 경쟁

구문 [5행~8행] Even when not in use, / *the mobile* (placed on the table) / acts as <u>an effective symbolic bodyguard</u>, <u>a protector against unwanted social contact</u>: ~.
( ) 부분은 the mobile을 후치 수식하는 과거분사구이며, 밑줄 친 두 개의 명사구는 동격을 나타낸다.

[9행~14행] <u>The idea</u>(S) of <u>one's social support network of friends and family being somehow "inside" the mobile phone</u> / <u>means</u>(V) // <u>that even just touching or holding the phone</u>(S') <u>gives</u>(V'1) a sense of being protected — and <u>sends</u>(V'2) a signal to others that one is not alone and vulnerable.(O)

The idea와 one's social ~ the mobile phone은 동격 관계이다. 전치사 of가

동격 관계를 나타내며, '~라는'으로 해석한다. that절은 동사 mean의 목적어 역할을 하며, that절의 주어인 동명사구(even just touching ~ the phone)에 두 개의 술부 gives ~ protected와 sends ~ vulnerable이 and로 연결되어 병렬구조를 이룬다.

어휘 **on one's own** 혼자서, 단독으로 **public** 공공의 **barrier** 장벽, 울타리 **alternative** 대안 **traditional** 전통적인 **unavailability** 접근[이용] 불가능 **mark** 표시하다 **territory** 영역; 영토 **symbolic** 상징적인 **social** 사회적인 **potential** 잠재적인; 잠재력 **intruder** 침입자; 불청객 **approach** 접근하다, 다가가다 **vulnerable** 연약한, 취약한; ~하기[받기] 쉬운 [선택지 어휘] **emerging** 최근 생겨난; 신생의, 떠오르는 **regarding** ~에 관하여

25 도표 이해 ③

소재 아프리카 멸종 우려 동물 종(種)의 수

해설 멸종이 우려되는 파충류는 총 48종으로, 이는 포유류, 조류, 어류에 이어 네 번째로 많은 수이다. 따라서 정답은 ③이다.

해석 〈아프리카 멸종 우려 동물 종(種)의 수〉

주제문 IUCN(세계자연보호연맹)은 멸종 위기에 처한 동물 종(種)을 심각성에 따라 '취약한 상태', '위험한 상태', '상당히 위험한 상태'의 세 가지 범주로 분류하는 기준을 세웠다. 위 그래프는 아프리카 내에서 각 강(綱)에 속한 종의 수를 보여준다. ① 아프리카에서 멸종이 우려되는 포유류 289종 중, 위험한 상태와 상당히 위험한 상태로 각각 63종이 같은 수로 기록되었다. ② 조류는 이 그래프에서 두 번째로 큰 강을 형성하는데, 총 207종의 멸종 우려 조류 중 37종이 상당히 위험한 상태로 기록되었다. ③ 다섯 개의 모든 강 중에서 세 번째로 많은 강은 48종의 멸종 우려 아프리카 파충류로 구성되며, 이 중 2종은 상당히 위험한 상태이다. ④ 멸종 우려 양서류의 종수는 멸종 우려 파충류 종수의 절반에 못 미치며, 양서류에 상당히 위험한 상태인 종은 없다. ⑤ 어류 강에서는 상당히 위험한 상태의 종이 위험한 상태의 종이나 취약한 상태의 종보다 더 많은 부분을 차지한다.

구문 [9행~11행] Birds make up the second largest class in this graph / **with** *37 of the 207 total threatened bird species* **listed** as critically endangered.

「with + 목적어(명사(구)) + 분사」 구조의 분사구문으로 부대상황을 나타내며, 목적어와 분사의 관계가 수동이므로 과거분사(listed)가 쓰였다.

어휘 **conservation** 보호 **standard** 기준, 규범 **sort** 분류하다 **threatened** (야생 동물이) 멸종 위기에 있는 **extinction** 멸종, 소멸 **category** 범주, 부문 **severity** 심함; 격렬함 **endangered** 위험에 처한; (동식물이) 멸종될 위기에 처한 *cf.* **endanger** 위험에 빠뜨리다 **critically** 위태롭게; 비판적으로 **class** (생물 분류에서) 강(綱) **mammal** 포유동물 **make up** 형성하다 **consist of** ~으로 구성되다 **reptile** 파충류 **amphibian** 양서류 **portion** 부분

26 내용 불일치 ④

소재 영국의 동화 작가이자 삽화가인 Martin Handford

해설 Handford는 'Wally'라는 캐릭터를 만들고 첫 책을 출판했으며, 이후 일곱 권을 더 출판했다고 했으므로 시리즈는 총 여덟 권이 된다. 따라서 ④가 일치하지 않는 내용이다.

해석 ① 1956년에 런던에서 태어난 Martin Handford는 영국의 동화 작가이자 삽화가이다. 그는 네 살 무렵에 그림을 그리기 시작했고 나중에는 ② 그의 어린 시절 동안 가지고 놀던 장난감 병정에서 영감을 얻었다. ③ 대학을 졸업한 후, Martin은 많은 고객을 위해 군중 장면을 그리는 것을 전문으로 하는 프리랜서 삽화가로 일했다. 1986년에 Handford는 미술 감독으로부터 자신의 그림에 넣을 독특한 캐릭터를 고안해 달라고 요청받았다. 많은 생각 끝에, 그는 'Wally'라는 이름의 캐릭터인, 각 장소에 등장하곤 하며 항상 빨간색과 흰색이 섞인 옷을 입고 있는 배낭여행객을 만들었으며, 책을 출판했다. ④ 그는 이어서 〈Wally를 찾아라〉 책을 일곱 권 더 출판했고 Wally는 최소 17개국에서 출판이 허가되었다. ⑤ 그의 〈Wally를 찾아라〉 시리즈는 엄청난 성공을 거두었고, 그는 1980년대 중반에 전 세계적으로 유명해졌다.

구문 [10행~13행] After much thinking, / he invented *a character* (named "Wally"), *a backpacking tourist* [**who** would appear in each location and always dresses in red and white], and published a book.

(V1: invented, V2: published; a character = a backpacking tourist)

두 개의 술부(invented ~ white, published a book)가 and로 대등하게 연결된 형태이다. 주격 관계대명사 who가 이끄는 절이 선행사 a backpacking tourist를 수식하고 있다.

어휘 **author** 작가 **illustrator** 삽화가 **inspiration** 영감 **freelance** 프리랜서[자유 계약자]로 일하는; 프리랜서로 일하다 **specialize in** ~을 전문으로 하다 **crowd** 군중, 무리 **numerous** 많은 *cf.* **numerical** 수의, 수와 관련된 **come up with** 생각해내다, 제안하다 **invent** 고안하다, 발명하다 **appear** 나타나다 **location** 장소 **license** (책의) 출판을 허가하다; 승낙; 면허

27 안내문 불일치 ⑤

소재 동창회 축제

해설 안내문의 소제목과 선택지를 활용하여 필요한 정보를 빠르게 훑어 확인해야 한다. 무료 식사권이 포함된 재회 패키지 혜택을 받는 졸업생은 1976, 1991, 1996, 2006년 졸업생들이므로 ⑤는 안내문과 내용이 일치하지 않는다.

해석

동창회 축제

① 본 동문연합은 10월 7일 토요일 오후 3시부터 6시에 동창회관에서 열리는 올해의 동창회 축제에 모든 동창생들과 지역 공동체, 학생, 교수님, 교직원들이 참석하도록 특별 초대를 하고자 합니다.

동창회 축제는 다음과 같은 행사들을 포함합니다.

- 야외 바비큐
- 라이브 음악과 오락
- ② 페이스페인팅, 바운스 하우스, 게임 등이 있는 어린이 공간
- ③ 다양한 대학, 학부, 캠퍼스 프로그램을 대표하는 부스들이 특색을 이루는 동문 마을

더 있습니다.

④ 참석하는 선착순 200명은 새로운 로고 선물을 무료로 받게 됩니다.

(올해의) 재회의 해는?

⑤ 여러분이 1976, 1991, 1996, 2006년 졸업생이라면 특별 선물과 2인 무료 식사권을 포함하는 재회 패키지를 받을 수 있습니다.

구문 [12행~14행] *Alumni Village* (**featuring** *booths* (**representing** various colleges, departments, and campus programs)).

featuring 이하의 분사구 전체가 앞의 Alumni Village를 수식하고, 그 안에서 representing 이하의 분사구가 booths를 수식하는 형태이다.

어휘 **homecoming** 동창회; 귀향, 귀국 **alumni** (**alumnus**의 복수형) 졸업생들, 동창생들 **extend** 주다, 베풀다; 확대하다, 연장하다 **faculty** 대학 교수단; 능력 **entertainment** 오락 **feature** 특색을 이루다; 특별히 포함하다 **booth** (칸막이를 한) 작은 공간, 부스 **represent** 대표하다 **eligible** 자격이 있는 **reunion** (오랫동안 못 본 사람들의 친목) 모임, 재회 **complimentary** 무료의; 칭찬하는

28 안내문 일치 ②

소재 수족관 비공개 장소 투어

해설 투어 활동 중에 먹이를 준비하는 구역을 방문해서 식단이 어떻게 관리되는지 알아보는 것이 있으므로 ②가 정답이다.

해석

비공개 장소 투어

수족관의 상어들에게 가깝게 다가갈 수 있는 기회를 놓치지 마세요. 전문가와 함께 일반에게는 공개되지 않는, 상어들이 있는 곳을 탐험하면서 이 믿을 수 없는 바다의 포식자들에 관한 진실을 발견하세요.

활동
- ① 여러분 바로 밑에서 상어들이 조용히 헤엄치는 곳인 먹이 주는 다리 위를 걸어 보세요.
- 수족관 직원들이 상어들을 어떻게 보살피는지 배워보세요.
- ② 먹이를 준비하는 구역을 방문하여 식단이 어떻게 계획되고 감시되는지 알아보세요.

가격
어른 50달러
연장자 (65세 이상) 47달러
어린이 (8~11세) 41달러
- ③ 8세 이상의 어린이들은 어른과 함께 올 수 있습니다.
- ④ 가격에는 수족관 입장, 비공개 장소 접근이 포함된 안내 여행, 그리고 수족관 기념품이 포함되어 있습니다.

⑤ 문의나 예약을 원하시면 월요일에서 금요일, 오전 9시부터 오후 4시 30분 사이에 410-573-3344로 Central Reservations에 연락해 주세요.

구문 [8행~9행] Walk on *the feeding bridge*, // **where** sharks swim silently just inches beneath you
where는 앞에 쓰인 the feeding bridge를 선행사로 받는 관계부사의 계속적 용법으로 쓰였다.

어휘 **behind-the-scenes** 비밀[비공식]의; 배후의 **aquarium** 수족관 **expert** 전문가 **incredible** 믿을 수 없는, 믿기 힘든 **predator** 포식자, 약탈자 **senior** 연장자, 노인 **accompany** 동반하다, 동행하다 **admission** 입장(료); 입학; 승인 **access** 접근 **souvenir** 기념품

29 밑줄 어법 ③

소재 건강 유지의 생활화와 마라톤 열풍

해설 ③ 분사구문의 의미상 주어는 others(= marathons)로, '마라톤 경주'가 참가자들을 '끌어들이는' 것이므로 others와 draw는 능동 관계이다. 따라서 drawn은 현재분사인 drawing으로 고쳐야 한다.

오답 분석 ① 「a large number of + 복수명사 + 복수동사」이므로 work out은 적절히 쓰였다. ② 「so + 형용사 + that ~」 구조가 바르게 쓰였다. ④ few는 셀 수 있는 명사(runners)와 함께 쓰인다. ⑤ alike가 부사로 적절히 쓰였다. young and old alike는 '노소(老少)를 막론하고'란 뜻이다.

해석 건강을 유지하는 것이 생활화되면서 많은 수의 사람이 이제는 정기적으로 헬스클럽에서 운동을 하는데, 근력 운동을 하거나, 러닝머신에서 뛰거나, 자전거를 타거나 크로스트레이닝 기구를 사용한다. 주제문 그리고 장거리 마라톤 경주도 매우 인기가 많아져서 주최 측은 종종 참가할 수 있는 사람들의 수를 제한해야 한다. 미국에서는 보스턴 마라톤과 뉴욕 마라톤이 가장 유명하지만, 다른 도시들과 심지어 작은 마을에서도 열리는 다른 것(=마라톤)들이 많이 있는데, 이 대회들은 수천 명의 참가자들을 끌어들인다. 마라톤 주자들 가운데 우승하기를 바라는 사람은 거의 없다. 대부분은 그저 완주하는 것을 목표로 한다. 대부분의 마라톤 경주는 노소(老少)를 막론하고 심지어 휠체어를 탄 사람들에게까지, 달리고 싶은 누구에게나 열려 있다.

어휘 **keep fit** 건강을 유지하다 **a way of life** 생활양식[방식] **work out** 운동하다 **weight training** 근력 운동 **run on a treadmill** 러닝머신에서 뛰다 **cross-training** 크로스트레이닝(몇 가지 운동을 결합하여 행하는 트레이닝 방법) **organizer** 주최자; 조직자 **limit** 제한하다 **participate** 참가하다 *cf.* **participant** 참가자 **draw (drew-drawn)** 끌어당기다; 그리다 **aim to-v** v하는 것을 목표로 하다 **wheelchair** 휠체어

30 밑줄 어휘 ③

소재 유적 보호를 위한 영국의 '오염자 비용 부담' 원칙

해설 오염자 비용 부담 원칙의 목적은 아직 연구되지 않은 유적을 보호하기 위한 것이라고 했다. 따라서 이 원칙이 오염자로 간주하는 것은 이미 '개발된' 지역이 아니라 아직 '개발되지 않은' 지역에 공사를 계획하는 회사로 보는 것이 문맥상 적절하므로 ③은 undeveloped가 되어야 한다.

해석 상대적으로 작은 면적을 감안하면, 영국은 28개의 유네스코 세계 문화유산을 포함해 ① 엄청난 수의 주요 역사 유적지를 가지고 있다. 세계 문화유산의 보호를 받지 못하는 많은 유적은 어떠한가? 주제문 영국에서 어떤 주요 공사라도 계획하는 건설 회사는 '오염자 비용 부담'의 원칙을 ② 따라야 하는데, 이 원칙의 목적은 고고학자들이 아직 연구할 기회를 갖지 못한 어떤 유적이든 보호하는 것이다. 그 원칙은 ③ 개발된(→ 개발되지 않은) 지역에 공사 계획을 세우는 어떠한 회사든 오염자로 간주한다. 그것(=오염자 비용 부담의 원칙)은 개발 ④ 이전에 건설회사가 고고학자에게 유적을 조사하도록 비용을 지불해야 한다고 명시한다. 그것은 역사적 중요성을 지닌 어떤 것도 새로운 빌딩과 건축물에 의해 ⑤ 파괴되지 않도록 하는 것을 목표로 한다.

구문 [5행~8행] *Construction companies* (planning any major work in England)(S) have to follow(V) *the "polluter pays" principle*(O), // **whose** purpose is to protect *any sites* [that archaeologists have not yet had *the chance* (to study)].
현재분사구(planning ~ England)의 수식을 받아 주어 부분이 길어졌다. whose 이하는 앞의 명사구 the "polluter pays" principle을 보충 설명한다. to study는 형용사적 용법으로 앞의 the chance를 수식한다.

[9행~10행] The principle **views** *any company* [that plans to build in undeveloped areas](A) **as** a polluter(B).
「view[see] A as B」는 'A를 B로 간주하다'라는 의미이다. 「consider A B」, 「regard A as B」, 「think of A as B」가 모두 같은 뜻으로 쓰인다.

어휘 **considering** ~을 감안[고려]하면 **relatively** 상대적으로 **historical site** 역사 유적지 **including** ~을 포함하여 **World Heritage Site** 세계 문화유산 **construction** 건설, 공사 **principle** 원칙 **polluter** 오염 유발자 *cf.* **pollution** 오염 **archaeologist** 고고학자 **examine** 조사하다, 검사하다 **prior to** ~이전에 **ensure** 반드시 ~하게 하다, 보장하다

31 빈칸 추론 ②

소재 Piaget가 관찰한 아동의 미성숙한 사고

해설 심리학자 Piaget가 관찰한 아이들의 특징에 관한 글이다. 빈칸에는 아이들의 정의감이 '어떠한지'에 관한 내용이 들어가야 한다. 빈칸 다음의 예시에서 아이들이 어떤 행동을 한 사람의 의도보다 결과에만 초점을 둔다고 설명하며 아이들의 미숙함을 지적하고 있으므로 정답은 ② '원시적인'이다. 글 앞부분의 '아이들이 어른처럼 생각하지 못한다(He observed ~ adults at all.)'는 내용과 빈칸 앞의 also(또한, 역시)라는 표현을 통해서도 빈칸에 미숙함을 표현하는 단어가 들어가야 함을 알 수 있다.

해석 선구적인 심리학자인 Jean Piaget(장 피아제)는 자신의 이력 대부분을 아이들과 보냈다. 아이들의 말을 들어주고, 아이들을 관찰하며, 아이들에 관해 글을 쓰고, 같은 일을 하는 세계의 심리학자들의 작업을 연구하며 보냈다. 주제문 그는 아이들이 결코 어른처럼 생각하지 않는다는 것을 관찰했다. 예를 들어, 아주 어린 아이들은 종종 달이 자신을 따라온다고, 밤에 창문을 통해 꿈이 들어온다고 믿는다. Piaget가 관찰한 바에 따르면, 아이들의 정의감 역시 다소 원시적이다(=발달하지 못했다). 왜냐하면 그것(=아이들의 정의감)은 손해를 입힌 사람의 의도가 아니라, 단지 발생한 손해만 계산에 넣기 때문이다. 이것이 어머니를 돕다가 찻잔 3개를 깨뜨린 여자아이가, 자신이 화가 나서 그냥 찻잔 하나를 깨뜨리는 것보다 더 큰 벌을 받을 만하다고 생각하게 되는 이유다.
① 복잡한 ③ 무조건적인 ④ 뛰어난 ⑤ 충분한

구문 [8행~11행] Their sense of justice, / observed Piaget, / is also rather primitive // since it(= their sense of justice) takes into account / only *the damage* (caused), and (it does) not (take into account) *the intention* (of *the one* [who caused it(= the damage)]).

주절의 동사 observed는 명사절 (that) their sense of justice is also rather primitive를 목적어로 취한다. 또한, since가 이끄는 절 내의 동사(takes into account)는 두 개의 목적어를 취하는데, 각각 뒤에 수식어구가 온다.

[11행~14행] **This is why** *a girl* [who breaks three teacups / while helping her mother] **would think** // she deserves more punishment / than if she **were to** break just one teacup in anger.

앞 문장에 원인이 나온 뒤, 그 결과를 설명할 때 「This is why S′+V′~.」가 쓰이고 '이것이 ~하는 이유이다'라고 해석한다. 「if S′+were to-v ~, S+조동사 과거형+동사원형 ...」은 실현 가능성이 낮은 미래의 일을 가정하며 '만약 ~하게 된다면 …할 텐데'란 뜻이다.

어휘 **pioneering** 선구적인, 개척의 **psychologist** 심리학자 **career** 이력, 경력; 직업 **observe** 관찰하다; 준수하다 **sense of justice** 정의감 **take into account** ~을 계산에 넣다, 고려하다 **damage** 손해, 손상; 손해를 입히다 **intention** 의도, 목적 **deserve** ~을 받을 만하다

32 빈칸 추론 ④

소재 패턴 인식의 달인 M. C. Escher

해설 M. C. Escher가 벽의 소용돌이 장식에서 얼굴을 찾아내고, 구름이나 나뭇결을 보며 동물 모양을 찾아냈다는 내용에서 규칙적이고 반복되는 형태에서 예상치 못한 것을 그려내는 능력인 ④ '패턴 인식'에 그가 통달했음을 추론할 수 있다.

해석 패턴 인식의 위대한 달인 중 한 명이 그래픽 아티스트 M. C. Escher였는데, 그는 이 기술을 매일 연습했던 것 같다. 그의 아들 George Escher에 따르면, "아래층 작은 화장실 벽은 녹색, 노란색, 빨간색과 갈색의 불규칙적인 소용돌이로 장식되어 있었습니다. 아버지께서는 연필을 가져다가 여기선 선을, 저기선 음영을 강조하곤 하셨으며, '웃는, 슬픈, 혹은 심각한' 얼굴을 찾곤 했습니다. 여러 달에 걸쳐서 벽은 '얼굴로 생명을 얻게 되었습니다.' 아버지는 또한 구름이나 나뭇결과 같은 무작위적인 것 같은 형태에서 동물 모양을 식별하는 것을 즐기셨습니다!" 그의 맞물리는 동물들을 볼 때 우리는 형태가 아무리 복잡해도, 항상 아래에는 단순하고 반복되는 대칭적 형태가 있음을 깨닫는다. 주제문 Escher의 천재성은 규칙적이고 반복되는 다각형 속에서 물고기, 새, 도마뱀, 천사, 악마와 다른 예상치 못한 놀라운 것들을 본 것, 그리고 이러한 것들을 우리 또한 볼 수 있는 방법을 가르쳐준 것이었다.

① 환상 예술 ② 즉각적인 통찰 ③ 선택적 주의 ⑤ 수학적 정확성

구문 [14행~18행] Escher's genius was to see in a regular, repeating polygon the possibility of fish, ~ and other unexpected surprises — and to teach us how to see these things, too.

was 다음의 보어 to see ~ surprises와 to teach ~ too가 and로 연결되어 병렬구조를 이룬다. the possibility ~ surprises는 to see의 목적어이다.

어휘 **apparently** 겉보기에는, 외관상 **irregular** 불규칙한 **swirl** 소용돌이 **emphasize** 강조하다 **shade** 색조, 음영 **over the course of** ~ 동안, ~에 걸쳐서 **identify** 확인하다, 식별하다 **seemingly** 겉보기에는 **random** 무작위의 **wood grain** 나뭇결 **complicated** 복잡한 **figure** 형태, 형상 **symmetrical** 대칭적인(↔ **asymmetrical** 비대칭적인) **underneath** 아래에 **lizard** 도마뱀 [선택지 어휘] **selective** 선택적인 **recognition** 인식 **accuracy** 정확성

33 빈칸 추론 ④

소재 bigwig의 어원과 의미

해설 빈칸은 bigwig가 '어떤' 사람을 놀리는 표현인지에 관한 것이다. 옛날에는 목욕을 자주 하지 못해 가발을 썼는데 자기가 중요하다고 생각하는 사람일수록 큰 가발을 사서 썼다(The more ~ people's heads.)는 내용에서 bigwig는 ④ '자기가 중요하다고 생각하는 사람'을 의미한다는 것을 추론할 수 있다.

해석 17세기 유럽에서는 목욕이 드물었다. 아주 부유한 사람들도 일 년에 오직 서너 번만 목욕을 했다. 감지 않은 머리는 악취가 나고 이와 벌레가 들끓어, 사람들은 머리를 짧게 자르고 천이나 가발로 머리를 덮었다. 부자들은 울이나 실크로 만든 최신 유행의 가발을 구입했으며, 더 크고 점점 더 비싼 가발이 유행이었다. 더 중요한 사람일수록, 혹은 스스로 그렇다고 생각할수록, 가발이 더 컸다. 어떤 가발은 너무 커서 마치 사람 머리 위에 작은 소가 앉아 있는 것처럼 보였다. 주제문 이것이 우리가 'bigwig(거물)'라는 단어를 갖게 된 연유이며, 이 단어는 자기가 중요하다고 생각하는 사람을 놀리는 표현이다. bigwig라고 생각되는 사람에게 "당신이 bigwig입니다."라고 말하지 마라. 오직 bigwig의 뒤에서, 친구들에게 그렇게 말하라.

① 당신보다 많이 가진 사람
② 보기 흉한 가발을 쓴 사람
③ 머리카락이 거의 없거나 아예 없는 사람
⑤ 당신에 대해 험담하는 사람

구문 [10행~12행] This is (*the case*[*situation*]) **where** we got the word "*bigwig*," // **which** is *an expression* [**that** makes fun of *people* [**who** think they're important]].

관계부사 where 앞에 선행사 the case 또는 the situation이 생략된 것으로 본다. which, that, who는 모두 관계대명사로 각각 앞의 선행사를 보충설명하거나 수식한다.

[12행~13행] Don't say "you're a bigwig" to *a person* [(who) you think is a bigwig].

[ ] 부분은 앞의 a person을 수식하는 관계사절로, 주격 관계대명사 who가 생략되었으며 밑줄 친 you think는 삽입절이다. 생각, 희망(think, hope 등)을 나타내는 동사를 포함한 삽입절 앞에 오는 주격 관계대명사는 종종 생략된다.

어휘 **rare** 드문, 희귀한 **take a bath** 목욕하다 **unwashed** 씻지 않은, 더러운 **stink** 악취가 나다 **attract** 끌어들이다 **wig** 가발 **fashionable** 유행하는, 유행을 따르는 *cf.* **fashion** 유행; 양식 **increasingly** 점점 더 **costly** 많은 돈이 드는, 값비싼 **consider** ~로 생각하다[여기다]; 고려하다 **make fun of** ~을 놀리다

34 빈칸 추론 ②

소재 소행성과의 충돌을 피하기 위한 전략

해설 우주선을 소행성 옆에 보내서 인력의 힘을 이용해 수년에 걸쳐 소행성의 경로를 이동시킬 것이라고 했으므로 과학자들이 고안한 전략의 목표는 ② '소행성의 방향을 서서히 바꾸는 것'임을 알 수 있다. 마지막 문장의 the asteroid would be safely moved off its course over many years가 빈칸 추론의 결정적인 힌트가 된다.

해석 과학자들은 2029년에 소행성 하나가 지구와 충돌할 확률이 38분의 1이라고 추정했다. 이는 분명히 걱정을 일으키는 요인이다. 주제문 운 좋게도 과학자들은 충돌을 피할 전략을 개발했다. 그 전략은 소행성을 파괴하여 그 조각들이 지구에 쏟아져 내리는 위험을 감수하기보다 소행성의 방향을 서서히 바꾸는 것을 목표로 한다. 아주 적은 연료만 소비하는 원자력 엔진을 쓰면 우주선이 수년 동안 그 소행성 옆에서 이동하게 될 것이다. 인력의 힘 때문에 이 우주선의 질량은 그 소행성을 잡아당길 것이다. 그 힘은 약하겠지만, 우주에는 저항력이 없어서 그 소행성은 수년간에 걸쳐 그것의 (충돌) 경로에서 벗어나도록 안전하게 이동할 것이다.

① 대기권에서 전소시키는 것
③ 핵폭탄을 폭발시켜서 소행성의 궤도를 바꾸는 것
④ 우주선을 소행성에 충돌시켜서 (소행성의) 경로를 막는 것
⑤ 지구와 충돌하지 않도록 소행성의 속도를 바꾸는 것

구문 [5행~7행] **Rather than** destroy the asteroid and risk its pieces falling down on Earth, // the strategy aims to gradually change the asteroid's direction.
「A rather than B」는 'B하기보다는 A하다'란 뜻으로 이 문장에서는 rather than B가 A보다 앞에 위치했다.

어휘 **estimate** 추정하다; 평가하다 **asteroid** 소행성 **collide with** ~에 충돌하다[부딪히다] *cf.* **collision** 충돌 **concern** 걱정; 관심 **strategy** 전략 **crash** 충돌 (사고); 붕괴 **risk** ~의 위험을 무릅쓰다; 위험 **aim** ~을 목표로 하다; 목표 **nuclear-powered** 원자력을 동력으로 하는 **consume** 소비하다 **fuel** 연료 **gravity** 인력, 중력 **resistance** 저항(력) **course** 경로; 수업 [선택지 어휘] **atmosphere** 대기; 분위기 **alter** 바꾸다 **orbit** 《천문》 궤도 **explode** 폭발시키다

35 무관한 문장 ④

소재 영화가 역사 이해에 주는 도움

해설 영화가 전해주는 생생한 이미지를 통해 과거의 역사를 더 잘 이해할 수 있다는 내용의 글이다. 따라서 ④의 영화가 공부와 여가 활동을 균형 있게 하는 방법이라는 일반적인 내용이 글의 중간에 들어가는 것은 자연스럽지 않다.

해석 주제문 영화는 역사에 대한 당신의 지식을 깊이 있게 할 수 있다. 예를 들어 만약 당신이 머릿속에 그것(= 흑사병)에 관한 생생한 몇몇 이미지를 갖고 있지 않다면, 달리 어떤 방법으로 1300년대 유럽의 흑사병에 관한 강의를 완전히 이해할 수 있겠는가? 교과서에 그 질병을 이해하는 데 도움을 주는 지도나 삽화가 있을지 모른다. 강사가 그 당시에 살아 있는 게 어땠을지 느낌을 어떻게든 전달해주는 대단한 이야기꾼일지도 모른다. 그러나 만약 당신이 〈제7의 봉인〉이라는 스웨덴 영화감독 Ingmar Bergman(잉마르 베르히만)의 고전 영화를 본다면, 그 역사적 시기에 대해 훨씬 더 효과적으로 이해할 수 있을 것이다. 영화를 보는 것은 공부와 여가 활동을 균형 있게 하는 훌륭한 방법일 것이다. 제작된 모든 위대한 역사 영화들이 있다면, 다른 어느 곳에서 이보다 더 생생한 과거의 재현을 구하기는 어려울 것이다.

구문 [6행~8행] Your lecturer may be *a great storyteller* [**who** manages to convey a feeling of what it was like to be alive back then].
a feeling은 of 뒤에 나오는 명사절과 동격을 나타낸다. 「what it was like to-v」는 'v하는 것이 어땠는지'란 뜻으로 여기서 it이 to-v를 받는 가주어 역할을 한다.

[8행~11행] But **if** you **were to see** *The Seventh Seal*, a classic film ~ Ingmar Bergman, / you **would have** a much more powerful sense of the historical period.
「If S' + were to-v ~, S + 조동사 과거형 + 동사원형 ....」은 앞으로 일어날 가능성이 희박할 때 쓰는데, 정중하게 제안이나 요청을 할 때도 쓴다. '만약 ~한다면 …할 텐데'라고 해석한다.

[13행~15행] **With** *all of the great historical movies* [that have been made], / **it** would be difficult **to get** more vivid representations of the past anywhere else.
with가 이끄는 전명구가 가정법 과거의 조건절을 대신하며 '만약 ~이 있다면'으로 해석한다. 주격 관계대명사 that이 이끄는 절이 all ~ movies를 수식한다. it은 가주어이고 to get ~ else가 진주어이며, would be는 「조동사 과거형 + 동사원형」 형태로 가정법 과거 시제를 나타낸다.

어휘 **deepen** (지식·이해를) 깊게 하다; 깊어지다 **comprehend** (충분히) 이해하다 **say** 가령, 예를 들면 **lecture** 강의 *cf.* **lecturer** 강사 **lifelike** 실물과 똑같은 **illustration** 삽화; 실례 **storyteller** 이야기꾼, 작가 **manage to-v** v를 어떻게든[간신히] 해내다 **convey** (감정·생각 등을) 전달하다; 운반하다 **seal** 봉인(하다) **sense** 이해; 의미; 감각 **historical** 역사의 **vivid** 생생한; 선명한 **representation** 표현, 묘사

36 글의 순서 ⑤

소재 '해야 한다'는 표현을 하는 것의 의의

해설 이 글은 사람들이 무언가를 '해야 한다'고 말은 하지만 실제로 행동은 하지 않는다는 주어진 글의 내용과 (B)의 그럼에도 그렇게 말하는 것은 어떤 면에서 의미 있는 방법이라는 내용으로 나눌 수 있다. (A)의 Furthermore는 첨가의 연결사로 (B)의 내용과 연결되는 추가 의미를 제시하고 있다. 한편, (C)는 순접의 연결사 And로 시작되며 주어진 글과 내용이 연결된다. 따라서 정답은 ⑤ '(C)-(B)-(A)'이다.

해석 "나는 저축을 더 많이 해야 해."(아니면 공부를 더 많이 해야 해, 운동을 더 많이 해야 해, 가족, 친구들과 함께 더 많은 시간을 보내야 해 등)라고 말하기는 쉽다. 그러나 우리의 행동은 말이 하는 것보다 우리에 대해 더 많은 것을 말해준다.

(C) 그리고 저축을 더 많이 해야 한다거나 혹은 그 비슷한 무엇이든 그렇게 말하는 사람들 중, 실제로 자기 습관에 변화를 주는 사람이 거의 없는 게 아마도 사실일 것이다.

(B) 주제문 그러나 그런 '해야 한다'와 같은 표현을 하는 것은 더 괜찮은 사람이 되는 의미 있는 한 방법일 수 있다. 많은 사람들이 더 잘 먹고 운동도 더 많이 하겠다는 새해 결심을 하지만, 흡연을 시작하겠다거나 텔레비전을 더 많이 보길 원한다고 말하는 사람은 거의 없다.

(A) 게다가 사람들이 "나는 [A, B, C 등 어떤 것을] 더 많이 해야 해."라고 말할 때 그것은 대개 "나는 내가 시작하도록 동기를 부여해줄 제안, 조언, 전략 또는 (다른) 어떤 것에든 열려 있어."란 의미로 이해된다.

구문 [9행~10행] However, **it** can be *a meaningful way* (to be a better person) / **to make** such "should" statements.
it은 가주어 to make 이하가 진주어이다.

[14행~16행] And **it**'s probably true // **that** *few people* [who say (that) they should be saving more money or whatever] actually make any changes in their habits.
가주어 it은 that절(that few people ~ habits)의 내용을 받는다.

어휘 **furthermore** 게다가, 더욱이(= **moreover**) **generally** 일반적으로, 보통 **be open to** ~에 열려 있다, ~을 기꺼이 고려하다 **suggestion** 제안 **motivate A to-v** A가 v하도록 동기를 부여하다 **meaningful** 의미 있는, 유의미한 **statement** 표현, 진술 **resolution** 결심, 다짐; 해결, 해답 **probably** 아마 **or whatever** 혹은 그 비슷한 무엇이든

37 글의 순서 ④

소재 새가 흙 목욕을 하는 목적

해설 주어진 글은 새들이 흙 목욕을 하는 동작이 물에서 목욕하는 모습과 비슷하다는 내용이다. 그 뒤에는 물에서 하는 목욕의 목적과는 다른 흙 목욕의 목적을 다룬 (C)가 이어져야 자연스럽다. (A)는 (C)에서 언급한 해충 제거에 대한 부가 설명이므로 (C) 뒤에 오며, (B)는 해충을 제거하는 목적 외의 다른 목적에 대해 이야기하고 있으므로 마지막에 온다. 따라서 알맞은 글의 순서는 ④ '(C)-(A)-(B)'이다.

해석 새들이 깃털에 흙먼지를 뒤집어쓴 다음 털어내고 부리로 깃털을 정리할 때 하는 동작은 마치 그들이 물에서 목욕할 때 하는 동작처럼 보인다.

(C) 그러나 그 목적이 꼭 같지는 않다. 주제문 새들은 깃털 속에서 기어 다니는 해충들을 몸에서 없애려고 흙 목욕을 한다. 이와 진드기는 새들에게 흔한 문제로 깃털 속에 매우 많을 수 있다.

(A) 흙 목욕을 하는 새는 당신이 흙과 먼지를 없애려고 모래로 손을 문지르는 것과 매우 흡사하다. 거친 흙먼지는 새들이 그 벌레들을 없앨 수 있게 도와준다.

(B) 그 외에도, 새들이 또 다른 목적을 위해 흙 목욕을 한다는 학설이 있다. 그것은 새들이 (깃털에 있는) 지나치게 많은 기름기와 수분을 제거함으로써 깃털을 보송보송하게 유지하기 위해 한다는 것이다. 그러나 아직 이러한 이론을 뒷받침할 설득력 있는 증거는 없다.

구문 [1행~4행] The gestures [(which[that]) birds make ● / when they put dust on their feathers ~] look like *the movements* [(which[that]) they make ● / when bathing in water].
The gestures와 the movements는 각각 목적격 관계사가 생략되어 있는 관계사절의 수식을 받는다. ●는 관계사절에서 원래 목적어가 있던 자리이다.

어휘 **gesture** 동작; 몸짓 **dust** (흙) 먼지 **feather** 깃털 **arrange** 정리하다; 마련하다 **beak** (새의) 부리 **bathe** 목욕하다 **get A off** A를 ~에서 제거하다 **dirt** 때, 먼지 **rough** 거친; 대강의 **get rid of** ~을 제거하다 *cf.* **rid A of B** A에서 B를 제거하다 **fluffy** 보송보송한, 솜털 같은 **excess** 지나친, 과도한 **convincing** 설득력 있는 **evidence** 증거 **theory** 학설, 이론 **parasite** 해충 **louse** (복수형 **lice**) 이, 머릿니 **crawl** 기어가다

38 문장 넣기 ④

소재 고대 시대 실피움 식물의 인기와 멸종 이유

해설 주어진 문장은 실피움의 수요가 상당해서 사람들이 많은 돈을 지불했다는 내용으로, 이 식물이 여러 가지 용도로 쓰였다는 내용과 큰 수익을 얻고자 씨를 맺기도 전에 서둘러 수확했다는 내용 사이에 들어가는 것이 적절하다. 따라서 정답은 ④이다.

해석 주제문 고대 리비아의 도시 키레네는 실피움(silphium)으로 유명했는데, (그것은) 고대 그리스인과 로마인 모두에 의해 아주 소중히 여겨졌던 식물이다. 고대인들은 실피움을 상추처럼 신선하게 먹었고, 실피움의 강하고 매운 맛 때문에 수프나 스튜에 첨가했다. 그 식물은 또한 위장병에서부터 입 냄새에 이르는 다양한 문제들을 치료하는 데 쓰여 수요가 상당했다. 그것(=실피움)은 또한 매우 좋은 냄새가 나서, 다양한 향수의 필수 성분이 되었다. 그것에 대한 수요는 무척이나 커서 그것의 새로운 수송물이 키레네로부터 도착할 때마다 사람들은 줄을 서서 엄청난 값을 치르곤 했다. 불행히도, 벌어들일 수 있을 것 같은 어마어마한 수익이 키레네 사람들을 실피움이 씨를 맺기도 전에 수확하도록 유혹했다. 이것이 바로 이 놀라운 식물이 서기 100년경에 멸종된 이유이다.

구문 [1행~3행] It was in such *high demand* that whenever a fresh shipment of it arrived from Cyrene, // people would line up and pay huge prices.
「such ~ that ...」은 '너무 ~해서 …하다'라는 뜻의 구문이다. such 뒤에는 「형용사+명사」로 구성된 명사구가 오며, 이어지는 that절은 결과를 나타낸다.
[4행~6행] The ancient Libyan city of Cyrene was famed for *silphium*, *a plant* [(that was) highly prized by the ancient Greeks and Romans alike].
여기서 「A of B」는 A와 B가 동격임을 나타낸다. silphium과 a plant 이하 역시 동격이다.

어휘 **demand** 수요; 요구 (사항); 필요로 하다 **line up** 줄을 서다 **ancient** 고대의 *cf.* **the ancients** 고대인(특히 그리스인과 로마인을 지칭함) **Libyan** 리비아(사람)의 **Cyrene** 키레네(고대 그리스의 식민 도시) **be famed for** ~으로 유명하다 **prize** 소중히 여기다; 상(품) **alike** (앞에 나온 두 집단) 모두 **flavor** 맛 **treat** 치료하다; 다루다; 대우하다 **a wide range of** 다양한 **stomach** 위, 복부 **bad breath** 입 냄새 **essential** 필수적인; 본질적인 **component** (구성) 요소 **perfume** 향수 **make a profit** 돈을 벌다, 이익을 얻다 *cf.* **profit** 이익, 수익 **tempt A to-v** A가 v하도록 유혹하다 **harvest** 수확하다 **seed** 씨가 맺다; 씨앗 **extinct** 멸종된

39 문장 넣기 ③

소재 식품의 교차 오염을 막는 방법

해설 주어진 문장은 교차 오염을 막는 방법에 대한 예시가 시작되는 문장으로, 교차 오염을 막기 위해 식품과 접촉한 모든 것을 씻으라는 일반적인 내용과 (고기를 양념에 재운) 접시를 재사용하기 전에 뜨거운 비눗물로 세척하라는 문장 사이인 ③에 들어가는 것이 문맥상 적절하다.

해석 주제문 육류, 가금육, 그리고 생선은 종종 높은 수치의 박테리아를 가지고 있기 때문에 특별한 취급을 요한다. 게다가 그것들은 습기가 있고 영양이 풍부한 환경을 제공하는데, 이는 세균 증식에 이상적이다. 주제문 교차 오염을 방지하기 위해 그런 음식들과 접촉하게 된 어떤 것이든 씻어라. 예를 들어, 하나의 접시에서 날고기를 양념에 재운 후, 그것을 조리한 뒤에 다시 그 고기를 같은 접시에 놓지 마라. 그것을 재사용하기 전에 뜨거운 비눗물에 세척하라. 그렇지 않으면 날고기로부터 불가피하게 접시에 남아있는 박테리아가 조리된 음식 혹은 다른 음식을 오염시키고 그 속에서 증식할 수 있는데, 이는 교차 오염의 전형적인 예이다. 마찬가지로, 예를 들어 도마 위에서 닭고기 껍질을 벗긴 후 도마를 (그리고 당신의 손을) 씻어라. 그렇게 하지 않고 샐러드용 생채소를 썰기 위해 그 오염된 도마를 사용한다면, 그 채소는 그 가금육으로부터 나온 박테리아에 오염될 수 있다.

구문 [15행~18행] **If you don't**, / and you use the contaminated board / to cut up raw vegetables for a salad, // the vegetables can be contaminated / by bacteria from the poultry.
If you don't를 앞 구절의 내용으로 보충하면 If you don't wash a cutting board (and your hands) after skinning chicken on it이 된다. you use the contaminated board ~는 If에 연결된다.

어휘 **raw** 날것의 **poultry** 가금류(닭, 오리, 거위 등)의 고기 **additionally** 게다가 **nutritious** 영양이 풍부한 **ideal for** ~에 이상적인 **growth** 증가; 성장 **cross-contamination** 교차 오염 *cf.* **contaminate** 오염시키다 **inevitably** 불가피하게 **remain** 남다; 계속 ~이다 **classic** 전형적인, 대표적인; 최고 수준의 **cutting board** 도마 **skin** 껍질을 벗기다; 피부; 껍질

40 요약문 완성 ④

소재 개인보다 집단일 때의 노력 증가

해설 실험에서 실내 자전거를 탄 피실험자들이 혼자 자전거를 탈 때보다 다른 사람들이 '함께(company)' 있는 공간에서 자전거를 탈 때 더 좋은 기록을 낸 것으로 보아 '더 많이(more)' 노력했음을 알 수 있다.

해석 Indiana 대학의 Norman Triplett은 사회심리학 분야에서 수십 건의 실험을 수행했다. 실험에서 그는 자전거를 타는 사람들이 실내 자전거를 가능한 한 빠른 속도로 타도록 시켰는데, 때로는 주의를 흩뜨리는 것 없이 그들을 실험실에 홀로 두었고, 다른 때에는 모터식 사이클에 맞추도록 그들의 속도를 조정했고, 때때로 그들이 자전거를 타는 다른 사람들이 있는 곳에서 타도록 요청했다. 그의 관찰에서 전반적으로 Triplett은 어떤 자전거 타는 사람이 혼자일 때는 2분 49초에 1마일을 탔지만, 보조를 맞춰주는 네 명의 자전거 타는 사람들과 함께 탈 때는 용케도 같은 마일을 2분 37초 만에 탔음에 주목했다. 마찬가지로 그는 혼자 탈 때는 33분 17초에 10마일을 탔지만 몇몇 보조를 맞춰주는 사람들과 함께 탈 때는 같은 거리를 2분 더 빨리 탔다.

⬇

> 실험에 따르면 자전거를 타는 사람들은 다른 사람들과 (B) 함께 있을 때 (A) 더 많은 노력을 기울이는 경향이 있었다.

구문 [3행~8행] In the experiments, he **pushed** cyclists **to ride** / as fast as they could on stationary bikes, / [occasionally **leaving** them alone in the lab and free from distraction], [at other times **pacing** them against a motor-driven cycle], and [sometimes **asking** them to ride in the presence of other cyclists].
「push+O+C(to-v) (O가 v하도록 강요하다[시키다])」 구문이 사용되었다. 세 개의 [ ] 부분은 각각 leaving, pacing, asking이 이끄는 분사구문으로 콤마(,)와 and로 연결되어 병렬구조를 이룬다. alone in the lab과 free from distraction은 them의 상태를 설명해주는 형용사구 보어이다.
[8행~13행] Across his observations, Triplett noticed // that one cyclist rode a mile in 2 minutes 49 seconds / when (he was) alone, / but managed to ride the same mile in 2 minutes 37 seconds / when he

was riding with four pacing cyclists;
that절에서 동사 rode와 managed to ride가 but으로 연결되어 병렬구조를 이룬다. when alone에서 when과 alone 사이에 he was가 생략되어 있다.

어휘 **conduct** 수행하다; 행동하다; 지휘하다 **dozens of** 수십의; 많은 **experiment** 실험 **social psychology** 사회심리학 **stationary bike** 실내 자전거 *cf.* **stationary** 정지된, 고정된 **occasionally** 때때로 **leave A alone** A를 홀로 두다 **lab** 실험실(= **laboratory**) **free from** ~이 없는 **distraction** 주의 산만 **pace** 보조를 맞추다; 조정하다 **motor-driven** 모터로 움직이는 **in the presence of** ~이 있는 곳에 **observation** 관찰 **notice** 알아차리다, 주목하다 **manage to-v** 용케[간신히] v해내다 **exert** 노력하다; (권력 · 영향력을) 가하다[행사하다]

41~42 장문 41 ① 42 ④

소재 승자가 문제를 다루는 방법

해설 41. 일이 잘못되었을 때 다른 사람이나 상황을 탓하며 책임을 회피하기보다 문제에 책임을 지고 스스로 해결 방법을 모색하는 것이 성공에 이르는 길이라는 내용의 글이다. 이를 제목으로 가장 잘 표현한 것은 ① '자신의 성공을 만들어내기 위해 주도권을 잡아라'이다.
② 승자처럼 생각하라: 다른 사람들보다 힘을 얻어라
③ 다른 사람들을 탓하는 것이 문제를 해결할 수 없는 이유
④ 자신에게 가혹하게 하지 말고 자신을 사랑해주자
⑤ 인생에서 성공하는 법: 더 많이 승리하고 더 적게 패배하라

42. 빈칸이 포함된 문장을 읽고 자신의 문제를 스스로 책임지려면 '무엇'에 집중해야 하는지 찾아본다. 뒤이어 소개되는 승자들의 사고방식(putting your mind ~ what happens)이나 마지막 문장(Step up ~ to success.)에서 남을 탓하기보다 최선을 다해 해결책을 찾아보고 문제를 성공의 기회로 활용하라고 했으므로 빈칸에는 ④ '어떻게 그 문제를 해결할 수 있는지'가 가장 적절하다.
① 누가 승자인 것처럼 보이는지
② 당신이 지금 진정으로 무엇을 원하는지
③ 사람들이 당신에게 무엇을 기대하는지
⑤ 당신이 어떻게 증거를 이용하여 뒷받침할 수 있는지

해석 당신이 누군가를 실망시키거나 일이 당신이 원했던 대로 되지 않을 때, 다른 누군가 혹은 다른 무언가를 '탓하고' 싶은 유혹을 강하게 느낀다. 예를 들어, 당신이 약속에 늦으면, "내 잘못이 아니야. 교통체증이 정말 심했어!"라고 말하기 쉽다. 그러나 일단 잘못되어 가는 일에 대해 다른 사람들이나 상황을 탓하는 습관을 들이면, 당신은 자기 자신의 결과에 대한 힘을 잃게 된다.
주제문 비난할 목표물 찾기를 그만두고 당신이 어떻게 그 문제를 해결할 수 있는지에 초점을 맞추기 시작할 때, 당신은 자신의 상황과 삶에서 일어나는 일에 책임질 수 있다. 이것이 승자가 생각하는 방식이다. 당신이 교통체증 때문에 종종 늦는다면, 아마도 당신은 돌아서 갈 더 효과적인 경로들을 시도해야 할지 모른다. 아니면 예상치 못한 지연에 대비해 시간을 확보하기 위해 약속 장소로 훨씬 더 일찍 출발할 것을 고려해야 할지도 모른다. 승자가 되는 것이란 이런 것이다. 즉, 어떤 일이 일어나더라도 당신이 더 성공할 수 있게 당신의 지성과 재능을 이용하는 것이다. 승자라고 해서 인생에서 문제가 더 적은 게 아니다. 그들도 다른 사람들만큼 많은 어려움을 다룬다. 그들은 문제를 배워서 다음에 더 현명하게 행동할 도전과 기회로 활용하는 데 (남보다) 더 뛰어날 뿐이다. 주제문 그러므로 잘못을 찾느라 주위를 두리번거리는 것을 그만두라. 앞으로 나아가 이렇게 말하라. "나는 이 문제를 해결할 수 있어. 이 문제는 내 것이야!"라고. 그런 다음 그것을 성공을 향한 발판으로 이용하라.

구문 [19행~21행] ~: **putting** *your mind and talents* **to work** / to ^{V}make ^{O}you ^{C}more successful / no matter what happens.
= whatever: 무엇이 ~하더라도
앞에 나온 문장을 부연 설명하는 명사구다. 「put A to work」는 'A가 일을 하게 하다[시키다]'란 뜻이고, to make 이하는 '~하기 위해서'란 뜻으로 '목적'을 나타내는 to부정사구이다.

어휘 **let down** 실망시키다 **it is tempting to-v** v하고 싶은 유혹을 느끼다 **point the finger at** ~을 탓하다, ~에게 손가락질하다 **nightmare** 악몽 (같은 일) **get into the habit of v-ing** v하는 습관을 들이다 **blame** 나무라다, 비난하다 **go wrong** (일이) 잘못되다 **outcome** 결과 **take charge of** ~의 책임을 지다 **circumstance** 《주로 복수형》 상황, 배경 **target** 목표물; 목표로 하다 **get around** 돌아서 가다, 우회하다 **unexpected** 예기치 않은, 뜻밖의 **deal with** ~을 다루다, 처리하다 **step up** 앞으로 나아가다 **stepping-stone** 발판, 디딤돌 [선택지 어휘] **take control** 주도권을 잡다; 관리[통제]하다 **be hard on** ~을 심하게[가혹하게] 대하다 **remedy** 고치다, 개선하다; 해결[개선]책; 치료(약)

43~45 장문 43 ④ 44 ③ 45 ③

소재 대가 없는 친절에 관련된 일화

해설 43. Bryan Anderson이 시골 길가에서 타이어가 펑크 나 곤경에 처해 있는 노부인을 도와준 이야기인 (A) 다음에 노부인이 작은 카페에 들러 종업원의 친절한 태도에 감명 받는 이야기인 (D)가 이어져야 한다. 그 후 노부인이 식사비를 계산하는 과정에서 여종업원에게 돈을 남기고 가는 (B)가 이어져야 하고, 마지막으로 그 여종업원이 Bryan Anderson의 아내였다는 사실이 밝혀지는 (C)가 와야 한다.
44. (c)는 카페 여종업원을 가리키지만 나머지는 모두 노부인을 가리킨다.
45. (B)에서 노부인은 100달러짜리 지폐로 지불한 뒤 종업원이 거스름돈을 가지러 잠시 자리를 비운 틈에 나갔으므로 ③이 글의 내용과 일치하지 않는다.

해석 (A) 한 남자가 차를 운전하고 있을 때 시골의 길가에서 오도 가도 못하고 있는 노부인을 보았다. 그래서 그는 차를 멈추고 내렸다. ① 그는 그녀가 두려워하고 있는 것을 알아차릴 수 있었고, 그래서 그녀를 달래려고 했다. "저는 당신을 돕기 위해서 왔으니 걱정 마세요. 제 이름은 Bryan Anderson입니다." 그녀의 타이어가 펑크가 나 있었고 그래서 그는 차 아래로 기어 들어가야 했다. 그 일을 마쳤을 때, 그 노부인은 그가 도와준 것에 대해 얼마를 지불해야 하느냐고 물었다. Bryan은 미소를 지으며 ② "저에게 정말 갚고 싶으시다면, 다음에 도움이 필요한 사람을 만났을 때 그 사람에게 필요한 도움을 주세요."라고 말했다.
(D) 도로 아래로 몇 마일을 가서 그녀는 작은 카페를 발견했다. 그녀는 간단히 요기를 하기 위해 들어갔다. 그 카페는 초라해 보였다. 그때 (d) 그녀(=노부인)는 임신한 지 거의 8개월쯤 되어 보이는 종업원을 보았다. 그 종업원은 하루 종일 서서 시간을 보냈음에도 상냥하고 친절한 미소를 지었다. ⑤ 그 노부인은 어떻게 그렇게 가난한 사람이 낯선 사람에게 그렇게 잘해줄 수 있는가에 대해 궁금해 했다. 그런 뒤 (e) 그녀(=노부인)는 Bryan을 떠올렸다.
(B) 그 노부인은 식사를 끝내고 100달러짜리 지폐로 지불했다. 그 종업원은 거스름돈을 가져오기 위해 자리를 비웠고, ③ 그녀가 돌아왔을 때 그 부인은 가고 없었다. 그 종업원은 (a) 그녀(=노부인)가 어디에 있을까 의아해했다. 그때 그녀는 냅킨 위에 무언가 쓰여 있는 것을 보았다. 거기에는 "당신은 내게 어떤 것도 빚지지 않았어요. 지금 내가 당신을 돕는 것처럼 전에 어떤 사람이 나를 도와주었어요."라고 쓰여 있었다. 그 종업원은 냅킨 아래에 100달러짜리 지폐가 네 장이나 더 있는 것을 발견했다.
(C) 그날 밤, 그 종업원은 집에 일찍 들어갔다. 그녀는 그 부인과 (b) 그녀(=노부인)가 남긴 돈에 대해 생각을 하고 있었다. 그 부인은 그녀와 그녀의 남편이 그것을 얼마나 필요로 했는지 어떻게 알 수 있었을까? 다음 달 출산 예정인 아이 때문에 돈이 궁해질 참이었다. (c) 그녀(=카페 종업원)는 남편이 그것에 대해 걱정하고 있다는 것을 알았고, 그래서 그에게 기쁘게 그 좋은 소식을 전했다. 그런 뒤 그녀는 그에게 키스를 하고 속삭였다. ④ "사랑해요, Bryan Anderson."

구문 [(B) 2행~3행] The waitress left to get change // and when she came back, / the lady **was gone**.
수동태 형식의 was gone은 '가버려서 (현재 여기에) 없다'는 완료의 의미를 나타낸다. gone을 서술적 용법으로 쓰인 형용사로 '(사람이) 떠난'의 뜻으로 보면 이해하기가 쉽다.

어휘 (A) **countryside** 시골 지역 **frightened** 두려워하는, 겁먹은 **crawl** (엎드려) 기다; 몹시 느리게 가다 **owe** 빚지다; 신세를 지다 **assistance** 도움, 원조 (B) **change** 거스름돈; 바꾸다 **wonder** 의아하게 여기다; 놀라다 (C) **badly** 몹시, 심히 **due** ~하기로 예정된; ~때문에; (돈을) 지불해야 하는 **whisper** 속삭이다 (D) **spot** 발견하다; 얼룩지게 하다; 장소; 점; 얼룩 **grab a bite to eat** 간단히 요기하다 **pregnant** 임신한 **on A's feet** A가 (일어)서서

실전 모의고사 03

본문 p.41

18 ⑤	19 ②	20 ③	21 ③	22 ⑤	23 ④	24 ②	25 ③	26 ①	27 ③
28 ⑤	29 ③	30 ②	31 ⑤	32 ③	33 ①	34 ③	35 ③	36 ④	37 ②
38 ④	39 ①	40 ④	41 ④	42 ⑤	43 ④	44 ④	45 ③		

18 글의 목적 ⑤

소재 글쓰기 센터 지도 교사 자리 제안

해설 앞부분에서 안부를 물은 후, 글쓰기 센터의 후보자로 가장 먼저 Jeremy(편지 수신인)가 떠올랐다고 하면서 글쓰기 개인 교사로서의 업무와 보상에 대해 소개하고 이에 관심이 있다면 연락을 달라고 했다. 따라서 글의 목적으로 가장 적절한 것은 ⑤이다.

해석 Jeremy에게

잘 지내니? 네 졸업 논문이 잘 되어가고 있기를 바란다. 네가 해야 할 모든 일들로 매우 바쁠 게 분명하지만 나는 네가 그걸 처리할 수 있을 거라고 확신해. 언제나 넌 글쓰기에 뛰어난 재능을 가진 우수한 학생이었지. 주제문 사실 글쓰기 센터의 후보자를 고려할 때 네 이름이 제일 먼저 생각났단다. 너도 이미 알고 있을지 모르겠지만, 학생 글쓰기 센터는 보고서와 그 외의 글쓰기와 관련된 과제를 하는 학생들에게 도움을 제공한단다. 개인 지도 교사로서 너는 학생들과 함께 일하고 그들의 글쓰기를 향상시키는 법에 대해 조언을 하게 될 거야. 보답으로, 개인 지도 교사는 귀중한 교육 경험뿐만 아니라 상당한 시급을 받게 된단다. 주제문 이것이 네가 관심을 가질 만한 것으로 여겨진다면 내게 알려다오.

Susan Kim

어휘 **thesis** (졸업) 논문 **come along** (원하는 대로) 되어 가다 **come to mind** 생각나다, 떠오르다 **candidate** 후보자, 지원자 **assistance** 도움 **assignment** (연구) 과제, 숙제 **alongside** 함께, 나란히 **in return** 보답으로; 그 대신에 **decent** 상당한, 나쁘지 않은; 알맞은 **wage** 급료, 임금

19 심경 변화 ②

소재 손님맞이

해설 손님이 올 것을 잊고 있다가 허둥지둥(In a panic) 손님을 맞이할 준비를 하던 'I'는 이후 관리인들이 손님이 묵을 방을 깔끔히 치워둔 것을 보고 안도의 한숨(a sigh of relief)을 쉰다. 따라서 심경 변화로 가장 적절한 것은 ② '초조한 → 안도하는'이다.

해석 나는 관리인들이 "손님께서 도착하셨습니다!"라고 외치는 소리를 듣기 전까지 손님이 올 것이라는 사실을 완전히 잊고 있었다. 손님이 묵을 방은 엉망인 상태였다. 서둘러! 서둘러야 해! 나는 허둥지둥 내 머리, 턱수염 그리고 옷에 묻은 먼지를 털어내고, 나의 손님을 맞이하러 갔다. 나는 악수를 하면서, 마치 오후 내내 편안하게 휴식을 취하고 있었던 것처럼 침착하게 보이려고 노력했다. 우리가 함께 저녁을 먹고 대화를 나누고서 마침내 나는 그를 그의 방으로 안내해야 했다. 방을 보았을 때 나는 안도의 한숨을 내쉬었다. 관리인들이 방을 충분히 깔끔하게 정리해둔 것이었다. 그리고 밤 동안 바퀴벌레들이 조용히 있어 준다면, 나의 손님은 편안하게 하룻밤을 쉴 수 있을 것이다.

① 우울한 → 화가 난
③ 기쁜 → 고마워하는
④ 평온한 → 짜증이 난
⑤ 기대하는 → 실망한

구문 [1행~2행] I **had** completely **forgotten** (that) he was coming // until I heard the housekeepers call: "The guest has arrived!"

(O: (that) he was coming / V′: heard / O′: the housekeepers / C′: call)

과거완료(had forgotten)가 쓰여 '(그때까지) 죽 잊고 있었다'는 '계속'의 의미를 나타낸다. until이 이끄는 절의 동사 heard는 지각동사이므로 목적격보어에 원형부정사(v)나 현재분사(v-ing) 형태가 올 수 있다.

[5행~7행] I tried to look **as** calm **as if** I **had been resting** comfortably all afternoon // **as** I went through the shaking of hands.

「as+형용사 원급+as」는 동등비교 구문으로 '~만큼 …한'의 뜻이다. 「as if+가정법 과거완료」는 과거 사실의 반대(실제로 휴식을 취하고 있지 않았음)를 나타낸다. 세 번째 as는 '~하면서'라는 의미의 접속사이다.

어휘 **in an awful state** 엉망인 상태의 **in a panic** 허둥지둥, 공황상태에서 **go through** ~을 경험하다[겪다] **dine** 식사를 하다, 만찬을 들다 **converse** 대화를 나누다 **show A to B** A를 B로 안내하다 **breathe a sigh of relief** 안도의 한숨을 쉬다 **cockroach** 바퀴벌레

20 필자 주장 ③

소재 식품 성분 표시에 관한 정책 수정의 필요성

해설 필자의 주장이 담긴 주제문을 찾아야 한다. '자연산'이란 말이 식품 성분 표시에 무분별하게 쓰인다는 문제를 지적한 후, 이를 바로잡기 위해 FDA가 관련 정책을 정비할 필요가 있다는 필자의 주장이 마지막 문장의 needs to 이하에 잘 드러나 있다. 따라서 필자의 주장으로 가장 적절한 것은 ③이다.

해석 많은 식품의 통조림과 상자에 '자연산'이라는 말이 큰 글씨로 적혀 있다. 하지만 이 말은 이따금 소비자들에게 안에 있는 식품에 대한 잘못된 생각을 전달한다. 비록 법은 모든 식품의 성분 표시가 진실한 정보를 제공할 것을 요구하지만, 항상 그렇게 되는 것은 아니다. '자연산'이라는 말은 식품 성분 표시를 담당하는 기관인 FDA(미국 식품의약국)에 의해 규정되어 있지 않다. 그래서 어떤 식품 업자라도 포장에 그 말을 사용할 수 있다. 가장 질이 낮은 정크 푸드조차도 틀림없이 그 안에 자연적인 어떤 것을 포함하고 있다. 따라서 이런 식품을 만드는 제조업자들은 포장에 '자연산'이라는 말을 사용할 수 있다. 주제문 FDA는 식품 성분 표시에 관한 현재의 정책을 수정하고, 포장에 있는 정보가 실제 내용물을 반영해야 한다고 요구하는 법을 만들 필요가 있다.

구문 [5행~7행] The word "natural" has not been defined by the FDA, the agency in charge of food labels.

콤마(,)는 the FDA와 the agency in charge of food labels가 동격 관계임을 나타낸다.

[10행~13행] The FDA needs / to modify its current policy on food labeling and (to) make *a law* (**requiring** that the information on the package / (should) **reflect** the actual contents).

동사 needs의 목적어인 두 개의 to부정사구(to modify ~, (to) make ~)가 접속사 and로 연결되어 있다. requiring 이하는 a law를 수식하는 현재분사구이며, 요구를 나타내는 동사 require의 목적어절의 내용이 '~해야 한다'는 당위성을 내포하고 있으므로 동사는 '(should) 동사원형'을 쓴다.

어휘 **require** 요구하다, 필요로 하다 **label** 성분 표시; 꼬리표; (상)표 **define** 규정하다; 정의하다 **in charge of** ~을 담당하고[책임지고] 있는 **junk food** 정크 푸드(건강에 좋지 않은 것으로 여겨지는 인스턴트 음식이나 패스트푸드) **certain** 틀림없는, 확실한; 어떤 **modify** 수정[변경]하다 **current** 현재의, 현행의; 흐름 **policy** 정책, 방침 **reflect** 반영하다; 반사하다 **content** 내용(물); 목차; 만족하는

21 밑줄 함의 ③

소재 Wrigley의 특별한 사업 재능

해설 Wrigley는 비누를 팔면서 베이킹파우더를 무료로 주었고, 베이킹파우더의 수요가 더 크다는 것을 확인한 후에는 베이킹파우더 판매로 사업을 전환했다. 그러다가 무료로 제공한 껌이 인기를 얻자 다시 껌 사업으로 방향을 바꿔 성공하게 되었다. 이러한 Wrigley의 재능은 ③ '사업 기회를 재빨리 포착하는 능력'으로 이해할 수 있다.

해석 29세에 William Wrigley는 자신의 사업을 시작했다. 주제문 무한한 열정과 에너지 말고도, 그는 특별한 재능 하나가 있었다. 그는 비누 판매를 시작했다. Wrigley 비누를 취급하는 상인에 대한 장려책으로 그는 무료 베이킹파우더를 상인에게 제공했다. 베이킹파우더가 비누보다 더 인기가 있다는 것이 밝혀지자, 그는 재빨리 베이킹파우더 사업으로 전환했다. 그러고 나서 Wrigley는 베이킹파우더 한 통에 무료 껌을 상인들에게 제공하는 아이디어를 생각해냈다. 또 다시 그 제공(품)이 큰 성공을 거두었다. 이제 그는 회사의 방향을 바꿀 시기라고 결론을 내렸다. 망설임 없이 그는 자신의 이름이 들어간 껌을 판매하기 시작했다. 곧, 그의 제품은 매우 인기를 얻었다.

① 다른 사업체들과 협력하는 능력
② 적은 자본으로 창업하는 자신감
④ 고객의 마음에 드는 낮은 가격을 정하는 권한
⑤ 사업 실패에 대한 두려움을 극복하려는 결의

어휘 **besides** ~외에; 게다가 **unlimited** 무제한의 **enthusiasm** 열정, 의욕 **possess** 소유하다 **incentive** 장려[우대]책 **merchant** 상인 **switch** 바꾸다 **hesitation** 망설임, 주저함 [선택지 어휘] **capacity** 능력 **cooperate** 협동하다 **confidence** 자신감 **capital** 자본; 수도; 대문자 **capture** 포착하다; 붙잡다 **appeal** 마음에 들다; 간청하다; 호소하다

22 글의 요지 ⑤

소재 친구를 사귀는 방법

해설 친구를 사귀는 방법에 대해 질문을 던진 뒤 답을 하는 구조의 글이다. 중반부에 친구를 사귀는 올바른 태도를 가져야 한다는 내용(So the trick ~ the right attitude.)에 이어서 편안하고 자신감 있는 태도를 보이는 방법이 구체적으로 나열되어 있으므로, 글의 요지로 가장 적절한 것은 ⑤이다.

해석 새 친구를 사귀는 적절한 방법이 있을까? 그렇다. 주제문 당신이 필요한 친구를 이미 모두 가진 것처럼 행동하라. 이것은 이상한 충고처럼 보일지 모른다. 그러나 어떤 이유에서인지, 십 대들은 친구가 되길 간절히 원하는 것처럼 보이는 사람들에 대해 관심을 잃는다. 아마도 십 대들은 당신이 그들과 친구가 되고 싶어 하면 당신에게 분명 뭔가 잘못된 게 있을 거라고 생각한다. 주제문 따라서 비결은 올바른 태도를 보이는 것이다. 완전히 여유롭고 자신감 있게 행동하라. 느긋하지만 (상대방을) 존중하는 태도를 지녀라. 자신감은 넘치지만 록 스타인 양 거만하지 않도록 하라. 호기심이 많지만 어린 강아지처럼 행동하지 마라. 공손하지만 너무 멀지 않게 느껴지도록 하라. 그리고 당신이 기분 좋다는 것을 보여줄 만큼 충분히 미소를 짓되, 정신이 이상한 것처럼 보일 정도로 웃지는 마라. 당신의 태도를 잘 조절하면 새로운 친구는 쉽게 다가올 것이다.

구문 [10행~12행] And smile **enough to show** that you feel good, // but (do) **not** (smile) **so much as** / (enough) to suggest (that) you're crazy.

「enough to-v」는 'v할 만큼 충분히'란 뜻이다. 「not so much as」는 '~정도는 아닌, ~처럼 많지는 않은'이란 뜻으로 as much as(~처럼 많이)의 부정형이다.

어휘 **proper** 적절한, 제대로 된 **turn A off** A가 관심을 잃게[끄게] 하다 **desperate to-v** v하길 간절히 원하는 **figure** 생각[판단]하다; 숫자; 모양, 형태 **attitude** 태도 **at ease** 편안한 **confident** 자신감 있는 **relaxed** 느긋한, 여유 있는 **respectful** 존중하는, 존경심을 보이는 **arrogance** 거만, 오만 **distant** 거리를 두는, 다정하지 않은; 먼 **suggest** 시사[암시]하다; 제안하다 **tune** 조절[조정]하다; 곡조, 선율

23 글의 주제 ④

소재 어린이 칭찬 방법

해설 어린이를 칭찬할 때는 진심이 담긴 칭찬을 해야 하고, 포괄적인 칭찬보다는 특정 과업에 대해 구체적인 칭찬을 하는 것이 좋다고 조언하는 내용이므로 글의 주제로 가장 적절한 것은 ④ '어린이를 칭찬하는 효과적인 방법'이다.

해석 우리는 어른의 칭찬이 어린이들에게 도움이 될 수 있다고 알고 있지만, 심리학자들은 부적절한 칭찬은 어린이들에게 상처를 줄 수도 있다고 우리에게 말한다. 보통 헛스윙을 하는 리틀 리그의 야구 선수가 파울볼을 날린다고 가정해보자. "좋은 시도였어."가 진심 어린 적절한 칭찬이다. 그러나 "아주 좋아!" 같은 언급은 당신이 그 아이가 경기를 잘할 수 있다고 생각하지 않는다는 메시지를 보낸다. 좋은 점수에 대한 지나친 칭찬은 학습한 내용보다 점수가 더 중요한 것처럼 보이게 만들 수 있다. 그리고 "그 퍼즐 맞춘 거 잘했어."와 같이 특정 과업에 대한 칭찬이 "똑똑한 아이구나."와 같은 언급보다 더 의의가 많은 것임을 명심하라. 주제문 어린이들의 노력을 칭찬하여 그들을 격려하되, 반드시 당신의 칭찬이 진실되고 건설적이게 하라.

① 어린이를 칭찬하는 것의 장점과 단점
② 어린이의 자신감을 발달시키는 방법
③ 칭찬으로 전달되는 숨겨진 메시지
⑤ 어린이를 너무 많이 칭찬하는 것의 위험

구문 [5행~7행] But a comment like "That's terrific!" sends the message that you don't think // (that) the child is capable of playing well.

that ~ well은 the message를 부연 설명하는 동격절이다. think와 the child 사이에 명사절 접속사 that이 생략되어 있다.

[7행~9행] *Too much praise* (for good grades) can **make** grades **seem** more important than what is learned.
(S: Too much praise, V: make, O: grades, C: seem ~)

make는 사역동사로 목적격보어로 원형부정사가 오며 'O가 v하게 하다'로 해석한다.

어휘 **praise** 칭찬 **psychologist** 심리학자 **inappropriate** 부적절한 (↔ **appropriate** 적절한) **swing and miss** 헛스윙하다 **foul ball** 파울볼 **sincere** 진심 어린, 진정한 **comment** 언급, 논평 **terrific** 아주 좋은, 멋진 **be capable of** ~을 할 수 있다 **grade** 성적; 학년; 등급 **specific** 구체적인; 특정한 **task** 임무, 과제 **put together** 조립하다; 합하다 **encourage** 격려하다 **constructive** 건설적인 [선택지 어휘] **pros and cons** 장단점; 찬반양론 **confidence** 자신(감); 신뢰 **convey** 전달하다

24 글의 제목 ②

소재 유대감을 키워주는 대면 소통

해설 대면 소통은 진정한 대화를 발전시키고 신뢰와 유대를 강화시키는 힘이 있으므로 이를 회피하지 말라는 내용의 글이다. 따라서 이 글의 제목으로 가장 적절한 것은 ② '대면 소통이 유대를 만든다'이다.

해석 기술상으로 추진되는 업무의 이 현대 시대에, 전자 장치를 통한 의사소통을 위해 실제 물리적인 인간의 교류에 대한 생각을 피하는 것은 쉬울 수 있다. 우리는 이메일을 보내고 소셜 미디어를 사용하고 문자를 보내고 전화로 이야기하지만, 이 모든 것들이 한 가지 일반적인 구성요소인 실제의, 대면식 인간 교류를 놓치고 있음을 자주 망각한다. 주제문 누군가와 실제 대화를 해나가는 것은 당신이 그들에게 결코 대면하여 말을 걸게 되지 않는다면 훨씬 더 어렵다. 당신의 팀에 관해서는, 당신들은 적어도 서로를 향해 적절한 정도의 신뢰를 쌓을 필요가 생기게 될 것이므로, 주제문 대면 교류가 서로 의지하며 함께 일하게 될 두 사람 간의 신뢰의 유대를 더욱 강화하는 데 도움이 될 수 있을 때에 왜 이것(=대면 교류)을 포기하는가? 직접 교류를 피하는 것은 이러한 자연스러운 과정이 자연스럽게 전개되지 못하도록 명백히 방해할 수 있다.

① 신뢰를 쌓기 위해 대화를 이용하는 방법
③ 대면 소통의 장점과 단점
④ 온라인 소통 대(對) 대면 소통
⑤ 대면 소통: 장벽 허물기

구문 [7행~9행] Developing a real conversation with someone(S) is(V) **far** more difficult // if you never **get to speak** to them face to face.
동명사구 Developing ~ someone이 주어이고 is가 동사이다. far는 비교급을 강조하는 표현 중 하나로 '훨씬'의 의미를 가진다. get to-v는 'v하게 되다'의 뜻이다.

어휘 **drive** 추진시키다; 몰다 **push aside** ~에 대한 생각을 피하다; 옆으로 옮기다 **interaction** 상호작용, 교류 **via** ~을 통하여 **device** 장치, 기구 **component** 구성요소 **face-to-face** 대면하는 **when it comes to A** A에 관한 한 **decent** 괜찮은, 적절한; 품위 있는, 예의 바른 **serve** 도움이 되다, 기여하다 **strengthen** 강화하다 **bond** 유대 **rely on** ~에 의지하다 **in-person** 직접의 **definitely** 명백히, 확실히 **hinder** 방해하다 **run its course** 자연스럽게 전개되다 [선택지 어휘] **barrier** 장애물, 장벽

25 도표 이해 ③

소재 대학과 기업 간 소셜 미디어 사용 비교

해설 500개의 기업 중 19퍼센트가 온라인 비디오를 이용하고 있는데, 이는 게시판(27퍼센트)과 소셜 네트워킹(21퍼센트)에 이어 세 번째로 높은 이용률이다. 따라서 ③은 도표와 일치하지 않는다.

해석 **〈대학과 기업 간 소셜 미디어 사용 비교〉**

주제문 위 도표는 대학 입학처와 Inc. 500, 즉 미국에서 가장 빠르게 성장하고 있는 500개 기업에서 사용되는 다양한 유형의 소셜 미디어의 비율을 비교한 것이다. ① 대학의 29퍼센트는 블로그를 사용하였는데 이는 대학에서 가장 많이 선택한 것으로, 소셜 네트워킹이 23퍼센트, 게시판이 21퍼센트로 그 뒤를 이었다. ② 한편 500개 기업은 17퍼센트만이 블로그를 사용한 데 반해, 가장 많이 선택한 것은 게시판으로 그보다 10퍼센트 포인트 더 많은 수가 사용했다. ③ 500개 기업은 온라인 비디오를 대학보다 5퍼센트 포인트 더 많이 사용하였고, 이것은 기업이 네 번째로 많이 사용한 소셜 미디어 형식이었다. ④ 팟캐스팅(인터넷이나 휴대용 디지털 기기로 콘텐츠를 다운로드하는 시스템)은 500개 기업이 가장 적게 사용한 소셜 미디어 형식으로, 단 5퍼센트만 사용하였다. ⑤ 한편, 대학에서는 10퍼센트가 팟캐스팅을 사용했고, 3퍼센트만이 위키(인터넷 사용자들이 내용을 편집할 수 있는 웹사이트)를 사용하였다.

구문 [12행~14행] Podcasting was the least used form of *social media* (used by the Inc. 500), **with** *only 5% of them* **using** it.
「with + 목적어(명사(구)) + 분사」 구문은 부대상황을 나타내는 분사구문으로, 목적어와 분사의 관계가 능동이므로 현재분사(using)가 쓰였다.

어휘 **compare** 비교하다 **proportion** 비율 **admission** 입학; 입장; 승인 **corporation** (큰 규모의) 기업 **meanwhile** 한편; 그 동안에

26 내용 불일치 ①

소재 chuck wagon(취사 마차)의 이용

해설 chuck wagon은 대평원을 이동하는 이주민들에게 음식을 공급하는 마차에 붙여진 이름이라고 했으므로 ①이 글의 내용과 일치하지 않는다.

해석 ① 'Chuck wagon(취사 마차)'은 마차 행렬로 북미 대평원을 가로질러 이동하는 이주자들을 위해 음식과 취사도구를 운반하던 마차에 붙여진 이름이었다. ② 취사 마차는 먼 지역에 있는 카우보이와 벌목꾼들에게 음식을 공급하기 위해 이동하기도 했다. 마차 요리사는 냉장 보관 없이 서부의 여름 더위 속에서 두 달 동안 견뎌낼 충분한 음식을 운반해야 했다. ③ 따라서 신선한 야채와 달걀은 절대 운반되지 않았다. 오직 건조 음식만이 그러한 조건에서 견뎌낼 수 있었다. ④ 훌륭한 취사 마차 요리사는 콩, 감자, 빵, 쌀과 같은 고칼로리 음식으로 만든 한 솥 스튜로 카우보이들을 잘 먹였다. ⑤ 현대에 취사 마차는 일부 요리 경연대회, 행사 그리고 '취사 마차 경주'로 알려진 일종의 경마에서도 사용된다.

어휘 **chuck wagon** (목장용) 취사 마차 **supply** (복수형) 보급품[물자]; 공급하다 **settler** 이주민; 정착자 **wagon train** (서부 개척 시대의 기차처럼 길게 늘어선) 마차 행렬 **feed (fed-fed)** 음식을 먹이다 **logger** 벌목꾼 **remote** 멀리 떨어진; 원격의 **refrigeration** 냉장 (보관) **stew** 스튜(고기와 채소를 넣고 끓인 국물 있는 요리)

27 안내문 불일치 ③

소재 한국에 관한 영상 콘테스트 안내

해설 영어나 한국어로 된 영상을 선호하긴 하지만, 다른 언어로 된 영상도 한국어나 영어로 자세한 설명을 붙여 출품할 수 있다고 했으므로 안내문의 내용과 일치하지 않는 것은 ③이다.

해석

한국에 관한 영상 콘테스트

① 한국인 친구나 한국 음식에 관한 흥미 있는 영상을 만들 수 있다고 생각한다면 이 영상 콘테스트에 참가하고 싶으실 겁니다.

조건:
- ② 영상은 3분을 초과하면 안 됩니다.
- ③ 영어나 한국어로 제작된 영상이면 더 좋습니다.
(다른 언어로 된 영상은 반드시 한국어나 영어로 된 자세한 설명이 있어야 합니다.)

지원 방법:
- ④ 영상을 YouTube나 다른 합법적인 영상 공유 사이트에 업로드하세요.
- 외무부의 홈페이지 www.mofa.go.kr에서 지원서를 다운로드하고 2020년 8월 9일 오후 5시까지 제출해주세요.

수상작은 2020년 9월 30일에 발표될 것입니다. ⑤ 수상자에게는 개별적으로 통지될 것입니다.

어휘 **description** 설명, 서술; 묘사 **upload** 업로드하다 **legal** 합법적인 **application form** 지원서, 지원 양식 **the Ministry of Foreign Affairs** 외무부 **submit** 제출하다 **entry** 출품작 **notify** 알리다 **individually** 개별적으로, 개인적으로

28 안내문 일치 ⑤

소재 수학 경시대회 안내

해설 적정 등록비가 수납될 때까지 등록이 완료된 것으로 여겨지지 않는다는 것은 등록비를 납부해야 등록이 완료된다는 것과 같은 의미이다. 따라서 ⑤가 안내문의 내용과 일치한다.

해석

MIC 수학 경시대회

MIC 수학 경시대회는 고등학생을 대상으로 하는 행사입니다. ① 그것(=MIC 수학 경시대회)은 MIC 대학의 학부생들에 의해 조직되어 1981년 이래로 MIC 대학에서 매년 개최되고 있습니다. MIC 수학 경시대회가 모든 참가자들에게 도전적이고 흥미 있는 하루를 제공할 수 있기를 바랍니다.

② 경시대회 부문:
대수학, 기하학, 미적분학
(③ 모든 시험은 높은 수준의 비판적 사고를 필요로 하는 어려운 문제들을 출제합니다.)

온라인 등록:
- 등록 기한 (학생당 6달러): 2021년 2월 1일
- ④ 추가 등록 기한 (학생당 10달러): 2021년 2월 8일

⑤ 적정 등록비 수납까지 등록은 완료된 것으로 여겨지지 않습니다.(=등록비를 납부해야 등록이 완료됩니다.)

문의할 내용이나 하실 말씀이 있으면 mic.eure@email.com으로 경시대회 관리자들에게 이메일을 보내시기 바랍니다.

구문 [4행~6행] **Organized** by MIC undergraduate students, it **has been held** annually at MIC University since 1981.
Organized ~ students는 과거분사로 시작된 수동의 분사구문으로 의미상의 주어

는 it(=The MIC Mathematics Tournament)이다. 대회가 과거부터 현재까지 지속적으로 개최되어 온 것이고 주어와 동사의 관계가 수동이므로, 현재완료 수동태(has been held)가 쓰였다.

어휘 **undergraduate** 학부생 **annually** 해마다 **challenging** 도전적인; 어려운 **participant** 참가자 **category** 부문; 범주 **involve** ~을 필요로 하다[수반하다]; 연루시키다 **critical** 비판적인; 중요한 **registration** 등록 **deadline** 마감 기한 **consider** 여기다, 간주하다 **complete** 완료된; 완전한; 완료하다

29 밑줄 어법 ③

소재 감정을 가진 존재인 과학자

해설 ③ 문맥상 과학자들도 예술가들만큼 열정이 있다는 내용이어야 하므로 동등 비교를 나타내는 「as+원급+as(~만큼 …한)」 구문이 쓰여야 한다. 따라서 than은 as로 바꾸어 써야 한다.

오답 분석 ① 문맥상 동사 lessen을 수식하는 '많이'라는 뜻의 부사가 들어가야 하는 자리이므로 much가 바르게 쓰였다. 「as+원급+as possible」은 '가능한 한 ~하게'라는 뜻이다. ② 앞에 나오는 명사 men을 수식하는 분사로, men과 investigate의 관계가 능동이므로 현재분사를 쓴 것은 적절하다. ④ 문맥상 the universe를 받으므로 단수형 소유대명사 its가 바르게 쓰였다. ⑤ but 뒤에 생략된 주어는 These people, 즉 과학자들이며 이해할 대상도 과학자들 자신이므로 재귀대명사 themselves로 표현한 것은 적절하다.

해석 감정적인 편견을 통제하는 것은 최고의 과학자들이 자신의 감정이 연구에 미치는 영향을 가능한 한 많이 줄이기 위해 배우는 기술이다. 순수한 이성이라는 도구만을 사용하여 연구실에서 자연 세계를 연구하는 흰 가운을 입은 사람에 대한 생각은 잘못된 생각이다. 주제문 최고의 과학자들은 감정이 없는 존재가 아니라, 정확히 그 반대이다. 예술가들이 자신의 작품에 대해 열정적인 것만큼 최고의 과학자들도 (연구하고 있는) 자신의 주제에 대해 열정으로 가득 차 있다. 그들은 객관적인 사실에 만족하지 않는다. 그들은 모든 그것의 아름다움 속에서 만물을 바라보고자 한다. 이들은 비록 과학을 사용하지만, 그들의 심장과 영혼으로부터 분리된 정신을 가지고 있는 것이 아니라 그들 자신과 그들이 사는 세상을 이해할 길을 찾고 있는 전인적 인간이다.

어휘 **bias** 편견, 편향, 선입견 **lessen** 줄이다, 작게 하다 **reason** 이성, 사고력; 이유 **emotionless** 감정이 없는; 무감동의 **be filled with** ~로 가득 차다 **passion** 열정 **enthusiastic** 열성적인, 열심인 **cold fact** 있는 그대로의 사실 **universe** 만물; 우주; 세계 **inhabit** 살다, 거주하다

30 네모 어휘 ②

소재 꿈의 비논리성

해설 (A) 꿈에서는 과거의 일이 현재처럼 나타나기도 한다는 내용이 이어지므로 시간 개념이 '달라진다'는 뜻의 altered가 적절하다. fix는 '고정시키다'의 뜻이다.
(B) 현실에서 동시에(at the same time) 일어나는 것이 불가능한 일도 꿈에서는 '동시에' 일어난다는 의미가 알맞다. spontaneously는 '자발적으로'란 의미이다.
(C) 꿈에서는 공간적 법칙이 적용되지 않아 '먼' 장소로 순식간에 이동할 수 있다는 문맥이므로 distant가 알맞다. nearby는 '근처의, 가까운'의 뜻이다.

해석 주제문 꿈은 우리가 깨어 있는 현실을 지배하는 논리의 법칙을 따르지 않는다. 예를 들어, 시간의 범주가 (A) 달라진다. 죽었다고 알고 있는 사람이 살아 있는 모습을 보기도 하고, 실제로는 여러 해 전에 일어났던 일에 휘말리기도 한다. 현실에서는 도저히 동시에 일어날 수 없는 두 가지 이상의 사건이 (B) 동시에 일어나는 꿈을 꾸기도 한다. 또한, 꿈은 공간적 법칙에도 거의 주의를 기울이지 않는다. 우리가 순식간에 (C) 먼 곳으로 이동하거나, 동시에 두 장소에 있거나, 두 사람을 하나로 합치는 것은 간단하다. 실로, 꿈에서 우리는 논리가 전혀 힘이 없는 새로운 세계를 창조한다.

구문 [9행~11행] **It**'s simple *for us* / **to move** to a distant place in an instant, **to be** in two places at once, or **to fuse** two persons into one.

가주어 It이 or로 연결된 세 개의 진주어(to move ~, to be ~, to fuse ~)를 대신하는 구문이다. for us는 의미상 주어를 나타낸다.

어휘 **logic** 논리 **govern** 지배하다, 통치하다 **waking** 깨어 있는 **category** 범주 **be[become, get] involved in** ~에 휘말리다, 연루되다 **occur** (일이) 일어나다, 생기다 **possibly** 《부정문에서》 도저히, 아무리 해도 **at the same time** 동시에 **pay attention to A** A에 주의를 기울이다 **in an instant** 즉시, 눈 깜짝할 사이에 **at once** 동시에; 즉시 **fuse A into B** A를 B로 합치다 **indeed** 실로, 참으로

31 빈칸 추론 ⑤

소재 미국의 자동차 제조업과 옥수수 수출업의 경쟁 관계

해설 미국의 자동차 제조업과 옥수수 수출업의 관계에 관한 내용이다. 빈칸 뒤에 정부가 자동차 제조업체를 지원하면 옥수수 재배 농부가 피해를 본다(If Detroit factories ~ Iowa farmers will suffer.)는 내용이 나오므로 둘은 ⑤ '경쟁' 관계임을 알 수 있다.

해석 미국에서 자동차가 생산되는 한 방식은 디트로이트 공장에서 그것들을 조립하는 것이다. 또 하나의 방식은 아이오와에서 그것들을 기르는 것이다. 그게 어떤 방식으로 작동하는가? 아주 간단하다. 우선, 아이오와의 농부가 옥수수를 재배하면 옥수수는 배에 실려 해외로 운송되고, 곧 그 배는 외국에서 만든 새 자동차를 가득 싣고 돌아온다. 주제문 경제학자 David Freedman에 의하면, 그것이 디트로이트 자동차 공장 노동자와 아이오와 농부가 사실상 서로 경쟁하는 이유이다. 만약 디트로이트 공장이 관세 및 무역 장벽을 통해 증대된 정부의 보호를 받게 되면, 이는 수입차 판매 감소로 이어져서 아이오와 농부들은 (옥수수 수출 감소로) 어려움을 겪게 된다. 그렇기 때문에 자동차 제조업체에 대한 더 많은 정부 지원이 반드시 모든 사람의 이익과 들어맞는 것은 아니다.

① 조화 ② 거래 ③ 동업자 관계 ④ 일치

구문 [1행~2행] *One way* [that automobiles are produced in the in the States] / is by building them(=automobiles) in factories in Detroit.
(S: One way, V: is)

문장의 주어인 One way가 관계부사 that이 이끄는 절의 수식을 받아 길어진 형태이다.

어휘 **automobile** 자동차 **load A onto[into] B** A를 B에 싣다 *cf.* **load A (up) with B** A에게 B를 가득 안겨주다 **overseas** 해외로; 외국의 **economist** 경제학자 **protection** 보호 **tariff** 관세《외국 물품에 부과하는 세금》 **trade barrier** 무역 장벽 **import** 수입하다(↔ **export**) **assistance** 지원, 도움 **manufacturer** 제조자[업체] **not necessarily** 반드시 ~은 아닌 **interest** 이익; 이자; 흥미 [선택지 어휘] **be in partnership with** ~와 동업자[동반자] 관계이다 **be in competition with** ~와 경쟁하다

32 빈칸 추론 ③

소재 모방에 불과한 유아기의 몸짓언어

해설 빈칸 문장이 that is(다시 말해)로 시작하므로 앞 내용을 재진술하고 있음을 알 수 있다. 빈칸 앞 문장에서 아기들이 함께 놀이에 참여한 것처럼 보이는 행동은 모방에 불과한 것이라고 했고 빈칸 뒤에서도 놀이 활동 시 친구들은 대개 '장난감'으로 다뤄지고, 웃는 것도 독립적인 반응이라고 했다. 이러한 내용을 종합해볼 때, 아기들의 몸짓언어는 ③ '진정한 사회적 상호 작용'이라고 볼 수 없다고 추론할 수 있다.

해석 만약 당신이 함께 앉아 서로를 향해 웃고 있는 두 아기를 본다면, 가장 먼저 무슨 생각을 떠올리겠는가? 부모들은 좀 더 큰 아이들과 어른들 사이에서라면 친근한 인사로 여겨질 수 있는 몸짓언어를 (아기들이) 주고받고 있는 것을 자신들이 보고 있다고 종종 생각한다. 주제문 그러나 이렇게 매우 어린 단계에서는, 서로 놀이에 참여한 것처럼 보이는 아기들의 행동은 모방에 불과한 것일 가능성이 크다. 다시 말해, 그것은 진정한 사회적 상호 작용이 아니다. 생의 가장 초기 단계에서의 놀이 활동은 보통 개별적으로 이루어지는 것으로, 다른 아기들은 대개 '장난감'으로 다뤄진다. 미소는 독립적인 반응일지도 모르는데, 아기가 흥미로운 사물을 보고 느끼는 즐거움을 나타낸다. 한 아기가 울기 시작하면 곁에 있는 아기도 종종 안절부절못하게 되지만, 이것은 진정한 공감이라기보다 불쾌한 소리 때문에 일어나는 불안일 가능성이 더 크다.

① 단순한 역할놀이 ② 개별적인 행동 ④ 지적 발달 ⑤ 솔직한 감정 표현

구문 [11행~13행] A smile may be an independent reaction, / **reflecting** *the amusement* [(that) a baby feels ●] / at the sight of an interesting object.
reflecting 이하는 A smile을 의미상 주어로 하는 부대상황의 분사구문이다. a baby feels는 the amusement를 수식하는 관계대명사절로 the amusement는 feels의 목적어에 해당한다.

어휘 **exchange** 교환(하다) **consider** ~로 여기다[생각하다]; 고려하다 **engage A in B** A를 B에 참여시키다 **be likely to-v** v할 가능성이 있다, v하기 쉽다 **nothing more than** ~에 불과한, ~에 지나지 않는 **imitation** 모방, 모조품 **individually** 개별적으로, 각각 따로 *cf.* **individual** 각각의; 개인의 **treat A as B** A를 B로 여기다 **largely** 주로, 대체로 **independent** 독립적인; 별개의 **amusement** 즐거움, 재미 **companion** 친구; 동행 **discomfort** 불편; 불쾌, 불안 **unpleasant** 불쾌한, 싫은 **genuine** 진심의; 진짜인, 진품의 **sympathy** 동정(심); 공감 [선택지 어휘] **role playing** 역할놀이 **interaction** 상호 작용 **intellectual** 지적인; 지능의

33 빈칸 추론 ①

소재 스트레스가 남녀의 감정 판단에 미치는 영향

해설 스트레스가 남성과 여성의 뇌에 미치는 영향이 정반대라는 내용의 글이다. 빈칸 문장은 스트레스가 '어떤' 능력에 영향을 미치는가에 관한 내용으로, 빈칸 이후에 타인의 감정을 정확히 판단하는 뇌의 능력이 남성에게서는 저하되었고 여성에게서는 증가했다고 했으므로, 빈칸에는 ① '감정을 정확하게 읽어내는'이 들어가는 것이 가장 적절하다.

해석 주제문 어느 신경학 실험에서 스트레스에 대한 남성의 반응이 한 가지 특정 측면에서 여성의 반응과 정반대인 것으로 나타났다. 참가자들은 처음에 의도적으로 매우 스트레스를 받은 다음, 사진 속 얼굴에 나타난 감정을 판단하도록 요청받았다. 남성과 여성의 감정을 정확하게 읽어내는 능력에 스트레스가 영향을 미치는 방식에는 현저한 차이가 있었다. (스트레스를 받은 상황에서) 여성은 더 정확해졌고 남성은 더 나빠졌다. 뇌에서 '얼굴표정을 판단하는' 부위의 활동이 남성에게서는 느려졌는데, 이것은 스트레스가 타인의 감정을 정확하게 판단하는 남성의 능력을 저하시킴을 나타낸다. 그러나 스트레스를 받는 것은 여성의 뇌가 그 '얼굴 표정을 읽는' 부위에 불을 밝히게 했다(=그 부위의 활동을 활발하게 했다). 이것은 스트레스를 많이 받는 상황에서 타인과 유대감을 형성하는 것이 여성에게 있어 진화상의 생존 욕구임을 나타낸다.
② 미래를 정확히 예측하는
③ 갈등에서 무사히 벗어나는
④ 자신의 스트레스 수준을 빠르게 낮추는
⑤ 다른 사람의 감정에 직접적으로 영향을 미치는

구문 [6행~7행] There was a striking difference / between *the way* [stress affected *their ability* (to interpret emotions correctly)].
[ ] 부분은 관계부사절로, 선행사 the way와 관계부사 how는 같이 쓰이지 않으므로 how가 생략되었다.
[9행~12행] *Activity* (in the "face-assessing" part of the brain) slowed down in the men, / **indicating that** stress reduces *their ability* (to correctly assess other people's feelings).
분사구문인 indicating that ~은 which indicates that ~으로 바꿔서 생각하면 이해하기 쉽다. 이때 which는 앞의 절 전체를 가리킨다.
[13행~15행] This indicates // that **it**'s an evolutionary survival impulse in women / **to bond** with others in times of great stress.
it은 가주어이고 to bond ~ great stress가 진주어이다.

어휘 **experiment** 실험(하다) **response to** ~에 대한 반응 **the opposite of** ~의 정반대의 것 **respect** 측면; 존경 **deliberately** 의도적으로, 고의로 **striking** 현저한, 눈에 띄는 **accurate** 정확한 *cf.* **accurately** 정확하게 **assess** 판단하다, 평가하다(=evaluate) **indicate** 나타내다, 보여주다; 가리키다 **light up** 불을 밝히다, 환하게 하다 **evolutionary** 진화의; 발전의 **impulse** 욕구, 충동 **bond with** ~와 유대감을 형성하다

34 빈칸 추론 ③

소재 농경의 옛 풍미와 현대의 풍요로움

해설 바로 앞 문장에서 농경의 '구식 풍미와 현대의 풍요로움을 둘 다 가질 수는 없다', 즉 일거양득 할 수 없다고 했으므로, 이에 어울리는 속담은 ③ '케이크를 갖기도 하고 먹기도 할 수는 없다.'이다.

해석 농경의 현대화의 결과, 오늘날의 농장은 대단히 공장처럼 보인다. 식량 생산과 유사 농경 사업은 국가에 식량을 공급할 잠재력을 갖고 있다. 그러나 모든 사람들이 농장에서 일어난 변화에 만족하는 것은 아니다. 어떤 사람들은 농장 공장의 닭에서 나온 계란에는 구식 유형의 풍미가 결여돼 있다고 말한다. 과일과 채소는 더 이상은 맛 때문에 재배되지 않고 기계식 추수를 견딜 수 있는 능력 때문에 재배된다. 구식의 풍미와 현대의 풍요로움 간의 선택은 하기 쉬운 것은 아니다. 많은 사람들은 차라리 구식을 유지하려는 반면 다른 사람들은 새로운 방식을 선호한다. 주제문 분명한 점은 구식 풍미와 현대의 풍요로움을 둘 다 가질 수는 없다는 것이다. 속담에 이르기를, "케이크를 갖기도 하고 먹기도 할 수는 없다."
① 필요는 발명의 어머니이다.
② 선행은 선행으로 보답 받는다. (가는 말이 고우면 오는 말도 곱다.)
④ 울타리 반대편의 풀이 더 푸르다. (남의 떡이 더 커 보인다.)
⑤ 당신이 아는 악마가 당신이 모르는 악마보다 낫다. (구관이 명관이다.)

구문 [8행~10행] Fruits and vegetables are **no longer** grown for flavor (A) **but** for *their ability* (to stand mechanical harvesting) (B).
「not A but B (A가 아니라 B)」 구문의 변형으로, no longer는 '더 이상 ~ 않다'의 뜻이다.

어휘 **modernization** 현대화 **agriculture** 농업 *cf.* **agricultural** 농업의 **potential** 잠재적인 **feed** 먹이다; 공급하다 **take place** 일어나다, 발생하다 **lack** 부족하다, 결핍되다 **old-fashioned** 구식의 **flavor** 맛, 풍미 **stand** 견디다 **mechanical** 기계의 **abundance** 풍요로움, 풍부 **keep to** ~에서 벗어나지 않다 **proverb** 속담 [선택지 어휘] **deserve** ~을 받을 만하다

35 무관한 문장 ③

소재 국가에 따른 지진 피해 차이

해설 비슷한 시기에 두 국가에서 일어난 지진의 피해가 차이나는 이유를 설명한 글이다. 칠레의 지진 규모가 더 컸음에도 불구하고 아이티에 비해 피해가 적었던 이유는 재난에 대한 대비가 달랐기 때문이었다. 인구과밀과 관련한 인명 피해를 언급한 ③은 얼핏 보면 앞 문장의 사망자 수와 연관된 것처럼 보이지만, 뒤에 이어지는 문장들은 국가의 부와 정치 수준에서 피해의 차이가 비롯되었다는 내용이므로 ③은 문맥에서 벗어난 문장이다.

해석 소규모 지진이 때로 대규모 지진에 비해 더 많은 피해를 야기하는 건 왜인가? 2010년 2월 27일, 칠레가 세계에서 규모가 가장 큰 지진 중 하나에 의해 타격을 받았다. 그 지진은 리히터 척도 8.8을 기록했고, 이것은 NASA(미 항공우주국)가 주장하길 지축이 움직일 정도로 강력한 것이다. 이런 사실을 고려할 때, 이 재난으로 인한 사망자 수가 단지 800명에 그쳤다는 것은 정말 놀랍다. 반면, 아이티에서는 불과 몇 주 전에 훨씬 약한 지진이 20만 명의 목숨을 앗아갔다. 인구과밀은 자연재해보다 생명에 훨씬 큰 위협이 될 수 있다. 주제문 이 커다란 차이의 이유는 간단하다. 칠레는 잘 운영되는 현대 민주국가로, 국가의 부(富)와 법률이 재난을 견딜 수 있도록 건물이 건축되는 것을 보장하고 있다. 반면에, 아이티는 오랫동안 몹시 가난했고, 정부는 부패했으며, 건물은 수준 이하였다.

구문 [4행~6행] **It** registered *8.8 on the Richter scale*, // **which** (NASA claims) is strong enough to push Earth off its axis.
It은 앞서 언급된 one of the world's biggest-ever earthquakes를 뜻하고, which의 선행사는 8.8 on the Richter scale이다. NASA claims는 삽입절이다.

어휘 **earthquake** 지진 **strike** (세게) 치다; 타격을 주다 **register** (기계가 저절로) 기록하다; 등록하다 **claim** 주장하다 **push A off B** A를 B에서 밀어 떨어뜨리다 **axis** (중심) 축 **considering** ~을 고려[생각]하면 **astonish** 깜짝 놀라게 하다 **death toll** (재난 · 전쟁 등에 의한) 사망자 수 **overpopulation** 인구과밀 **threat** 위협 **well-functioning** 제대로 기능하는 **modern** 현대의 **democracy** 민주국가; 민주주의 **guarantee** 보장하다; 보장, 보증서 **construct** 건설하다 **withstand** 견뎌내다 **desperately** 몹시; 절망적으로; 필사적으로 **corrupt** 부패한 **substandard** 수준 이하의, 열악한

36 글의 순서 ④

소재 성공 경험이 원숭이에게 미치는 영향

해설 주어진 글에 글의 주제가 제시되어 있으므로 그에 대한 부연설명을 논리적인 순서로 연결한다. 주어진 글에서 성공을 하면 원숭이의 뇌에 강력한 영향을 준다고 하였는데, 그 구체적인 내용에 해당하는 것이 (C)에 나와 있다. 또한 지시어구를 파악하는 것도 순서를 결정하는 데 도움이 되는데 (C)의 made a mistake를 받는 (A)의 its mistake와, (A)의 dopamine in the brain을 지칭하는 (B)의 this pleasure-giving chemical을 통해 ④ '(C)－(A)－(B)'의 흐름을 추론할 수 있다.

해석 주제문 원숭이에게 간단한 시각 작업을 하도록 훈련시키던 연구자들은 성공이 원숭이의 뇌에 강력한 영향을 준다는 것을 발견했다.

(C) 원숭이가 작업을 정확하게 수행했을 때, 뇌의 신경 과정이 더 빨라졌고 그것의 다음 과제에서 원숭이의 (과제 수행) 성과는 급상승했다. 그러나 원숭이가 실수를 하면 다음 과제에서 잘하지 못했다. 심지어 이전의 과제를 완전히 익힌 다음인데도 말이다.

(A) 바꿔 말해, 원숭이가 한 실수가 원숭이에게 핸디캡이 되었던 것이다. 수석 연구원이 말하길, 성공이 원숭이에게 벅찬 기쁨을 가져다주는데 이는 뇌 속 도파민의 급격한 증가 덕분이라고 한다.

(B) 인간뿐 아니라 원숭이에게도, 이 기쁨을 주는 화학물질은 보상으로 작용할 뿐만 아니라 또 다른 성공으로 이어지게 하는 자극이 되는 힘으로서의 역할을 한다.

구문 [1행~3행] Researchers(S) [who were **training** *monkeys* **to do** simple visual tasks] found(V) // that success **had a** *strong* **effect on** the monkeys' brains(O).

주격 관계대명사 who가 이끄는 관계사절의 수식을 받아 주어가 길어졌다. 「train+O+C(to-v)」는 'O가 v하도록 훈련시키다'란 뜻이다. 목적어 역할을 하는 that절 내의 「have a(n) ~ effect on ...」은 '…에 ~한 영향을 미치다'란 뜻이다.

[8행~10행] For monkeys, **as well as** humans, / this pleasure-giving chemical / acts **not only** as a reward / **but also** as *a stimulating force* [that leads to further success].

「B as well as A」, 「not only A but also B」는 모두 B를 더 강조하여 'A뿐만 아니라 B 역시'란 뜻이다.

어휘 **visual** 시각의, (눈으로) 보는 **task** 과제, 과업 **handicap** 핸디캡[불리한 조건]을 붙이다; (신체적 · 정신적) 장애 **a surge of** ~의 쇄도, 치밀어 오름 **sudden** 급격한, 갑작스러운 **chemical** 화학물질; 화학적인 **reward** 보상(하다), 보답(하다) **stimulating** 자극이 되는, 고무적인 **further** (**far**의 비교급) 더 이상의, 추가의 **neural** 신경의 **performance** 성과; 수행; 연기 **soar** 치솟다, 급증하다 **master** 완전히 익히다 **previous** 이전의

37 글의 순서 ②

소재 산불 이후 생태계의 회복과 변화

해설 주어진 글에서 산불 이후 생태계의 회복과 변화를 알아보기 위한 연구를 시작했다는 내용이 나오고 난 뒤, 산불로 훼손된 생태계가 회복되는 과정이 소개되고 있다. 글의 내용상 (B) 산불이 일부 지역만 파괴하고 다른 지역은 남겨 놓는다는 일반적인 원칙을 제시하고, 이것을 This phenomenon으로 받는 (A)가 이어져 산불 피해가 적은 지역에서 시작되는 생태계의 복원 과정이 나오고, (C)의 생태계가 복원된 뒤의 모습을 묘사하는 순서로 전개되는 것이 자연스러우므로 정답은 ② '(B)－(A)－(C)'이다.

해석 주제문 옐로스톤 국립공원의 73만 9천 에이커의 산림을 파괴한 1988년 산불 이후, 연구자들은 어떻게 생태계가 회복됐고 변화했는지 알아보기 위하여 생태계를 연구하기 시작했다.

(B) 그들은 산불의 영향이 여러 생태계에서 달라지지만, 몇 가지 일반적인 원칙이 적용된다는 것을 발견했다. 바람과 이용 가능한 연료에 따라, 산불은 일부는 훼손되지 않은 채 남겨두고 어떤 지역은 파괴하면서 모자이크 모양으로 타오른다.

(A) 이 현상은 (생태계) 회복에 매우 중요한데, 왜냐하면 훼손되지 않거나 약간만 타버린 산림 지역은 파괴된 지역에 다시 씨를 뿌리기 때문이다. 이것이 바로 1988년 산불 이후에 일어난 일이다.

(C) 땅까지 타버린 잔디는 땅속 뿌리로부터 다시 생성되었다. 들판은 곧 화려하고 붉은 잡초로 가득해졌고 어떤 희귀하고 작은 식물들도 잘 자라났다.

구문 [9행~10행] They found // **that**, while the effects of fire vary in different ecosystems, // some general principles apply.

found의 목적어 역할을 하는 that절은 「while이 이끄는 부사절＋주절」의 구조로 되어 있다. 여기서 while은 '양보'의 접속사로 쓰였다.

어휘 **wildfire** 산불 **acre** 에이커(약 4,047㎡, 땅을 재는 단위) **ecosystem** 생태계 **recover** 회복하다 **phenomenon** (복수형 **phenomena**) 현상 **critical** 매우 중요한, 결정적인 **untouched** 손상되지 않은; 손대지 않은 **patch** 땅 한 뙈기; 헝겊조각 **re-seed** 다시 씨를 뿌리다 **vary** 달라지다; 서로 다르다 **principle** 원칙 **apply** 적용되다; 지원하다 **depending on** ~에 따라 **available** 이용 가능한 **fuel** 연료 **mosaic** 모자이크 모양 **regenerate** 재생시키다, 재건하다 **bloom** 꽃; 개화; 꽃이 피다 **thrive** 번성하다

38 문장 넣기 ④

소재 장애인을 돕는 로봇 개발

해설 주어진 문장은 로봇이 물건을 옮기거나 현관에 나가 손님을 맞이하는 일을 할 수 있다는 내용이므로 집 안에서 자유롭게 이동할 수 있는 로봇이 개발되고 있다는 내용 다음에 들어가는 것이 적절하다. 따라서 정답은 ④이다.

해석 주제문 몇 가지 종류의 음성 작동 로봇이 장애인을 돕는 데 곧 이용 가능할지도 모른다. 이런 로봇 중 하나는 이미 개발되었는데, 탁상용 기계 장치다. 그것은 사람의 이를 닦아주거나 수프 깡통을 열어주는 것을 포함하여, 움직이지 않고 가만히 서있는 사람에 의해 행해질 수 있는 여러 가지 가사 일을 할 수 있다. 또한, 집 안에서 이 방에서 저 방으로 자유롭게 이동할 수 있는 로봇이 장애인을 위해 개발 중에 있다. 그것은 생활용품을 가져오거나 현관에 나가 손님을 맞이하는 것 같은 일을 할 수 있다. 또 다른 종류의 로봇은 장애인이 있는 사무실에서 유용할 것이다. 이 유형의 로봇은 서류 수납장을 열거나 컴퓨터에 USB를 꽂는 것 같은 사무를 하게 될 것이다.

어휘 **fetch** 가지고 오다; 불러오다 **voice-operated** 음성으로 작동되는 **disabled person** 장애인(=**person with a disability**) **desktop** 탁상용의 **chore** 가사, 허드렛일 **stand still** 움직이지 않고 가만히 서있다 **cabinet** 수납장, 캐비닛

39 문장 넣기 ①

소재 사회적 관행으로 하는 말

해설 주어진 문장의 these subjects는 첫 문장의 the weather, ~ or Myrna Loy's last picture를 가리키고, 이러한 주제들이 정보 제공의 가치가 없지만 아무 말도 안 하는 것은 무례하다는 내용이 ① 다음에 나와 있으므로 주어진 문장이 ①에 들어가야 흐름이 자연스럽다.

해석 티파티나 디너파티에 참석할 때, 우리 모두는 날씨든, Chicago White Sox의 (경기) 성적이든, Thomas Mann의 최신 서적이든 또는 Myrna Loy의 최신 영화든 그 어떤 것에 관해서든 말을 해야만 한다. 이러한 주제들에 대한 언급 중 유익한 것이

거의 없다는 것이 이러한 대화들의 전형적인 성격이다. 그럼에도 불구하고, 계속해서 아무 말도 안 하는 것은 '무례한' 것으로 여겨진다. 사실상, "좋은 아침입니다.", "날씨가 좋네요.", "다음번에 시내에 오면 한번 봅시다."와 같은 환영 인사와 작별 인사의 문제에 있어서 이러한 것들을 말하지 않는 것은 사교적인 실수로 여겨진다. 단지 말하지 않는 것이 예의에 어긋나기 때문에 우리가 말을 하는 수없이 많은 일상 상황들이 있다. 모든 사교 집단은 이러한 종류의 말에 대한 자기만의 형식이 있다. 주제문 이러한 사회적 관행들로부터 침묵을 방지하는 것이 그 자체로 말의 중요한 기능이며, 우리가 사회 안에서 '할 말이 있을' 때만 말하는 것이 완전히 불가능하다는 것을 추론하는 것이 가능하다.

구문 [1행~2행] It is typical of these conversations / that few of *the remarks* (made on these subjects) are informative.
It은 뒤에 나오는 that ~ informative를 받는 가주어이다. ( ) 부분은 과거분사 made가 이끄는 분사구로 앞에 있는 명사 the remarks를 수식한다.

[14행~18행] From these social practices / it(가주어) is possible / to infer **that**(진주어) the prevention of silence is itself an important function of speech, / and **that** it(가주어) is completely impossible / for us(의미상 주어) in society to talk only when we "have something to say."(진주어)
첫 번째 가주어 it의 진주어는 to infer ~ something to say이고, 두 번째 that절 안의 가주어 it의 진주어는 to talk ~ something to say이다. to infer의 목적어로 쓰인 두 개의 that절이 and로 연결되어 병렬구조를 이루고 있다.

어휘 **typical** 전형적인; 보통의 **remark** 언급(하다), 발언(하다) **informative** 유익한; 정보를 제공하는 **latest** 최신의, 최근의 **be regarded as** ~로 여겨지다 **rude** 무례한(= impolite) **remain** 계속 ~이다; 남다 **farewell** 작별(인사); 작별의 **social** 사교적인; 사회의 **numberless** 수없이 많은 **practice** 관행; 실행(하다); 연습(하다) **infer** 추론하다 **prevention** 방지, 예방(법) **function** 기능(하다) **completely** 완전히

40 요약문 완성 ④

소재 활동성 인식과 수명 사이의 관계

해설 과거에 자신이 또래보다 활동성이 떨어진다고 생각했던 사람들이 실제 활동량과 관계없이 사망 가능성이 더 높았던 것으로 나타났다는 연구 결과에 관한 글이다. 이는 활동적이지(active) 않다고 생각하는 것만으로도 수명을 단축시킬(shorten) 수 있다는 문장으로 요약할 수 있다.

해석 Stanford 대학의 Alia Crum과 그녀의 동료들은 20년이 넘는 시간을 거슬러 올라가 6만 명이 넘는 미국 성인들의 설문조사를 분석했다. 이 연구는 몇 가지 질문에 집중했다. "당신은 당신 나이의 다른 사람들보다 더 자주 걸어서 혹은 자전거를 타고 일터로 가고 있다고, 혹은 집 청소를 더 많이 한다고, 혹은 계단으로 더 빨리 다닌다고 하시겠습니까?" 신체적 활동, 나이, 체질량 지수, 만성 질병과 같은 요인에 대해 통제하기 위해 통계 모형을 이용하고 나서 그들은 2020년의 사망 기록을 보았는데, 이는 첫 번째 연구가 행해진 지 25년 후였다. 주제문 연구자들은 자신의 또래보다 신체 활동을 덜 수행한다고 생각했던 사람들이 (신체 활동을) 더 많이 한다고 생각했던 사람들보다 그 기간에 사망했을 가능성이 71퍼센트 더 높았음을 발견했다. 심지어 두 집단 모두 비슷한 활동 수준을 보였을 때조차도 말이다.

⬇

당신이 주변 사람들만큼 (A) 활동적이지 않다고 생각하는 것이 실제로 당신의 수명을 (B) 단축시킬 수 있다.

구문 [7행~11행] **Using** statistical models / to control for *factors* (like physical activity, age, body mass index and chronic illnesses), / they then looked at the death records in 2020, // **which** was 25 years after the first study took place.
Using ~ illnesses는 After they used ~ illnesses의 의미를 갖는 분사구문이다. which는 앞의 절(they then ~ in 2020) 내용 전체를 받는다.

[11행~15행] The researchers found // that *people*(S') [who thought // they performed fewer body activities than their peers] were(V') 71 percent more likely to die in that period / than *those* [who thought // **they did more**]~
목적어절의 주어 people이 관계사절의 수식을 받아 길어졌다. they did more는 they performed more body activities를 간단히 쓴 것으로, did는 performed를 받는 대동사이다.

어휘 **colleague** 동료 **analyze** 분석하다 **survey** 설문조사 **date back** (시대를) 거슬러 올라가다 **stair** 계단 **statistical** 통계의 **model** 모형 **factor** 요소, 요인 **body mass index** 체질량 지수 **chronic** 만성의 **take place** 일어나다, 발생하다 **peer** 또래, 동년배 **life span** 수명

41~42 장문 41 ④ 42 ⑤

소재 철저한 여행 준비

해설 41. 여행을 갈 때 짐은 시간을 충분히 들여서 꼼꼼하게 싸고, 예상치 못한 최악의 상황을 상정하여 이에 대비해 두라는 내용의 글이므로 제목으로 가장 적절한 것은 ④ '당신의 여행에 대한 모든 세부사항에 대비하라'이다.
① 여행을 즐기는 법을 배워라
② 해외여행으로 얻을 수 있는 것
③ 인생은 여행과 같으니 미리 계획하라
⑤ 첫 번째 계획이 실패할 경우에 대비하여 제2안을 개발하라

42. 필자는 작은 가방과 큰 가방을 준비하여, 작은 가방에는 필수품을 넣어 기내에 함께 가지고 탄다. 이는 큰 가방 하나만 준비했다가 잃어버렸을 경우의 '재앙'을 피하기 위한 방법이므로, 두 개의 가방 중 하나만 잃어버렸을 때는 '불편함' 정도만 있을 것이다. 따라서 (e) disaster를 (an) inconvenience로 바꿔 써야 한다.

해석 주제문 여행을 가기 위해 짐을 쌀 때, 전문적인 여행자들은 몇 단계를 습관이 될 때까지 반복하여 수행한다. 첫째로, 그들은 다가오는 여행을 위해 필요로 할 모든 것의 목록을 만든다. 그들은 자신의 (a) 기억력을 신뢰하지 않는다. 그들은 그것을 전부 적는다. 둘째로, 그들은 짐을 싸기 전에 미리 갖고 갈 모든 것을 펼쳐놓는다. (b) 준비는 전문가의 특징이다. 셋째로, 그들은 예정된 시간보다 한참 전에 공항을 향해 떠날 준비가 되도록 완전히 짐을 싼다. 전문적인 여행자들은 당신에게 충분한 시간이 허용되지 않아서 당신이 패닉 상태에서 짐을 싸면, 나중에 여행에서 불필요한 불편을 초래할 수 있는 물품들을 깜박하게 된다는 것을 알고 있다. 주제문 잘 여행하고 당신이 목적지에 도착할 가능성을 증가시키기 위해 쓸 수 있는 기법 중 하나는 (c) 예상치 못한 상황에 대비하는 것이다. 이것을 하려면 자문해보라. "이 여행에서 일어날 수 있는 가능한 최악의 일이 뭘까?" 전문 연사이자 세미나 리더로서 나에게 일어날 수 있는 최악의 일은 내 수하물이 분실되어 내가 연설 업무를 위해 필요한 옷과 세미나 자료 없이 도착하는 것일 것이다. 이러한 상황에 대비해 조심하기 위해 나는 내 모든 (d) 필수품을 작은 가방에 넣고 그것을 기내에 함께 가지고 가 결코 내 시야에서 벗어나지 않도록 한다. 큰 가방은 검사를 받을 수 있지만, 수송 중에 잃어버려도 손실은 그저 (e) 재앙(→ 불편)일 뿐이다. 이러한 사전 계획의 습관 때문에, 나는 수하물 연착이나 분실로 인해 해결할 수 없는 문제를 한 번도 겪어본 적이 없다.

구문 [14행~17행] **One** of *the techniques* [that you can use to travel well and increase the likelihood = that you will arrive at your destination] **is** to prepare for an unexpected situation.
주어는 One (of the techniques)이고 동사는 is이다. [ ]는 that이 이끄는 관계대명사절로 the techniques를 수식한다. [ ] 절에서 to 다음으로 동사원형 travel과 increase가 공통으로 이어지며 병렬구조를 이룬다. that you ~ destination은 the likelihood에 대한 동격절이다.

어휘 **over and over** 계속해서 **upcoming** 다가오는 **lay out** 펼치다 **in advance** 미리 **mark** 표시, 특징 **scheduled** 예정된 **inconvenience** 불편 **likelihood** 가능성 **destination** 목적지, 행선지 **luggage** 수하물 **engagement** 업무; 약속; 참여 **guard against** ~에 대비해 조심하다 **essential** 필수적인 것 **on board** 기내에, 탑승한 **in transit** 수송 중에 **baggage** 수하물

43~45 장문

43 ④ 44 ④ 45 ③

소재 책을 좋아하는 Lisa

해설 43. Lisa가 도서관에서 도서관 카드를 발급받는 (A) 다음에는 좋아하는 책을 빌리러 도서관 접수대로 갔다가 도서관 카드를 분실했음을 알게 되는 (D)가 와야 한다. 그 다음에는 집에 도착해서 한 소녀가 자신의 도서관 카드를 발견해 가져다 준 것을 알게 되는 (B)가 이어지고, 마지막에는 엄마와 다시 도서관에 책을 빌리러 간 Lisa가 도서관 카드를 찾아 준 소녀를 만나게 되는 (C)가 와야 내용의 전개가 자연스럽다. 따라서 알맞은 글의 순서는 ④ '(D)-(B)-(C)'이다.

44. (d)는 Lisa의 도서관 카드를 찾아준 소녀이고 나머지는 모두 Lisa를 가리킨다.

45. (C)에서 Lisa가 분실했던 도서관 카드를 찾은 후에 도서관에 가자는 엄마의 제안에 함께 도서관에 갔으므로 ③은 글의 내용과 일치하지 않는다.

해석 (A) Lisa는 책 읽기를 좋아했다. 엄마가 그녀를 서점으로 데리고 갈 때마다 그녀는 두 권의 책을 사곤 했다. 그녀가 잠자리에 들 때쯤, Lisa는 이미 그중에 한 권을 읽었다. 다음날 엄마는 Lisa에게 "네게 너 자신의 도서관 카드를 갖게 하는 것이 필요한 것 같구나."라고 말했다. "와! 저는 언제나 도서관 카드를 갖고 싶었어요."라고 Lisa가 외쳤다. 다음날 ① 방과 후에 엄마는 (a) 그녀(=Lisa)가 도서관 카드를 얻게 하려고 도서관에 데리고 갔다. 접수대에서 일하는 여성은 엄마에게 서류를 작성할 것을 요청했고 그다음에는 Lisa에게 이름을 활자체로 쓰라고 했다. 그러고 나서 그녀는 Lisa에게 카드로 그녀가 얼마나 많은 책을 빌릴 수 있는지를 알려주었다. Lisa는 신바람이 났다.
(D) Lisa가 가장 좋아하는 책은 추리 소설이었다. Lisa는 다음 날 반납해야 할 세 권의 책이 있었다. 그러나 그녀가 도서관 접수대로 왔을 때, 그녀는 카드를 가지고 있지 않았다. Lisa는 "아, 이런! 저는 도서관 카드를 찾을 수가 없어요!"라고 접수대의 여성에게 말했다. 그 여성은 ⑤ "미안하지만, 카드가 없으면 어떤 책도 빌려줄 수가 없구나."라고 말했다. (e) 그녀(=Lisa)는 무척 슬퍼하면서 도서관을 떠났다.
(B) Lisa가 집에 돌아왔을 때, 엄마는 Lisa에게 한 소녀가 (b) 그녀(=Lisa)의 도서관 카드를 가지고 왔는데 그 아이가 그것을 도서관 근처 인도에서 발견했다고 말했다고 알려주었다. "내가 들고 갔던 책 중 하나에서 그것이 떨어졌던 게 분명해요."라고 Lisa가 말했다. "그 소녀가 네 카드를 발견해서 다행이었어."라고 엄마가 말했다. ② "넌 매우 조심해야 해. 도서관 카드를 갖는 것은 커다란 책임이란다." Lisa는 "그걸 제 지갑에 보관해야겠어요."라고 말했다.
(C) ③ 엄마는 "도서관에 돌아가서 네가 원했던 책들을 가지러 가자."라고 말했다. "좋아요."라고 Lisa가 말했다. 그들이 도서관에 갔을 때 엄마 역시 책 몇 권을 가져가기로 결정했다. 그들이 도서관에 있는 동안 엄마는 Lisa에게 (c) 그녀(=Lisa)의 카드를 발견했던 소녀가 원형 테이블에 앉아있다고 말했다. ④ Lisa는 그녀에게 다가가서 "내 카드를 찾아줘서 고마워."라고 말했다. (d) 그녀(=a girl)는 자기가 도움이 되어 기쁘다고 Lisa에게 말했고, 그들은 함께 추리 소설을 찾았다. Lisa는 책과 카드와 그리고 새 친구도 갖게 되었다.

구문 [(B) 4행~5행] It **must have dropped** out of one of *the books* [I was carrying], ~
「must have p.p.」 구문은 '(과거에) ~했음에 틀림이 없다'는 뜻으로 과거 사실에 대한 단정적 추측을 표현한다.

[(C) 4행~6행] While they were in the library, // Mom told(V) Lisa(IO) / (that) *the girl* [that found her card] was sitting at the round table.(DO)
접속사 that이 생략된 명사절이 told의 직접목적어로 쓰였다. [ ] 부분은 that절의 주어인 the girl을 수식한다.

어휘 **(A) fill out** (서류를) 작성하다 **print** 활자체로 쓰다 **(B) sidewalk** 보도, 인도 **responsibility** 책임 **wallet** 지갑 **(C) mystery** 추리 소설 **(D) return** 반납하다, 되돌려주다; 돌아가다[오다]

실전 모의고사 04

본문 p.55

18 ④	19 ③	20 ③	21 ④	22 ⑤	23 ④	24 ③	25 ④	26 ③	27 ⑤
28 ④	29 ⑤	30 ④	31 ①	32 ②	33 ③	34 ③	35 ④	36 ②	37 ②
38 ④	39 ③	40 ④	41 ⑤	42 ②	43 ④	44 ③	45 ④		

18 글의 목적 ④

소재 자선 행사 자원봉사자 모집

해설 글을 끝까지 읽고 글쓴이의 진짜 의도를 파악해야 한다. 자선 행사 소개에 이어 여러 자원봉사 업무를 나열한 뒤 자원봉사 참여를 권유하는 말로 글을 맺고 있다. 따라서 글의 목적으로 가장 적절한 것은 ④이다.

해석 달리기 주자들은 주목해 주십시오.
Trout Community Fun Run을 다시 한 번 할 시간이 다 되어 갑니다! 이 재미있고 즐거운 자선 달리기는 지역 기업들이 후원하고 지역 사회 수천 명의 사람들이 참여하는 연례행사입니다. 이 행사는 6월 17일 토요일, 오전 11시에 진행될 것입니다. 하지만 행사의 성공은 여러분과 같은 분들의 너그러움과 지원에 달려 있습니다. 주제문 저희는 사람들을 등록시키고, 간식 부스를 관리하고, 기부금을 모을 직원들이 필요합니다. 올해에는 훨씬 더 많은 참가자가 있을 것으로 예상되기 때문에 인파 관리를 도와줄 분들도 필요합니다. 만약 과거에 이 행사를 즐기셨다면, 다른 모든 분들을 위해 (자원봉사에) 참여하셔서 행사를 즐겁게 만드시는 건 어떨까요? 그곳에서 여러분을 뵙길 바랍니다!
주최자 Jake Thompson

구문 [3행~6행] This entertaining and fun charity run / is *a yearly event* (sponsored by local businesses [and] attended by thousands from the community).
과거분사 sponsored와 attended가 이끄는 두 개의 형용사구가 and로 병렬 연결되어 a yearly event를 뒤에서 수식하고 있다.

어휘 **charity** 자선; 자선 단체 **yearly** 연간의, 1년에 한 번씩 있는 **sponsor** 후원하다; 후원(자) **attend** 참석하다, 참여하다; 주의를 기울이다 **rely on** ~에 달려 있다; ~에 의지[의존]하다 **generosity** 너그러움, 관용 **sign A up** A를 등록[가입]시키다 **donation** 기부(금), 기증(품) **crowd** 인파, 군중 **participant** 참가자 **get involved** ~에 참여[관여]하다 **organizer** 주최자; 조직자

19 심경 변화 ③

소재 캠프에 남겨진 Willie

해설 Willie는 아버지가 자신을 캠프에 홀로 남겨두고 떠난다는 생각에 울며 겁에 질린(frightened) 상태였지만, 지도원인 Matthew가 들려주는 캠프의 여러 가지 재미있는 활동 이야기에 눈물을 그치고 귀를 기울인 것에서 호기심이 생긴(curious) 것을 알 수 있다. 따라서 정답은 ③이다.

해석 아버지 없이 캠프에 홀로 남겨질 생각에 Willie는 울기 시작했다. Willie 방의 담당 지도원이 될 18세 대학생인 Matthew가 이를 알아채고 Willie에게 다가갔다. 그는 팔을 Willie의 어깨에 두르며 말했다. "Willie, 내 옆에 앉을래? 너한테 우리 캠프 얘기를 해줄게." Matthew는 Willie에게 그들이 하는 게임, 매일 저녁에 하는 캠프파이어, 수영, 그리고 그들이 먹는 맛있는 식사에 대해 이야기해 주었다. 그러자 눈물이 흐르던 것이 멈추었다. 소년은 눈을 빛내며 그의 말에 귀를 기울였다. 그것은 아마 Willie가 모험 이야기를 들을 때마다 눈물범벅이 되는 대신 귀를 쫑긋 세우는 아이이기 때문이었을 것이다.
① 안도하는 → 걱정하는
② 기쁜 → 짜증이 난
④ 감사하는 → 당황한
⑤ 기대에 찬 → 실망한

구문 [2행~4행] Matthew, *an eighteen-year-old college student* [who **was to be** Willie's cabin counselor], / noticed and walked over to him.
주격 관계대명사 who가 이끄는 [ ] 부분은 앞의 an ~ student를 수식한다. was to be 부분에서 be to-v는 'v할 예정이다'의 의미로 쓰였다.

어휘 **cabin** 오두막집; (배의) 객실, 선실 **counselor** 지도원, 지도 교사; 상담사 **flow** (액체가) 흐르다; 흐름 **adventure** 모험(심); 도전 **be all ears** 열심히 귀를 기울이다 **be all tears** 눈물에 젖어 있다

20 필자 주장 ③

소재 차이를 존중하는 것

해설 사람들 사이의 차이를 존중해야 하는 이유에 관한 글이다. 글 후반부의 조동사 should를 포함한 문장에서 자신의 지각적 한계를 인정하고 다른 사람들과 교류함으로써 발전할 수 있다고 하였고, 마지막 문장에서 차이를 존중하는 것의 중요성을 다시 한번 강조하고 있으므로, 필자의 주장으로 가장 적절한 것은 ③이다.

해석 차이(사람들 간의 정신적, 정서적, 심리적 차이)에 가치를 두는 것은 시너지의 본질이다. 그리고 그러한 차이에 가치를 두는 데 있어서의 핵심은 모든 사람이 세상을 있는 그대로 보는 것이 아니라 자기 자신에 맞게 본다는 것을 깨닫는 것이다. 당신이 세상을 있는 그대로 본다고 생각한다면, 왜 차이에 가치를 두고 싶겠는가? 당신은 다른 모든 사람들이 중요하지 않은 사소한 것에 파묻혀 있는 반면, 당신은 더 큰 그림을 본다고 생각한다. 그게 당신의 생각이라면, 당신은 결코 효과적으로 상호 의존적인, 혹은 심지어 효과적으로 독립적인 사람이 될 수 없을 것이다. 주제문 진정으로 유능해지고 싶다면, 당신이 가진 지각적 한계를 인정하고 다른 사람들의 마음, 정신과의 교류를 통해 이용할 수 있는 풍요로운 자원의 진가를 알아보는 겸손과 존경심을 갖춰야 한다. 차이를 존중하라. 왜냐하면 그러한 차이가 당신의 지식과 현실에 대한 이해를 더해주기 때문이다.

구문 [3행~5행] And the key to valuing those differences(S) is(V) / to realize that all people **see** the world not **as** ***it is***, but **as** ***they are***.(C)
to realize 이하는 보어인 to부정사구이며 realize의 목적어인 that절이 이어져 길어졌다. 「see A as B」는 'A를 B로 보다[여기다]'의 뜻이다. 여기서 it is는 the world is를 의미하고, they are는 the people are를 의미한다.
[5행~6행] If you think you see the world as it is, **why** would you want to value differences?
why ~ difference?는 수사의문문으로서, 강한 부정의 의미(= you wouldn't want to value differences)를 내포한다.

어휘 **essence** 본질, 정수 *cf.* **essential** 본질적인; 필수적인 **bury** 묻다; (~ 속에) 푹 파묻다 **interdependent** 상호 의존적인 **humility** 겸손 **perceptual** 지각(력)의, 지각과 관련된 **limitation** 《주로 복수형》 (능력 등의) 한계; 제한 **appreciate** 진가를 알아보다, 인정하다; 고마워하다; 감상하다 **interaction** 교류; 상호 작용 **add to** ~을 늘리다

21 밑줄 함의 ④

소재 고장 났다고 오해한 기압계

해설 기압계가 없어졌을 뿐만 아니라 그의 집도 없어진 것을 알았다는 글 마지막 부분의 내용에서 기압계 바늘이 허리케인을 가리켰던 것이 그대로 실현되었음을 알 수 있다. 즉, 밑줄 친 부분의 의미로 가장 적절한 것은 ④ '그곳에 정말로 허리케인이 있었다'이다.

해석 롱아일랜드에 살던 한 남자가 어느 날 자신을 위해 아주 훌륭한 기압계를 구입함으로써 평생의 야망을 충족시킬 수 있었다. 그 기기가 집에 도착했을 때, 그는 (기압계의) 가리키는 바늘이 '허리케인'이라고 표시된 부분을 가리키며 꼼짝도 않는 것처럼 보이는 것을 알고는 아주 실망했다. 그 기압계를 세게 여러 번 흔든 다음에, 그것의 새 주인은 앉아서 그 기기를 산 가게에 항의 편지를 썼다. 그 다음 날 아침 뉴욕에 있는 사무실로 가는 길에 그는 그 편지를 부쳤다. 그날 저녁 그가 롱아일랜드 집에 돌아왔을 때, 그는 그 기압계가 없어졌을 뿐만 아니라 그의 집도 없어진 것을 알았다. 그 기압계의 바늘이 옳았다.

① 기압계가 방금 발견되었다.
② 기압계가 다시 작동하기 시작했다.
③ 기압계의 바늘이 없어졌다.
⑤ 허리케인의 경로가 갑자기 바뀌었다.

구문 [11행~13행] That evening / he returned to Long Island / **to** V'**find** not only O'1the barometer C'1missing but also O'2his house C'2(missing).

to find ~ house는 to부정사의 부사적 용법으로 '결과'를 나타낸다. 즉, 롱아일랜드로 돌아와서 기압계와 집이 없어진 것을 발견하게 되었다는 의미이다. 「find+O+C(형용사)」는 'O가 ~한 것을 알게 되다'의 의미이며, 「not only A but also B」의 상관접속사로 연결되었다. his house 뒤에는 반복되는 missing이 생략되었다.

어휘 **ambition** 야망, 야심 **barometer** 기압계 **instrument** 기기, 도구; 악기 **extremely** 극도로; 몹시 **indicate** 가리키다; 표시하다; 나타내다 **appear** ~인 것처럼 보이다; 나타나다 **stuck** 움직일 수 없는; 갇힌 **sector** 영역, 구역 **vigorously** 세게 **a letter of complaint** 항의 편지 [선택지 어휘] **shift** 바꾸다; 이동하다

22 글의 요지 ⑤

소재 분노를 다루는 방법

해설 화가 났을 때 시간을 충분히 갖고 분노의 진짜 근원과 이유를 파악하게 되면 엉뚱한 사람에게 잘못된 방식으로 반응하는 것을 피할 수 있다는 내용의 글이다. 따라서 글의 요지로 가장 적절한 것은 ⑤이다.

해석 관습적인 지혜는 우리의 분노를 표출하기 전에 10까지 세라고 말한다. 지연은 훌륭한 전략이다. 주제문 그러나 요점은 이 지연 동안 단지 숫자를 세는 게 아니라, 대신에 왜 우리가 화가 났는지를 규정해보라는 것이다. 이 기법은 우리가 문제에 더욱 적합한 반응을 내놓을 수 있게 해준다. 우리의 분노 이유를 확인하는 것은 우리가 우리 자신에게 정말로 화가 났을 때 다른 사람들을 마구 몰아세우는 대신에 적확한 사람에게 반응할 수 있게 해준다. 우리의 분노 이유를 알아차리는 데 시간을 쓰는 것은 우리가 잘못된 사람에게 잘못된 방식으로 반응하는 것을 피할 수 있게 해줄 것이다. 그러면 우리의 반응은 분노의 진짜 근원으로 향해질 수 있고 분노의 진짜 이유를 다룰 수 있게 된다.

구문 [3행~4행] However, the point is not simply **to count** during this delay (A) but instead **to define** why we are angry (B).

「not A but B (A가 아니라 B인)」 구문이다. A와 B 자리에 모두 to부정사가 위치하여 병렬구조를 이룬다.

[9행~11행] Taking *time* (to discern the reason for our anger) (S) will enable (V) us (O) to avoid responding in the wrong way / to the wrong person (C).

Taking ~ anger는 동명사 주어이며 동사는 will enable이다. ( )는 time을 수식하는 형용사적 용법의 to부정사구이다.

어휘 **conventional** 관습적인 **wisdom** 지혜 **suggest** 말하다, 암시하다 **delay** 지연, 연기 **strategy** 전략 **define** 정의하다, 규정하다 **enable** 가능하게 하다 **response** 반응 *cf.* **respond** 반응하다 **identify** 확인하다 **lash out at** ~을 마구 몰아세우다 **discern** 알아차리다; 분간하다 **direct** ~로 향하다; 겨냥하다 **source** 근원, 원천 **address** (문제 등을) 다루다, 처리하다; 연설하다

23 글의 주제 ④

소재 문제 해결에 도움이 되는 글쓰기

해설 문제에 직면했을 때 생각만 하지 말고 글을 쓰는 것이 문제 해결에 도움이 된다는 내용의 글이다. 글쓰기는 생각과는 다른 사고 과정을 요구하기 때문에 새로운 방식으로 문제를 보고 해결책에 다가갈 수 있다고 했으므로, 글의 주제로 가장 적절한 것은 ④ '문제 해결을 위한 효과적인 도구로서의 글쓰기'이다.

해석 때때로 우리는 우리의 진짜 생각과 감정을 글로 담아내고서야 그것들을 인식한다. 주제문 글쓰기는 당신 자신과 당신 주변의 세계를 배우는 한 방법이다. 그것은 당신의 생각을 집중시키게 만들며 문제 해결 기회를 제공한다. 다음번에 당신이 문제에 직면해 있음을 깨닫게 될 때, 그것에 대해 글을 써보아라. 일기는 잠재적인 해결책에 대해 브레인스토밍을 할 뿐만 아니라 문제에 대해 알려진 것을 기록할 자리를 제공한다. 글의 형식으로 아이디어를 표현하는 것은 생각과는 다른 사고 과정을 요구한다. 우리는 글을 쓰기 위하여 새로운 방식으로 생각해야 하는데, 이것이 우리가 문제를 다르게 보고 좀 더 빠르게 해결책에 도달하게 해줄 수 있다. 일기 쓰기는 생각과 자기표현의 새로운 방식에 영감을 불어넣는 데 도움이 될 수 있는 다양한 기법과 연습을 빠르게 드러내줄 것이다.

① 글쓰기 능력을 향상시키는 몇 가지 방법들
② 매일 글을 쓰는 것의 심리적 이점
③ 학습 방법으로서의 글쓰기의 유용성
⑤ 글쓰기의 요소를 이해하는 것의 중요성

구문 [1행~2행] Sometimes we're not aware of our true thoughts and feelings (A) until we capture them with the written word (B).

「not A until B」는 직역하면 'B할 때까지 A하지 않다'의 의미로, 바꾸어 말하면 'B하고 서야 비로소 A하다'로 해석할 수 있다.

[7행~9행] A journal provides *a place* (to record what is known about the problem (A) **as well as** to brainstorm potential solutions (B)).

「A as well as B」는 'B뿐만 아니라 A도'의 뜻이며, A와 B 자리에 모두 to부정사구가 왔다. 두 개의 to부정사구는 앞의 명사 a place를 수식한다.

[9행~11행] Expressing ideas in written form (S) requires (V) a different thought process / than does (V) thinking (S).

Expressing ~ form은 동명사구 주어이며 requires가 동사이다. than 다음에 「동사+주어」 어순으로 도치가 일어났으며, 대동사 does는 requires a thought process를 지칭한다.

어휘 **be aware of** ~을 알다, ~을 인식하다 **capture** (글로 감정 등을) 담아내다, 포착하다; 포획하다 **confront** 직면하다, 맞서다 **journal** 일기 **record** 기록하다; 녹음하다 **brainstorm** 브레인스토밍하다 **potential** 잠재적인; 잠재력 **reveal** 드러내다, 밝히다 **inspire** 영감을 주다 [선택지 어휘] **psychological** 심리적인, 정신적인 **benefit** 이점, 혜택; 이익이 되다 **element** 요소, 성분; 《화학》 원소

24 글의 제목 ③

소재 퇴직에 대비한 재정 계획

해설 글의 도입에서 퇴직 후의 생활을 위해서는 가능한 한 미리 계획을 세워야 한다는

주제문을 제시한 뒤 구체적인 재정 관리 방법을 설명하고 있으므로, 글의 제목으로는 ③ '퇴직 전 재정 계획'이 가장 적절하다.

해석 주제문 퇴직 후에 당신의 꿈을 펼치고자 한다면 당신은 가능한 한 멀리 계획을 미리 세워야 하는데, 최소한 직장에서의 마지막 날로부터 5년 전에는 계획을 세워야 한다. 우선 가능한 한 많은 자본력을 가지려면, 당신의 돈을 회사 주식, 부동산, 정부 채권(= 국채), 그리고 이자율이 높은 은행 계좌와 같이 각기 다른 다양한 계획에 투자하는 것이 적극적으로 권장된다. 돈을 더 적게 쓰고 더 많이 저축하는 것부터 시작하고 불필요한 물건을 사는 것을 멈춰라. 은행 대출을 받는 것을 피하고, 높은 이자 수수료를 내지 않으려면 신용카드 잔금은 반드시 제때 갚아라. 그리고 노후 생활에 대해 제대로 보장받도록 확실히 하려면 생명보험과 의료보험 증권을 갱신하라.

① 조기 퇴직은 너무 위험한가?
② 5년 더 일찍 퇴직하는 법
④ 은퇴 이후, 퇴직했지만 일하기
⑤ 만일에 대비해 저축하는 올바른 방법

구문 [3행~8행] First of all, **it** is strongly recommended // **that** you invest your money in a range of different schemes, (such as company shares, real estate, government bonds, and high-interest bank accounts), / **to give** you as much financial strength as possible.

가주어 it은 that you invest ~ bank accounts까지의 내용을 받는다. such as ~ bank accounts는 different schemes를 부연 설명하는 삽입구이고, to give 이하는 to부정사의 부사적 용법으로 '목적'을 나타낸다.

어휘 **retirement** 퇴직, 은퇴 **ahead** 미리 **in advance** 미리, 앞서 **invest** 투자하다 **a range of** 다양한 **scheme** (운영) 계획, 제도 **share** 주식; 몫; 공유하다 **real estate** 부동산 **bond** 채권; 유대 **account** 계좌; 장부; 계정 **financial** 재정적인 **take out a loan** 대출을 받다 **pay off** (빌린 돈을) 갚다 **balance** 잔고, 잔액; 균형 **interest** 이자; 이익; 흥미 **insurance policy** 보험 증권[증서] **medical** 의료의 **cover** (보험으로) 보장하다; 가리다, 덮다 [선택지 어휘] **risky** 위험한 **for a rainy day** 만일에 대비하여

25 도표 이해 ④

소재 과학자와 기술자가 처음 미국에 온 이유

해설 18~34세의 연령층에서는 과학 기반 시설이나 전문적 기반 시설의 이유로 미국에 온 사람의 비율이 6.2퍼센트이며, 이는 5.5퍼센트인 그 밖의 이유보다 높으므로 가장 낮은 수치가 아니다. 따라서 ④가 정답이다.

해석 〈과학자와 기술자가 처음 미국에 이민 온 이유〉

주제문 위 도표는 (미국에) 이주해 있는 과학자들과 기술자들이 처음 입국한 나이와 당시 미국에 온 주된 이유라고 말한 것들을 보여준다. ① 18세 이전에 미국에 온 사람들은 거의 70퍼센트가 가족과 관련된 이유 때문에 왔지만, 이 수치는 더 높은 연령에 (미국에) 들어온 응답자에서는 상당히 더 낮았다. ② 18~34세 사이에 온 과학자들과 기술자들은 교육의 기회가 가장 중요한 이유였으며, 가족과 관련된 이유, 그 다음으로 일자리나 경제적인 기회가 뒤를 이었다. ③ 35세 이상일 때 온 사람들은 주로 가족과 관련된 이유와 일자리나 경제적인 기회 때문에 왔다. ④ 과학 기반 시설이나 전문적 기반 시설은 세 개의 모든 그룹에서 다섯 개의 범주 중에 가장 적게 선택되었다. ⑤ 마지막으로, 각 연령별 그룹에서 설문조사한 사람들 중 5.5~12퍼센트는 그 밖의 이유로 미국에 왔다.

어휘 **immigrant** (다른 나라로 온) 이민자, 이주민 **significantly** 상당히, 크게; 중요하게 **mainly** 주로 **infrastructure** 사회[공공] 기반 시설 **category** 범주, 부문 **survey** 설문조사하다

26 내용 불일치 ③

소재 Clara Barton의 생애

해설 전쟁 후 Abraham Lincoln은 Barton을 부상병을 돕는 간호사 대표가 아니라, 실종 병사를 찾는 임무의 책임자로 임명하였다. 따라서 ③이 정답이다.

해석 1821년 크리스마스 날 매사추세츠에서 태어난 Clara Barton은 미국 적십자사의 설립자이다. 자신의 오빠가 헛간 지붕에서 추락해 크게 다친 후 ① 스스로 의학과 간호학을 공부하기 시작했을 때 그녀는 고작 열한 살이었다. 30년 후, ② 미국 남북전쟁이 한창일 때 그녀는 의료 구호품 단체를 세우고 전방에서 부상자들을 간호했는데, 그것이 그녀가 '전쟁터의 천사'라는 별명을 얻게 해주었다. 전쟁이 끝났을 때, ③ Abraham Lincoln은 Barton을 실종 병사를 찾는 임무의 책임자로 임명했다. ④ 1870년에 그녀는 유럽으로 건너가 보불전쟁 동안 적십자사에서 일했다. 고국으로 돌아오자마자, ⑤ 그녀는 미국 적십자사를 설립했고, 83세의 나이로 은퇴했던 해인 1904년까지 회장을 역임했다.

구문 [5행~9행] Thirty years later, **with** *the Civil War* **raging**, / she established a medical supplies agency and nursed the wounded at the front line, // **which** earned her the nickname the "Angel of the Battlefield."

「with+(대)명사+분사」는 동시상황을 나타내며 '남북전쟁이 한창인 중에'라는 의미이다. the Civil War가 맹렬히 계속되고 있다(rage)는 뜻이므로, 능동 관계를 나타내는 현재분사 raging이 쓰였다. 관계대명사 which는 밑줄 친 부분을 받는다.

[12행~15행] **Upon** returning home, ~ until *1904*, [**when** she retired at the age of eighty-three].

「on[upon] v-ing」 구문은 '~하자마자'의 의미로, 밑줄 친 부분은 Immediately after she returned home으로 바꾸어 쓸 수 있다. when 이하는 1904를 보충 설명하는 관계부사절이다.

어휘 **founder** 설립자, 창립자 *cf.* **found** 설립하다(= **establish**) **medicine** 의학; 약 *cf.* **medical** 의학[의료]의 **seriously** 심하게, 엄청나게 **injured** 다친, 상처를 입은 **the Civil War** 미국 남북전쟁 **rage** (전쟁·언쟁 등이) 맹렬히 계속되다; 격렬한 분노 **agency** 단체; 대리점 **the wounded** 부상자 **battlefield** 전쟁터 **appoint A (as) B** A를 B로 임명[지명]하다 **sail to** ~로 항해하다 **the Franco-Prussian War** 보불(普佛)전쟁《프로이센과 프랑스 간의 전쟁》 **retire** 은퇴하다, 퇴직하다

27 안내문 불일치 ⑤

소재 피트니스 센터 무료 행사 안내

해설 소제목과 선택지를 활용하여 필요한 정보를 빠르게 훑어 확인해야 한다. 상품 추첨에 참여하려면 한 주간 무료 체험 프로그램에 등록하라고 했으므로 ⑤가 안내문과 일치하지 않는다.

해석

Free Fun Fitness Week

당신과 행운의 친구 한 분을 Free Fun Fitness Week에 초대합니다!

상품을 받으세요!
① 행운의 아홉 분께 3천 달러 이상의 개인 훈련 프로그램이 제공됩니다!

다음 중 하나를 받을 수 있습니다.
– 400달러 가격인 한 달 간의 무료 개인 훈련
– ② 320달러 가격인 두 달 간의 무료 온라인 개인 훈련
– ③ 280달러 가격인 세 달 간의 무료 단체 수업

④ 저희 훈련 프로그램은 개인별 식단과 운동 계획을 이용하여 여러분이 집중하고자 하는 모든 문제되는 부분(의 근육)을 강화할 수 있도록 도와드릴 것입니다.

⑤ 추첨에 참여하려면 한 주간 무료 체험 프로그램에 참가하시기만 하면 됩니다!
자리가 한정되어 있어 매우 빠르게 사라지니 서두르세요.

어휘 **personal** 개인적인, 개인의 *cf.* **personalized** 개인이 원하는 대로 할 수 있는 **valued** 가격이 사정된 **enter into the drawing** 추첨에 참여하다 **extremely** 매우, 몹시

28 안내문 일치 ④

소재 과학 박물관 안내

해설 입장료(admission) 안내 내용에서 매달 마지막 일요일은 입장료가 무료라고 했으므로 ④가 안내문의 내용과 일치한다.

해석

Wilson 박물관

발명품, 아이디어, 혁신 탐구에 여러분을 초대합니다. ① Wilson 박물관은 약간의 최신 연구물들과 인공지능의 역사, 홀로그래피를 보여주는 특별한 갤러리를 특징으로 합니다.

개장 시간
- 주요 공휴일을 제외한 매일 오전 10시~오후 5시
- ② **7, 8월 한정:** 목요일에는 오전 10시~오후 7시

입장료
- 성인: 10달러
  18세 미만과 학생, 65세 이상의 연장자: 5달러
  ③ 5세 미만 어린이: 무료
- ④ 매달 마지막 일요일은 무료입장
- 박물관에 입장하신 분들에게는, IT업계의 초청 연사를 모시는 저녁 프로그램이 무료입니다.

교육용 방문
교육 프로그램은 8명 이상의 단체가 이용하실 수 있습니다. ⑤ 모든 단체는 사전 예약이 필요합니다.

어휘 **explore** 탐구하다 **innovation** 혁신 **feature** 특징으로 하다 **artificial intelligence** 인공지능 **holography** 홀로그래피《레이저 광선을 이용한 입체 사진술》 **admission** 입장(료) **community** 집단; 공동 사회 **advance reservation** 사전 예약

29 밑줄 어법 ⑤

소재 한국인의 수면 부족의 문제점

해설 ⑤ 문맥상 압박감 때문에 우리가 잠을 '빼앗기는' 것이므로 We와 deprive(빼앗다)는 수동 관계이다. 따라서 과거분사 형태인 deprived of가 되어야 한다.

오답 분석 ① 전치사 by의 목적어이므로 동명사 형태가 적절히 쓰였다. ② '권장되는' 수면 시간이므로 amount와 recommend는 수동 관계이다. 따라서 과거분사를 쓴 것은 옳다. ③ much는 비교급 less를 강조하는 부사로 적절히 쓰였다. 이외에 비교급을 강조하는 부사로는 far, even, still 등이 있다. ④ 준부정어 only가 문두에 나와 '주어-동사'의 어순이 바뀐 것은 적절하다. 이 문장과 같이 동사가 현재완료시제인 경우, 「have+주어+p.p.」의 어순이 된다.

해석 잠을 잘 자는 것은 우리의 건강과 행복을 위해 매우 중요해서 전문가들은 우리가 하루에 7~9시간 사이의 잠을 잘 필요가 있다고 말한다. 그것은 면역체계를 강화시킴으로써 질병과 우울증을 예방하는 데 도움을 준다. 주제문 그러나 우리 중 너무나 많은 사람이 권장된 양(= 시간)보다 더 적게 잠을 잔다. 실제로 한국인들은 OECD 국가들 가운데 '가장 많이 깨어 있는' 국민으로, 보통 다른 나라 사람들이 자는 것보다 훨씬 더 적게 잠을 잔다. 최근에서야 건강 전문가들이 우리의 수면 부족을 진지하게 받아들이기 시작했다. 우리는 학교와 직장에서 경쟁하는 압박감 때문에 잠을 빼앗긴다. 그러나 우리가 휴식을 취하기보다 계속해서 일하면, 우리는 생산성을 잃을 뿐 아니라 더욱 불행해진다.

어휘 **well-being** (건강·안전 등에 대한) 행복; 복지 **expert** 전문가 **depression** 우울(증) **strengthen** 강화하다 **immune system** 면역체계 **in general** 보통, 대개 **take A seriously** A를 심각[진지]하게 생각하다 **lack** 부족 **deprive of** ~을 빼앗다 **pressure** 압박(감); 압력 **compete** 경쟁하다 **productivity** 생산성

30 밑줄 어휘 ④

소재 선물로서 손편지의 가치

해설 정성이 들어간 편지가 값비싼 물건보다 선물로서 더 적합하다는 내용의 글이다. 우리는 우리를 가장 사랑해주는 이들을 (소중히 해야 하는데도) 당연하게 받아들이는 경우가 많기 때문에, 그들을 소중히 생각한다는 것을 상기시켜주는 편지를 보내는 것이 좋다는 문맥이 되어야 하므로 ④ least는 most로 고쳐야 한다.

해석 우리는 어렸을 때 최고의 선물은 손으로 만든 것이라고 배운다. 주제문 손으로 만든 선물과 함께 오는 것은 선물 그 자체뿐만 아니라, (그 보다) 더 중요하게도, 상대방이 그것(선물)에 들인 ① 귀중한 시간도 있다. 이러한 점에서, 편지는 (상대방이 투자한) 시간뿐만 아니라 편지가 필요로 하는 있는 그대로의 감정과 생각 때문에 값을 매길 수 없는 것에 ② 완벽하게 들어맞는다. 극단적으로 말하자면, 오로지 다이아몬드 목걸이와 금반지만이 교환되는 관계는 오직 편지만이 교환되는 관계 앞에서 ③ 무색해질 것이다. 우리를 가장 사랑하는 사람들은 우리가 ④ 가장 덜(→ 가장 많이) 당연시하는 사람들인 경향이 있기 때문에, 당신이 그들을 소중하게 생각한다는 것을 예고 없이 상기시키는 것(= 편지)을 보내는 것은 전혀 나쁘지 않다. 내가 장담하건대 그것은 ⑤ 값비싼 선물보다 더 소중히 여겨질 것이다.

구문 [2행~4행] What comes with a handmade gift (S) is (V) **not only** the (C) gift itself **but**, more importantly, *the invaluable time* [(that) the other person put ● into it].

「not only A but (also) B」는 'A뿐만 아니라 B도'라는 뜻으로 A와 B는 문법적으로 성격이 대등해야 한다. 여기서 A는 the gift itself이고 B는 the invaluable time이 된다. the invaluable time 뒤에는 목적격 관계대명사가 생략되었으며 ●는 원래 목적어가 위치했던 자리이다.

[8행~11행] ~, *a relationship* (S) [**where** nothing but diamond necklaces and gold rings are exchanged] / would pale (V) in comparison to *a relationship* [**where** nothing but letters are exchanged].

두 개의 a relationship은 각각 바로 뒤의 where가 이끄는 관계부사절의 수식을 받고 있다. 관계부사 where의 선행사로 항상 물리적인 어떤 '장소'만 오는 것은 아니다.

어휘 **invaluable** 귀중한, 값을 헤아릴 수 없는 **in this respect** 이 점에서는 **fit the bill** 꼭 들어맞다, 알맞다 **priceless** 값을 매길 수 없는, 매우 귀중한 **raw** 있는 그대로 보여주는; 가공되지 않은; 날것의 **to an extreme** 극도로 **pale** 무색해지다; 창백해지다; 창백한; 색이 엷은 **in comparison to** ~와 비교할 때 **nothing but** 오직, 그저 ~일 뿐인 **take A for granted** A를 당연시하다 **reminder** (이미 잊었거나 잊고 싶은 것을) 상기시키는 것 **think the world of** ~을 소중히 여기다; ~을 몹시 좋아하다 **cherish** 소중히 여기다; 아끼다 **luxurious** 호화로운, 고급의

31 빈칸 추론 ①

소재 팀워크의 본질

해설 빈칸 앞 문장에서 팀의 일원으로 일한다는 것은 '우리'를 위해 '나'의 일부를 완전히 포기하는 것이라고 했으므로, 팀워크의 본질은 ① '희생'이라 할 수 있다. 또한 no commitment, selfishness는 모두 팀워크의 정신에 어긋나는 것으로 제시되었으므로, 이와 반대되는 단어인 sacrifice가 빈칸에 적절함을 알 수 있다.

해석 직장에서 많은 사람들은 개인적 목표는 갖고 있지만 회사의 임무에 대한 헌신은 없다. 그들은 사무실에서 슈퍼스타가 되기를 원하거나 승진을 쫓지만, 팀의 생각을 지지하지 않고, 자신들이 팀을 발전시키도록 고용된 것이지 팀과 경쟁하라고 고용된 것이 아니라는 것을 필연적으로 이해하지 못한다. 주제문 궁극적으로 나는 그 모든 것은 결국 이기심으로 요약된다고 생각하고, 그 단어가 가혹하게 들리기는 하지만 우리는 그것의 실체를 확인하는 것이 좋은데, 그렇지 않으면 그것을 바로잡을 수 없다. 만약 여러분이 팀을 신뢰하지 않는다면 개인 사업을 시작해서 자신의 꿈을 오로지 혼자서만 추구하라. 팀을 신뢰하지 않는다면 팀에 합류하지 마라. 이유는 여러분이 그렇게 하면(= 팀에

합류하면) 온전히 팀 안에서의 '우리'를 위해 팀 안에서의 '나'의 일부를 완전히 포기해야 하기 때문이다! 주제문 팀워크의 진정한 본질은 정말로 희생임을 깨달아야 한다.
② 선견지명 ③ 신뢰 ④ 인내심 ⑤ 융통성

구문 [5행~6행] ~ they were hired to enhance the team and not (to) compete with the team.
to부정사구는 '목적(~하기 위해)'의 의미로 쓰였다. to 다음의 동사원형 enhance와 not compete가 병렬구조를 이룬다.

[8행~9행] ~ and **as harsh as that word sounds**, we'd better identify it **or** we won't be able to correct it.
as harsh as that word sounds 부분은 '~하겠지만'의 뜻으로 쓰인 양보의 부사절이다. 접속사 or는 '그렇지 않으면'의 뜻으로 쓰였다.

어휘 **commitment** 헌신, 열심 **mission** 임무 **corporation** 기업, 회사 **promotion** 승진; 촉진; 홍보 **concept** 개념, 생각 **inevitably** 불가피하게 **enhance** 향상시키다, 높이다 **ultimately** 궁극적으로 **come down to** 결국 ~이 되다 **selfishness** 이기적임 **harsh** 가혹한 **identify** 확인하다 **sole** 혼자, 단독의 *cf.* **solely** 오로지; 혼자서 **exclusively** 오로지; 독점적으로 **give up on** ~을 단념하다

32 빈칸 추론 ②

소재 푸에르토리코 사람들의 삶에서 음식의 의미

해설 빈칸 뒤에 나오는 예시를 통해 여성의 결혼생활에서 기대되는 부분이 '무엇'인지 추론해야 한다. 이것은 충분히 부양받았다는 신호이며, 체중이 감소한 기혼 여성들에 대해 사람들이 부정적인 반응을 보였다는 것에서, 빈칸에는 ② '체중 증가'가 가장 적절함을 알 수 있다.

해석 주제문 푸에르토리코 사람들의 삶에서 음식은 중요한 역할을 한다. 다른 나라에서와 달리 (푸에르토리코에서) 훌륭한 어머니이자 아내가 남편과 자식에 대한 사랑을 표현하는 한 가지 방식은 그들에게 많은 양의 음식을 제공하고 (그들이) 먹은 음식의 양에 대해 관심을 보이는 것이다. 푸에르토리코 사람들의 삶에서 더 특이한 부분은 체중 증가인데, 그것은 여성의 사회생활, 특히 결혼에서 기대되는 부분이다. 그것은 특히 그녀의 가족들에게 있어, 그녀가 충분히 부양받는다는 신호이다. 체중이 감소하는 여성들은 부정적인 반응을 얻는다. 남편과 이혼하고 체중이 170에서 140파운드로 줄어든 어느 여성은 이렇게 말했다. "내가 체중이 줄자 사람들이 이렇게 말했어요. '당신은 너무 말랐어요! 무슨 일이 생긴 거죠?' 아주 많은 사람이 내게 살찐 것이 나빠 보이지 않았으며, (몸에) 굴곡이 있었을 때 내가 더 좋아 보인다고 말했어요."
① 음식 제공 ③ 특별한 요리법 ④ 맛에 대한 민감성 ⑤ 변함없는 인내

구문 [2행~6행] *one way* [in which a good mother and wife expresses her love / for her husband and children] is by **presenting** ~ food and **showing** ~ eaten.
(S: one way, S′: a good mother and wife, V′: expresses, O′: her love, V: is, C: by presenting ~ food and showing ~ eaten)
전치사 by의 목적어로 쓰인 presenting ~ food와 showing ~ eaten이 and로 연결된 병렬구조이다.

어휘 **integral** 없어서는 안 될, 필수적인 **present A with B** A에게 B를 제시하다[보여주다] **concern** 관심; 걱정, 염려 **amount** 양; 총계 **adequately** 충분하게, 적당하게 **provide for** ~을 부양하다 **negative** 부정적인 **decline** 줄어들다; 감소 **divorce** 이혼하다 **skinny** 깡마른, 바짝 여윈 [선택지 어휘] **recipe** 요리법 **sensitivity** 민감성; 예민함 **unfailing** 언제나 변함없는

33 빈칸 추론 ③

소재 건강한 현실 탈출구로서의 독서

해설 소설을 읽는 것은 현실 경험에 못지않게 두뇌에 자극을 제공하고, 잠시 실생활에서 벗어나 다른 세상으로 이동하며 긴장을 풀 기회를 주므로 독자에게 ③ '건강한 탈출'을 제공한다고 할 수 있다.

해석 주제문 소설을 읽는 것은 건강한 탈출을 제공한다. 〈뉴욕 타임스〉 선데이 리뷰에 실린 기사에서 Annie Murphy Hall은 소설 작품을 읽는 것이 우리 두뇌에 어떻게 영향을 미치는지를 논한다. Murphy는 말한다. "두뇌는 경험에 대해 읽는 것과 그것을 실생활에서 마주치는 것 간에 그다지 구별을 두지 않는 것 같습니다." 정말로 읽기는 현실에 대한 생생한 모의실험, 즉 "컴퓨터 시뮬레이션이 컴퓨터상에서 작동하는 것과 마찬가지로 독자의 정신에서 작동하는" 것(= 모의실험)을 만든다. 우리의 아이들은 독서할 때 다른 세상으로 이동된다. 소설을 읽는 것은 어린이들이 매일의 걱정에서 벗어나 휴식을 취하는 데 도움을 주고 그들에게 플러그를 뽑고 긴장을 풀 기회를 제공한다. 끊임없이 환상의 세계에서 사는 것은 해롭겠지만, 한두 시간의 유예된 현실이 바로 의사들이 명한 그것일지 모른다!
① 삶의 교훈 ② 독서 기술 ④ 생생한 상상력 ⑤ 어린이들을 위한 영감

구문 [4행~7행] The brain, (it seems), does not make much of a distinction between reading about an experience and encountering it in real life.
(A: reading about an experience, B: encountering it in real life)
it seems는 삽입절이다. make a distinction between A and B는 'A와 B를 구별하다'의 뜻이다. A와 B 자리에 모두 동명사로 시작되는 명사구가 위치해 있다.

어휘 **article** 기사 **distinction** 구별 **encounter** 우연히 마주치다 **vivid** 생생한, 선명한 **simulation** 모의실험 **transport** 수송하다, 옮기다 **unplug** 플러그를 뽑다 **constantly** 끊임없이, 항상 **suspend** 중단하다, 유예하다 [선택지 어휘] **inspiration** 영감

34 빈칸 추론 ③

소재 관계 지속성을 보여주는 단어 연상 테스트

해설 단어 연상 테스트로 '무엇'을 할 수 있는지를 파악하며 글을 읽는다. 마지막 문장(the higher ~ a year)에서 파트너를 좋지 않은 단어와 더 많이 연관시킬수록 관계가 깨질 가능성이 더 크다고 했다. 이는 단어 연상 테스트로 관계의 지속 여부를 알 수 있다는 것을 의미하므로 정답은 ③ '어떤 관계가 지속될 것인지 아닌지를 나타낼'이다. 이처럼 실험 내용을 소개하는 글은 '결과'에 주목하여 읽도록 한다.

해석 주제문 간단한 단어 연상 테스트가 어떤 관계가 지속될 것인지 아닌지를 나타낼 수 있다. 이 테스트는 아무 생각을 하지 않는 무의식적 단계에서 효과가 있기 때문에, 실제로 타인에 대해 당신이 마음 깊이 그리고 가장 지속적으로 느끼는 감정을 드러낸다. 테스트에서 단어들은 모니터 상에 한 번에 하나씩 휙 지나가게 되는데, 당신은 그 단어가 당신의 파트너와 관련이 있는지 없는지를 매우 빨리 확인해야 한다. 그 단어들은 세 가지 범주로 나뉜다. 즉, '사랑'과 '물' 같이 '좋은 단어들'과 '상처'와 '절규' 같이 '좋지 않은 단어들', 반려동물의 이름이나 개인적 특징 같이 '파트너(와 관련된) 단어들'이 그것이다. 이 테스트를 발명한 사람들은 그 결과가 일관되며 분명하다고 말한다. 즉, 당신이 당신의 파트너와 연관시키는 '좋지 않은 단어들'의 수가 많을수록, 당신이 1년 안에 (그 사람과) 헤어질 가능성이 더 크다는 것이다.
① 어떤 사람이 말로 하지 않은 의도를 드러낼
② 속이고 거짓말한 확실한 증거를 제공해 줄
④ 장기적인 관계에 대한 당신의 믿음을 확인시켜 줄
⑤ 빠르고 분명하게 생각하는 것의 중요성을 우리에게 가르쳐 줄

구문 [11행~14행] ~ : **the higher** the number of "*bad words*" [(that) you associate ● with your partner], / **the higher** the likelihood that you'll break up within a year.
(the likelihood = that you'll break up within a year)
「the 비교급 ~, the 비교급 ...」은 '~할수록, 더욱 더 …한'의 의미이다. [ ] 부분은 목적격 관계대명사가 생략된 관계대명사절로 bad words를 수식한다. the likelihood는 이어지는 that절과 동격을 이룬다.

어휘 **association** 연상, 연관 *cf.* **associate A with B** A를 B와 연관시키다 **work on** ~에 효과가 있다 **automatic** 무의식적인; 자동적인 **reveal** 드러내다, 밝히다 **persistent** 지속적인; 끈질긴 **flash** 휙 지나치다; 번쩍임 **relate to** ~와 관련이 있다 **category** 범주 **trait** 특성 **consistent** 일관된, 한결같은 **likelihood** 가능성 **break up (with)** (~와) 헤어지다 [선택지 어휘] **unspoken** 말로 하지 않은 **intention** 의도 **solid evidence** 확실한 증거 **cheat** 속이다 **long-term** 장기적인

35 무관한 문장 ④

소재 학교의 행복 요인: 우정

해설 많은 아이들이 학교에서 가장 행복한 이유로 '우정'을 꼽는다는 내용의 글이다. 학교에서 아이들을 행복하게 만드는 요인에 관한 설문 조사 결과를 설명하는 중간에 고등학교 때 우정이 가장 오래간다는 내용인 ④가 들어가는 것은 적절하지 않다.

해석 학교에서 당신을 행복하게 만드는 것은 무엇인가? 당신이 가장 좋아하는 선생님? 어떤 특정한 수업? 시험에서 만점을 받는 것? 당신의 우정은 어떤가? 주제문 아이들이 학교에 관해 자신이 좋아하는 것이 무엇이냐는 질문을 받으면, 한 가지가 나머지 것들보다 월등하게 두드러진다. 그리고 그것은 바로 우정이다. 요크셔 지역의 학생 3,457명에 대한 설문 조사에서 62.8퍼센트의 아이들이 자신이 학교에서 행복하다고 느꼈을 때 그것은 우정 때문이었다고 답했다. '우정'은 단짝 친구들에 대한 긴밀한 애착뿐 아니라 급우들과 선생님들에 대한 친밀한 관계로도 정의되었다. 많은 우정 가운데 고등학교에서 형성된 우정이 가장 지속적이고 강력하다. 많은 아이들이 우정 외에도, 안전하다고 느끼는 것, 그리고 다른 사람들에게 사랑받는 것을 학교에서 행복한 이유로 꼽았다.

어휘 **particular** 특정한; 특별한 **stand out** 두드러지다, 부각되다 **define A as B** A를 B로 정의하다 **attachment** 애정, 애착; 부착[부가]물 **buddy** 친구 **friendly** 친한; 상냥한; 우호적인 **connection** 관계; 연결; 연관성 **lasting** 지속적인 **in addition to** ~이외에; 게다가 **cite** (이유 · 예를) 들다; (구절 등을) 인용하다

36 글의 순서 ②

소재 독개미를 먹고 독을 갖게 된 개구리

해설 주어진 문장은 남미에 서식하는 독개구리가 독을 스스로 만들지 않는다는 사실을 발견했다는 내용이다. 이어서 그 독은 개구리가 먹는 개미에게서 온다는 내용의 (B)가 나온 뒤 (B)의 마지막에 언급된 the deadly poison을 설명한 (A)가 그다음에 이어지고, (A)의 마지막에 언급된 개구리 위의 내용물을 조사한 결과인 (C)가 마지막에 오는 것이 적절하다. 따라서 정답은 ② '(B)-(A)-(C)'이다.

해석 주제문 어느 미국 과학자는 남미의 어떤 작고 화려하며 독이 있는 개구리가 실제로는 스스로 독을 만들어내지 않는다는 사실을 발견했다.

(B) 그녀는 독을 만드는 것은 그 개구리가 먹는 개미란 것을 확신한다. 그녀는 개구리가 태어날 때는 해롭지 않다는 것과 오직 다 자란 개구리의 피부만이 치명적인 독으로 덮여 있다는 것을 발견했다.

(A) 사실 그 독은 너무나 치명적이어서 개구리 한 마리가 백 마리의 쥐를 죽일 수 있고 사람을 불구로 만들 수도 있다. 연구의 일부로서, 그 과학자는 개구리 수백 마리의 위(胃) 안에 있는 내용물을 조사했다.

(C) 그 위(胃)에서 매우 강한 독성 물질을 만들어내는 여러 개미를 포함하여 135종의 개미들이 드러났다. 그녀는 이 개미들이 가장 (독이) 치명적인 개구리가 먹는 먹이의 70퍼센트를 차지한다는 것을 발견했다.

구문 [8행~9행] She is confident // that **it**'s *the ants* [(that) the frogs eat] **that** produce the poison.

「It is ~ that ...」 강조구문이 쓰여 원래 문장 The ants the frog eat produce the poison.에서 주어인 the ants the frogs eat을 강조한다.

어휘 **poisonous** 독성이 있는 *cf.* **poison** 독(약) **deadly** 치명적인 **disable** 불구로 만들다; 망가뜨리다 **examine** 조사하다; 시험하다 **content** 내용(물); 함량 **confident** 확신하는 **harmless** 무해한 **mature** 다 자란; 성숙한 **coat** (막 같은 것을) 덮다 **species** 《생물》 종(種) **including** ~을 포함하여 **toxic** 유독성의 **substance** 물질 **make up** ~을 차지하다; 보충하다 **diet** 음식; 식이요법, 다이어트

37 글의 순서 ②

소재 정보 가속화로 인한 문제점

해설 주어진 글은 정보 속도의 전염성으로 인해 정보가 빨라지고 있다는 내용이다. 따라서 이를 부연 설명하는 짧은 뉴스 기사의 예가 제시된 (B)가 그 뒤에 오고, 이러한 정보 환경에서 맥락과 이해가 부족해지는 문제점에 대해 언급한 (A)가 이어지는 것이 자연스럽다. (A)가 사람들이 많은 양의 정보를 훑어보게 된다는 내용으로 끝나므로, 이렇게 훑어보는 정보 중 많은 것이 기억되지 않는다는 내용의 (C)가 그 뒤에 와야 한다. 따라서 정답은 ② '(B)-(A)-(C)'이다.

해석 속도는 전염성이 있다. 잡지와 신문 같이 속도가 더 느린 매체는 인터넷과 텔레비전 같이 속도가 가장 빠른 매체를 모방한다.

(B) 더 명백한 메시지와 더 적은 분석으로 기사는 점점 더 짧아진다. 굉장히 짧은 뉴스 기사들은 계속해서 업데이트되고 있다. 모든 사람이 10초는 할애하지만, 누가 몇 분을 할애하겠는가? 정보의 단순화와 가속화에 대한 우려가 가장 빠르고 가장 간편한 매체에 우선권을 준다.

(A) 주제문 이처럼 정신없이 바쁜 정보 환경에서 잃게 되는 것은 맥락과 이해이다. 시간의 압박은 정보 소비자들로 하여금 다수의 채널을 대충 훑어보고 흥미롭거나 중요한 것을 찾아 많은 양의 정보를 흡수한 뒤 거르도록 강요한다.

(C) 하지만 그들은 자신들이 훑어봤던 것 중 많은 것을 반드시 기억하는 것은 아니다. 마지막 정보가 그것의 이전 정보를 의식으로부터 밀어낸다.

구문 [16행~18행] But they do **not necessarily** remember / much of what they scanned; the last piece of data(S) pushes out(V) (from consciousness) *the piece of data*(O) (previous to **it**).

not necessarily는 '반드시 ~은 아닌'이라는 의미의 부분부정이고, remember의 목적어는 much of what they scanned이다. 부사구 from consciousness를 괄호로 묶어 생각하면 pushes out의 목적어인 the piece of data ~를 파악하기 쉽다. 문장 끝의 it은 the last piece of data를 가리킨다.

어휘 **contagious** 전염성의 **imitate** 모방하다 **lost** 잃은 **context** 맥락; 문맥 **scan** 대충 훑어보다 **take in** ~을 섭취[흡수]하다 **filter** 거르다, 여과하다; 필터, 여과 장치 **article** 기사 **analysis** 분석 **constantly** 계속해서, 끊임없이 **spare** 할애하다; 남는, 여분의 **simplify** 단순화하다 **give the edge to** ~에게 우선권[우위]을 주다 **compact** 간편한; 소형의; 조밀한 **consciousness** 의식 **previous** 이전의

38 문장 넣기 ④

소재 점유권과 소유권의 차이

해설 주어진 문장의 this reason은 피아노를 10년간 관리해오고 있는 누군가가 피아노를 소유한 사람은 자신이라고 생각할 수도 있다는 가정을 가리키며, the terms "possession" and "ownership"을 ④ 다음 문장에서 they로 받아 두 용어의 의미 차이를 설명하고 있으므로 주어진 문장은 ④에 들어가야 옳다.

해석 '점유는 법에서 90%의 승산이 있다.(가진 사람이 임자다.)'는 단지 어떤 것을 점유하고 있는 것만으로도 법적으로 그것을 소유하는 것과 거의 같다는 것을 시사하는 속담이다. 그러므로 그것(= 속담)은 만약 사람들이 어떤 것을 계속 가지고 있기만 하면 실제 소유주가 그것을 돌려받기 어려울 것이라서 그 물건이 그들(= 물건을 계속 점유한 사람들)의 것이 된다는 생각을 심어준다. 10년 동안 당신을 대신해서 피아노를 관리해오고 있는 누군가에게서 당신의 피아노를 돌려받는 것이 얼마나 어려울지를 상상해보라. 그 사람은 자신이 피아노를 소유하고 있다고 생각할지도 모른다. 이런 이유로 '점유권'과 '소유권'이라는 용어가 때때로 혼동될 수 있다. 주제문 그러나 이 용어들은 법률 용어로는 절대로 같은 것이 아니다. 예를 들어, 당신이 차를 친구에게 빌려주면 현재는 당신의 친구가 그 차를 '점유'하고 있으나 당신은 여전히 법적으로 그것을 '소유'하고 있다.

구문 [3행~5행] "Possession is nine-tenths of the law"(S) is(V) *a saying*(C) [that suggests // that just having a thing in your possession(S′) **is**(V′) almost **the same as** legally owning it(C′)].

여기서 suggest는 '(~해야 한다고) 제안하다'라는 당위의 뜻이 아니라 '시사하다, 암시하다'란 뜻으로 쓰였으므로, that절 내의 동사가 「(should) 동사원형」이 아니라 is가 쓰였다. the same as는 '~와 같은 것'이란 의미이다.

[5행~8행] Thus, it gives people **the idea** / **that** if they just hold onto a thing, // it will be hard for the real owner to get it back, // **which** will make the thing theirs.

the idea와 that절은 동격이다. that절은 「if가 이끄는 절, S+V ~」의 구조로 길어진 형태이며, which는 앞의 절(if ~ back)의 내용을 받는 계속적 용법으로 쓰였다.

[8행~10행] Just imagine // how hard it would be to get your piano back from *somebody* [who **has been looking** after it for you for ten years].

how가 이끄는 절이 imagine의 목적어로 쓰였다. 「have been v-ing」는 현재까지 동작이 '계속'되어 왔음을 강조하며 for ten years처럼 기간을 나타내는 부사구와 함께 잘 쓰인다.

어휘 **possession** 점유; 소지품 *cf.* **possess** 가지다 **ownership** 소유(권) *cf.* **own** 소유하다; 자신의 *cf.* **owner** 소유주, 주인 **confused** 혼란스러운 **suggest** 시사[암시]하다; 제안하다 **legally** 합법적으로 *cf.* **legal** 합법적인; 법률(상)의 **hold onto** ~을 계속 가지고 있다 **look after** ~을 돌보다 **definitely** 절대로, 확실히 **term** 용어; 학기; 기간

39 문장 넣기 ③

소재 신체 언어의 문화 차이

해설 ③ 앞의 '신체 언어 관찰이 성격 파악에 도움이 된다'는 내용과 ③ 뒤의 '예를 들어 인터뷰 받는 사람이 눈을 피하면 문화 차이로 인해 교활하다는 오해를 받을 수 있다'는 내용은 논리적으로 연결되지 않는다. However로 시작하며 '오해를 불러일으킬 수 있는 신체 언어의 문화 차이가 있다'는 내용의 주어진 문장이 ③에 들어가면 For example로 시작하는 ③ 다음 문장이 주어진 문장에 대한 예시로 자연스럽게 연결된다.

해석 일터와 일상생활 둘 다에서 사람들의 행동을 관찰한 바를 보면 대부분의 사람들은 호감 가는 특징과 호감 가지 않는 특징을 다 가지고 있다. 어떤 사람의 성격에 대한 강한 인상은 종종 신체 언어를 관찰함으로써 형성될 수 있다. 많은 예에서 이것은 도움이 될 수 있다. 주제문 그러나 많은 경우 우리가 어떤 사람에 대해 잘못된 가정을 내리도록 유도할 수 있는 신체 언어의 미묘한 문화 차이가 있다. 예를 들어, 어떤 문화에서 사람들은 존경을 표현하기 위해 인터뷰하는 사람의 눈을 쳐다보지 않으려 한다. 불운하게도 다른 문화에서 인터뷰를 하는 사람은 이것을 인터뷰를 받는 사람이 '무언가를 숨기고 있다'는 증거로, 혹은 그들이 '내 눈도 못 보는 교활한 사람'이라는 증거로 오해한다. 신체 언어의 문화적 차이들에 대한 지식수준을 향상시키는 것이 국제적인 능숙함을 쌓는 데 도움이 될 수 있다.

구문 [11행~15행] Unfortunately, this, in other cultures, is often misread by interviewers / as evidence **that** the interviewee is "hiding something," or as evidence **that** they are *a "shifty character* [who couldn't look me in the eye]."

두 개의 that절은 각각 앞의 evidence와 동격인 명사절이다.

어휘 **subtle** 미묘한; 교묘한 **assumption** 가정, 추정 **observation** 관찰 **favorable** 호감이 가는(↔ **unfavorable**) **characteristic** 특징 **character** 성격; 특징; 인물; 글자 **misread** (**misread-misread**) 잘못 해석하다, 오해하다 **shifty** 교활한, 수상쩍은 **aid** 돕다 **competence** 능숙함; 능력

40 요약문 완성 ④

소재 음식의 소리가 미각에 미치는 영향

해설 실험에서 피실험자들은 과자의 바사삭 소리가 더 크게 들리고 주파수가 높아지면 과자를 더욱 바삭거린다고 느꼈으므로, '소리(sound)'가 우리가 음식을 어떻게 '인식하는지(perceive)'에 영향을 미친다는 결론을 내릴 수 있다.

해석 먹는 것은 생존에 필수적이다. 그래서 우리 몸이 '맛'의 감각을 '냄새'의 감각에 연결시킴으로써 그것을 '연장'하려 하는 것이 놀랍지 않다. 그것은 합리적인 것 같다. 결국 좋은 음식은 보통 냄새도 좋으니까. 주제문 그러나 우리가 음식에 대해 어떻게 느끼는지에 영향을 미치는 다른 요소가 있다. Oxford 대학은 피실험자들이 칩을 먹는 동안 잡음 제거 헤드폰을 착용하고 마이크 앞에 앉아 있는 실험을 진행했다. 자원자들이 바사삭 소리를 들을 수 있는 유일한 방법은 헤드폰 안에 있는 확성기를 통하는 것이었고, 이것은 심리학자들이 제어했다. 바사삭 소리가 보통 수준으로 재생되면, 칩을 먹는 사람들은 칩이 보통 바삭하다고 생각했다. 소리가 더 커지거나 고주파가 증가하면, 그들은 그것이 더욱 바삭하다고 평가했다. 그리고 바사삭 소리나 고주파가 낮춰지면, 칩은 덜 바삭한 것 같았다.

⬇

음식의 냄새뿐만 아니라 (A) 소리도 우리가 먹는 것을 우리가 어떻게 (B) 인식하는지에 영향을 미친다.

구문 [1행~3행] So it's not surprising / that our body will "extend" the sense of "taste" / **by linking** *it* **to** the sense of "smell."

「by v-ing」는 '~함으로써'의 뜻이며, 「link A to B」는 'A를 B에 연결시키다'의 의미이다. 여기서 it은 the sense of "taste"를 지칭한다.

[9행~11행] *The only way* [the volunteers could hear the crunch] / was via *the loudspeakers* (inside the headphones) — **which** the psychologists controlled.

[ ] 부분은 The only way를 수식하는 관계부사절로, the way를 수식할 때는 관계부사 how를 함께 쓸 수 없으므로 how가 생략되었다. which는 the loudspeakers inside the headphones를 지칭하는 목적격 관계대명사이다.

어휘 **extend** 연장시키다 **reasonable** 합리적인 **after all** 결국 **factor** 요소 **subject** 피실험자, 대상; 주제; 과목 **microphone** 마이크 **volunteer** 자원자 **crunch** 아삭아삭 씹는 소리 **via** ~을 통하여 **loudspeaker** 확성기 **psychologist** 심리학자 **crisp** 바삭바삭한 **high frequency** 고주파 **lower** 낮추다 **have an influence on** ~에 영향을 미치다 **judge** 판단하다 [선택지 어휘] **appearance** 모습, 외모; 출현 **texture** 질감, 감촉 **identify** 알아보다, 식별하다

41~42 장문 41 ⑤ 42 ②

소재 자기 인식을 바탕으로 유혹에 대비하기

해설 41. 유혹에 굴복하지 않고 자제심을 기르기 위해 유혹의 영향력을 사전에 예측하고 자기 분석을 통하여 이에 효과적으로 대비하라는 내용의 글이므로 제목으로 가장 적절한 것은 ⑤ '유혹을 사전에 예방하여 극복하라'이다.

① 유혹을 피하지 말고 맞서라
② 유혹에 저항하기 위해 무엇이 우리를 강하게 만들어줄까?
③ 유혹: 당신이 생각하는 것보다 저항하기 더 힘들다
④ 열정: 우리가 유혹에 굴복하는 이유

42. Odysseus는 자신의 몸을 배에 묶어둠으로써 강력함이 아니라 무력함을 계획한 것이므로 (b)의 powerfulness를 powerlessness로 바꿔 써야 한다.

해석 트로이 전쟁이 끝나고 집으로 가는 오랜 여정 길에, 영웅 Odysseus(오디세우스)는 바다 님프 사이렌들과 마주했다. 그들은 너무나 아름답게 노래해서 선원들은 다가가서 배를 주변의 바위에 충돌시키지 않을 수 없었다. Odysseus는 자신의 몸을 배의 막대에 묶고, 선원들의 귀는 밀랍으로 채워 넣고, 그들에게 자신의 얼굴 표정을 무시하라고 엄격한 지시를 내렸다. 그들이 위험한 해역으로 항해할 때 그곳에 이 (a) 약삭빠른 영웅이 서 있었다. 사이렌들은 그를 불렀고, 그는 그들의 노래를 들었다. 그는 자신의 부하들에게 자신을 풀어달라고 애원했지만, 그의 부하들은 그의 간청을 들을 수 없었다. 그를 파멸로부터 구해준 것은 바로 그의 계획된 (b) 강력함(→ 무력함)이었다. 그는 죽지 않고 사이렌들의 노래의 아름다움을 들은 최초의 인간이 되었다. Odysseus는 자신의 (c) 약점을 예상했고 자신의 예측된 열망이 파괴적인 결말에 도달하는 것을 막기 위해 조치를 취했다. 사이렌들의 드라마는 (d) 자제심 전투에 관한 것이다. 매일이 그러한 전투와 같다. 당신이 직장의 자판기에서 산 캔디바를 먹는다면, 당신은 지갑에 어떤 동전도 두지 않겠다는 선택을 할 수 있다. 이러한 작은 변화가 당신 식단에서 큰 향상을 이룰 수 있다. 우리의

유혹은 강력하고 부단하지만, 우리가 (e) 굴복할 운명인 것은 아니다. 주제문 우리가 그것들의 영향을 예측할 수 있기 때문에, 규율이 더해진 자기인식은 만족스럽고 도덕적인 삶을 영위하기 위한 전투에서 승리하는 전략을 제공할 수 있다.

구문 [3행~5행] They sang **so** beautifully // **that** sailors were compelled to approach [and] crashed their ships / on the surrounding rocks.
「so ~ that ...」 구문은 '너무 ~해서 …하다'의 뜻이다. 「be compelled to-v」는 '할 수 없이 v하다'의 뜻이다. that절에서 과거동사 were와 crashed가 병렬구조를 이룬다.

[12행~13행] **It was** *precisely his planned powerlessness* **that** saved him from destruction.
「It was ~ that ...」 강조구문이 쓰여 precisely ~ powerlessness가 강조되었으며 '…한 것은 바로 ~이다'의 뜻이다.

어휘 **nymph** 님프, 정령 **sailor** 선원 (= crew) **compel** ~하게 만들다, 강요하다 **pole** 막대 **instruction** 지시 **cunning** 약삭빠른; 교활한; 교묘한 **beg** 간청[애원]하다 **set A free** A를 풀어주다 **plea** 애원, 간청 **precisely** 바로, 정확히 **destruction** 파멸, 파괴 *cf.* **destructive** 파괴적인 **anticipate** 예상하다 **take steps** 조치를 취하다 **predictable** 예측할 수 있는 **vending machine** 자판기 **temptation** 유혹 **constant** 끊임없는, 부단한 **be destined to-v** v할 운명이다 **surrender** 굴복하다 **self-knowledge** 자기인식 **discipline** 규율, 훈육 **moral** 도덕의

43~45 장문 43 ④ 44 ③ 45 ④

소재 가장 좋아했던 자신의 귀와 꼬리 때문에 위험에 빠진 토끼

해설 43. (A)는 한 토끼가 샘물에 비친 자기 모습에 감탄했다는 내용으로, 바로 뒤에는 뒷다리를 보기 전까지 계속 자신의 귀와 꼬리에 감탄하는 토끼의 행동이 묘사된 (D)가 오는 것이 적절하다. 이어서 자신의 뒷다리가 마음에 들지 않아 불평하던 중 사냥꾼과 사냥개에게 쫓기게 되는 (B)가 오고, 귀와 꼬리 때문에 사냥개에게 붙잡히고 말았다는 (C)가 이어져야 내용의 흐름이 자연스럽다.

44. (c)는 토끼의 뒷다리(her legs)를 가리키나 나머지는 모두 토끼의 귀와 꼬리(her ears and tail)를 가리킨다.

45. (C)에서 토끼는 자신의 몸에서 가장 좋아하던 부분인 귀와 꼬리 때문에 사냥개에게 잡히게 되었다. 따라서 ④가 글의 내용과 일치하지 않는다.

해석 (A) 어느 날 작은 토끼가 맑은 샘에서 물을 마시다가 물에 비친 자신을 보게 되었다. 토끼는 (a) 자기가 본 것(= her ears and tail)에 아주 만족해서 귀를 위아래로 세우기도 하고 꼬리를 좌우로 흔들면서 꽤 오랫동안 머물렀다.
(D) ⑤ "오, 토끼파이야!" 토끼는 (그게 자기 별명이라서) 혼자 이렇게 중얼거렸다. "네 부드럽고 하얀 귀는 정말 예쁘구나! 귀를 그렇게 하니까 얼마나 귀여운지! 그게 네 오밀조밀 작은 얼굴과 사랑스러운 눈을 어찌나 돋보이게 해주는지! 그리고 네 복슬복슬한 하얀 꼬리말이야. 정말 완벽해! 그런 꼬리는 숲속의 모든 자매 토끼들의 부러움의 대상이고말고!" 그렇게 토끼는 계속해서 (e) 그녀가 가진 것(= her ears and tail)에 감탄하며 칭찬을 아끼지 않았다. 그러다 몸을 뻗어 자신의 뒷다리를 보게 되었다.
(B) ① 뒷다리를 위아래로 쳐다보면서 토끼는 얼굴을 찌푸렸다. "내 몸의 나머지 부분도 내 꼬리와 귀처럼 예쁘면 좋을 텐데! (b) 그것들(= her ears and tail)은 바로 나를 가장 만족시키는 부분이거든! 그런데 이 다리는, 휴! 이 다리로 빨리 달리고 높이 뛰는 것도 부끄러워. 만약 누군가 (c) 그것들(= her legs)이 내 몸에 얼마나 꼭 맞는 모양인지 말하더라도 난 상관하지 않아! 내게 있어 다리는 보기 흉하고 못생긴 존재일 뿐이야. 아예 다리가 없었으면 좋겠어!" 토끼는 자신을 흠모하기도 하고 도대체 자기 다리를 어떻게 하면 좋을지 생각하기도 하면서 ② 샘물가에 머물러 있었다. 바로 그때, 갑자기 사냥꾼과 개 짖는 소리가 들려왔다.
(C) 그들이 토끼 냄새를 맡았던 거다. 토끼는 힘껏 뛰어올라 개가 달릴 수 있는 것보다 훨씬 더 빨리 언덕을 가로질러 껑충껑충 열심히 달렸다. 1마일 정도를 달리자 ③ 토끼는 가시덤불을 발견하고 그 안에 기어 들어가 가만히 있으려고 했지만 ④ 복슬복슬한 하얀 꼬리가, 밝은 하얀 표지판처럼 덤불 바로 바깥에 나와 있었다. 사냥개가 다시 다가왔다. 토끼는 반대편으로 뛰어나가려고 했으나 부드러운 귀가 가시덤불에 걸려 사냥개가 토끼의 꼬리를 붙잡았다! 주제문 토끼를 이렇게 끔찍한 궁지에 걸려들게 한 건 바로 (d) 그것들(= her ears and tail)이었다.

구문 [(B) 2행~3행] "**If only** the rest of me **could be** as cute as my tail and my ears! ~"
[(B) 8행] **I wish** I **didn't have** them at all!
「If only+가정법 과거」, 「I wish+가정법 과거」는 현재 실현 불가능한 일에 대한 소망을 나타내는 표현이다. If only를 쓰면 '~하기만 한다면 좋을 텐데'로 소망의 뜻이 더 강조된다.

[(B) 10행~12행] At that moment, / suddenly came(V) *the sound*(S) (of hunters and barking dogs).
주어가 길고 상대적으로 술부가 짧을 경우, 문장의 균형을 맞추기 위해 주어와 동사를 흔히 도치시킨다.

[(C) 8행~9행] ~ and the dogs had her **by** her tail!
by는 동작의 대상이 되는 신체의 일부를 나타낼 때 쓰인다.
e.g. I caught her **by** the shoulder. (나는 그녀의 어깨를 잡았다.)

[(C) 9행~10행] **It was** *they*(S') **that** caused(V') her(O') to be caught in this terrible trap(C').
「It was[is] ~ that ...」 강조구문으로 주어인 they를 강조하고 있다. 「cause+O+C(to-v)」는 'O가 v하게 만들다'의 의미이다.

어휘 **(A) spring** 샘; 튀어 오르다 **reflect** 비추다; 반영하다 **pleased** 만족한, 기쁜 **for quite some time** 오랫동안, 한동안 **(B) frown** (얼굴을) 찌푸리다, 찡그리다 **rest** 나머지; 휴식(하다) **ashamed** 부끄러운 **unshapely** 보기 흉한, 못생긴(= ugly-looking) **admire** 흠모하다; 감탄하다; 칭찬하다 (= praise) **on earth** 《강조》 도대체 **(C) pick up** (냄새 · 소리 등을) 알아차리다, 감지하다; (차에) 태우러 가다; 집어 올리다 **scent** 냄새 **bound** 껑충껑충 달리다 **thorny** 가시가 있는 *cf.* **thorn** 가시덤불, 가시 **crawl** 기어가다 **fluffy** 솜털이 보송보송한, 솜털 같은 **trap** (빠져나갈 수 없는) 궁지, 덫 **(D) say[talk] to oneself** 혼잣말하다 **highlight** 돋보이게 하다, 강조하다 **delicate** 섬세한; 연약한, 다치기 쉬운 **asset** 가진 것, 자산 **catch sight of** ~을 보게 되다, ~을 얼핏 보다

실전 모의고사 05

본문 p.69

18 ④	19 ⑤	20 ③	21 ④	22 ①	23 ②	24 ③	25 ⑤	26 ⑤	27 ⑤
28 ②	29 ⑤	30 ⑤	31 ⑤	32 ③	33 ③	34 ⑤	35 ④	36 ④	37 ③
38 ⑤	39 ③	40 ⑤	41 ③	42 ④	43 ②	44 ⑤	45 ④		

18 글의 목적 ④

소재 작가가 쓴 책의 도움을 받은 것에 대한 감사

해설 첫 문장에 글의 목적이 잘 드러나 있다. 작가가 쓴 책의 내용 덕분에 고모에게 진정한 위로를 드릴 수 있었다며 감사를 표현하고 있으므로, 글의 목적으로 가장 적절한 것은 ④이다.

해석 Hall 씨께,

주제문 약 1년 전쯤에 저는 귀하의 소책자, 〈모든 경우에 대해 편지를 쓰는 법〉을 읽었고 그 책이 최근 저에게 얼마나 큰 도움을 주었는지 말씀드리고 싶습니다. 사실, 저희 고모가 사랑하는 고양이가 오랜 병을 앓다가 얼마 전에 죽고 나서 저는 뭐라도 말씀드려야 한다고 생각했어요. 그런데 뭐라고 말씀드리지요? 전 Allie라는 이름의 그 고양이를 잘 몰랐지만 Peggy 고모가 그 고양이를 얼마나 많이 사랑했는지는 알았어요. 그때 당신의 소책자에서 위로 편지를 쓰는 것에 대해 이야기한 것이 떠올랐고, 저는 Allie에 관해 기억하고 있는 작은 이야기 하나를 Peggy 고모에게 썼어요. Peggy 고모는 나중에 '고모를 다시 미소 짓게 해줘서' 제게 고맙다는 답신을 주셨어요. 고모는 제 편지가 고모가 Allie와 함께 했던 시절의 많은 다른 행복한 추억을 떠올리는 데 도움을 주었다고 말씀하셨어요.
Martin Garrix 드림

어휘 **booklet** 소책자 **occasion** (특별한) 경우, 때 **beloved** 사랑하는; 인기 많은 **illness** (특정 종류의) 병, 질환 **condolence** 위로, 애도

19 분위기 추론 ⑤

소재 수업 중에 쓰러진 선생님

해설 선생님이 수업 중에 갑작스럽게 쓰러진 사건을 묘사한 글이다. 선생님이 쓰러진 후 학생들이 소리 지르며 앞으로 몰려간 모습에서 '놀라고 긴급한(shocking and urgent)' 상황임을 알 수 있다. 따라서 정답은 ⑤이다.

해석 학생들은 허리를 꼿꼿이 세우고 책상에 앉아 있었다. Morgan 선생님의 얼굴이 백지장처럼 하얘졌고, 그녀는 거친 숨을 들이마시며 입이 물 밖으로 나온 물고기처럼 열렸다 닫혔다 했다. 분필이 칠판에 글쓰기를 멈추고 잠시 공중에서 춤을 추더니 갑자기 바닥에 떨어져 두 조각이 났다. 그런 다음 아주 크게 '쿵!'하는 소리가 들렸고, 앞줄에 앉은 누군가가 "Morgan 선생님께서 쓰러지셨어! Morgan 선생님께서 바닥에 쓰러지셨어!"라고 외쳤다. 이것은 무엇보다도 가장 놀라운 뉴스였다. 전 학급이 그 즉시 벌떡 일어나 (상황을) 더 잘 보려고 앞으로 달려 나갔다. 주제문 그리고 거기에 정말 선생님이 계셨다. Morgan 선생님이 의식을 잃은 채 바닥에 바로 누워 있었던 것이다.

① 활기차고 축제 분위기인 ② 심각하고 엄숙한
③ 낙담시키고 절망적인 ④ 지루하고 단조로운

구문 [11행~13행] And **there** indeed **she was**: *Ms. Morgan* (flat on her back on the floor, unconscious).
There나 Here 등은 보통 「There[Here]+V+S」의 도치구문으로 쓰이나, 주어가 대명사일 때는 도치가 일어나지 않는다. ( ) 부분은 형용사구로 앞에 있는 Ms. Morgan을 수식한다.

어휘 **pure** 순전한; 깨끗한 **draw in a breath of air** 숨을 들이마시다 **for a moment** 잠시 동안 **in mid-air** 공중에 **thump** 쿵 하는 소리; ~을 주먹으로 치다 **fall down** 넘어지다; 무너지다 **sensational** 매우 놀라게 하는; 선정적인 **at once** 즉시; 동시에 **get[have, take] a good look** 잘[자세히] 보다 **flat on one's back** (등을 대고) 바로 누운 **unconscious** 의식을 잃은; 무의식적인

20 필자 주장 ③

소재 아이가 저지른 성가신 일을 다루는 부모의 태도

해설 아이가 의도치 않게 성가신 일을 저지를 때 부모가 취해야 할 태도에 대해 조언하는 글이다. 글의 중반부(Instead of ~ viewpoint)에 본인의 불편함에 대해 생각하기보다 아이의 관점에서 보라는 필자의 주장이 드러나 있으므로 정답은 ③이다.

해석 아이들은 성가신 일을 저지르는데, 악의가 있어서가 아니라 어른들처럼 생각하지 않기 때문이다. 만약 아이들이 저지른 온갖 엉망진창의 상태가 당신을 괴롭히게 내버려둔다면 당신은 비참한 하루를 보낼 것이다. 당신이 주방에 들어서자 당신의 두 살짜리 아이가 싱크대에서 온 바닥에 물을 튀기는 것을 본다. 당신은 '난 불쌍해'란 생각에 으레 빠져들 수 있다. 그러나 더 바람직한 선택이 여기 있다. 주제문 당신 자신의 불편함에 대해 먼저 생각하는 대신, 즉시 당신 아이의 관점을 클릭하여 들어가라. "이거 재미있군. 접시와 물을 가지고 네가 얼마나 많은 걸 할 수 있는지 보자."라고. 이런 식으로 당신은 아이가 하고 있는 것이 (성장) 발달적으로 적절하다는 것을 유념하게 될 것이다. 당신이 몇 분 더 기다리면 아이는 다른 일을 시작할 것이다. 당신 자신에게서 벗어나 아이 속으로 들어가는 것은 정신적 부담을 덜어준다. 당신은 바닥의 물도, 당신 머릿속의 엉망진창인 상태도 치우지 않아도 된다.

구문 [4행~5행] As you enter the kitchen, // you see(V) *your two-year-old* (at the sink)(O) splashing water all over the floor(C).
「지각동사(see, watch, feel, hear 등)+O+C」의 구조이다. 지각동사는 목적격보어 자리에 현재분사(v-ing) 또는 원형부정사(v)를 취할 수 있다.

어휘 **annoying** 성가신, 짜증스런 **maliciously** 악의를 갖고, 심술궂게 **miserable** 비참한 **mess** 엉망진창인 상태, 난장판 **splash** (물을) 튀기다, 첨벙첨벙하다 **sink into** (생각에) 잠기다, 빠져들다 **mindset** (고정된) 사고방식; 태도 **inconvenience** 불편(↔ **convenience** 편의, 편리) **viewpoint** 관점, 견해(= **point of view**) **developmentally** (성장) 발달적으로 **appropriate** 적절한, 알맞은 **go on to** (새로운 것을) 시작하다; ~로 넘어가다 **get out of** ~에서 벗어나다[빠져나오다] **strain** 부담, 압박(감) **along with** ~와 마찬가지로; ~와 함께

21 글의 요지 ④

소재 영어 학습에 있어 어휘력의 중요성

해설 영어에서 어휘 학습의 중요성에 대해 기술한 글이다. 두 번째 문장(Memorizing vocabulary ~ important thing.)에서 어휘를 외우는 것이 중요하다는 주제문을 제시하고, 마지막 문장(The best way ~ speak them aloud.)에서 어휘를 더 많이 암기하고 말해 보는 것이 영어를 더 잘할 수 있는 최상의 방법이라 했다. 따라서 요지로 가장 적절한 것은 ④이다.

해석 학생들에게 외국어로서의 영어 학습을 더 재미있게 만들어 주고 싶다면, 문법을 제쳐놓는 것에서부터 시작할 수 있다. 주제문 어휘와 전체 문장을 암기하는 것이 가장 중요한 일이다. 좋은 어휘력을 갖췄다면, 당신이 만드는 문장이 완벽하지 않더라도 어떻게든 의사소통이 가능하다. 한편, 문법은 잘 이해하고 있는데 어휘가 부족하다면, (상대방의 말을) 이해하고 (자신의 생각을 상대방에게) 이해시키는 데 어려움을 겪을 것이다. (언어를 배우는) 학생은 더 많은 어휘를 이해할수록, 말을 하려는 용기가 더 생길 것이다. 주제문 언어를 더 잘하는 최상의 방법은 더 많은 단어를 학습하고, 그 단어들을 생각해내서 소리 내어 말하는 것이다.

구문 [9행~10행] **The more** vocabulary a student understands, / **the more** encouraged they'll be to speak. (= As a student understands more vocabulary, they'll be more encouraged to speak.)
「the+비교급 ~, the+비교급 ....」은 '~할수록, 더욱 더 …하다'란 뜻이다.

어휘 **leave aside** ~을 제쳐놓다, 따로 두다 **grammar** 문법 **vocabulary** 어휘 **complete** 완전한; 완결된 **get by** 그럭저럭 해내다 **grasp** 이해, 파악; 움켜잡기; 완전히 이해하다; 움켜쥐다 **poor** 형편없는; 가난한 **struggle** 애쓰다, 분투하다; 싸우다 **encourage A to-v** A가 v하도록 용기를 북돋다[격려하다] **aloud** 소리 내어; 크게

22 글의 주제 ①

소재 관리자로서 나쁜 소식을 전하는 자세

해설 주제문인 첫 번째 문장에서 관리자로서 직원들에게 나쁜 소식을 잘 전하는 방법을 아는 것의 중요성을 언급한 후 구체적인 방법에 대해 설명하고 있으므로, 글의 주제로 가장 적절한 것은 ① '직원들에게 나쁜 소식을 전하는 방법들'이다.

해석 주제문 유능한 관리자나 고용주가 되는 것의 일부는 나쁜 소식을 잘 전하는 사람이 되는 방법을 아는 것과 관련이 있다. 무엇보다, 그 소식을 전해 받는 사람과 얼굴을 마주하고 나쁜 소식을 직접 전해야 한다. 직원들에게 올해 급여 인상을 받지 못할 거라든가, 그들이 실수를 저질렀다든지 또는 기대보다 실적이 좋지 않다는 것을 알리기 위해 메모를 쓸 수는 없다. 당신이 그 문제에 대해 어떻게 느끼는지와, 개인적으로 유감스럽게 생각하며 그들과 공감한다는 것을 보여주어야 한다. 당신이 전하는 나쁜 소식에 대한 그들의 반응에 귀 기울일 준비가 되어 있음을 보여준다면, 당신은 분명히 그들의 분노를 사지 않을 것이다. 당신이 전하는 소식을 납득하고, 그들이 아마도 느낄 감정을 다스릴 수 있도록 사람들에게 시간을 주어라.
② 동료에 대한 공감을 표하는 방법
③ 나쁜 소식을 전해야 하는 일련의 이유
④ 직원들이 대처해야만 하는 피할 수 없는 나쁜 소식들
⑤ 직원들이 나쁜 소식에 대처하는 효과적인 방법들

구문 [1행~2행] Part of being an effective manager or employer (S) involves (V) knowing how to be a good bearer of bad news (O).
Part of being ~ employer가 주어이고, 동사 involves는 knowing 이하를 목적어로 취한다.
[4행~7행] You can't write memos to tell staff (IO) // **that** they will not get raises this year (DO1), // **that** they have made an error (DO2), [or] **that** they are not performing as well as expected (DO3).
세 개의 that절은 tell의 직접목적어이며 접속사 or로 연결되어 병렬구조를 이룬다.

어휘 **effective** 유능한; 효과적인 **involve** 수반[포함]하다; 관련시키다 **bearer** 전달자, 나르는 사람 **break the news** 나쁜 소식을 전하다 **face to face** 서로 얼굴을 맞대고 **raise** (임금 등의) 인상; 높이다 **personally** 개인적으로 **sympathize** 공감하다; 동정하다 *cf.* **sympathy** 공감; 동정 **indicate** 보여주다, 나타내다 **reaction** 반응 **save** (불쾌한 일을) 피하다 **digest** 납득[이해]하다; (음식물을) 소화하다 [선택지 어휘] **convey** 전달하다 **inevitable** 피할 수 없는 **deal with** 대처하다, 처리하다(= cope with)

23 글의 제목 ②

소재 생활에 쓰이는 우주 기술

해설 두 번째 문장(But much of ~ masses)에서 NASA가 개발한 우주 기술이 대중적으로 쓰이게 되었다는 주제문을 제시한 후, 이어지는 내용에서 휴대전화 카메라, MRI와 같은 예시가 주제를 뒷받침하고 있으므로, 글의 제목으로는 ② '지상으로 가져온 우주 기술'이 가장 적절하다.

해석 NASA의 주된 목적은 우주를 탐사하고 더 잘 이해하는 것이다. 주제문 하지만 NASA가 별에 도달하기 위해 개발한 기술 중 많은 것들이 대중들에게 영감을 주었으며, 예를 들어 보다 영양가 높은 유아용 분유, 해로운 자외선을 차단하는 선글라스, 그리고 더 많은 것들과 같은 혁신을 이끌었다. 모든 휴대전화 카메라의 3분의 1이 원래 NASA의 우주선을 위해 개발된 기술을 사용한다. 그리고 1960년대에, 달의 사진의 화질을 높이고 싶어 한 NASA 과학자들은 디지털 이미지 처리 기술을 발명했다. 그 기술은 나중에 많은 다른 용도를 찾았는데, 특히 의학 분야에서 자기공명영상(MRI)과 같은 몸의 영상 촬영 기술을 가능하게 하는데 도움이 되었다.
① 우주 탐사에 이로운 것
③ 우주 탐사는 비용만큼의 가치가 있는가?
④ 일상용품에서 기인한 NASA의 발명품들
⑤ NASA는 우주 탐사의 새로운 시대를 열었다

구문 [2행~6행] But much of *the technology* [(which[that]) NASA developed ● in reaching for the stars] / has inspired the masses, / **leading** to innovations / such as more nutritious infant formula, *sunglasses* [**that** block harmful ultraviolet light], and many more.
첫 번째 [ ] 부분은 선행사 the technology를 수식하고 있으며, 목적격 관계대명사 which 또는 that이 생략되었다. ●는 developed의 원래 목적어인 the technology가 있었던 자리이다. leading ~ many more는 부대상황을 나타내는 분사구문이다. 두 번째 [ ] 부분은 관계사절로, 앞에 있는 sunglasses를 수식하고 있다.

어휘 **primary** 주된, 주요한 **explore** 탐사[탐구]하다 *cf.* **exploration** 탐사; 탐구 **cosmos** 우주 **reach** 도달하다 **inspire** 영감을 주다 **mass** 대중; 무리; 덩어리 **lead to** ~로 이어지다 **innovation** 혁신; 획기적인 것 **nutritious** 영양가가 높은 **ultraviolet light** 자외선 **spacecraft** 우주선 **enhance** 질을 높이다, 향상시키다 **invent** 발명하다 **application** 적용; 용도; 지원; (약 등을) 바름 **field** 분야; 들판 **enable** 가능하게 하다 **magnetic** 자석의, 자기의 **resonance** ((과학)) 공명; (소리의) 울림 [선택지 어휘] **benefit** 이롭다, 이익이 되다; 혜택, 이익 **originate from** ~에서 생겨나다 **daily goods** 일상용품 **era** 시대

24 도표 이해 ③

소재 다양한 여가 활동에 보내는 시간 통계

해설 15~19세의 연령층이 하루 중 독서에 소비하는 시간은 평균 0.1시간이고 컴퓨터로 여가를 보내는 시간은 평균 0.3시간이다. 컴퓨터 사용에 0.1시간을 소비하는 그룹은 65세 이상의 연령층이다. ③의 they는 the younger group을 가리키므로 도표의 내용과 일치하지 않는다.

해석 **〈다양한 여가 활동에 보내는 하루 평균 시간 (미국, 2018년)〉**
주제문 위의 그래프는 2018년에 미국의 15~19세의 연령층과 65세 이상의 연령층이 다양한 여가 활동에 보내는 하루 평균 시간을 보여준다. ① 두 연령층 모두 TV 시청에 가장 많은 시간을 보냈는데, 65세 이상은 하루에 3.8시간, 15~19세의 연령층은 2.3시간을 보냈다. ② 더 나이 든 그룹(= 65세 이상의 연령층)은 두 번째로 많은 시간인 하루에 한 시간을 독서에 소비했다. ③ 더 젊은 그룹(= 15~19세의 연령층)은 독서에 하루 평균 0.1시간만을 소비하였는데, 이는 이들이 여가에 컴퓨터를 사용하며 보낸 시간과 같다. ④ 더 나이 든 그룹(= 65세 이상의 연령층)은 스포츠, 운동, 오락 활동에 0.2시간을 보냈고, 이것은 더 젊은 연령층이 같은 활동에 보낸 시간보다 적다. ⑤ 하지만 더 나이 든 그룹은 휴식과 사색에 더 젊은 그룹보다 네 배 더 많은 시간을 소비하였다.

구문 [8행~10행] The younger group averaged only 0.1 hours per day reading, / equal to *the time* [(that) they spent ● using a computer for leisure].

they spent 앞에는 선행사 the time을 수식하는 목적격 관계대명사가 생략되었다. ●은 spent의 원래 목적어가 있던 자리이다.

어휘 **average** 평균(의); 보통(의); 평균 ~이 되다 **leisure** 여가 **portion** (더 큰 것의) 부분[일부] **recreation** 오락; 휴양

25 내용 불일치 ⑤

소재 지구 최후의 날 비행기

해설 가끔 연료 탱크 호스가 유리창에 부딪히는 경우가 있지만 큰 피해는 없었다고 했으므로 ⑤가 글의 내용과 일치하지 않는다.

해석 ① '지구 최후의 날 비행기'라고 알려진 특수 보잉 747기는 미국에 엄청난 타격을 주는 공격이 있을 경우, 떠다니는 펜타곤(미 국방부 본부)의 역할을 할 수 있다. ② 이 비행기는 거의 36시간 동안 공중에 떠 있을 정도로 충분한 음식과 물, 연료를 실을 수 있다. ③ 비행기는 48명에서 112명까지의 승무원으로 운영되는데, 이것은 공군 역사상 어떠한 항공기 승무원보다 많은 수이다. 그것은 1970년대에 만들어졌으며, ④ 핵전쟁 중에도 비행을 계속할 수 있도록 설계되었는데, 이것이 이 비행기가 공중에서 연료를 재공급 받을 수 있는 이유이다. ⑤ 때때로, 공중에 떠 있는 연료 탱크의 연료 호스가 조종사의 앞 유리를 마치 성난 거대한 뱀처럼 세게 칠 때도 있었지만, 심각한 손상을 일으킨 적은 없었다.

어휘 **doomsday** 최후의 심판일 **serve as** ~의 역할을 하다 **headquarters** 본부, 본사 **in the event of** ~할 경우에, 만약 ~하면 **devastating** 엄청난 타격을 주는; 엄청나게 충격적인 **fuel** 연료; ~에 연료를 공급하다 *cf.* **refuel** 연료를 재공급하다 **airborne** 공중에 떠있는 *cf.* **in midair** 공중에 **aircraft** 항공기 **nuclear war** 핵전쟁 **on occasion(s)** 때때로, 가끔 **smash** (세게) 부딪치다, 충돌하다 **windshield** 앞 유리, 바람막이 창

26 안내문 불일치 ⑤

소재 국립 난초 정원 가이드 투어

해설 가이드 투어는 무료지만 난초 정원의 입장료는 유료이므로 ⑤가 안내문과 일치하지 않는 내용이다.

해석

5월 17일 (토): 국립 난초 정원 가이드 투어

싱가포르 식물원 국립 난초 정원에 있는 난초의 아름다움과 다채로움을 탐사해 보세요. 1,000종의 순종과 2,000종의 교배종이 현재 정원 보유 품종의 구성이며, ① 600종 이상의 순종과 교배종이 전시되어 있습니다.

② 이 도보 투어는 자원봉사자들에 의해 시행되며 매달 세 번째 토요일에 열립니다.
- 시간: ③ 오전 9시, 10시, 11시 (영어) 그리고 오후 4시 (표준 중국어)
- 투어 시간: 1시간
- ④ 등록: 투어 15분 전에 선착순으로 관광 안내소에서 등록합니다.
- 비용: ⑤ 투어는 무료이나 난초 정원의 입장료는 적용됩니다. 성인 5달러, 학생 1달러, 60세 이상 연장자 및 12세 미만의 어린이는 무료입장
- 연락처: 관광객 서비스 6471-7361

어휘 **diversity** 다양성 **botanic** 식물(학)의 **hybrid** 교배종, 잡종 **on display** 전시된 **conduct** 시행하다, 실시하다 **Mandarin** 표준 중국어 **registration** 기재, 등록; (우편물의) 등기 *cf.* **register** 기재하다, 등록하다 **prior to** ~에 앞서 **on a first-come-first-served basis** 선착순으로 **admission** 입장(료)

27 안내문 일치 ⑤

소재 캠퍼스 버스 운행 안내

해설 마지막 문장에서 1년, 9개월, 한 학기 주차권을 소지한 교직원은 요청하면 무료로 승차권을 발급받을 수 있다고 했으므로 ⑤가 안내문의 내용과 일치한다.

해석

버스 운행

① Nebraska 대학 링컨 캠퍼스에서는 가을과 봄 학기 동안 월요일부터 금요일까지 버스 노선을 운행합니다.

운송 정보
- 본 웹사이트에서 노선도와 시간표를 인쇄하세요.
- ② 버스는 모든 정류장에 정차하지 않습니다. 정류장에서 기다리고 있어야 하며, 운전기사가 여러분이 내린다는 것을 알도록 해야 합니다.

버스 승차권

③ 학생과 교원/직원은 모두 운송 서비스를 이용하기 위해서 다음에 있는 것 모두를 필요로 합니다.

1. StarTran 승차권
2. NCard

④ 학생은 학생 회비를 통해 지급되는 승차권을 발급받게 됩니다. 이 버스 승차권과 이후의 모든 운송 개선책들은 학생회에서 지원합니다.

⑤ 교원/직원들은 요청하는 즉시 (1년/9개월/학기 주차권 소지자에게) 무료로 승차권이 발급됩니다.

어휘 **operate** 운영하다; 작동하다 **semester** 학기 **transit** 공공여객 운송 (기관의 노선) **route map** 노선도 **faculty** 교원; 능력, 재능 **issue** 발행하다 **student fees** 학생 회비 **the student body** 학생회 **upon request** 요청하는 즉시 **permit** 허가증; 허락하다

28 네모 어법 ②

소재 코골이 치료

해설 (A) 주장 · 요구 · 제안 · 명령 등의 동사가 that절을 목적어로 취하고 그 내용이 '~해야 한다'는 당위성의 의미를 가질 때 that절의 동사는 「should+동사원형」이 되며, should는 일반적으로 생략된다. 따라서 should가 생략된 동사원형 call이 알맞다.
(B) 앞부분에 나온 not only와 연결되도록 (B)에는 but (also)가 필요하다. 「not only A but (also) B」는 'A 뿐만 아니라 B도'의 뜻이다.
(C) 「wish+S+V」 구문에서 현재 사실을 반대로 가정, 상상할 때는 동사의 과거형이 사용되며, 과거 사실을 반대로 가정, 상상할 때는 과거완료형이 사용된다. years ago라는 과거 부사구에서 과거 사실과 반대되는 가정임을 알 수 있으므로 과거완료형이 와야 한다.

해석 나는 성공적이지 못한 나의 코골이 치료를 많이 시도해 왔기에 아내가 Bronner 박사의 코골이 치료에 대해 듣고 그(= 박사)에게 전화를 걸어 예약을 잡아보라고 제안했을 때, 나는 즉시 그렇게 했다. Bronner 박사의 클리닉에서 나는 어느 유명한 수면 클리닉에서 환자들을 박사에게 위탁했을 뿐 아니라, 박사의 발명품을 시도해본 많은 사람이 극적인 결과를 경험했다는 사실을 알게 되었다. 그는 나에게 구강 장치를 설치했고 그 결과는 정말 놀라웠다! 주제문 나의 코골이가 치료되었으며, 나의 아내는 이제 내가 내던 그 끔찍한 소음 때문에 깨어나는 일 없이 밤새 잠을 잘 수 있다는 사실에 매우 기뻐한다. 잠 못 이루는 밤을 수년 동안 보낸 후, 우리 둘은 이제 쉽게 잠을 잔다! 우리 부부는 내가 이 장치를 수년 전에 설치했더라면 하고 아쉬워한다.

어휘 **treatment** 치료 **snore** 코를 골다 **appointment** 예약, 약속; 임명 **refer A to B** A를 B에 위탁하다[맡기다] **dramatic** 극적인; 과장된 **fit A with B** B를 A에 설치하다 **oral** 입의, 구두(口頭)의 **appliance** 장치, 기구 **awful** 끔찍한, 지독한 **restless** 잠 못 이루는; 불안한

29 밑줄 어휘 ⑤

소재 부시먼족의 경제 체제

해설 부시먼족은 자원이 부족하여 분업과 공유에 기반을 둔 경제 체제를 갖게 되었다는 내용의 글이다. 이 집단은 혁신과 변화보다는 전통과 안정성, 연속성을 중시하므로 삶이 예측 불가능한 것이 아니라 예측 가능한 방식으로 전개되리라는 것을 알 수 있다. 따라서 ⑤의 unpredictable을 predictable로 바꿔 써야 한다.

해석 전통적인 경제 체제에서 무엇을 어떻게 생산할지 그리고 누구를 위해 생산할지의 질문은 전통에 의해 답변되었다. 칼라하리 부시먼족은 세계에서 가장 혹독한 환경 중 하나에서 사는데, 그곳에서는 심지어 가장 기본적인 자원조차도 공급이 ① 제한되어 있다. 생존하고 충분한 식량을 갖기 위해, 부시먼족은 ② 성별에 기반을 둔 분업을 개발했다. 여성들은 식량 채집을 수행하고 남성들은 사냥을 수행한다. 식량은 그런 후 부족 전체와 나눈다. 이러한 유형의 체제에서 안정성과 연속성이 혁신과 변화보다 ③ 선호된다. 이 체제에서 노인, 어린이, 약자와 장애인은 집단에 의해 돌봄을 받는다. 집단은 그들이 가진 몇 안 되는 소유물을 공유하며, 사유 재산은 ④ 생소한 개념이다. 대개 이 체제의 모든 사람들은 자신이 공동체와 맺고 있는 관계를 이해하며, 그 결과 삶은 꽤 ⑤ 예측 불가능한(→ 예측 가능한) 방식으로 진행된다.

구문 [1행~3행] In a traditional economic system, the questions **of** what and how to produce [and] whom to produce for are answered by tradition.
the questions가 주어이고 동사는 are answered이다. of의 목적어는 두 밑줄 친 부분으로 병렬구조를 이루며, 「의문사+to부정사」 형태의 명사구이다.

어휘 **harsh** 혹독한; 가혹한 **resource** 자원 **supply** 공급 **division of labor** 분업 **based on** ~에 기반을 두어 **gender** 성별 **tribe** 부족 **stability** 안정성 **continuity** 지속성, 연속성 **favor** 선호하다; 찬성하다; 지지하다 **innovation** 혁신 **possession** 소유물 **private property** 사유 재산 *cf.* **property** 재산 **alien** 생소한; 이질적인 **for the most part** 대개 **fairly** 꽤

30 지칭 대상 ⑤

소재 Edward의 새 이웃의 소음 문제

해설 나머지는 모두 Edward를 가리키지만 ⑤는 아래층에 새로 이사 온 이웃을 가리킨다.

해석 주제문 쿵쿵 두드리는 소리가 Edward를 미치게 했다. ① 그(= Edward)의 아래층 아파트로 이사 온 새 이웃은 벽과 창이 흔들릴 정도로 큰 소리로 음악을 연주하고 있었다. 그래서 ② 그(= Edward)는 아래층으로 내려가 새 입주자에게 제발 소리를 줄여달라고 부탁했다. 그(= 새 이웃)는 놀라고 당황한 것 같았고 "죄송해요. 소리가 그렇게 시끄러운지 몰랐습니다."라고 말했다. 그 후 Edward는 자신에게 뿌듯함을 느끼며 그의 아파트로 돌아왔는데, ③ 그(= Edward)가 단호한 입장을 취해 새 이웃에게 시끄러운 음악 소리는 용인되지 않을 거라는 걸 알렸기 때문이었다. 그날 남은 밤 동안과 그 다음 날 낮에는 조용했고, ④ 그(= Edward)는 계속해서 자신에 대해 뿌듯해했다. 그러나 그날 밤, 그는 아래층에서 똑같이 쿵쿵거리는 소리에 잠이 깼다. 또 ⑤ 그(= 새 이웃)였다.

구문 [3행~4행] ~, was playing music *loud* **enough to shake** the walls and windows.
「enough to-v」는 'v할 수 있을 정도로, v하기에 충분한'이란 뜻이다.

어휘 **pounding** 쿵쿵 두드리는 소리 **drive A crazy** A를 미치게 하다 **tenant** 입주자, 세입자 **turn down** (소리·온도 등을) 줄이다; 거절하다 **embarrassed** 당황한 **take a firm stand** 단호한 입장을 취하다 **tolerate** 용인하다, 참다 **pleased** 만족해하는, 기뻐하는 **awaken** 깨우다; (잠에서) 깨다 **thump** 쿵쿵거리다; 치다, 두드리다

31 빈칸 추론 ⑤

소재 예술의 의도성

해설 두 번째 문장에서 art가 들어간 단어는 '계획된 무언가(something that was planned)라는 발상'을 담고 있다고 했다. 이어지는 예시도 우연히 선택한 바위와 의도적으로(deliberately) 골라온 바위는 다르다는 내용이므로, 빈칸 문장은 예술이 ⑤ '의도'와 관련 있다는 내용이 되어야 한다.

해석 '예술(art)'은 문자 그대로 '제작, 즉 특별히 만들어진 무언가'를 의미한다. '기교 있는(artful), 장인(artisan), 예술적인(artistic)'은 서로 관련되어 있으며, 또한 계획된 무엇이라는 발상을 담고 있다. 예술에 대한 사전적 정의에는 노력(effort), 배치(arrangement)와 같은 단어들이 포함된다. 그 단어들 모두, 숲에서 당신이 우연히 앉게 된 바위와 당신이 숲에서 가져와서 당신 정원에 둥그렇게 앉을 자리를 만들려고 다른 바위들과 배치한 바위 사이에는 차이가 있다는 생각을 뒷받침해 준다. 후자는 예술이다, 왜냐하면 당신은 '예술가' 혹은 '제작자'로서의 당신의 마음에 들도록 사물을 의도적으로 집합시켰기 때문이다. 주제문 예술은 제작물 그 자체만큼이나 제작자의 의도와 깊은 관계가 있는 게 분명하다.
① 스타일 ② 기량 ③ 감정 ④ 창조성

구문 [5행~9행] They all support the idea that there's a difference / between *a rock* [(that) you happen to sit on in a forest], [and] *a rock* [that you carry out ~ other rocks / to create a circle of seats].
the idea와 that절 전체가 동격을 이루고 있다. that절에 「difference between A and B」가 쓰여 두 개의 a rock을 비교한다. a rock은 각각 목적격 관계대명사절의 수식을 받는다.

어휘 **literally** 문자 그대로; 그야말로 **production** 제작; 생산(량) *cf.* **product** 제작[생산]물, 제품 **related (to)** (~에) 관련된 **contain** 포함하다 **dictionary definition** 사전적 정의 **arrangement** 배치, 배열 *cf.* **arrange** 배열하다; 마련하다 **happen to-v** 우연히 v하다 **latter** (둘 중에서) 후자(의) **deliberately** 의도적으로, 고의로 **assemble** 집합시키다, 모으다 **have much[nothing] to do with** ~와 깊은 관련이 있다[아무 관련이 없다]

32 빈칸 추론 ③

소재 가상현실 기술

해설 가상현실 기술로 체험할 수 있는 것에 관해 설명하는 글이다. 빈칸 뒤에 산 위를 날거나 머나먼 행성을 탐사하는 등 현실에선 불가능한 일을 직접 경험할 수 있다는 내용이 이어지고 있으므로, 빈칸에는 ③ '불가능한 것이 가능한 것이 된다'가 가장 적절하다.

해석 화성의 표면을 걷는다고 상상해 보라. 당신은 한때 물이 흘렀을지도 모르는 수로(水路)를 따라가고, 온갖 크기의 바위로 덮인 평평한 평원을 가로질러 걷는다. 불가능해 보이는가? 주제문 가상현실(VR)은 신이 나는 현실 세계만큼이나 환상적인 컴퓨터 세상을 모든 면에서 보거나 듣고, 그 안에서 돌아다니도록 해주는 기술이다. 비디오 게임이나 컴퓨터 예술과는 달리, 가상현실은 컴퓨터 화면을 없애고 당신이 3차원의 인공적인 세계로 들어갈 수 있게 해준다. 당신이 해야 할 일은 특수 비디오 안경과 전선이 연결된 장갑을 끼는 것이 전부인데, 그러면 불가능한 것이 가능한 것이 된다. 당신은 산에 오르거나 그 위를 날 수 있고, 머나먼 행성을 탐험하거나 분자를 가지고 놀 수 있으며, 3차원으로 그림을 그리거나 집을 가로질러 다니면서 디자인할 수 있다.
① 당신의 과거를 느낄 수 있다
② 그것은 지구 전체의 모형이다
④ 당신은 사물들을 정확하게 측정할 것이다
⑤ 그것은 가상 세계가 아닌 현실 세계이다

구문 [4행~7행] Virtual reality (VR) is *a technology* [that **allows** you to look at, (to) listen to, [and] (to) move around inside *a computer world* every bit [(which is) as fantastic as the wildest reality]].
첫 번째 [ ]는 a technology를 수식하는 관계사절이고 「allow+O+C(to-v) (O가 v하게 하다)」의 구조로 세 개의 to부정사구가 and로 연결되어 있다. 두 번째 [ ]는 a computer world를 수식한다.

어휘 **surface** 표면 **channel** (강바닥 등의) 수로(水路); 경로 **plain** 평지, 평야; 분명한 **virtual** 가상의; 사실상의 *cf.* **virtual reality** (컴퓨터를 이용해 만든) 가상현실 **every bit** 어느 모로 보나; 전적으로 **wild** 신이 나는; 야생의; 거친 **eliminate** 제거하다 **three-dimensional** 3차원의 *cf.* **dimension** 차원 **artificial** 인공의, 인위적인 **goggles** (보호) 안경 **wired** 유선의 [선택지 어휘] **miniature** 축소 모형, 미니어처; 아주 작은 **measure** 측정하다; (길이·치수 등이) ~이다 **accurately** 정확하게

33 빈칸 추론 ③

소재 감정을 말로 표현하는 것의 효과

해설 감정을 말함으로써 그 감정을 변화시킬 수 있다는 내용의 글이다. 빈칸 이전의 내용에서 화를 변화시키고 두려움의 크기를 변화시킨 것은 모두 감정을 말로 표현함으로써 가능했음을 알 수 있다. 따라서 정답은 ③ '감정을 말함으로써 그 감정이 바뀌는데'이다.

해석 당신이 예전 여자 친구에게 오랫동안 화가 나 있었고 어느 날 그녀를 우연히 만났다고 하자. 당신은 멈춰 서서 이야기를 나누다 갑자기 이렇게 말한다. "나는 너에게 정말 화가 나 있어."라고. 자, 당신이 (방금) 뭘 했는지 생각해보라. 당신은 화를 변화시켰다. 그 화는 더 이상 당신의 머릿속에서 그렇게 커다랗고 보기 싫은 모습으로 존재하는 것이 아니다. 공개되었으니, 이제 그것은 뭔가 다른 게 되었다. 즉, 두 사람 모두 직시할 수 있고 심지어는 웃어넘길지도 모르는 뭔가가 말이다. 두려움을 말하면 그 크기가 달라진다. 당신이 그것을 말하는 방식에 따라 두려움이 줄어들거나 커질 수 있다. 그것은 "저는 길을 잃었어요."라고 누군가에게 말하는 것이 어떻게 집에 다시 돌아오는 길을 찾는 커다란 밑거름이 되는지와 같다. 주제문 그리고 감정을 말함으로써 그 감정이 바뀌는데, 그것(= 감정을 말하는 것)이 우리를 다른 사람들과 연결해주고 더 넓은 시각을 갖게 해주기 때문이다.

① 함께 있는 것은 친밀함을 증진하는데
② 도움을 요청함으로써 우리 자신을 돕는데
④ 감정 조절이 우리의 건강에 도움이 될 수 있는데
⑤ 정확한 정보가 이해로 이어질 수 있는데

어휘 **let's say that** (예를 들어) ~라고 해보자 **for ages** 오랫동안 **happen to-v** 우연히 v하다 **chat** 이야기하다, 잡담하다 **anger** 화, 분노 **exist** 존재하다 **(out) in the open** 공개된, 밝혀진 **state** (정식으로) 말하다; (문서에) 명시하다 **depending on** ~에 따라 **connect A to B** A를 B와 연결하다 **perspective** 시각, 관점(= **point of view**) [선택지 어휘] **closeness** 친밀감, 가까움 **transform** 변화시키다 **manage** 조절하다; 관리하다 **mood** 감정, 기분; 분위기 **lead to** (결과 등으로) 이어지다 **understanding** 이해(심)

34 빈칸 추론 ⑤

소재 음식 앞에서 사라지는 침팬지의 학습 능력

해설 침팬지는 실험자의 빈손을 가리켜야 실험자의 다른 손에 있는 상품을 손에 넣을 수 있다. 그러나 실험자가 먹을 것을 들고 있으면, 빈손을 가리키는 것이 게임의 규칙임에도 불구하고 침팬지는 절대로 그렇게 하지 못한다. 이는 침팬지들이 ⑤ '열망하는 것을 이겨내기 위해 그들의 지능을 사용할' 수 없기 때문이다. 즉, 음식에 관해서는 침팬지들은 이성적으로 행동할 수 없다는 내용의 글이다.

해석 여기에 연구자들이 침팬지들을 가르치는 묘책이 있다. 연구자들은 한 손에 침팬지들이 원하는 것을 잡고 있다. 그러나 그들은 침팬지가 연구자의 다른 손을 가리켜야만 그 물품을 침팬지에게 줄 것이다. 침팬지들은 이 작은 게임을 재빨리 학습하고 연구자의 오른손으로부터 자신의 상품을 가져가기 위해 왼손을 가리키거나 그와 반대로 한다. 그러나 바라는 물품이 먹을 것이면 이러한 학습 능력은 사라진다. 침팬지들이 먹이(예를 들어 즙이 풍부한 바나나)를 볼 때 그들은 게임은 완전히 잊어버리고 그것을 향해 바로 간다. 심지어 수십 번의 실패를 한 후에도 그들은 좌절감이 점점 심해지는 가운데 그들이 바라는 먹이가 있는 손을 계속해서 가리키고 얻지 못한다. 주제문 침팬지들은 그야말로 열망하는 것을 이겨내기 위해 그들의 지능을 사용할 수 없다.

① 선택을 할 시간을 가질
② 행동 계획을 세우고 행동할
③ 모든 선택을 근거하여 판단할 정해진 규준을 개발할
④ 올바른 결정을 하기 위해 정보를 모을

구문 [10행~12행] Even after dozens of failures / they **keep pointing**, (with growing frustration), **at** the hand with *the food* [(which[that]) they desire] and **don't get**.

「keep v-ing」는 '계속해서 v하다'의 뜻이다. with growing frustration은 삽입구이며 pointing과 at이 연결된다. [ ]는 앞에 목적격 관계대명사 which[that]가 생략되어 the food를 수식한다. 문장의 동사 keep과 don't get이 병렬구조를 이룬다.

어휘 **trick** 비결, 묘책 **vice versa** 그 반대도 마찬가지이다 **disappear** 사라지다 **juicy** 즙이 많은 **dozens of** 수십의 **frustration** 좌절(감), 불만 **simply** 그야말로 [선택지 어휘] **criteria** 《**criterion**의 복수형》 규준, 표준 **intelligence** 지능

35 무관한 문장 ④

소재 옛 삶의 기억창고 역할을 하는 책

해설 주제문인 첫 문장 뒤에 주제를 뒷받침하는 콜카타 유대인의 이야기가 예시로 이어지고 있다. 그들의 문화유산이 담긴 책만 남게 되고 그 책들을 통해 그들에 대한 기억을 간직하게 된다는 내용인데, ④는 독서를 통해 다른 관습에 익숙해진다는 내용이므로 글의 흐름에서 벗어난다.

해석 주제문 책은 지나간 삶의 창고다. 예를 들면, 콜카타 유대인의 이야기가 있다. 원래 바그다드에서 온 무역상이었던 그들은 1700년대 후반, 인도의 콜카타에 정착했고, 그들 자신만의 독특한 관습과 요리법, 생활방식을 가진 활기찬 공동체를 설립했다. 오늘날에는 오직 소수의 나이 든 콜카타 유대인들만이 남아 있고, 그들 역시 그들의 교회당, 빵가게, 그리고 상점들과 함께 곧 사라질 것이다. 그들에 관해 남겨질 것은 그들의 책뿐이다. 그들이 발간했던 회고록과 요리책, 그리고 그들이 수집했던 그 외의 서적들(만이 남을 것이다). 다양한 책을 읽는 것은 다른 관습에 익숙해지는 한 방법이다. 이 책들이 없다면 우리는 콜카타 유대인들에 대한 기억을 잃을 것이다.

구문 [12행~13행] **Without** these, we **would lose** the memory of the Jews of Kolkata.

「Without ~, S+조동사 과거형+동사원형 ...」은 현재 사실을 반대로 가정하며, '~이 없다면 …할 텐데'란 뜻이다.

어휘 **storehouse** 창고 **Jew** 유대인 *cf.* **Jewish** 유대인의 **originally** 원래 **trader** 무역상, 상인 **settle** 정착하다 **establish** 설립하다 **vibrant** 활기찬, 생기가 넘치는 **community** 공동체 **custom** 관습, 풍습 **cuisine** 요리(법) **a handful of** 소수의; 한 줌의 *cf.* **handful** 한 줌, 한 움큼 **elderly** 나이든 **familiar with** ~에 익숙한[친숙한]

36 글의 순서 ④

소재 풍력 터빈의 문제점과 해결 방안

해설 풍력 터빈 속으로 새와 박쥐 등이 날아 들어와 죽는 경우가 있는데, 터빈의 색깔을 바꿈으로써 이를 예방할 수 있다는 내용의 글이다. 주어진 문장에서 생물이 풍력 터빈에 걸려 죽는 문제가 제기된 후 (C)의 해결책이 이어지는 것이 자연스럽다. (C)가 터빈 색상인 흰색에 대해 언급하는 내용으로 끝나므로, 흰색이 문제를 발생시키는 이유를 설명하는 (A)가 다음에 와야 한다. (B)는 (A)의 마지막에 제시된 보라색에 대해 언급하면서 색깔 변경과 같은 작은 변화를 통한 문제 해결 가능성으로 마무리 짓고 있으므로 정답은 ④ '(C)-(A)-(B)'이다.

해석 풍력 터빈은 환경에 무척 이롭지만, 새, 박쥐 그리고 대기 중에서 시간을 보내는 다른 동물들에게는 매우 위험하다.

(C) 주제문 새로운 연구는 이러한 위험이 터빈의 색을 바꿈으로써 해결될 수 있다고 결론 내린다. 당신에게는 터빈 색상의 현재 추세인 흰색이 문제가 될 수 있다고 보이지 않을 수 있다.

(A) 하지만 그 연구에 따르면 흰색 터빈이 벌레를 끌어들이는데, 이것이 벌레를 먹고 사는 새와 박쥐를 종종 죽게 한다고 한다. 흰색, 밝은 회색 그리고 노란색이 (벌레에게) 가장 매력적인 색깔이었던 반면 보라색은 정반대였다.

(B) 이것이 모든 터빈이 이제 보라색으로 칠해져야 한다는 것을 의미하지는 않지만, 색깔 변경과 같은 간단한 것으로 새와 박쥐가 풍력 터빈 속으로 날아드는 것을 예방할 수 있음을 나타낸다.

구문 [4행~6행] But the study says // that *white turbines attract bugs*, // **which** often leads *the birds and bats* [that eat them] to their death.

which는 계속적 용법의 관계대명사로 앞에 나온 절 white turbines attract bugs를 대신한다.

어휘 **wind turbine** 풍력 발전용 터빈 **highly** 매우, 대단히 **beneficial** 유익한, 이로운 **creature** 생물, 동물 **attract** 끌어들이다 *cf.* **attractive** 매혹적인 **lead A to B** A를 B로 유도하다[이끌다] **opposite** 정반대(의) **indicate** 나타내다, 가리키다 **prevent A from v-ing** A가 v하는 것을 막다 **conclude** 결론을 내리다 **unlikely** ~할 것 같지 않은, 있음직하지 않은 **current** 현재의; 통용되는 **trend** 동향, 추세

37 글의 순서 ③

소재 식단이 몸에 미치는 영향

해설 식사 후 가끔 피곤한 것은 걱정할 필요가 없다는 주어진 글의 내용과 반대되는 내용, 즉 식후 피곤함이 계속되면 식단을 바꿀 필요가 있다는 내용이 역접의 연결사(however)로 이어진 (B)가 가장 먼저 나온다. 그 뒤에는 설탕 함량이 높은 음식이 극도의 피곤함을 느끼게 한다는 문제를 제기하는 (C)가 나오고, 그 문제를 피하는 권장 식단을 소개하는 (A)가 마지막에 이어지는 것이 자연스럽다.

해석 밥을 먹은 후에 심하게 졸린 것이 정상은 아니다. 그러나 식사 후 이따금 아주 피곤한 것에 대해 걱정할 필요는 없다.

(B) 주제문 그러나 만약 그런 일이 매일 일어나고 있다면, 당신은 식단을 바꿀 필요가 있을 수 있다. 피로감은 당신의 몸에 문제가 있다는 것을 보여주는 데 도움이 되는 느낌이다.

(C) 설탕 함량이 높은 음식을 먹고 그 에너지를 소모할 만큼 충분히 운동하지 않는다면 당신의 혈당 수치는 로켓처럼 치솟는다. 그런 다음, 곧바로 그 수치는 다시 급격히 떨어지게 되는데 이렇게 말도 안 되게 널뛰는 혈당 수치가 당신이 매우 피곤함을 느끼도록 만든다.

(A) 이러한 문제를 피하기 위해서는, 특히 과일이나 채소, 견과류, 통밀로 만든 시리얼과 같이 당분과 지방 함량은 적고 복합 탄수화물이 높은, 더 가벼운(= 소화가 잘 되는) 음식을 선택하라. 이 음식들은 소화하기도 쉽고, 아무리 많은 일을 하더라도 당신의 몸이 에너지를 많이 만들어 내도록 도와준다!

구문 [11행~12행] Tiredness is *a useful feeling* [**that** can indicate // (that) there is a problem with your body].

(can indicate: V′, (that) there is a problem with your body: O′)

a useful feeling은 주격 관계사 that이 이끄는 절의 수식을 받으며, 관계사절의 동사 can indicate 뒤에는 목적어인 명사절을 이끄는 접속사 that이 생략되었다.

어휘 **normal** 정상의, 보통의(↔ **abnormal** 비정상의) **extremely** 매우; 극단적으로 **once in a while** 가끔 **light food** 소화가 잘되는 음식 **low in A** A가 적은(↔ **high in A** A가 많은[풍부한]) **wholegrain** 통밀로 만든 **digest** 소화하다 **generate** 발생시키다 **no matter how** 아무리 ~해도 **diet** 식단; 식품; 다이어트 **burn** (에너지 · 연료 등을) 소모하다[쓰다] **crash down** 폭락하다; 무너지다 **seesaw** 널뛰다, 변동[요동]하다; 시소 (놀이) **leave** (어떤 상태 등에) 있게 만들다[두다]; 떠나다 **wear out** 지치다, 기진맥진하다; 닳다

38 문장 넣기 ⑤

소재 19세기의 도로

해설 주어진 문장은 통나무 때문에 말이 미끄러지거나 넘어지는 사고에 관한 내용이므로, 통나무를 깐 후에도 다른 문제가 있었다는 내용과 때로 말의 발이 통나무 사이에 끼기도 했다는 내용 사이에 오는 것이 적절하다. 따라서 정답은 ⑤이다.

해석 주제문 현대의 도로는 과거의 것과 상당히 다르다. 일반적인 19세기의 도로나 거리는 6~8피트(약 2미터) 폭의 흙길이었다. 봄에 비가 내리면 이 길들은 진흙탕이 되었고 물웅덩이로 가득했다. 더운 여름에는 길들이 완전히 말라버려 누군가가 그곳을 걸을 때마다 거대한 먼지 구름이 일었다. 이 시기에 둥그런 통나무를 흙(길) 전체에 나란히 깔면서 도로가 개선되기 시작했다. 이렇게 통나무로 덮인 도로는 먼지와 웅덩이로 인한 문제는 적었으나 다른 문제가 있었다. 종종, 통나무가 마차의 무게를 견디지 못하고 굴러서 말들이 미끄러져 넘어졌다. 때로 말의 발이 통나무 사이의 틈에 끼기도 했는데, 이것은 (말이) 크게 넘어져 뼈가 부러지게 했다.

어휘 **under the weight of** ~의 무게로; ~의 중압을 받고 **coach** (대형 4륜) 마차 **cause A to-v** A가 v하게 하다 **slip** 미끄러지다 **stumble** 넘어지다; 휘청거리다 **vastly** 상당히, 엄청나게 **average** 일반적인; 평균의 **dirt** 먼지; 흙 **muddy** 진창인, 진흙투성이인 **puddle** 물웅덩이 **dry up** 바싹 마르다, 말라붙다 **dust** 흙먼지; 가루 **improve** 개선하다 **period** 시기, 기간 **lay** 깔다, 놓다; (알을) 낳다 **side by side** 나란히, 함께 **across** 전체에 걸쳐; 가로질러 **get trapped** 끼이다; 덫에 걸리다, 갇히다 **gap** 틈, 간격

39 문장 넣기 ③

소재 인간과 동물이 식량을 구하는 방법의 차이

해설 인간과 동물 모두 자연으로부터 식량을 구하지만 인간은 자연으로부터 직접 구하기보다는 다른 사람을 거쳐 얻는다는 내용이다. 주어진 문장은 지난 한 해 동안 본인이 얼마나 많은 것을 자연에서 직접 얻었는지 묻는 내용으로, 이에 대한 대답에 해당하는 문장 앞인 ③에 와야 한다.

해석 많은 동물들은 대부분의 깨어 있는 시간을 먹이를 찾고 그것을 먹는 데 보낸다. 그들(= 동물들)은 먹을 것을 찾아 자신들의 환경을 탐색한다. 어떤 동물들은 혼자서 찾고 다른 동물들은 함께 찾지만, 주제문 일반적으로 동물들은 자연으로부터 직접 먹이를 얻는다. 인간의 식량 또한 자연에서 비롯하지만, 대부분의 사람들은 이제 자신들의 식량을 다른 사람들로부터 얻는다. 지난 한 해 동안, 당신이 먹은 것 중 얼마나 많은 부분을 식물로부터 따거나 동물들을 사냥하고 죽여서 자연으로부터 직접 얻었는가? 전부는 아닐지라도 아마 여러분이 먹은 것의 대부분은 다른 사람들에 의해 식량이 준비되고 판매되는 슈퍼마켓, 혹은 어떤 사람들에 의해 재배된 식량이 다른 사람들에 의해 요리되고 대접되는 식당이나 구내식당에서 왔을 것이다. 그러한 모든 시설들이 갑자기 사라지고 사람들이 자신의 식량을 자연으로부터 직접 얻어야 한다면, 우리들 대부분은 그것을 어떻게 시작해야 할지 모를 것이다. 많은 사람들이 굶주려 죽을 것이다.

구문 [14행~17행] If all those institutions **were to** suddenly vanish / and people **had to get** their food directly from nature, // most of us **would not know** how to go about it.

가정법 과거 구문으로 현재 사실을 반대로 가정하거나 있을 법하지 않은 일을 나타낸다. 「If+주어+과거동사[were to-v] ~, 주어+조동사 과거형+동사원형 ....」의 형태이며 '만약 ~라면 …할 것이다'란 뜻이다.

어휘 **portion** 부분, 일부 **majority** 대부분, 대다수 **in general** 일반적으로 **originate** 비롯하다; 시작하다 **cafeteria** 구내식당 **institution** 시설, 기관, 협회 **vanish** 없어지다, 사라지다 **go about** ~을 시작하다 **starve** 굶어 죽다, 굶주리다

40 요약문 완성 ⑤

소재 고정관념으로 인한 창의성 저하

해설 압정 한 상자와 성냥을 이용해 초를 벽에 붙여보라는 요청에 실험 참가자들은 각각의 물건을 본래의 '익숙한(familiarity)' 용도로만 생각했기 때문에 압정 상자를 촛대로 사용할 수 있다는 새로운 활용법을 상상하는 능력이 '막힌(blocked)' 것이다.

해석 한 실험에서 심리학자 Karl Duncker는 벽을 마주보도록 배치된 테이블에 참가자들을 앉게 했다. 그는 각각의 사람들에게 초 한 개, 압정 한 상자, 성냥을 주었고, 그들에게 초를 벽에 붙여보라고 요청했다. 몇몇 참가자들은 압정을 사용하여 초를 벽에 바로 꽂으려고 시도했다. 다른 사람들은 녹인 촛농을 이용하여 초를 벽에 붙이려고 시도했지만, 압정은 너무 짧았고 녹인 촛농은 벽에 붙도록 굳지 않았다. 오직 소수의 참가자들만이 압정 상자를 이용할 생각을 했다. 이러한 거의 몇 안 되는 창조적인 사고자들은 압정으로 상자를 벽에 고정시켰고, 그것을 촛대로 효과적으로 바꿔놓았다. 주제문 Duncker는 참가자들이 압정 상자의 전통적인 기능에 너무 집중해서 그것을 문제에 대한 가능한 해결책으로 생각할 수 없었음을 깨달았다.

⬇

이 실험에서 참가자들은 상자의 의도된 용도에 대한 (A) 익숙함이 새로운 용도를 상상하는 능력을 (B) 막았기 때문에 임무를 완수하는 데 어려움을 겪었다.

구문 [13행~16행] Duncker realized // that participants were **so** focused on the tack box's traditional function **that** they couldn't **think of** it **as** a possible solution to the problem.

「so ~ that ...」 구문은 '너무 ~해서 …하다'의 뜻이고, 「think of A as B」는 'A를 B로 생각하다'의 뜻이다.

어휘 **experiment** 실험 **participant** 참가자 **position** 두다, 배치하다 **match** 성냥 **attach A to B** A를 B에 붙이다 **pin** (핀으로) 꽂다, 고정시키다 **directly** 직접 **attempt** 시도하다 **stick A to B** A를 B에 붙이다 **melt** 녹이다 **wax** 밀랍, 왁스 **bind** 굳다, 엉기다 **a handful of** 소수의; 한 줌의 **effectively** 효과적으로 **transform** 변형시키다, 바꿔놓다 **candleholder** 촛대 **function** 기능 **complete** 완수하다 **intend** 의도하다

41~42 장문 41 ③ 42 ④

소재 현대인의 끝없는 욕망

해설 41. 역사상 가장 많은 부와 기회가 있는 사회에 살면서도 만족하지 못하는 현대인의 문제를 지적하는 글이다. 두 번째 단락의 첫 번째 문장(The trick ~ more *isn't* better.)에 드러난 글의 주제인 '더 많은 것을 갖는 것이 더 좋다는 생각을 버려야 한다'를 가장 잘 반영한 제목은 ③ '승산 없는 생각: '더 많을수록 더 좋다''이다.

① 덜 쓰고 더 갖기
② 더 원하는 것이 바로 인생
④ 현대 사회와 현대의 욕망
⑤ 현대의 욕망과 사회 갈등

42. 빈칸 뒤 두 문장의 더 많은 것을 원하는 끊임없는 욕망이 우리를 해친다는 내용에서 현대인의 만족하지 못하는 특성을 알 수 있으므로, 빈칸에 가장 적절한 단어는 ④ '불만족스러운'이다.

① 건강하지 못한 ② 똑똑한 ③ 진보적인 ⑤ 게으른

해석 우리는 역사상 다른 어떤 사회보다 (지금) 우리 사회에서 더 많은 부와 기회를 가지고 있다. 주제문 그러나 사실 우리는 역사상 가장 불만족스러운 사람들 중 하나이기도 하다. 많은 것을 갖는 것이 그 자체로 해로운 것은 아니다. 우리를 해치는 것은 바로 '점점 더 많은 것'을 원하는 끊임없는 욕망이다. 우리는 무언가를 손에 넣자마자 바로 더 좋은 것을 원하기 시작한다. 이것은 우리가 가진 많은 축복들에 감사하는 우리의 능력을 갉아먹는다. 예를 들어, 나는 한 부부를 아는데, 그들은 좋은 지역에 아름다운 집을 구입했다. 그들은 그곳에 정착할 때까지 그 집을 좋아했다. 그런 다음 그들은 더 좋은 지역에 더 큰 집을 샀어야 했다고 생각하기 시작했고 이런 사고방식이 그들로 하여금 자신의 집을 진정으로 좋아하는 것을 방해했다.
주제문 이러한 성향을 극복하는 방법은 더 많은 것이 더 좋은 것은 '아니라는' 것을 우리 자신에게 확신시키는 것이다. 문제는 우리가 가지지 않은 것에 있는 게 아니라 그것을 갖고자 하는 욕망에 있다. 행복의 훌륭한 측정법 한 가지는 당신이 가진 것과 당신이 원하는 것 사이에 얼마나 많은 차이가 있느냐 하는 것이다. 당신은 당신이 더 많이 가지면 '정말로' 행복해질 거라고 생각하면서 평생을 보낼 수도 있다. 아니면 당신은 더 적게 원하기로 의식적인 결정을 내릴 수도 있다. 이 후자의 전략이 훨씬 더 쉽고 더 충족감을 준다.

구문 [5행~6행] **It's** *the unceasing desire for more and more* **that**'s hurting us.

「It is[was] ~ that ...」 강조구문으로 원래 문장의 주어가 강조되었으며 '우리를 해치는 것은 바로 끊임없는 욕망이다'라고 해석한다.

[11행~14행] Then they started thinking // (that) they **should have bought** a bigger house in a better area, // and this way of thinking **stopped** *them* **from** truly **enjoying** their home.

「should have p.p.」는 '(과거에) ~했어야 하는데 (안 해서 유감이다).'라는 현재의 후회를 나타낸다. 「stop A from v-ing」는 'A가 v하는 것을 방해하다[막다]'라는 뜻이다.

어휘 **opportunity** 기회 **on record** 역사상; 공식적으로 **harmful** 해로운 **in itself** 그 자체로 **unceasing** 끊임없는 **desire** 욕망 **eat into** ~을 갉아먹다[축내다] **appreciate** 고마워하다; 진가를 알아보다 **blessing** 축복 **settle in** (새로운 곳에) 정착하다 **trick** 비결; 속임수 **tendency** 성향; 추세 **convince** 확신시키다; 납득시키다 **longing to-v** v하려는 욕망 **measure** 측정(법); 척도; 측정하다 **make a decision to-v** v하기로 결정을 내리다 **conscious** 의식적인 **latter** 후자의 **strategy** 전략, 계획 **infinitely** 《비교급 앞에서》 훨씬; 무한히 **fulfilling** 충족감[성취감]을 주는

43~45 장문 43 ② 44 ⑤ 45 ④

소재 장애가 있는 동생을 생각하는 소년의 마음

해설 43. (C)의 what the boy said surprised Paul과 그 뒤의 소년이 한 말의 내용은 (A)의 마지막 부분에 나온 Paul의 예상과 반대되는 것이므로, (C)가 (A) 바로 뒤에 이어져야 하고, (D)는 소년이 집에 도착해서 동생을 데리고 나온 이후의 상황이므로, (B)의 뒤에 와야 한다. 따라서 ② '(C)-(B)-(D)'의 순서가 가장 적절하다.

44. (e)는 Paul을 가리키며 나머지는 모두 소년을 가리킨다.

45. (D)에서 Paul이 소년에게 차에 타보고 싶은지 물어본 것을 알 수 있다.

해석 (A) ① Paul은 크리스마스 선물로 형에게서 자동차를 한 대 받았다. 크리스마스 이브에 Paul이 사무실에서 나왔을 때 한 소년이 넋을 잃고 보면서 빛나는 새 차 옆으로 걸어오고 있었다. "아저씨 차예요?"라고 그는 물었다. Paul은 고개를 끄덕였다. "아저씨의 형이 아저씨에게 크리스마스 선물로 준 거란다." 그 소년은 깜짝 놀랐다. "아저씨 형이 이 차를 아저씨에게 주었고, 아저씨는 한 푼도 안 들었다는 뜻이에요? 와, 저도…." (a) 그(= 소년)는 망설였다. 물론 Paul은 그가 무엇을 바라게 될지 알고 있었다. 그(= 소년)는 그와 같은 형을 갖기를 바랄 것이다.
(C) 그러나 그 소년이 한 말은 Paul을 놀라게 했다. "저도…." 소년은 계속 말을 했다. "③ 그런 형이 되었으면 좋겠어요." Paul은 깜짝 놀라서 그 소년을 쳐다보았다. ④ 그 다음 충동적으로 "아저씨 자동차를 타고 싶니?"라고 말했다. "네, 타고 싶어요."라고 (d) 그(= 소년)가 말했다. 자동차를 타고 잠시 후, 그 소년은 돌아서서 빛나는 눈빛으로 "아저씨, 우리 집 앞까지 태워주실 수 있으세요?"라고 말했다.
(B) Paul은 옅은 미소를 지었다. 그는 그 소년이 무엇을 원하는지 안다고 생각했다. (b) 그(= 소년)는 이웃들에게 큰 자동차를 타고 집으로 올 수 있다는 것을 보여주고 싶었을 것이다. 하지만 Paul은 또 틀렸다. "저기 계단 두 개 가 있는 곳에 세워 주실래요?"라고 그 소년은 부탁했다. 그는 계단을 올라갔다. 그리고 잠시 후 Paul은 그가 돌아오는 소리를 들었는데, ② 그가 빨리 오는 것은 아니었다. (c) 그(= 소년)는 장애가 있는 동생을 데리고 왔다. 그는 아래쪽 계단에 동생을 앉히고는 자동차를 가리켰다.
(D) "내가 위에서 말했던 (e) 그 아저씨(= Paul)가 저기 있어. 아저씨의 형이 저 차를 크리스마스 선물로 아저씨에게 줬고, 아저씨는 한 푼도 들지 않았대. 그리고 언젠가 나도 너에게 저런 차를 줄 거야. 그러면 너는 내가 말한 크리스마스 윈도우에 있는 온갖 아름다운 것들을 혼자서도 볼 수 있을 거야." ⑤ Paul은 차에서 나와서 그 장애가 있는 소년을 자기 차의 앞좌석에 앉혔다. 반짝이는 눈을 한 그의 형도 차에 올라타 그의 옆에 앉았고, 그들 셋은 기억에 남을 만한 휴일의 드라이브를 시작했다. 주제문 그해 크리스마스이브에 Paul은 '크리스마스 정신'의 진정한 의미를 알게 되었다.

구문 [(A) 2행~4행] On Christmas Eve when Paul came out of his office, / a boy was walking around the shiny new car, / **admiring** it.
admiring it은 동시동작을 나타내는 분사구문으로 '~하면서'라고 해석한다.

어휘 **(A) admire** 감탄하며 바라보다; 존경하다 **nod** 고개를 끄덕이다 **astound** 깜짝 놀라게 하다 **hesitate** 망설이다, 주저하다 **(B) handicapped** 신체[정신]적 장애가 있는 **bottom** 아래의; 밑바닥 **(C) astonishment** 깜짝 놀람 **impulsively** 충동적으로 **glow** 빛나다, 반짝이다 **(D) beside** ~옆에 **memorable** 기억할 만한 **spirit** 정신; 영혼

실전 모의고사 06

본문 p.83

18 ①	19 ②	20 ①	21 ②	22 ④	23 ①	24 ⑤	25 ⑤	26 ④	27 ②
28 ④	29 ③	30 ②	31 ⑤	32 ⑤	33 ④	34 ②	35 ④	36 ④	37 ⑤
38 ⑤	39 ⑤	40 ④	41 ④	42 ②	43 ④	44 ③	45 ④		

18 글의 목적 ①

소재 농구 캠프 참가 권유

해설 농구 캠프에 아들을 참여시키려는 사람에게 그 농구 캠프의 장점에 대해 언급하며 실망하지 않을 것이라고 하고 있다. 따라서 글의 목적으로 가장 적절한 것은 ①이다.

해석 Linda 씨께,

지난번 보내주신 편지를 받으니 매우 반가웠고, 잘 지내고 계시다니 기쁩니다. 주제문 어쩌면 Maple 중학교의 농구 캠프에 아드님을 등록시킬 수도 있다고 말씀하셨기 때문에 제 아들의 경험을 공유해 드리고 싶습니다. 낮은 기대에도 불구하고, 제 아들 Dan은 그 농구 캠프에 꽤 만족했습니다. 저희는 일주일 기간에 200달러를 지불했고, 전혀 후회하지 않습니다. Dan과 다른 아이들은 날마다 많은 시간을 코트에서 농구를 하며 보냈고, 제 아들은 공통의 관심사를 가지고 있는 몇몇 친구들을 사귀었습니다. 게다가, 제 아들은 일대일 교육 시간이 자신의 경기를 정말로 향상시켰다고 말했으며, 그것(= 농구 캠프)에 관해 계속해서 말합니다. 주제문 다시 말해, 당신은 이 캠프에 실망하지 않으실 것입니다.

조만간 연락드리겠습니다.

Samantha

어휘 **register** 등록하다 **despite** ~에도 불구하고 **satisfy** 만족시키다 **session** 기간, 시간 **regret** 후회(하다); 유감(으로 생각하다) **plenty of** 많은 **court** (농구 등을 하는) 코트; 법정; 궁궐 **one-on-one** 일대일의 **instruction** 교육, 지도; (자세한) 설명(서); 지시 **improve** 향상시키다; 나아지다 **disappoint** 실망시키다, 낙담시키다

19 심경 변화 ②

소재 딸의 오디션

해설 심경을 묻는 유형이므로 등장인물이 처한 상황을 파악해야 하며, 사건의 추이와 함께 심경과 관련된 어구에도 주의하여 판단한다. Brian은 처음에는 오디션 현장에서 딸이 잘하지 못할까봐 걱정했지만, But then 이후, 딸이 실수하지 않고 최고의 연기를 보여주자 미소를 지으며 안도했으므로 Brian의 심경 변화로는 ② '걱정하는 → 안도하는'이 적절하다.

해석 딸이 무대에서 연기하는 것을 보는 것은 Brian에게 절대 쉬운 일이 아니었다. 학교에서 연극 책임 선생님으로서, 이런 상황에서 그는 부모이자 감독이었다. 설상가상으로, 그의 딸이 최근 독감에 걸려서 그는 딸이 평소만큼 잘하지 못할까 봐 걱정했다. 주제문 그는 딸에게 그 배역을 줄 수 없을 거라고 생각했기 때문에 땀을 약간 흘리기 시작했다. 그러나 그때 그는 딸의 오디션을 더 주의를 기울여 들었다. 그녀는 어떤 실수도 하지 않고 있었고 그녀의 노래는 만족스러웠고 자신감이 넘쳤다. 사실상, 그녀는 이제껏 최고의 연기를 보여주고 있었다. 주제문 그는 천천히 숨을 내쉬고 옅은 미소를 지으며 의자에 편안히 앉았다. 그는 공정함을 유지하면서 여전히 딸을 행복하게 할 수 있을 것이다. 이번에는 그녀가 주연을 맡을 만했고 모두가 그것을 알고 있었다.

① 자신감 있는 → 두려워하는
③ 단호한 → 혼란스러워하는
④ 격분한 → 기쁜
⑤ 초조한 → 무관심한

구문 [1행~2행] **Watching** his daughter **perform** on stage (S) / **was** (V) never easy for Brian (C).

동명사구가 주어로 쓰였고, 「watch+O(his daughter)+원형부정사(perform)」의 구조로 'O가 v하는 것을 보다'의 의미를 나타낸다. 동명사(구) 주어는 단수 취급을 하므로 단수동사인 was가 사용되었다.

[4행~6행] Even worse, / his daughter had caught a bad cold recently, // so he was concerned // (that) she wouldn't do **as well as** she usually did.

여기서 「as well as ...」는 '…만큼 잘'의 의미를 가진 원급 비교 표현이다.

어휘 **perform** 연기[공연]하다; 수행[실행]하다 **director** 감독, 연출자; 책임자 **catch a cold** 감기에 걸리다 **concerned** 걱정하는 **sweat** 땀(을 흘리다); 수고, 노력 **part** 배역, 역할 **pleasing** 만족스러운, 즐거운 **as a matter of fact** 사실상, 사실은 **sit back** (보통 의자에) 편안히 앉다 **fair** 공정한 **deserve** ~할[받을] 만하다, ~할 가치가 있다 **lead role** 주연, 주인공 역할

20 필자 주장 ①

소재 정부와 언론의 관계

해설 필자의 주장이 담긴 주제문을 찾아야 한다. 정부와 언론이 상충되는 목적을 가지고 있더라도 그러한 갈등을 없애지 말고 서로가 거리를 두고 기능을 해야 한다는 내용으로, 필자의 주장은 역접의 접속사 but 이후에 조동사 should를 사용한 두 개의 문장(the basic conflicts ~ removed., The government ~ at arm's length.)에서 알 수 있다. 따라서 정답은 ①이다.

해석 정부와 언론은 상충되는 목적을 갖는다. 그들의 인식은 다르며, 그들은 다른 방식으로 상황을 바라본다. 하지만 이것은 나쁜 것이 아니다. 그 차이는 해소되어서는 안 된다. 비록 이런 길이 자주 불완전하고 불만족스럽다 할지라도, 정부는 계속 자기의 길을 가야 하며, 언론도 자기의 길을 가야 한다. 확실히 개선은 있을 수 있다. 주제문 하지만 기본적인 갈등이 제거되어서는 안 된다. 정부와 언론은 어느 정도 거리를 두고 기능해야 한다. 만약 그들이 떨어져 있지 않으면, 만약 그들의 목적이 인위적이고 부자연스러운 합의로 형성이 되면, 그 국가는 해를 입는 것이다.

구문 [4행~7행] The government should continue on its course / and the media (should continue) on theirs, // **as imperfect and unsatisfactory as these courses often are**.

as imperfect ~ often are는 「(as) 형용사 as+S+V」 형태의 as가 이끄는 양보의 부사절로, '(al)though these courses often are imperfect and unsatisfactory'와 같은 의미이다.

어휘 **press** 언론, 신문; 누르다 **conflicting** 상충[상반]되는, 모순되는 *cf.* **conflict** 갈등, 충돌; 상충하다, 모순되다 **perception** 인식; 지각, 자각; 통찰력 **resolve** 해소[제거]하다; 해결하다; 결심하다 **imperfect** 불완전한 **unsatisfactory** 불만족스러운 **improvement** 개선, 호전; 향상 **remove** 제거하다, 없애다; 치우다 **function** 기능하다, 작용하다; 기능 **at arm's length** 어느 정도 거리를 두고 **apart** 떨어져; 따로 **artificial** 인위적인; 인공[인조]의 **agreement** 합의, 동의

21 밑줄 함의 ②

소재 내적 이미지를 활용한 목표 달성

해설 골프 선수가 샷을 칠 때 공이 나아가야 할 방향을 마음속에 그려봄으로써 잘 칠 수 있으며 이는 삶의 목표를 이루는 데에도 적용된다고 했으므로, flight simulators(모의 비행 장치)의 의미로 가장 적절한 것은 ② '목표를 달성하기 위해 내적 이미지를 사용하는 것'이다.

해석 한 골프 대회의 챔피언이 어떻게 성공했는가를 질문 받을 때, 그는 그의 삶에서 모의 비행 장치를 어떻게 사용하는지 설명한다. 그 골프 선수는 "골프를 치는 동안에 여러분이 생각한 것이 아마도 시합의 가장 중요한 부분일 것입니다."라고 말한다. 그는 그것을 규칙적으로 연습하는 것을 강조한다. "잘 치는 비결은 공을 치기 전에 그 공이 가기를 바라는 곳으로 그 공이 가는 것을 보는 것입니다." 챔피언은 공이 가야 할 곳으로 정확히 가는 것을 상상하면서 완벽한 샷의 이미지를 마음속에 자신 있게 지녀야 한다. 이러한 원리는 삶에서도 적용이 된다. 여러분은 자신이 인생에서 하고 싶은 것을 정확하게 알아야 한다. 주제문 여러분은 목표를 정하고 그것을 정확히 어떻게 이룰지 결정할 필요가 있다. 그 다음에 여러분은 항상 그것을 마음속에 그려야 한다. 그리고 나서야 여러분의 목표를 성취할 수 있을 것이다.

① 인생의 큰 그림을 보는 것
③ 현실적인 목표를 설정하고 그것에 집중하는 것
④ 성공과 실패를 미리 상상해보는 것
⑤ 긍정적인 사고의 힘을 이해하는 것

구문 [3행~4행] **What** you think / while playing golf is probably the most important single part of your game.
(S: What you think / while playing golf, V: is, C: the most important single part of your game)

what이 이끄는 명사절이 주어이며 while playing golf는 시간을 나타내는 부사절로, 접속사 while 다음에 you are가 생략되어 있다.

[13행~14행] **Only then** will you be able to accomplish your objective.
(조동사: will, S: you, V: be able to accomplish)

부정어구 Only then이 문두로 나오면서 「부정어구+(조)동사+주어」 어순으로 도치되었다.

어휘 **flight simulator** (조종사 훈련용) 모의 비행장치 **on a regular basis** 정기적으로 **shot** (한번) 치기, 타격 **confidently** 자신 있게 **be supposed to-v** v해야 한다, v하기로 되어 있다 **principle** 원리 **precisely** 정확히, 엄밀하게 **set a goal** 목표를 세우다 **determine** 결정하다 **visualize** 마음속에 그려 보다, 상상하다 **objective** 목표; 객관적인 [선택지 어휘] **mental** 내적인, 정신의 **in advance** 미리

22 글의 요지 ④

소재 문학 연구 방법

해설 문학 연구가 문학의 역사적 배경 연구에 치우친 것을 비판하고, 작품 자체에 대한 분석과 비평을 통해 문학을 이해해야 한다고 주장하는 내용의 글이다. 글의 중반부(This over-emphasis ~ literature itself.)에 문학 작품의 배경 연구보다는 문학 작품 자체를 해석해야 한다는 요지가 잘 드러나 있으므로 정답은 ④이다.

해석 수년간 문학 연구는 문학의 역사적 배경에 몰두해 있었다. 작품 자체에 대한 분석과 비평은 이러한 작품이 만들어진 환경에 대한 연구에 쏟아진 엄청난 노력에 비하면 보잘것없었다. 주제문 이렇게 작품이 만들어진 시대의 사회적, 정치적 현실에 대한 지나친 강조는 작품 자체를 진정으로 즐기는 것을 방해했을지 모른다. 사실, 문학 연구를 위한 자연스럽고 논리적인 출발점은 문학 작품 자체에 대한 해석이다. 오직 시, 소설, 희곡과 에세이 등 그 자체만이 작가의 삶과 작가가 활동했던 사회적, 정치적, 그리고 역사적 환경에 대한 우리의 관심을 정당화한다.

구문 [2행~6행] *Analysis and criticism* (of the works (*themselves*)) were trivial / in comparison to *the enormous effort* (expended on the study of *the circumstances* [in which these works were produced]).
(S: Analysis and criticism, V: were, C: trivial)

themselves는 the works를 강조하는 재귀대명사이다. expended ~ were produced는 in comparison to(~에 비하면)에 이어지는 명사구 the enormous effort를 수식하는 과거분사구이다.

[6행~9행] *This over-emphasis* (on the social and political realities of *the period* [in which a work was produced]) **may have prevented** *real enjoyment* (of the work (*itself*)).
(S: This over-emphasis, V: may have prevented, O: real enjoyment)

주어인 This over-emphasis가 전명구(on the social ~ produced)의 수식을 받아 길어졌다. 「may have p.p.」는 '~했을지도 모른다'란 뜻으로 과거에 대한 불확실한 추측을 나타낸다. 재귀대명사 itself는 강조를 위한 것으로 생략해도 무방하다.

어휘 **literary** 문학의; 문학적인 *cf.* **literature** 문학 **absorbed in** ~에 사로잡힌[몰두한] **historical** 역사적인, 역사와 관련된 *cf.* **historic** 역사적으로 중요한 **setting** 배경, 환경 **analysis** 분석 **trivial** 보잘것없는, 하찮은 **in comparison to** ~과 비교하여 **enormous** 엄청난, 막대한 **expend** (시간·노력 등을) 쏟다, 들이다 **circumstance** 《주로 복수형》 환경, 상황 **emphasis** 강조 **political** 정치적인 **logical** 논리적인 **scholarship** 연구, 학문; 장학금 **justify** 정당화하다

23 글의 주제 ①

소재 인터넷 정보의 문제점

해설 인터넷의 정보는 정제되지 않고 부정확하며 신뢰도가 떨어질 가능성이 있다는 내용의 글이므로 주제로 가장 적절한 것은 ① '인터넷 정보의 문제점'이다.

해석 당신은 어디에서 정보를 얻는가? 당신은 정보를 찾기 시작할 최고의 장소는 인터넷이라고 말할지 모른다. 인터넷의 발명 이전에 우리는 정보를 책에서 얻었다. 책에서 얻은 정보는 일반적으로 정제되고 다듬어진 것이었다. 그러나 오늘날 당신은 권위자들에 의해 걸러지지 않은 온갖 종류의 정보를 다운로드 받을 수 있다. 인터넷은 사람들이 자신의 개인적인 생각과 그 밖의 글 조각들을 익명으로 게시하는 것을 대단히 쉽게 만들었다. 주제문 그 결과 부정확하고 신뢰할 수 없는 정보가 많아졌다. 근거 없는 출처와 편향된 분석에 기반을 둔 연구로 문제가 발생한다. 인터넷의 현혹시키는 정보는 편견을 유발할 수 있다. 당신은 아는 것이 힘이라는 말을 들어봤을 것이다. 그러나 오직 신뢰성 있는 정보만이 힘이라는 것을 알아야 한다.

② 온라인에 가짜 정보를 만드는 것의 영향
③ 인터넷에서의 정보 사용 윤리
④ 인터넷 정보 검색 요령
⑤ 인터넷 정보의 장점과 단점

구문 [8행~10행] The Internet has made it very easy *for people* to anonymously post their personal ideas and other pieces of writings.

it은 가목적어이고 to anonymously post ~ writings가 진목적어이다. for people은 to anonymously post에 대한 의미상 주어이다. 정리하면 「make+가목적어(it)+목적격보어(형용사)+의미상 주어(for 목적격)+진목적어(to-v)」는 '~가 v하는 것을 (형용사)하게 만들다'의 뜻이다.

[14행~15행] You **may have heard** // that knowledge is power.
「may have p.p.」는 과거 사실에 대한 불확실한 추측을 나타내며 '~했을지도 모른다'로 해석한다.

어휘 **invention** 발명(품) **acquire** 얻다, 획득하다 **typically** 일반적으로, 전형적으로 **refined** 정제된; 세련된 **polished** 다듬어진; 세련된 **all sorts of** 온갖 종류의 **filter** 여과시키다, 거르다 **authority** 권위(자) **anonymously** 익명으로 **post** 게시하다 **inaccurate** 부정확한 **unreliable** 신뢰할 수 없는 (↔ **reliable** 신뢰할 수 있는) **based on** ~에 기반을 둔 **unfounded** 근거 없는 **source** 출처, 원천, 근원 **biased** 편향된 **analysis** 《복수형 **analyses**》 분석 **misleading** 현혹시키는, 오해를 불러일으키는 **prejudice** 편견 [선택지 어휘] **impact** 영향 **ethics** 윤리, 도덕 원리

24 글의 제목 ⑤

소재 인간이 수집을 하는 이유

해설 인간이 수집을 하는 이유에 관한 글이다. 세 번째 문장(but one theory ~ is unfinished)에서 인간이 삶에서 결여된 무언가 때문에 물건을 수집한다는 이유를 제시하고 이어지는 내용에서 이를 자세히 설명하고 있으므로, 제목으로 가장 적절한 것은 ⑤ '사람들은 왜 물건을 수집하는가?'이다.

해석 우리 인간은 물건 모으기를 좋아한다. 우리는 장난감, 동전, 조개껍데기 등 간단히 말해서 재미있고 호기심을 끄는 것은 무엇이든 모은다. 물건을 모으려는 우리의 강한 욕망에는 많은 이유가 있을 수 있지만, 주제문 한 이론에 따르면 이 욕망은 누군가의 과거에 무언가가 아직 끝나지 않았다는 느낌에서 생겨난다고 한다. 수집은 우리의 삶에서 빠진 무언가를 완성하고 있는 것처럼 느끼게 할 수 있다. 수집하는 동안 우리는 사람들이 보통 명상이나 기도, 낭만적인 사랑과 연관 짓는 그러한 종류의 느낌을 경험하면서, 일종의 숭배에 빠진다. 이것은 거의 마치 특별한 물건들로 이루어진 당신만의 수집품을 갖는다는 것이 불확실성과 상실에 대한 일종의 심리적인 보호인 것 같다.

① 당신은 어떤 물건을 수집해야 하는가?
② 초보자를 위한 훌륭한 수집품
③ 수집가가 되기 위한 방법과 비법
④ 수집 가치가 있는 물건을 쉽게 구하는 방법

구문 [4행~6행] ~, but one theory says // that this desire stems from a feeling that *something* (in one's past) is unfinished.

a feeling과 that절은 동격을 이룬다.

[8행~11행] While we are collecting, // we are engaged in a kind of worship, / **experiencing** *the kind of feeling* [**that** people usually associate ● with meditation or prayer or romantic love].

현재분사 experiencing은 동시상황을 나타내는 분사구문을 이끈다. that이 이끄는 관계대명사절의 수식을 받는 선행사 the kind of feeling은 「associate A with B」에서 A가 앞으로 나온 것이다.

어휘 **seashell** 조개껍데기 **in short** 간단히 말하면 **cause** 이유, 원인 **theory** 이론 **desire** 욕망 **stem from** ~에서 생겨나다 **as though** 마치 ~인 것처럼(= as if) **complete** 완성하다; 완전한 **missing** (원래 있던 것이) 빠진; 없어진 **be engaged in** ~에 참여하다; ~에 종사하다 **worship** 숭배 **associate A with B** A와 B를 연관 짓다 **meditation** 명상 **prayer** 기도 **romantic** 낭만적인 **psychological** 심리적인 **uncertainty** 불확실성 **loss** 상실 [선택지 어휘] **collectible** 《보통 복수형》 수집할 가치가 있는 물건; 모을 수 있는

25 도표 이해 ⑤

소재 중고 타이어 순환

해설 글의 내용을 도표에서 찾아 꼼꼼히 비교해야 한다. 재사용을 위한 수출과 재생 타이어가 되는 비율은 총 24%로 전체 중고 타이어 사용의 4분의 1인 25%를 넘지 않으므로 ⑤가 도표의 내용과 일치하지 않는다.

해석 〈중고 타이어의 순환〉

10년 전에 중고 타이어는 대부분 결국 쓰레기 매립지에서 끝을 맺었다. 주제문 오늘날 낡은 타이어는 다른 경로를 따라 경제 순환으로 돌아갈 수 있다. ① 이들 타이어의 30퍼센트 가량이 에너지 재생에 사용되는데, 타이어를 전기로 전환하는 발전소나 폐타이어를 사용해 만든 연료(TDF) 시장에서 쓰인다. ② 30퍼센트에 조금 못 미치는 (타이어가) 새 도로를 위한 아스팔트 포장과 같은 곳에 재활용된다. ③ 재활용이나 에너지 재생에 투입되는 타이어의 비율은 50퍼센트를 넘는다. ④ 유감스럽게도, 매립이 여전히 중고 타이어의 18퍼센트를 차지한다. ⑤ 중고 타이어의 4분의 1 이상이 재사용을 위해 수출되거나 재생 타이어가 된다.

어휘 **used** 중고의 **circuit** 순환 **end up** 결국 ~으로 끝나다, 결국 ~이 되다 **landfill** 쓰레기 매립(지) **take a route** 경로를 타다 **economic cycle** 경제[경기] 순환 **recovery** 재생, 회수; (건강의) 회복 **power plant** 발전소 **convert A to B** A를 B로 변환시키다[바꾸다] **derive** ~에서 얻다[끌어내다] **asphalt** 아스팔트 **pave** (도로를) 포장하다 **account for** 차지하다; 설명하다 **export** 수출하다; 수출 **retread** 재생 타이어(를 만들다)

26 내용 불일치 ④

소재 Hans von Bulow의 생애

해설 Hans von Bulow는 Munich(뮌헨)에서 Liszt가 아닌 Wagner의 두 작품의 초연 지휘를 맡았다. 따라서 ④가 글의 내용과 일치하지 않는다.

해석 Hans von Bulow는 1830년에 드레스덴에서 태어났다. ① 젊었을 때 Bulow는 Friedrich Wieck 문하에서 피아노를 배웠고, 그 후에는 바이마르에서 Franz Liszt로부터 배웠다. ② 나중에 베를린에서 그는 Stern and Marx 음악 학교의 수석 피아노 교사가 되었으며 Liszt(리스트)와 Wagner(바그너)의 '신독일파' 작품을 옹호했다. ③ 1850년대부터 그는 전문적인 피아니스트로서 유럽, 잉글랜드, 그리고 미국에서 순회공연을 했다. 그는 그 시대의 사실상 모든 주요 작품을 알고 있었다고 한다. ④ 그는 1864년에 뮌헨 궁정의 음악 감독이 되었고, 그곳에서 Wagner의 초연 작품 두 곡을 지휘했다. 그는 1878년에서 1880년까지 하노버에서 지휘했고 ⑤ 1880년에서 1885년까지 마이닝겐에서 지휘했으며, 그곳에서 그의 오케스트라는 유럽에서 가장 훌륭한 오케스트라 중 하나가 되었다. 그의 (작품) 해석은 완전함과 정서적 힘으로 널리 존중받았다.

구문 [12행~14행] He conducted at *Hannover* from 1878 to 1880 and at *Meiningen* from 1880 to 1885, // **where** his orchestra became one of the finest in Europe.

관계부사 where는 Hannover와 Meiningen을 지칭하며, where로 시작되는 관계부사절이 그곳에서 있었던 일에 대해 설명하고 있다.

어휘 **principal** 주요한, 제일의; 교장 **champion** 옹호하다; 우승자 **expert** 전문적인, 전문가의; 전문가 **virtually** 사실상, 거의; 《컴퓨터》 가상으로 **court** 궁정; 법정 **conduct** 지휘하다; 이끌다 **interpretation** 해석 **integrity** 완전한 상태; 진실성 **emotional** 정서의, 감정의

27 안내문 불일치 ②

소재 책과 데이트를 하는 모임

해설 소제목과 선택지를 활용하여 필요한 정보를 빠르게 훑어 확인해야 한다. 등록은 사전에 온라인과 전화로 가능하다고 했으므로 ②가 안내문의 내용과 일치하지 않는다.

해석

책과 데이트를 하는 모임

여러분들이 사랑하는 책을 공유하고,
어쩌면 새로운 사랑을 발견할 수 있는 새로운 방법

- ① 매월 셋째 주 일요일 오후 6시부터 7시 30분에 열립니다.
- ② 등록은 프로그램이 시작되기 24시간 이전에 온라인으로 가능하며, 또는 프로그램 시작 전까지 전화 702-338-4565를 통해서 할 수 있습니다.

자주 묻는 질문:

어떻게 진행되나요?
공유하고 싶은 책을 몇 권 잡으세요. ③ 어떤 장르의 책이든 환영합니다.

누가 참석하나요?
④ 20대 초반부터 60대 초반에 이르는 연령대의 고객들을 맞았습니다. 1월에는 39명의 참석자가 있었습니다!

그 다음에는 어떻게 되나요?
⑤ 각 책 데이트는 4분으로 시간이 정해지는데, 모든 참석자들이 만나서 자신들이 읽은 것에 대해 대화를 나눌 수 있는 기회를 드립니다.

어휘 **take place** 개최되다, 일어나다 **registration** 등록 **available** 이용 가능한 **grab** (갑자기) 잡다, 잡아채다 **host** 접대하다 **range** (활동 범위 · 관심

· 연구 등이) (…에) 이르다, 걸치다 **attendee** 참석자 **time** 시간을 재다; 시간을 정하다 **allow A to-v** A가 v하도록 허락[허용]하다

28 안내문 일치 ④

소재 소설 쓰기 경연대회

해설 지침에서 단편소설의 길이를 1,800자에서 4,000자 사이로 규정하고 있으므로 ④가 안내문의 내용과 일치한다.

해석

> **〈The Story〉의 소설 쓰기 경연 대회가 지금 열렸습니다. 오늘 응모하세요!**
>
> 혹시 여러분이 글쓰기를 좋아한다면 저희는 하나의 멋진 소설을 찾고 있습니다. 〈The Story〉에서는 10대가 쓴 독창적이고 미출간된 소설을 검토할 예정입니다. ① 저희는 문학, 판타지, 공상 과학, 로맨스, 공포물을 포함하는 모든 장르의 위대한 소설에 관심이 있습니다.
>
> **상품**
> - ② 500달러와 우승작이 게재된 잡지 25권
> - ③ 〈The Story〉의 편집자와 함께 출판을 위해 자신의 작품을 편집할 수 있는 기회
>
> **지침:**
> - ④ 단편소설은 1,800에서 4,000자 사이여야 하며 저자의 고유한 창작물이어야 하고 미출간된 작품이어야 합니다.
> - 참가 양식이나 비용은 없습니다.
> - ⑤ 〈The Story〉사는 당사가 정한 양식으로 그 소설을 출판할 권리를 갖게 됩니다.
>
> **마감 기한**
> 6월 30일

어휘 **submit** 제출하다 **consider** 검토하다; 고려하다; 여기다 **original** 독창적인; 최초의; 원본 **genre** 장르 **literary** 문학 **sci-fi** 공상 과학 소설 **horror** 공포 **feature** 특집으로 크게 다루다; 특징을 이루다; 특징 **edit** 편집하다 *cf.* **editor** 편집자 **reserve** (권한 등을) 갖다[보유하다]; 예약하다 **publish** 출판하다 *cf.* **publication** 출판 **deadline** 마감 기한

29 밑줄 어법 ③

소재 교과목 통합학습

해설 ③ 주절에 '주장'을 나타내는 동사 insist가 쓰였지만 목적어인 that절이 '~해야 한다'는 당위성이 아니라 단순 사실을 나타내므로 「(should) 동사원형」이 아닌 일반동사가 와야 한다. that절의 주어가 동명사구(integrating ~ math)이므로 단수 취급하여 works가 되어야 한다.

오답 분석 ① 주어가 The traditional idea이므로 단수동사 is가 알맞게 쓰였다.
② the alternative view와 동격인 명사절을 이끄는 접속사 that이 적절히 쓰였다.
④ 「make+O+C」 구조로 목적격보어 자리에 형용사 available을 쓴 것은 적절하다.
⑤ encourage는 목적격보어로 to부정사를 쓴다.

해석 ESL(제2외국어로서의 영어) 학생들에게 영어를 가르치는 것에 관한 전통적인 견해는 학생들이 영어로 과학이나 수학을 공부하기 전에 영어에 능숙해져야 한다는 것이다. 주제문 그러나 교육 전문가와 경험 많은 교사들이 참가한 최근 국제학회 및 연구는 과학, 수학, 언어 학습의 통합이 학생의 전반적인 숙달과 수행을 강화할 수 있다는 대안적 견해를 촉진했다. 사실, 많은 관련 교사들이 영어 교육을 과학, 수학과 통합하는 것이 자신들의 학급의 학생들에게 확실히 효과가 있다고 주장한다. 그 교사들은 자신들의 성과를 온라인에서 이용할 수 있도록 했다. 이러한 행동은 다른 학교와 다른 교사들이 과학, 수학, 영어 습득을 통합하는 비슷한 전략을 채택하도록 권장한다.

어휘 **proficient** 능숙한 **conference** 학회, 회의 **alternative** 대안적인; 대안 **integration** 통합 *cf.* **integrate A with B** A를 B와 통합하다 **strengthen** 강화하다 **overall** 전반적인 **performance** 수행; 성적; 성과 **concerned** 관계가 있는; 걱정하는 **insist** 주장하다 **instruction** 교육; 지시, 설명 **available** 이용할 수 있는 **adopt** 채택하다; 입양하다 **acquisition** 습득, 취득

30 네모 어휘 ②

소재 몸을 잘 돌보는 것의 중요성

해설 (A) 자전거가 '닳기' 전까지 계속 탈 것이라는 의미가 문맥상 적절하므로 '(낡아) 떨어지다'라는 뜻의 wears out이 적절하다. work out은 '일이 잘 풀리다; 운동하다'라는 뜻이다.
(B) with는 '~이 있다면', without은 '~이 없다면'의 의미로 가정법 과거의 조건을 나타내는 부분이다. 문맥상 '조심한다면' 몸이 오랫동안 건강을 유지할 수 있다고 해야 적절하므로 With가 와야 한다.
(C) 몸을 소홀히 하면 '회복하는' 데 많은 돈이 들 것이라는 문맥이 적절하므로 restore가 와야 한다. damage는 '손상을 입히다'라는 뜻이다.

해석 당신이 올해 크리스마스 선물로 자전거를 받았다고 하자. 만약 당신이 현명하다면 당신은 그것이 (A) 낡기 전에 수년 동안 자전거 타는 것을 즐길 것이다. 그러나 당신이 그다지 현명하지 못하다면 오래지 않아 그것은 녹이 슬고 망가져 쓸모없는 것이 되어 잊히고 말 것이다. 당신의 몸도 마찬가지이다. 주제문 결국, 몸은 그저 기계가 아니라, 세상에서 가장 좋으며 가장 유용한 것(= 기계)이다. 주의를 (B) 한다면 그것(= 몸)은 적어도 80년은 지속하겠지만, 만약 당신이 몸을 소홀히 하고 함부로 다룬다면 그것은 곧 당신을 몹시 실망시킬 것이다. 몸과 자전거의 주요한 차이점은, 당신이 언제든 또 다른 두 발 자전거를 살 수 있다는 것이다. 그러나 당신의 몸을 소홀히 다뤄 망가진다면 적은 돈으로는 몸을 (C) 회복시키기에 충분하지 않을 것이다.

구문 [7행~9행] **With** care, / it **should** last at least 80 years, // but it **will** soon **fail** you badly // if you **neglect** and **abuse** it.
「With ~, 가정법 과거」 구문이다. 부사구인 With care에 '만약 조심히 다룬다면'이라는 조건의 뜻이 들어 있으며 if절을 대신한다. but 이하의 문장은 「주절+조건의 부사절」로 이루어진 문장으로 주절이 미래 시제이지만 조건의 부사절에서는 현재시제가 미래시제를 대신하므로 시제를 일치시키지 않고 현재시제 neglect, abuse가 쓰였다.

어휘 **suppose** 가정하다; 추측하다 **rusty** 녹이 슨 **the same goes for** ~도 마찬가지이다 **last** 오래가다, 지속하다 **at least** 적어도 **badly** 몹시, 심하게 **neglect** (돌보지 않고) 방치하다; 방치, 소홀 **abuse** (몸 등을) 혹사하다; 남용[오용]하다 **two-wheeler** 자전거; 2륜 마차 **ruin** 망치다; 파멸시키다; 《복수형》 폐허

31 빈칸 추론 ⑤

소재 스토리텔링이 갖는 설득의 힘

해설 Obama 미국 전 대통령이 자신의 어머니 이야기를 들어 건강보험 개혁안을 통과시킬 수 있었다는 사례를 통해 이야기가 사람들의 마음을 움직이는 힘이 있음을 보여주는 내용의 글이다. 따라서 빈칸에는 ⑤ '스토리텔링'이 가장 적절하다.

해석 미국 전 대통령 Barack Obama는 훌륭한 연설가로 유명하다. 건강보험 개혁을 위한 그의 캠페인 중에 그는 암으로 돌아가신 자신의 어머니 이야기를 자주 했고, 그 이야기는 사람들을 감동시켜 울리기에 충분했다. 그는 말했다. "어머니는 암과 싸우는 데 모든 것을 바쳤어야 했습니다. 하지만 그 대신에 어머니는 어머니의 병원비를 지불하지 않으려는 보험회사와 싸우셔야 했습니다." 자신의 어머니가 죽어가면서 벌였던 투쟁을 생생하게 묘사한 덕분에 Obama는 많은 지지를 얻었고, 마침내 그의 건강보험 개혁안을 법률로 통과시켰다. 우리는 사람들을 이끌어가는 데 있어서의 스토리텔링(이야기하기)의 힘을 오래 전부터 알고 있다. 주제문 Barack Obama가 보여주었듯이, 그것(= 스토리텔링)은 위대한 사회적 변화를 일으키는 데 도움이 될 수 있다.
① 공포 ② 직관 ③ 의지 ④ 단순함

구문 [5행~6행] "She **should have been** *devoting* everything(A) *to* fighting the cancer(B)," // he said.

「should have p.p.」는 '~했어야 하는데 하지 못했다'라는 의미로 과거 사실에 대한 후회를 나타낸다. 「devote A to B」는 'B에 A를 바치다, 쏟다'라는 뜻이다.

[8행~11행] Painting a vivid picture **of** his mother's dying struggle / helped Obama to win much support, // and he eventually turned his health care reform bill into law.
(S1, V1, O1, C1, S2, V2, O2)

and로 연결된 두 개의 절은 각각 「help A to-v(A가 v하는 것을 돕다)」, 「turn A into B(A를 B로 바꿔 놓다)」의 구조이다.

어휘 **former** (시간적으로) 전의, 앞의 **be renowned as[for]** ~로서[로] 유명하다 **campaign for[against]** ~을 찬성하는[반대하는] (사회 · 정치적) 운동 **health care** 《미》 건강보험; 의료서비스 **reform** 개혁(하다) **cancer** 암 **move A to-v** A가 감동하여 v하게 하다 **insurance** 보험 **get out of** (책임을) 회피하다 **bill** 청구서, 계산서; (국회에 제출된) 법안 **vivid** 생생한 **struggle** 투쟁(하다); 노력(하다) **win support** 지지를 얻다 **eventually** 마침내, 결국 **bring about** ~을 일으키다[초래하다] **social** 사회의

32 빈칸 추론 ⑤

소재 반복되는 일에서 얻는 교훈

해설 빈칸 다음의 예에서 반복되는 사건들이 소중한 교훈을 얻을 기회라고 말하고 있다. 또한 뒤에 이어지는 영화의 예시에서도 주인공은 똑같이 반복되는 일상을 겪다가 마침내 자신이 변해야 한다는 교훈을 얻었으므로, 빈칸에는 ⑤ '일상에서 반복해서 일어나는' 것들로부터 교훈을 얻는다는 내용이 들어가는 것이 적절하다.

해석 주제문 당신은 일상생활에서 반복해서 일어나는 것들로부터 배우는 교훈이 있다는 것을 알아챈 적이 있는가? 당신은 마치 다른 몸과 다른 이름을 가진 똑같은 사람과 몇 번이나 사랑에 빠지는 것처럼 보일 수 있다. 당신은 어디에서 일하든지 계속해서 똑같은 유형의 상사를 만나거나 동료들과 똑같은 불화를 겪을지도 모른다. 결국 당신은 이것들이 소중한 교훈을 배울 기회라는 것을 깨닫게 될 것이다. 예를 들면, 사랑하는 사람들에게 더 잘 대해주라는 것, 또는 동료와 잘 어울리는 법과 같은 것이다. 1993년에 나온 〈Groundhog Day〉라는 영화에서 Bill Murray는 이기적이고 지루해하는 TV 기상 예보관을 연기하는데, 그는 계속해서 (매일) 똑같은 하루를 맞는다. 똑같은 사건들이 되풀이되고 똑같은 일들이 그에게 계속 일어난다. 마침내 그는 그 반복을 깨고 자유롭고 행복해지려면 자기 자신이 변해야만 한다는 것을 배우게 된다.
① 실패에서 대개 유래되는
② 당신을 더욱 현명하고 강하게 만드는
③ 적절한 시기에 제시되는
④ 너무 늦게 습득될 것 같은

구문 [14행~16행] At last he learns // that to break the cycle and (to) be free and happy, / he himself must change.
that 이하는 learn의 목적어 역할을 하는 명사절이다. to break ~ happy는 '목적'을 나타내는 to부정사구로, he himself must change에 연결되는 내용이다.

어휘 **notice** 알아차리다, 인지하다 **lesson** 교훈; 수업 **run into** (우연히) 만나다; 충돌하다 **conflict** 충돌, 대립; 말다툼 **co-worker** 동료(= **colleague**) **valuable** 소중한 **treat** 다루다; 간주하다; 치료하다 **get along with** ~와 잘 지내다 **play a role** 역할을 하다 **weatherman** 기상 예보관 **cycle** 순환; 회전 [선택지 어휘] **failure** 실패 **present** 제시하다 **be likely to-v** v할 것 같다

33 빈칸 추론 ④

소재 창의력을 저해하는 현대 교육과정

해설 나이가 들수록 사람들의 창의력 테스트 점수가 떨어진다는 연구 결과를 언급한 후에 그 원인에 대해 질문을 던지고 있다. 그 질문에 대해 빈칸을 포함한 문장 뒤에서 현대의 학교는 말 잘 듣고 통제된 기계처럼 행동하는 공장 직원들을 양성할 목적으로 생겨났다고 했다. 이는 학교 교육과정에 창의력이 고려되지 않았다는 것과 일맥상통하므로 ④ '학교 교육과정 전반에 걸쳐 무시되어'가 빈칸에 가장 적절하다.

해석 1968년 NASA(미 항공우주국)의 한 과학자가 다섯 살짜리 아이들 1,600명을 대상으로 창의력 테스트를 실시했고, 98퍼센트가 그것을 통과했다. 5년 후 그 아이들은 다시 테스트를 받았다. 놀랍게도 이 열 살짜리 아이 중 30%만이 테스트를 통과했다. 2만 8천 명의 성인에게 동일한 테스트를 실시한 결과, 고작 2%만이 테스트를 통과했다. 주제문 이 결과로 그 과학자는 창의적이지 않은 사고가 습득된다는 결론을 내렸다. 그러나 어떤 방식으로? 왜 우리는 덜 창의적이게 될까? 그것은 아마도 창의력이 학교 교육과정 전반에 걸쳐 무시되어 왔기 때문일 것이다. '현대적' 학교는 200년도 더 전인 산업혁명 때 생겨났고, 말 잘 듣는 공장 노동자를 양산하는 목적으로 고안되었다. 사실 현대의 교육제도는 한때 '공장 모델'이라고 불렸는데, 왜냐하면 그것이 아이들이 잘 통제된 기계처럼 행동하도록 하는 데 기반을 두었기 때문이다.
① 통제된 관점에서 연구되어
② 무능한 교사들에 의해 저해되어
③ 정부에 의해 더 심각하게 고려되어
⑤ 성격의 측면으로 간주되어

구문 [10행~13행] "Modern" schools were born in the Industrial Revolution, / more than 200 years ago, / and were designed / for the purpose **of** producing obedient factory workers.
(S1, V1, V2)

전치사 of는 the purpose와 producing obedient factory workers를 동격으로 연결하고 있다.

어휘 **creativity** 창의력, 창조력 *cf.* **creative** 창의[창조]적인 **incredibly** 놀랍게도, 믿을 수 없을 정도로 **lead A to-v** A가 v하는 결과를 이끌다 **conclude** 결론짓다; 끝내다 **acquire** 습득하다, 얻다 **the Industrial Revolution** 산업혁명(기) **design** 고안하다; 설계하다 **for the purpose of** ~의 목적으로 **obedient** 말 잘 듣는, 순종적인 **be based on** ~에 기초하다[기반을 두다] **regulate** 통제[규제]하다 [선택지 어휘] **perspective** 관점, 시각(= **point of view**) **incompetent** 무능한(↔ **competent** 유능한; 능숙한) **curriculum** 교육과정 **regard as** ~으로 여기다 **aspect** 측면 **personality** 성격, 개성

34 빈칸 추론 ②

소재 유비무환(有備無患)

해설 등장인물은 빗속에서 곤경에 처했지만 핸드폰은 충전하지 않아서 방전되었고, 우산은 고장 난 상태로 방치됐고, 재킷은 이웃에게 빌려준 후 돌려받지 않아 사용할 수 없다. 즉, 평소에 제대로 대비나 관리를 하지 않아 더욱 어려운 상황에 처한 것이다. 여기에 어울리는 모토는 ② '목마르기 전에 우물을 파라'이다.

해석 당신은 폭풍우 속에서 어둡고 구불구불한 길을 따라 운전하고 있다. 뼈에 스미는 으스스한 가을비다. 당신은 모퉁이를 돌다가 불운하게도 유리 한 무더기를 덮고 있던 나뭇잎이 쌓인 부분에 부딪친다. 얼마 안 되어 당신의 타이어에 구멍이 나고 당신은 자신이 길에 발이 묶인 신세임을 깨닫는다. 당신은 핸드폰에 손을 뻗지만 배터리가 나갔음을 깨닫는다. 당신은 사무실을 나서기 전에 그것을 충전했어야 했다. 빗속으로 향하기 전에, 당신은 우산에 손을 뻗지만 그것이 지난번의 바람이 많이 불던 폭풍으로 부서졌음을 깨닫는다. 당신은 그것을 교체해놨어야 했다. 당신은 빗속으로 나가 트렁크를 열고, 당신이 이웃에게 재킷을 빌려주고 결코 돌려받지 못했기 때문에 재킷이 없다는 것을 깨닫는다. 이제 무엇을 할 것인가? 어린 시절의 보이스카우트 모토를 기억하는가? 주제문 목마르기 전에 우물을 파라.
① 우물에서 뜨거운 물을 찾지 마라
③ 목마른 사람이 우물을 판다
④ 물을 찾을 때까지 계속 우물을 파라
⑤ 삽으로 우물을 파는 것은 불가능하다

구문 [5행~6행] ~ and you **find** *yourself* **stranded** on the road.
「find+O+C(p.p.)」는 'O가 ~된 것을 알게 되다'의 뜻이다. yourself와 같은 재귀대명사는 주어와 같은 대상을 지칭하는 목적어 자리에 쓴다.

[7행~8행] You **should have charged** it before you left the office.
「should have p.p.」는 '~했어야 했는데(하지 못했다)'는 과거의 후회를 나타낸다.

어휘 **winding** 구불구불한 **chilling** 으스스한 **soak** 흠뻑 적시다 **patch** 부분, 작은 땅 **unfortunately** 불운하게도 **pile** 무더기 **blow out** (타이어가) 갑자기 구멍이 나다 **strand** 오도 가도 못 하게 하다, 발을 묶다 **charge** 충전하다 **replace** 교체하다 **missing** 없어진 **motto** 모토, 좌우명

35 무관한 문장 ④

소재 바하사 인도네시아어의 다양한 "아니요" 표현

해설 인도네시아 원주민 언어인 바하사어에는 '예'라고 말하지만 실제로는 '아니요'를 의미하는 단어가 매우 많아서 외국인들이 의사소통에 어려움을 겪을 수도 있다는 내용이다. 반면 ④는 인도네시아인들이 다른 지방 언어에도 능하다는 내용이므로 글의 흐름과 무관하다.

해석 주제문 세계의 어떤 지역에서는, 영어권 국가에서 온 방문객들이 만약 대답으로 "아니요"라고 답하는 게 무례하다는 걸 모른다면 곤경에 처할 수도 있다. 세계에서 그런 지역의 하나가 인도네시아인데 그곳의 원주민 언어인 바하사 인도네시아어는 "예"라고 말하면서도 실제로는 "아니요"를 의미하는 단어가 열두 개나 된다. 만약 당신이 바하사어에 능통하지 않다면, 당신은 동의하지 않는다는 정확한 메시지를 전달하지 못할 것이다. 적절한 번역으로도 "아니요"의 정확한 어조를 전달하지 못할 수 있고, 당신의 말을 듣는 사람이 당신을 오해할 수도 있다. 그러나 대부분 인도네시아인이 종종 바하사어 외에도 지역 사회 안에서 흔히 사용되는 다른 지방 언어에 능통하다. 인도네시아인에게 "아니요"라고 말하는 것은 공손하지 못한 것이기 때문에 방문객들은 그들의 긍정적인 대답이 "예"를 의미한다고 여겨서는 안 된다.

구문 [1행~4행] ~, *visitors* (from English-speaking countries) may find themselves in trouble // if they aren't aware // that **it**'s not polite to give "no" as an answer.
that절의 it은 밑줄 친 to부정사구를 대신하는 가주어이다.

어휘 **aware** 알고 있는 **native** 태어난 곳의; 원주민의 **unless** ~하지 않는 한(= **if ~ not**) **fluent** 유창한 **convey** (생각·감정 등을) 전달하다 **disagreement** 불일치, 의견 차이 **proper** 적절한 **translation** 번역 **tone** 어조, 말투 **misunderstand** 오해하다 **aside from** ~을 제외하고 **regional** 지방[지역]의 **local** 지역의 **community** (공동) 사회, 공동체

36 글의 순서 ④

소재 감정 표현에 관한 문화적 차이

해설 감정 표현의 문화적 차이를 일본인과 유럽인을 비교하면서 설명하는 글이다. (C)의 This stereotype이 가리키는 내용은 주어진 글의 마지막 문장의 내용이다. (A)의 in fact는 앞 문장과 유사한 내용을 이끄는 연결사이며, 그 내용은 (C)에 언급된 일본인의 무표정에 대해 부연설명하고 있다. (B)의 대조의 연결사 on the other hand를 통해 (A)의 유럽인과 북미인의 풍부한 감정 표현에 대한 내용과 (B)의 일본인의 감정 표현 자제에 대한 내용이 자연스럽게 연결된다. 따라서 정답은 ④ '(C)-(A)-(B)'이다.

해석 주제문 감정에 관해서라면, 우리는 종종 문화적 차이에 주목한다. 아시아 사람들에 대한 유럽인들의 태도가 좋은 예이다. 오랫동안 영국과 다른 유럽권에서는 아시아인들이 신비스러운 존재로 흔히 묘사되어 왔다.

(C) 이러한 고정관념은 유럽인 여행자들이 그 지역(아시아) 사람들의 감정을 읽기 어렵다고 여기는 사실에서 왔다. 예를 들면, 그들은 일본인의 무표정이 자신들(= 유럽인)의 감정과는 매우 다른 감정을 숨길지도 모른다고 생각했다.

(A) 실제로 일본인들은 유럽과 북미 사람들보다 자신의 감정을 숨기기 위해 더 열심히 노력한다. 유럽과 북미에서 사람들은 감정을 드러내는 생생한 얼굴 표정을 장려한다. 무표정은 일반적으로 아둔하거나 정직하지 못한 것으로 여겨진다.

(B) 반면, 일본에서 과도한 감정 표현은 종종 무례한 것으로 여겨지며, 일본인들은 결과적으로 자신의 감정 표현을 최소화하려고 노력한다.

구문 **when it comes to A** A에 관해서라면 **cultural** 문화의 **attitude** 태도 **describe** 묘사하다 **mysterious** 신비스러운 **encourage** 장려하다 **vivid** 생생한, 선명한 **expression** 표정; 표현 **regard A as B** A를 B로 간주하다[여기다] **dull** 아둔한; 무딘 **dishonest** 부정직한 **excessive** 지나친, 과도한 **display** 표현; 전시 **perceive** 인식[인지]하다 **rude** 무례한 **consequently** 그 결과(로서) **make an effort to-v** v하려고 노력하다 **minimize** 최소화하다(↔ **maximize** 최대화하다) **stereotype** 고정관념 **local** 주민, 현지인; 현지의 **wonder** ~인가 하고 생각하다 **whether** ~인지 어떤지

37 글의 순서 ⑤

소재 기회비용과 인플레이션으로 인한 이자의 발생

해설 돈을 빌려주면 기회비용과 인플레이션으로 인해 위험이 발생한다는 주어진 글 다음에는 For example로 시작하며 돈을 빌려줘서 사고 싶던 물건을 원하는 때에 못 사고 웃돈을 줘야 살 수 있게 되는 예가 제시된 (C)가 와야 한다. also와 함께 돈을 돌려받지 못할 또 다른 위험을 제시한 (B)가 그 다음으로 나오고, 이로 인해 이자의 필요성이 발생했다는 (B)의 마지막 부분과 은행에서 이자를 주는 이유를 설명한 (A)가 연결된다. 따라서 정답은 ⑤ '(C)-(B)-(A)'이다.

해석 당신이 친구에게 지갑에 있는 돈을 빌려준다면, 당신의 기회비용은 그것의 즉각적인 사용을 희생시킨 것이다. 당신의 친구가 결국 당신에게 돈을 갚을 때, 돈은 인플레이션 때문에 구매력을 상실했을 것이다.

(C) 예를 들어, 당신이 돈을 빌려줬을 때 50달러가 나가던 의자가 친구가 당신에게 돈을 갚은 2년 후에는 55달러가 나갈지도 모르는데, 이는 당신이 의자가 처음 필요했을 때 그것을 살 수 없었을 뿐만 아니라, 지금 그것을 구매하기 위해 그것이 당신에게 더 많은 비용을 들게 할 것임을 의미한다.

(B) 당신의 친구가 코스타리카로 이사 가서 당신의 돈을 갚는 것을 '잊어버릴' 위험도 있다. 주제문 결과적으로 사람들이 돈을 빌려줄 때, 그들은 많은 경우 기회비용과 인플레이션을 상쇄하기 위해 추가적인 지불(이자)로 보상을 받기를 요구한다.

(A) 당신이 돈을 저축 예금에 넣어둘 때, 당신은 마찬가지의 이유로 이자 받기를 기대한다. 그렇지 않으면 당신은 그저 돈을 매트리스 아래에 채워 넣을 것이다.

구문 [10행~11행] There is also the risk that your friend will move to Costa Rica and "**forget**" **to pay** you back.
that ~ back은 the risk에 대한 동격절이다. 「forget to-v」는 '~할 것을 잊다'의 뜻이다.

[15행~19행] ~, *the chair* [that cost $50 when you loaned the money] might cost $55 two years later ~, / meaning **not only** were you unable to buy the chair when you first needed it, **but** it will cost you more to buy it now.
[ ] 부분은 주어 the chair를 수식한다. meaning 이하는 분사구문이다. 부정어 표현이 앞으로 나오면 「동사+주어」 어순으로 도치되므로 not only 다음에 were you와 같은 어순이 쓰였다. 「not only A but (also) B」는 'A뿐만 아니라 B도'의 뜻이다.

어휘 **opportunity cost** 기회비용 **sacrifice** 희생 **immediate** 즉각적인 **inflation** 인플레이션, 통화 팽창 **deposit** 예금하다, 두다 **savings account** 저축 예금 (계좌) **interest** 이자 **otherwise** 그렇지 않으면 **stuff** 채워 넣다 **reward** 보상을 주다 **additional** 추가적인 **offset** 상쇄[벌충]하다 **loan** 빌려주다 (= **lend**)

38 문장 넣기 ⑤

소재 예비 아빠가 살찌는 이유

해설 주어진 문장은 찬장에 먹을 것이 갑자기 늘어나면 남편들도 먹고 싶은 유혹이 생긴다는 내용이므로, 임신한 여성들이 평소보다 더 많은 간식을 보관한다는 내용과 간식 먹을 기회가 풍부해지는 것이 예비 아빠들이 살이 찌는 더 그럴싸한 이유가 된다는 내용 사이에 오는 것이 적절하다. 따라서 정답은 ⑤이다.

해석 임신 동안 체중이 느는 것은 여성들만이 아니다. 주제문 한 조사는 예비 아빠 중 25퍼센트가 그들 배우자의 임신 동안 체중이 또한 늘었다는 것을 발견했다. 그들이 제시하는 살이 찌는 이유 중 하나는 '내 배우자를 위한 동정심 때문에 먹는 것'이었다. 바꿔 말하면, 예비 아빠들이 자신의 체중을 늘림으로써 그들 배우자(= 아내)가 체중 증가에 대해 기

분이 나아지게끔 하려고 더 많이 먹는다는 것이다. 그뿐 아니라, 임신한 여성들은 간식을 간절히 원하는 경향이 있어서 집에 평소보다 더 많은 간식을 보관해 둔다. 찬장에 갑자기 바로 먹을 수 있는 음식이 가득 차면 남자들이 그것을 먹고 싶은 유혹을 느끼는 것은 그리 놀랄 일이 아니다. '동정심' 때문에 먹는다기보다 간식을 먹을 기회의 이러한 새로운 풍부함이 예비 아빠들의 체중 증가에 대한 더 그럴듯한 이유가 된다.

구문 [1행~3행] **It**'s hardly surprising // that men are tempted to eat // if the cupboards are suddenly filled with ready-to-eat foods.
it은 밑줄 친 that절 전체 내용을 받는 가주어이다. that절 내에 조건절(if ~)이 포함된 구문이다.

어휘 **hardly** 거의 ~아니다 **be tempted to-v** v하고 싶어지다, v하도록 유혹당하다 **cupboard** 찬장 **be filled with** ~으로 가득 차다 **ready-to-eat** 바로 먹을 수 있는, 인스턴트의 **gain weight** 체중이 늘다(↔ **lose weight** 체중이 줄다) **pregnancy** 임신 *cf.* **pregnant** 임신한 **father-to-be** 예비 아빠(= **would-be father**) **out of sympathy** 동정심 때문에 **tend to-v** v하는 경향이 있다 **crave** 간절히 원하다 **abundance** 풍부 **opportunity** 기회 **likely** ~할 것 같은; 그럴듯한

39 문장 넣기 ⑤

소재 연기와 스포츠에서의 행위의 차이

해설 주어진 문장의 By contrast로 미루어 앞 문장에는 관객들이 보는 것과 실제 행동 사이에 차이가 있는 것에 관한 내용이 있어야 한다. 따라서 어려운 행동을 하는 것처럼 보이나 실제로는 그렇지 않은 배우들의 연기에 대한 이야기가 나온 후인 ⑤에 들어가는 것이 가장 적절하다.

해석 배우들은 대본에 쓰인 연기를 하며, 그것들은 다른 사람들에 의해 만들어지고 그 안에서 모든 사람들이 계획된 결과를 이루어내기 위해 협력한다. 영화와 모든 형태의 드라마에서의 긴장감은 관객들에게 영향을 끼치지만, 일반적으로 참여자들(= 배우들)에게는 영향을 끼치지 않는다. 하지만 경기에서 선수들은 양쪽 팀이 경쟁하면서 각 팀이 다른, 실은 반대되는 결과를 만들기 위해 노력하며 대본에 없는 행위를 보인다. 주제문 **스크린에서 위험하고 어려운 행동을 하는 것처럼 보이는 배우들은 실제로는 그것들을 거의 하지 않는다.** 그들의 대역배우들이 실제로 위험한 일을 하고, 그 행위는 일반적으로 실제로 위험한 것보다 더욱 위험해 보이게 한다. 주제문 대조적으로, 야구, 미식축구, 그리고 농구 선수들은 정말로 관중이 보기에 그들이 하는 동작을 수행한다. 그들이 하는 것은 실제이며 그들의 노력의 결과는 관객과 참여자들(= 선수들) 모두에게 미리 알려져 있지 않다.

구문 [3행~5행] Actors give *scripted performances*, // which are designed by others and in which all cooperate to achieve a planned outcome.
which ~ others와 in which ~ outcome은 scripted performances를 보충 설명하며 병렬구조를 이룬다.
[7행~10행] But *players* (in games) give *unscripted performances* [in which two sides compete, / **with** *each* **trying** to produce a different — indeed the opposite — outcome].
「전치사+관계대명사」 형태인 in which가 이끄는 절은 unscripted performances를 수식한다. 콤마(,) 뒤의 with ~ outcome은 「with+O+v-ing」 구문으로 'O가 v하면서 [v하여, v한 채로]'라고 해석한다.

어휘 **spectator** 관객, 관중(= **audience**) **script** 대본[원고](을 쓰다) **design** 만들다; 설계하다 **cooperate** 협력[협동]하다; 협조하다 **outcome** 결과; 성과 **tension** 긴장감 **indeed** 실로, 참으로 **appear** ~인 것처럼 보이다; 나타나다 **hazard** 위험한 것; 위험 (요소) **in advance** 미리, 사전에

40 요약문 완성 ④

소재 우울증 극복 방법

해설 이 글의 두 심리학자는 우울하면 자신에게 집중하지 말고 다른 사람들을 위해 무언가를 하라고 했으므로, 우울증을 극복하는 효과적인 방법은 '자신에게만 몰두(self-absorbed)'하지 말고 다른 사람들에게 '인정을 베푸는(compassionate)' 것이라고 요약할 수 있다.

해석 마음이 울적한가? 유명한 두 심리학자의 충고를 받아들여 보면 어떨까? 심리학자 Carl Menninger는 한번은 자신의 강의 중 하나에서 청중들로부터 받은 질문에 답하고 있었다. 누가 물었다. "어떤 사람이 우울함을 느끼면 그에게 뭘 하라고 충고하시겠습니까?" 대부분의 사람들은 그가 "즉시 가서 의사를 만나세요."라고 말할 거라고 생각했지만 그는 그러지 않았다. 놀랍게도 Menninger 박사는 대답했다. "집을 걸어 잠그고, 철로를 건넌 다음, 곤경에 처한 사람을 찾아내서 그 사람을 도와주세요. 주제문 **자신에게 집중하지 마세요. 대신에 다른 사람들의 삶에 관여하세요.**" 한번은 심리학자 Alfred Adler가 자신의 의뢰인들에게 비슷한 충고를 제시했다. 그는 단 14일이면 우울증에 걸린 누구라도 치유할 수 있다고 주장했다. Adler는 자신의 의뢰인들에게 말하곤 했다. 주제문 **"2주 동안 매일 다른 사람을 위해 무언가를 하면 당신의 우울증은 사라질 겁니다."**

⬇

위의 두 심리학자에 따르면, 우울증을 극복하는 효과적인 방법은 (A) 자신에게만 몰두하지 말고 다른 사람들에게 (B) 인정을 베푸는 것이다.

구문 [5행~6행] "What **would** you **advise** a person to do // **if** that person **felt** depressed?"
「If+주어+과거동사, 주어+would+동사원형」의 가정법 과거 문형이다.

어휘 **feel down** 마음이 울적하다 **lecture** 강의 **depressed** 우울한 **to A's surprise** A가 놀랍게도 **reply** 대답하다 **railroad track** 철로, 선로 **get involved in** ~에 관여하다 **used to-v** (예전에는) v하곤 했다 **overcome** 극복하다 [선택지 어휘] **indifferent** 무관심한 **self-confident** 자신감 있는 **self-willed** 고집이 센

41~42 장문 41 ④ 42 ②

소재 우정의 조건과 의미

해설 41. 우정은 평등해야 하고, 공유하는 경험과 활동이 있어야 하고, 수단이 아닌 목적 그 자체여야 하고, 돈으로 사고팔 수 없으며, 끊임없이 관심을 기울이고 가꿔나가야 한다는 내용의 글이다. 우정의 조건과 의미를 상술하고 있으므로 제목은 ④ '우정: 조건과 의미'가 가장 적절하다.

① 친구들은 어떻게 의사소통하는가?
② 좋은 친구는 찾기 어렵다
③ 시간의 경과에 따른 우정의 변화 방식
⑤ 건강한 우정을 발전시키는 것의 중요성

42. 우정은 강과 같이 어떤 방향으로 나아가야만 의미가 있다고 했으므로 '가변적인 것'이어야 함을 알 수 있다. 부정어 not이 있으므로 '가변적인 것'의 의미를 표현하려면 not an invariable thing이 되어야 한다. 따라서 (b)의 (a) variable을 (an) invariable로 바꿔 써야 한다.

해석 우정의 본질은 평등이다. 진정한 우정은 단지 힘과 선물만이 아니다. 그것은 또한 (a) 공통의 관심과 감정과 생각에 기반을 두어야 한다. 확실한 것은 공유할 것이 없는 가장된 우정은 잘 되지 않는다는 것이다. 우정은 (b) 가변적인(→ 불변의) 것이 아니다. 그것은 강과 같아서, 어떤 방향으로 향하는 경우에만 의미가 있다. 그것은 항상 발전하고, 확장되고, 새로운 경험을 흡수해야 한다. 누군가가 옛날에 말했듯이, "잉글랜드인은 친구를 두지 않는다. 그들은 어떤 일에 대한 친구를 가지는 것이다." (c) 공유된 활동 혹은 필요가 우정의 이면에 있다. 세상에는 정말 많은 사람들이 있다. 왜 단지 이 한 사람과만 시간을 보내는가? 함께 있는 게 즐겁기 때문에, 그들이 '매우 재밌고' 즐겁고 지지해주고 친절한 것이다. 우리 모두가 알게 되듯이, 이것은 많은 경우 그것의 가장 강력한 표현을 그들과 함께 게임을 하는 데서 찾아낸다. 친구들은 (d) 계산적이면 안 된다. 진짜 친구는 당신에게 그들의 진정한 모습을 보여준다. 우정은 윤리학의 중심 규칙을 따른다. 즉, "사람을 목적 그 자체로 대하고 목적의 수단으로 대해서는 안 된다." 친구가 '당신을 이용하고 있다고' 느낀다면 우정은 끝난다. 진정한 사랑과 아름다움을 사거나 팔 수 없듯이 우정도 구매할 수 없다. 대리점에 가서 친구를 구매하거나 고용할 수 없는 반면, 특정 업무를 위해 어떤 사람의 정신이나 신체는 확실히 고용할 수 있다. 그러므로 우정은 두 명의 동등한 사람들이 장기적으로 서로를 좋아하는 것에 관한 문제이다. 우리는 우정에서 열심히 노력해야 한다. 그것은 자연스럽게 오지도 않고 끊임없는 (e) 관심이 없으면 남아있지도 않는다. 친

구들은 과수원에 비유될 수 있다. 그들을 주의 깊게 심고 가지치기하고 보호해야 한다.

구문 [29행~30행] ~ it **neither** comes naturally **nor** remains without constant attention.
A B

「neither A nor B」는 'A도 아니고 B도 아니다'의 뜻이다.

어휘 **equality** 평등 **be based on** ~에 기반을 두다 **pretend** 가장하다 **variable** 가변적인 **only if** 오직 ~한 경우에만 **head** 향하다 **expand** 확장하다 **absorb** 흡수하다 **put it** 말하다, 표현하다 **company** 함께 있음 **supportive** 지지하는 **calculating** 계산적인, 타산적인; 계산용의 **ethics** 윤리학 **namely** 즉, 다시 말해 **end** 목적 **in oneself** 그 자체로는 **means** 수단 **purchase** 구매하다 **agency** 대리점 **hire** 고용하다 **particular** 특정한, 특별한 **long-term** 장기적인 **constant** 부단한, 끊임없는 **orchard** 과수원

43~45 장문 43 ④ 44 ③ 45 ④

소재 시작하는 것의 중요성

해설 43. (A)는 현재 가진 것으로 할 수 있는 것이 많지 않다고 생각하는 사람에게 그것은 변명일 뿐이라고 깨우쳐주는 내용으로, 이를 부연설명하기 위해 예시로 시작하는 (C)가 이어지는 것이 적절하다. 친구가 해준 Tony의 이야기를 (C)의 마지막에 언급했으므로 다음에는 접시닦이로 시작해(D), 레스토랑 주방장까지 되었다는(B) 순서로 Tony의 일화가 이어지는 것이 적절하다.

44. (c)는 Bernard를 가리키지만 나머지는 모두 Tony를 가리킨다.

45. (D)에서 Tony는 접시닦이 일에 지원했음을 알 수 있으므로 ④가 일치하지 않는 내용이다.

해석 (A) 만약 당신이 삶의 어느 위치에 와 있는지 걱정된다면, 그리고 당신이 생각하기에 자신의 그 꿈에 조금도 가까이 다가가고 있지 않다면, 당신 자신에게 이렇게 물어보라. "내가 바로 지금 가지고 있는 것으로 나는 지금 무엇을 하고 있는가?" 그에 대한 대답이 "별로 많지 않아. 내가 가진 것이 많은 것을 하기에 충분하지 않거든."이라고 한다면 유일한 문제는 바로 당신이다. 세상은 변명이 아닌 노력에 보답하기 때문이다.

(C) 예를 들어, 그들의 멋진 직업과 훌륭한 업적 때문에 당신이 존경하는 사람들에 대해 생각해보라. 음, 한 가지 확실한 것은 그들이 모두 어디에선가 시작하려고 노력했다는 점이고, 그것이 바로 다음 기회 그리고 또 다음 기회를 이끌었다는 점이다. 사람들이 "어느 곳에도 일자리가 없어요!"라고 말하는 것을 들으면, 나는 매우 성공한 식당 주인인 나의 친구 Bernard가 언젠가 내게 들려준 이야기가 생각난다. Bernard는 내게 Tony라는 이름의 (c) 자신(= Bernard)의 오랜 친구가 ③ 뉴욕에서 어떻게 첫 직장을 갖게 되었는지를 들려주었다.

(D) 그는 이탈리아에서 (뉴욕에) 막 도착해서 돈도 없었고 영어도 할 줄 몰라서 ④ 접시닦이로 일하는 것에 지원하려고 이탈리아 레스토랑을 찾아갔다. 기다리라는 말을 들은 후, (d) 그(= Tony)는 화장실에 가서 솔을 발견하고는 ⑤ 타일과 변기를 티 하나 없이 깨끗해질 때까지 닦았다. 그가 면접을 볼 때쯤에는 (이미) 레스토랑에 있던 모든 사람들이 화장실에서 일어난 일에 대해 묻고 있었다. 그들은 곧 그것이 "(e) 저(= Tony)는 열심히 일하는 사람이고 청소라는 것을 진지하게 생각합니다."라고 말하는 Tony의 방식이라는 것을 알게 되었다.

(B) 그렇게 (a) 그(= Tony)는 직장을 얻었다. 한 달 뒤, 보조 요리사가 그만두자 Tony는 그 레스토랑 주인이 이제껏 고용했던 중 ① 최고의 요리사가 되는 여정을 시작했다. ② 그 레스토랑 주인이 바로 Bernard이며, Tony는 그 오랜 친구이다. Tony의 여정과 관련해 (b) 그(= Tony)로부터 배울 수 있는 교훈은, 간단히 말해서 당신이 할 수 있는 어느 곳에서든 시작하라는 것이다. 주제문 당신 앞에 있는 무엇에든지 최선을 다하면, 기회는 당신의 문을 두드리기 시작할 것이다. 그것은 '한 가지가 또 다른 것을 이끈다'란 원칙을 실천에 옮기는 것이다.

구문 [(B) 2행~3행] ~ and Tony was on his way to becoming ***the best** chef* [**that** the restaurant's owner **had ever had**].

「최상급+that+완료시제」는 최상급 표현 중 하나로 '이제껏 ~한 것 중 가장 …한'이란 뜻이다. 여기에서 that은 목적격 관계대명사로 선행사 the best chef를 수식한다.

[(B) 7행~9행] **Put your best into** *whatever is there in front of you*, and opportunities will start knocking on your door.

「put one's best into A」는 'A에 최선을 다하다'란 뜻이다. whatever ~ you가 전치사 into의 목적어 역할을 한다. 「명령문, and+S+V.」는 '~해라, 그러면 …할 것이다'의 의미이다.

어휘 **(A) reward** 보상하다; 보수 **excuse** 변명; 용서하다 **(B) prep cook** 보조 요리사 **on one's way to** ~로 가는 길[도중]에 **chef** 요리사, 주방장 **owner** 주인 **regarding** ~와 관해 **put A into action** A를 실천에 옮기다 **principle** 원칙 **(C) admire** 존경하다; 칭찬하다 **achievement** 업적, 성취 **for sure** 확실히 **make an effort to-v** v하기 위해 노력하다[애쓰다] **lead to** ~로 이어지다; ~을 이끌다 **(D) apply for** ~에 지원하다 **scrub** 문질러 닦다, 청소하다 **spotless** 티끌 하나 없는 *cf.* **spot** 점, 얼룩; (특정한) 장소

실전 모의고사 07

본문 p.97

18 ③	19 ②	20 ④	21 ①	22 ⑤	23 ②	24 ②	25 ③	26 ④	27 ⑤
28 ④	29 ④	30 ⑤	31 ②	32 ②	33 ①	34 ③	35 ③	36 ⑤	37 ③
38 ④	39 ③	40 ①	41 ②	42 ③	43 ④	44 ③	45 ③		

18 글의 목적 ③

소재 분실물 찾기

해설 프로그램에 참여하던 중 딸이 부주의로 금목걸이를 잃어버려서 그것을 찾기 위해 도움을 요청하는 편지글이므로 정답은 ③이다. 글의 중반 'So, if anyone should happen to find a necklace ~ please contact me.'에 글의 목적이 잘 드러나 있다.

해석 관계자 분께,
제 가족과 저는 최근에 귀사의 가족을 위한 '나무꼭대기 모험' 과정 중 하나에 참여했고 그것이 분명히 재미있고 신났었지만 작은 문제가 있었습니다. 그런데, 확실히 짚고 가자면 여기에 책임은 전적으로 저에게 있습니다. 짚라인이나 외줄 그네를 시도할 때 장신구류를 착용해서는 안 된다고 안내원이 분명하게 말했지만 제 딸이 주의 깊게 듣지 않았던 것 같습니다. 집에 돌아오자마자 그 애는 금목걸이를 잃어버린 것을 알아챘습니다. 그것이 할머니의 선물이었기 때문에 아이는 당연히 속상해하고 있습니다. 주제문 그래서 어느 분이 혹시라도 짚라인 아래 숲속에서 목걸이를 우연히 발견한다면 제게 연락주시기 바랍니다. 귀사의 도움에 깊이 감사드릴 것이고 수고에 대해 기꺼이 작은 보상도 드릴 것입니다. 미리 귀사의 도움에 감사드리며 이렇게 멋진 프로그램을 계속 잘 운영하시길 바랍니다!
Chaerin Lee 드림

구문 [12행~14행] So, if anyone **should** happen to find a necklace in the woods beneath the zip line, // please contact me.
조건절에서 should는 실현 가능성이 적은 사항을 가정하며 '혹시라도 ~라면'의 뜻이다.

어휘 **to whom it may concern** (불특정 상대에 대한 편지 등의 첫머리에 써서) 관계자 분(들)께 **let me be clear** 확실하게 짚고 넘어갑시다 **fault** 책임; 잘못 **entirely** 전적으로, 완전히 **attempt** 시도[도전]하다; 시도 **understandably** 당연히 **reward** 보상 **keep up the good work** 계속 잘하다

19 심경 변화 ②

소재 수영 대회 참가

해설 글 초반부의 'My heart beats fast, my knees begin to tremble.'에 경기 시작 전의 초조한 심경이 드러나고, 마지막 문장의 'Wow, I am not last! I am almost first. I did it.'에는 예상 밖의 좋은 결과에 흥분하고 신난 모습이 드러난다. 따라서 'I'의 심경 변화로 가장 적절한 것은 ② '초조한 → 신나는'이다.

해석 나는 수영장 옆에서 대기하고 있다. 주제문 몇 분 후, 나는 내 첫 경주를 시작할 것이다. 내 심장이 빨리 뛰고 무릎이 떨리기 시작한다. 잘 해내고 싶지만 난 꼴찌로 들어올 것이다. 난 그걸 알고 있다. 난 그리 뛰어난 수영선수가 아니다. 내가 할 수 있는 거라곤 최선을 다하는 것뿐이다. 마침내 그들이 모든 50미터 자유형 경기 참가자들을 부른다. 나는 속이 울렁거리지만 일어선다. 나는 2조에 있지만 그것은 내 기분에 도움이 되지 않는다. 첫 번째 조가 가고 두 번째 조가 물에 뛰어들 준비를 하고 있다. 호각이 울린다. 휘이이잇! 우리는 출발한다! 첨벙! 텀벙, 참방, 텀벙, 참방. 나는 벽을 붙잡고 주위를 바라본다. 내가 꼴찌가 아니다. 사실은 거의 모두가 내 뒤에 있다. 누군가가 내게 2등을 뜻하는 파란 막대를 건네준다. 주제문 와, 내가 꼴찌가 아니야! 거의 1등이야. 내가 해냈어.
① 슬픈 → 행복한
③ 만족한 → 실망한
④ 지루해하는 → 기쁜
⑤ 두려워하는 → 화가 난

어휘 **tremble** (몸을) 떨다 **freestyle** 자유형(의) **feel sick** 울렁거리다, 멀미가 나다. **whistle** 호각 **splash** 물 튀기는 소리, 첨벙 **splish** 첨벙(의성어로 유머러스한 표현)(= splash) **splosh** (물속에서) 참방거리다; 참방(거리는 소리) **grab** 붙잡다 **stick** 막대; 찌르다

20 필자 주장 ④

소재 아프리카 원조를 바라보는 입장

해설 아프리카가 자립하도록 돕는 것이 가난과 저개발에 대한 근본적인 해결책이라는 내용의 글이다. 글의 주제문인 마지막 문장(They believe, as I do, ~ for Africa.)에서 아프리카 국가들이 원조에 의존하지 않는 것(non-reliance on aid)이 아프리카 문제를 해결하는 열쇠라고 강조하고 있으므로 정답은 ④이다.

해석 원조는 아프리카가 처한 곤경에 대한 해결책이 아니라고 주장하는 것이 유행이 되고 있는데, 이 주장은 단점과 장점을 가지고 있다. 단점은 원조가 생명을 직접적으로 구한다는 사실에 있는데, 특히 그것이 HIV(에이즈 바이러스)나 말라리아 같은 질병을 목표로 할 때에 그렇다. 반면에, 이 주장의 장점은 원조 '단독'으로는 아프리카의 빈곤이나 저개발을 뒤집을 수 없다는 사실에 있다. 나는 아프리카 거버넌스 이니셔티브(Africa Governance Initiative)에 동참하는 국가들에 의해 이뤄져온 발전에 대해 매우 자랑스럽게 생각하는데, 이는 르완다와 시에라리온의 재건 프로그램을 지원한다. 회원국의 지도자들은 부패를 종식하고 투자자를 보호하는 것에 대해 진지하다. 주제문 나와 마찬가지로 그들은 훌륭한 통치와 튼튼한 경제, 그리고 원조에 의존하지 않는 것이 아프리카의 회복과 번영을 위한 열쇠라고 생각한다.

구문 [8행~11행] I am incredibly proud of *the progress* [**that** has been achieved by *those countries* (working with *the Africa Governance Initiative*, // **which** supports reconstruction programs in Rwanda and Sierra Leone)].
[ ] 부분은 주격 관계대명사 that이 이끄는 관계사절로 선행사 the progress를 수식한다. ( ) 부분은 those countries를 수식하며, which는 계속적 용법으로 쓰인 주격 관계대명사로 선행사인 the Africa Governance Initiative를 부연 설명한다.

어휘 **trendy** 최신 유행의 **argue (that)** (~라고) 주장하다 *cf.* **argument** 주장; 논쟁 **aid** 원조, 지원 **weakness** 단점, 약점 **lie in** (생각·문제 등이) ~에 있다 **target** 목표로 삼다, 겨냥하다; 목표 **reverse** 뒤집다, 뒤바꾸다 **poverty** 빈곤, 가난 **underdevelopment** 저개발, 낙후 **governance** 통치 **initiative** 계획; 자주성 **reconstruction** 재건, 복원 **corruption** 부패, 타락 **investor** 투자자 *cf.* **invest** 투자하다 **non-reliance** 독립(↔ **reliance** 의존) **recovery** (경제·건강 등의) 회복 **prosperity** 번영, 번성

21 밑줄 함의 ①

소재 미국의 초기 통나무집

해설 미국의 초기 통나무집은 벽 사이의 틈을 통해 바람이 들어왔고, 틈새를 채워도 바람을 완전히 막을 수 없었다는 내용이다. 따라서 '바람이 항상 승리했다'는 것은 ① '바람이 벽을 통과해 들어왔다'는 의미이다.

해석 주제문 통나무 오두막집은 완성이 덜 된 구조를 가진 작은 통나무집이다. 통나무집은 유럽에서 고대의 역사를 갖고 있으며, 미국에서는 많은 경우 정착민들이 만든 1세대 가정집 건축물과 연관된다. 거실, 식당과 침실은 미국의 대부분의 19세기 통나무집에 존재하지 않았다. 내벽이 없이 단지 방 한 개만 있었다. 바닥은 진흙으로 만들어졌다. 이러한 오두막집은 추위로부터의 보호가 전혀 안 되고 습기가 흙바닥을 통해 올라오지 못하게 막아줄 방도가 없어서 매우 추웠다. 게다가 통나무 벽 사이의 틈을 통해 바람이 불어 들어왔다. 이를 막기 위해 정착민들은 진흙과 지푸라기로 시멘트를 만들었지만 좀처럼 모든 틈새를 채울 수가 없었다. 바람이 항상 승리했다.

② 통나무집 근처에서는 항상 바람이 불었다
③ 벽의 갈라진 틈이 더 넓어졌다
④ 집은 약한 바람으로 둘러싸여 있었다
⑤ 바람이 집의 습기를 말려주었다

구문 [8행~10행] These cabins were very cold / **with** no protection from the cold and no way to **keep** the damp **from** coming up / through the earthen floor.
밑줄 친 두 어구가 병렬구조를 이루며 공통적으로 with의 목적어 역할을 한다. 「keep[prevent, stop]+O+from v-ing」는 'O가 v하지 못하게 막다'의 뜻이다.

[11행~13행] To prevent this, settlers(S1) **made**(V1) a cement(A) **out of** mud and straw(B), // but rarely could(조동사) they(S2) fill(V2) every gap.
「make A out of B」는 'B로 A를 만들다'의 뜻이다. but 이하의 절은 부정어가 문두에 와서 「부정어(rarely)+조동사(could)+주어(they)+동사(fill)」의 어순으로 도치되었다.

어휘 **log** 통나무 **cabin** 오두막집 **structure** 구조 **ancient** 고대의 **be associated with** ~와 연관되다 **settler** 정착민 **exist** 존재하다 **be made of** ~로 만들어지다 **mud** 진흙 **damp** 습기, 물기; 축축한 **earthen** 흙의 **what is more** 게다가 **blow (blew-blown)** 불다; 날려 보내다 **prevent** 막다, 예방하다 **straw** 지푸라기 **rarely** 좀처럼 ~ 않다 [선택지 어휘] **crack** 갈라진 틈 **humidity** 습기

22 글의 요지 ⑤

소재 자녀의 성공에 도움이 되는 생산적인 피드백

해설 부모의 피드백이 아이에게 미치는 영향에 관한 내용의 글이다. 글의 도입에서 생산적인 피드백의 예를 보여준 뒤, 글 중반부의 주제문(Parents can help ~ providing productive feedback.)에서 구체적이고 객관적이며 정확한 피드백이 자녀의 성공에 도움이 된다고 했으므로 글의 요지로 가장 적절한 것은 ⑤이다.

해석 부모가 자식에게 피드백을 제공하는 상황을 상상해보라. "Mary, 난 네가 영화를 보러 가지 못해 실망한 마음을 다스린 방식이 맘에 들어. 네가 약간 기분이 상했을 거란 거 알아. 넌 네 감정을 잘 다스렸어. 넌 나한테 화났다고 말하고 나서 다른 방으로 가서 해야 할 공예 과제를 찾아냈지." 여기서 부모는 아이가 한 일을 정확히 아이에게 지적했다. 이러한 종류의 피드백은 아이에게 교훈적이다. 그것은 좋은 문제 해결 능력과 좋은 의사소통 능력을 강화시켜준다. 주제문 부모들은 생산적인 피드백을 제공함으로써 그들의 자녀가 성공하는 것을 도울 수 있다. 이것은 우리가 다른 사람의 수행과 행동에 대해 하는 평가이며, (이 평가는) 직접적이고 구체적이며, 객관적이고 정확하다. 그것은 합리적이며, 부정적인 행동뿐만 아니라 긍정적인 행동에 대해서도 제공된다.

구문 [12행~14행] This is *an evaluation* [(that[which]) we make of another person's performance and behavior] [that is direct, specific, objective, and accurate].
an evaluation은 목적격 관계대명사가 생략된 절(we make ~ behavior)과 주격 관계대명사절(that is ~ accurate)의 수식을 받는다.

[15행~16행] ~ and it is provided for positive **as well as** for negative behavior.
「A as well as B」는 'B뿐만 아니라 A도'의 뜻이다. behavior가 positive와 negative에 공통으로 걸린다.

어휘 **provide** 제공하다 **handle** 다루다, 처리하다 **disappointment** 실망 **upset** 속상한 **craft** 공예 **point out** 지적하다 **instructive** 교훈적인, 유익한 **reinforce** 강화하다 **productive** 생산적인 **evaluation** 평가 **performance** 수행 **behavior** 행동 **specific** 구체적인 **objective** 객관적인; 목적, 목표 **accurate** 정확한 **rational** 합리적인; 이성적인

23 글의 주제 ②

소재 벌떼 감소가 농업에 미친 영향

해설 글의 도입에서 벌떼 감소로 인해 영향을 받은 중국 쓰촨성의 농업 상황을 설명한 후, 전 세계적으로 벌떼 수 감소로 인해 흉작이 되고 있다는 주제문(All over the world, ~ crops to fail.)과 이를 뒷받침하는 구체적인 예시가 이어지고 있다. 따라서 글의 주제로 가장 적절한 것은 ② '벌의 소멸과 그로 인해 일어날 수 있는 영향'이다.

해석 중국 쓰촨성의 농부들은 과실수의 가루받이를 위해 꿀벌에 더는 의존할 수 없다. 대신, 일꾼들이 손으로 그 일을 해오고 있다. 중국 농부들의 그러한 경험은 단지 진행되고 있는 환경적, 농업적 재앙의 괴로운 수많은 징후 중 하나에 불과하다. 주제문 전 세계적으로, 불가사의하게 벌떼들이 죽어가고 있으며 이로 인해 작물은 흉작이 되고 있다. 미국의 벌떼 중 30퍼센트가 재작년에 사라진 이후, 작년 겨울에는 35퍼센트가 사라졌다. 유럽 전역뿐만 아니라 호주, 브라질, 인도, 그리고 남아프리카 같은 나라들에 이르기까지 광범위하게 벌 개체 수 상실은 똑같이 충격적이다. 영국 양봉협회에서는 꿀벌을 필요로 하는 사과, 배, 아몬드, 그리고 다른 모든 농작물들과 함께, 꿀벌이 영국에서 10년 내에 완전히 사라질 수도 있다고 경고했다.

① 꿀벌 수분과 유기농업의 장점
③ 양봉 기술의 최근의 발전
④ 농작물 수분 방법의 전 세계적인 비교
⑤ 임박한 농업 위기 대처 전략

어휘 **no longer** 더 이상 ~않다 **rely on** ~에 의존하다; ~을 믿다 **pollinate** 수분(受粉)하다, 가루받이하다 *cf.* **pollination** 수분, 가루받이 **environmental** 환경적인 **agricultural** 농업의 **in the making** 발달[발전] 중의 **colony** (동식물의) 집단, 군집; 식민지 **crop** 농작물 **collapse** 사라지다; 쓰러지다 **loss** 상실; 손실, 손해 **devastating** 충격적인; 파괴적인 **widespread** 넓게 퍼진 **throughout** 전체에 걸쳐, 도처에 **association** 협회; 연합 **entirely** 완전히 **along with** ~와 함께 [선택지 어휘] **merit** 장점 **impending** 곧 닥칠, 임박한

24 글의 제목 ②

소재 지금 실천하는 것의 중요성

해설 사람들은 언젠가 미래에 조건이 충족하면 하고 싶은 일의 목록을 마음속에 품고 살지만 이는 아무 결과도 만들어내지 못하고 심적 부담만 될 뿐이므로, 생각만 하지 말고 오늘 당장 행동에 옮기라고 권하는 글이다. 따라서 제목으로 가장 적절한 것은 ② '꿈꾸는 자가 되지 말고 행동하는 자가 되어라'이다.

해석 대부분의 사람들은 '언젠가는' 목록을 가지고 있다. 그들이 언젠가 …할 때 할 일들 말이다. 언젠가 시간이 더 생길 때, 가족들을 저 대(大)휴가에 데려갈 것이다. 언젠가 돈이 더 생길 때, 그들에게 의미 있는 대의들에 기부하기 시작할 것이다. 그리고 목록은 계속해서 이어진다. 그리고 이 모든 '언젠가는'이 짐이 된다. 주제문 그 굴레를 벗어던지는 가장 빠른 방법은 '언젠가'를 오늘로 만드는 것이다. 엉덩이를 대고 앉아있는 동안엔 시간의 모래에 족적을 남길 수 없다. 당신은 현재 시간의 모래에 엉덩이 자국을 내고 있는 사람을 알고 있다. 그들에겐 꿈도 야망도 많지만, 불행히도 그중 어느 것도 어떤 실제 행동을 수반하지 않는다.

① 추구할 현실적인 목표를 세워라
③ 임무를 분할하여 정복하라
④ 항상 당신의 강점에 집중하라
⑤ 중요한 것을 먼저 하려고 노력하라

구문 [12행~14행] They have lots of dreams and ambitions, // but unfortunately none of **them** are accompanied by any real action.
none of them에서 them은 lots of dreams and ambitions를 지칭한다.

어휘 grand 웅장한, 대(大)- contribute to ~에 기여[기부]하다 cause 대의명분 on and on 계속해서 burden 짐, 부담 throw off 벗어던지다 footprint 발자국 butt 엉덩이 currently 현재 ambition 야망, 포부 be accompanied by ~을 동반하다 [선택지 어휘] realistic 현실적인; 사실적인 conquer 정복하다; 이기다

25 도표 이해 ③

소재 동물군에 따른 미국의 육류 수출 통계

해설 쇠고기와 돼지고기 수출량은 2013년 중반까지 그 차이가 줄어들어 마침내 같아졌다가 2014년부터는 다시 크게 벌어졌으므로 ③이 정답이다.

해석 **〈동물군(群)에 따른 미국의 육류 수출(2003~2019)〉**

주제문 이 도표는 2003년부터 2019년까지 쇠고기(소), 돼지고기(돼지), 가금류 고기(닭, 칠면조)인 세 동물군(群)에 대해, 천 미터톤 단위로 측정한 미국의 육류 수출량을 보여준다. ① 전 기간에 걸쳐 가금류 수출량이 쇠고기와 돼지고기의 수출량보다 더 많았다. ② 쇠고기 수출량에서는 2013년에 시작하여 2014년에 끝난 아주 급격한 감소가 있었다. ③ 2014년 이후 쇠고기 수출량과 돼지고기 수출량의 차이가 줄어들었다. ④ 돼지고기 수출량은 2017년까지 꾸준한 성장세를 보였고, 2017년에서 2018년 사이에 갑작스런 상승 움직임을 보였다. ⑤ 2018년에는 세 개의 수출 범주에서 모두 하락세를 보였고 어느 하나도 성장세를 회복하지 못했다.

어휘 export 수출(량); 수출하다 chart 도표, 차트 illustrate (삽화로) 보여주다 measure 측정하다 poultry (닭, 오리 등의) 가금류 period 기간, 시기 sharp 급격한; 날카로운 gap 차이, 틈, 간격 steady 꾸준한, 한결같은 sudden 갑작스런; 불시, 돌연 upward 상승하는; 위쪽을 향한 decline 하락, 감소; 줄어들다 category 범주 regain 회복하다, 되찾다

26 내용 불일치 ④

소재 코모도왕도마뱀(Komodo dragon)의 특징

해설 코모도왕도마뱀의 시각 범위는 300미터에 이르지만 밤에는 잘 보지 못한다고 했으므로 ④가 글의 내용과 일치하지 않는다.

해석 ① 코모도왕도마뱀은 인도네시아의 코모도, 린카, 플로레스, 길리 모탕 섬이 원산지인 도마뱀의 일종이다. 그것은 현존하는 가장 큰 도마뱀 종이고 ② 다 자라면 평균적으로 길이는 2~3미터 사이이며 무게는 약 70킬로그램에 이른다. ③ 큰 귓구멍에도 불구하고 그것은 제한된 청각 범위를 가져서 매우 낮은 소리와 매우 높은 소리는 모두 감지하지 못한다. 그것(= 코모도왕도마뱀)은 색을 보며 ④ 시각 범위는 300미터에 이르지만, 밤에는 잘 보지 못하며 움직이지 않는 물체를 그리 쉽게 감지하지 못한다. 다른 많은 파충류처럼 ⑤ 코모도왕도마뱀은 매우 민감한 혀를 가지고 있어서 그 혀를 이용해 움직임, 냄새, 온도 변화, 그리고 환경의 다른 중요한 징후들을 감지한다.

어휘 species (동식물) 종(種) lizard 도마뱀 native to (동식물이) ~ 원산의; (사람이) ~ 출신의 in existence 현존하는 average 평균 ~이 되다; 평균(의); 보통(의) in length 길이가 ~인 in weight 무게가 ~인 despite ~에도 불구하고 limited 제한된 range 범위, 폭 detect 감지하다; 발견하다 low-pitched (소리가) 낮은(↔ high-pitched) extend to (범위·영향 등이) ~까지 이르다 object 물체; 대상; 목적 sensitive 민감한 signal 징후, 조짐; 신호를 보내다

27 안내문 불일치 ⑤

소재 SFA 학생 디자인 콘테스트 장학금 안내

해설 소제목과 선택지를 활용하여 필요한 정보를 빠르게 훑어 확인해야 한다. 자격 요건의 마지막 문장에서 팀은 최대 3명까지라고 했으므로 ⑤가 안내문의 내용과 일치하지 않는다.

해석

장학금: SFA 학생 디자인 콘테스트

자신의 연구실을 디자인하는 것이 어떤 것일까 상상해본 적이 있습니까? 이것이 바로 과학가구협회(SFA)가 기대하는 것입니다. ① 모든 연구실 장비나 가구에 대한 혁신적인 디자인을 받습니다.

응모 방법:

- ② 4월 1일 이전이나 당일까지 필수 정보가 모두 제공되어야 하고 출품작/개요가 접수되어야 합니다. 디자인을 요약하는 개요는 250자 이내여야 합니다.
- ③ 이 경선에는 참가비가 없습니다.

상금: 6,000달러
수상이 가능한 수: 3
자격 요건: ④ 고등학교 3학년 학생이어야 합니다. ⑤ 학생들은 개별적으로 또는 최대 참가자 3명으로 구성된 팀의 구성원으로 작업할 수 있습니다.

구문 [9행~11행] All required information must be provided // and your entry/abstract (must be) received / on or before April 1.
수동태 문장으로 and 뒤에 오는 절의 received 앞에는 앞 절에 쓰인 must be가 생략되었다.

어휘 scholarship 장학금 lab 연구실(= laboratory) innovative 혁신적인 equipment 장비, 용품 entry 출품작; 참가 abstract 개요 summarize 요약하다 award (부상이 딸린) 상 requirement 필요조건, 요건; (보통 복수형) 필요한 것, 필수품 senior (고등학교의) 마지막 학년의 individually 개별적으로; 개인적으로 consist of ~으로 구성되다 maximum 최대

28 안내문 일치 ④

소재 인디언 국립 박물관 안내

해설 박물관에 주차는 불가하지만 근처에 여러 주차장이 있다고 했으므로 ④가 안내문의 내용과 일치한다.

해석

인디언 국립 박물관

① 이 박물관의 영구적 그리고 일시적 전시품들은 음악, 무용 공연을 포함한 많은 공공 프로그램들과 함께 미 원주민의 다양성을 탐구할 수 있도록 해줍니다.

개관 시간과 입장료

② 박물관은 평일에는 오전 10시부터 오후 5시까지이며, 목요일에는 오전 10시부터 오후 8시까지 개관합니다. 입장료는 무료입니다.

오시는 길

③ 박물관은 스미소니언 항공우주 박물관과 미 국회의사당 건물 사이의 National Mall에 위치해 있습니다.

- **지하철**
  랑팡 플라자(파랑/주황색 라인)역에서 내려 메릴랜드 애버뉴/스미소니언 박물관 방향 출구
- **버스**
  30, 32, 34번 서던 애버뉴에서 하차
- **주차**
  ④ 주차는 불가하나 근처에 몇 군데의 주차장이 있습니다.

보안

⑤ 스미소니언 박물관의 최신 보안 절차를 스미소니언 웹사이트에서 확인하세요.

어휘 permanent 영구적인 temporary 일시적인, 임시의 exhibition 전시품; 전시회 explore 탐험[탐구]하다 diversity 다양성 admission 입장(료) locate 위치하다; 찾아내다 security 보안 procedure 절차

29 밑줄 어법 ④

소재 사피어-워프의 가설

해설 ④ 「find+O+C」 구문으로 목적어는 to부정사구(to agree ~ independently)이고 목적격보어는 hard이다. 그런데 SVOC 구조의 목적어 자리에는 to부정사구를 쓰지 못한다는 원칙에 따라 가목적어 it을 두고 진목적어인 to부정사구는 목적격보어 뒤로 보내므로 them을 가목적어 it으로 고쳐야 한다.

오답 분석 ① Questions가 문장의 주어이므로 복수동사인 have가 바르게 쓰였다. ② 동사인 think와 behave를 수식하므로 부사인 differently가 적절히 쓰였다. ③ 「name A after B」는 'B의 이름을 따서 A라고 부르다'란 뜻이다. 여기서는 A가 문장 주어로 쓰였는데 A에 해당하는 The hypothesis와 name의 관계는 '수동'이므로 was named는 수동태로 바르게 쓰였다. ⑤ suggest의 목적어절(language ~ thought)을 이끄는 접속사 that이 올바르게 쓰였다.

해석 언어와 우리가 사고하는 방식 간의 관계를 둘러싼 의문은 수 세기 동안 철학자와 언어학자들에게 생각할 거리가 되어왔다. 예를 들어, 다른 나라 말을 하는 사람들은 그들의 언어 때문에 다르게 생각하고 행동할까? 주제문 사피어-워프의 가설에 따르면 (이 질문에 대한) 답은 '그렇다'이다. 그 가설은 미국의 인류학자 Edward Sapir와 Benjamin Whorf의 이름을 딴 것으로, 그들은 인간의 사고는 언어에 의해 형성된다고 강력하게 주장했다. 당시의 사람들은 우리가 모두 언어에 의해 통제받고 있어 독립적으로 사고할 수 없다는 가설에 동의하기 어렵다고 생각했다. 그러나 호피 인디언 언어에 관한 Sapir와 Whorf의 연구는 언어가 적어도 부분적으로는 사고를 결정짓는다는 것을 시사한다.

구문 [1행~3행] *Questions* (surrounding language and its relationship to *the way* [we think]) have been food for thought / to philosophers and linguists / for centuries.
(S: Questions, V: have been, O: food for thought)
현재분사구(surrounding ~ think)가 Questions를 수식하여 주어가 길어졌다. we think는 관계부사 how가 이끄는 관계사절로 선행사 the way를 수식하는데, how와 the way는 함께 쓸 수 없으므로 관계부사가 생략되었다.

[12행~15행] But *Sapir and Whorf's studies* (of the Hopi Indian language) **do suggest** // that language **does** at least partially **determine** thought.
(S: Sapir and Whorf's studies, V: do suggest, S′: language, V′: does ~ determine, O′: thought)
조동사 do와 does는 본동사(suggest, determine)의 뜻을 강조하는 역할을 한다.

어휘 **relationship** 관계; 관련성 **philosopher** 철학자 **linguist** 언어학자 **anthropologist** 인류학자 **argue** 주장하다 **independently** 독립적으로 **suggest** 시사하다; 제안하다 **partially** 부분적으로 **determine** 결정하다

30 밑줄 어휘 ⑤

소재 추울수록 눈이 내리지 않는 이유

해설 전체 문맥상 온도가 낮을수록 공기 중의 수분의 양이 줄어들어 눈이나 비가 내리지 않을 뿐 아니라 수분이 부족해 건조할 수 있다는 내용이 적절하므로, 가장 추운 남극 대륙에 대한 설명인 ⑤는 '가장 습한(wettest)'이 아니라 '가장 건조한(driest)'이 되어야 한다.

해석 가장 추운 겨울날에는 절대로 눈이 내리지 않는 것 같다. 날씨가 너무 ① 추워져서 눈이 내리지 않을 수 있을까? 주제문 공기가 차가워질수록 공기가 담을 수 있는 증발된 물(=수증기)은 더 적어져서, 영하 40도 이하의 온도는 눈을 만들어내는 것을 매우 ② 어렵게 만든다. 아주 낮은 온도에서는 본질적으로 공기 중에 수분이 없다. 이것은 그것(= 수분) 대부분이 ③ 더 높은 온도에서 이미 응결되어 비나 눈의 형태로 다시 지상에 내렸기 때문이다. 온도가 올라감에 따라, 공기 중 수분의 양이 ④ 증가한다. 그것이 남극 대륙이 지구상에서 가장 추운 지역이면서도 또한 ⑤ 가장 습한(→ 가장 건조한) 대륙인 이유이다.

구문 [3행~5행] Well, **the colder** the air is, **the less** evaporated water it can hold, / and *any temperature* [lower than 40 degrees below zero] makes **it** very hard **to produce snow**.
(S: any temperature, V: makes, O: it, C: very hard)
「the 비교급 ~, the 비교급 ...」은 '~하면 할수록 더 …하다'라는 의미이다. and 이후의 주어는 any ~ zero이며, it은 가목적어로 진목적어인 to부정사구를 대신한다.

어휘 **evaporate** (액체가) 증발하다 **degree** (온도 단위인) 도; 정도; 학위 **below zero** 영하 **essentially** 본질적으로, 근본적으로 **moisture** 수분, 습기 **condensed** 응결된, 응축된 **Antarctica** 남극 대륙 **continent** 대륙

31 빈칸 추론 ②

소재 천재들의 지식 시각화 능력

해설 빈칸 이후에 제시된 예시들을 보면, 레오나르도 다 빈치는 생생한 도해를 사용했고 갈릴레오 갈릴레이는 도표를 활용했으며 아인슈타인은 그림을 그려서 자신의 생각을 표현했으므로 이러한 천재들이 가진 능력은 생각을 눈에 보이도록 ② '시각화하는' 능력임을 알 수 있다.

해석 주제문 창의적인 천재들은 그들의 생각을 시각화해주는 특별한 능력을 개발한다. 이러한 능력은 그들에게 정보를 다른 방식으로 보여줄 수 있는 융통성을 부여한다. 르네상스 시대에 있었던 창의성의 폭발은 Leonardo da Vinci(레오나르도 다 빈치)의 생생한 도해의 개발과 직접적으로 결부되어 있었다. Galileo Galilei(갈릴레오 갈릴레이)는 그의 동시대인들이 좀 더 관습적인 수단을 사용하던 동안 도표를 통해 자신의 생각을 보여주었다. 마찬가지로 Albert Einstein(알버트 아인슈타인)은 순수하게 수학적인, 혹은 언어적인 선을 따르기보다 공간적 형태의 측면에서 사고했다. 많은 경우 그는 단지 자신이 머릿속으로 문제를 보는 방식을 보여주려고 그림을 그리곤 했다. 사실 그는 말과 숫자가 글로 혹은 말로 표현될 때, 자신의 사고 과정에 중대한 역할을 하지 않는다고 믿었다.
① 논리적인 ③ 단순한 ④ 흥미로운 ⑤ 개념의

구문 [9행~11행] Similarly, Albert Einstein thought in terms of spatial forms **rather than** along purely mathematical or verbal lines.
「A rather than B」는 'B라기보다는 오히려 A'의 뜻이다. A와 B 자리에 모두 전명구가 위치해 있다.

[11행~12행] Oftentimes he **would** draw just to illustrate how he saw the problem in his head.
would는 과거 습관을 나타내는 표현으로 '~하곤 했다'의 뜻이다. 밑줄 친 부분은 illustrate의 목적어 역할을 하는 명사절이다.

어휘 **flexibility** 융통성 **explosion** 폭발 **the Renaissance** 르네상스 **intimately** 직접적으로, 친밀히 **be tied to** ~에 결부되다 **graphic** 그림[회화]의; 생생한 **illustration** 삽화, 도해 *cf.* **illustrate** 분명히 보여주다 **contemporary** 동시대인; 동시대의 **conventional** 관습적인 **means** 수단 **in terms of** ~의 측면에서 **spatial** 공간의 **verbal** 말의, 언어의 **play a role** 역할을 하다 **significant** 중요한

32 빈칸 추론 ②

소재 샤워가 해로울 수 있는 이유

해설 샤워기에서 증식하는 박테리아로 인해 샤워를 하는 것이 꼭 좋지만은 않을 수도 있다는 연구결과를 설명하는 글이다. 세 번째 문장(The researchers ~ harm you.)이 빈칸을 추론하는 단서가 된다. 박테리아가 있는 샤워기에서 맨 처음 분사되는 물이 가장 위험할 수 있다고 했으므로, 빈칸이 포함된 문장은 ② '물이 처음 나오기 시작할 때' 샤워기 아래에 서 있지 말라는 조언이 되어야 한다.

해석 주제문 믿기 어렵겠지만, 샤워를 하는 것이 당신에게 항상 좋지는 않을 수도 있다. Colorado 대학의 연구자들은 샤워기 꼭지에서 해로운 박테리아가 매우 잘 증식한다는 것을 발견했다. 연구자들은 또한 박테리아가 있는 샤워기에서는, 그것에서 처음으로 분사되는 물이 당신에게 해로울 가능성이 가장 크다고 말했다. 그 샤워기는 박테리아를 공기 중에 분사하면서 에어로졸(분무기)처럼 작동하는데, 그것은 우리가 매일 하는 샤워가 우리가 그렇다고 생각하고 싶어 하는 것처럼 깨끗하고 건강한 필수요건이 아닐 수도 있다는 의미이다. 미국 전역의 수백 가구에서 50가지의 서로 다른 종류의 샤워기가 검사되었다.

이들 중 3분의 1에서 폐 손상을 일으킬 수 있는, 매우 높은 박테리아 수치가 나왔다. 수석 연구자인 Leonie Baum은 다음과 같은 조언을 했다. "수많은 박테리아가 당신 몸속에 침투하는 것을 막으려면 물이 처음 나오기 시작할 때 샤워기 아래에 서 있지 마세요."라고.
① 샤워기가 사용하기에 너무 낡았다면
③ 물이 따뜻해지기 전에
④ 목욕을 마친 후에는
⑤ 머리를 감을 때에는

구문 [1행~2행] Believe it or not, it seems // that taking a shower (S′) might **not always** be (V′) good (C′) for you.

「it seems that ~」은 '~인 것 같다'란 의미이다. not always는 '항상 ~인 것은 아닌'이란 뜻으로 부분부정을 나타낸다.

[7행~10행] The shower acts like an aerosol, / **spraying** the bacteria into the air, // **which** means // that our daily shower (S′) may not be (V′) *the clean-and-healthy necessity* [that we like to think it is] (C′).

spraying ~ the air는 앞의 절과 동시에 일어나는 일을 나타내는 분사구문으로 '~하면서'로 해석한다. which 이하는 앞 절 전체를 보충 설명하는 계속적 용법의 관계사절이다. [ ] 부분은 the clean-and-healthy necessity를 수식하며, we like to think it(= our daily shower) is the clean-and-healthy necessity의 의미로 이해하면 된다.

어휘 **believe it or not** 믿기 어렵겠지만, 믿거나 말거나 **researcher** 연구자 **harmful** 해로운 *cf.* **harm** 해치다, 손상하다; 피해 **bacteria** 박테리아, 세균 **spray** 스프레이, 분무; 분사하다, 뿌리다 **be likely to-v** v할 가능성이 있다, v할 것 같다 **aerosol** 에어로졸, 분무기 **daily** 매일의; 하루에 **necessity** 필수요건; 필수품; 필요성 **lung** 폐, 허파 **following** 다음의, 다음에 언급되는 **avoid** 피하다 [선택지 어휘] **run** (액체가) 흐르다

33 빈칸 추론 ①

소재 협업에서 리더의 역할

해설 빈칸 바로 뒤의 문장에서 협업 시 최종 의사결정을 내릴 수 있는 책임자가 있어야 한다고 언급했고, 마지막 문장에서 회의를 주관하는 사람이 집단의 나머지 사람들이 따를 만한 결정을 내려야 한다고 했다. 이를 종합하면, 협업을 효과적으로 하는 리더를 설명하는 빈칸에는 ① '팀을 이끄는 데 있어 강력한 역할을 맡는다'가 들어가는 것이 적절하다.

해석 리더들이 직원들로 하여금 (서로) 협업하게 하려 할 때면 또 다른 문제에 직면한다. 바로 과도하게 협업을 하는 것이다. (그럴 때) 협력은 생산성을 촉진하는 것 대신 저하시키는 것이 된다. 주제문 협업을 효과적으로 하는 리더들은 팀을 이끄는 데 있어 강력한 역할을 맡는다. 팀원들에게는 창의력을 발휘할 (수 있는) 자유가 필요하지만, 최종 판단을 내리고 논쟁을 종식할 수 있는 책임자 또한 반드시 있어야 한다. 팀이 모이면, 사람들은 아이디어를 제안하고 서로에게 이의를 제기할 것이다. 그들은 최상의 아이디어가 승리할 때까지 언성을 높이고 심지어는 격렬하게 논쟁할 수도 있다. 그러나 시간 내에 분명한 합의점에 이르지 못하면 그 회의를 주관하는 사람이 집단의 나머지 사람들이 수용할 만한 결정을 내려야 한다.
② 모든 참여자의 의견에 귀를 기울인다
③ 팀원들 사이에서 업무를 공평하게 분배한다
④ 팀원들이 각자의 속도에 맞춰 일하도록 한다
⑤ 다양한 경영 기법을 사용한다

어휘 **collaborate** 협력하다 *cf.* **collaboration** 협력 **collaborative** 협력하는 **face** 직면하다 **aid** 촉진하다; 돕다; 도움 **productivity** 생산성 **effective** 효과적인, 유효한; 유능한 **in charge** ~을 맡고 있는, ~의 담당인 **propose** 제안하다; 청혼하다 **challenge** 이의를 제기하다; 도전하다 **furiously** 격렬하게; 격노하여 **obvious** 명확한 **reach** ~에 이르다; 뻗다 [선택지 어휘] **direct** 이끌다; 지도하다 **distribute** 분배하다; 유통시키다 **evenly** 고르게 **at one's own pace** 자신만의 속도로 **management** 경영, 관리

34 빈칸 추론 ③

소재 음식을 먹는 시간과 체중 증가의 관계

해설 암컷 원숭이들을 대상으로 한 검사를 통해 음식을 먹는 시간과 체중 증가는 아무 관련이 없음이 밝혀졌으므로 늦은 밤에 먹고 싶은 충동이 느껴져도 체중 증가에 대해 걱정할 필요가 없다는 내용의 글이다. 빈칸에는 걱정하지 않아도 되는 이유가 나오는 것이 적절하므로 ③ '당신의 몸은 실제로 지금이 하루 중 몇 시인지 알지 못한다'가 문맥상 적절하다.

해석 미국 오리건 보건과학대학의 과학자들이 47마리의 암컷 원숭이들에게 검사들을 시행했다. 그들의 연구는 원래 암컷의 호르몬과 체중 증가 간의 관계에 관해 더 많은 것을 알아내기 위해 계획되었다. 주제문 하지만 뜻밖에도 연구자들은 그 동물들이 먹는 시간과 체중 증가의 정도 간에 그 어떠한 연관성도 발견하지 못했다. "우리는 늦은 밤에 먹는 것이 체중 증가를 야기할 것이기 때문에 그 시간에 먹는 것을 피해야 한다고 들어왔습니다. 하지만 그것은 사실 다소 도시 괴담일지도 모릅니다."라고 Cameron 박사는 말했다. "저는 그것이 사람들이 다이어트에 관심을 갖기 시작했을 때로 거슬러 올라간다고 생각합니다. TV를 시청하는 밤에 사람들은 기름기가 많은 간식을 먹을 가능성이 더 높습니다. 그것을 피하기 위해서 그들은 언제 먹어야 할지에 제약을 두지요."라고 그가 덧붙였다. 그러므로 당신이 밤늦게 주방으로 몰래 들어가고 싶은 충동이 느껴진다면 걱정하지 마라. 당신의 몸은 실제로 지금이 하루 중 몇 시인지 알지 못한다.
① 섭식 장애를 이겨내는 간단한 방법들이 있다
② 당신은 당신을 비만이 되게 하는 호르몬을 쉽게 고칠 수 있다
④ 당신이 얼마나 체중이 증가하는지는 무엇을 먹는지에 달려 있지 않다
⑤ 체중 측정만으로는 체지방의 정도를 알아낼 수 없다

구문 [15행~16행] So if you feel *the urge* (to creep into the kitchen late at night), don't worry.
the urge는 to부정사구(to creep ~ at night)의 수식을 받는다. 「an urge to-v」는 'v하고 싶은 충동'으로 해석한다.

어휘 **carry out** 시행하다 **unexpectedly** 뜻밖에, 예상외로 **somewhat** 다소, 어느 정도 **date back to A** (시기 따위가) A까지 거슬러 올라가다 **restriction** 제약, 제한, 규제 **urge** (강한) 충동, 욕구; 강력히 권고하다 **creep into** ~에 몰래 들어가다[다가가다] [선택지 어휘] **eating disorder** 섭식 장애 **obese** 비만의, 뚱뚱한 **measurement** 측정, 측량; 치수 **determine** 알아내다, 밝히다; 결정하다 **status** 상태; 지위, 신분

35 무관한 문장 ③

소재 사람마다 다른 동기 부여 원천

해설 사람마다 다른 것에 의해 동기 부여를 받으며, 동기 부여가 없으면 부정적인 결과를 초래하므로 사람들이 하는 업무에도 이러한 점을 반영해야 한다는 흐름의 글이다. 주제의 핵심이 되는 어구가 '동기 부여'인데, ③은 근로자들의 업무 만족도를 높이는 일반적인 방법에 관한 내용이므로 글의 흐름과 무관하다.

해석 각기 다른 사람들은 각기 다른 것에 동기 부여를 받는다. 정치인들은 권력을 좇고, 은행가들은 큰 이윤을 추구한다. 다른 이들은 도덕적인 이상에 의해 동기를 부여받을지도 모른다. 주제문 중요한 건 모든 사람이 무엇인가에 의해 동기 부여를 받는다는 사실이고, 동기 부여의 결여는 지루함, 좌절, 불행, 게으름을 야기한다. 일을 하는 데 계속해서 생산적이려면, 일에서 보상받는 방식이 당신에게 동기를 부여하는 것과 밀접하게 관련되어야 한다. 사원들의 기술과 업무 습득 방식을 존중해 주는 것이 행복과 생산성을 고무하는 비결이다. 예를 들어, 당신이 안전에 의해 동기 부여를 받는다면, 고위험 직종에서 일하는 건 좋은 생각이 아니다. 마찬가지로, 여가 시간을 갖는 데서 동기 부여를 받는 사람이라면 그 사람을 오랜 시간 일하게 하는 것은 실수다. 왜냐하면 봉급을 올려도 그들의 생산성은 떨어질 것이기 때문이다.

구문 [7행~8행] ~, **how** you are compensated for your work (S) should be closely tied (V) / to **what** motivates you.
how가 이끄는 의문사절이 문장의 주어이고, what은 선행사를 포함한 관계대명사로 전치사 to의 목적어절을 이끈다.

어휘 **motivate** 동기를 부여하다 *cf.* **motivation** 동기 부여, 자극 **politician** 정치인 **chase after** 뒤쫓다; 추구하다 **profit** 이윤, 이익 **moral** 도덕적인 **ideal** 이상; 이상적인 **lack** 결여, 결핍; 부족하다 **boredom** 지루함, 따분함 **frustration** 좌절감 **idleness** 게으름 **productive** 생산적인 *cf.* **productivity** 생산성 **compensate** 보상하다 **tie** 관련시키다; 묶다 **encourage** 고무하다, 장려하다 **security** 안전; 보안 **high-risk** 위험성이 큰 **likewise** 마찬가지로, 똑같이 **slide** (가치 · 이익 등이) 떨어지다; 미끄러지다

36 글의 순서 ⑤

소재 우정에 대한 문화권별 기대의 차이

해설 문화마다 친구에 대한 기대가 달라 문제가 생길 수 있다는 주제를 제시한 주어진 글 뒤에 이를 뒷받침하는 구체적인 예시가 이어지는 구조이다. (C) 첫 문장의 설명은 주어진 글의 의미를 좀 더 이해하기 쉽게 설명하고 있으며, 그에 대한 예시로 멕시코의 문화를 제시한다. (B)에서는 이와 대조되는 북미의 문화를 설명하고, (A)에서는 (B)의 북미 문화에 대한 추가 설명과 함께 이러한 문화의 차이가 오해를 유발한다는 사실을 다시 언급하고 있다. 따라서 글의 순서로는 ⑤ '(C)-(B)-(A)'가 가장 적절하다.

해석 주제문 친구라면 무엇을 해야 하는가에 관해 서로 상충하는 생각이 있을 때 다문화(多文化) 간 어려움이 일어날 수 있다.

(C) 어떤 문화권에서는 어떤 친구라도 할 수 있는 평범한 부탁으로 여겨지는 것이 다른 곳에서는 매우 무례한 것으로 간주될 수 있다. 예를 들어, 멕시코에서는 친구에게 일자리를 부탁하거나 돈을 빌려달라고 요청하는 것이 괜찮다.

(B) 그러나 북미 대부분에서는 일반적인 사회 관습보다는 개인적 우정 자체에 많이 의존한다. 일반적으로, 당신이 오랫동안 알고 지내던 아주 친한 친구를 제외하고는, 누구에게도 어려운 부탁을 하는 게 용인되지 않는다.

(A) 그리고 아주 친한 친구의 경우라도, 그러한 부탁을 받거나 부탁을 할 때 사람들은 여전히 불편함을 느낀다. 우정에 대한 기대가 일치하지 않는 상황에서 어떻게 오해가 발생할 수 있는지를 쉽게 볼 수 있다.

구문 [14행~16행] What one culture considers ● to be *a routine favor* [that any friend can ask] may be considered terribly rude elsewhere.

관계대명사 What이 이끄는 긴 주어 내에서 동사 역할을 하는 consider가 취하는 구조는 「consider+O+C(to-v)」로 여기에서 목적어 역할을 하는 what이 문두로 나갔다. that절은 앞의 명사 a routine favor를 수식한다.

어휘 **cross-cultural** 여러 문화가 섞인 **conflicting** 상충하는, 모순되는 **be supposed to-v** v해야 한다, v하기로 되어 있다 **uncomfortable** 불편한 **favor** 부탁; 호의 *cf.* **ask a favor of** ~에게 부탁을 하다 **misunderstanding** 오해 **arise** (문제 등이) 생기다; (태양이) 솟아오르다 **match** 일치하다; 어울리다; 시합 **broad** 일반적인; 넓은 **social customs** 사회 관습 **acceptable** 용인되는, 받아들여지는 **except** ~을 제외하고 **consider** 여기다, 생각하다 **routine** 일상적인, 판에 박힌; 일상 **loan A B** A에게 B를 빌려주다

37 글의 순서 ③

소재 상처를 부인하는 본능

해설 주어진 글은 동물들이 다쳤을 때 재빨리 일어나려 한다는 내용이다. 그 뒤에 이러한 행동의 이유를 설명하는 (B)가 온 뒤 인간도 감정적인 측면에서 이러한 행동을 한다는 (C)가 이어지며, 마지막으로 이러한 동물과 인간의 행동을 한데 묶어 설명하는 (A)가 오는 것이 자연스럽다. 따라서 정답은 ③ '(B)-(C)-(A)'이다.

해석 어떤 동물이 다쳤을 때, 그것이 할 수 있다면 가장 먼저 할 일은 재빨리 일어나는 것이다.

(B) 이러한 행동이 아마 더한 통증을 야기할 것이라는 사실에도 불구하고 일어나고자 하는 본능이 그 동물을 몰아붙이는데, 왜냐하면 일어나려는 동작을 전혀 취하지 않는 또 다른 선택사항은 무방비 상태의 그 동물을 죽여서 먹어치울 포식자를 불러들이는 것이기 때문이다.

(C) 감정적인 면에서 우리도 (동물들과) 똑같이 한다. 흔히 이제 막 부상 또는 큰 충격이나 상실을 겪은 사람은 "어떻게 지내니?"라는 질문을 받을 때 "좋아"라고 대답할 것이다.

(A) 이것을 단지 부인이라고 규정하는 것은 보다 심오한 사실을 놓치는 것이다. 주제문 동물이든 사람이든 유기체들은 공격을 피하기 위해 괜찮아 '보이려고' 노력할 뿐만 아니라 괜찮은 상태에 '있으려고' 노력한다.

구문 [7행~11행] Despite the fact that this action will probably cause further pain, / *the instinct* (to get up) drives the animal // because the alternative, taking no action to get up, invites *predators* [who will kill and eat the defenseless one].

동격절 that this action ~ further pain은 the fact의 내용을 부연 설명한다. because절에서 taking no action to get up도 앞에 나온 the alternative를 부연 설명하는 동격 구문이며, the defenseless one에서 one은 animal을 지칭한다.

어휘 **injured** 다친, 부상을 입은 *cf.* **injury** 부상 **label** 라벨을 붙이다; (상)표 **denial** 부인, 부정 **organism** 유기체, 생물 **attack** 공격 **despite** ~에도 불구하고 **instinct** 본능 **drive** (특정한 방식의 행동을 하도록) 몰아붙이다[만들다]; 운전하다 **alternative** 대안, 선택 가능한 것 **predator** 포식자 **defenseless** 무방비의; 방어할 수 없는 **suffer** (상실 등을) 겪다; 고통 받다

38 문장 넣기 ④

소재 사람의 세 가지 얼굴

해설 사람에게 세 가지 종류의 얼굴이 있다고 한 뒤, 이를 하나씩 설명하고 있다. 주어진 문장의 It은 나이가 들면 바뀌고 화장이나 성형수술로도 바뀔 수 있다고 했으므로 우리의 원래 얼굴("foundation" face)을 말한다. 따라서 주어진 문장은 ④에 들어가는 것이 적절하다.

해석 많은 문화권에는 한 사람의 얼굴은 그 사람의 영혼이 비친 모습이라는 믿음을 표현하는 고유의 속담이 있다. 이러한 속담의 인기야말로 인간이 얼굴에 매료되었음을 말해준다. 주제문 특히 흥미로운 한 가지는 우리가 실제로는 '세 가지' 얼굴에 대해 이야기하고 있다는 것이다. 첫 번째 얼굴은 우리가 '근본' 얼굴이라고 부를 수 있는 것, 즉 우리가 타고난 얼굴이다. 이 얼굴은 우리가 나이 들면서 변하고 화장이나 성형수술로 달라질 수 있지만, 이것은 우리가 어떻게 생겼는지에 대한 본질이다. 또 다른 얼굴은 우리가 마음대로 바꿀 수 있는 얼굴인데, 예를 들면 우리가 미소를 짓거나, 인상을 찌푸리거나, 놀란 표정 등을 짓기로 마음먹는 때의 얼굴이다. 마지막으로, 우리가 처할지도 모르는 상황이나 우리가 받아들이고 있는 메시지에 따라 변화하는 것(=얼굴)이 있다.

구문 [4행~5행] Many cultures have *original proverbs* (expressing the belief that one's face is a reflection of one's soul).

original proverbs는 expressing이 이끄는 현재분사구의 수식을 받는다. the belief와 that절은 동격이다.

[13행~15행] Finally, / there's *the one* [that changes / according to *the situations* [(which) we may be in], or *the messages* [(which) we're receiving]].

that은 선행사 the one을 수식하는 관계사절을 이끄는 주격 관계대명사이다. the situations와 the messages는 각각 목적격 관계대명사가 생략된 관계사절의 수식을 받는다.

어휘 **age** 나이를 먹다; 나이 **alter** 바꾸다, 변경하다 **cosmetic surgery** 미용 성형수술(=**plastic surgery**) **essence** 본질, 정수 **original** 고유의; 독창적인 **proverb** 속담, 격언 **belief** 믿음, 생각 **reflection** (거울 등에 비친) 상[모습] **popularity** 인기 **fascination** 매료, 매혹 *cf.* **fascinating** 대단히 흥미로운, 매력적인 **foundation** 근본, 기반 **be born with** ~을 타고나다 **at will** 마음대로, 의지대로 **frown** 얼굴을 찌푸리다 **according to** ~에 따라

39 문장 넣기 ③

소재 Randall Arauz가 종식시킨 코스타리카의 상어 지느러미 사냥

해설 주어진 문장은 shark finning(상어 지느러미 사냥)에 대한 구체적인 설명으로, 상어 사냥에 대해 처음 언급한 내용(He found that Chinese fishing boats ~)과 상어 지느러미만 잘라내고 상어는 바다에 버리는 이유를 설명하는 내용(It's cheaper to throw ~) 사이에 오는 것이 적절하다. 따라서 정답은 ③이다.

해석 주제문 코스타리카의 생물학자인 Randall Arauz는 '생태계 보존 활동의 노벨상'이라 불리는 골드만상을 수상했는데, (그가) 무자비하며 환경에 막대한 피해를 주는 한 산업에 국제적 이목을 집중시켰기 때문이다. 그는 거북이의 죽음과 관련된 어획 관행을 조사하던 중 훨씬 더 중대한 문제를 발견했다. 그가 중국 어선들이 코스타리카 영해에서 상어 사냥을 하고 있다는 사실을 알게 된 것이다. 좀 더 구체적으로 말하면, 중국 어선들은 '상어 지느러미 사냥'을 하고 있었는데, 그것은 상어의 지느러미 부분을 잘라낸 다음 상어를 다시 바다에 내버려 비참하게 죽게 만드는 것이었다. 이렇게 상어를 바다에 다시 버리는 것이 비용이 더 저렴한데, 상어 지느러미만으로 상당한 값어치가 있기 때문이다. 실제로 상어 지느러미는 중국에서 킬로그램당 100달러에 팔리는데, 중국은 상어 지느러미 수프에 대한 욕구가 매우 큰 곳이다. Arauz는 코스타리카에서의 상어 지느러미 사냥을 간신히 종결시켰고, 코스타리카는 이제 상어 보호에 있어서 세계적인 선두 주자가 되었다.

어휘 **specifically** 구체적으로 말하면; 명확히 **ecological** 생태계의, 생태학의 **activism** 활동주의 **cruel** 무자비한, 잔혹한 **environmentally** 환경적으로 **disastrous** 피해를 주는, 처참한 **industry** 산업 **investigate** 조사하다 **practice** 관행, 관례; 실천 **associate A with B** A를 B와 연관 짓다 **worth a fortune** 값어치가 매우 큰 **sell for** ~의 가격으로 팔다 **appetite for** ~에 대한 욕구[식욕] **manage to-v** 간신히[용케] v해내다, 어떻게든 v하다

40 요약문 완성 ①

소재 확률보다 친숙한 것에 더 높은 가능성을 기대하는 경향

해설 사람들은 예컨대 1, 2, 3, 4, 5, 6이 적혀 있는 복권보다 5, 18, 19, 31, 35, 45가 적힌 복권이 당첨 '가능성(probability)'이 더 높다고 판단하는데, 후자가 그들에게 친숙한 복권의 모습과 더 '닮았기(resemble)' 때문이라는 내용이므로 정답은 ①이다.

해석 여러분이 밖에서 한 친구와 함께 걸어가다가 두 장의 복권을 발견한다고 생각해 보자. 여러분은 각각 한 장씩 복권을 갖기로 결정한다. 여러분의 친구는 두 장의 복권 중 어느 것을 갖기를 원하는지 여러분이 결정할 수 있다고 친절하게 말한다. 한 장의 복권에는 1, 2, 3, 4, 5, 6이라는 숫자들이 쓰여 있다. 다른 한 장의 복권에는 5, 18, 19, 31, 35, 45라는 숫자들이 쓰여 있다. 여러분은 어느 복권을 갖기로 선택하겠는가? 통계적으로는 두 복권 모두 동일한 당첨 확률을 갖고 있다. 그것들은 둘 다 동일한 당첨 가능성을 가지고 있으므로 어느 복권을 선택하느냐는 중요하지 않다. 그러나 많은 사람들이 첫 번째 복권보다는 두 번째 복권을 선택할 것이다. 이것은 왜일까? 주제문 우리가 두 번째 복권을 당첨되는 복권의 더 전형적인 모습으로 본다는 것이다. 즉, 여러분은 그것들이 둘 다 동일한 가능성을 가지고 있다는 사실을 무시하고, 그 대신 여러분이 생각하기에 당첨되는 복권과 그것이 얼마나 유사한지에 근거하여 결정을 내린다.

⬇

> 사람들은 한 사건이 이미 낯익은 것과 얼마나 많이 (B) 닮아 있는가에 근거하여 그것의 (A) 가능성을 판단하는 경향이 있다.

구문 [8행~10행] So it doesn't matter which ticket you choose // because **they** both have the same chance of winning.
it은 가주어이고 which ~ choose 부분이 진주어이며, because절에서 they는 the (two) tickets를 가리킨다.

[14행~16행] That is, you ignore the fact that they both have an equal chance / and instead make the decision / based **on** how similar (you think) it is to a winning ticket.
문장의 동사는 ignore와 make가 병렬구조를 이루고 있다. how ~ ticket은 전치사 on의 목적어로, 「의문사(how similar)+주어(it)+동사(is)」 어순의 간접의문문이다. you think는 삽입절이며, to는 similar에 이어진다. (similar to: ~와 유사한)

어휘 **lottery ticket** 복권 **statistically** 통계상으로 **probability** 확률, 가망, 개연성 **matter** 중요하다 **chance** 가능성, 기회 **representative** 전형적인, 대표하는; 대표자, 대리인 **tendency** 경향, 추세 **on the basis of** ~에 근거하여
[선택지 어휘] **influence** 영향을 미치다; 영향 **frequency** 빈도 **benefit** 유익하다; 이익, 혜택

41~42 장문 41 ② 42 ③

소재 인간의 가축 사용이 감소한 이유

해설 41. 가축은 인류 역사 초기부터 유용하게 사용되었으나, 인구가 증가하고 동물에 비해 값싼 인간의 노동력이 풍부하게 유입되면서 가축이 상대적으로 사치재가 되어 수가 점차 줄게 되었다는 내용의 글이다. 즉, 인간의 가축 이용이 줄어든 이유를 설명하는 글이므로, 제목으로 가장 적절한 것은 ② '왜 인간은 많은 경우 동물 사용을 포기하는가?'이다.
① 인간의 노동은 동물로 인해 증가되어왔다
③ 동물의 가축화는 어디에서 시작되었는가?
④ 가축이 초기 농경을 변모시킨 방식
⑤ 가축과 인간의 관계

42. 가축이 사라지고 인간의 노동력으로 대체된 이유는 인간의 노동이 '더' 비쌌기 때문이 아니라 '덜' 비쌌기 때문일 것이므로 (c)의 more를 less로 바꿔 써야 한다.

해석 가축은 인류가 이용할 수 있었던 가장 초기의 가장 효과적인 '기계'이다. 그들은 인간의 등과 팔에서 부담을 가져간다. 식량원(고기와 우유의 단백질)으로서나 물건을 나르고 물을 길어 올리고 곡식을 가는 수단으로서나 동물은 인간의 생활수준을 상당히 (a) 끌어올릴 수 있다. 주제문 그들이 너무나 명백히도 대단히 도움이 되므로, 우리는 수백 년 동안 인간이 기르는 동물의 숫자와 품질을 높이려 한 것을 발견하게 되리라고 기대할지도 모른다. 놀랍게도 이것은 대개 사실이 아니었다. 일본에서 가축은 대략 1600년까지의 기간에 꽤 (b) 널리 사용되었다. 다수의 말과 황소가 있었다. 그 후에 인구가 증가함에 따라, 동물은 서서히 인간의 노동력으로 대체되었다. 19세기 후반 무렵에 일본 중부의 쌀 집중 재배 지역에는 대형 가축이 사실상 없었다. 모든 땅은 작물을 재배하기 위해 사용되고 있었으므로, 동물들이 길러질 곳은 없었다. 어떤 경우든 인간의 노동이 (c) 더(→ 덜) 비쌌다. 이런 일이 발생한 것은 아시아만은 아니었다. 서유럽의 많은 지역에서 (d) 동일한 패턴을 볼 수 있다. 예를 들어, 프랑스에서는 황소, 말, 양, 염소에 관해 1인당 이용 가능한 동물 에너지가 18세기보다 13세기에 더 높았다. 사람들은 더 이상 그것들을 기를 '여유'가 없었다. 동물이 인간에 의해 대체되는 것은 자연 법칙인 것 같다. 동물들은 여러 방면에서 (e) 사치품이다. 오직 상대적으로 부유한 사람들만이 그것들을 가질 여유가 있다. 빈곤이 그들을 점차 몰아낸다. 아들이 당나귀나 황소를 대체하거나, 물건을 등에 지고 나르거나, 혹은 동물을 데리고 쟁기질하기보다는 삽을 쓸 것이다.

구문 [18행~20행] All the land **was being used** to grow crops, // so there was *nowhere* for the animals (**to be kept**).
「be being p.p.」는 '~되고 있다, ~되는 중이다'의 뜻이다. for the animals는 to be kept의 의미상 주어이다. '동물들이 길러지는 것'이므로 수동의 to부정사(to be p.p.)가 사용되었다.

어휘 **domesticate** 길들이다, 사육하다 *cf.* **domesticated animal** 가축(= **domestic animal**) **strain** 부담, 중압감 **considerably** 상당히 **protein** 단백질 **grind** 갈다 **grain** 곡물 **obviously** 명확히 **up to** ~까지 **ox** (복수형 **oxen**) 황소 **gradually** 점차 **practically** 사실상 **intensive** 집중적인 **in terms of** ~의 측면에서 **cannot afford to-v** v할 여유가 없다 **replace** 교체하다 **luxury** 사치(품) **relatively** 상대적으로, 비교적 **well off** 부유한 **poverty** 가난, 빈곤 **drive A out** A를 몰아내다 **shovel** 삽
[선택지 어휘] **transform** 변형시키다; (특히 더 좋게) 완전히 바꾸어 놓다

43~45 장문 43 ④ 44 ③ 45 ③

소재 지혜를 얻고자 철학자 Pi에게 찾아간 소년

해설 43. (A)는 한 소년이 지혜를 얻는 방법을 알기 위해 유명한 철학자를 찾아갔다는 내용으로 마지막에 노인이 답을 알고 싶으면 자신과 함께 가자고 했으므로, 뒤에는 소년

이 노인을 따라 바닷가로 갔다는 내용의 (D)가 이어져야 자연스럽다. (D)에서 노인이 소년을 물속으로 힘껏 눌렀다는 내용이 나오므로 발버둥을 치며 숨 막혀 하는 소년의 모습이 나오는 (B)가 이어지고, (B)에서 노인이 한 질문에 대한 소년의 대답이 이어지는 (C)가 마지막에 오는 것이 적절하다.

44. (c)는 소년을 가리키고 나머지는 모두 철학자 Pi를 가리킨다.

45. (C)에서 소년은 마침내 지혜를 얻은 것이 아니라 지혜를 얻기 위해 어떻게 해야 하는지를 알게 된 것이다.

해석 (A) 옛날 옛적에 한 어린 소년이 있었는데 그 아이의 유일한 꿈은 자신의 영웅인 Pi처럼 되는 것이었다. Pi는 (a) 그(= Pi)의 위대한 지혜와 친절함으로 전국에 걸쳐 명성이 높은 철학자였다. 소년은 그의 조언을 구하기 위해 그 위대한 노인을 찾아가기로 했다. 그들이 만났을 때, 소년은 어떻게 하면 그도 위대한 지혜의 재능을 얻을 수 있을지 Pi에게 물었다. 그 철학자는 이렇게 대답했다. "지금은 네게 정답을 알려주지 않을 것이다. 그러나 나와 함께 간다면 그걸 알게 될 거다."
(D) ④ 노인은 소년의 손을 잡고 바닷가까지 걸었다. 그곳에서 ⑤ Pi는 옷을 다 입은 채로 파도를 향해 곧장 걸어가더니 그 학생에게도 따라오라고 불렀다. (d) 그(= Pi)는 종종 자신을 따르는 사람들에게 어떤 주장을 증명해 보이려고 할 때 이 같은 뜻밖의 일을 했다. 소년은 고분고분하게 바닷속으로 걸어 들어가 물이 턱까지 차오를 정도의 깊이에 서 있는 Pi와 만났다. 말 한마디 없이 Pi는 자신의 손을 그 소년의 어깨 위에 굳게 올려놓더니 상냥한 미소를 지으며 (e) 그(= Pi)는 온 힘을 다해 (소년을) 내리눌렀다.
(B) ① 한 사람이 다른 사람의 머리를 물 아래로 내리눌렀으니 당연히 엄청난 발버둥이 있었다. 그러나 그 소년은 죽음이 닥치기 전에 풀려났다. 숨을 거칠게 몰아쉬며, ② 소년은 곧장 복수하기로 마음먹었다. 소년은 노인을 찾아 주변을 둘러보았고, 자신이 본 것을 믿을 수 없었다. Pi는 이미 해변에 돌아가서 가만히 지켜보고 있었던 것이다. 소년은 해변에 있는 (b) 그(= Pi) 옆으로 비틀거리며 걸어가서 눈물을 글썽이며 소리쳤다. "당신은 저를 죽이려고 했어요! 왜죠?" 노인의 대답은 또 다른 질문이었다. "물속에서 네가 곧 죽을 거라고 생각했을 때, 네가 세상의 그 무엇보다 더 갈구한 것은 무엇이었느냐?"
(C) 소년은 그 질문이 또 다른 속임수일지 모른다고 생각해서 잠시 머뭇거린 후 곧 진실을 인정했다. (c) 그(= 소년)는 조용히 말했다. "숨을 쉬고 싶었어요." Pi는 그제야 어린 학생에게 아름다운 미소를 지으며 위로하는 목소리로 말했다. "얘야, 알겠니? ③ 네가 숨쉬기를 원했던 것만큼 지혜의 재능을 간절히 원할 때 너의 재능을 갖게 될 거란다."

어휘 (A) **philosopher** 철학자 **renowned** 명성 있는, 유명한 **throughout** ~의 도처에; ~동안 죽 **counsel** 조언, 충고; 조언하다 **acquire** 얻다, 획득하다 (B) **release** 풀어주다, 놓아주다 **determine to-v** v하기로 결심하다 **revenge** 복수 **stumble** 비틀거리며 걷다; 발을 헛디디다 **tearfully** 울먹이며, 눈물을 흘리며 **desire** 갈구하다, 원하다 (C) **trick** 속임수 **hesitate** 망설이다 **admit** 인정하다 **comforting** 위로가 되는 (D) **take A by the hand** A의 손을 잡다 **obediently** 고분고분하게 **with all one's might** 힘껏, 온힘을 다해

실전 모의고사 08

본문 p.111

18 ⑤	19 ④	20 ①	21 ⑤	22 ④	23 ⑤	24 ⑤	25 ④	26 ③	27 ①
28 ②	29 ④	30 ⑤	31 ①	32 ③	33 ③	34 ④	35 ③	36 ⑤	37 ②
38 ⑤	39 ④	40 ④	41 ②	42 ①	43 ③	44 ④	45 ⑤		

18 글의 목적 ⑤

소재 드론의 성능 문의

해설 글을 전체적으로 보고 글쓴이의 진짜 의도를 파악해야 한다. 첫 문장에서 드론에 관한 문의임을 밝혀주면서 시작한다. However(그러나)부터 드론의 성능에 관해 질문하며, 마지막 문장에서 앞서 문의한 정보를 제공해 준다면 감사하겠다는 것으로 보아, 글의 목적으로 가장 적절한 것은 ⑤이다.

해석 고객 지원팀에게:
전 귀사의 웹사이트에 있는 Raven X7 드론에 관하여 글을 씁니다. 광고에 따르면, Raven X7은 3킬로그램까지 운반하면서 날 수 있습니다. 주제문 하지만 다른 드론을 사용한 제 경험이 이것에 의문을 갖게 합니다. 전 Raven X7에 무게가 1킬로그램을 조금 넘는 몇 개의 간단한 카메라 장비를 갖추게 해야 할 것입니다. 이것이 드론의 비행 거리에 영향을 미칠까요? 또한, 온라인에서 드론의 최대 비행 높이를 찾을 수가 없습니다. 땅에서 적어도 50미터 위로 비행할 수 있으면 좋겠습니다. 주제문 당신이 이 정보를 제게 제공해 주실 수 있다면 정말 감사하겠습니다.
Mark Spencer

구문 [7행~9행] I will need to equip the Raven X7 with *some simple camera equipment* (weighing just over a kilogram).
( )는 형용사구로 앞의 명사 some simple camera equipment를 수식한다.

어휘 **support** 지원, 지지; 지원[지지]하다 **in regard to** ~에 관련하여[대하여] **drone** 드론, 무인항공기 **advertisement** 광고 *cf.* **advertise** 광고하다, 선전하다 **up to** (특정한 수 · 정도) 까지 **equip A with B** A에게 B를 갖추게 하다 *cf.* **equipment** 장비, 용품 **weigh** 무게가 ~이다 **affect** 영향을 미치다 **range** 거리, 범위 **maximum** 최대[최고]의 **height** 높이; 키 **at least** 적어도, 최소한 **appreciate** 감사하다; 이해하다; 진가를 알아보다; 감상하다

19 심경 추론 ④

소재 억지로 다녔던 중국어 학교

해설 방과 후에 친구들과 함께 놀지 못하고 어머니의 손에 이끌려 인상이 무서운 교장 선생님이 있는 중국어 학교에 다녀야 했던 어린 화자의 모습이 그려져 있다. 이 상황에서 'I'의 심경을 가장 잘 나타내는 것은 ④ '좌절하고 무서워하는'이다.

해석 매일 오후 5시가 되면 우리 또래의 4, 5학년 친구들과 함께 놀거나 집에서 살짝 빠져나가 공터로 가서 귀신놀이를 하거나 동물 뼈를 찾아다니는 대신에 나와 동생은 중국어 학교에 다녀야 했다. 주제문 아무리 발버둥치고 소리치며 애원해 보아도 어머니를 달리 설득할 수 없었으며, 어머니는 우리의 유산인 언어를 반드시 익히도록 하겠다고 굳게 마음먹고 계셨다. 결심을 하시고는 우리들을 집에서 학교까지의 일곱 블록이나 되는 길고도 험한 길을 끌고 간 뒤에 얼굴이 비참하게 눈물범벅이 된 우리들을 그 근엄한 교장 선생님 앞에 떨구어 놓으셨다. 그 교장선생님에 대한 내 유일한 기억은 선생님이 손을 등 뒤에 감춘 채로 끊임없이 앞뒤로 몸을 흔들었다는 것이다. 나에게 선생님은 무서운 괴물이었고, 언젠가 우리가 그의 손을 보게 된다면 우리는 커다란 곤경에 빠지게 될 거라는 것을 나는 알고 있었다.

① 질투 나고 화난 ② 지루하고 무관심한
③ 만족하고 결심한 ⑤ 동정적이고 슬퍼하는

구문 [1행~4행] Every day at 5 p.m., / instead of **playing** with our fourth- and fifth-grade friends [or] **sneaking** out to the empty lot / to hunt ghosts and animal bones, / my brother and I had to go to Chinese school.
(M1: Every day at 5 p.m., M2: instead of ~ bones, S: my brother and I, V: had to go)
시간의 부사구와 「instead of+동명사구(~ 대신에)」의 부사구가 먼저 나오고 나서 주어인 my brother and I가 이어지는 문장 형태이다. 자연스럽게 앞에서부터 해석해 나가는 것이 좋다.

어휘 **sneak out** 살짝 나가다 **lot** 부지, 지역 **plead** 애원하다 **convince** 설득시키다 **heritage** (국가 · 사회의) 유산 **hilly** 험한, 언덕이 많은 **miserable** 비참한 **tearful** 울먹이는 **stern** 근엄한, 엄중한 **principal** 교장; 주요한 **constantly** 끊임없이, 계속 **rock** (전후좌우로 부드럽게) 흔들다 **back and forth** 앞뒤로 **horrifying** 무서운, 끔찍한 **be in trouble** 곤경에 빠지다

20 필자 주장 ①

소재 자존감

해설 글의 앞부분에서 다른 사람들에게 인정받기 위해 경쟁하는 것은 실망과 좌절을 가져올 수 있다고 지적하고 있다. 뒷부분에서는 자기 자신에 대한 믿음을 갖게 되면 다른 사람들의 지나친 기대를 견뎌내기 쉽고 인생에서의 여러 긍정적인 결과를 얻게 된다고 말하고 있다. 즉, 필자는 자신에 대한 존중심을 가져야 한다고 주장하고 있으므로 정답은 ①이다.

해석 당신의 성공이나 실패를 다른 사람의 의견에 좌우되게 하는 것은 잘못이다. 부모님, 선생님, 친구, 동료나 그 외의 다른 사람에게 깊은 인상을 주려고 경쟁하는 것은 궁극적으로는 만족을 주지 못할 것이다. 당신은 그들의 모든 희망과 이상에 따를 수 없으며, 당신의 성과가 그들의 인정을 받지 못한 것을 알게 되면, 아마 실망하고 좌절할 것이다. 만약 당신이 어느 누구의 의견에도 기대지 않는, 당신이 할 수 있는 것에 대한 강한 믿음을 가지고 (어떤 일을) 시작한다면, 어느 것으로도 만족하지 않는 사람들을 견뎌내기가 훨씬 더 쉬울 것이다. 게다가, 확고한 자부심을 갖는 것은 실제로 인생에서 좋은 건강, 높은 의욕과 위대한 업적에 대한 당신의 역할을 키워준다.

구문 [2행~4행] **Competing** to impress your parents, teachers, peers, co-workers, or anybody else / will be ultimately unrewarding.
문장의 주어는 Competing ~ anybody else 전체이다. 동명사구 주어이므로 '~하는 것'으로 해석한다. to impress ~ else는 to부정사의 부사적 용법 중 '목적'을 나타내며 '~하기 위해'로 해석한다.

[7행~10행] If you start with *a strong belief* in what you can do [**that** depends on no one else's mind], // you will have a much easier time tolerating *those* [for **whom** nothing is enough].
that 이하의 주격 관계대명사절이 a strong belief를 수식한다. 「have a(n) easy[hard] time+v-ing」는 'v하기 쉽다[어렵다]'란 뜻이고, tolerating은 관계대명사절의 수식을 받는 those 이하를 목적어로 취한다.

어휘 **compete** 경쟁하다, 겨루다 **peer** (나이, 지위, 능력 등이) 동등한 사람, 또래 **unrewarding** 만족을 주지 못하는, 보람이 없는 **conform to A** A에 따르다; (규칙, 관습 등에) 맞게 하다 **ideal** 이상, 이상적인 목표 **frustrated** 좌절감을 느끼는 **accomplishment** 성과, 성취 **win** 얻다, 획득하다; 이기다 **approval**

인정; 찬성 **tolerate** 참다, 견디다; 너그럽게 봐주다 **firm** 확고한; 굳은 **self-esteem** 자부심, 자존심 **share** (개인의) 몫; 역할, 공헌

21 글의 요지 ⑤

소재 지역 농산물 구매 장려

해설 지역 농산물 구매를 장려하는 글이다. 글 중반부의 주제문(For those who ~ the local economy.)을 통해 자신이 사는 지역에서 재배된 식품을 구매하는 것이 음식에 대한 통제권을 높이고 지역 경제에 도움이 된다고 했으므로, 글의 요지로 가장 적절한 것은 ⑤이다.

해석 점점 더 많은 사람이 자신이 먹는 음식에 대해 걱정하고 있다. 누가 그것을 재배했는지, 그것에 어떤 농약이 사용되었는지, 또는 농장에서 상점까지 어떤 경로로 그것이 운송되었는지를 알기란 종종 불가능하다. 주제문 자신의 입에 넣는 것(먹을거리)에 대해 더 많은 통제권을 원하는 사람이라면 지역에서 재배한 식품이 좋은 대안이 된다. 그리고 지역에서 구매하는 것은 그 지역 경제에도 더 좋다. 평균적으로 농부는 지불된 각 식품(가격의) 1달러 중 단 20센트만 받고 나머지 금액은 운송, 가공, 포장, 냉동, 그리고 마케팅으로 가버린다. 소비자에게 직접 식품을 판매하는 농부는 자기 농산물의 모든 소매가격을 받는다. 즉, 지불된 각 식품(가격의) 1달러 당 100센트(= 1달러)를 받는 것이다.

구문 [2행~4행] **It** is often impossible / **to find out** who grew it, (O'1) / what pesticides were used on it, (O'2) / or which route it travelled from farm to store. (O'3)

It은 가주어이며 뒤에 나오는 to부정사구(to find out ~ to store) 전체가 진주어이다. 세 개의 명사절이 find out의 목적어로 쓰였다.

[7행~10행] Farmers on average receive only 20 cents of each food dollar spent, / **with** *the rest* **going** to transportation, processing, packaging, refrigeration, and marketing.

「with+(대)명사+분사」는 동시상황을 나타낸다. (대)명사와 분사의 관계가 능동이면 현재분사가, 수동이면 과거분사가 쓰인다. 남은 금액(the rest)이 운송, 가공 등을 하는 데 '나가는' 것이므로 현재분사(going)가 쓰였다.

어휘 **concerned about** ~에 대해 걱정하는 **find out** 알아내다 **pesticide** 농약, 살충제 **route** 경로, 길 **locally** 지역에서; 지역적으로 *cf.* **local** 지역의, 현지의 **make sense** 일리가 있다; 이치에 맞다 **on average** 평균적으로 **receive** 받다 **transportation** 운송, 수송 **processing** 가공 **packaging** 포장 **refrigeration** 냉장, 냉동 **directly** 직접 **retail** 소매(의) **value** 가격; 가치 **produce** 농산물; 생산물; 생산하다

22 글의 주제 ④

소재 가격이 음식 만족도에 미치는 영향

해설 연구 및 실험에 관한 글은 실험 결과의 시사점이 주제가 될 수 있는데, 더 높은 가격을 지불한 사람들이 음식 맛을 높게 평가했다는 내용의 문장(The diners ~ 11% tastier.)이 이에 해당된다. 따라서 이 글의 주제로는 ④ '가격이 음식 만족도 평가에 미치는 영향'이 가장 적절하다.

해석 David Just 박사와 Ozge Sigirci, 그리고 〈Slim by Design: Mindless Eating Solutions for Everyday Life〉의 저자인 Brian Wansink 박사로 이루어진 연구자들에 의해 행해진 연구에서, 한 이탈리아의 무제한 뷔페식당에서 식사를 한 139명의 손님들에게 4달러와 8달러 중 하나를 점심 뷔페 가격으로 청구했다. 그 뷔페는 피자, 샐러드, 브레드스틱, 파스타, 그리고 스프를 제공했다. 식사를 마친 후, 손님들은 9점 만점을 기준으로 자신들이 식사를 얼마나 맛있게 먹었는가를 평가하도록 요청받았다. 주제문 그 뷔페에 더 높은 가격을 지불한 손님들이 11퍼센트 더 그 음식이 맛있다고 평가했다. 이러한 연구 결과를 근거로 연구자들은 비록 값싼 무제한 뷔페가 인기가 있긴 하지만, 사람들은 '돈을 낸 만큼 얻는다'는 심리를 고수하는 경향이 있어서 (값싼) 음식을 질적으로 더 낮게 평가할 것이기 때문에, 뷔페 주인들에게 낮은 뷔페 가격을 정하기 전에 다시 한 번 생각해 볼 것을 권장한다.

① 뷔페 음식 가격에 적용되는 과학적 원리
② 뷔페 음식 가격을 낮게 유지하는 전략
③ 음식 맛에 대한 객관적인 평가의 필요성
⑤ 가격이 낮은 음식의 질에 대한 염려

구문 [7행~9행] **After finishing their meal,** / the diners **were asked to *rate*** / how much they enjoyed the dining experience / on a 9-point scale.

After finishing their meal은 접속사를 생략하지 않은 능동 분사구문이다. were asked to rate는 「ask+O+C(to-v) (O가 v할 것을 요청하다)」의 수동형이며, 밑줄 친 how ~ experience는 의문사가 이끄는 명사절로 rate의 목적어 역할을 한다. 전명구 on a 9-point scale이 rate를 수식하고 있다.

어휘 **conduct** 수행(하다); 행동(하다); 지휘하다; 안내하다 **diner** 식사하는 사람[손님] *cf.* **dining** 식사; 정찬 **charge** (요금을) 청구[부과]하다 **rate** 평가하다; 등급을 매기다; 속도; 비율; 요금 **scale** 기준, 척도; 규모, 범위 **recommend** 권장[권고]하다; 추천하다 **tend to-v** v하는 경향이 있다 **stick to A** A를 고수하다, A에 집착하다 **mentality** 심리, 사고방식; 정신력 [선택지 어휘] **principle** 원리, 원칙 **objective** 객관적인 **assessment** 평가 (의견) **concern** 염려, 걱정; 관심

23 글의 제목 ⑤

소재 초등학교에서의 아이들 생일 축하

해설 설탕의 부정적인 영향을 깨닫고 달콤한 음식으로 하는 생일 축하에서 초점을 바꾸려고 노력한다는 글의 주제문(Recognizing ~ celebration.) 이후로 생일을 맞은 아이를 위한 학교에서의 여러 축하 아이디어들과 그것들의 긍정적 효과를 설명하고 있다. 이를 제목으로 가장 잘 표현한 것은 ⑤ '아이들을 위한 축하에서 초점 바꾸기'이다.

해석 지난 30년 동안 초등학교에서의 생일 축하는 학급 전체를 위해 컵케이크 위에 쌓인 단것을 제공하는 것을 중심으로 한 거대한 경쟁으로 부풀어 확대되었다. 주제문 설탕이 아이들에게 미치는 부정적인 영향을 깨닫고 많은 학구에서는 축하의 초점을 바꾸려고 노력해왔다. 만일 여러분의 학교가 생일 축하에 대한 그들의 관행을 아직 바꾸지 않고 있다면 다른 학교들이 채택하고 있는 몇 가지 아이디어는 다음을 포함한다. 각각의 아이가 (생일을 맞이한) 아이에 대해 특별한 점을 하나씩 쓰는 '나를 축하해 줘' 책이나 카드, 온종일 쓰는 학교의 특별한 생일 왕관, 하루 동안 보조교사나 줄 반장이나 활동 선택자가 되기 등이다. 달콤한 음식에서 초점이 벗어나는 것은 결과적으로 더 건강한 교실과 온종일 축하할 수 있는 아이들을 만든다. 교사들은 이런 아이디어가 아이들을 집중하게 하고 배울 준비가 되게 하기 때문에 종종 이를 지지한다.

① 아이들을 위한 정말 멋진 기획들
② 보상으로 사탕류를 주는 것의 문제점
③ 자녀의 마음을 감동하게 하는 건강에 좋은 선물들
④ 아이들을 위한 축하: 가치 있는 전통

구문 [8행~11행] ~, *a few ideas* [**that** other schools have adopted] (S) include (V) *a "celebrate me" book or card* [**where** each kid writes *one thing* [**that** is special about that child]]; ~.

주어는 a few ideas이고 동사는 include이다. 첫 번째 that은 목적격 관계대명사로 a few ideas를 수식하는 관계사절을 이끈다. a "celebrate me" book or card는 관계부사 where가 이끄는 절의 수식을 받으며 where는 in which로 바꾸어 쓸 수 있다. 두 번째 that은 주격 관계대명사로 one thing을 수식하는 관계사절을 이끈다.

어휘 **decade** 10년 **balloon into** ~로 부풀어 확대되다 **sugary treats** 단것(과자, 사탕 등) **stack** 쌓다; 쌓이다; 무더기, 더미 **school district** (미국의) 학구, 학군 **practice** 관행; 실천; 연습 **adopt** 채택하다; 차용하다; 입양하다 **supportive** 지지[지원]하는; 협력적인

24 도표 이해 ⑤

소재 국가와 도시의 인구 증가율 비교

해설 도시들 중에서 가장 낮은 인구 증가율을 보인 곳은 바르샤바이고, 두 번째로 낮은 곳이 모스크바이다. 따라서 정답은 ⑤이다.

해석 **〈가장 빠르게 성장하는 도시 인구 증가율 대비 국가 인구 증가율(2010~2020)〉**
주제문 위 그래프는 2010년부터 2020년까지 일곱 국가의 인구 증가율과 그 국가에서 가장 빠르게 성장하는 도시의 인구 증가율을 함께 보여준다. ① 일곱 국가 중 세 곳을 제외한 모든 곳에서 2010년에서 2020년 사이에 인구 증가를 보였다. ② 같은 기간, 스페인은 일곱 국가 중에서 가장 높은 인구 증가율을 보였으며, 일곱 도시 중에서 팔마데마요르카도 그러했다. ③ 그 기간에 팔마데마요르카, 피닉스, 화성의 인구는 각각 20퍼센트 넘게 증가했다. ④ 가와사키와 뮌헨의 증가율은 둘 다 10퍼센트 정도인데, 그 도시가 속한 국가인 일본과 독일은 인구에 거의 변화가 없었다. ⑤ 도시들 중에서 모스크바는 그 기간에 가장 낮은 증가율을 기록했고, 바르샤바는 두 번째로 낮았다.

구문 [6행~8행] Spain showed the highest rate of population growth / out of the seven countries, // as **did** Palma de Mallorca, of the seven cities.
(did: V´, Palma de Mallorca: S´)
여기서 as는 '~와 같이, ~처럼'을 뜻하는 접속사로, 이런 경우 이어지는 절에서는 도치가 일어날 수 있다. did는 앞 절의 showed the highest rate of population growth를 대신하는 대동사이다.

어휘 **national** 국가의, 전국적인 **population** 인구 **growth rate** 성장률 **alongside** ~와 함께; ~옆에, 나란히 **period** 기간 **register** 기록하다; 등록하다

25 내용 불일치 ④

소재 Albrecht Dürer의 삶

해설 끝에서 세 번째 문장(After 1512, his work was sponsored by emperor Maximilian I.)에서 1512년 이후 황제로부터 후원을 받았다고 했으므로 이와 반대되는 내용인 ④가 일치하지 않는다.

해석 ① Albrecht Dürer는 독일 르네상스 시대의 화가이자 판화 제작자였다. 그는 1471년 5월에 뉘른베르크에서 그의 부모님의 둘째 아들로 태어났다. 역사가들은 현재 생각하기를 그가 적어도 열세 명 그리고 어쩌면 열일곱 명이나 되는 형제자매가 있었다고 여긴다. ② 그의 아버지는 Dürer에게 어린 나이에 금을 다루는 것과 그림의 기초를 가르친 성공한 금세공인이었다. ③ 20대에 Dürer는 이미 자신의 고품질 목판화로 유명해지고 있었다. 일생 동안, 그는 Raphael, Giovanni Bellini, 그리고 Leonardo da Vinci를 포함하여 그 시대의 많은 위대한 예술가들과 어울렸다. ④ 1512년 이후, 그의 작품은 Maximilian 1세 황제로부터 후원을 받았다. Dürer의 작품은 조각품, 초상화와 자화상, 그리고 수채화를 포함한다. ⑤ 더욱이, 그가 고전적인 테마를 북유럽 예술에 도입한 것은 그를 북유럽 르네상스의 가장 중요한 인물 중 한 명으로 만들었다.

구문 [14행~17행] Moreover, / his introduction of classical themes into Northern European art / **has made him one of *the most important figures* (of the Northern Renaissance)**.
(has made: V, him: O, one of ~: C)
「make+목적어(him)+목적격보어(one of ~ Renaissance)」의 구조로, 목적어와 목적격보어는 동격의 의미를 나타낸다.

어휘 **printmaker** 판화 제작자 **possibly** 어쩌면, 아마 **sibling** 형제자매 **goldsmith** 금세공인 **woodcut** 목판(화) **associate with** ~와 어울리다 **era** 시대, 시기 **sponsor** 후원하다; 후원자 **emperor** 황제, 제왕 **carving** 조각품; 조각술 **portrait** 초상(화); 인물 사진; (상세한) 묘사 *cf.* **self-portrait** 자화상 **watercolor** 수채화; 그림물감 **moreover** 더욱이, 게다가 **classical** 고전적인; 고전(주의)의; 클래식의 **figure** (중요한) 인물; 모습; 숫자; 도형 **Northern Renaissance** 북유럽 르네상스

26 안내문 불일치 ③

소재 드라마 동아리 소개

해설 드라마 동아리 가입 혜택으로 뉴스레터인 〈Actors in Action〉을 받아볼 수 있다고는 했지만 직접 제작한다는 내용은 언급되지 않았으므로 ③이 안내문과 일치하지 않는다.

해석

Parker 고등학교 드라마 동아리

① 본 동아리의 목적은 여기 우리 학교의 드라마 프로그램과 배우들을 지원하고, 다양한 드라마 관련 행사들에 관한 정보를 공유하며, 연극 공연의 열정적인 지지자들이 여기 모여 공유하는 자리를 갖는 데 있습니다.

드라마 동아리에 가입하세요!

② 여러분이 이 드라마 동아리에 가입하기 위해 연기 동아리의 단원이거나 드라마 수업에 등록해야 할 필요는 없습니다.

회비: 연간 회비는 5달러입니다.
혜택:
- 회원은 공연 입장권을 할인받습니다.
- ③ 드라마 뉴스레터인 〈Actors in Action〉을 받아볼 수 있습니다.

활동과 행사:
- ④ 학기 중 매월 두 번째 화요일의 정기 미팅(오후 3시 20분에 시작합니다.)
- ⑤ 학교와 지역 사회에 유익한 봉사 활동
- 휴일 파티

구문 [2행~7행] The purpose of the club is to support the drama program and actors here at our school, to share information about various drama-related events, and to have a place for theater enthusiasts here to meet and share!
문장의 보어로 쓰인 3개의 to부정사구가 and로 연결되어 병렬구조를 이룬다.

어휘 **enthusiast** 열성적인 지지자 **enroll** 등록하다 **annual** 연간의, 매년의 **due** (보통 복수형으로) 회비 (= fee) **benefit** 혜택, 이익; ~에게 이롭다

27 안내문 일치 ①

소재 동물원 체험학습 안내

해설 두 번째 문장(Thank you ~ each student)에 학생들의 입장료를 제공해 준 것에 대해 학부모 단체에 감사하는 내용이 있으므로 ①이 안내문의 내용과 일치한다.

해석

체험학습

5월 10일 수요일에 우리 학교는 중앙 동물원으로 체험학습을 갑니다. ① 모든 학생들의 입장료를 제공해 주신 학부모 단체에 감사의 말씀을 드립니다.

아셔야 할 것들:
- ② (학생들의) 형제자매와 부모님은 언제나 환영하지만 입장료는 지불하셔야 합니다.
- ③ 여행 당일 자녀의 점심 도시락을 싸서 준비해 주셔야 합니다.
- 야외(활동)에 적당한 옷을 입혀 아이를 보내주시기 바랍니다.

저희와 함께 참여하시려면:
- ④ 버스에는 교사와 학생들에게만 충분한 자리가 있으니 따로 운전해서 오셔야 합니다.

⑤ **출발 시간:** 오전 9시 15분
귀가 시간: 오후 3시 15분

어휘 **admission** 입장(료) **sack lunch** 간단한 점심 도시락 가방 **outdoor** 야외의 **separately** 따로따로, 각기 **departure** 출발

28 밑줄 어법 ②

소재 잠을 푹 자는 것의 필요성

해설 ② 동명사구 주어(Catching up on ~ lie-ins)는 단수 취급하므로 don't를 단수형 조동사인 doesn't로 고쳐야 한다.

오답 분석 ① to부정사가 '목적'을 나타내는 부사적 용법으로 쓰였다. ③ 뒤의 명사 alertness를 꾸며주는 과거분사가 적절하게 쓰였다. alertness가 '감소되는' 것이므로 과거분사 형태가 온다. ④ '~하도록'의 의미를 나타내는 so that이 문맥상 적절하다. ⑤ '때'를 나타내는 부사절을 이끄는 접속사로 뒤에는 they are가 생략되었다.

해석 주제문 당신의 나이와 상관없이, 당신의 몸과 마음이 최상의 상태로 기능하도록 유지하기 위해서는 매일 밤 잠을 푹 잘 필요가 있다. 짧은 낮잠이나 주말 늦잠으로 밀린 잠을 보충하는 것은 별로 도움이 되지 않는데, 당신에게 필요한 것은 규칙적이고, 깊고, 평소보다 긴 잠이기 때문이다. Mayo 클리닉의 전문가들은 불충분한 수면이 기억력 문제, 둔한 반응 시간, 줄어든 각성도를 야기한다고 말한다. 전문가들은 또한, 장기간의 수면 부족은 당신의 신체적, 정신적 건강에 해를 입힌다고 말한다. 밤에 잠을 푹 자는 것은 당신이 바이러스와 박테리아로부터 더 잘 보호받도록 면역체계를 향상시킨다. 게다가 전문가들은 수면이 부족한 운전자들과 노동자들이 운전 중이나 기계를 작동할 때 잠이 들어서 심각한 사고를 일으킬 가능성이 더 크다고 말한다.

구문 [5행] ~, because **it's** *regular, deep, extended sleep* (O′) **that** you (S′) need (V′).

「it is ~ that ...」 강조구문으로 it is와 that 사이에 강조하려는 어구가 온다. 여기서는 목적어(regular, deep, extended sleep)를 강조하고 있다.

어휘 **function** 기능하다; 기능 **catch up on** ~을 만회하다 **lie-in** 늦잠 **extended** (보통 때보다) 늘어난[길어진] **insufficient** 불충분한(↔ **sufficient** 충분한) **reaction** 반응 **alertness** 각성도 **long-term** 장기간의 **boost** 향상시키다 **immune system** 면역 체계 **deprive** 빼앗다 **be prone to-v** v할 가능성이 있다, v하기 쉽다 **at the wheel** 운전 중인, 운전대에 앉은 *cf.* **wheel** (자동차의) 핸들; 바퀴 **machinery** 기계(류)

29 밑줄 어휘 ④

소재 노화에 따른 건강 문제에 대한 오해

해설 후반부(There are ~ the younger years.) 내용은 노화로 인한 신체적 변화가 있을 수 있지만 젊을 때 잘 관리하면 건강을 유지할 수 있다는 내용이다. 따라서 ④가 포함된 문장은 노화로 인한 신체 변화가 반드시 '건강하지 않은' 생활방식으로 이어지는 것은 아니라는 의미가 되어야 한다. 따라서 ④는 '건강한(healthy)'이 아닌 '건강하지 않은(unhealthy)'이 되어야 한다.

해석 사람들이 노화를 떠올릴 때는 대부분 신체 건강의 변화를 먼저 생각하는 경향이 있다. 많은 사람이 노화를 수많은 약, 질병, 혼자서 제대로 기능을 ① 할 수 없음, 죽기를 기다리는 몸과 연관 짓는다. 주제문 하지만 이는 ② 오해이며, 특히 사람들이 더 오래, 더 건강하게, 더 생산적인 삶을 살아가는 오늘날의 사회에서 그러하다. 성년기에는 다음의 세 단계가 있다. 성년 초기(20, 30대), 중년(40, 50대), 그리고 노년(60대 이상)이다. 이중 어느 단계에서든 사람들이 노화와 관련된 문제들 때문에 고통을 ③ 겪는 대상이 되는 것은 아니다. 노화와 함께 일어나는 신체적 변화는 있으나, 이것이 반드시 노년에 ④ 건강한(→ 건강하지 않은) 생활방식으로 이어지는 건 아니다. 말년에 당신의 몸이 ⑤ 잘 작동하게 하는 주요 요인은 당신이 젊은 시절에 그것을 얼마나 잘 다뤘는가에 있다.

구문 [14행~16행] *A major factor* (S) (in how well your body functions in later years) is (V) how well you treat it in the younger years (C).

factor in은 '~에서의 요인'이란 뜻이다. 전치사 in의 목적어 역할을 하는 명사절(how well ~ later years) 때문에 주어가 길어졌다. 보어 자리에도 how가 이끄는 명사절이 왔다. 의문사가 이끄는 명사절의 어순은 「의문사(how well)+주어(you)+동사(treat) ~」가 된다.

어휘 **aging** 노화 **physical** 신체의 **associate A with B** A를 B와 연관 짓다 **numerous** (수가) 많은 **medication** 약, 약물 치료 **function** (제대로) 기능하다; 기능 **on one's own** 혼자서, 단독으로 **misconception** 오해 **productive** 생산적인 **adulthood** 성년, 성인기 **be subjected to A** A의 대상이다; A를 당하다[받다] **suffer** (고통·질병 등을) 겪다 **due to** ~때문에 **take place** (사건 등이) 일어나다; (행사 등이) 개최되다 **not necessarily** 반드시 ~은 아닌 **lead to** ~로 이어지다 **major** 주요한 **factor** 요인 **treat** 다루다

30 지칭 대상 ⑤

소재 중국 호랑이의 멸종 위기

해설 나머지는 모두 호랑이(tigers)를 가리키나 ⑤는 법률(laws)을 가리킨다. 엄격하게 시행되어야 하는 것은 법률이다.

해석 불과 백 년 전 아시아의 야생에는 적어도 10만 마리의 호랑이가 있었다. 이제 ① 그들(= 호랑이)의 수가 3천 마리 이하로 줄었다고 세계야생생물기금은 밝힌다. 주제문 그 단체는 심각하게 멸종 위기에 처한 이들 동물들을 구하기 위한 조치를 즉각 취하지 않으면 ② 그들(= 호랑이)이 2030년쯤 야생에서 멸종될 것이라고 경고한다. 1950년대와 1960년대에 중국은 발전이라는 명목으로 ③ 그들(= 호랑이)에 대한 몰살 운동에 참여했다. 이후에 국제적인 압박 속에서 중국은 호랑이를 보호하는 법을 도입했지만, 법은 일관되게 시행되지 않았다. 이제 중국은 ④ 그들(= 호랑이)의 더 나은 보호와 호랑이 신체 부위에 대한 불법 거래를 막기 위한 더 많은 노력을 약속한다. 어느 동물 보호 운동가는 "중국에는 이미 적절한 보호법들이 있어요. 지금 우리에게 필요한 것은 ⑤ 그것들(= 법률)이 엄격하게 시행되는 겁니다."라며 여전히 회의적이다.

구문 [2행~3행] Now **the number of** them (S) has fallen (V) / to fewer than 3,000, ~

「the number of+복수명사+단수동사」는 '~의 수'란 뜻이다. 수 일치에 주의한다.

[4행~6행] The organization (S) warns (V) // that they will be extinct in the wild by 2030 // unless *immediate action* is taken (**to save** these extremely endangered animals) (O).

that 이하의 절이 문장의 목적어이다. unless(~하지 않는 한)가 이끄는 절의 주어 immediate action을 수식하는 to부정사구가 길어져 동사 뒤로 보내졌다.

[14행~15행] **What** we need now (S) is (V) *for them* **to be strictly enforced** (C).

What이 이끄는 명사절이 문장의 주어이며 '~하는 것'으로 해석한다. for them은 보어로 쓰인 to부정사구의 의미상 주어이다.

어휘 **at least** 적어도, 최소한 **wildlife** 야생 생물 **extinct** 멸종한; 사라진 **immediate** 즉각적인 **extremely** 심각하게, 극도로 **endangered** 멸종 위기에 처한 **in the name of** ~라는 명목으로 **progress** 발전, 진보 **engage in** (활동에) 참여하다 **campaign against** ~에 반대하는 운동[캠페인] **under pressure (from)** (~로부터의) 압박 속에서 **consistently** 일관되게 **enforce** 시행[집행]하다; 강요하다 **illegal** 불법의(↔ **legal** 합법적인) **skeptical** 회의적인, 의심 많은 **adequate** 적절한 **strictly** 엄격히

31 빈칸 추론 ①

소재 활동에 주목하는 것과 즐거움의 관계

해설 싫어하는 활동에 참여하게 된 피실험자들은 활동에서 더 많은 새로운 요소에 주목하라는 지시를 받을수록 (비록 싫어하는 활동이었지만) 활동에 대한 만족도가 높아졌다는 연구 결과를 통해 어떤 일이라도 ① '유념하여(mindfully)' 수행하면 좋아할 수 있게 된다는 것을 알 수 있다.

해석 한 연구에서 우리는 사람들에게 싫어하는 활동에 참여해달라고 요청했다. 축구 시청을 싫어하는 사람들은 축구를 보게 됐다. 클래식 혹은 랩 음악을 싫어하는 사람들은 그것을 듣게 됐다. 미술을 좋아하지 않는 사람들은 그림을 보는 데 시간을 써야 했다. 각각의 경우에 우리는 네 그룹을 만들었다. 한 그룹은 그 활동을 그냥 했고, 한 그룹은 그것에 대해 새로운 것 한 가지에 주목하라는 말을 들었고, 한 그룹은 세 가지 새로운 것에 주목하라는 말을 들었고, 마지막 그룹은 여섯 개의 새로운 것에 주목하라는 말을 들었다. 그들

이 더 많은 것에 주목하면 할수록 그 활동을 더욱 좋아했다. 주제문 이 연구는 거의 어떤 활동도 유념하여 시도되면 재밌고 즐거울 수 있음을 우리에게 보여준다.
② 반복하여 ③ 집합적으로 ④ 즉시 ⑤ 예측할 수 없게

구문 [2행~3행] *Those* [who hated watching football] **were to** watch football.
[ ]는 주어 Those를 수식한다. those who는 '~한 사람들'이라는 뜻이다. 「be to-v」는 'v할 예정이다, v해야 한다' 등의 뜻이다.

어휘 **engage in** ~에 참여하다 **notice** 주목하다, 알아차리다 **pleasurable** 즐거운 **undertake** 착수하다, 시도하다

32 빈칸 추론 ③

소재 바이오연료의 비환경친화성

해설 빈칸이 포함된 문장이 However로 시작하므로 앞 내용과 역접 관계인 내용이 들어가야 한다. 앞부분은 바이오연료가 온실가스 배출을 줄이는 데 효과적이라는 내용이므로 이와 반대되는 내용인 ③ '보기보다 기후 친화적이지 않다'가 정답이다. 빈칸 이후에 제시된 야자유를 얻기 위해 열대우림을 제거함으로써 대기 중 탄소량이 증가했다는 예시에서도 정답을 확인할 수 있다.

해석 '지속 가능한 자원 관리를 위한 국제 패널'에 의한 최근 연구는 바이오연료가 온실가스 배출을 줄이는 효과적인 수단임을 인정한다. 주제문 그러나 그 연구는 또한, 어떤 바이오연료는 보기보다 기후 친화적이지 않다는 점을 지적했다. 바이오연료를 제조하는 데 사용되는 천연원료에 따라, 바이오연료는 (온실가스) 배출을 줄일 수도 있고, 문제를 더 악화시킬 수도 있다. 예를 들어, 그 연구에서 언급하는 바에 따르면 에탄올 연료를 생산하는 데 사탕수수를 이용한 브라질 및 다른 나라들에서는 최대 100%까지 (온실가스) 배출 감소를 이뤄냈다. 그러나 인도네시아, 말레이시아 같은 동남아 국가에서는 야자유로 만든 바이오 디젤 생산으로 (온실가스) 배출이 크게 증가했다. 주된 문제점은 기름을 얻기 위한 야자수를 기르려고 열대우림이 제거되는 것인데, 이렇게 되면 대기 중 탄소량이 크게 증가한다.
① 국가마다 서로 다르다
② 화석연료보다 더 비용 효율적이다
④ 지리적 영역에 너무 의존적이다(특정 지역에서만 생산된다)
⑤ 다양한 천연원료에서 얻는다

구문 [8행~11행] For example, the study notes // that emissions reductions (of up to 100%) have been achieved / in *Brazil and other countries* [**that** use sugarcane / **to produce** ethanol fuel].
(S′: emissions reductions (of up to 100%), V′: have been achieved)
주절의 동사 notes의 목적어 역할을 하는 that절이 길어진 형태이다. 주격 관계대명사 that이 이끄는 절(that use ~ fuel)은 선행사(Brazil and other countries)를 수식하며, to produce ~는 '목적'을 나타내는 to부정사구이다.

[14행~16행] The main problem is // that rainforests are cleared / to grow the palm trees for the oil, // **which** greatly adds to carbon in the atmosphere.
(S: The main problem, V: is, C: that rainforests are cleared / to grow the palm trees for the oil)
주절의 동사 is의 보어 역할을 하는 that절이 길어진 형태이다. which가 이끄는 계속적 용법의 관계대명사절은 that절 전체 내용을 보충 설명한다.

어휘 **panel** 패널, 위원단 **sustainable** (환경을 파괴하지 않고) 지속 가능한 **management** 관리, 경영 **acknowledge** 인정하다 **biofuel** 바이오연료, 생체연료 *cf.* **fossil fuel** 화석연료 **means** 수단, 방법 **greenhouse gas** 온실가스 **emission** (가스 등의) 배출 **note** 지적하다; 주목하다; 언급하다 **manufacture** 제조하다, 생산하다 **sugarcane** 사탕수수 **ethanol** 에탄올 **production** 생산(량) **bio-diesel** (식물 기름을 이용한) 바이오 디젤 **palm oil** 야자유 **rainforest** 열대우림 **carbon** 탄소 **atmosphere** 대기; 분위기 [선택지 어휘] **cost-efficient** 비용 효율적인 **climate-friendly** 기후 친화적인 **geographical** 지리적인 **obtain** 얻다, 획득하다

33 빈칸 추론 ③

소재 승리는 포기하지 않는 것의 결과

해설 이 글은 한 미식축구 선수의 이야기를 예로 들며 경기에서 지고 있는 마지막 순간까지도 포기하지 않고 최선을 다할 때 승리를 일구어낼 수 있다는 교훈을 전하고 있다. 따라서 빈칸 문장은 승리가 ③ '모든 것(= 상황)이 지는 것처럼 보일 때에도 포기하지 않는 것'의 결과라는 내용이 되어야 한다.

해석 주제문 모든 스포츠팬이 알고 있는 것은 대다수의 사람들이 경기가 끝났다고 생각할 때조차도 (실제로) 경기는 좀처럼 끝나지 않는다는 것이다. 예를 들어, 공격수인 Adam Vinatieri는 2002년 12월에 마이애미 돌핀스와의 경기에서 뉴잉글랜드 패트리어츠 미식축구팀에 승리를 안겨주기 위해 고군분투했다. 돌핀스가 패트리어츠를 대파하고 있었고, Vinatieri가 마지막 순간에 결정적인 필드 골을 찼을 때는 많은 팬들이 다 끝났다고 생각하며 이미 경기장을 떠나고 있었다. 계속 싸우는 그의 끈질김에 대한 팬들의 믿음이 "Vinatieri가 찰 때까지 끝난 것이 아니다"라는 말을 만들어 냈다. 그리고 놀랍게도 Vinatieri는 2004년 슈퍼볼에서 다시 한 번 패트리어츠를 위해 마지막 순간에 결승골을 차 넣었다. 주제문 Vinatieri의 선례는, 승리란 대개 모든 것(= 상황)이 지는 것처럼 보이는 때에도 포기하지 않는 것의 결과라는 것을 보여준다.
① 단 하나의 실수도 하지 않는 것
② 경쟁자보다 더 열심히 훈련하는 것
④ 자신이 팀 동료들보다 낫다고 여기지 않는 것
⑤ 더 강한 상대와 계속 경쟁하는 것

구문 [1행~2행] *Something* [(that) every sports fan knows] is // that the game is rarely over, // even when the majority think it is (over).
(S: Something, V: is, C: that the game is rarely over, // even when the majority think it is (over))
주어 Something은 목적격 관계사가 생략된 절의 수식을 받으며 보어인 that절과 의미상 동격을 이룬다. 보어인 that절은 다시 주절(the game ~ over)과 부사절(even when ~ it is)로 이루어져 있으며, it is 뒤에는 over가 생략되었다.

어휘 **rarely** 좀처럼 ~하지 않는, 드물게 **majority** 대다수, 대부분 **defeat** 패배(시키다) **crucial** 결정적인, 중대한 **field goal** 필드 골(미식축구에서 필드에서 차서 골대를 넘겨 얻은 득점) **lead to** ~의 결과를 가져오다; ~을 유발하다 **incredibly** 놀랍게도, 믿을 수 없을 만큼 **Super Bowl** 슈퍼볼(미국 프로 미식축구의 우승팀 결정전) [선택지 어휘] **appear** ~인 것 같이 보이다; 나타나다 **lost** (경기에서) 진; 길을 잃은 **place A above B** A를 B보다 중시하다[우위에 두다] **continuously** 계속해서, 연달아 **opponent** 상대

34 빈칸 추론 ④

소재 영어 문장에 행위자가 있어야 하는 이유

해설 빈칸 다음에 예문으로 나온 'It is raining.'에서 알 수 있듯이 영어는 자연적으로 발생하는 일을 표현할 때 의미가 없는 주어 it을 필요로 한다고 했으므로 빈칸에는 ④ '주어 없이 자연적으로 일어나는 사건을 나타낼 수 없다'는 내용이 들어가야 적절하다.

해석 주제문 '자연적으로 일어난 사건'이라는 개념은 중국인과 다른 많은 비서양인에게 그런 것(= 친숙하거나 용인되는 것)만큼 미국인에게는 친숙하거나 용인되지 않는다. 사건은 그저 발생하거나 자연적으로 일어나지 않는다. 그것에 책임이 있는 원인이나 행위자를 필요로 한다. 미국인은 누가 책임을 지는지, 즉 누가 그 일을 행했는지 또는 누가 그 일이 행해지게 했는지를 결정하고 나서야 사건의 발생에 대한 진술에 만족해한다. '아니 땐 굴뚝에 연기 나랴'는 각각의 결과 내지는 사건이 어떤 요인에 의해 야기된다는 것을 의미한다. 영어는 미국인(과 영국인)의 이런 사고의 특징을 반영한다. 예를 들어, 영어에서는 주어 없이 자연적으로 일어나는 사건을 나타낼 수 없다. 'Is raining.'이라는 진술을 허용하는 로망스어군과는 달리, 영어 화자는 'It is raining.'이라고 말하기 위해 가주어를 만들어 내야만 한다. 이 영어 진술에서 'it'은 주어 자리를 채우는데, 이 자리는 일반적으로 동사의 행위자와 연관된다.
① 수동태 동사 다음에 목적어를 두지 않는다
② 어떤 행동이 없을 때는 주어를 필요로 하지 않는다
③ 한 문장 속에서 주어와 목적어를 도치할 수 있다
⑤ 어떤 단어의 도움 없이도 생각을 전달할 수 있다

구문 [1행~3행] The idea of a "natural happening" is not **as** *familiar or acceptable* for Americans // **as** it(= the idea) is (familiar or acceptable) for the Chinese and many other non-Westerners.
「as+형용사 원급+as~」 구문으로 as it is 다음에는 앞에 나온 형용사 familiar or acceptable이 생략된 것으로 보면 이해하기가 쉽다. 대명사 it은 앞에 나온 명사 The idea를 가리킨다.

어휘 **happening** 일, 사건 **familiar** 친숙한 **acceptable** 받아들일 수 있는 **agent** 행위자; 대리인 **hold responsible** 책임을 지다 **statement** 진술 **occurrence** (사건의) 발생; 사건 **determine** 결정하다 **factor** 요인 **reflect** 반영하다, 나타내다 **dummy subject** 《문법》 가주어 **associate** 연합하다 [선택지 어휘] **object** 《문법》 목적어; 대상; 목표 **passive** 수동의 **reverse** 바꿔 넣다, 거꾸로 하다

35 무관한 문장 ③

소재 회색큰다람쥐의 대이동

해설 이 글은 회색큰다람쥐의 이동에 관한 내용으로 그 규모와 경로, 이동 모습을 설명하고 있다. 반면 ③은 회색큰다람쥐가 영국에 온 유래를 설명하고 있으므로 전체 글의 흐름과 어울리지 않는다.

해석 주제문 사라져버린 이상한 자연현상 중 하나는 가끔 있는 회색큰다람쥐의 대이동이었다. 극심한 기근을 가져온 과도한 개체 수 증가로 인해, 수백만 마리의 다람쥐가 이러한 이동에 참여했다. 5억 마리가 1843년 위스콘신 남부 지역을 지나 이동한 것으로 추정되었다. 그리고 최초의 회색큰다람쥐는 부자들에게 재미를 주려고 영국으로 데려와졌는데, 아마 19세기 초였을 것이다. 엄청난 수가 이동하면서 그들은 가는 길마다 곡식을 먹어 치웠고, 심지어 거대한 강을 가까스로 헤엄쳐 건너기도 했다. 현재 이 다람쥐의 개체 수는 (이전보다) 훨씬 적어지긴 했지만, 계속 증가하고 있다. 이동은 여전히 일어나고 있지만, 과거에 그랬던 것처럼 눈에 띄지는 않는다.

어휘 **phenomenon** 현상 《복수형 **phenomena**》 **disappear** 사라지다 **occasional** 가끔의 **mass** 대규모의, 대량의 **emigration** (타지로의) 이주 **squirrel** 다람쥐 **excessive** 과도한, 지나친 **build-up** 증가, 증진 **population** 개체 수, 인구 **extreme** 극도의, 심한 **hunger** 기근, 굶주림 **involve** 참여시키다; 포함하다 **estimate** 추정하다; 평가하다 **migrate** 이주하다 **amuse** 즐겁게 해주다 **devour** 먹어치우다; 게걸스럽게 먹다 **crop** 농작물 **manage to-v** 가까스로 v하다 **mighty** 거대한; 강력한 **noticeable** 눈에 띄는, 주목할 만한

36 글의 순서 ⑤

소재 재봉틀 발명에 영감을 준 꿈

해설 주어진 글은 Elias Howe가 재봉틀을 발명하기 위해 수년간 궁리했다는 내용이다. 꿈속에서 야만인들이 Howe에게 재봉틀을 만들라고 강요했다는 (C)와 그것을 만들지 못해 야만인들에게 죽임을 당할 뻔했다는 (B)가 차례로 이어지는 것이 자연스럽다. (A)는 잠에서 깬 후 그가 꿈에서 얻은 아이디어를 이용하여 성공적으로 재봉틀을 만들었다는 내용이므로 마지막에 오는 것이 적절하다. 따라서 정답은 ⑤ '(C)-(B)-(A)'이다.

해석 Elias Howe는 재봉틀을 발명하기 전 좌절감을 주었던 수년간 그의 아이디어를 실현할 방법을 도무지 찾을 수가 없었다.
(C) 그러던 어느 날 밤 그는 야만인들이 그를 붙잡아 자신들에게 재봉틀을 만들어 주지 않으면 그를 죽이겠다고 말하는 꿈을 꾸었다. 그는 필사적으로 작업했지만, 그 기계를 만들 수 없었다.
(B) 그래서 야만인들은 Howe를 둘러싸고는 그들의 창을 높이 치켜들었는데, 그들이 그렇게 했을 때, Howe는 그 창끝에 이상한 눈 모양의 구멍이 있는 것을 보았다. 그때 그는 잠에서 깼다.
(A) 누워서 여전히 그 꿈으로 인해 놀란 채로, 그는 이상한 곳에 구멍이 있던 그 창을 떠올려보고는 갑자기 깨달았다. '내 기계에도 저런 바늘이 필요해!' 주제문 그렇게 Howe의 아이디어를 세계에서 가장 성공적인 발명품 중 하나로 바꿔 놓은 것은 바로 꿈이었다.

구문 [4행~6행] As he lay there, / still **frightened** by the dream, // he (S) recalled (V1) *those spears* (with the oddly placed holes) (O1) and suddenly realized (V2): ~.
동시상황을 나타내는 분사구문(still frightened by the dream)이 삽입된 구조이다. 분사구문의 의미상 주어가 문장의 주어 he와 같으므로 생략되었다.

어휘 **frustrating** 좌절감을 주는 **invent** 발명하다 *cf.* **invention** 발명(품) **sewing machine** 재봉틀 *cf.* **sew** 바느질하다 **lie (lay-lain)** 눕다; 놓여 있다 **frighten** 놀라게[겁먹게] 하다 **recall** 기억해 내다; (물건을) 회수하다 **spear** 창 **oddly** 이상하게 **turn A into B** A를 B로 바꿔 놓다 **savage** 야만인; 야만적인 **surround** 둘러싸다 **eye-shaped** 눈 모양의 **tip** (뾰족한) 끝; 조언; 팁, 봉사료 **capture** 붙잡다; (마음·관심을) 사로잡다 **murder** 죽이다 **desperately** 필사적으로; 절망적으로

37 글의 순서 ②

소재 의사소통에서 비언어적 단서의 중요성

해설 (B)의 such wordless signals는 주어진 글의 nonverbal cues를 가리키므로 (B)가 주어진 글 다음에 나와야 한다. (A)의 These messages는 (B)의 strong messages를 가리키므로 (A)가 그 다음에 나와야 하며, (C)의 these mixed signals는 (A)의 마지막에 언급된 우리의 입에서 나오는 것과 우리의 몸짓이 서로 다르다는 것을 가리키므로 (C)가 마지막에 나와야 한다. 따라서 정답은 ② '(B)-(A)-(C)'이다.

해석 훌륭한 언어적 의사소통은 모든 성공적인 관계의 기초라고 알려져 있다. 주제문 그러나 우리가 의사소통할 때 가장 크게 말하는 것은 바로 우리의 비언어적인 단서들이라는 것을 아는 것은 중요하다.
(B) 우리가 다른 사람들과 소통할 때, 우리는 계속해서 그러한 말 없는 신호를 주고받는다. 우리의 비언어적인 행동의 모든 것, 다시 말해, 우리가 만드는 몸짓, 우리가 앉는 방식, 우리가 얼마나 가까이 서있는가는 강한 메시지를 보낸다.
(A) 이러한 메시지는 여러분이 말하는 것을 멈출 때에도 멈추지 않는다. 여러분이 아무 말도 하지 않을 때도 여전히 비언어적으로 소통하고 있는 것이다. 자주 우리의 입에서 나오는 것과 우리의 몸짓을 통해 의사소통하는 것은 둘이 전적으로 다르다.
(C) 이러한 혼합된 신호에 직면했을 때, 듣는 사람은 언어적인 메시지를 믿을지 비언어적인 메시지를 믿을지를 선택해야 하는데, 비언어적인 메시지는 어떤 주어진 순간 우리의 진정한 감정과 의도를 무심코 누설하는 자연스럽고 무의식적인 언어이기 때문에 듣는 사람은 대부분의 경우에 비언어적인 메시지를 선택할 것이다.

구문 [3행~5행] **It**'s important **to recognize**, though, // that **it's** *our nonverbal cues* **that** speak the loudest, // when we communicate.
첫 번째 It은 진주어인 to부정사구(to recognize ~ communicate)를 받는 가주어이다. to recognize의 목적어로 쓰인 that절 안에는 「it is ~ that ...」 강조용법이 쓰여 our nonverbal cues를 강조하고 있다.

어휘 **verbal** 언어의(↔ **nonverbal** 비언어적인, 말을 쓰지 않는) **foundation** 기초, 토대 **recognize** 알다, 인지하다; 인정하다 **cue** 단서, 신호 **silent** 말을 안 하는, 조용한 **interact** 소통하다, 상호작용하다 **be faced with** ~에 직면하다 **whether** ~인지 어떤지 **unconscious** 무의식의 **broadcast** 무심코 누설하다; 널리 알리다; 방송하다 **intention** 의도

38 문장 넣기 ⑤

소재 명절 우울증 문제

해설 주어진 문장은 많은 사람들이 감정을 해결하기 위해 과식과 과음을 한다는 내용이므로, 먹을 음식이 많은 명절에 그렇게 하기(= 과식과 과음을 하기) 쉽다는 마지막 문장(It's easy ~ to drink.) 앞에 오는 것이 적절하다. 따라서 정답은 ⑤이다.

해석 주요 명절 기간과 관련된 문제들에는 어떤 것들이 있을까? 주제문 한 가지 흔한 문제는 이 기간에 우울증 때문에 도움을 구하는 사람들이 급증한다는 것이다. 이것은 명절

이 노인이나 미혼남녀, 그리고 가족이 없는 사람들의 외로움과 고립을 강화시킨다는 사실과 관련이 있다. 스트레스를 일으키는 것으로 알려진 일들도 이러한 명절 동안 증가한다. 사야 할 선물, 준비해야 할 음식이 있고, 가게에서 길게 줄을 서야 하며, 어딜 가든 교통이 혼잡하다. 이 모든 것에 둘러싸여서 사람들은 압박을 느낄 수밖에 없다. 많은 사람이 자신의 감정에 대처하기 위해 과식과 과음을 한다. 먹을 모든 명절 음식과 마실 모든 명절 음료가 이렇게 많은 때에 그렇게 하기 쉽다.

구문 [1행~2행] Many people(S) find(V) themselves(O) overeating and drinking(C) / to cope with their feelings.
많은 사람들이 과식과 과음을 하고 있는 자신을 발견한다는 의미로, 목적격보어 자리에는 동작이 진행 중임을 강조하기 위해 현재분사가 쓰였다. to cope 이하의 to부정사는 '목적'을 나타낸다.

[12행~13행] **Surrounded** by all this, / people can't help but feel under pressure.
(= Because[As] they are surrounded by all this)
사람들(people)이 상황에 둘러싸여 있는 것이므로 과거분사 Surrounded가 쓰였으며, 내용상 '이유'를 나타내는 분사구문이다.

[13행~15행] **It**'s *easy* (to do) // when there's *all that holiday food* (to eat) and *all those holiday drinks* (to drink).
It은 앞 문장의 overeating and drinking을 지칭한다. to do는 형용사 easy를 수식하는 부사의 역할을 하고, to eat과 to drink는 각각 앞의 명사구를 수식하는 형용사 역할을 한다.

어휘 **overeat** 과식하다 **cope with** ~에 대처하다; ~을 다루다 **associate A with B** A와 B를 관련짓다 **sharp** (변화가) 급격한; 날카로운 **seek** 구하다, 청하다; 찾다 **depression** 우울증; 불황, 불경기 **be related to** ~와 관련이 있다 **intensify** 강하게 하다 **isolation** 고립 **the elderly** 노인 **chaos** 혼돈, 혼란 **surround** 둘러싸다 **cannot help but v** v하지 않을 수 없다(= **cannot help v-ing**) **under pressure** 압박을 받는

39 문장 넣기 ④

소재 교역의 발달

해설 주어진 문장은 '이러한 교역의 증가'라는 표현으로 시작하는데, 이는 ④의 앞 문장에 제국의 출현으로 교역의 중요성이 더해졌다는 내용과 의미상 연결된다. 또한 주어진 문장에서 상인 계급의 출현을 언급했는데, ④ 다음 문장의 '이러한 새로운 경제 행위자들'이 상인 계급을 지칭하므로 주어진 문장은 ④에 들어가는 것이 가장 적절하다.

해석 주제문 인간이 존재했던 기간 동안 교역이 있었다. 처음에 교역은 간단한 문제였다. 예를 들어 한 가족 내의 사람들이 그들의 이웃들과 먹을 것을 교환했다. 시간이 흐르면서 사람들이 먼 곳에서 온 새로운 제품에 노출되고 그것에 대한 취향을 발전시켰을 때 교역은 확장됐다. 부족이 왕국이 되고 왕국이 제국이 됨에 따라, 교역은 중요성을 더했다. 이러한 교역의 증가는 영향력 있는 상인 계급의 출현으로 이어졌다. 이러한 새로운 경제 행위자들은 수익을 찾아서 역경에 용감히 맞섰고, 그들의 활동은 근대 세계 형성에 도움이 되었다. 비록 교역의 규모는 역사 전체에서 믿을 수 없을 정도로 커졌지만, 변하지 않은 것은 교역이 항상 개인 간에 일어난다는 점이다.

어휘 **emergence** 출현, 발생 **influential** 영향력 있는 **merchant** 상인 **expand** 확장하다 **be exposed to** ~에 노출되다 **tribe** 부족 **empire** 제국 **grow in importance** 중요성을 더하다 **agent** 행위자 **brave** 용감히 직면하다; 용감한 **hardship** 역경, 고난 **in search of** ~을 찾아서 **profit** 수익 **scale** 규모 **incredibly** 믿을 수 없을 정도로, 엄청나게 **throughout** ~ 전체에

40 요약문 완성 ④

소재 은메달리스트와 동메달리스트의 행복감 차이

해설 올림픽 대회의 은메달리스트는 금메달을 딸 수도 있었던 '긍정적인(positive)' 상황에 더욱 근접했다가 실패했기 때문에 이를 상상할 때 기분이 '더 안 좋아지는(worse)' 것이고, 반대로 동메달리스트는 메달을 따지 못할 수도 있는 상황에서 벗어나 메달을 땄기 때문에 더 행복감을 느끼는 것이다. 따라서 은메달리스트의 경우를 일반화한 요약문의 빈칸에는 ④가 들어가는 것이 가장 적절하다.

해석 더 행복한 학생들이 점수도 더 잘 받을까? 최고의 자리에 오른 한 명의 선수가 가장 행복한 사람인가? 올림픽 대회의 동메달리스트와 은메달리스트들을 생각해보라. 누가 더 행복할거라고 생각하는가? 그러한 시합에서 금메달리스트와 그밖의 모든 사람들 간에 질적 차이가 있다. 오직 금메달리스트만이 시합에서 승리했고, 영광을 획득했으며, 대단히 수익성이 높은 협찬을 기대할 수 있다. 그러한 시합의 은메달리스트는 금메달을 따는 데 동메달리스트보다 더 가까이 갔으므로 무슨 일이 있을 수 있었는지에 대한 생각으로 괴로움을 당할 가능성이 더 높다. 대조적으로, 동메달리스트는 아무 것도 얻지 못하는 상황에 위험할 정도로 근접했으므로 이러한 불운을 피했던 것에 대해 특히 기쁠 것이다. 주제문 은메달리스트가 "금메달을 딸 수도 있었는데"라는 이유로 기분이 상한 반면 동메달리스트가 "적어도 메달은 땄어"라는 이유로 만족하면, 은메달리스트는 동메달리스트보다 행복감을 덜 느낄 수 있다.

↓

다른 사람들보다 객관적으로 형편이 더 나은 사람이 훨씬 더 (B) 긍정적인 결과를 상상할 수 있으면 기분이 (A) 더 안 좋아질 수 있다.

구문 [3행~4행] ~ **who** do you suppose **is happier**?
do you suppose가 주절이며 who is happier는 suppose의 목적어인 간접의문문이다. do you suppose와 같이 답변이 'yes/no'로 나오지 않는 경우 간접의문문의 의문사를 문장의 맨 앞에 쓴다.

[8행~12행] *The silver medalist*(S) (in such a competition) has come(V1) closer to winning gold than **has the bronze medalist** / and so is more likely to be tormented(V2) / by thoughts of what might have happened.
than 다음의 has the bronze medalist는 주어와 동사의 어순이 도치되었으며, 대동사 has는 has come close to winning gold를 뜻한다.

[12행~15행] In contrast, the bronze medalist ~ may therefore be especially pleased at **having avoided** this misfortune.
at 다음의 동명사를 완료동명사(having p.p.) 형태로 썼는데, 이는 주절의 동사(may be pleased)보다 더 앞선 상황을 나타낸다.

어휘 **crowned** 최고의 자리에 오른; 왕관을 쓴 **bronze** 청동 **competition** 대회, 시합; 경쟁 **qualitative** 질적인 **attain** 획득하다 **highly** 매우, 대단히 **profitable** 수익성이 있는 **sponsorship** 후원, 협찬 **be likely to-v** v할 것 같다, v하기 쉽다 **torment** 괴롭히다, 학대하다 **in contrast** 대조적으로 **misfortune** 불운 **gratify** 만족시키다 **objectively** 객관적으로 **better off** 형편이 더 나은 **outcome** 결과

41~42 장문 41 ② 42 ①

소재 실패를 바라보는 올바른 시각

해설 41. 마지막 문단에 글의 요지가 담겨 있다. 문학작품 속 비극적 인물의 실패에 대해 너그러운 것처럼 실제 삶에서도 다른 사람의 문제와 실패에 대해 섣불리 판단해서는 안 된다는 내용이므로, 이를 제목으로 가장 잘 표현한 것은 ② '인내심을 가지고 다른 사람들의 실패를 바라보자'이다.
① 왜 우리는 자신을 매우 가혹하게 판단하는가?
③ 성공에 필수적인 것: 자신의 실패 수용하기
④ 이야기에 공통적으로 있는 것: 비극
⑤ 위대한 비극적 등장인물에게서 존경에 대해 배우자

42. 빈칸을 포함한 문장은 앞에 나온 질문(So, what ~ understanding?)에 대한 답(Perhaps it's ~ our teachers.)을 다시 반복한 것이다. 문학 속 비극적 등장인물들이 존중과 이해를 얻는 건 우리가 그렇게 교육을 받았기 때문이라는 내용이므로, respect and understanding을 포괄하는 ① '동정'이 빈칸에 적절하다. 문학 속 등장인물은 존중과 이해를 얻는데 보통 사람들은 그렇지 못하다는 의미이다.
② 자부심 ③ 행복 ④ 열정 ⑤ 기회

해석 실패하는 것에 대한 두려움은 매우 흔한 두려움이다. 이 두려움의 주요 원인은 만일 우리가 실패할 경우 사람들이 말할지도 모르는 것에 대해 우리가 매우 많이 걱정하기 때문이다. 사람들이 당신을 비웃고 당신을 거부할 거라는 생각이 실패 그 자체에 대한 생각보다 훨씬 더 두려울 수 있다.
예술과 문학 속 위대한 비극적 인물들이 매우 형편없는 대접을 받는다고 상상해 보라! Shakespeare(셰익스피어)의 〈햄릿〉을 예로 들어 보자. 수백 년 동안 독자와 관객들은 이해심을 가지고 Hamlet을 보아 왔는데, 이는 희곡에서 그를 복잡한 인간으로 나타내기 때문이다. 그는 약점을 갖고 있으며 때로 잘못된 행동을 하기도 하지만, 우리는 그를 동정하며 계속해서 그의 편에 선다. 그러나 만일 오늘날 Hamlet이 살아 있다면 그만큼 존경을 얻을 것 같지 않다. 특히 블로거와 다른 '네티즌들'은 아마도 온라인상에서 그에 대해 험담을 할 것이며, 그의 비극을 오로지 그의 책임으로 돌릴 것이다.
실제 삶에서, 실패하는 사람들은 아주 혹독한 대접을 받는 것 같다. 그렇다면 무엇이 Hamlet과 기타 문학의 다른 비극적 인물들에게 존중과 이해를 가져다주는가? 아마도 그것은 우리가 그들을 고귀하게 보도록, 그들의 창작자들과 우리 선생님들로부터 교육을 받았기 때문일 것이다. 우리는 그들에게 보통 사람들도 받을 만하지만 좀처럼 받지 못하는 정도의 동정을 주라고 부추김을 받는다. 주제문 위대한 비극적 이야기들은 우리에게 재앙이 일어나는 것이 얼마나 쉬운지, 올바른 삶을 이끌어 나가기가 얼마나 어려운지, 왜 우리가 다른 사람들의 문제와 실수를 너무 성급하게 혹은 너무 가혹하게 판단해서는 안 되는지를 느끼게 해준다.

구문 [3행~5행] The idea that people will laugh at you and reject you / can be **even** *scarier* / than the thought of failure itself.
(S: The idea, =: that절, V: can be)
that절과 The idea가 동격을 이루고 있다. even은 비교급을 수식하는 부사로 쓰여 '훨씬'으로 해석한다.

[13행~14행] **Were he** alive today, however, // it's unlikely (that) he **would get** as much respect.
「If+S'+were ~, S+조동사 과거형+동사원형 ...」은 '만약 ~라면 …할 텐데'란 의미이다. if가 생략되어 if절의 주어(he)와 동사(were)의 위치가 바뀌었다. 주절에 it's unlikely (that)이 함께 쓰여 '추측'의 의미가 더 강해졌다.

[25행~29행] Great tragic stories make us sense // O'1 how easy it is for disasters to happen to us, O'2 how hard it is to lead a good life, and O'3 why we shouldn't judge others too quickly or too harshly / for their problems and mistakes.
(S: Great tragic stories, V: make, O: us, C: sense)
sense(~라고 느끼다)의 목적어 역할을 하는 명사절 3개가 and로 연결된 구조이다. how가 이끄는 절은 「it is+(for 의미상 주어)+to-v」의 형태로 가주어 it이 진주어인 to부정사구를 대신한다. for disasters는 to happen의 의미상 주어이다.

어휘 **major** 주요한; 다수의 **reject** 거부하다, 거절하다 **tragic** 비극적인, 비극의 *cf.* **tragedy** 비극 **character** 등장인물; 성격, 특징; 문자 **literature** 문학 **audience** 관객, 청중 **understanding** 이해(심) **represent A as B** A를 B로 나타내다 **human being** 인간 **weakness** 약점 **remain** 남다; 머무르다 **on one's side** ~의 편인 **feel for** ~에게 동정심을 느끼다 (= **feel sympathy for**) **it is unlikely (that)** ~일 것 같지 않다, ~할 가능성이 없다 *cf.* **likely** ~할 것 같은 **as much** 그 만큼, 그 정도 **blame A for B** B를 A의 책임[탓]으로 돌리다, B로 인해 A를 탓하다 **noble** 고귀한; 귀족의; 귀족 **encourage to-v** v하도록 장려하다 **ordinary** 보통의, 평범한 **deserve** (마땅히) 받을 가치가 있다 **harshly** 가혹하게, 냉혹하게 [선택지 어휘] **embrace** 수용하다; 품다; 포옹하다 **have in common** 공통적으로 지니다

43~45 장문

43 ③ 44 ④ 45 ⑤

소재 물에 빠진 친구를 구한 일화

해설 43. (A)에 Tyler의 옆 자리에 있던 Gary가 Tyler에게 모래성을 만들자고 제안하는 내용이 나오므로, 모래성을 만드는 내용인 (C)가 가장 먼저 이어진다. 파도에 뛰어든 Gary가 손을 흔들며 도움을 청하는 것을 Tyler가 본 것이 (C)의 마지막 장면이므로, Tyler가 행동하고 구조원이 Gary를 구조하는 (D)가 이어지고, Gary의 어머니가 Tyler와 그의 어머니를 저녁 식사에 초대하는 (B)가 마지막에 나온다. 따라서 글의 순서는 ③ '(C)-(D)-(B)'가 가장 적절하다.
44. (d)는 수영 수업을 배운 Tyler를 가리키고 나머지는 모두 Gary를 지칭한다.
45. (D)에서 Gary를 해변으로 데려온 것은 인명구조원이므로 ⑤는 글의 내용과 일치하지 않는다.

해석 (A) 초여름이었고, 날씨는 정말 더웠다. ① Tyler와 그의 어머니는 해변에 왔다. 어머니는 물 근처 모래 위의 좋은 장소를 발견했다. 그들은 담요를 깔고 몇 개의 의자를 설치했다. Tyler 정도의 나이의 (a) 한 소년(= Gary)이 그들 가까이 앉아 있었다. 그는 다가와서 그의 이름이 Gary이며 ② Tyler에게 (b) 그(= Gary)와 함께 모래성을 쌓고 싶은지를 물었다. Tyler는 "물론이지."라고 말을 했다. 그의 어머니는 Tyler의 어머니에게 학교, 일, 어머니들이 보통 이야기하는 것에 대해 말을 걸기 시작했다.
(C) 그 소년들은 큰 모래성을 만들었다. 그들은 물로 향하기로 결정했다. "조심해."라고 Gary의 어머니가 외쳤다. "조심할게요."라고 Gary가 되받아 외쳤다. 그 소년들은 물에 들어갔다 나왔다 하고 웃으면서 파도 사이로 뛰어들었다. 그들은 좋은 시간을 보내고 있었다. 갑자기 그들은 큰 파도로 뛰어들기 위해 달렸지만, Tyler는 Gary를 발견할 수가 없었다. Tyler는 주위를 돌아다보고 마침내 (c) 그(= Gary)가 손을 흔들며 도와달라고 외치는 것을 보았다.
(D) Tyler는 즉시 행동을 시작했고, 지역 수영장에서 (d) 그(= Tyler)의 수영 수업 동안에 그가 배운 인명 구조 기술을 기억해냈다. '나는 Gary에게 가야 해.'라고 Tyler는 생각했다. ④ Tyler는 Gary가 있는 곳까지 수영해서 (e) 그(= Gary)를 자신의 팔로 감싸고 그에게 꽉 잡으라고 말을 했다. 바로 그때 인명구조원이 그들을 보았다. 그는 물로 달려들어가서 (Gary 구하는 일을) 이어받았다. ⑤ 그는 Tyler로부터 Gary를 받아 그를 안전하게 해변으로 되돌아오게 할 수 있었다.
(B) Gary의 어머니는 아주 겁을 먹었고, Tyler의 빠른 행동이 없었다면 Gary는 익사했을지도 모른다는 것을 알았다. Gary와 그의 어머니는 Tyler에게 그의 빠른 생각과 뛰어난 수영 기술에 대해 감사를 표현했다. 그날 밤 ③ Gary의 어머니는 Tyler와 그의 어머니를 저녁 식사에 초대했다. "제 감사함의 대접입니다."라고 Gary 엄마가 말했다. 그 소년들은 친구가 되었을 뿐 아니라 그의 어머니들도 친구가 되었다!

구문 [(D) 1행~3행] Tyler **sprang** into action and **remembered** *the lifesaving skills* [(that[which]) he **had learned** / during his swimming class / at the local pool].
(V1: sprang, V2: remembered)
[ ] 부분은 관계대명사절로 the lifesaving skills를 수식한다. 수영 수업 시간에 인명 구조 기술을 배운 것이 본동사(sprang, remembered)보다 앞선 시점이므로 관계사절의 동사는 대과거(had p.p.)로 썼다.

어휘 **(A) spot** 장소, 지점; 발견하다 **blanket** 담요 **sand castle** 모래성 **(B) scared** 겁먹은, 두려워하는 **drown** 익사하다, 물에 빠지다 **(C) head for** ~로 향하다, 나아가다 **yell** 외치다 **(D) spring into action** 갑자기 행동하기 시작하다 **lifesaving** 구명의, 구조의 **hold on tight** 꼭 잡다 **lifeguard** 인명 구조원 **take over** 인수하다

실전 모의고사 09

본문 p.125

18 ④	19 ②	20 ④	21 ③	22 ⑤	23 ①	24 ⑤	25 ④	26 ⑤	27 ①
28 ④	29 ①	30 ②	31 ⑤	32 ③	33 ②	34 ③	35 ④	36 ③	37 ⑤
38 ③	39 ③	40 ②	41 ④	42 ⑤	43 ③	44 ⑤	45 ⑤		

18 글의 목적 ④

소재 새로운 동물 보호소 설립 요청

해설 편지 도입부에서는 유기 동물과 관련한 자신의 경험을 소개한 이후, 중반부부터 새로운 동물 보호소의 설립이 필요한 이유를 밝히며 동물 보호소 설립을 요청하고 있다. 따라서 글의 목적으로 가장 적절한 것은 ④이다.

해석 Green 시장님께,
제 편지를 읽으실 시간을 내주셔서 감사드립니다. 저는 학교 선생님으로부터 제가 그런 것처럼 시장님도 고양이와 강아지를 매우 좋아하신다는 것을 알게 됐습니다. 사실, 전 두 마리의 강아지가 있고, 그 두 마리 모두 Ravenwood 동물 보호소에서 입양했습니다. 엄마께선 동물 보호소가 가능한 한 많은 강아지들을 구조한다고 말씀하십니다. 하지만 여전히, 우리 도시 거리에는 (누구도) 원하지 않는 집 없는 수백 마리의 강아지와 고양이가 있습니다. 저는 사람들이 이 문제를 (해결하도록) 돕고 싶어 하지만 방법을 모른다고 생각합니다. 주제문 **우리 도시는 이 문제를 해결하기 위해 더 많은 보호소가 필요합니다. 당신은 우리 시의 시장이시므로 가능하시면 우리 지역에 새로운 동물 보호소를 설립하는 것을 고려해주셨으면 좋겠습니다.** 동물들은 우리를 위해 매우 많은 것들을 하지만 지낼 곳에 관해서는 우리에게 의지하기도 합니다. 우리는 옳은 일을 해야 합니다.
Cindy Park 올림

구문 [4행~6행] In fact, I have *two dogs*, // **both of which** I adopted from Ravenwood Animal Shelter.
「부정대명사+of+목적격 관계대명사」인 both of which는 and both of them을 의미하며, which는 앞의 two dogs를 선행사로 한다.

어휘 **mayor** 시장 **adopt** 입양하다; 채택하다 **animal shelter** 동물 보호소 *cf.* **shelter** 보호소; 피신처; 주거지 **issue** (걱정거리가 되는) 문제; 주제, 쟁점 **perhaps** 《정중한 부탁 · 제의》 가능하시다면, 아마도 **establish** 설립하다, 수립하다 **depend on** ~에 의지[의존] 하다; ~에 달려 있다

19 심경 변화 ②

소재 망가진 채소밭

해설 심경을 묻는 유형이므로 등장인물이 처한 상황을 파악해야 한다. 사건의 추이와 함께 심경과 관련된 어구에도 주의하여 판단한다. Mary는 자신이 가꾼 채소밭을 보고 미소를 지으며 만족해했지만, 이웃의 개가 갑자기 채소밭의 울타리를 넘어 식물들을 쓰러뜨려 엉망으로 만든 상황이므로 Mary의 심경 변화로는 ② '기쁜 → 충격을 받은'이 적절하다.

해석 주제문 **Mary는 자신의 노력에 대한 결과를 보고는 미소를 지었다.** 많은 시간이 걸리는 고된 작업이었지만, 그녀의 채소밭은 이제 아주 멋져 보였다. 허브의 신선한 향은 그녀가 요리할 수 있는 모든 훌륭한 조리법에 대해 생각하는 동안 그녀의 기운을 북돋웠다. 그리고 토마토 묘목에 내리쬐는 햇살은 잡지에 나오는 것처럼 보였다. Mary가 자신의 완성물의 사진을 찍기 위해 준비할 때, 이웃 주민의 개가 갑자기 채소밭의 울타리를 뛰어넘었다. 그 개가 흙을 박차고 식물들을 쓰러뜨리면서 채소밭으로 돌진하는 동안 Mary는 입을 크게 벌린 채 그 자리에 얼어붙었다. 그녀는 상황의 난감함에 작은 비명을 질렀다. 상황이 끝났을 때, Mary는 믿을 수 없었다. 주제문 **그녀의 모든 노력이 엉망이 되어 있었다.**
① 즐거워하는 → 부러워하는
③ 초조한 → 좌절한
④ 깜짝 놀란 → 창피한
⑤ 만족한 → 무관심한

구문 [3행~5행] *The fresh smells* (from the herbs) / lifted her spirits // as she thought about *all the great recipes* [(that) she could cook].
( ) 부분은 전명구로 The fresh smells를 수식한다. 생략된 목적격 관계대명사 that이 이끄는 관계사절이 선행사 all the great recipes를 수식한다.

[9행~11행] Mary stood frozen in place / **with** *her mouth* **wide open** // as the dog rushed into the garden, / **kicking up dirt and knocking over plants.**
「with+(대)명사+형용사」는 '…을 ~한 채로'의 의미이며, kicking up ~ over plants는 '~하면서'의 뜻인 분사구문으로 동시상황을 나타낸다.

어휘 **effort** 노력, 수고 **vegetable garden** 채소밭 **lift one's spirit** 기운을 돋우다 **accomplishment** 완성, 마무리; 성과; 업적 **rush** 돌진하다; 급속히 움직이다, 서두르다 **knock over** 쓰러뜨리다, 때려눕히다 **helplessness** 난감함; 무력함; 어쩔 도리가 없는 것 **ruin** 엉망으로 만들다, 망치다

20 필자 주장 ④

소재 화가 난 아이를 다루는 방법

해설 아이들이 화를 내는 것은 자연스러운 것이므로 이를 인정하고 그것이 긍정적인 방향으로 향할 수 있도록 해야 한다는 내용의 글로, 중반부의 We have to free ourselves ~.와 마지막 문장인 We must acknowledge ~.에 필자의 주장이 잘 나타나 있다. 따라서 정답은 ④이다.

해석 많은 어른들이 아이들의 화 때문에 괴로워하며 혼란스러워한다. 이것은 화난 아이와 마주할 때 우리 스스로 분노와 좌절감의 감정이 너무나 쉽게 치밀어 오르기 때문이다. 우리는 우리 대부분이 어릴 때 분노 관리 기술을 전혀 배우지 않았다는 것을 염두에 두어야 한다. 아마도 당신은 화를 내면 좋은 사람이 아니라고 믿게 되었을 것이다. 당신은 오직 나쁜 아이들만이 화를 내며, 분노를 드러내는 것은 매우 나쁘다는 메시지를 습득한 것이다. 우리는 이처럼 자신을 파괴하는 견해로부터 스스로를 자유롭게 해야 한다. 주제문 **화난 감정을 갖고 있는 아이를 적절하게 다루기 위해서는 먼저 분노를 인간이라는 것의 자연스러운 일부로 받아들여야 한다. 우리는 아이의 분노를 비판 없이 인정해야 하며, 아이가 그것(= 분노)을 긍정적인 결과로 향하게 할 수 있도록 도와주어야 한다.**

구문 [10행~12행] **To properly handle** *children* [who have angry feelings], / one must first accept anger / as a natural part of being human.
To properly handle ~은 '목적'을 나타내는 to부정사구로, 부사 properly가 handle을 수식하고 있다.

어휘 **distressed** 괴로워하는 **confused** 혼란스러운, 당황한 **rage** 분노, 격분 **stir up** (화 등의 감정이) 치밀어 오르다 **bear in mind** 명심하다, 유념하다 **self-damaging** 자신을 파괴하는, 자신에게 해로운 **properly** 적절하게 **handle** 다루다, 처리하다 **acknowledge** (사실로) 인정하다; 승인하다; 감사하다 **judgment** 비판; 판단; 견해 **direct** (주의 · 노력 등을) 향하게 하다; 가리키다; 지도하다 **outcome** 결과

21 밑줄 함의 ③

소재 인간관계에서 사소한 것의 중요성

해설 작은 쥐 한 마리가 큰 비행기를 꼼짝 못하게 만드는 것처럼, 인간관계에서도 작은 것을 무시하고 지나치지 말고 세심하게 관리해야 한다는 내용의 글이다. 따라서 밑줄 친 부분의 의미로 가장 적절한 것은 ③ '세부사항에 주의를 기울이다'이다.

해석 주말 동안 칸쿤에 있는 멕시코 리조트행 스위스 제트기가 취리히에서 하루 동안 이륙을 못하게 됐다. 승무원들은 항공기의 입국 비행 동안 나타난 쥐를 수색했다. 케이블을 갉아먹었다면 안전상의 위험을 야기했을 그 쥐가 발견될 때까지 약 200명의 승객들이 하룻밤 동안 비행기에 탑승할 수 없었다. 이 이야기는 당신이 다른 사람들과 맺는 관계에 대한 좋은 비유이다. 주제문 가장 작은 것이 당신이 당신의 자녀, 파트너들, 혹은 고객들과 맺는 관계에 손상을 입힐 수 있다. 인간관계에서는 작게 생각하는 것이 중요하다. 작게 생각하는 것은 당신이 사람들을 대할 때 자주 무시하는 것에 신경을 쓰는 것을 의미한다. 당신의 작은 몸짓이나 행동이 지속되는 인상을 남길 수 있다는 것을 명심하라. 당신의 인간관계에 쥐가 있는가? 당신은 그것을 없애야 한다.

① 다른 사람들에게 예의를 갖추다
② 자신의 실수에서 배우다
④ 예상치 못한 사건에 대비하다
⑤ 열린 마음으로 사물을 보다

구문 [4행~7행] About 200 passengers couldn't board the plane overnight // until the mouse, [which posed a safety risk / if it chewed on cables], was found.
(S′: the mouse, V′: was found)
until이 이끄는 부사절에서 주어는 the mouse이고 동사는 was found이며, which ~ on cables는 the mouse를 부연 설명한다.

[10행~12행] Thinking small means taking care of *something* [(that[which]) you often ignore / when you deal with people].
(S: Thinking small, V: means, O: taking care of something)
[ ] 부분은 something을 수식하며, 목적격 관계대명사 that[which]가 생략되었다.

어휘 **bound for** ~행(行)의 **ground** 이륙을 못하게 하다; (자녀에 대한 벌로) 외출하지 못하게 하다 **crew** 승무원 **appearance** 출현, 나타남; 외모 **aircraft** 항공기 **incoming** 들어오는 **flight** 비행; 항공편 **passenger** 승객 **board** 탑승하다 **overnight** 하룻밤 동안 **pose a risk** 위험을 끼치다, 해가 되다 **chew** 씹다 **analogy** 비유 **client** 고객 **deal with** ~을 대하다; ~을 다루다 **lasting** 지속적인 **impression** 인상; 감명 **get rid of** ~을 없애다

22 글의 요지 ⑤

소재 우정

해설 물건은 붙들어둘 수 있을지라도 친구는 자신의 삶을 사는 주체이므로 억지로 붙들어둘 수 없으므로, 이미 죽어버린 우정이라면 그것을 받아들이고 다른 관계를 추구하라는 내용의 글이다. 따라서 글의 요지로 가장 적절한 것은 ⑤이다.

해석 "무언가를 사랑한다면 그것을 (자유롭게) 풀어줘라. 그것이 돌아오면 그것은 당신의 것이다. 그렇지 않으면 (당신의 것이) 절대 아니었던 거다."라는 오래된 속담이 있다. 다음번에 당신이 누군가의 우정을 붙들고자 하는 유혹을 느낄 때 이 속담을 기억하라. 당신은 당신의 개를 줄에 매고, 당신의 자전거를 차고에 넣고 잠가둘 수 있지만, 당신의 친구들에게는 자기 자신의 삶을 살 자유가 있어야 한다. 여러분 두 사람이 여러분의 경험을 공유하고 서로의 개성을 존중할 수 있다면 멋진 일이다. 그렇지 않으면, 여러분은 좋은 지인일 수 있으나 진정으로 좋은 친구는 아니다. 이미 죽어버린 우정을 붙들려고 애쓰는 것은 비탄의 원인이 될 수 있을 뿐이다. 주제문 고통을 받아들이고, 왜 그런 일이 일어났는지를 이해하려고 노력하고, 넘어가라. 저 밖에 다른 사람들이 있으며, 그들이 일단 당신과의 우정의 기회를 보게 되면, 들어와서 당신이 느낄지 모르는 어떠한 공허함도 채워줄 것이다.

구문 [3행~4행] Remember this saying // **the next time** you're tempted to hold onto someone's friendship.
the next time은 '~하는 다음번에'의 뜻으로 접속사 역할을 한다.

[10행~11행] Trying to hold onto *a friendship* [that has already died] can only be a cause of heartache.
(S: Trying to hold onto a friendship [that has already died], V: can only be)
동명사구 주어이며, a friendship은 관계사절의 수식을 받는다.

어휘 **proverb** 속담(= **saying**) **set A free** A를 풀어주다, 석방하다 **be tempted to-v** v하라고 유혹받다; v하고 싶다 **hold onto** ~에 매달리다, ~을 꼭 잡다 **leash** (개 등을 매어 두는) 가죽끈[줄], 사슬 **garage** 차고 **individuality** 개성, 개체성 **acquaintance** 지인(知人), 아는 사람 **heartache** 비탄, 심적 고통 **move on** 넘어가다 **emptiness** 공허, 허무

23 글의 주제 ①

소재 포도주 보관 조건

해설 세 번째 문장(Darkness, stillness, ~ good shape.)에서 어두움, 정지 상태, 습도와 적절한 온도가 포도주 보관에 중요하다고 한 뒤 이 요소들을 구체적으로 설명하고 있으므로, 이 글의 주제로는 ① '포도주 수명에 영향을 미치는 요소들'이 가장 적절하다.

해석 주제문 제대로 보관되면, 고급 포도주는 수년 간 지속될 수 있으며 맛의 스타일(character)과 맛과 향의 조화(complexity)가 계속 향상될 수 있다. 많은 난파선에서 아주 오래된 포도주가 바다 밑바닥의 거의 완벽한 저장 환경 덕분에 마시기에 아주 좋은 상태로 발견되어 왔다. 주제문 어두움, 정지 상태, 습도, 알맞은 온도는 좋은 포도주를 좋은 상태로 보관하는 데 필수적이다. 서늘한 섭씨 13~15도의 알맞은 온도는 (포도주) 보관에 특히 중요한 요소인데, 왜냐하면 포도주에 맛의 스타일(character)을 부여하는 복잡한 유기 화학 반응이 이 범위의 온도에서 일어나기 때문이다. 습도 또한 중요한데, 습도는 70퍼센트 정도에서 유지되어야 한다. 낮은 습도는 코르크 마개가 말라 쪼그라들게 하는데, 이것은 산소와 박테리아가 병 안으로 들어가게 하여 그 안에서 포도주를 재빨리 상하게 만들어 버린다.

② 포도주 보관에 있어 온도의 역할
③ 포도주 생산 연도의 중요성
④ 포도주 맛의 스타일에 미치는 박테리아의 영향
⑤ 포도주 맛을 향상시키는 데 있어 화학 반응의 이점

구문 [1행] (Being) **Stored** correctly, / fine wine can last for many years ~.
= If it(= fine wine) is stored correctly,
문장의 주어 fine wine과 store가 수동 관계이므로 과거분사 Stored가 쓰였다.

[11행~12행] Also important is *humidity*, // **which** must be kept at around 70%.
(C: important, V: is, S: humidity)
보어가 앞으로 나가면서 주어, 동사가 도치된 형태이다. 여기서는 humidity의 보충설명(which ~ 70%)이 길어져 도치가 일어났다.

어휘 **store** 보관[저장]하다 *cf.* **storage** 보관, 저장 **complexity** 복합성, 복잡성 *cf.* **complex** 복잡한 **condition** 상태; 조건 **shipwreck** 난파(선) **stillness** 고요; 움직이지 않음 **humidity** 습도 **temperature** 온도 **vital** 필수적인 **Celsius** 섭씨의 **particularly** 특히 **factor** 요소, 요인 **organic reaction** 유기 (화학) 반응 **range** 범위, 폭 **cause A to-v** A가 v하게 하다 **cork** 코르크 마개 **shrink** 오그라들다 **spoil** (음식이) 상하다; 못쓰게 만들다, 망치다

24 글의 제목 ⑤

소재 습지의 홍수 방지 역할

해설 20세기 내내 습지는 쓸모없는 땅으로 여겨져 이익을 낼 수 있는 곳으로 개발되어 왔으나 이는 큰 실수라고 하면서 습지가 홍수를 예방하는 역할을 한 사례를 보여주고 있으므로, 글의 제목으로 가장 적절한 것은 ⑤ '습지: 효과적인 홍수 방지책'이다.

해석 당연히 습지는 자연적으로 물기가 매우 많은 지역이다. 20세기 내내 습지는 대개 좋은 땅을 낭비하는 것으로 여겨져 골프 코스나 쇼핑센터, 그리고 그 밖에 '더 이익이 나는' 곳으로 개발되었다. 그러한 관점은 중대한 실수였다. 2006년에 단 하루 동안 13.3인

치의 비가 매사추세츠 주(州)의 뉴베리포트에 내렸다. 근처 헤이버힐에는 (비가) 10인치 만 내렸는데도 심각한 홍수와 파괴를 겪었고, 뉴베리포트는 그렇지 않았다. 두 도시 모두 메리맥 강변에 있는데 왜 이렇게 큰 차이가 생긴 것일까? 그것은 헤이버힐은 습지를 메워 개발했었던 반면 뉴베리포트는 습지를 자연 상태 그대로 보존했기 때문이었다. 주제문 습지는 거대한 스펀지 같은 작용을 한다. 즉, 범람하는 강들로부터 엄청난 양의 물을 빠르게 흡수하고, 물이 안전하게 퍼져나갈 수 있도록 하는 것이다.

① 습지에 관한 상반된 견해
② 습지의 가치 측정하기
③ 사라져 가는 습지를 복구하는 방법
④ 습지와 생물의 다양성 사이의 관계

구문 [11행~13행] It was because Haverhill (S′) had covered and developed (V′) its wetlands (O′), // while Newburyport (S″) had allowed (V″) its wetlands (O″) to remain untouched (C″).

「allow+O+C(to-v)」는 'O가 v하게 하다'란 뜻이다. untouched는 remain의 보어로 쓰인 과거분사이다.

어휘 **wetland** 습지(대) **throughout** ~내내; 곳곳에 **consider** (~을 …로) 여기다; 고려하다 **profitable** 수익성이 있는; 이득이 되는 **destruction** 파괴 **untouched** 본래 그대로의, 손을 대지 않은 **absorb** 흡수하다 **overflow** 범람하다, 넘쳐흐르다 **spread** 퍼지다; 퍼뜨리다 [선택지 어휘] **conflicting** 상충하는; 모순되는 **measure** 측정하다 **restore** 복구하다 **link** 관련성, 관계; 연결 **biodiversity** 생물의 다양성 **effective** 효과적인 **prevention** 방지, 예방

25 도표 이해 ④

소재 국가별 기부 및 자원봉사 여부 조사 결과

해설 아시아 국가인 한국, 일본, 중국 중 돈의 기부는 한국이 가장 많이 했으나 자원봉사는 일본이 한국보다 더 높은 비율을 차지하고 있으므로, 시간 면(in terms of time)에서는 일본의 자선 기부(charitable giving) 수준이 더 높다. 따라서 ④는 도표와 일치하지 않는다.

해석 〈기부 혹은 자원봉사〉

주제문 이 그래프는 사람들에게 지난달에 돈을 기부하거나 자원봉사를 했는지 여부를 물은 설문 결과를 여러 나라별로 비교한 것이다. ① 기부에 대해서 상위 3개 국가는 네덜란드, 영국, 호주로, 적어도 70퍼센트의 사람들이 돈을 기부했다. ② (조사에 참여한) 모든 국가의 설문 결과는 자원봉사를 하는 것보다 돈을 기부하는 것에 대한 전반적인 선호를 보여준다. ③ 미국은 돈 기부자로서는 3위 안에 들지 못했지만, 자원봉사에서는 가장 높은 비율을 기록했다. ④ 아시아 국가 중에는 한국이 시간과 돈 면에서 모두 가장 높은 자선 기부 수준을 기록했다. ⑤ 가장 인색한 국가는 중국으로 자원봉사와 기부 모두에서 단연코 가장 낮은 수준이었다.

어휘 **donate** 기부[기증]하다 *cf.* **donor** 기부[기증]자 **volunteer** 자원봉사하다; 자원봉사자 **previous** 이전의 **indicate** 보여주다, 나타내다; 암시하다 **preference** 선호(도), 애호 **A rather than B** B(라기)보다는 A **record** 기록하다; 녹음하다 **charitable** 자선의; 관대한 **in terms of** ~면에서, ~에 관하여 **generous** 너그러운, 관대한 **by far** (비교급 · 최상급을 강조하여) 단연코, 훨씬

26 내용 불일치 ⑤

소재 Carl Ludwig Luz Long의 생애

해설 선택지를 먼저 읽은 후, 본문을 읽으며 해당 내용이 나올 때마다 선택지와의 일치 여부를 확인한다. 마지막에서 세 번째 문장에서 Long이 전쟁에서 당한 부상으로 인하여 3일 후에 사망했다고 했으므로, ⑤에서 '원인 불명'이라는 표현이 글의 내용과 일치하지 않는다.

해석 Carl Ludwig Luz Long은 1913년 4월 27일에 태어난 ① 독일의 올림픽 멀리뛰기 선수였다. 그는 독일 멀리뛰기 선수권 대회에서 여섯 번, 즉 1933년, 1934년, 1936년, 1937년, 1938년 그리고 1939년에 우승을 하면서 자신의 종목에서 꽤 성공적이었다. 그는 1936년 ② 베를린 하계 올림픽에서 은메달을 딴 것으로도 기억된다. 그 대회 동안, 그는 ③ 미국의 멀리뛰기 선수 Jesse Owens와 친구가 되었고, 둘은 그 후 수년 동안 계속 연락을 유지했다. Jesse Owens는 직접 Long의 아들의 결혼식에 참석하기도 했다. 시합에 참가하지 않을 때, Long은 Leipzig 대학에서 법학을 공부했고, 졸업 후 그는 ④ 함부르크에서 변호사로 개업했다. 유감스럽게도, Long이 제2차 세계대전 중 부상을 당하고 ⑤ 부상으로 인해 겨우 3일 만에 사망하면서 그의 생은 갑자기 막을 내렸다. 그러나 그의 유산은 계속 살아 있다. 그의 죽음 이후에, 그는 베를린 올림픽에서 메달과 함께 스포츠 정신을 훌륭하게 보여준 것으로 존경받았다.

구문 [13행~15행] Sadly, / Long's life was cut short // when he was injured during World War II / and died just three days later from the wounds.

when이 이끄는 부사절의 동사 was injured와 died는 접속사 and로 연결되어 병렬구조를 이루고 있다.

어휘 **long jumper** 멀리뛰기 선수 *cf.* **long jump** 멀리뛰기 **championship** 선수권 (대회) **remain** 여전히 ~이다; 남다, 잔존하다 **in contact** 연락[접촉]하는 **compete** (경기에) 참가하다; 경쟁하다 **practice** (전문직을) 개업하다; 연습[실습]하다 **cut short** 갑자기 끝내다 **wound** 부상, 상처; 부상[상처]을 입히다 **legacy** 유산; 물려받은 것 **live on** 계속 살아 있다; ~을 먹고 살다 **honor** 존경[존중]하다; 영예[명예](를 주다) **sportsmanship** 스포츠 정신

27 안내문 불일치 ①

소재 동문 체육대회 안내

해설 녹색과 흰색의 운동복은 학생들이 재학 시절 입었던 것으로 설명되어 있을 뿐, 체육대회 복장에 대한 언급은 없으므로 ①이 안내문의 내용과 일치하지 않는다.

해석

동문 체육대회

매년 Steven 대학의 동문 선수들은 학교 동문 체육대회에 모여 ① 녹색과 흰색의 Steven 학교 운동복을 자랑스럽게 입었던 그 시절의 운동기술을 되살리고 있습니다.

일정

② 동창생들은 연례 동문 체육대회 30주년을 맞이하여 2020년 12월 10일 토요일에 모입니다.

③ 오전 10:30	라크로스 경기 (여자)
③ 오전 11:30	라크로스 경기 (남자)
④ 오후 12:30	Pirate 수영장에서의 바비큐 파티
오후 1:30	농구 경기 (남자)
오후 2:30	농구 경기 (여자)

대학 구내매점 특별 개장 시간

⑤ 대학 구내매점이 동문 체육대회 동안 오전 10시부터 오후 2시까지 문을 엽니다. 잠시 들러서 여러분과 친구들을 위해 Steven 대학 로고가 새겨진 최신 운동복을 구입하시기 바랍니다.

구문 [2행~6행] Each year, Steven alumni athletes gather for our Alumni Games, / **reviving** athletic skills from *the days* [**when** they proudly wore the Steven green and white].

reviving은 부대상황을 나타내는 분사구문을 이끈다. when은 선행사 the days를 수식하는 관계부사절을 이끈다.

어휘 **alumni** (alumnus의 복수형) 동창생들, 동문들 **athlete** 운동선수 **gather** 모이다; 모으다 **revive** 되살리다, 부활시키다 **annual** 매년의, 연례의 **lacrosse** 라크로스(각각 10명의 선수로 이뤄진 두 팀이 그물채 같은 것으로 공을 던지거나 잡는 하키와 비슷한 경기) **logo** 로고; (티셔츠 등에 인쇄된) 문자 **stop by** ~에 잠시 들르다 **sportswear** 운동복

28 안내문 일치 ④

소재 Belleville 벼룩시장 소개

해설 판매자 자격으로 신상품 판매 소매상과 중고품 판매자를 모두 명시하고 있으므로 정답은 ④이다.

해석

> Belleville 벼룩시장
> 2020년 7월 5일 | 오전 9시~오후 5시
> (① 판매자 도착 시간: 오전 6:30~8:00)
> 주소: 120 Park Ave. Belleville, NJ 07201
>
> ② 한 달에 한 번 열리는 이 벼룩시장은 새로운 상품들을 특징으로 하는데, 몇 가지 예를 들자면 보석류, 스포츠 수집품, 모자, 핸드백, 선물용품들이 있습니다. 시장에는 여러분이 찾고 계신 것을 발견할 수 있는 널찍한 중고품 판매 공간이 있습니다. ③ 이 행사는 실외에서 열리지만 비가 오는 경우에는 실내에서 열립니다.
>
> **판매자 자격이 있는 분:**
> - ④ 소매상 (신상품 판매)
> - 미술품, 공예품, 사진 전시가
> - ④ 중고품 판매자, 중고 물품 세일 (중고품 판매)
>
> ⑤ *이곳은 실외 벼룩시장이므로 실외 공간을 얻기 위해 신청서는 필요 없습니다.*

구문 [10행~11행] This event **will be held** outdoors [but] (this event will be held) indoors **if** it **rains**.
if절은 조건의 부사절이므로 현재시제로 미래시제를 대신하였다.

어휘 **flea market** 벼룩시장 **vendor** 판매자, 노점상 **merchandise** 상품 **collectible** (보통 복수형) 수집할 가치가 있는 것, 수집 대상물 **to name a few** 두서너 가지 예만 들자면 **garage sale** 중고 물품 판매 **outdoors** 실외에서 (↔ **indoors** 실내에서) **eligible** 자격이 있는 **retail** 소매상 **craft** 공예 **exhibitor** 출품자, 참가자 **secondhand** 중고품의; 간접적인 **application** 신청(서), 지원(서)

29 밑줄 어법 ①

소재 천문학자 Carl Sagan의 어린 시절 꿈

해설 ① 과거에 했던 것을 기억한다는 의미일 때는 remember 뒤에 v-ing 형태가 온다. 과거에 별에 대해 물어본 것을 기억한다는 내용이므로 to ask는 asking으로 고쳐야 한다.

오답 분석 ② 분사구문의 생략된 주어는 주절과 동일한 Sagan이다. 주어가 감정을 느끼지 못했다는 문맥이므로 과거분사 Unsatisfied가 적절히 쓰였다. ③ 과거의 특정한 시점(then)까지 계속된 상태를 나타내고 있으므로 과거완료(had p.p.)가 적절히 쓰였다. ④ 전치사 by의 목적어 looking과 and로 연결된 병렬구조이므로 wishing은 어법상 올바르다. ⑤ a dream을 선행사로 받으며 관계사절에서 surrendered의 목적어 역할을 하는 관계대명사 which가 적절히 쓰였다.

해석 주제문 어린 시절, 천문학자 Carl Sagan은 이미 하늘에 대해 생각하고 있었다. "별이 무엇인지 친구들에게 물어보았던 일이 기억납니다."라고 그는 말한다. "그들은 별은 하늘의 빛이라고 얘기해 주었죠." 이 대답이 만족스럽지 못해서 Sagan은 별이란 매우 멀리 떨어져 있는 항성이라고 되어 있는 책을 한 권 찾아냈다. "그때까지 나의 우주는 내가 사는 동네였죠."라고 그는 말한다. "이제 난 우주의 엄청난 크기를 느끼게 되었고 별 그리고 행성과 사랑에 빠졌습니다." 그의 사랑은 Edgar Rice Burroughs가 쓴, 단지 화성을 바라보고 그곳에 가기를 바람으로써 화성에 갈 수 있었던 한 사람에 대한 이야기를 읽으면서 더욱 깊어졌다. 어린 Sagan은 (하늘을) 올려다보며 그의 온 마음을 다하여 그도 그곳에 갈 수 있기를 소망했다. 그것은 그가 절대 포기하지 않은 꿈이었다.

구문 [4행~6행] **Unsatisfied** with this answer, / Sagan found *a book* [**that** told him **that** the stars were greatly distant suns].
(told: V′, him: IO′, that ~ suns: DO′)
Unsatisfied ~ answer는 Because he was unsatisfied ~ answer를 의미하는 분사구문이다. 첫 번째 that 이하는 a book을 수식해주는 주격 관계대명사절이며, 두 번째 that 이하는 동사 told의 직접목적어 역할을 하는 명사절이다.

어휘 **astronomer** 천문학자 **distant** 먼, 떨어진 **sun** 항성(스스로 빛을 내는 천체) **incredible** 엄청난, 놀라운 **planet** 행성 **surrender** 포기하다; 항복하다; 넘겨주다

30 네모 어휘 ②

소재 John Doe라는 이름 사용의 유래와 목적

해설 (A) 신원 미상의 남성을 '가리키다, 지칭하다'란 문맥이므로 refer가 적절하다. appeal은 '호소하다, 간청하다'란 뜻이다.
(B) John Doe라는 이름이 가상의 소작인을 '나타내는' 데 쓰였다는 문맥이므로 represent가 와야 한다. release는 '풀어주다, 해방하다'라는 뜻이다.
(C) '사생활을 보호하기 위해서'란 문맥이므로 protect가 적절하다. invade는 '침해하다, 침범하다'란 뜻이다.

해석 왜 'John Doe'라는 이름이 신원 미상의 남성을 (A) 가리키는 데 사용되는 걸까? 추리소설을 읽거나 경찰과 강도가 나오는 영화를 본 사람이라면 누구나 신원이 확인되지 않은 혹은 신원을 확인할 수 없는 남성 피해자나 용의자를 묘사하기 위해 John Doe라는 이름이 사용되는 것을 들어본 적이 있을 것이다. 일찍이 17세기 중반에 그 이름은 영국 법정에서 소유권이 애매하거나 논란이 벌어진 토지에서 쫓겨난 가상의 소작인을 (B) 나타내기 위해 사용되었다. 주제문 John Doe(무명의 여성인 경우엔 Jane Doe)는 북미 법정에서 신원을 알 수 없을 때마다 혹은 공개적으로 이름을 밝힐 수 없는 사람의 사생활을 (C) 보호하기 위해 널리 사용된다.

구문 [2행~5행] *Anyone* [**who** has read a detective novel or seen a cops-and-robbers movie] / has heard the name John Doe **used** to describe an unidentified or unidentifiable male victim or suspect.
(Anyone: S, has heard: V, the name John Doe: O, used ~ suspect: C)
the name John Doe와 use가 수동 관계이므로 목적격보어 자리에 과거분사 used가 쓰였다.

[6행~9행] As early as the mid-17th century, / the name was used in British courts / **to represent** *imaginary tenants* (**being** evicted from *land* [**whose** ownership was ambiguous or disputed]).
to represent 이하는 '목적'을 나타내는 부사적 용법의 to부정사구이다. being 이하는 imaginary tenants를 수식하는 분사구로서, 이 분사구 안에서 whose가 이끄는 소유격 관계대명사절이 land를 한정하고 있다.

어휘 **unidentified** 신원 미상의, 정체불명의 **detective** 탐정의; 탐정 **victim** 피해자, 희생자 **suspect** 용의자; 의심하다 **court** 법정; 궁정; 뜰; (테니스 · 배구 등의) 코트 **imaginary** 가공의, 상상의 **tenant** 소작인; 세입자 **ownership** 소유(권) **ambiguous** 애매한, 모호한 **dispute** 논란을 벌이다; 반박하다; 분쟁 **unnamed** 이름이 없는, 무명의 **in public** 공개적으로, 사람들 앞에서

31 빈칸 추론 ⑤

소재 동물의 다양한 의사소통 방법

해설 빈칸 이하에 제시된 예를 보면 벌은 춤으로 정보를 알리고, 수컷 큰가시고기는 특별한 헤엄으로 구애하고, 사슴은 분비물로 영역을 표시하고, 까마귀는 상황에 맞는 다양한 소리 신호를 사용하고, 개와 인간도 신체적 표현을 사용하는데, 이는 모두 ⑤ '의사소통'의 형태이다.

해석 주제문 모든 살아있는 생물은 어떤 형태의 의사소통을 관리한다. 벌들이 자신의 벌집에서 춤추는 패턴은 멀리 있는 꽃의 들판으로 가는 길을 가리키거나 꽃가루와 꿀의 성공적인 채집을 알리는 데 도움이 된다. 수컷 큰가시고기 물고기는 구애 기간 동안 정기적으로 거꾸로 헤엄친다. 수컷 사슴들은 그들 자신의 신체 분비물을 경계석 혹은 경계 나무에 문질러서 영역 소유권을 표시한다. 수백 년에 걸쳐서 관찰자들은 까마귀들이 특정한 상황에서 특정한 소리를 사용한다는 것에 주목했다. 경고음, 집합 명령, 조난 신호와 많

은 다른 것들이 주목받았다. 모든 사람들은 겁에 질린 개가 꼬리를 다리 사이에 두고 당황하여 달리는 것을 본 적이 있다. 우리 역시 우리의 말을 강조하기 위해 몸짓, 표정, 자세와 동작을 사용한다.
① 위협 ② 갈등 ③ 관심 ④ 동지애

구문 [12행~13행] Everyone has **seen** *a frightened dog* **put** his tail between his legs and **run** in panic.
「지각동사 see+O+C(원형부정사) (O가 ~하는 것을 보다)」 구문이다. 동사원형으로 시작되는 두 밑줄 친 부분은 a frightened dog의 상태를 설명하는 목적격보어로서 병렬구조를 이룬다.

어휘 **hive** 벌집 **announce** 알리다, 발표하다 **pollen** 꽃가루 **nectar** (꽃의) 꿀 **upside-down** 거꾸로의 **courtship** 구애 (기간) **territorial** 영역의, 영토의 **ownership** 소유권 **rub** 문지르다 **secretion** 분비물 **boundary** 경계(선) **note** ~에 주목하다 **circumstances** 상황 **alarm call** 경고음 **assembly** 집합 **distress** 고통, 조난 **frightened** 겁먹은 **posture** 자세 **give A point** A에 역점을 두다, A를 강조하다

32 빈칸 추론 ③

소재 체중 증가를 야기하는 수면 부족

해설 수면 부족으로 인한 호르몬 불균형이 과식하게 만든다는 내용과 렘(REM) 수면 시간이 부족하면 밤에 열량이 충분히 소모되지 못한다는 내용을 종합해 볼 때, 수면 부족이 결국 체중을 증가시킴을 알 수 있다. 따라서 빈칸에는 이와 일맥상통하는 내용인 ③ '당신의 허리둘레를 망칠'이 가장 적절하다.

해석 수면 부족은 단순히 당신의 기분을 나쁘게 하는 것 이상을 할 수 있다. 주제문 그것은 실제로 당신의 허리둘레를 망칠 수 있다. 최근의 연구에 따르면, 우리가 충분한 수면을 취하지 않으면 에너지를 아끼려고 우리의 신진대사가 느려진다. 그것은 코르티솔이라는 호르몬의 분비를 야기하는데, 이것은 식욕을 증가시킨다. 악순환으로, 수면 손실은 또한 우리 몸이 그렐린(배고픔을 알려주는 또 다른 호르몬)을 더 많이 분비하게 하고, 렙틴(당신의 위장이 꽉 찼다고 말해 주는 호르몬)은 더 적게 분비하게 한다. 호르몬의 불균형으로 당신의 몸은 과식하게 될 수 있다. 말할 것도 없이, 더 많은 시간 깨어 있으면 군것질할 시간도 더 많아진다. 게다가 수면 부족이 사람들을 더 살찌게 하는 또 다른 요인이 있다. 잠자는 동안 신체가 소모하는 칼로리의 대부분은 깊이 잠든 단계인 렘(REM) 수면 동안에 소모된다. 그리고 잠을 더 적게 자는 것은 렘(REM) 수면 시간이 더 적다는 것을 뜻한다.
① 당신을 새벽까지 깨어 있게 할
② 당신의 심박동수에 영향을 줄
④ 당신을 완전히 지치게 할
⑤ 당신의 마음을 안개 속에 둘(= 집중력을 잃게 할)

어휘 **lack** 부족, 결핍 **release** 방출, 유출; 방출하다 **appetite** 식욕; 욕구 **vicious cycle** 악순환 **loss** 손실, 상실 **signal** 신호를 보내다; 징후, 조짐 **out of balance** 불균형 **set to-v** v할 것 같은[준비가 된] **majority** 대부분, 대다수 **burn** 소모하다; (연료가) 타다 [선택지 어휘] **dawn** 새벽 **heart rate** 심박동수 **ruin** 망치다; 파멸시키다 **dog-tired** 지쳐 죽을 지경인, 기진맥진한

33 빈칸 추론 ②

소재 러들링 언어 놀이

해설 빈칸이 포함된 문장은 러들링(ludling)이 무엇인지 설명하는 내용이다. 이어지는 예시에서 이것이 원래의 단어(finger, dog)를 새로운 규칙에 따라 배열해서 새 단어(inger-fay, og-day)로 만드는 언어 놀이임을 알 수 있으므로, 빈칸에는 ② '기존의 단어에서 새로운 단어를 만들어내는'이 가장 적절하다.

해석 주제문 아이들은 아무 의미도 없는 운(음조가 비슷한 글자)과 언어 놀이를 좋아한다. 아이들은 특히 '러들링(ludling)'을 좋아하는데, 이것은 기존의 단어에서 새로운 단어를 만들어내는 비밀스러운 '실마리'나 규칙이 있는 언어 놀이다. 영어권에서 널리 친숙한 러들링 중 하나는 '피그 라틴'이라고 불리는 '비밀' 언어다. 핵심은 단지 단어의 첫 소리를 맨 끝으로 옮기고 '-ay'를 덧붙이는 것이다. 그렇게 해서 finger는 inger-fay로, dog은 og-day 등으로 모습을 바꾸게 된다. 당신이 피그 라틴으로 말할 때, 만약 사람들이 게임의 실마리를 알지 못한다면, 당신은 사람들이 당신(의 말)을 이해할 수 없는 방식으로 원래의 영어를 왜곡하게 된다. 이것이 러들링이 아이들에게 그렇게 인기 있는 이유다. 아이들은 '외부인'들로부터 비밀을 꼭꼭 숨긴 채, 친구들과 비밀을 공유하는 걸 좋아한다.
① 친근한 동물들과 대화하는
③ 영어를 할 줄 모르는 아이들에게 말을 거는
④ 당신 자신과 다른 이들에 관한 비밀을 만드는
⑤ 다른 사람들이 당신에 대해 뭐라고 말하는지 알아내는

어휘 **rhyme** 운, 라임 **key** (이해의) 실마리; 비결; 핵심; 열쇠 **rule** 규칙 **A is disguised as B** A가 B의 모습을 하다 *cf.* **disguise** 가장[변장]하다; 변장 **and so on** (기타) 등등(= **and so forth**) **distort** 왜곡하다; 비틀다 **original** 원래의; 독창적인 **popular** 인기 있는; 대중적인 [선택지 어휘] **existing** 기존의, 현재 사용하는

34 빈칸 추론 ③

소재 재능을 이루는 여러 가지 기본 능력

해설 빈칸 문장이 Similarly로 시작하므로 빈칸 문장의 내용은 앞서 서술된 내용과 유사할 것이다. 앞부분에서 무언가를 잘하는 재능은 한 가지 능력만을 갖춰서가 아니라 협력적으로 작용하는 여러 능력 때문이라고 하였다. 이어지는 빵 덩어리와 재료의 예시에서, 재료가 가지는 무한한 가능성에 대해 언급하였으므로, 이상적인 직업을 찾기 위해서는 이 재료에 해당하는 것들, 즉 ③ '결합하여 당신의 재능을 구성하는 기본적인 능력들'에 관심을 기울여야 할 것이다.

해석 어떤 사람이 수학이나 (다른) 사람들과 함께 문제를 해결하는 것, 또는 글쓰기를 잘한다면, 그들은 단 한 가지 능력을 소유한 것이 아니라, 협력하여 작용하는 여러 가지 능력을 소유한 것이다. 때때로 빵 덩어리를 보는 것은 쉽지만 그 재료는 지나치기 쉽다. 생각해보면, 한 덩어리의 빵으로는 샌드위치와 프렌치토스트 만들기, 그리고 새들에게 먹이주기처럼 할 수 있는 일이 조금 밖에 없다. 하지만 밀가루, 이스트, 물, 기름, 그리고 소금과 같은 기본 재료들을 혼합하면 무한한 가능성들이 있다. 슈퍼마켓의 어디에나 이러한 몇 안 되는 재료들로 만들어진 수백 가지 제품들이 있다. 주제문 마찬가지로 당신이 이상적인 직업을 찾도록 도와주는 방식으로 타고난 능력을 평가하는 옳은 방법은 가장 깊은 수준, 즉 결합하여 당신의 재능을 구성하는 기본적인 능력들에 진지하게 관심을 기울이는 것이다.
① 모든 기본기의 숙달
② 효율적인 다중작업 능력의 발전
④ 재료를 혼합하는 과정에 대한 이해
⑤ 가능한 한 많은 정보를 이용한 심도 있는 준비

구문 [11행~14행] Similarly, *the correct way* (to evaluate your innate abilities / in *a way* [**that** helps you find your ideal career]) / is to get down to the deepest level, *the basic abilities* [**that** combine to make up your talents].
(S: the correct way, V: is, C: to get down ~)
the correct way가 to evaluate ~ ideal career의 수식을 받아 주어가 길어졌다. that이 이끄는 두 개의 주격 관계대명사절은 각각 a way와 the basic abilities를 수식한다. the deepest level과 the basic ~ your talents는 동격을 이룬다.

어휘 **possess** 소유하다 **in concert** 협력하여; 일제히 **ingredient** 재료 **limitless** 무제한의; 방대한 **possibility** 가능성 **combine** 혼합[결합]하다 **evaluate** 평가하다, 감정하다 **innate** 타고난, 선천적인 **get down to** ~에 진지하게 관심을 기울이다; ~을 시작하다 [선택지 어휘] **mastery** 숙달, 통달; 지배(력) **underlying** 밑에 있는; 근본적인(= **fundamental**) **multitasking** 다중작업; 동시에 여러 가지 일을 하는 능력 **advanced** 고급[상급]의; 선진의 **preparation** 준비

35 무관한 문장 ④

소재 기억력 감퇴 예방법

해설 신체 활동을 통해 기억력 감퇴를 막을 수 있지만, 스트레스는 뇌 세포와 기억력에 해롭다는 내용의 글이다. 따라서 스트레스가 면역력을 높인다는 긍정적 영향을 언급한 ④는 글의 흐름에서 벗어난다.

해석 주제문 많은 사람들이 노화로 인한 기억력 감소는 불가피하다고 생각하지만 실제로 이것은 사실이 아니다. 우리는 규칙적인 신체 활동을 통해 기억력 감퇴를 예방할 수 있다. 연구들은 활발한 활동 중에 발생한 뇌로 가는 증가된 혈액 공급이 우리의 건강 상태뿐 아니라 기억력도 향상시킨다고 한다. 하지만 어떻게 해서라도 피해야 하는 한 가지는 스트레스다. 스트레스는 우리 몸이 코르티솔이라는 호르몬을 방출하게 하는데, 이것은 뇌 세포에 유해하며 기억력에도 그러하다. 번지점프를 하기 전 느끼는 것과 같은 급격한 스트레스는 실제로 면역 체계를 강화한다. 따라서 명상이나 운동, 혹은 편안한 취미 활동을 통해 스트레스를 줄이는 것이 기억력을 유지하는 데 도움이 될 수 있다.

구문 [4행~7행] Studies have shown // that *the increased blood supply to the brain* [which occurs during vigorous activity] / improves our memories **as well as** our level of fitness.
(S′: the increased blood supply to the brain, V′: improves, B: our memories, A: our level of fitness)

which가 이끄는 주격 관계사절이 that절 내의 주어를 수식하여 길어진 형태이다. 「B as well as A」는 'A뿐 아니라 B도'란 뜻으로 「not only A but also B」로 바꿔 쓸 수 있다.

[8행~10행] Stress makes our bodies produce *a hormone* (called cortisol), // **which** is harmful to brain cells and thus (is harmful) to memory.
(S: Stress, V: makes, O: our bodies, C: produce a hormone)

make가 SVOC 구조를 이룰 때, 원형부정사를 목적격보어로 취할 수 있다. 계속적 용법으로 쓰인 which가 이끄는 관계대명사절은 선행사 a hormone called cortisol을 부연 설명한다.

어휘 **unavoidable** 불가피한, 피할 수 없는 *cf.* **avoid** 피하다 **aging** 노화 **decrease** 감소, 감퇴 **blood supply** 혈액 공급 **occur** 일어나다, 발생하다 **vigorous** 활발한 **fitness** 건강 **at any cost** 어떻게 해서라도, 어떤 희생을 치르더라도 **cell** 세포 **acute** 격렬한, 심한; 예리한 **boost** 강화하다; 밀어 올리다 **immune system** 면역 체계 **meditation** 명상 **preserve** 유지하다; 보존하다 **capacity** 능력, 역량

36 글의 순서 ③

소재 미래를 계획하는 동물의 행동

해설 인간이 미래를 위한 계획을 세우는 유일한 동물이라는 일반적인 추측에 대해 캘리포니아덤불어치의 행동에 대한 연구를 토대로 반론을 제시하는 내용의 글이다. (B)의 this general assumption은 주어진 글의 내용이며, (B)는 그 추측에 대한 반대 의견을 소개하는 문장이다. (A)의 the bird's ~가 지칭하는 새는 (C)에 처음 나온 a mere bird — the Western scrub jay이므로, 이 근거들을 종합하면 글의 순서는 ③ '(B)-(C)-(A)'가 된다.

해석 새는 종종 기후가 더 따뜻한 지역으로 이동하며, 곰은 겨울철 기근에 대비해 미리 겨울잠을 잔다. 사람들은 이러한 동물들과 다른 동물의 행동이 자연의 변화 조짐에 대한 그저 '아무 생각 없는' 본능적 반응이라고 생각하는 경향이 있다.

(B) 동물이 영리하지 않고 우리가 하는 것처럼 생각하지 못한다는 이러한 일반적 추측에도 불구하고, 주제문 최근의 한 연구는 인간이 미래를 위한 계획을 세우는 유일한 동물이 아닐 수도 있음을 암시한다.

(C) 실제로 Cambridge 대학의 연구자인 Caroline Raby는 새에 불과한 캘리포니아덤불어치가 바로 그렇게 한다고 믿고 있다. 그 어치는 먹이가 부족할 때 가까운 곳에 있는 은신처에 먹이를 저장한다.

(A) 그 새의 행동을 연구한 뒤 Raby와 동료들은 그 행동이 '추울 때 음식을 묻어 두어라'고 하는 단지 본능 이상의 것이라고 확신한다.

구문 [10행~13행] Despite this general assumption **that** animals aren't smart / and don't think like we do, / a recent study suggests // **that** human beings may not be *the* only *animals* [**that** plan for the future].
(this general assumption = that절)

첫 번째 that은 this general assumption과 동격인 명사절을 이끌고, 두 번째 that은 suggests의 목적어인 명사절을 이끌며, 세 번째 that은 the animals를 선행사로 하는 주격 관계대명사절을 이끈다.

어휘 **migrate** 이동[이주]하다 **climate** 기후 **hibernate** 겨울잠을 자다 **in advance of** ~에 대비해 미리, ~보다 앞서 **famine** 기근; 가뭄 **merely** 단지, 그저 *cf.* **mere** 한낱 ~에 불과한, 단지 ~인 **dumb** 우둔한; 말을 못하는 **instinctive** 본능의 *cf.* **instinct** 본능; 직감 **colleague** 동료 **convinced** 확신하는 **bury** (파)묻다 **despite** ~에도 불구하고 **assumption** 추측, 가정 **recent** 최근의 **suggest** 암시하다, 시사하다; 제안하다 **handy** 가까운 곳에 있는; 유용한, 편리한 **scarce** 부족한, 드문

37 글의 순서 ⑤

소재 미국 정부의 태양열 에너지 이용 장려책

해설 친환경적인 태양열 시스템과 이를 장려하는 정부 지원에 관한 글이다. 주어진 글의 마지막에 나온 지원(supporting)에 대한 예시를 나타내는 연결사 for example로 시작하는 (C)가 먼저 나오고, (C)의 마지막에 나온 인센티브(incentives)의 구체적 예시로 태양열 시스템 설치비 지원을 설명한 (B)가 이어진다. 마지막으로 (설치 후에 발생하는) 여분의 에너지를 정부가 되사는 계획을 설명하는 (A)가 온다. 따라서 글의 순서로는 ⑤ '(C)-(B)-(A)'가 적절하다.

해석 당신의 집 지붕에 태양열 에너지 시스템을 설치하는 것은 화석연료로부터의 독립을 이루고 가정의 온실가스 배출을 줄이는 큰 도약이다. 주제문 미래를 생각하는 국가들은 이것이 얼마나 중요한지 이해하고 있으며 따라서 태양열 에너지로의 전환을 지원하고 있다.

(C) 예를 들어, 미국에서는 연방 정부와 주(州) 정부가 현재 태양열 시스템을 설치하는 가구 소유주에게 상당한 인센티브를 제공하고 있다.

(B) 연방 정부의 '태양열 융자 제도'에서 당신이 새로운 (태양열) 시스템을 설치하는 데 드는 비용의 보조금을 주게 되며, 주 정부는 당신의 태양열 시스템이 재빨리 이익이 되도록 도울 것이다.

(A) 주 정부는 '에너지 되사기 계획'을 통해 이것을 할 것인데, 그것은 가정의 태양열 시스템으로 생산된 여분의 전기에 대해 가구 소유주에게 금전적인 지급을 해주는 것이다.

구문 [1행~4행] Installing a solar energy system / on the roof of your home / is a great leap forward / in achieving independence from fossil fuels and (in) reducing your domestic greenhouse gas emissions.
(S: Installing a solar energy system / on the roof of your home, V: is)

길어진 동명사구(installing ~ home)가 주어이다. 전치사 in의 목적어인 두 개의 동명사구 achieving ~ fuels와 reducing ~ emissions가 and로 병렬 연결되어 있다.

[8행~10행] States will do this / through *their Energy Buyback Scheme*, // which **pays** homeowners **for** *any surplus electricity* (produced by their solar power system).

계속적 용법으로 쓰인 관계대명사절(which ~ system)은 선행사인 their Energy Buyback Scheme을 보충 설명한다. 「pay A for B」는 'A에게 B를 지불하다'란 뜻이며, 분사구(produced ~ system)가 명사 any surplus electricity를 수식하고 있다.

어휘 **install** 설치하다 **solar energy system** 태양열 에너지 시스템 **leap** 도약; 급증 **independence** 독립 **fossil fuel** 화석 연료 **domestic** 가정(용)의; 국내의 **greenhouse gas** 온실가스 **emission** (가스 등의) 배출 **forward-thinking** 장래를 고려하는 **switch** 전환, 변경; 스위치 **buyback** 되사기 **scheme** (운영) 계획, 제도 **surplus** 잉여(의), 과잉(의); 흑자 **electricity** 전기 **federal government** (미) (각 주에 대한) 연방 정부 *cf.* **state government** (미) 주(州) 정부 **credit** 융자(금); 신용 거래 **pay for** itself 비용만큼 돈이 절약되다, 본전을 뽑다 **substantial** 상당한 **incentive** 인센티브, (어떤 행동을 장려하는) 장려책, 장려금

38 문장 넣기 ③

소재 신화의 특징

해설 ③ 이전에는 과학과 기술의 시대 이전에는 신화가 세상에 대한 설명을 제공했다는 신화의 '설명적(explanatory)' 기능에 대해 설명하고 있다. ③ 이후로는 신화의 극적 요소와 구전적 특징으로 인해 성공을 거두었다는 내용으로 주제 전환이 일어났다. 주어진 문장은 신화가 구조적이고 재미있어서 인기를 얻었다는 내용으로, ③ 바로 다음 문장의 this dramatic element가 주어진 문장의 내용을 받아 자연스럽게 이어진다. 따라서 주어진 문장은 ③에 들어가는 것이 가장 적절하다.

해석 주제문 신화의 설명적 요소는 그것의 구조에 중요하다. 다른 어떤 종교와 마찬가지로, 고대 그리스 신화는 답할 수 없는 것처럼 보이는 질문에 확정적인 답을 제공하는 것을 추구했다. 고대인들은 과학적, 기술적 지식에 의한 제약을 받지 않았기 때문에, 그들은 이러한 현상들을 설명하는 몇 가지 이야기들을 자유롭게 개발했다. 주제문 동시에 신화는 처음과 중간과 끝이 있는 재미있는 이야기여서 사람들은 그것을 듣기를 원했다. 고대인들의 구전은 부분적으로 이러한 이야기들의 이 극적 요소 때문에 번성했다. 사람들은 신화를 들었고, 그것을 다시 얘기했고, 얘기한 다음에는 그것을 암기했고, 마침내 그것을 적었다. 그 점이 그것(= 신화)이 오늘날에도 여전히 존재하는 이유이다.

어휘 **myth** 신화(= mythology) **entertaining** 재미있는 **explanatory** 설명적인 **element** 요소 **religion** 종교 **classical** 고대 그리스 · 로마의; 고전적인 **seek** 추구하다; 찾다 **definitive** 확정적인 **seemingly** 겉으로 보기에 **constrain** 제한[제약]하다 **phenomena** (**phenomenon**의 복수형) 현상 **oral tradition** 구전(口傳) **ancient** 고대인 **thrive** 번성하다; 잘 자라다 **in part** 부분적으로 **existence** 존재

39 문장 넣기 ③

소재 이삿짐 상자 관리 방법

해설 주어진 문장은 하나의 중요 목록을 사용하여 모든 이삿짐 상자를 관리할 수 있다는 내용이므로, 이 문장 뒤에는 그 목록을 이용하는 구체적인 방법이 나와야 한다. 따라서 주어진 문장은 ③에 들어가는 것이 가장 적절하다.

해석 주제문 집을 이사할 때 무엇이 어느 상자에 들어 있는지를 파악하기 위한 체계를 마련하라. 굵은 매직 마커로 각 상자의 모든 네 옆면에 그 상자가 들어갈 방을 적어 놓으면, 당신은 상자가 어디로 가야 하는지 점검하는 수고를 덜 수 있을 것이다. 그런 다음 상자의 윗면에는 상자 속에 무엇이 들어 있는지, 예를 들면 '컵, 접시, 칼, 요리책'처럼 적을 수 있으나 '모든 것'의 목록을 작성하려고 하면 매우 성가실 수 있다는 것을 기억하라. 대신에 당신은 단 하나의 중요 목록으로 당신의 모든 상자를 관리할 수 있다. 각 방마다 부엌(kitchen)에는 K, 욕실(bathroom)에는 BTH와 같이 암호를 배정하고 당신의 목록에 코드와 각 상자의 숫자를 기록하라. 그런 다음 목록에 당신이 원하는 만큼 상자 내용물의 항목을 적을 수 있다. 즉, 만약 당신에게 욕실 물건이 든 상자가 세 개 있다면 당신의 목록은 이렇게 쓰여 있을 것이다. 'BTH1 : 수건', 'BTH2 : 모발 관리 제품', 'BTH3 : 전기 제품'.

구문 [4행~7행] With a thick magic marker, / **label**(V1) each box(O1) on all four sides **with** *the room* [(which) it goes in], // and this(S2) will save(V2) you(IO2) *the trouble*(DO2) (of checking where it goes).

「label A with B」는 'A에 B라는 라벨을 붙이다'라는 의미이다. the room은 목적격 관계대명사가 생략된 관계대명사절의 수식을 받는다. the trouble은 전명구 of checking ~ goes의 수식을 받으며, 여기에서 명사절 where is goes는 check의 목적어로 쓰였다.

어휘 **alternatively** 그 대신에 **manage** 관리하다 **master list** 중요 리스트[목록] *cf.* **list** 목록을 작성하다; 목록 **set up** 마련하다; 세우다 **keep track of** ~을 계속 파악하고 있다; ~을 추적하다 **trouble** 수고; 문제, 곤란 **annoying** 성가신, 짜증스러운 **assign** 배정[할당]하다 **content** 내용(물) **read** 쓰여 있다; 읽다 **electrical** 전기의; 전기를 이용하는

40 요약문 완성 ②

소재 자문화와 타문화의 수용력 차이

해설 순풍을 받으며 항해할 때는 바람이 있음을 눈치 채지 못하지만 역풍으로 항해할 때에 바람의 힘을 느끼는 것처럼, 자문화의 영향력은 거의 '인식하지(realize)' 못하지만 타문화를 맞닥뜨렸을 때는 그 힘을 매우 강하게 느끼고 익숙하지 않은 것에 '저항하게(resist)' 된다는 내용의 글이다. 따라서 정답은 ②이다.

해석 당신의 신념, 태도, 행동 그리고 편견은 당신이 가장 동일시하는 집단으로부터 배우게 된다. 당신 자신의 문화 내에서 산다는 것은 순풍을 받으며 항해하는 것과 같다. 바람이 당신을 함께 실어 날라 주는 것이며, 바람이 거기에 있다는 것을 거의 눈치 채지 못한다. 주제문 그러나 역풍으로 항해를 해야만 할 때마다 당신은 그것(= 바람)의 힘을 느낀다. 이것은 우리가 다른 문화를 대면하게 될 때 일어나는 일이다. 다른 문화의 바람은 우리의 얼굴에 정면으로 불어온다. 유럽을 방문하는 북미인들은 조그만 자동차와 좁은 도로를 이상하게 여길지도 모른다. 북미를 방문하고 있을 때, 아시아인들은 누군가의 집에 들어가기 전에 더러운 신발을 벗고 싶은 충동과 싸우고 있는 자신을 발견할지도 모른다. 그들은 또한 왜 그렇게 많은 사람들이 공원의 잔디밭을 맨발로 걸어 다니는 것을 즐거워하는지 의아하게 생각할지도 모른다.

⬇

우리는 자문화의 영향은 거의 (A) 인식하지 못하는 반면, 타문화의 힘은 매우 강력해서 우리가 익숙하지 않은 것에 (B) 저항할지도 모른다.

어휘 **prejudice** 편견, 선입견 **identify with** ~와 동일시하다 **along** 함께 **hardly** 거의 ~아니다 **force** 힘; 강요하다 **odd** 이상한; 홀수의 **instinct** 본능 **remove** 벗다; 제거하다 **wonder** 의아하게 여기다; 놀라다; 경탄 **barefoot** 맨발의; 맨발로 **overwhelming** 압도적인, 매우 강력한 **be accustomed to** ~에 익숙하다 [선택지 어휘] **analyze** 분석하다 **deny** 부정하다 **absorb** 흡수하다 **disregard** 무시하다

41~42 장문 41 ④ 42 ⑤

소재 온라인 자가진단의 문제점

해설 41. 온라인 자가진단에 의존하는 경향이 확산되고 있는데, 실제 연구 결과를 보면 온라인 자가진단은 대단히 부정확하고 건강 불안증을 증가시키는 등의 문제점이 많으므로 의사와 상담하는 것이 최선이라는 내용의 글이다. 따라서 제목으로 가장 적절한 것은 ④ '온라인 자가진단의 문제는 무엇인가?'이다.

① 인터넷이 건강 불안증의 도화선인가?
② 온라인 검색 행동과 그것의 영향
③ 당신의 건강에 대해 염려하는 것이 당신을 아프게 할 수 있다
⑤ 우리는 왜 우리의 증상을 인터넷에서 찾아보는가?

42. 온라인에서 집요하게 증상을 조사하고 심각한 질병으로 자가진단하는 것은 건강 불안증을 감소시키는 것이 아니라 증가시킬 수 있으므로 (e)의 reduce를 increase로 바꿔 써야 한다.

해석 당신이 아프다고 해 보자. 당신은 피로, 근육통, 메스꺼움을 겪고 있고 두통도 있다. 당신의 첫 번째 행동 방침은 무엇인가? 의사에게 전화하는 것인가, 인터넷에 의지하는 것인가? 당신의 답변이 후자라면, 당신은 (a) 혼자가 아니다. 한 인터넷 연구는 응답자의 4분의 3이 의사를 만나기 전에 그들의 증상을 진단하기 위해 웹사이트를 이용한다는 것을 발견했다. 인터넷 자가진단이 왜 그렇게 놀라울 정도로 (b) 인기를 얻게 되었는지를 이해하기는 쉽다. 우리는 힘이 있다고, 우리의 건강관리를 거의 제어하고 있다고 느낀다. 마우스 클릭으로 우리는 의학적 지식의 (c) 무한한 공급에 접근할 수 있으며, 병원 방문 일정을 짜는 데 요구되는 시간과 돈과 에너지를 절약한다. 그것은 완벽한 해답처럼 보인다. 주제문 하지만 온라인 자가진단은 부정확하며, 패닉을 유도하고, 신뢰성이 없다. 동일한

연구에서 의사들이 면밀히 검사를 한 사람들 중 90%는 그들의 자가진단이 (d) 틀렸다는 것을 알아냈다. 그리고 응답자 중 절반이 넘는 사람들이 인터넷 진단이 그들로 하여금 패닉을 일으키게 했다고 말했다. 그들은 집요하게 증상을 조사하고 심각한 질병으로 자가진단하려 할 것이다. 이는 건강 불안증을 (e) 감소시킬(→ 증가시킬) 수 있다. 인터넷 자가진단이 인생의 의학적 질문에 대한 실용적인 해결책처럼 보이지만, 당신의 의사와 상담하는 것이 항상 최선이다. 결국 한 시간의 인터넷 조사가 의대에서의 몇 년의 세월과 정말로 경쟁이 될 수 있겠는가? 당신 혹은 당신 자녀의 건강에 관한 한 아무리 주의해도 결코 지나치지 않다.

구문 [11행~14행] With the click of a mouse, / we can have access to an unlimited supply of medical knowledge, / V saving IO us DO *the time, money, and energy* [(which[that] scheduling a doctor's visit requires ●].
saving 이하는 분사구문이다. 「save+사람+사물」은 '~에게 …을 덜어주다[면하게 하다]'의 뜻이다. [ ] 부분은 목적격 관계대명사 which[that]가 생략된 관계사절로 the time, money, and energy를 수식한다. 관계사절에서 scheduling a doctor's visit이 동명사 주어이고 동사는 requires이다.

어휘 **fatigue** 피로 **soreness** 아픔, 고통 **nausea** 메스꺼움 **course of action** 행동 방침 **turn to** ~에 의지하다 **the latter** 후자 **respondent** 응답자 **diagnose** 진단하다 *cf.* **self-diagnosis** 자가진단 **symptom** 증상 **physician** 의사 **inaccurate** 부정확한 **induce** 유도하다 **unreliable** 신뢰할 수 없는 **follow up** 면밀히 조사하다; 잇따라 ~하다 **obsessively** 집요하게 **practical** 실용적인 **compete** 경쟁하다 **when it comes to A** A에 관한 한 [선택지 어휘] **trigger** 계기, 도화선; 방아쇠; 촉발하다

43~45 장문 43 ③ 44 ⑤ 45 ⑤

소재 말 목장을 갖겠다는 소년의 꿈

해설 43. Monty Roberts가 장래희망에 관한 글에서 목장을 소유하는 것에 대해 상세히 적었다는 이야기인 (A)에 이어서 Monty의 글에 적힌 꿈이 현실성이 없다고 지적하는 선생님의 이야기인 (C)가 와야 한다. 그럼에도 불구하고 글에 적힌 꿈의 내용을 바꾸지 않는 (D) 이후에 훗날 자신의 꿈을 이룬 Monty가 목장을 방문했던 그 선생님과의 일화를 사람들에게 말하는 (B)가 와야 한다.
44. (e)는 Monty Roberts를 가리키지만 나머지는 모두 선생님을 가리킨다.
45. (D)에서 Monty는 자신이 F를 받더라도 꿈을 지킬 거라고 말하며 똑같은 과제를 제출했으므로 ⑤가 일치하지 않는다.

해석 (A) Monty Roberts는 이리저리 이동하는 ① 말 조련사의 아들이었다. 그가 고등학교에서 최고학년이 되었을 때 그의 선생님은 그에게 그가 커서 되고 싶고 하고 싶은 것에 대해 글을 쓸 것을 요구했다. ② 그는 자기 꿈에 대해 대단히 상세히 썼고 거대한 목장의 그림을 그리기까지 했다. 그리고 그는 200에이커의 꿈의 목장 위에 자리할 4,000제곱피트 주택의 상세한 평면도를 그렸다.
(C) 그는 과제에 열정을 쏟았고 선생님에게 그것을 제출했다. 그것을 돌려받았을 때, 첫 페이지에는 "방과 후 나를 보러 오거라."라고 쓰인 쪽지와 함께 커다란 빨간 F가 있었다. 꿈을 가진 소년은 그 선생님을 보러 갔고 (b) 그(= 선생님)에게 물었다. "왜 제가 F를 받았죠?" (c) 그(= 선생님)는 말했다. "④ 이건 너에게는 비현실적인 꿈이야. 말 목장을 소유하는 것은 엄청난 돈이 필요해. 너는 절대로 이걸 갖지 못할 거다."
(D) 그리고 교사는 덧붙였다. "네가 이 글을 다시 쓴다면 네 점수를 재고하겠다." 소년은 집으로 가서 아버지에게 조언을 구했다. 아버지가 말했다. "아들아, 보렴. (d) 그(= 선생님)의 말을 심각하게 받아들이지 말거라. 그러나 이것은 아주 중요한 결정이란다." ⑤ 결국, 소년은 전혀 다른 게 없는 똑같은 글을 제출했다. (e) 그(= Monty Roberts)는 말했다. "선생님은 계속 F를 주셔도 돼요. 전 계속 제 꿈을 지키겠어요."
(B) 그리고 장면이 전환되어, 이제 Monty는 모여 있는 집단에게 몸을 돌려 말한다. "저는 여러분이 여기 저의 말 목장에 있기 때문에 여러분에게 이 이야기를 합니다. ③ 저는 여전히 그 학교 과제를 가지고 있습니다." 그는 덧붙인다. "최고의 부분은 두 해 전 여름에 그 학교 선생님이 저의 목장에 30명의 아이들을 데려왔다는 것입니다. (a) 그(= 선생님)는 떠날 때 말씀하셨습니다. "나는 수많은 아이들의 꿈을 훔쳤단다. 다행히 너는 네 꿈을 포기하지 않을 힘을 가지고 있었지."

구문 [(A) 2행~4행] When he was a senior in high school, // his teacher asked him to write an essay about **what** he hoped to be and do // when he grew up.
전치사 about의 목적어인 what 이하 절에서 동사 hoped의 목적어로 to be와 (to) do가 병렬구조를 이루고 있다.

어휘 **(A) travel** 이동하다; 여행하다 **diagram** 그림, 도표 **floor plan** (건물의) 평면도 **(B) scene** 장면; 경치 **assemble** 모이다; 조립하다 **ranch** 목장 **(C) put one's heart into** ~에 골몰[열중]하다 **assignment** 과제 **receive** 받다 **unrealistic** 비현실적인 **require** 필요로 하다; 요구하다 **(D) reconsider** 재고하다 **state** 말하다, 진술하다; 상태; 지위

실전 모의고사 10

본문 p.139

18 ③	19 ③	20 ④	21 ③	22 ④	23 ⑤	24 ⑤	25 ④	26 ⑤	27 ⑤
28 ④	29 ④	30 ②	31 ③	32 ①	33 ⑤	34 ①	35 ③	36 ④	37 ③
38 ③	39 ④	40 ⑤	41 ④	42 ②	43 ②	44 ⑤	45 ②		

18 글의 목적 ③

소재 개인 지도 교사 모집

해설 앞부분에서 Sunshine Tutoring의 프로그램을 소개한 뒤, 개인 지도 교사 공석에 대해 언급하며 독자들에게 공석을 채울 것을 독려하는 글이다. 따라서 글의 목적으로 가장 적절한 것은 ③이다.

해석 장래의 개인 지도 선생님들께,
15년이 넘도록, Sunshine Tutoring은 초중등 학생들에게 그들이 성공하기 위해 필요한 수단들을 제공해 왔습니다. 상을 받은 저희의 컴퓨터 기반 읽기, 쓰기 그리고 수학 프로그램 시스템은 어디에서도 최고입니다. 물론, 진정한 마법은 저희의 훌륭하고 헌신적인 개인 지도 교사들로부터 옵니다. 여기가 여러분이 참여하실 곳입니다! 주제문 Sunshine Tutoring에는 현재 개인 지도 교사를 위한 공석이 있습니다. 여러분께서 어린 학습자들을 일대일로 가르칠 기회를 원하신다면, 지금이 기회입니다. 모든 수업 자료와 교육이 제공되고, 학생들은 면밀한 테스트 후에 개인 지도 교사와 짝이 지어집니다. 주변에서 가장 훌륭한 개인 교습 학원의 일원이 되세요! 더 많은 정보를 위해서는 www.sunshineacademy.com을 오늘 방문하십시오.
감사합니다.

구문 [2행~4행] For over 15 years, / Sunshine Tutoring has **provided** elementary and middle school students(A) **with** *the tools*(B) [(which[that]) they need ● to succeed].
「provide A with B」는 'A에게 B를 제공하다'라는 뜻이다. [ ] 부분은 목적격 관계대명사 which 또는 that이 생략된 관계대명사절로 선행사 the tools를 수식한다.

어휘 **tutor** 개인 지도 교사; 개인 교습을 하다 **tool** 수단, 도구; 공구, 연장 **award-winning** 상을 받은 **dedicated** 헌신적인 **opening** 공석, 빈자리; 구멍, 틈 **one-on-one** 일대일(로) **material** (수업) 자료; 재료; 물질의, 물질적인 **training** (특정 직업에 필요한) 교육, 훈련, 연수 **match with** ~와 짝을 맞추다

19 분위기 추론 ③

소재 왕의 행렬을 기다리는 사람들

해설 왕의 행렬을 보기 위해 모여든 사람들이 기대에 차서 웅성거리는 장면을 묘사하고 있다. 왕의 행렬이 올 도로를 지켜보고 있는 군중들의 모습에서 '들뜨고 기대에 찬 (exciting and expectant)' 분위기를 느낄 수 있으므로 정답은 ③이다.

해석 외딴 마을과 고립된 고지대에서 온 방문객들이 도착하기 시작했을 때 태양은 정면으로 그들을 향하고 있었다. 캐스터브리지의 모든 노동자는 가장 깨끗한 셔츠를 입고 있었다. 갑자기 군중 중에서 키 큰 사람들은 고개를 돌리고, 키 작은 사람들은 발끝을 세웠다. 주제문 줄을 따라서 소곤거리는 소리가 번져가기 시작했다. 왕의 행렬이 다가오고 있는 것이다! 아직 철로가 캐스터브리지까지 이르지 못해, 런던에서부터 남은 여정은 도로를 따라 걸어야 했다. 주제문 그래서 종이 울리고 사람들이 수군거리는 가운데, 모두 기다리며 멀리 뻗어 있는 런던 도로를 바라보았다. 왕이 온다는 것을 거의 믿을 수 없다는 듯이.
① 고요하고 평화로운
② 희망적이고 매혹적인
④ 영광스럽고 의기양양한
⑤ 실망스럽고 지루한

구문 [9행~13행] Thus, amid the ringing of bells and the chattering of tongues, / everybody waited and watched the far-stretching London highway, / hardly **believing** that the king would ever come.
believing 이하는 주절의 동사(waited and watched)와 부대상황을 나타내는 분사구문이다.

어휘 **full-faced** 정면을 향한 **confront** 직면하다, 마주하다 **remote** 외딴; (거리 · 시간이) 먼 **upland** 《주로 복수형》 고지대 **crowd** (길거리에 모인) 군중, 무리 **stand on tip-toe** 발끝으로 서다 **whisper** 속삭임, 소곤거리는 소리; 속삭이다 **royal** 국왕[여왕]의 **approach** 다가오다 **remainder** 나머지 **amid** (흥분 · 공포 등이 느껴지는) 가운데 **chatter** 수다를 떨다; 재잘거림 **far-stretching** 멀리 뻗은 [선택지 어휘] **expectant** 기대하는 **triumphant** 의기양양한; 큰 승리를 거둔

20 필자 주장 ④

소재 대학 운동 시설 설립 요청

해설 대학에서 학생들을 위한 운동 시설이나 프로그램을 전혀 지원하지 않아서 학생들이 운동할 공간이 없다는 내용의 글이다. 마지막 문장(It's time ~ this problem.)에 이 문제에 대한 조치가 필요하다는 필자의 주장이 드러나 있으므로 정답은 ④이다.

해석 전국 곳곳에서 사람들이 수영, 조깅, 요가를 하고 벨리 댄스 수업을 듣는 등 건강을 유지하기 위해 무엇이든지 하고 있습니다. 신문, 잡지와 웹사이트에서는 우리가 건강 혁명의 한가운데 있다고 주장합니다. 이런 긍정적인 추세와는 정반대로, 우리 대학은 운동 시설과 스포츠 프로그램에 대한 재정적 지원 및 부지를 제공하는 것을 계속 거부하고 있습니다. 올해 들어 지금까지, 행정관계자들은 축구장 주위에 육상 트랙을 설치해 달라는 요청을 거절했으며, 사용하지 않는 대학 부지에 수영장을 건설하겠다는 어느 기부자의 제의도 거절했고, 심지어 학생들을 위한 댄스 프로그램을 시작하는 것조차 거절했습니다. 따라서 학생들은 자신의 방 안을 제외하고는 어디에서도 운동할 곳이 없습니다! 주제문 대학의 행정관계자들이 이 문제에 대해 무언가 긍정적인 조치를 취해야 할 때입니다.

구문 [7행~11행] ~, the administrators(S) have denied(V1) *a request* (for a running track around the football field), / (have) rejected(V2) *a donor's offer* (to build a swimming pool on unused college land), / and (have) even refused(V3) to begin a dance program for students.
주어는 the administrators이고 세 개의 동사구가 and로 병렬 연결되어 있으며 두 번째와 세 번째 동사 앞에는 완료시제의 have가 생략되어 있다.
[13행~14행] **It's time** (that) college administrators **did** something positive about this problem.
「It is time (that)+가정법 과거」는 '(마땅히 ~할 때가 되었는데 안 하고 있을 때) 이제 ~할 때다'란 뜻이다. that절의 동사는 「should+동사원형」으로도 바꿔 쓸 수 있다.
e.g. **It is time** that you **thought**[**should think**] of your future.
(네 장래에 대해 생각해봐야 할 때이다.)

어휘 **all over** 곳곳에, 전역에 **keep fit** 건강을 유지하다 *cf.* **fitness** 건강, 신체 단련 **claim (that)** (~이 사실이라고) 주장하다 **in the middle of**

~의 한가운데에, ~의 중간[도중]에 **in direct opposition to** ~와 정반대로 **trend** 추세, 동향 **financial** 재정의, 금융의 **facility** 시설, 설비 **so far** 지금까지 **administrator** 행정관, 관리인 **deny** 거부[거절]하다; 부인[부정]하다 **request** 요청; 요청하다 **donor** 기부자 **nowhere** 어디에도 (~ 없다)

21 글의 요지 ③

소재 비언어적 단서를 통한 거짓말 감지

해설 평균적으로 사람들이 거짓말을 많이 하는 것에 비해 그것을 알아낼 수 있는 확률은 낮은데, 이러한 문제를 해결하기 위해 상대방의 비언어적인 단서들에 주의를 기울이는 것이 도움이 된다는 내용이므로 ③이 글의 요지로 적절하다.

해석 누군가가 당신에게 거짓말을 하고 있다고 생각해 본 적이 있는가? 당신의 직관이 아마도 옳았을 것인데, 사람들은 10분의 대화를 하는 동안 평균적으로 두세 번 거짓말을 하기 때문이다. 훨씬 더 놀랄 만한 것은 사람들 중 91퍼센트가 가정과 직장에서 정기적으로 거짓말을 한다는 것이다. 하지만 우리는 그러한 거짓말들을 겨우 절반 정도만 알아낼 수 있는데 이것은 동전 던지기나 다름없는 것(확률)이다. 얼굴 표정, 손짓, 신체 움직임과 목소리 톤과 같은 비언어적 행동을 풀어내고 해석하는 방법을 배우는 것이 의사소통의 필수적인 부분이다. 사람과 사람 사이의 의사소통의 93퍼센트가 비언어적인 것인데도, 우리는 자주 모든 우리의 상호작용의 근거를 언어적인 내용에만 둔다. 주제문 그러한 비언어적 단서들에 주의를 기울임으로써, 당신과 함께 있는 사람이 당신을 속이려 하는 것인지 아닌지를 더 이상 속수무책으로 궁금해하지 않게 될 것이다.

구문 [6행~9행] Learning how to decode and interpret *nonverbal behavior* (such as facial expressions, gestures, physical movements and vocal tone) / is an integral part of communication.
(S: Learning ~ vocal tone, V: is, C: an integral part of communication)

how to decode ~ vocal tone은 동명사 Learning의 목적어이며, ( ) 부분은 앞의 nonverbal behavior를 수식한다. 동명사구 주어이므로 동사는 단수동사 is를 썼다.

[12행~14행] By paying attention to such nonverbal cues, / you will no longer wonder helplessly // **if** *the person* [(whom) you are with] is trying to deceive you.

여기서 if는 '~인지 아닌지'의 의미이며, 동사 will wonder의 목적어 역할을 하는 명사절을 이끈다. [ ] 부분은 목적격 관계대명사가 생략된 관계대명사절로 선행사 the person을 수식한다.

어휘 **lie** 거짓말(하다); 눕다 **intuition** 직관(력), 직감 **on average** 평균적으로 **frightening** 놀랄 만한; 무서운, 두려운 **regularly** 정기적으로 **detect** 알아내다, 탐지하다 **no better than** ~이나 다름없는 **toss** 던지기; 던지다 **decode** 풀다; 해독하다 **interpret** 해석[이해]하다 **nonverbal** 비언어적인(↔ **verbal** 언어적인; 구두의) **physical** 신체의 **vocal** 목소리의 **integral** 필수적인 **interpersonal** 사람과 사람 사이의 **base A on B** A의 근거를 B에 두다 **interaction** 상호작용 **content** 내용 **pay attention to A** A에 주의를 기울이다 **cue** 단서; 신호 **no longer** 더 이상 ~않다 **wonder** 궁금해하다; 경탄, 경이(감) **helplessly** 속수무책으로, 속절없이 **deceive** 속이다, 기만하다

22 글의 주제 ④

소재 유산 관광의 특성

해설 유산 관광(heritage tourism)은 수요가 공급을 만들어내는 다른 산업들과는 달리 공급(유산)이 수요(관광객)에 선행하며 유형과 무형의 요소가 있음을 설명하는 내용이다. 유산 관광의 특성을 개괄적으로 설명하고 있으므로 주제로 가장 적절한 것은 ④ '유산 관광의 독특한 특성들의 개요'이다.

해석 유산 관광에서는 공급이 보통 수요에 선행한다. 일부 관광 유형을 포함하여 대부분의 다른 산업에서는 일반적으로 수요가 공급에 선행한다. 유산 공급은 물질적 대상을 포함하는데, 무엇보다도 특히 역사적으로 중요한 건물, 차량, 도시와 소도시, 시골의 문화적 경치, 역사 유적지, 박물관과 이동이 쉬운 유물들이 있다. 그것은 또한 이전 세대들로부터 전승되어 오늘날 어떤 형태로 감상되고 사용되거나 소비되는 문화와 역사의 무형 요소도 포함한다. 무형 유산의 가장 좋은 예 중 일부는 음악과 춤, 문화 전통, 사회관습, 언어, 사회적 연결망, 조리법과 요리, 세계관, 이민과 문화적 다양성, 생활 방식, 시와 미술, 그리고 문학을 포함한다. 주제문 이러한 과거의 유무형의 특색들은 결합되어 관광업을 위한 가장 중요한 명소의 토대 중 하나를 형성하며, 정말로 관광 상품의 많은 부분을 구현한다.

① 유산 관광이 선호되는 이유
② 관광 상품 개발의 필요성
③ 미래 세대를 위한 유산 관광의 전망
⑤ 문화유산 보존과 증진의 중요성

구문 [15행~18행] These intangible and tangible features of the past / combine to make one of the most prominent attraction bases for tourism, [and] indeed embody much of the tourism product.
(S: These intangible and tangible features of the past, V1: combine, V2: embody)

These ~ of the past 부분이 주어이며 동사는 combine과 embody가 병렬구조를 이루고 있다.

어휘 **heritage** (국가 · 사회의) 유산 **supply** 공급 **precede** 선행하다 **demand** 수요; 요구 **industry** 산업 **material** 물질의; 유형의 **object** 대상; 물체 **notably** 특히; 현저히 **historic** 역사적으로 중요한 *cf.* **historical** 역사상의, 역사와 관련된 **vehicle** 차량; 운송 수단 **rural** 시골의 **portable** 휴대[이동]가 쉬운; 휴대용 제품 **encompass** (많은 것을) 포함하다; 에워싸다 **pass down from** ~로부터 전하다 **appreciate** 감상하다; 진가를 인정하다 **foodways** 식생활 습관; 조리법 **cuisine** 요리(법) **worldview** 세계관 **immigration** 이민, 이주 **tangible** 유형의, 만질 수 있는 **feature** 특징 **prominent** 중요한; 유명한 **embody** 구현[상징]하다 [선택지 어휘] **prospect** 전망; 가망, 가능성 **conserve** 보존하다 **promote** 증진하다; 장려하다; 승진시키다

23 글의 제목 ⑤

소재 아동 탈수증

해설 아이들에게 나타나는 탈수증의 증상(Some of the common symptoms ~.)과 원인(The most common cause ~.)에 대해 설명하고 있으므로, 글의 제목으로 가장 적절한 것은 ⑤ '아동 탈수증: 원인과 증상'이다.

해석 주제문 탈수증은 체액의 극심한 손실로 정의되는 의학적 질병이다. 아이들은 어른들보다 탈수증으로 고통 받을 가능성이 더 크다. 아동 탈수증의 흔한 증상에는 무기력함, 땀을 많이 흘리는 것, 화장실에 너무 자주 가는 것, 구토를 심하게 하는 것, 혹은 이들 증상이 함께 나타나는 것이 있다. 아동 탈수증의 가장 흔한 원인은 독감 같은 바이러스나 박테리아에 의해 생기는 감염이다. 아이들은 더러운 것을 만지고 손을 잘 씻지 않는 경향이 있기 때문에 이러한 전염병에 더 자주 걸린다. 탈수증은 아이들에게 특히 해로운데, 아이들은 어른들보다 더 약하고 자신을 잘 돌보지 못하기 때문이다.

① 아동 탈수증의 응급 처치
② 체액 손실을 사전에 예방하는 법
③ 노인에게 있어서 탈수증의 위험
④ 수분 섭취: 가장 좋은 탈수증 치료법

구문 [7행~9행] *The most common causes* (of dehydration in children) are *infections* (caused by viruses such as the flu or by bacteria).
(S: The most common causes, V: are, C: infections)

caused by viruses ~ or by bacteria는 infections를 수식하는 과거분사구이다.

어휘 **dehydration** 탈수(증) **condition** 질병; 조건 **define** 정의하다 **extreme** 극심한, 극도의 **loss** 손실 **body fluid** (혈액 · 림프액 등의) 체액 *cf.* **fluid** 유체((액체 · 기체의 총칭)) **be likely to-v** v할 가능성이 있다;

v하기 쉽다 **suffer from** ~로 고통 받다 **symptom** 증상 **vomit** 토하다 **combination** 결합 **infection** 감염; 전염병 **flu** 독감, 인플루엔자 **tend to-v** v하는 경향이 있다 [선택지 어휘] **first aid** 응급 처치 **prevent** 예방하다 **in advance** 미리, 앞서 **cure** 치료(법); 치료하다

24 도표 이해 ⑤

소재 이공계에서 수여된 석사 학위 수

해설 2010년에서 2019년까지 가장 낮은 증가율을 보인 분야는 자연 과학(physical sciences) 분야이므로 정답은 ⑤이다.

해석 〈분야별 이공계 석사 학위 (2010~2019)〉

주제문 위 그래프는 2010년에서 2019년까지 이공계에서 수여된 석사 학위 수를 보여준다. ① 이 기간 동안, 공학 분야에서 수여된 석사 학위는 나머지 어떤 분야보다 더 많았고, 그 수는 2019년에 최고조에 달했다. ② 컴퓨터 공학 분야에서 수여된 석사 학위가 2위를 차지했고 주어진 기간 내내 15,000건 이상에 머물렀다. ③ 그와 동시에, 생명 과학과 농업 과학 분야의 석사 학위 수는 2010년에 10,000건을 갓 넘었던 것에서 2019년에는 거의 15,000건에 이르도록 점차 증가했다. ④ 자연 과학 분야의 석사 학위는 2010년에 수학 분야의 그것(= 석사 학위)보다 조금 더 흔했지만(= 많았지만), 2019년 무렵에는 5,000건을 약간 넘는 정도로 동일했다. ⑤ 이 기간을 통틀어, 수학 분야에서 석사 학위가 가장 적게 수여되었고, 2010년에서 2019년까지 가장 낮은 증가율을 보였다.

어휘 **master's degree** 석사 학위 **field** 분야 **award** 수여하다; 상 **peak** 최고조에 달하다; 최고조; (산의) 정상 **remain** 머무르다; 남다; 계속 ~이다 **throughout** 내내, ~동안 쭉 **agricultural** 농업의 **physical science** 자연 과학 **common** 흔한, 보통의 **tie** 동점을 이루다; 묶다 **rate** 비율; 속도; 요금; 평가하다

25 내용 불일치 ④

소재 소설가 Jane Austen

해설 Jane Austen의 작품 중 4편의 소설만이 사후가 아닌 생전에 출판되었다고 했으므로 ④는 글의 내용과 일치하지 않는다.

해석 Jane Austen은 1775년에서 1817년까지 살았던 영국 최초의 여성 소설가였다. ① Jane은 대가족 속에서 성장했다. 그녀는 여섯 명의 오빠와 한 명의 언니 Cassandra가 있었는데, 그녀는 Jane의 소설 아이디어에 도움이 되는 조력자였다. ② 그 둘은 등장인물들과 그들의 역할, 그들의 삶을 토론하고, 결과적으로 그들(= 등장인물들)이 그들(= Jane과 Cassandra)에게 '사실적으로' 보이도록 만들었다. Jane의 유일한 교육적 배경은 친척과 Reading Ladies Boarding School에 짧게 출석한 데서 나왔다. 그녀는 소녀 시절에 이야기를 썼다. 결혼하지 않은 채로 살면서 그녀는 ③ 그 당시 사회에서의 여성의 위치를 보여주는 소설을 창작했다. 그녀의 작품들은 많은 수정을 거친 후에야 출판되었다. ④ 그녀가 살아있는 동안 그녀의 소설 중 단지 4편만 출판되었다. Jane은 41세의 이른 나이에 죽었지만, ⑤ 그녀의 소설은 영문학의 학문적인 연구 프로그램의 중요한 부분으로 남아있다.

구문 [4행~6행] The two would discuss(V1) the characters, their roles, their lives, [and] in turn make(V2) them(O) seem as 'real'(C) to them.

동사 discuss와 make가 병렬구조를 이루고 있다. 사역동사 make 다음에 목적격 보어로 원형부정사 seem이 나왔다. 첫 번째 대명사 them은 the characters를 가리키고, 두 번째 them은 the two(= Jane and Cassandra)를 가리킨다.

어휘 **assistant** 조력자, 조수 **in turn** 결과적으로; 차례차례 **relative** 친척 **attendance** 출석 **boarding school** 기숙학교 **unwed** 미혼의 **revision** 수정, 개정 **academic** 학문의; 학구적인 **literature** 문학

26 안내문 불일치 ⑤

소재 길 잃은 반려동물 발견자 안전 수칙

해설 전문가의 도움 없이 상처 입은 고양이를 만지지 말라고 했고, 사람이 길 잃은 고양이에게 물리거나 할큄을 당했을 경우 즉시 치료를 받아야 한다고 했으므로 ⑤가 안내문의 내용과 일치하지 않는다.

해석

길 잃은 반려동물 안전 정보

반려동물들은 달아나 그들의 가족들에게서 떨어지게 될 수 있습니다. 여러분이 길 잃은 반려동물을 발견한다면 www.petsafety.org에서 여러분 지역의 보호소를 찾아서 조언을 구하기 위해 즉시 전화하시기 바랍니다.

길 잃은 고양이를 발견했을 때 할 일

- ① 고양이에게 음식과 물을 제공합니다.
- ② 고양이를 강제로 여러분의 차에 태우려고 하지 마세요.
- 전문가의 도움 없이 상처 입은 고양이를 만지지 마세요.
- ③ 고양이를 보호소로 데려가도록 조치해서 그 고양이가 마이크로칩을 검사받아 보호소의 잃어버린 동물 명단에 포함될 수 있도록 해주세요.
- ④ 그 고양이를 다른 반려동물들과 떨어지게 하여 잠재적인 싸움이나 질병의 확산이 일어나지 않도록 하세요.
- ⑤ 여러분이 물리거나 할큄을 당한다면 그 상처가 경미하더라도 즉시 치료를 받으세요.

구문 [12행~14행] Arrange for the cat to go to a shelter // so it can be scanned for a microchip / [and] (can be) included in the shelter's lost pet listings.

included는 앞에 나온 can be에 이어지는 수동태에 쓰인 과거분사로, 등위접속사 and에 의해 병렬 연결되어 있다.

어휘 **break loose** 도주하다; 속박에서 벗어나다 **local** 지역의 **shelter** 보호소 **arrange for** 조치하다; 준비하다 **scan** 검사하다; 훑어보다 **keep A away from B** A를 B에 가까이 하지 않게 하다 **potential** 잠재적인; 잠재력 **spread** 확산, 전파; 퍼지다 **medical attention** 치료 **minor** 작은, 가벼운 (↔ **major** 중요한)

27 안내문 일치 ⑤

소재 청년 연설 대회 안내

해설 마지막 문장에서 연설은 5분에서 30초 내외 길이어야 하며, 그보다 짧거나 긴 연설은 감점을 받을 것이라고 했으므로 ⑤가 안내문의 내용과 일치한다.

해석

청년 연설 대회

① 매년 농업국은 군(郡) 단위에서 시작하는 청년 연설 대회를 주관합니다. ② 2020년의 주제는 '식품 안전은 미국 국민들에게 있어 중요한 문제이다. 플로리다 농업국은 어떻게 하면 미래를 위한 수준 높은 해결책을 계속해서 제시할 수 있을 것인가?'입니다.

규칙

- ③ 참가자들은 최소 14세이어야 하며 2020년 9월 19일 당일 또는 그 이전에 18세를 넘으면 안 됩니다.
- 참가자는 직접 연설문을 준비하고 발표해야 합니다. ④ 어떠한 형태의 화상 회의 또는 시각 자료도 허용되지 않습니다.
- ⑤ 연설은 5분을 기준으로 30초 내외이며 (기준 시간보다) 너무 짧거나 긴 연설은 감점을 받게 됩니다.

어휘 **bureau** 국(局), 부서 **sponsor** 주관하다; 후원하다 **county** 군(郡), 카운티(주 아래의 지역 단위) **agriculture** 농업 **quality** 양질의; 품질; 특성 **competitor** (시합) 참가자; 경쟁자 **personally** 직접; 개인적으로 **video**

10

conferencing 화상 회의 visual aids 시각 자료 result in (결과적으로) ~을 낳다[야기하다] subtract 빼다, 감하다

28 네모 어법 ④

소재 바넘 효과

해설 (A) 사람들이 '자기 자신'에 대해 일반적이고 애매하게 묘사하는 것을 정확하다고 받아들이는 경향이 있다는 문맥이므로 재귀대명사인 themselves가 와야 한다.
(B) 「make+O+C」 구조이다. 문맥상 목적어와 목적격보어의 관계가 수동(이끌리다)이 되어야 하므로 attracted가 알맞다.
(C) be동사의 보어 역할을 하는 명사절을 이끌며 뒤에 주어, 동사가 완전한 절이 오므로 접속사 that이 알맞다. what은 선행사를 포함하는 관계대명사이므로 이어지는 절이 불완전하다.

해석 왜 별점과 손금 보기가 그렇게 오랫동안 인기를 끌어왔을까? 주제문 (이를 설명 할 수 있는) 한 가지 설명은 '바넘 효과'이다. 이것은 사람들이 자신에 대해 매우 일반적이거나 막연하게 묘사하는 것을 정확하다고 받아들이는 경향이다. 이는 P. T. Barnum의 이름을 따서 명명되었는데, 그는 멋진 서커스 공연에 '모든 사람들이 그 요소에 끌리는 어떤 것이 조금씩 들어 있다'고 믿었다. 별점이나 손금을 보면 이런 말을 자주 듣는다. "당신은 사용하지 않은 능력이 많이 있네요. 당신은 가끔 수줍어하지요." 사람들은 그런 말들이 어찌나 '정확한지'에 자주 놀라곤 한다. 비결은 그런 일반적인 말이 거의 누구에게나 다 정확하게 들린다는 것이다.

어휘 palm reading 손금 보기 tendency 경향, 추세 vague 애매한, 막연한 characterization (성격) 묘사; 특징짓기 accurate 정확한 name after ~의 이름을 따서 명명하다 element 요소, 성분; 원소 at times 가끔, 때때로 amazed 놀란, 경탄한 trick 비결; 속임수

29 밑줄 어휘 ④

소재 스포츠 연출의 특성

해설 스포츠 방송 제작은 복잡성과 많은 변수 때문에 고도로 조직되고 통제된 제작이 필요하다는 내용의 글이다. 제작자가 행사 안팎의 예측할 수 없는 일들(unpredictable occurrences)에 대응해야 한다는 것은 불확실성과 의미가 통하므로, ④ certainty는 uncertainty(불확실성)로 고쳐야 한다.

해석 주제문 텔레비전으로 방송되는 스포츠의 연출은 고도로 조직되고 통제된 제작을 포함한다. 스포츠 행사 제작과 관련된 ① 복잡성 때문에 가능한 한 많은 변수를 통제하는 것이 중요하다. 제작 스태프에는 보통 제작자, 감독, 실황 방송 아나운서, 카메라 기사, 영상과 음향 조절 기사, 그리고 기술자들 사이의 계급에 따른 업무 ② 분배가 일반적으로 포함된다. 각각의 개인에게는 분명하게 규정된 책임이 있고, 그것은 그들이 장비의 어떤 결함에도 불구하고 (그 책임을) ③ 이행할 것으로 기대되는 것이다. 유연성도 훌륭한 자질이긴 하지만, 각각은 기술과 이전의 경험에 따라 특정한 역할에 고용된다. (일과) 관련된 압박은 시간제한뿐 아니라 ④ 확실성(→ 불확실성)에서도 오는데, 그 이유는 제작자들은 행사 내부적인 것과 외부적인 것 둘 다에서 예측할 수 없는 사건에 대응해야 하기 때문이다. 따라서 경기 그 자체는 ⑤ 대본이 없을 수 있지만, 스포츠 행사의 제작은 가능한 한 조직화된다.

구문 [8행~10행] Each individual has *clearly defined responsibilities*, // **which** they are expected to fulfill / despite any deficiencies in equipment.
which 이하는 clearly defined responsibilities를 보충 설명하는 관계대명사절이다.

[13행~16행] *The pressures* (involved) come / **not just** from time limitations **but also** from uncertainty, // as producers have to react to unpredictable occurrences / both within the event and external to **it**.
「not just A but also B」는 'A뿐만 아니라 B도'라는 의미이다. it은 앞에 나온 the event를 의미한다.

어휘 presentation 연출 involve 포함하다; 관련시키다 production 제작; 생산 complexity 복잡성 variable 변수; 가변적인 hierarchical 계급[계층]에 따른 division of labor 분업 typically 보통, 일반적으로 operator (장치) 조작자, 기사 define 규정하다 fulfill 이행하다, 수행하다 deficiency 결함; 결핍 equipment 장비, 설비 previous 이전의 flexibility 유연성 desired 훌륭한, 바람직한 pressure 압박; 압력 limitation 제한, 한정 certainty 확실성 occurrence 사건; 발생 external 외부의 unscripted 대본이 없는

30 지칭 대상 ②

소재 발음하기 어려운 이름을 제대로 말하려고 노력한 Sid 삼촌

해설 나머지는 모두 Theo를 지칭하나 ②는 필자의 삼촌인 Sid를 가리킨다. 식료품점을 방문한 것은 필자의 삼촌인 Sid이다. 참고로 Sid는 식료품점 공급업자이며, 그가 방문하는 식료품점의 주인이 그리스 사람인 Theo이다.

해석 주제문 어떤 이름들은 발음하기 어려울 수 있다. 그러나 많은 사람들은 누군가의 이름을 제대로 말하는 법을 배우려고 노력조차 하지 않는다. 식료품점 공급업자인 나의 삼촌 Sid Levy에게는 Theodoros Andriopoulos(테오도로스 안드리오폴로스)라는 이름의 고객이 있었다. 대부분의 사람들은 ① 그(= Theo)를 그냥 Theo라고 불렀다. 그러나 Sid 삼촌은 ② 그(= Sid)가 (식료품점을) 방문하기 전에 그 이름을 말하는 정확한 방법을 배우는 데 특별한 노력을 기울였다. Sid 삼촌이 Theo의 식료품점에 들어서서 완벽한 그리스 억양으로 "안녕하세요, Theodoros Andriopoulos 씨."라고 말하자 ③ 그(= Theo)는 충격을 받았다. 한동안 ④ 그(= Theo)로부터 아무런 대답이 없었다. 마침내 ⑤ 그(= Theo)는 그의 두 눈에 눈물을 글썽이면서 "나의 친구여, 내가 조국을 떠난 지 20년이 되었지만 내 이름을 우리 가족이 불러주던 것처럼 똑같이 말해주는 걸 들어보기는 처음입니다."라고 말했다.

구문 [12행~15행] ~, "My friend, / in the 20 years since I left my country, / this(S) is(V) *the only time*(C) [(when) I've heard(V') my name(O') spoken(C') // just like my family used to say it]."
선행사(the only time)를 수식하는 관계부사절에서 관계부사가 생략된 형태이다. 「hear+O+C」의 목적격보어 자리에 과거분사 spoken이 쓰였으므로 '이름이 불리는 걸 듣다'란 뜻이다.

어휘 pronounce 발음하다; 선언[선고]하다 make an effort to-v v하려고 노력하다 properly 제대로, 적절히 supplier 공급업자, 공급업체 Greek 그리스(인)의 accent 억양, 말씨; 강세 for a while 한동안 used to-v (예전에는) v하곤 했다; v이었다

31 빈칸 추론 ③

소재 노래를 이용한 사과하기

해설 빈칸 문장을 먼저 읽고, 누군가에게 사과하기 위한 노래를 고를 때 '무엇'이 중요한지를 찾도록 한다. 빈칸 바로 앞 문장에서 당신이 처한 상황이나 사과하려는 사람과의 관계에 그 노래가 적절하다면, 사과를 더 효과적으로 만들어 줄 것이라고 했으므로 빈칸에 들어갈 정답은 ③ '연관성'이다.

해석 주제문 사과에 당신만의 특별한 느낌을 더할 수 있는 많은 창의적인 방법이 있고, 노래를 이용하는 것은 가장 좋은 방법 중 하나이다. 예를 들어, (그룹) 시카고의 'Hard to Say I'm Sorry(미안하다고 말하기 어려워)'라는 노래는 더 좋은 파트너가 되겠다고 약속하는 것에 관한 아름다운 가사를 담고 있다. 당신은 편지에 그 노래를 포함시킴으로써 당신의 사과를 더 효과적으로 만들 수 있다. 다음으로 당신이 나누는 (당신이) 가장 좋아하는 노래와 그것을 어떻게 사과에 끌어들일 수 있을지, 혹은 어떻게 선물로 줄지를 생각해 보되 그 노래를 상황과 연관시켜야 함을 기억하라. 아마도 그것은 당신이 첫 데이트에서 당신의 파트너와 춤추었던 노래일 수도 있다. 아니면 잊지 못할 휴가 때 둘이 함께 그 노래를 들었을지도 모른다. 그것이 어떤 중요한 면에서 당신들의 관계나 그 상황에 적절하다면 음악이나 가사를 더하는 것은 당신의 사과를 더 괜찮게 만들어줄 것이다. 연관성

이 "미안해"라고 말하기 위한 노래를 선택할 때 성공의 열쇠이다.
① 정직성 ② 인내심 ④ 신속함 ⑤ 용기

구문 [7행~9행] ~, think about *a favorite song* [that you share ●] and how you can **bring** it into your apology or (how you can) **offer** it as a gift, ~.

think about의 목적어로 a favorite song과 how가 이끄는 명사절이 and로 연결되어 있으며, 명사절 안에서 동사 bring과 offer가 접속사 or로 병렬 연결되어 있다.

어휘 **touch** (일을 하는 방식에 따른) 느낌; 솜씨; 감촉 **apology** 사과 **bring A into B** A를 B에 끌어들이다 **relate** 연관시키다 **memorable** 잊지 못할 **lyric** (복수형) (노래의) 가사

32 빈칸 추론 ①

소재 오랜 시간과 인내를 통한 관찰과 발견

해설 빈칸 이하의 문장에서는 오랫동안 수면 아래를 관찰한 과학자, 동물을 이해하기 위해 오랜 시간을 관찰한 과학자, 반복하여 표본을 관찰하도록 훈련받는 과학자 등의 예시가 나오는데, 이들이 알려주는 관찰의 비결은 바로 ① '시간과 인내'이다.

해석 주제문 관찰은 과학의 견고한 토대이며, 많은 과학자들은 그것의 비결이 시간과 인내에 있다고 믿는다. Karl von Frisch는 벌의 춤 언어를 연구했는데, 자신의 관찰 능력이 단순히 누워있는 것에서 나왔다고 썼다. "수면 바로 아래에 있는 점액질 녹색 돌 위와 돌 사이에서 볼 수 있는 생물들을 관찰하면서, 무심한 행인은 전혀 아무것도 못 보는 곳에서 오랫동안 고생한 관찰자에게 놀라운 세계가 스스로의 모습을 드러낼지도 모른다는 것을 저는 발견했습니다." Konrad Lorenz의 거위, 물고기와 다른 동물 연구는 그들의 숨겨진 세계를 드러냈는데, 그는 또한 관찰에 대한 사랑을 집중시킬 필요에 대해 논평했다. "동물들과 그들의 행동을 진짜로 이해하기 위해 여러분은 무언가를 볼 수 있을 정도로 충분히 오랜 시간 그것들을 봐야 합니다." Harvard의 지질학자 Nathaniel Shaler와 같은 다른 과학자들은 예컨대 어떤 물고기는 양면의 비늘 패턴이 다르다는 사실이 명확해질 때까지 반복하여 표본을 보도록 하는 훈련을 받았다.
② 비전과 열정 ③ 조화와 균형 ④ 정직과 근면 ⑤ 분석과 비교

구문 [6행~8행] Watching *living things* [(which[that]) I could see ● on and between the slimy green stones just below the surface of the water], ~.
Watching ~ the water는 분사구문이며, '~을 보면서'의 뜻이다. [ ]는 앞에 목적격 관계대명사 which[that]가 생략되어 living things를 수식한다.

[15행~20행] Other scientists, ~ were given *exercises* [that forced them to look at a specimen over and over // until some facts, for example, that in some fish the scale pattern differs on the two sides, became obvious].
[ ]는 exercises를 수식한다. 「force+O+C(to-v)」는 'O가 v하도록 강요하다, v하게 만들다'의 뜻이다. until절에서 주어는 some facts이고 동사는 became이며, that ~ sides는 some facts에 대한 동격절이다.

어휘 **solid** 견고한; 고체의 **foundation** 토대, 기반 **lie in** ~에 있다 **lie down** 눕다 **slimy** 점액질의 **surface** 표면 **reveal** 드러내다 **casual** 무심한; 평상시의 **passer-by** 행인 **goose** 거위 **comment** 논평하다 **geologist** 지질학자 **exercise** 훈련; 연습 **specimen** 표본, 견본 **over and over** 반복해서 **scale** 비늘 **differ** 다르다 **obvious** 명확한

33 빈칸 추론 ⑤

소재 걸음걸이와 삶에 대한 태도의 상관관계

해설 첫 문장에서 심리학자들이 느린 걸음걸이를 삶에 대한 부정적 태도와 관련짓는다고 한 뒤, 빈칸 이후에 걷는 속도와 자세에 따라 자신감의 정도가 다르다는 내용을 제시하고 있다. 마지막 두 문장(If you ~ you feel.)에서 걸음걸이를 바꾸면 마음가짐도 바뀐다고 했으므로, 빈칸에 가장 적절한 말은 ⑤ '당신이 움직이는 방식이 당신을 변화시킬 수 있다'이다.

해석 몇몇 심리학자는 맥 빠진 자세와 느릿느릿한 걸음걸이를 삶에 대한 부정적 태도와 관련짓는다. 주제문 주위를 둘러보면 당신이 움직이는 방식이 당신을 변화시킬 수 있다는 것을 알게 될 것이다. 아주 우울한 사람들은 매우 천천히 걸으며 거의 발을 들어 올리지 않는다. 그들은 자신감이 전혀 없다. 보통 사람들은 '보통' 걸음으로 걷는다. 그들은 기분이 좋지도 우울하지도 않다. 그다음으로는 자신감 넘치는 세 번째 집단이 있다. 이 사람들의 평균보다 빠른 걸음걸이와 훌륭한 자세는 이렇게 선언한다. "나는 '정말로' 어딘가에 가고 있어. 그리고 그곳에 도착하면 내가 해야 할 일이 무엇이든 나는 잘 해낼 거야."라고. 그들이 걷는 방식을 따라 하기만 하면 당신은 자신감을 키울 수 있을 것이다. 한번 해보라. 어깨를 뒤로 젖히고 발걸음에 속도를 내고서 얼마나 다른 기분이 드는지 살펴보라.
① 당신에게 맞는 걸음걸이가 가장 좋다
② 성공에는 자신감이 중요하다
③ 천천히 그리고 꾸준히 하면 이긴다
④ 우리는 걸음걸이가 서로 다르다

구문 [2행~3행] **Look** around // **and** you'll see // that *the way* [you move] can change you.
「명령문+and」는 '~해라, 그러면 …이다'란 뜻이다. the way는 '~하는 방식'이란 뜻으로 how로 바꿔 쓸 수 있다.

[10행~11행] And I will succeed at **whatever** I have to do // when I get there.
whatever는 '~하는 것은 무엇이든지 (모두)'란 뜻으로 anything that과 같으며, 여기서는 whatever가 이끄는 명사절이 succeed at의 목적어로 쓰였다.

어휘 **psychologist** 심리학자 **link A to B** A를 B와 관련짓다[연결시키다] **posture** 자세 **pace** (움직임의) 속도 **attitude** 태도 **depressed** 우울한 **hardly** 거의 ~않다 **self-confidence** 자신감 *cf.* **confident** 자신감 있는; 확신하는 **average** 보통(의); 평균(의) **neither A nor B** A도 아니고 B도 아니다 **declare** 분명히 말하다; 선언하다; 신고하다 **succeed** 성공하다; 뒤를 잇다 [선택지 어휘] **matter** 중요하다; 문제; 물질 **steady** 꾸준한

34 빈칸 추론 ①

소재 침대의 집먼지진드기 제거 방법

해설 빈칸에는 과학자들이 장려하는 생각이 '무엇'인지 들어가야 한다. 집먼지진드기는 인간의 땀을 마시고 사는데, 침대 시트나 담요를 정리하지 않고 어지른 채로 내버려두면 통풍을 통해 땀이 마르게 되어 집먼지진드기가 살 수 없게 된다(If sheets ~ to survive.)는 내용이 이어지므로 정답은 ① '아침에 일어난 후 침대를 정리하지 않는 것'이다.

해석 주제문 영국 Kingston 대학의 과학자들은 아침에 일어난 후 침대를 정리하지 않는 것이 건강에 더 좋을지 모른다는 생각을 장려하고 있다. 그 과학자들은 집먼지진드기 전문가들인데, 집먼지진드기는 우리 침대, 베개, 소파, 쿠션이나 (그들이) 마실 인간의 땀을 찾을 수 있는 곳이면 어디든 살기 좋아하는 아주 작은 생물이다. 잠이 들었을 때, 우리는 집먼지진드기의 배설물을 쉽게 흡입하게 되는데, 이것은 심각한 알레르기와 천식을 일으킬 수 있다. 하지만 그 과학자들이 지적한대로 집먼지진드기는 축축하고 땀에 젖은 곳에서만 생존할 수 있다. 침대 시트나 담요를 아침에 어지른 채로 내버려두면, 공기가 그 속과 매트리스 속을 통과해 순환해서 당신이 흘린 땀을 말려준다. 이렇게 하면 집먼지진드기가 생존하는 데 필요한 것을 빼앗음으로써 집먼지진드기를 죽이게 된다.
② 가능한 한 자주 침대 시트를 세탁하는 것
③ 침대보다 바닥에서 자는 것
④ 방을 옷가지로 어지르지 않는 것
⑤ 밤에는 침실 창문을 닫아두는 것

구문 [1행~3행] *Scientists* (at Kingston University in England) are promoting the idea that **not making** your bed after you get up may be better for your health.

10

the idea와 동격인 절(that not ~ your health)의 주어는 동명사구(not ~ get up)이다. 동명사를 부정할 때는 그 바로 앞에 not, never 등의 부정어를 쓴다.

[12행~14행] This kills the dust mites / by robbing **them** of what **they** need to survive.
them과 they는 the dust mites를 지칭하며, 전치사 of의 목적어는 what이 이끄는 명사절이다. 「rob A of B」는 'A에게서 B를 빼앗다'는 의미이다.

어휘 **promote** 장려하다; 촉진하다; 홍보하다; 승진시키다 **expert** 전문가 **dust mite** 집먼지진드기 **microscopic** 현미경으로 봐야만 보이는, 미세한 **pillow** 베개 **sweat** 땀 *cf.* **sweaty** 땀에 젖은 **inhale** 숨을 들이마시다 (↔ **exhale** 숨을 내쉬다) **poo** (어린이들이 쓰는 말) 응가, 배설물 **severe** 심각한 **allergy** 알레르기 **asthma** 천식 **point out** 지적하다; 알려주다 **moist** 축축한, 습한 **in a mess** 어질러져서 *cf.* **mess up** ~을 엉망으로 만들다[망치다] **circulate** 순환하다 **survive** 살아남다 [선택지 어휘] **make one's bed** 잠자리를 정리하다; 잠자리를 준비하다

35 무관한 문장 ③

소재 인터넷 무료 다운로드의 나쁜 점

해설 무료로 파일이나 소프트웨어를 다운받는 과정에서 침투한 소프트웨어가 개인의 인터넷 서핑 습관, 방문 사이트를 감시하고, 이를 이용해 광고를 보내거나 개인 정보를 유출시킬 수 있다는 내용이다. 한편 ③은 온라인을 이용한 판촉 광고가 과거에 비해 빨라졌고 가격도 적당해졌다는 내용으로 글의 흐름과 무관하다.

해석 주제문 인터넷에서 무료 파일이나 소프트웨어, 특히 게임과 음악, 영화를 매우 인기 있는 파일 공유 사이트에서 다운받는다면, 당신이 원래 예상했던 것 이상의 것도 받을 가능성이 있다. 공짜로 내려 받는 프로그램들은 다운로드 과정 동안 당신의 PC에 조용히 침투할 수 있고, 일단 거기에 들어오면 몰래 여러 가지를 할 수 있다. 그 소프트웨어는 당신의 서핑 습관을 추적하고, 당신이 방문한 사이트들을 기록하며, 당신의 인터넷 연결을 이용해 원격으로 연결된 기지에 보고하고, 당신을 표적으로 하는 광고를 전달할 수 있다. 한때는 온라인 광고는 비용이 많이 들었지만, 오늘날 온라인으로 기업을 홍보하는 것은 빠르기도 하고 비용도 감당할 수 있을 정도이다. 예를 들어, 만일 당신이 좋아하는 밴드를 검색한다면, 그 소프트웨어는 당신에게 그 밴드의 곧 있을 콘서트 광고를 전달할지도 모른다. 그 소프트웨어는 또한 당신의 컴퓨터에 저장된 사적인 정보를 수집하고, 당신의 컴퓨터가 원격으로 사용되도록 할 수도 있다.

구문 [15행~17행] It can also collect *private information* (stored on your computer) and **allow** your computer **to be used** remotely.
and로 동사 collect와 allow를 병렬연결하고 있다. 「allow+O+C(to-v)」는 'O가 v하게 하다'의 의미이며, your computer와 to use의 관계가 수동이므로 to be used가 쓰였다.

어휘 **(the) chances are (that)** ~할 가능성이 충분하다; 아마 ~일 것이다 **freeload** (남의 것을) 거저 쓰다; (음식물을) 공짜로 얻어먹다 **process** 과정, 처리 **track** 추적하다; 길; 자국 **record** 기록하다; 녹음하다 **remote** 원격의; 먼 *cf.* **remotely** 원격으로, 멀리서 **base** 기지, 본부; 기초, 토대 **affordable** (가격 등이) 감당할 수 있는 **upcoming** 다가오는, 곧 있을 **store** 저장하다; 가게

36 글의 순서 ④

소재 지진으로 무너진 학교에서 아들을 구한 아버지

해설 지진이 나서 아버지가 아들을 구하러 학교에 갔지만 학교가 이미 무너졌다는 주어진 글 다음에는 아버지가 손으로 폐허를 파헤치기 시작했다는 (C)가 알맞다. 이를 사람들이 만류했지만 아버지는 멈추지 않았다는 (A)가 그다음에 나오고, 이렇게 38시간을 판 끝에 아들의 목소리가 들렸다는 (A)의 마지막 부분 다음에는 아들과 14명의 학생들을 구조했다는 (B)가 이어지는 것이 자연스럽다. 따라서 정답은 ④ '(C)-(A)-(B)'이다.

해석 1988년 12월에 심한 지진이 아르메니아를 강타했다. Armand라는 이름의 한 소년이 지진이 났을 때 학교에 있었다. Armand의 아버지는 아들을 구조하려고 그의 학교로 서둘러 갔지만, 학교가 파괴된 것을 발견했을 뿐이었다.

(C) 그는 아들의 교실이 학교의 뒤편 구석에 있었다는 것을 알고 있어서, 무더기 위로 올라가서 교실이 있던 곳을 파헤치려고 손으로 파기 시작했다.

(A) 사람들이 그를 만류하려고 애쓰며 그에게 소용없는 짓이라고 말하려 할 때마다, 그는 대답하곤 했다. "함께 할 게 아니면 날 혼자 내버려둬요!" 38시간 동안 손으로 판 후에, 그는 약한 목소리를 들었다. "아빠, 아빠 맞아요?"

(B) 그의 아들과 14명의 그의 반 친구들이 무너진 벽 아래에 생존해 있었다. 그는 그들이 견뎌냈던 어둠으로부터 낮의 빛 속으로 그들 모두를 들어올렸다. Armand는 친구들을 향해 말했다. "봤지? 우리 아빠는 우리를 잊지 않을 거라고 했잖아."

구문 [3행~5행] Armand's father rushed to the son's school to rescue him, / **only to** V **find** O the school C destroyed.
only to-v는 '(~했지만 결국) v하기만 했다'의 뜻이다. 「find+O+C」는 'O가 ~인 것을 알아내다'의 뜻인데, 학교가 '파괴되는' 것이므로 목적격보어는 수동을 나타내는 과거분사가 왔다.

어휘 **severe** 심한 **earthquake** 지진(= **quake**) **strike** (재난이 갑자기) 발생하다; 치다 **rush** 급히 움직이다, 서두르다 **rescue** 구조하다 **destroy** 파괴하다 **every time** ~할 때마다 **dig** 파다 **collapse** 무너뜨리다, 붕괴시키다 **endure** 견디다, 참다 **pile** 무더기 **uncover** 파내다; ~의 뚜껑을 열다

37 글의 순서 ③

소재 중국어 방 논증

해설 '중국어 방 논증'이라는 사고 실험(생각으로만 진행하는 실험)에 대한 내용으로, 주어진 문장에서 실험의 목적을 말한 뒤에 '실험 과정 → 실험 결과 → 결과의 의의' 순서로 전개되고 있다. 각 문장의 연결 관계를 파악하는 데 도움이 되는 지시어구를 통해서도 순서를 추론할 수 있다. (B)의 The argument는 주어진 글의 Chinese Room Argument를 받아 실험 과정을 설명하는 도입 문장을 이끌고 있다. (C)의 The result는 (B)에서 설명한 실험 과정에 대한 결과이다. (A)의 So는 (C) 문장의 that절을 받는다. 따라서 글의 순서는 ③ '(B)-(C)-(A)'가 적절하다.

해석 주제문 '중국어 방 논증'은 John Searle이라는 영향력 있는 철학 교수에 의해 1980년에 만들어졌다. 그는 (컴퓨터) 프로그램이 컴퓨터에 지능을 부여할 수 없다는 것을 증명하려고 그것을 만들었다.

(B) 그 논증은 이렇게 전개된다. 당신이 어떤 방에 갇혀 있다고 생각해보라. 당신이 전혀 읽을 수 없는 중국어 글자가 방 안에 들어온다. 그리고 중국어 글자 하나를 다른 글자와 연결하는, 당신의 언어로 쓰인 지시가 들어온다.

(C) 그 결과로 당신은 중국어로 주어진 지시에 중국어로 반응할 수 있는 것처럼 보이지만, 실제로는 중국어를 한 마디도 이해할 수 없다.

(A) 컴퓨터도 이와 마찬가지다. 약간의 정보와 단순한 지시를 부여받은 컴퓨터는 그 지시를 따를 수는 있지만, 정보를 '이해하지는' 못한다.

구문 [11행~13행] Then come(V) instructions(S), / written in your language, / for relating one piece of Chinese to another.
주어를 보충 설명하는 과거분사구와 전명구가 이어져 길어졌기 때문에 주어와 동사가 도치된 형태이다.

어휘 **argument** 논증; 논쟁 **formulate** (세심히) 만들어 내다 **influential** 영향력 있는 **philosophy** 철학 **demonstrate** 증명[입증]하다 **provide A with B** A에게 B를 제공하다(= **provide B for A**) **intelligence** 지능 **instruction** 지시; 설명 **writing** 글자, 글씨; 글(쓰기) **relate** 관련짓다 **respond** 반응하다; 대답하다

38 문장 넣기 ③

소재 지휘법의 기본 원칙

해설 주어진 문장은 지휘법에 한 가지 외에는 별다른 원칙이 없기 때문에 다양한 지휘 스타일이 존재한다는 내용이다. Aside from this로 시작하므로 이 문장 앞부분에 어떤 지휘 원칙이 언급되었음을 알 수 있다. Therefore로 시작하는 문장에서 지휘의 유일한

원칙에 대해 언급했고, There is a particular distinction 이하에서 서로 다른 지휘 스타일을 소개하기 시작하므로, 주어진 문장은 두 내용 사이인 ③에 와야 한다.

해석 합창단원들과 오케스트라의 연주자들은 모두 지휘 기술에 의존한다. 기본적으로 지휘는 지휘자가 공연 중 '실시간'으로 연주자들에게 자신의 지시를 전달하는 방식이다. 주제문 따라서 지휘에 있어 유일한 원칙은 그것이 정확하고 유의미해야 한다는 것이다. 이것 외에는 '정확하게' 지휘하는 법에 대한 어떠한 원칙도 없는데, 이것이 바로 매우 다양한 지휘 스타일이 존재하는 이유이다. 오케스트라의 지휘와 합창단의 지휘에는 한 가지 특정한 차이점이 있다. 오케스트라의 지휘자들은 일반적으로 지휘봉을 사용하여 박자를 표현하고 연주자들이 얼마나 부드럽게 또는 강하게 연주해야 하는지를 전달한다. 반면, 합창단의 지휘자들은 지휘하는 데 지휘봉을 거의 사용하지 않지만 대신에 감정적인 음색과 음악적 형태에 초점을 맞추기 위해 표현을 풍부히 담아 그들의 얼굴과 손을 사용한다.

구문 [1행~3행] Aside from this, / there are no rules on how to conduct "correctly," // **which** is why so many different conducting styles exist.
which는 앞의 내용 전체(there are ~ "correctly")를 가리킨다.

어휘 **aside from** ~외에는, ~을 제외하고는 **conduct** 지휘하다; 수행하다 *cf.* **conductor** 지휘자 **exist** 존재하다 **choir** 합창단 *cf.* **choral** 합창의 **orchestra** 오케스트라, 관현악단 **rely on** ~에 의존하다 **basically** 기본적으로 **instruction** 지시; 설명 **precise** 정확한 **meaningful** 유의미한, 의미 있는 **particular** 특정한; 특별한 **distinction between A and B** A와 B의 차이 **typically** 일반적으로; 전형적으로 **baton** 지휘봉 **indicate** 나타내다, 보여주다 **convey** 전달하다 **rarely** 거의 ~않는 **expressively** 표현력 있게 **emotional** 감정의 **tone** 음색, 음조; 말투; 분위기

39 문장 넣기 ④

소재 완곡어법

해설 Similarly(마찬가지로)로 시작되는 주어진 문장이 정치 분야에서의 완곡어법을 말하고 있으므로, 주어진 문장 앞에는 정치 외 분야에서의 완곡어법이, 주어진 문장 다음에는 정치 분야의 완곡어법이 나올 것이다. ④ 앞에는 '쓰레기 수거인'에 대한 완곡어법이 나오고 ④ 이후로는 평화 협상에 필요한 완곡어법이 나오고 있으므로 주어진 문장은 ④에 들어가는 것이 알맞다.

해석 주제문 완곡어법은 불쾌하게 들릴지도 모르는 것을 말하는 것을 피하고자 쓰이는 단어나 어구를 나타내는 문학 용어이다. 그것은 보통 불편하게 들릴 만한 것을 말하는 예의 바른 방식이다. 예를 들어, 일부 사람들이 불편한 직업이라 생각하는 것을 숨기려는 노력으로, 동네 쓰레기 수거인은 '위생 엔지니어'라 불려왔다. 여기에는 잘못된 점이 없지만, 위생 엔지니어라는 용어는 엔지니어를 여전히 대단히 기술을 갖춘, 기술 지향 전문인으로 생각하는 누군가를 혼동시킬 수 있다. 마찬가지로, 정치에서 완곡어법 표현의 사용은 필수인데, 그것이 특히 평화 협상 동안 긴장된 상황을 진정시키는 데 도움이 되어서이다. 한 측이 대립하는 측의 군인 1만 명을 죽였다고 말한다면, 이는 상황을 긴장되게 만들 가능성이 있고 협상에 도움이 안 될 것이지만, 한 측이 1만 명의 사상자를 냈다면, 불편함이나 분노를 일으킬 개연성은 다소 떨어진다. 이와 같이 완곡어법은 쓴 약에 입힌 당의와 같은 방식으로 작동한다.

구문 [4행~6행] Euphemism is *a literary term* [**that** represents *a word or a phrase* [**that** is said to avoid saying *something* [**that** might sound offensive]]].
that은 모두 주격 관계대명사로 각각 앞의 명사구(a literary term, a word or a phrase, something)를 지칭한다. 관계사절 내에 관계사절이 포함된 구조이다.

어휘 **euphemistic** 완곡어법의 **politics** 정치(학) **must** 꼭 해야 하는 것 **tense** 긴장된 **negotiation** 협상 **literary** 문학의 **term** 용어; 학기; 기간 **represent** 나타내다 **phrase** 어구 **offensive** 불쾌한 **normally** 보통 **occupation** 직업 **neighborhood** 동네 **sanitary** 위생의 **oriented** ~을 지향하는 **opposing** 대립하는, 싸우는 **casualty** 사상자 **somewhat** 다소 **probable** 있을 것 같은, 개연성 있는 **rage** 분노 **sugar coating** 당의(당분으로 얇은 막을 싼 것)

40 요약문 완성 ⑤

소재 부정적 감정의 영향을 줄이는 방법

해설 기분이 좋지 않을 때 퍼즐을 하거나 시를 외우는 등의 '어려운(demanding)' 일에 생각을 집중하면 부정적인 감정에서 잠시 벗어나 그 영향을 '줄일(lessen)' 수 있다는 내용의 글이므로 정답은 ⑤이다.

해석 당신은 정말로 기분이 좋지 않을 때 낱말 맞히기 퍼즐을 하거나 스도쿠 퍼즐을 풀거나 시를 암기하는 것이 잠시 동안 당신의 감정을 완전히 잊게 할 수 있다는 것을 알아챈 적이 있는가? 그리고 당신 스스로 부과한 그 작은 과제를 끝내자마자 그 나쁜 감정이 바로 다시 되돌아오기 시작한다. 이것은 부정적인 감정이 정신적 에너지를 많이 소모하기 때문에 일어난다. 즉, 나쁜 감정은 뇌를 상당히 고갈시키는 원인이다. 주제문 도전적인 어떤 것에 생각을 집중하면 심적 자원(mental resources)이 그 '나쁜 감정 공장'에서 꺼내져 퍼즐을 풀거나 시를 암기하는 데 사용된다. 이것이 당신이 괴로운 감정 상태에서 일시적으로 벗어나는 것처럼 보이는 이유다.

⬇

> 부정적 감정의 영향을 (A) 줄이는 한 가지 방법은 당신의 뇌의 자원을 감정적 작용에서 가져와 정신적으로 (B) 부담이 큰 과제에 이용하는 것이다.

구문 [1행~4행] Have you ever noticed // **that** when you are in a really bad mood, / doing ~, solving ~, or memorizing a poem(S′) can make(V′) you(O′) completely forget your feelings for a while(C′)?
전체 문장의 목적어 역할을 하는 that절 내에 「when S′+V′ ~, S+V~.」의 구조가 쓰였다. that절의 주어(doing ~ a poem)가 동명사구로 길어진 형태이며 사역동사 make의 목적격보어로 원형부정사인 forget이 쓰였다.
[9행~12행] When ~ challenging, / mental resources(S) are pulled away(V1) from the "bad feelings factory" and (are) put to work(V2) / **to solve** the puzzle or **to memorize** the poem.
등위접속사 and로 동사구 두 개가 병렬 연결되어 있다. to solve the puzzle과 to memorize the poem은 '목적'을 나타내는 부사적 용법의 to부정사구이다.

어휘 **in a bad[good] mood** 기분이 안 좋은[좋은] **sudoku** 스도쿠(숫자 퍼즐 게임의 한 종류) **completely** 완전히 **task** 과제, 일 **emotion** 감정 *cf.* **emotional** 감정적인 **take up** 소모하다, 쓰다 **mental** 정신의, 마음의 **drain** 고갈(의 원인); 배수구; 물을 빼내다 **focus A on B** A를 B에 집중시키다 **challenging** 도전적인 **pull A away** A를 끌어내다[꺼내다] **put to work** 사용하다 **temporarily** 일시적으로 **escape from** ~에서 벗어나다[빠져 나오다] **state** 상태; 국가; 주(州) **apply A to B** A를 B에 사용[적용]하다 [선택지 어휘] **eliminate** 없애다, 제거하다 **investigate** 조사하다 **trivial** 사소한, 하찮은 **evaluate** 평가하다 **continuous** 지속적인 **demanding** 힘든, 부담이 큰; 요구가 많은

41~42 장문 41 ④ 42 ②

소재 가까운 사람과 비교하게 되는 이유

해설 41. 우리는 큰 부자나 성공한 사람들을 모두 다 부러워하는 것이 아니라, 우리와 가까운 사람들의 성공을 부러워한다는 내용의 글이다. 이를 제목으로 가장 잘 표현한 것은 ④ '우리가 우리 이웃들의 성공을 부러워하는 이유'이다.
① 자신의 삶에 만족하는 방법
② 성취는 별개로 존재하는가?
③ 성공은 다른 사람들의 평가에서 온다
⑤ 다른 사람들과 자신을 비교하는 것의 위험성

42. 빈칸 문장은 우리가 '누구'라고 생각하는 사람과 비교를 한다는 내용이다. 세 번째 문단에서 우리는 '성공한 모든 사람들'과 비교를 하는 것이 아니라 우리와 '가까운 사람들'과 비교한다고 했고, 부유한 사우디아라비아 왕자보다 부모님께 새 핸드폰을 선물 받은

반 친구가 더 부럽다는 예시를 들어 설명하고 있으므로 ② '우리와 동등한' 사람들과 비교한다는 내용이 가장 적절하다.
① 우리의 성장을 도와줄
③ 우리의 역할모델인
④ 가장 성공한
⑤ 자기 분야에서 전문가인

해석 현대문명은 우리 선조가 상상도 할 수 없었던 부유함의 복을 우리가 누리게 해주었다. 따라서 매우 많은 사람들이 자신이 가진 것과 자신의 현재 모습이 충분치 않다고 느끼는 것은 이상하다. 그러나 우리가 '충분하다'고 판단하는 방식 이면의 심리를 고려해보면 그것이 그렇게 이상해 보이지는 않을지도 모른다. 주제문 우리는 우리가 가진 것을 별개로 판단하지 않는다. 우리는 그것을 우리가 생각하기에 우리와 동등한 사람이 가진 것과 비교함으로써 판단한다.
우리는 우리와 함께 자라거나 함께 학교에 다니거나 함께 일하는 사람들만큼 혹은 그들보다 더 많이 가져야만 다행이라고 느낀다. 우리를 가장 괴롭히는 것은 바로 이러한 사람들(= 자신과 비슷한 사람들)이 성취한 것이다. 만약 당신이 키가 작은데 키 작은 사람들 사이에서 산다면, 당신은 당신의 키 때문에 몹시 괴롭지는 않을 것이다. 그러나 당신이 속한 집단의 사람들이 키가 갑자기 커지면, 비록 당신 자신은 1밀리미터도 키가 줄지 않았다 하더라도, 당신은 아마도 짜증이 나고 질투심을 느끼기 시작할 것이다.
우리가 어디서나 목격하는 엄청난 불평등을 고려해 볼 때, 우리가 우리보다 더 부유하거나 더 성공한 '모든 사람'에 대해 엄청난 부러움을 갖지 않는다는 것은 놀랄 만하다. 예를 들어, 사우디아라비아 왕자의 어마어마한 부와 특권이 우리를 패배자라고 느끼게 하지 않는다. 그러나 반 친구가 우리 부모님께서는 사주시지 않을 정말 멋진 휴대전화나 가방을 갖고 있으면 우리는 부러움에 배가 아픈 걸 느낄 수 있다. 우리 준거 집단의 구성원들은 우리가 우리 자신과 비교하는 거울이다. 그것이 바로, 가장 견디기 어려운 성공이 우리와 가까운 사람들의 성공인 이유이다.

구문 [7행~8행] We do it / by **comparing** it(A) **with** *that*(B) (of *the people* [(O′)whom (S′)we (V′)consider ● (C′)to be our equals]).
「compare A with B」는 'A와 B를 비교하다'란 뜻이다. 문맥상 it은 what we have, that은 what they(= the people whom we consider to be our equals) have를 받는다.
[9행~11행] We feel fortunate // **only if** we have as much as, or more than, / *the people* [(whom) we grow up with, go to school with, or work with] (have).
only if는 '~해야만'의 의미로 어떤 일이 가능한 유일한 상황을 말할 때 쓴다.
[18행~21행] **Given** *the great inequalities* [(which[that]) we see ● everywhere], / it(가주어)'s remarkable that we don't have *terrible feelings of envy* (about *everyone* [who is richer or more successful / than we are]).(진주어)
given은 여기서 '~을 고려할 때'란 의미의 전치사로 쓰였다.
[27행~29행] **That's why** the hardest successes to endure(S′) are(V′) those(C′) of *the people* [(whom) we're close to ●].
「That's why ~」는 '그것이 ~인 이유이다'란 뜻으로 앞에 언급한 이유에 따른 결과가 이어진다. to endure는 형용사 hardest를 수식하는 부사적 용법의 to부정사이다. those는 앞에 언급한 the successes를 가리킨다.

어휘 **civilization** 문명(사회) **bless A with B** A에게 B의 축복을 베풀다 **unimaginable** 상상도 할 수 없는 **ancestor** 조상 **psychology** 심리(학) **in isolation** 별개로; 홀로 **compare A with B** A를 B와 비교하다 (= **measure A with B**) **fortunate** 다행한, 운 좋은 **achievement** 이룬 것, 성취, 업적 **bother** 괴롭히다 **overly** 몹시, 매우 **annoyed** 성가신, 짜증나는 **envious** 부러워하는 *cf.* **envy** 부러움; 부러워하다 **height** 키; 높이 **given** ~을 고려할 때 **inequality** 불평등 **remarkable** 놀라운, 놀랄 만한 **enormous** 엄청난, 막대한 **privilege** 특권 **reference group** 준거 집단 (개인이 자기 태도 및 판단의 기준으로 여기는 특정 집단) **endure** 참다, 견디다

[선택지 어휘] **regard** 높은 평가; 존경; 안부 **role model** 역할모델(모범이 되는 사람) **expert** 전문가

43~45 장문 43 ② 44 ⑤ 45 ②

소재 봉사활동을 통한 우울증 극복

해설 43. Jessica가 우울증으로 힘들어하자 친구가 자원봉사를 권유하는 (A) 다음으로는 Jessica가 지역 프로그램에 등록해서 문맹자인 Marie를 가르치는 (C)가 오는 것이 적절하다. 함께 공부하면서 Marie가 자신감을 갖게 되고 아이에게 책을 읽어주는 (B)가 이어지고, 마지막으로 Jessica 자신도 우울증을 극복한 (D)가 오는 것이 적절하다.
44. (e)는 봉사활동을 통해 우울증을 극복하고 삶의 열정을 느낀 Jessica를 가리키지만 나머지는 모두 Marie를 가리킨다.
45. (B)에서 프로그램이 끝날 무렵 Tony가 책을 읽는 것을 도와준 것은 Marie 자신이므로 ②는 글의 내용과 일치하지 않는다.

해석 (A) 지난여름, Jessica는 자신이 심한 우울증에 빠져 있다는 것을 알았다. 어떤 것도 그녀의 흥미를 끌지 못했고, 일상은 공허하게 느껴졌다. 사람들은 그녀에게 그녀가 여름 우울증에 시달리고 있다고 말했다. 어느 날, 한 친구가 이러한 상황에 처한 그녀를 보고는 자원봉사 일을 해 볼 것을 권했다. Jessica는 처음에는 주저했지만, 나중에는 한 번 시도해 보기로 결심했다. 그 결과, Jessica는 평생 잊지 못할 교훈을 얻었다.
(C) Jessica는 지역 프로그램을 통해 등록한 뒤 읽고 쓸 수 있게 도와주는 자원봉사자가 되었다. 그녀의 첫 번째 학생 Marie는 ③ 세 아이를 혼자 키우는 마흔네 살의 어머니였다. 첫 수업에서, Jessica는 (c) 그녀(= Marie)가 어느 버스를 타야 하는지를 알지 못해서 가장 가까운 슈퍼마켓까지 5킬로미터를 걸어가는 것을 알게 되었다. 그녀는 또한 ④ 사야 할 물건 목록을 작성할 수 없기 때문에 일단 슈퍼마켓에 가고 나서도 어려움을 겪는다고 Jessica에게 말했다.
(B) 그들이 함께 공부하면서 읽는 법을 알게 되는 것은 Marie의 자신감을 키워주었다. ① 그녀는 빠른 진전을 보였고, (a) 그녀(= Marie) 혼자 버스를 타고 슈퍼마켓에 갈 수도 있었다. 이런 성공적인 외출 후에, 그녀는 얼마나 자신감을 느꼈는지 말했다. 그 프로그램이 끝날 때, ② (b) 그녀(= Marie)는 그녀의 막내아들 Tony가 책을 읽는 것을 돕기 시작했다. 그녀는 아들이 잠자리에 들기 전에 같이 앉아서 이야기를 읽곤 했다.
(D) (d) 그녀(= Marie)가 책을 읽을 때 아들의 눈이 기쁨으로 커지자 자부심이 온통 그녀의 얼굴 위에 나타났고, 그녀는 열심히 노력한 것이 어떻게 보답을 받는가를 깨닫기 시작했다. 그녀가 이 경험에 대해 이야기하자 Jessica도 자신이 자랑스러웠다. 그녀는 Marie를 도운 것이 정말로 보람 있다고 느꼈다. ⑤ 그녀의 우울증은 사라졌고, (e) 그녀(= Jessica)는 삶에 대한 새로운 열정을 느꼈다. 주제문 다른 사람들을 도운 것은 사실 그녀 자신을 도운 것이었다.

구문 [(A) 4행~6행] One day, when a friend saw her in this condition, // she recommended **that** Jessica (should) **try** volunteer work.
recommend처럼 제안, 주장, 명령, 요구의 뜻을 가지는 동사 뒤의 that절이 당위성(~해야 한다)을 의미하는 경우, 동사의 형태는 「(should) 동사원형」을 쓰며 should는 생략 가능하다.

어휘 **(A) depression** 우울(증), 의기소침; 불황 **daily** 매일 일어나는 **routine** 틀에 박힌 일, 일상적인 일 **suffer from** ~로 고통 받다 **blues** 우울; (재즈 음악의) 블루스 **volunteer work** 자원봉사 *cf.* **volunteer** 자원봉사하다; 자원봉사자 **reluctant** 주저하는, 마지못한 **give it a try** 시도하다, 한번 해보다 **(B) self-confidence** 자신감 **rapid** 빠른, 신속한 **progress** 진척, 발달 **(C) sign up** 등록하다; 서명하다 **local** 지역의 **literacy** 읽고 쓸 수 있는 능력(↔ **illiteracy** 문맹) **(D) excitement** 기쁨, 흥분 **pay off** 보상받다; 성과를 올리다; (빚을) 갚다 **rewarding** 보람 있는; 수익이 많이 나는 **vanish** 없어지다, 사라지다 **zeal** 열의, 열정

고난도 모의고사 11

본문 p.153

18 ⑤	19 ③	20 ③	21 ⑤	22 ⑤	23 ①	24 ②	25 ⑤	26 ④	27 ④
28 ⑤	29 ③	30 ③	31 ②	32 ①	33 ④	34 ③	35 ⑤	36 ③	37 ⑤
38 ⑤	39 ③	40 ①	41 ④	42 ⑤	43 ②	44 ②	45 ③		

18 글의 목적 ⑤

소재 견학 허가서 요청

해설 글을 전체적으로 보고 글쓴이의 진짜 의도를 파악해야 한다. 앞부분에서 환경 인식의 달의 목표를 소개한 후 자연 교육 프로그램 견학 계획을 설명하고, 자녀의 프로그램 참가에 대한 허가서를 학부모에게 요청하는 내용이다. 따라서 글의 목적으로 가장 적절한 것은 ⑤이다.

해석 친애하는 학부모님께,
5월은 Maple 학교에서 환경 인식의 달입니다. 이 달은 젊은이들에게 환경 관련 실천의 중요성을 교육하는 것을 목표로 한 교내 활동, 과제, 그리고 일일 견학의 달입니다. 책임감 있는 물 사용은 필수적으로 이것의 큰 부분을 이룹니다. 이것을 강조하기 위해, Yellow Garden의 하루 동안의 교육적인 자연 프로그램 견학이 5월 25일에 계획되어 있습니다. 주제문 첨부된 허가서에 기입하여 주시고 학생이 이것을 25일 전에 교실로 가져오게 하여 그들이 참가할 수 있게 해주십시오. 그 날은 습지 걷기가 포함되고 수질을 향상시키는 것에 관련된 많은 개념들과 지속 가능한 미래 용수를 만드는 것을 소개합니다. 만약 질문이나 우려되는 점이 있으시다면 제게 전화 주시거나 Yellow Garden 웹사이트 yellowgarden.org를 방문해 주세요.
Patricia Wilkins 올림

구문 [9행~12행] Please fill out the attached permission slip and **have** *your child* **bring** it to class before the 25th, so he or she can participate.
밑줄 친 두 개의 명령문이 병렬구조를 이룬다. have가 사역동사로 쓰여 「have+O+원형부정사(O가 …하게 하다)」의 형태를 가진다.

어휘 **environmental** 환경의, 환경과 관련된 **awareness** 인식; 의식 **aim** 목표하다; 목표 **practice** 실천, 실행; 연습 **responsible** 책임감 있는 **necessarily** 필수적으로, 반드시 **emphasize** 강조하다 **fill out** 기입하다, 작성하다 **attached** 첨부된, 덧붙여진 **permission slip** 허가서 **wetland** 습지 **sustainable** 지속 가능한

19 심경 변화 ③

소재 고모의 가르침

해설 필자는 처음에는 좋아하는 카드가 길에 떨어져 있는 것을 보고 매우 신이 났으나 (excited), 고모의 충고를 듣고 카드를 포기하게 되었는데, 이때 카드를 잃어버린 사람뿐만 아니라 자신의 감정도 배려해 주고 이해해 준 고모의 충고 방식에 큰 가르침을 받고 부끄러워하는(ashamed) 내용이다. 마지막 문장이 필자의 부끄러운 심정을 나타낸다. 따라서 정답은 ③ '신이 난 → 부끄러운'이다.

해석 나는 열 살이었고 고모와 함께 브루클린 52번가를 걷고 있었다. 우리가 철도역에 다가갔을 때 나는 우리 앞 보도 위에 적어도 100장의 배트맨 트레이딩 카드가 흩어져 있는 것을 보았다. 주제문 나의 행운에 압도되어서 (나는 배트맨 카드를 정말 좋아했다) 나는 탐욕스럽게 그것들을 주워 담았다. 그러나 거의 즉시 내 팔에 부드러운 당김이 있었다. "네가 얼마나 그 카드를 원하는지 알아." 고모가 말씀하셨다. "하지만 누군가가 그걸 어쩌다 떨어뜨렸을지도 모르고, 네가 그 사람이라면 똑같이 느낄 것처럼 그 사람도 카드가 없어진 걸 알면 슬플 거야." 보통 때라면 나는 분개하고 말씨름하며 불평하고 이 모든 일의 말도 안 되는 불의에 맞서 격분했을 것이다. 그 대신에, 나는 카드에서 손을 놓고 고개를 저은 후 고모에게 말했다. "그래요, 고모 말씀이 맞아요." 주제문 나는 고개를 들어 고모의 눈을 똑바로 쳐다볼 수도 없었다.
① 행복한 → 화난
② 무관심한 → 호기심 있는
④ 기쁜 → 우울한
⑤ 당혹스러운 → 실망한

구문 [2행~4행] As we approached a railway station, I saw(V) scattered before us on the sidewalk(C) at least a hundred Batman trading cards(O).
동사는 saw이고 과거분사로 이루어진 목적격보어(scattered before us on the sidewalk)가 목적어(at least a hundred Batman trading cards)보다 앞에 나와 있다.

어휘 **scattered** 흩어져 있는; 뿌려진 **trading card** 트레이딩 카드(스포츠 선수나 유명인의 모습이 인쇄되어 있는 카드로, 아이들이 수집하고 교환하기도 함) **overwhelmed** 압도된 **greedily** 탐욕스럽게 **scoop up** 주워 담다 **tug** 잡아당김 **by accident** 어쩌다, 우연히 **indignant** 분개한 **rage against** ~에 격분하다 **ridiculous** 말도 안 되는 [선택지 어휘] **perplexed** 당혹스러운

20 필자 주장 ③

소재 올바른 대화 자세

해설 대화할 때 상대방에게 무조건 피드백이나 충고를 주려 하지 말고, 상대방의 말을 끊지 않고 관심을 기울이며 잘 들어주는 것이 대화의 올바른 자세라고 하였으므로, 필자의 주장으로 가장 적절한 것은 ③이다.

해석 주제문 우리의 자녀가 됐건, 배우자가 됐건, 친구가 됐건, 다른 사람들이 우리와 함께 이야기를 나눌 때, 우리는 듣는 동안 권위적이기보다는 공감적이어야 한다. 우리는 많은 경우 각각의 상황에 피드백을 주거나 충고를 해야 한다고 느낄 때, 상황의 유머나 기쁨을 놓치게 된다. 우리가 매 상황에서 다른 사람들의 말을 끊어야 한다고 결정할 때, 그것은 사실상 일종의 자만심이다. 그것은 우리가 그들이 아는 것보다 더 잘 안다는 것을 암시한다. 원치 않는 충고는 좌절, 상처, 심지어 분노까지 유발할 수 있다. 모든 것이 가르침을 받을 만한 순간일 필요는 없다. 상대방의 말을 끊는 것을 선택할 때, 우리는 공유하는 우정과 신뢰를 깊게 할 기회를 상실할 수 있다. 기뻐할 때건 슬퍼할 때건, 우리의 완전한 관심을 주면서 그저 듣는 것이 온당할 것이다.

구문 [1행~3행] **Whether** it is our children, our spouse, or a friend, // when others share a story with us, // we should be empathetic(A) **rather than** authoritative(B) / while listening.
「whether A, B, or C」는 'A이든, B이든, C이든'의 뜻이다. our children, our spouse, a friend가 or로 연결되어 병렬구조를 이룬다. 「A rather than B」는 'B라기보다는 오히려 A'의 뜻이다.

[8행] It suggests // that we know better than they **do**.
do는 대동사이며 know를 지칭한다.

[10행] **Not everything** needs to be a teachable moment.
Not everything은 부분부정 표현으로 '전부 ~한 것은 아니다'의 뜻이다.

어휘 **spouse** 배우자 **empathetic** 공감할 수 있는 **authoritative** 권위적인 **pride** 자만; 자부심; 자존심 **interrupt** (말을) 중단시키다; 방해하다 **frustration** 좌절(감); 실패 **teachable** 가르침을 받을 만한 **talk over** (말을) 중단시키다 **rejoice** 대단히 기뻐하다 **mourn** 애도하다, 슬퍼하다 **do well to-v** v하는 것이 온당하다 **undivided** 완전한, 전적인; 분할되지 않은

21 밑줄 함의 ⑤

소재 캡사이신의 장단점

해설 캡사이신은 점막을 자극하고 위 질환을 증가시킬 수 있지만, 한편으로는 엔도르핀 방출을 자극하고 만성 질환에 따르는 통증을 감소시켜주는 장점도 있다. 이러한 양면적 특성을 '양날의 검(a double-edged sword)'으로 비유한 것이므로, 밑줄 친 부분은 ⑤ '고통과 질병을 유발하지만 정신적, 신체적 고통은 감소시키는' 작용을 의미한다.

해석 매운 음식에 들어가는 재료인 캡사이신은 끈적이는 독이다. 그것은 점막에 들러붙는데, 그것이 당신이 고추를 만진 후 어느 때든 눈을 문지르면 눈이 화끈거리는 이유이다. 대량으로 쓰면 캡사이신은 매우 해로울 수 있다. 과학자들은 연관관계에 대해 여전히 논쟁 중이지만, 고추가 거의 주식인 스리랑카 같은 곳의 사람들은 훨씬 높은 비율의 위 질환을 갖는 경향이 있다. 하지만 고추의 '매운' 성분인 캡사이신은 엔도르핀 방출도 자극하는데, 엔도르핀은 쾌감을 유발하고 스트레스의 기분은 감소시킨다. 게다가 캡사이신이 관절염과 당뇨병 같은 질환으로 유발되는 만성적인 통증을 줄이는 데 도움이 될 수 있다는 증거가 점점 많아지고 있다. 주제문 복합적이고 상충되어 보이는 작용들을 고려하여, 캡사이신은 양날의 검으로 불려왔다.

① 식욕은 증가시키지만 만성 질환을 유발하는
② 신체의 통증을 촉발하지만 정신 질환은 치유하는
③ 먹기는 힘들지만 먹은 후에는 건강에 좋은
④ 소량으로는 독이며 대량으로는 약

구문 [2행~4행] ~ it adheres to mucous membranes, // **which** is why your eyes burn // if you ever rub **them** / after handling peppers.
which는 앞부분 전체를 지칭하고, them은 your eyes를 지칭한다.

[11행~14행] Even more, there is a growing body of evidence that capsaicin may be helpful / in reducing *the chronic pain* (caused by conditions / such as arthritis and diabetes).
that ~ diabetes는 a growing body of evidence와 동격절이다. ( ) 부분은 수동의 의미로 the chronic pain을 수식한다.

어휘 **ingredient** (요리의) 재료 **sticky** 끈적끈적한 **adhere** 들러붙다 **rub** 문지르다 **handle** 만지다, 다루다 **pepper** 고추(류 식물) **quantity** 양 **debate** 논쟁하다 **connection** 관계; 연결 **staple** 주식(主食); 주요 산물 **rate** 비율 **stimulate** 자극하다 **release** 방출; 석방 **induce** 유발[초래]하다; 유도하다 **a body of** 많은 **chronic** 만성적인 **condition** 질환; 상태 **arthritis** 관절염 **diabetes** 당뇨병 **in light of** ~을 고려하여, ~에 비추어 **seemingly** 겉보기에는 **conflicting** 상충되는, 모순되는 **be referred to as A** A로 불리다 **a double-edged sword** 양날의 검 [선택지 어휘] **appetite** 식욕 **trigger** 유발하다, 일으키다; 방아쇠; 계기 **mental** 정신의

22 글의 요지 ⑤

소재 매스컴의 사회 문제 보도 증가

해설 가정 폭력, 아동 학대와 같은 사회 문제에 대한 언론의 보도가 늘어나고 있지만, 과거에는 경찰에 신고하지 않았던 것을 지금은 신고하여 보도되기 때문이지 실제로 이런 사건의 수가 증가한 것은 아니라는 내용이다. 따라서 글의 요지로 가장 적절한 것은 ⑤이다.

해석 얼핏 보기에, 어떤 문제를 다루는 매스컴 보도가 증가하는 것은 그 문제가 더 심각해지고 있다는 것을 의미하는 것처럼 보인다. 하지만 그것이 실제로 일어나고 있는 일인가? 예를 들어, 최근 몇 년 동안 우리는 가정 폭력과 아동 학대에 관해 더 많은 기사가 보도되고 보도 기사가 제작되는 것을 보았다. 이것은 심각한 문제이고, 매스컴은 이 문제에 대한 대중의 인식을 높이는 데 중요한 역할을 하지만, 이것이 현재 더 많은 여성과 아이들이 구타당하고 학대당하고 있다는 것을 반드시 의미하는 것은 아니다. 이것은 오히려 사건을 경찰에 신고하는 비율이 더 높아진 것을 나타내며, 이것이 결국, 훨씬 더 광범위한 매스컴 보도를 이끈다. 주제문 우리는 단지 사건에 대해 더 듣는 것이지, 그 수가 증가하는 것을 보는 것은 아니다.

구문 [4행~6행] ~, we(S) have seen(V) more and more articles(O1) published(C1) [and] news stories(O2) produced(C2) / about domestic violence and child abuse.
동사 have seen이 지각동사로 쓰여 SVOC 구조를 취하며, 목적어와 목적격보어의 관계가 문맥상 수동(기사가 '보도되고', 보도 기사가 '제작되는' 것)이므로 목적격보어에 과거분사가 쓰였다.

어휘 **at first glance** 얼핏 보기에; 첫눈에 **media coverage** 매스컴의 보도(량) **news story** (사실 그대로를 전하는) 보도 기사 **domestic violence** 가정 폭력 **child abuse** 아동 학대 *cf.* **abuse** 학대(하다); 오용(하다) **awareness** 인식, 의식, 자각 **assault** 구타하다, 폭행하다 **indicate** 나타내다, 가리키다 **incident** 사건, 일어난 일 **lead** 이끌다 **extensive** 광범위한 **merely** 단지 (~에 불과한)

23 글의 주제 ①

소재 운동 번아웃을 막는 방법

해설 운동을 처음 시작할 때는 동기부여가 잘 되어 지나치게 심한 빈도와 강도로 운동을 하게 되는데, 이러면 극도의 피로 상태인 번아웃(burnout)에 빠질 수 있다. 운동에도 중용의 미덕이 적용되기 때문에 중간 정도의 운동 프로그램부터 시작하여 그 지점부터 차근차근 발전시켜 나가는 것이 운동을 장기적으로 할 수 있는 전략이라고 소개하는 글이므로, 주제로 가장 적절한 것은 ① '운동 번아웃을 피하는 효과적인 방법'이다.

해석 운동을 시작하게 하는 동기부여는 처음엔 강력하며, 더욱 건강한 생활을 향한 첫 단계를 밟기 위해 필요한 것을 제공한다. 그러나 이러한 긍정적인 열의는 많은 경우 부정적으로 바뀌는데, 왜냐하면 사람이 성공의 또 다른 핵심 구성요소인 중용을 잊기 때문이다. 운동하는 사람이 열정적으로 시작하여 너무 빈번하거나 너무 격렬한 운동에 착수할 때, 그러면 불가피하게 그들은 에너지가 소진되어 완전히 그만두게 된다. 주제문 삶의 대부분의 것들과 마찬가지로, 운동에서 중용은 매우 중요하다. 중간 정도의 운동 프로그램은 개인마다 그리고 건강 수준마다 다르지만, 일반적으로 천천히 시작해서 거기에서부터 쌓아나가야 한다. 효과적인 운동 계획은 매주 안전한 방식으로 당신의 운동 강도를 천천히 증가시켜줄 것이다.

② 운동을 시작하는 다른 동기들
③ 규칙적인 운동이 정신 건강에 미치는 영향
④ 운동 강도를 결정하는 것의 어려움
⑤ 중간 수준 운동의 장점과 단점

구문 [6행~9행] When an exerciser starts eagerly [and] takes on *workouts* [that are far too frequent or far too intense], // then inevitably they burn out [and] quit altogether.
When절의 동사 starts와 takes on이 병렬구조를 이룬다. [ ] 부분은 workouts를 수식하는 관계사절이다. 주어 they 다음의 동사 burn out과 quit도 병렬구조를 이룬다.

어휘 **motivation** 동기부여 **enthusiasm** 열의, 열정, 열광 **turn** (~로) 변하다 **component** 구성요소 **moderation** 중용 **eagerly** 열심히, 열정적으로 **take on** 착수하다; (책임을) 떠맡다 **workout** 운동 **frequent** 빈번한 **intense** 강렬한 *cf.* **intensity** 강도 **inevitably** 불가피하게, 필연적으로 **burn out** 에너지를 소진하다 *cf.* **burnout** 번아웃(어떤 활동이 끝난 후 극도의 피로감으로 심신이 지친 상태) **altogether** 완전히 **as with** ~와 같이, 마찬가지로 **moderate** 중간의, 보통의 **vary** 서로 다르다; 달라지다 **fitness** 건강 **in general** 일반적으로 **manner** (일의) 방식; (사람의) 태도 [선택지 어휘] **motive** 동기, 이유 **merit** 장점(↔ **demerit** 단점)

24 글의 제목 ②

소재 좋은 아이디어를 만들어내는 조건

해설 100개의 아이디어를 생각해내면 그중 99개는 대개 실패하고, 실패하지 않은 아이디어도 다른 아이디어와 결합되어야 유용하게 쓰이는 경우가 대부분이기 때문에 수많은 아이디어를 만들어내는 것이 중요하다고 하였다. 즉, 수많은 아이디어 속에서 하나의 좋은 아이디어가 만들어진다는 내용이므로 제목으로 가장 적절한 것은 ② '아이디어: 양이 질을 낳는다'이다.

해석 사람들이 나에게 글을 보내거나 전화하여 그들의 새로운 아이디어를 판매하려고 노력할 때 나는 항상 놀란다. 나는 그들에게 묻는다. "그게 뭔가요?" 그들은 내가 그 아이디어에 돈을 지불할 때까지는 나에게 그것을 얘기해줄 수 없다고 말한다. 나는 그들에게 그들의 아이디어는 단독으로는 가치가 없다고 설명하려 애쓴다. 그들은 많은 경우 충격을 받는다. 그들은 자신이 아이디어를 생각했다는 바로 그 이유 때문에 그것이 가치를 가진다고 생각한다. 주제문 사실은 적어도 원래의 형태로는, 100개의 아이디어 중 99개가 잘 되지 않는다. 이것이 당신이 차이를 만들어내는 하나의 아이디어를 생각해내려면 많은 아이디어를 만들어내야 하는 이유이다. 그리고 정말로 잘 되는 그 하나의 아이디어는 어떤 가치 있는 목적을 성취하기 위해 다양한 다른 아이디어, 정보와 결합되고 재결합될 때에만 가치를 갖는다.

① 행동이 새로운 아이디어를 만든다
③ 좋은 아이디어는 창의력에서 나온다
④ 모든 새로운 아이디어는 옛 아이디어로 만들어진다
⑤ 호기심은 새로운 아이디어를 위한 상상력을 자극한다

구문 [8행~10행] **This is why** you have to generate a lot of ideas // if you are going to come up with *the one* [that makes a difference].
This is why ~는 '이것이 ~한 이유이다'라는 뜻이다. the one은 the idea를 지칭하며, [ ] 부분은 the one을 수식하는 관계사절이다.

[10행~13행] And *the one idea* [that **does** work] only has value // when it is combined and re-combined with a variety of other ideas and information / to achieve some worthy end.
[ ] 부분은 주어인 the one idea를 수식하는 관계사절이며 동사는 has이다. 관계사절에서 does는 동사 work를 강조하는 조동사로 '정말로'라는 뜻으로 쓰였다.

어휘 **of no value** 가치 없는 **by oneself** 단독으로, 혼자서 **at least** 적어도 **original** 원래의; 원본의; 독창적인 **form** 형태 **generate** 생성하다, 발생시키다 **come up with** 생각해내다 **be combined with** ~와 결합되다 **a variety of** 다양한 **achieve** 성취하다, 달성하다 **worthy** 가치 있는 **end** 목적 [선택지 어휘] **quantity** 양 **quality** (품)질 **fuel** 자극하다; 연료를 공급하다; 연료

25 도표 이해 ⑤

소재 성인 여성의 식자율 통계

해설 2017년에 남아시아 지역과 사하라 사막 이남 아프리카 지역 여성의 식자율이 50퍼센트를 넘었으므로 문맹률은 50퍼센트 미만이다. 따라서 ⑤가 잘못된 설명이다.

해석 **〈성인 여성 식자율 (2000~2017)〉**

주제문 위 그래프는 2000년부터 2017년까지의 성인 여성의 식자율을 지역별로 보여주고 있다. ① 동아시아와 태평양 지역의 비율은 2000년부터 2010년까지는 감소했지만, 2010년과 2017년 사이에는 소폭의 증가세를 보였다. ② 반면, 라틴아메리카와 카리브 해 지역의 비율뿐만 아니라 유럽과 중앙아시아 지역의 비율도 2000년대에는 증가했고 이후에는 거의 혹은 전혀 증가하지 않았다. ③ 그럼에도, 2017년에 유럽과 중앙아시아 지역의 성인 여성 식자율은 1위를 점했고, 라틴아메리카와 카리브 해 지역이 동아시아와 태평양 지역과 함께 2위를 점했다. ④ 한편, 남아시아 지역과 사하라 사막 이남 아프리카 지역의 비율은 연구 기간 동안 꾸준한 증가를 보였다. ⑤ 하지만 그 두 지역은 나머지 지역보다 매우 뒤처져 있어서, 2017년에 그 지역 여성의 절반 이상이 문맹이었다.

어휘 **literacy rate** 식자율(글을 아는 사람들의 비율) *cf.* **literate** 글을 (읽고 쓸 줄) 아는(↔ **illiterate** 문맹의) **region** 지역 **Pacific** 태평양 지역; 태평양의 **decline** 감소하다; 거절하다 **slight** 약간의 **Caribbean** 카리브 해 지역; 카리브 해의 **followed by** 뒤이어, 잇달아 **progress** 증가; 진보; 진척 **rank** 등급[순위](을 차지하다) **tie with** ~와 동점이 되다 **steady** 꾸준한; 한결같은 **improvement** 증가; 향상 **remain behind** 뒤처지다

26 내용 불일치 ④

소재 음악가 Glennie

해설 Glennie가 청각장애에 대한 질문에 불쾌한 반응을 보였다는 것에서 장애에 대해 언급하는 것을 싫어한다는 것을 알 수 있으므로 ④가 정답이다.

해석 1965년에 스코틀랜드 애버딘에서 태어난 Glennie는 ① 타악기 독주의 '제1인자'로 불린다. ② 그녀는 열두 살에 청각을 잃었고, 그때 타악기를 공부하기 시작했다. Glennie는 1985년에 프로로 데뷔를 했고, 그녀의 음악적 대담함이 드러나는 데는 오래 걸리지 않았다. 스스로 작곡도 하는 Glennie는 ③ 영화와 TV를 위한 음악을 작곡했다. Glennie는 언론 자료에 그녀의 ④ 귀가 들리지 않는 것에 대해 언급을 하지 않고 있으며, 음악 문제 말고 그것에 대해 질문을 받으면 불쾌하다고 반응하는 것으로 알려져 있다. 그녀는 심한 청각장애가 있지만, 어떤 소리는 느낄 수 있다. 그녀는 다리와 발에서 낮은 음을 느끼고, 얼굴, 목, 가슴에서 높은 음을 느낀다고 말한다. ⑤ Glennie는 청각은 촉각의 형태이고, '청각장애인'이든 아니든 모든 사람이 개별적 방식으로 소리를 처리한다고 주장한다.

구문 [8행~11행] Glennie does not mention her deafness in press materials, // and she has been known to react with annoyance // **when** (she was) **asked** about it / to the exclusion of musical matters.
when과 asked 사이에 she was가 생략되었다. 시간을 나타내는 접속사 when 다음에는 문맥을 통해 뜻을 알 수 있을 경우에 「주어+be동사」가 종종 생략된다.

어휘 **be referred to as A** A로 불리다 **first lady** 1인자, 지도적 입장의 여성 **instrument** 악기; 기구, 도구 **debut** 첫 무대, 데뷔 **adventurousness** 대담함, 저돌성 **composer** 작곡가 **deafness** 귀가 들리지 않는 것 **press** 언론; 누르다 **material** (주로 복수형) 자료; 재료 **annoyance** 불쾌함, 성가심 **to the exclusion of** ~을 제외하고 *cf.* **exclusion** 제외, 배제 **profoundly** 극심하게; 완전히; 깊이 **contend** 주장하다; 다투다, 겨루다 **process** 처리하다; 과정; 진행

27 안내문 불일치 ④

소재 Smith 자연 자전거 타기 투어

해설 보통 선택지 순서는 글의 순서와 같으므로 안내문을 읽으면서 선택지의 순서대로 일치 혹은 불일치 여부를 파악한다. 자전거를 5달러에 대여할 수 있다고 했지만 참가비에 대한 언급은 없으므로 ④가 안내문의 내용과 일치하지 않는다.

해석

Smith 자연 자전거 타기 투어

Smith 자연 자전거 타기 투어는 운동을 하면서 Smith 습지에 대해 알 수 있는 재미난 기회입니다.

① 9월 17일 금요일 오후 1시~5시

(자전거) 타기: ② 이는 평지 위를 달리는 20킬로미터 (자전거) 타기이고, 우리는 자연 명소들을 감상하기 위해 종종 멈출 것입니다.

③ **가이드:** Jim Hendricks 씨는 17년의 경력을 가진 공원 동식물 연구가입니다. 그는 또한 경험이 풍부한 자전거 운전자입니다.

준비해야 할 것: 자전거, 헬멧, 충분한 (양의) 물, 그리고 적절한 복장을 가져 오세요.
④ 자전거는 공원 입구 근처의 가판대에서 5달러에 대여할 수도 있습니다.

오후 12시 45분까지 ⑤ 방문자 센터 옆 Smith Wetlands의 남쪽 입구에서 만납시다.

어휘 **opportunity** 기회 **wetland** 습지대 **flat** 평평한 **frequently** 종종, 흔히 **appreciate** 감상하다; 진가를 알다; 이해하다; 감사하다 **attraction** 명소, 명물; 매력 **naturalist** 동식물 연구가 **experienced** 경험[경력]이 풍부한; 능숙한 **plenty of** 충분한, 많은 **appropriate** 적절한, 적합한 **rent** (사용료를 내고 단기간) 대여하다, 빌리다 **stand** 가판대 **entrance** (출)입구; 입장, 등장; 입학

28 안내문 일치 ⑤

소재 Greentree 현수교 공원 안내

해설 마지막 문장에서 아기를 데리고 다닐 때 다리 난간보다 낮은 높이에서만 데리고 다녀야 한다고 했으므로 ⑤가 안내문의 내용과 일치한다.

해석

Greentree 현수교 공원

① Greentree 현수교의 건설을 기념하기 위해 1914년에 세워진 이 역사적인 장소는 매년 7만 5천 명의 방문객을 맞이합니다.

주의

모든 안전 표시판을 잘 따르기 바랍니다.
② 안전하지 않은 행동은 공원에서의 퇴장 조치, 중상이나 치명상을 야기할 수 있습니다.

공원에서:

③ 지정된 코스의 오솔길이나 보도 위로 다녀야 합니다.
보도가 젖어있을 때에는 미끄러울 수 있습니다.
부모나 보호자들은 그들의 보호 하에 있는 사람들을 관리해야 합니다.

다리 위에서:

④ 떨어뜨린 물건들을 회수하려 하지 마세요. 공원의 직원들에게 알려주시기 바랍니다.
어린아이들의 손을 꼭 잡아야 합니다.
달리거나 뛰거나 고의로 다리를 흔들어서는 안 됩니다.
⑤ 아기들은 난간 높이 아래로만 데리고 다니거나 아기를 데리고 다닐 수 있도록 고안된 기구에 태워서 다녀야 합니다.

구문 [8행~9행] Unsafe behaviors may result in removal from the park (V, O1) or serious or fatal injury. (O2)
result in의 목적어로 removal ~ park와 serious ~ injury가 or로 연결되었다.

어휘 **suspension bridge** 현수교(양쪽 언덕에 줄이나 쇠사슬을 건너지르고, 거기에 의지하여 매달아 놓은 다리) **establish** 설립하다 **commemorate** (중요 인물 · 사건을) 기념하다 **historic** 역사적인, 역사적으로 중요한 *cf.* **historical** 역사상의 **observe** (법 · 규칙 등을) 준수하다; 관찰하다 **removal** 추방; 제거 **fatal** 치명적인 **designated** 지정된 **trail** 코스, 오솔길 **walkway** 보도, 통로 **slippery** 미끄러운 **supervise** 관리하다, 감독하다 **retrieve** 회수하다 **notify** 알리다 **intentionally** 의도적으로 **railing** 난간, 철책 **device** 기구, 장치

29 밑줄 어법 ③

소재 전파를 통한 외계 생명체 신호 감시

해설 ③ as 절에서 주어는 they이고 동사는 search이므로 동사 형태가 다시 나올 수 없다. 앞의 명사 civilization을 능동의 의미로 수식하는 sending으로 바꿔 써야 한다.

오답 분석 ① 주어는 The possibility이므로 단수형 동사 has가 옳게 쓰였다. ② Using ~ waves는 능동 의미의 분사구문으로 As they are using ~ waves에서 접속사와 주어, be동사가 생략된 것이다. ④ if는 명사절을 이끄는 접속사로 '~인지'의 뜻이며, if절은 동사 predict의 목적어 역할을 한다. ⑤ 뒤에 절이 왔으므로 접속사 because가 적절히 쓰였다.

해석 주제문 먼 별의 행성에 생명체가 있을 가능성은 오랫동안 SF 작가들과 영화 제작자들의 가장 좋아하는 주제였다. 이제 이 문제는 존경 받는 과학자들의 진지한 관심을 끌었다. 매우 약한 전파를 수신할 수 있는 특수 제작된 망원경을 사용하여, 그들은 우리 위의 하늘을 매일 밤낮으로 매분 살피고 있다. 이러한 전파망원경은 우주로 메시지를 보내는 멀고도 진보된 문명의 어떤 실마리라도 탐색할 때 수백만이 넘는 채널을 동시에 추적 관찰할 수 있다. 우리가 언제라도 우주 어느 곳의 지적 생명체로부터 발송된 신호를 받을지는 누구도 예측할 수 없다. 그러나 한 가지는 확실하다. 우리가 정말로 그러한 메시지를 받는다면, 우리는 과거에서 온 생각을 듣고 있는 게 될 거라는 점이다. 이것은 지구와 생명체를 포함하고 있을 수 있는 다른 행성을 떨어뜨려 놓는 엄청난 거리를 전파가 가는 데 오랜 시간이 걸리기 때문이다.

구문 [13행~14행] If we **do** receive such a message, // we'll be hearing thoughts from the past.
do는 동사 receive를 강조하기 위해 쓰였으며 '정말로'의 뜻이다.

[14행~17행] This is because **it takes** *radio waves* a long time **to travel** *the incredible distances* [that **separate** Earth **from** *other planets* [that may contain life]].
「it takes+O+(시간)+to-v」는 'O가 v하는 데 (시간)이 걸리다'의 뜻이다. that separate ~ life는 the incredible distances를 수식한다. 「separate A from B」는 'A를 B로부터 분리시키다'의 뜻이다.

어휘 **possibility** 가능성 **planet** 행성 **distant** 먼 **draw interest** 흥미를 끌다 **telescope** 망원경 **radio wave** 전파 **monitor** 추적 관찰하다 **simultaneously** 동시에 **clue** 단서, 실마리 **advanced** 진보한; 선진의 **civilization** 문명 **signal** 신호 **intelligent** 지능이 있는 **being** 존재 **incredible** 엄청난, 믿을 수 없을 정도의 **separate** 분리시키다

30 밑줄 어휘 ③

소재 선동가가 사람들을 선동하는 방법

해설 밴드웨건 기법은 선동가가 '다른 사람들도 다 하고 있으니 당신도 합류해야 한다'라고 현혹하는 것이므로 사람들의 독립심이 아니라 의존심에 호소하는 기법이다. 따라서 ③의 independence를 dependence로 바꿔 써야 한다.

해석 주제문 선동가는 인간의 ① 감정에 호소한다. 그는 청중을 (그가) 바라는 목표로 향하게 하기 위해 두려움, 희망, 분노, 좌절 혹은 동정심을 이용한다. 밴드웨건은 선동가가 쓸 수 있는 또 다른 장치이다. "모두가 그걸 하고 있어요. 그러니까 당신도 그걸 하셔야 해요." 물론 이 진술은 ② 과도한 단순화이다. 모두가 그걸 하고 있지는 않다. 밴드웨건은 ③ 독립심(→ 의존심)에 대한 우리의 필요에 대한 호소이다. "그러니까 밴드웨건에 올라타세요. 군중에 합류하고 만족과 안정감을 느끼세요." 선동가는 또한 자신이 무엇에 대해 말하고 있는지를 ④ 알고 있다는 인상을 준다. 그의 목소리는 강력하다. 그의 표정은 대담하다. 그의 몸짓은 결단력 있다. 여기서의 이론은 이와 같은 것이다. 이 사람이 그렇게 ⑤ 자신감이 있으면, 그가 옳은 것임에 틀림없다. 사람들은 승자를 지지하기를 선호하고, 그러한 방식은 사람을 승자처럼 보이게 만든다.

구문 [15행~16행] ~, and such a manner **makes** *a person* **look** like a winner.
사역동사 make는 「make+O+원형부정사 (O가 ~하게 하다)」의 구문으로 사용되었다.

어휘 **appeal to** ~에 호소하다 **frustration** 좌절 **sympathy** 동정심 **direct** 지휘하다, 안내하다; ~로 향하다 **bandwagon** (시류에) 편승; (행렬의) 악대 차(車) **device** 장치 **statement** 진술 **oversimplification** 지나친 단순화 **hop** (버스 등에) 타다; 깡충깡충 뛰다 **secure** 안전한, 안심하는 **bold** 대담한 **bodily** 몸의, 신체의 **decisive** 결단력 있는 **theory** 이론

31 빈칸 추론 

소재 비즈니스 편지를 쓰는 방법

해설 비즈니스 편지는 읽는 사람을 고려해야 하고, 사무적인 어조로 구체적인 예시를 사용하며, 기술 용어는 상대방이 잘 모를 수 있으니 주의해서 사용하고, 논리적으로 구성하고, 하나의 목적에만 전념하여 작성되어야 한다. 이것을 종합하면 비즈니스 편지는 ② '명확한' 특성을 갖는다고 할 수 있다.

해석 비즈니스 편지를 쓰는 것은 당신이 다른 분야에 있을 수 있는 다른 기업인과 소통하고 있음을 명심하는 한 어려울 필요가 없다. 당신의 편지 언어는 받는 사람에게 맞춰져야 한다. 이는 당신이 사무적인 어조로 써야 한다는 것을 의미한다. 읽는 사람이 공감할 수 있는 구체적인 예를 사용하라. 당신의 편지를 읽는 사람이 당신 사업의 기술 용어를 이해한다고 가정하지 마라. 명심하라, 대부분의 편지는 편지 수신인 외의 사람들도 읽을 수 있음을. 이 사람들은 당신이 사용하는 기술 언어에 익숙하지 않을 수 있다. 당신은 또한 읽는 사람이 당신이 말하는 바를 정확하게 이해하도록 당신의 생각을 논리적인 순서로 제시해야 한다. 당신의 편지는 임의적인 생각의 모음이어서는 안 된다. 그것은 그 목적에 있어서 하나에만 전념해야 한다. 간단히 말해서, 주제문 당신의 비즈니스 편지는 명확해야 한다.
① 간결한 ③ 정확한 ④ 전문적인 ⑤ 대화의

구문 [11행~13행] You should also present your ideas in a logical order *for the reader* **to understand** precisely what you are saying.
for the reader는 to understand에 대한 의미상 주어이다. 밑줄 친 부분은 명사절로 understand의 목적어로 사용되었으며, 관계대명사 what은 '~한 것'의 뜻이다.

어휘 **as long as** ~하는 한 **adapt** 맞추다, 조정하다 **recipient** 받는 사람, 수령인 **matter-of-fact** 사무적인 **tone** 어조 **specific** 구체적인, 특정한 **relate to** ~에 공감하다, ~을 이해하다 **assume** 가정하다 **term** 용어 **trade** 사업; 거래 **other than** ~ 외에 **present** 제시하다 **logical** 논리적인 **precisely** 정확히 **random** 임의의 **single-minded** (한 가지 목적에만) 전념하는, 한결같은

32 빈칸 추론 ①

소재 시험에서 좋은 점수를 받는 비결

해설 처음에는 좋은 점수를 받지 못했던 필자가 좋은 점수를 받게 된 비결은 스스로를 교수의 머릿속에 두어 보려 노력한 것이었으므로 빈칸에 들어갈 말은 ① '나의 선생님들처럼 생각하는 것'이다.

해석 생각하는 법을 배우는 것은 당신의 삶을 더 쉽게 만들어줄 것이다. 대학 시절의 첫 해에 나는 교재에서 중요성이 그다지 부여되지 않았던 모든 주제에서 최고가 되려고 노력하면서 시험 대비로 벼락치기를 지나치게 많이 했다. 여러분도 예상하셨다시피 나는 좋은 점수를 받지 못했다. 선생님들께서 확실히 제기할 질문들에 집중하는 것이 훨씬 더 나았을 텐데, 선생님들이 과제로 내주신 주요 수업에 주의를 기울였다면 내가 그것들을 알아챌 수도 있었을 것이다. 시험에 뭐가 나올지에 대한 최고의 통찰력을 얻기 위해 나는 그것(= 시험)을 고안한 강사들인 나의 선생님들이나 교수님들에게 시선을 돌렸다. 몇몇 분들은 나에게 시험 대비 공부 지침을 주시면서 이 일을 쉽게 해주셨다. 하지만 그들이 그렇게 하지 않으셔도, 나는 무엇이 나올지를 알아내려고 그들의 수업에서 나오는 신호를 포착하기 위해 노력했다. 나 자신을 강사의 머릿속에 두어 보려 노력하는 것은 개인적 관심이 가는 과목들에 집중하기 시작했을 때 훨씬 더 수월해졌고, 나는 대학 시절 동안 시험에서 성공을 거둘 수 있었다. 좋은 점수를 받는 내 비결은 나의 선생님들처럼 생각하는 것이었다.
② 과거의 시험을 찾아내는 것
③ 내 약점을 확인하는 것
④ 나의 시험 치는 기술을 향상시키는 것
⑤ 성취도가 최고인 학생들과 함께 공부하는 것

구문 [5행~8행] It(가주어) **would have been** much better to focus on *questions* [(which[that]) my teachers were certain to ask](진주어), // **which** I could have discerned // if I had paid attention to their main take-home lessons.
It은 가주어이고 to focus ~ ask가 진주어이다. 「would have p.p.」는 '~했을 것이다'의 뜻이다. which는 questions를 지칭하며, which 이하는 「If+S'+had p.p., S'+조동사 과거형+have p.p. (~했다면 …했을 텐데)」의 가정법 과거완료 표현이 쓰였다.

어휘 **cram** 벼락치기 공부를 하다 **discern** 알아차리다; 구별하다 **insight** 통찰력 **look to** ~으로 시선을 돌리다; ~에 기대를 걸다 **instructor** 강사 **cue** 신호 **figure out** 알아내다 **show up** 나타나다 **concentrate on** ~에 집중하다 **subject** 과목; 주제; 피실험자 [선택지 어휘] **track down** ~을 찾아내다 **identify** 확인하다

33 빈칸 추론 ④

소재 경험의 해석에 따른 현실 구성

해설 모든 경험은 중립적이며 그 의미를 해석하는 것은 개인이 쌓아온 역량과 경험에 달려 있다. 그래서 동일한 현상을 어떤 사람은 실패로 보지만 어떤 사람은 성공의 가능성으로 보고 도전한다. 따라서 빈칸 문장은 어떻게 ④ '자신의 경험을 해석하는 것을 선택'하느냐에 따라 자신의 현실이 구성된다는 의미가 되는 것이 가장 적절하다.

해석 모든 경험은 중립적이다. 그것들은 아무 의미도 없다. 당신이 사제면 어디서든 신의 증거를 본다. 당신이 무신론자면 어디서든 신의 부재를 본다. 미국의 다국적 기술 기업인 IBM은 세상의 누구도 개인용 컴퓨터를 갖고 있지 않음을 관찰했다. IBM은 이를 시장이 없다는 뜻으로 받아들였다. 대학 중퇴자인 Bill Gates와 Steve Jobs는 동일한 개인용 컴퓨터의 부재를 관찰하고 거대한 기회를 보았다. 한번은 Thomas Edison이 전구에 쓸 필라멘트 작업을 하는 동안 한 조수가 다가왔다. 조수는 Edison에게 왜 포기하지 않는지 물었다. "결국, 5천 번 실패하셨잖아요." 그는 말했다. Edison은 그를 보고 조수가 '실패'로 뭘 말하고자 하는지 이해하지 못하겠다고 그에게 말했다. Edison은 말했다. "나는 잘 되지 않는 5천 가지를 발견한 거예요." 주제문 당신은 자신의 경험을 해석하는 것을 선택함으로써 당신 자신의 현실을 구성한다.
① 최악의 시기에 최고를 봄
② 당신의 강점을 개발하는 데 주력
③ 시간과 에너지를 자신에게 바침
⑤ 문제를 예상하고 그에 대비

어휘 **neutral** 중립적인 **priest** 사제, 성직자 **atheist** 무신론자 **absence** 부재, 없음 **multinational** 다국적의 **dropout** 중퇴자 **massive** 거대한 **assistant** 조수 **bulb** 전구 **after all** 결국 **construct** 구성하다; 건설하다 [선택지 어휘] **dedicate A to B** A를 B에 바치다[전념하다] **interpret** 해석하다 **anticipate** 예상하다

34 빈칸 추론 ③

소재 인간의 성취에 영향을 미치는 문화적 가치와 신념

해설 주제문에 해당하는 빈칸 문장의 내용은 이어지는 예시를 통해 추론해내야 한다. 인체 해부를 반대하는 종교적 신념으로 인해 의학적 발전이 어려웠으나 14세기 이후에 서양에서는 인체 해부를 용인하는 사회적 분위기가 조성되었으며, 이로 인해 서양 의사들이 인체 해부를 여전히 금기시했던 아시아 문화권의 의사들을 능가하게 되었다고 했다. 이를 통해 사람이 성취할 수 있는 것이 ③ '자신이 속한 문화가 공유하는 가치나 신념'에 좌우된다는 것을 추론할 수 있다.

해석 주제문 사람이 인생에서 성취할 수 있는 것은 자신이 속한 문화가 공유하는 가치나 신념에 의해 상당히 좌우된다. 예를 들어, 의학적 발전은 인체를 잘라내는 것을 반대하는 종교적 규정에 의해 저지되어왔다. 이런 이유로, 인도와 중국의 의사들은 지금부터 2,000년도 전에 수준 높은 의학 지식을 발달시켰음에도 체내 구조와 장기의 기능을 연구할 기회가 전혀 없었다. 신체에 대한 이런 직접적인 접근 없이, 그들은 많은 중요한 발견들을 하지 못하게 됐다. 서양 의학도 이와 마찬가지로 사체를 검사하는 것의 금지로 인해 14세기에 상당히 들어설 때까지 (발전이) 더뎠지만, 나중에는 신체의 내부 작용을 분석하는 것이 점차로 허용되었다. 이리하여, 서양 의사들은 그들의 아시아 상대자들(= 의사들)을 따라잡았으며 그러고 나서는 능가하게 되었다.
① 자신이 속한 사회의 기술에 관한 기준
② 자신이 개척자 정신을 지녔는지 여부
④ 자신의 아이디어를 다른 이들에게 전달하는 능력
⑤ 결국에는 모든 것이 잘될 거라고 믿는지의 여부

구문 [5행~9행] For this reason, / *Indian and Chinese physicians*, // who **had developed** sophisticated medical knowledge / more than two thousand years ago, // never **had** *a chance* (to study the internal structure and function of organs).

주어를 부연 설명하는 관계사절(who ~ ago)의 시제가 주절의 시제보다 앞서므로 대과거(had p.p.)가 쓰였다.

[13행~15행] ~, but afterward it became increasingly permissible to analyze the body's internal workings.

it은 가주어로, 진주어 to analyze ~ internal workings를 대신한다.

어휘 **to a high degree** 고도로, 대단히 *cf.* **degree** 정도; 등급 **be capable of** ~할 수 있다 **accomplish** 이루다, 달성하다 **hold back** 저지하다, 방해하다 **religious** 종교적인 **sophisticated** (사람이) 수준 높은, 지적인; 정교한; 세련된 **internal** 내부의(↔ **external** 외부의) **function** 기능 **organ** 《생물》 장기, 기관 **access** 접근(하다) **prevent A from v-ing** A가 v하는 것을 막다 **medicine** 의학, 의술; 약(물) **prohibition** 금지 **examine** 검사하다, 조사하다; 시험하다 **permissible to-v** v하는 것이 허용된 **analyze** 분석하다 **workings** (기계 · 조직 등의) 작동, 작용 **catch up with** ~을 따라잡다 **surpass** 능가하다, 뛰어넘다 **counterpart** 대응 관계에 있는 사람[것], 상대 [선택지 어휘] **technological** 기술에 관한, 과학 기술의 **standard** 기준 **pioneer** 선구자, 개척자; 개척하다

35 무관한 문장 ⑤

소재 선진국 국민들의 기대수명 연장

해설 선진국 국민의 기대수명이 건강관리의 향상과 의학 치료의 발전 덕분에 더 늘어나고 있다는 내용의 글인데 반해, ⑤는 비만의 확산에 따른 건강상의 문제점에 관한 내용이므로 전체 글의 흐름에서 벗어난다.

해석 부유한 국가들이 계속해서 평화와 번영 속에 산다면 그 국가에서 새로 태어난 아기들은 이제 백 년 이상 사는 것을 기대해볼 수 있다. 20세기 이래 선진국 국민은 과거보다 30년가량 더 오래 살고 있다. 주제문 놀랍게도 이 장수 추세는 줄어들 기미를 보이지 않고 있다. 건강관리의 향상은 지속적으로 노화 속도를 늦추며, 기대수명에 정해진 상한선이 있다는 믿음에 이의를 제기하고 있다. 심장병, 암, 당뇨병과 같은 문제가 노인층에서 증가하고 있지만, 의학 치료의 발전은 또한 그들이 계속 더 오랫동안 살고 활동적이게 하는 것을 가능하게 하고 있다. 그러나 비만의 급속한 확산은 문제를 복잡하게 만들 수도 있다. 과체중은 주요한 건강상의 문제를 일으키는데, 특히 전형적인 서구의 '부자 나라' 식단으로 자란 아이들에게 나타날 수 있다.

구문 [9행~13행] While *problems* (such as heart disease, cancer, and diabetes) are rising in the elderly, // *advances* (in medical treatment) are also making it possible for them / to remain alive and active for longer.

가목적어 it은 to부정사구(to remain ~ for longer)를 대신한다. for them은 to부정사의 의미상 주어이다.

어휘 **prosperity** 번영, 번성 **newborn baby** 신생아 **population** 사람들; 인구 **developed country** 선진국 **longevity** 장수 **improvement** 향상, 증진; 개선 **aging** 노화 **challenge** 이의를 제기하다; 도전하다 **fixed** 고정된; 확고한 **ceiling** 상한[최대 한계]; 천장 **life expectancy** 기대수명 **diabetes** 당뇨병 **the elderly** 노인들 **advance in** ~에서의 발전[진보] **medical treatment** 의학 치료 **remain** 계속 ~이다; 남다 **obesity** 비만 **epidemic** (나쁜 것의) 급속한 확산[유행]; 전염병 **complicate** 복잡하게 만들다 **typical** 전형적인

36 글의 순서 ③

소재 '연상' 광고 기법

해설 광고 기법 중에 이미지를 활용하는 '연상'이 있다는 주어진 글 다음에는 그것의 예로 남성용 로션을 제시한 (B)가 나온다. Let's say는 '예를 들면'의 뜻이다. 이 광고가 로션 자체에 관한 정보는 거의 제시하지 않는다는 내용의 (B) 다음에는 '대신에(Instead)' 로션을 바른 남성을 쫓아가는 여성의 이미지를 제시한다는 (C)가 나온다. 광고하는 물건(로션)과 아이디어(매력) 간의 연관관계 생성이 연상 기법의 핵심임을 논한 (C) 다음에는 광고주들이 소비자들로 하여금 이러한 연관관계를 받아들이게 하려고 노력한다는 내용의 (A)가 나온다. 따라서 적절한 글의 순서는 ③ '(B)-(C)-(A)'이다.

해석 주제문 광고주들이 제품을 홍보하기 위해 사용하는 가장 흔한 기법 중 하나는 연상이다. 인간 심리에 호소하며, 이 기법은 제품 이면에 광범위한 아이디어를 생성하기 위해 이미지를 사용한다.

(B) 판매중인 상품이 남성용 로션이라고 예를 들어보자. 그것을 광고하는 상업광고가 로션에 대해 당신에게 말해주는 것은 거의 없을 것이다.

(C) 대신에 그것은 로션을 바른 운 좋은 남자 뒤를 쫓는 매력적인 여성들을 보여준다. 이 기법의 효과는 물건(로션)과 아이디어(매력)의 연관관계에 달려있다.

(A) 이러한 방식으로 광고주들은 소비자가 로션을 사용하면 더 매력적이게 될 거라고 믿게 만들기 위해 노력한다. 생산되는 것은 제품이 아니라 당신, 소비자이다.

구문 [1행~3행] One of *the most common techniques* [that advertisers use / to promote their products] / is association.

수식어구에 의해 주어가 길어진 형태로, 주어의 핵심이 One이므로 단수동사가 is가 왔다.

[8행~9행] What is being produced is **not** product, **but** you, the customer.

What이 이끄는 명사절이 주어이며, 보어는 「not A but B (A가 아니라 B)」의 상관 접속사로 연결되었다. you와 the customer는 동격이다.

어휘 **advertiser** 광고주 **promote** 홍보하다; 촉진하다 **association** 연상 **appeal to** ~에 호소하다 **a chain of** 일련의 **attractive** 매력적인 *cf.* **attractiveness** 매력 **commercial** 상업광고; 상업적인 **chase** 쫓다 **dependent** 달려있는, 의존하는

37 글의 순서 ⑤

소재 균형 있는 가격 책정의 중요성

해설 주어진 글은 가격 책정이 일의 가치에 대해 느끼는 감정에 영향을 미친다는 내용으로, 그 다음에 가격을 낮게 책정하거나 높게 책정하는 것의 문제점을 각각 언급한 (C), (B)가 이어지고, 균형 있게 가격 책정을 해야 한다는 결론을 제시하는 (A)가 마지막에 오는 것이 자연스럽다. (B)와 (C)의 관계에서는 (B)의 a different set of problems(다른 일련의 문제들)에서 (C) 다음에 (B)가 나와야 함을 알 수 있다. 따라서 정답은 ⑤ '(C)-(B)-(A)'이다.

해석 가격 책정은 이상한 일일 수 있다. 그것은 당신이 하는 일의 가치에 대해 당신이 느끼는 방식에 큰 영향을 미친다.

(C) 만일 당신이 너무 적게 청구하면, 당신은 결국 매우 적은 것을 위해 열심히 일한 셈이 될지도 모른다. 당신은 값이 싸서 그다지 귀하지 않게 인식될지도 모른다. 당신은 결국 많은 일을 하지만 당신의 사업이나 기술을 개발하고 성장시킬 시간은 없게 될지 모른다.

(B) 가격을 너무 높게 청구하는 것은 다른 일련의 문제들을 동반한다. 당신은 누구도 지불하지 않을(만큼 높은) 가격을 매기게 되거나, 혹은 당신이 요구한 높은 가격만큼 가치 있게 보여야 한다는 너무나 강한 압박 때문에 당신의 업무가 지장을 받을지도 모른다.

(A) 주제문 그러므로 당신과 당신의 고객 양측 모두를 위하여 올바른 균형을 찾는 것이 필수적이다. 당신은 당신이 고객들에게 청구하는 가격에 만족해야 하고 당신의 고객들도 그들 자신이 받고 있는 것으로 인지하는 가치에 만족해야 한다.

구문 [5행~6행] You need to feel satisfied with *the price* [(which[that]) you charge your customers ●], // and your customers must feel satisfied with *the value* [(which[that]) they perceive themselves to be receiving ●].

[ ]는 각각 앞의 명사 the price와 the value를 수식하는 관계대명사절로, ●는 관계대명사로 받아 생략된 목적어 자리이다. 두 관계대명사절 모두 목적격 관계대명사 which 또는 that이 생략되었다.

어휘 **influence** 영향(을 미치다) **value** 가치; 가격 *cf.* **valuable** 귀중한, 소중한; 값비싼 **essential** 필수의, 근본적인 **balance** 균형 **charge** (요금을) 청구하다 *cf.* **over-charge** (금액을) 너무 많이 청구하다 **perceive** 인지하다, 감지하다 **receive** 받다 **set a price** 가격을 책정하다 **intense** 극심한, 강렬한 **pressure** 압박, 부담; 압력 **appear** ~처럼 보이다; 나타나다 **demand** 요구하다; 요구; 수요 **end up (with)** 결국 ~하게 되다

38 문장 넣기 ⑤

소재 Gutenberg의 인쇄기가 가져온 혁명적 변화

해설 주어진 문장은 '인쇄기를 종교적 텍스트에만 쓰지 않고 시와 철학 등으로 범위를 넓혔다'는 내용이므로 이 앞에는 '인쇄기를 종교적 텍스트 인쇄에 쓴 상황'이 나와야 하는데 그것이 ⑤ 이전까지의 내용이다. ⑤ 다음 문장은 인쇄기가 새로운 사상을 전파하는 데 역할을 하여 종교 및 사회 개혁의 동력이 되었다는 내용인데, 이는 주어진 문장에 있는 '식자율 상승'으로 인해 가능했음을 추론할 수 있다. 따라서 주어진 문장은 ⑤에 들어가는 것이 가장 적절하다.

해석 1440년경에 Johannes Gutenberg(요하네스 구텐베르크)라는 이름의 독일인 대장장이이자 금세공인이 인쇄기의 혁명적인 버전을 도입했다. 이 기계는 개별적인 글자 틀(인쇄되는 작품에 따라 재배열될 수 있었다)을 판에 놓는 '가동 활자' 개념을 사용했다. 존재했던 최초의 인쇄기는 아니었지만, Gutenberg의 버전은 훨씬 더 효율적이었으며 하루에 3,000페이지가 넘는 텍스트를 생산할 수 있었다. 문학계에 미친 영향은 심오하기도 했고 즉각적이기도 했다. Gutenberg의 인쇄기는 역사상 처음으로 성경 사본을 대량 생산하기 시작했고, 이전에는 종교계와 귀족 계층의 구성원들이 보유했던 텍스트를 접할 수 있게 해주었다. 곧 인쇄기는 종교적 텍스트에만 한정되지 않게 됐고, 시와 철학 작품이 유럽 전역으로 나아갔는데, 이는 식자율에서 주목할 만한 증가를 촉발시켰다. 새로운 생각과 아이디어를 빠르고 효율적으로 대중에게 전달할 수 있는 능력은 또한 종교개혁에 힘을 보탰고, 유럽의 상류층 시민과 하류층 시민 간의 분할을 허물어뜨리는 데 도움이 되었다.

구문 [11행~13행] While (it was) not the first printing press in existence, // Gutenberg's version was(V1) **far** more efficient [and] could produce(V2) more than 3,000 pages of text a day.

While 다음에는 it(= Gutenberg's version) was가 생략되어 있다. far는 비교급을 강조하는 표현으로 '훨씬'의 뜻이다.

어휘 **press** 인쇄기 **poetry** (집합적) 시(詩) **philosophy** 철학 **spark** 촉발시키다; 불꽃을 일으키다; 불꽃 **notable** 주목할 만한 **literacy rate** 식자율(글을 읽고 쓸 줄 아는 비율) **goldsmith** 금세공인 **revolutionary** 혁명적인 **moveable type** 가동 활자 **mold** 주형, 틀 **rearrange** 재배열하다 **plate** (인쇄용) 판 **profound** 심오한 **mass-produce** 대량 생산하다 **formerly** 이전에 **reserve** (권한을) 갖다, 보유하다 **nobility** 귀족 **mass** 대중 **fuel** 부채질하다; 연료를 공급하다; 연료 **the Protestant Reformation** 종교개혁 **divide** 분할; 나누다 **upper-class** 상류층의 **lower-class** 하류층의

39 문장 넣기 ③

소재 아이가 가리키는 행동의 의미

해설 주어진 문장 속에 있는 a new reaction from your baby를 통해 아기의 반응 방식이 달라지는 부분에 주어진 문장이 들어가야 함을 알 수 있다. 따라서 물건을 가져다 달라는 아기의 가리킴에서 경험을 공유하기 위한 가리킴으로 바뀌는 ③에 주어진 문장이 들어가야 한다.

해석 주제문 (손으로) 가리키는 것은 아기가 자기 주변 사람들과 정보를 교환하게 해준다. 그것은 사회적이고 의사소통적인 행위이다. 아기는 혼자 있을 때는 결코 가리키지 않는다. 사실, 아기는 자신의 행동이 주목받는 것을 확실히 하기 위해, 가리키기 전에 먼저 적극적으로 당신의 관심을 끌려고 할 것이다. 6개월쯤 되면, 아기는 구체적인 욕구를 전달하기 위해 그들의 손이 닿지 않는 곳에 있는 물건을 가리키기 시작한다. 이런 형태의 가리킴은 '도구적 가리킴'이라고 불리며, 매우 구체적이고 의도적인 목적 달성을 위한 수단이 되는 행동을 나타낸다. 그 결과로 생기는 부모의 반응, 즉, 장난감을 주워 아기에게 건네는 것은 예상되고 확인된다. 하지만 몇 개월 내에 당신은 아기의 새로운 반응으로 인해 당황할 수도 있다. 당신이 아기가 가리키고 있던 장난감을 아기에게 건네줄 때, 아기가 불만스러워하는 것처럼 보이거나 그것을 밀어낼 수 있다. 좌절감을 느끼는 당신의 아이는 이번에는 당신이 자신의 행동을 이해하지 못했기 때문에 짜증을 내고 있다. 이 경우에, 아기는 무언가가 자신에게 주어지기를 요청하던 것이 아니라 그 장난감을 당신에게 보여줌으로써 경험을 공유하고 있었던 것이다.

구문 [10행~12행] This form of pointing(S) **is called**(V1) "instrumental pointing"(C1) / [and] represents(V2) a very specific and intentional means-to-an-end action(O2).

This form ~ "instrumental pointing"은 SVOC 구조를 수동태로 전환한 것으로, 본래 We call this form of pointing "instrumental pointing"에서 O(this form of pointing)가 주어가 되고 C("instrumental pointing")는 그 자리에 그대로 남은 형태이다.

[15행~16행] When you hand him *the toy* [(which[that]) he was pointing at], // he may look displeased or push it away.

[ ] 부분은 목적격 관계대명사 which 또는 that이 생략된 관계대명사절로 the toy를 수식한다.

어휘 **perplex** 당황하게 하다 **exchange** 교환하다 **communicative** 의사소통적인 **ensure** 확실히 하다, 보장하다 **object** 물건; 대상; 목적 **convey** 전달하다; 운반[수송]하다 **specific** 구체적인, 명확한 **desire** 욕구, 갈망; 바람 **instrumental** 도구적인; 수단이 되는; 악기[기악]의 **represent** 나타내다; 대표하다 **intentional** 의도적인 **means-to-an-end** 목적 달성을 위한 수단이 되는 **response** 반응; 대답 **predict** 예상[예측]하다 **confirm** 확인[확정]하다 **displeased** 불만스러운 **frustrated** 좌절감을 느끼는 **annoyed** 짜증 난

40 요약문 완성 ①

소재 객관적인 확률의 선택지 선호 현상

해설 예시로 나온 실험에서 검은 구슬 혹은 흰 구슬을 뽑으려 할 때, 검은 구슬을 둘 중 한 병에서 뽑겠다고 선택했으면 흰 구슬은 나머지 한 병에서 뽑겠다고 선택하는 것이 논리적일 것이다. 그러나 사람들은 확률이 '객관적(objective)'으로 명시되어 있는 병과 확률이 '알려지지 않은(unknown)' 병 중에서 검은 구슬도 흰 구슬도 확률이 명시된 병에서만 뽑으려 하는 모순된 모습을 보였다는 내용의 글이다.

해석 당신 앞에 두 개의 큰 병이 놓여 있다. 병 안의 내용물은 볼 수 없다. 왼쪽 병에는 10개의 검은 구슬과 10개의 흰 구슬이 담겨 있다. 오른쪽 병에는 20개의 구슬이 있지만 당신은 검은색 대 흰색의 비율은 알지 못한다. 이제 게임은 병들 중 하나로부터 검은 구슬을 뽑는 것이다. 다시 해보자. 이제 게임은 흰 구슬을 뽑는 것이다. 대부분의 사람들은 이러한 선택들에 직면했을 때 왼쪽 병을 선택한다. 그리고 바로 거기에 역설이 있다. 검은 구슬을 뽑으려고 할 때 왼쪽 병을 고르면, 그것은 당신의 확률이 그 병에서 더 낫다고 생각한다는 의미이다. 그러나 두 병 모두 두 가지 색밖에 없기 때문에, 흰색 구슬을 뽑을 가능성은 검은색 구슬을 뽑을 가능성과 상호보완적인 것이 분명하다. 논리적으로 보면, 당신이 왼쪽 병이 검은 구슬을 뽑기 위한 더 나은 선택이라고 생각한다면, 오른쪽 병이 흰 구슬을 뽑기 위한 더 나은 선택이 되어야 한다.

⬇

이 글에 따르면, 의사결정자는 (B) 알려지지 않은 확률의 선택지보다 (A) 객관적인 확률의 선택지를 선호한다.

구문 [9행~10행] And therein lies the paradox.

부사 therein이 문두로 나와 주어와 동사가 도치되었다.

[15행~18행] Logically, **if** you **thought** // the left-hand jar **was** the better choice for a black marble, // the right-hand jar **should be** the better choice for a white marble.

「If+S'+동사의 과거형, S+should+동사원형 (~한다면 …(해야) 할 것이다)」의 가정법 과거 문장이다.

어휘 **jar** 병, 항아리, 단지 **content** (주로 복수형) 내용물 **marble** 구슬; 대리석 **proportion** 비율 **draw** 뽑아내다 **confront** 직면하다; 맞서다 **therein lies** 바로 그 안에 ~이 있다 **paradox** 역설 **chances** 가능성, 확률 **odds** 가능성, 공산 **complementary** 상호보완적인 **logically** 논리적으로 **prefer A to B** B보다 A를 더 선호하다 **probability** 확률 [선택지 어휘] **precise** 정확한 **predictable** 예측할 수 있는 **subjective** 주관적인

41~42 장문 41 ④ 42 ⑤

소재 민주주의 제도의 한계점

해설 41. 이 글에 따르면 민주주의는 다수의 횡포에 따를 수 있고, 대표자와 정당이 자신을 선출해준 사람들을 무시하고 정책을 추진할 수도 있으며, 여러 당의 공약에 동의해도 투표는 한 당에만 할 수 있을 뿐이다. 즉, 민주주의 체제가 가진 한계를 논한 글이므로 제목으로 가장 적절한 것은 ④ '민주주의가 우리 모두를 위한 최선의 정치 체제인가?'이다.

① 민주주의의 더 깊은 뿌리는 무엇인가?
② 민주주의는 평등과 부를 보장하지 않는다
③ 민주주의의 승리는 영원히 보장되지 않는다
⑤ 민주주의는 어떻게 그것의 의미를 변화시켰고 그것의 목적을 상실했는가

42. (e)의 앞 문장 'People can write ~ little effect.'는 민주주의 체제에서 시민의 의견이 정치인에게 묵살되는 상황을 보여준다. 이에 대해 정치인은 "민주주의는 사람들이 계속 말하도록 하는 것이 아니라 말을 그만하도록 할 수 있는 경우에만 효과적이다"라고 논평할 것이다. 또한 역접의 접속사 but으로 보아 앞의 discussion(토의)과 반대 개념이 되어야 함을 알 수 있다. 따라서 (e)의 keep을 stop으로 바꿔 써야 한다.

해석 민주주의의 논리에 따르면 정부는 다수의 의지에 따라야 한다. 이 다수는 자주 바뀌고 편견이 있는 견해를 갖기 쉽다. 주제문 다수는 소수의 이익을 희생시켜 자신의 이익을 (a) 배타적으로 추구한다. 그것이 다수의 횡포라고 알려져 있는 것이다. 정치인을 선출한 대부분의 사람들이 동의하지 않더라도 국가를 위한 최선의 행위라고 자신이 느끼는 것을 하는 정치인에게 마찬가지의 위험이 있다. 대립하는 정당 사이에서 삶의 복잡성을 단일한 결정으로 (b) 축소시키는 데에 또 다른 어려움이 있다. 국가적 선거에서 정당들은 선거 공약으로 자신들의 아이디어를 제시한다. 많은 사람들은 반대 정당의 프로그램 각각에서 약간씩에 동의한다. 하지만 당신은 오직 한 측에만 투표할 수 있다. 집권하게 되었을 때 정치인들은 그들의 선거 공약을 언급한 후(사람들은 이를 대부분 읽지 않았다) 그들을 선출했던 사람들이 예상하지 못했던 정책을 추구할 수 있다. 사람들은 결과적으로 (c) 속았다고 느낀다. 게다가 집권당은 많은 경우 1~2년 후에 새로운 아이디어를 도입하는데, 이 당에 투표했던 사람들은 여기에 완전히 반대한다. 그들은 전쟁을 하거나, 그들의 가장 강력한 지지자들조차 (d) 용납할 수 없는 새로운 세금이나 형법을 도입한다. 사람들은 자신의 국회의원에게 글을 쓸 수도 있지만, 이것이 영향력이 거의 없다고 느낀다. 영국 노동당 수상 Clement Attlee가 솔직하게 인정했듯이, "민주주의는 토의에 의한 정부를 의미하지만 그것(= 민주주의)은 사람들이 말을 (e) 계속 하도록(→ 그만하도록) 할 수 있는 경우에만 효과적이다."

구문 [7행~10행] An equal danger lies in *politicians* (doing what (they feel) is best for the country), // even if most of *the people* [who elected them] do not agree with them.

( ) 부분은 politicians를 수식하는 현재분사구이다. 그 안에서 what ~ country는 doing의 목적어이며, they feel은 삽입절이다.

어휘 **logic** 논리 **democracy** 민주주의 **obey** 복종하다, 따르다 **will** 의지 **frequently** 자주 **prejudiced** 편견이 있는 **exclusively** 배타적으로, 독점적으로 **interests** 이익 **at the expense of** ~을 희생하여 **tyranny** 압제, 폭압, 횡포 **lie in** ~에 있다 **politician** 정치인 **elect** 선출하다 **oppose** 반대하다 **party** 정당 **put forward** 제안하다 **election promise** 선거 공약 **vote** 투표하다 **come to power** 집권하다 **refer to** 언급하다 **pursue** 추구하다 **policy** 정책 **anticipate** 예상하다 **consequently** 결과적으로 **cheat** 속이다 **furthermore** 게다가 **criminal law** 형법 **unacceptable** 받아들일 수 없는 **Member of Parliament** 국회의원 **Prime Minister** 수상 **candidly** 솔직히 **admit** 인정하다 **discussion** 토의 [선택지 어휘] **guarantee** 보장하다 **equality** 평등 **triumph** 승리 **assure** 보장하다

43~45 장문 43 ② 44 ② 45 ③

소재 할머니께 햇빛을 보여드리고픈 손녀

해설 43. Elsa가 할머니는 왜 정원에 나오지 않으시는지 엄마에게 묻자, 너무 나이가 드셔서 나오지 못하신다고 대답하는 (A) 다음에는 Elsa가 그런 할머니에게 햇빛을 가져다 드리려고 고민하는 (C)가 이어진다. 어느 날 정원에서 자기의 무릎에 있는 햇빛을 할머니에게 가져다 드리려고 할머니 방으로 달려가는 (B)가 그다음에 온다. 마지막으로, 할머니가 Elsa의 눈과 머리카락에 햇빛이 나타난다고 하자, Elsa가 정원에서 놀다가 햇빛을 배달하려고 할머니에게 달려가는 (D)가 온다. 따라서 글의 순서는 ② '(C)-(B)-(D)'가 가장 자연스럽다.

44. (b)는 Elsa를 가리키고, 나머지는 모두 할머니를 가리킨다.

45. (B)에서 Elsa는 햇빛을 자신의 옷에 담아 할머니 방으로 가져다 드리려 했지만, 가서 옷을 펼쳐보았을 때 햇빛이 없었다. 따라서 ③은 글의 내용과 일치하지 않는다.

해석 (A) 옛날에 Elsa라는 이름의 작은 소녀가 있었다. 그녀는 언덕에 있는 아주 작은 집에 살았다. 매일 태양이 정원을 환하게 비추었다. 하지만 ① 할머니 방의 창문은 집의 북쪽에 있었기 때문에 햇빛은 할머니 방으로는 결코 들지 않았다. 어느 날 Elsa가 어머니에게 말했다. "왜 할머니는 정원에 나오지 않으세요? 난 (a) 그녀(= 할머니)가 햇빛을 좋아하시는 것을 알고 있는데." ② "할머니는 정원을 걸어 오시기에는 너무 나이가 드셨단다."라고 그녀의 어머니가 말했다.

(C) ④ 그 후에 Elsa는 어떻게 그녀가 할머니에게 햇빛을 가져다 줄 수 있을까 생각하고 생각했다. 그녀가 정원에서 놀고 있을 때 그녀는 풀과 꽃이 머리를 끄덕이는 것을 보았다. 새들은 달콤하게 이 나무에서 저 나무로 날아다니면서 노래를 불렀다. 모든 것이 "우리는 해를 사랑해요. 우리는 밝고 따뜻한 해를 사랑해요."라고 말하는 듯 보였다. 그 아이는 "할머니도 그것을 사랑하실 거야. 내가 (c) 그녀(= 할머니)에게 햇빛을 가져다 드려야만 해."라고 생각했다.

(B) 어느 날 아침 그녀가 정원에 있을 때, 그녀는 황금빛 머리카락에 태양의 따뜻한 광선을 느꼈다. 그리고 그녀는 앉아서 그것(= 태양 광선)을 자기 무릎에서 보았다. "나는 그것을 옷 안에 담아서 할머니 방으로 가져가 갈 거야."라고 그녀는 생각했다. 그래서 그녀는 팔짝 뛰어올라 집으로 달려 들어갔다. "보세요, 할머니, 보세요! 제가 할머니를 위해서 햇빛을 좀 가져왔어요."라고 그녀가 외쳤다. 그리고 ③ (b) 그녀(= Elsa)가 옷을 펼쳤지만 보이는 광선은 없었다.

(D) "그것이 네 눈에서 나타나는구나, 아가야. 그리고 네 밝은 황금빛 머리카락에서도 그것이 빛나는구나. (d) 나(= 할머니)와 함께 네가 있으면 난 태양이 필요 없단다."라고 큰 미소를 지으며 할머니가 말했다. Elsa는 태양이 어떻게 자기 눈에서 나타날 수 있는지 이해하지 못했다. 그러나 그녀는 자기가 사랑하는 할머니를 행복하게 해드릴 수 있어서 기뻤다. 햇빛을 (e) 그녀(= 할머니)에게 빨리 배달하려고 Elsa는 ⑤ 할머니 방 근처의 정원에서 매일 아침 놀았다. 그리고 그녀는 자기의 눈과 머리카락의 햇빛을 가지고 할머니의 방으로 달려갔다.

어휘 (B) **ray** 광선 **golden** 황금빛의 **lap** 무릎(의자에 앉았을 때 허리부터 무릎까지의 부분) (C) **nod** (머리를) 끄덕이다; 꾸벅꾸벅 졸다 (D) **peep** 일부 나타나다, 드러나다; 엿보다

고난도 모의고사 12

본문 p.167

18 ① 19 ③ 20 ④ 21 ⑤ 22 ② 23 ③ 24 ① 25 ③ 26 ② 27 ③
28 ⑤ 29 ④ 30 ⑤ 31 ③ 32 ① 33 ⑤ 34 ③ 35 ④ 36 ① 37 ⑤
38 ④ 39 ④ 40 ④ 41 ⑤ 42 ⑤ 43 ④ 44 ④ 45 ②

18 글의 목적 ①

소재 학교 전시회 안내

해설 교감선생님이 학생들에게 개교 35주년 기념 전시회에 대해 안내하고 있으므로, 글의 목적으로 가장 적절한 것은 ①이다.

해석 학생 여러분 주목해주세요.
올해 2020년에 Sullivan 예술 디자인 학교가 35주년을 기념합니다. 주제문 경축의 일환으로 디자인 전시회가 학교의 남쪽 갤러리에서 월말에 열릴 것입니다. 그것은 과거의 디자인 경연에서 나온 최고의 출품작들을 포함할 것입니다. 이 작품들은 수백 개의 지원작들 중에서 선정되었으며 최고 영예를 수상했습니다. 조각에서 회화와 포스터에 이르기까지 모든 것이 전시될 것입니다. 현재의 유명 화가들이 여러분의 지금 모습처럼 아직 학생이었을 때의 작품을 볼 멋진 기회입니다. 부모님과 일반 대중을 포함하여 모든 분들이 오시는 것을 환영합니다. 기부금은 현관에서 받겠지만 요구되는 것은 결코 아닙니다. 그곳에서 모두를 뵙기를 고대합니다.
교감 Yuna Lee

구문 [7행~9행] These works were selected out of hundreds of applications [and] awarded the highest honor.
selected ~ applications와 awarded ~ honor가 병렬구조를 이루며, 둘 다 were에 이어지는 수동태 구문이다.

어휘 **mark** (중요 사건을) 기념하다; 표시하다 **exhibition** 전시회 **feature** 특별히 포함하다; 특징으로 삼다 **entry** 출품작 **application** 지원, 신청 **award** 수여하다; 상 **sculpture** 조각(품) **public** 대중의, 일반인의 **donation** 기부(금) **by no means** 결코 ~이 아닌 **look forward to** ~을 고대하다

19 심경 변화 ③

소재 눈 속에 갇혀 빠져나갈 수 없는 차

해설 차가 눈에 빠진 상황에서 다시 빠져나갈 준비를 수월하게 마쳤을 때는 마음이 놓였다가(relieved) 좁은 길을 빠져나갈 수 없다는 것을 깨달은 뒤 눈보라까지 휘몰아치자 막막함에 좌절했을(frustrated) 것이다. 따라서 'I'의 심경 변화로는 ③ '안도한 → 좌절한'이 가장 적절하다.

해석 나는 차의 앞쪽 끝을 잭으로 들어 올리고 그 아래 있는 눈을 치웠다. 그러는 동안에 Daniel은 차를 따뜻하게 유지해서 우리가 얼어 죽지 않게 하고, (차를 작동시키기 위한) 작업에 충분한 빛을 마련하려고 라디에이터에서 2피트 앞에 불을 지폈다. 주제문 핸들 조정은 놀라울 정도로 수월해서 우리는 몇 분 이내로 다시 떠날 준비가 되었다. 그런데 그때 우리는 좁은 길로 들어왔던 것보다 빠져나가는 것이 더 어렵다는 것을 알게 되었다. 빽빽한 나무들 때문에 어딘가에 끼어버리는 심각한 위험을 감수하지 않고서는 차를 돌릴 방법이 없었다. 게다가 휘몰아치는 눈보라 때문에 시야가 매우 흐려졌다. 주제문 우리가 더 할 수 있는 일은 아무것도 없었다.
① 애정 어린 → 감동한 ② 걱정스러운 → 기쁜
④ 화난 → 동정적인 ⑤ 슬픔에 잠긴 → 당황스러운

구문 [2행~5행] Daniel built a fire about two feet in front of the radiator / **to keep** the car warm [and] (**to keep**) us **from freezing** to death, / [and] **to furnish** enough light for the operation.
'목적'을 나타내는 부사적 용법의 to부정사구 to keep ~과 to furnish ~가 and로 연결되어 병렬구조를 이루고 있다. 「keep A from v-ing」는 'A가 v하지 못하게 하다'란 뜻이다.

[7행~8행] Then we discovered // that it(가주어) would be more difficult to get out of the lane(진주어) / than it(가주어) **had been** (difficult) to get in (the lane)(진주어).
비교급 문장으로, 공통된 부분(difficult, the lane)은 생략하는 것이 일반적이다. '차가 좁은 길에 빠진 것'이 먼저 일어난 일이므로 대과거(had p.p.)가 쓰였다. it은 가주어이고 두 개의 to부정사구가 각각의 진주어이다.

어휘 **in the meantime** 그러는 동안에 **radiator** 라디에이터, (자동차의) 냉각기 **freeze to death** 얼어 죽다 **furnish** (필요한 것을) 마련해 주다, 제공하다 **operation** (기계 등의) 작동; 수술 **lane** 좁은 길 **density** 빽빽함, 조밀함; 밀도 **get stuck** (옴짝달싹 못하게) 끼다, 빠지다 **whirl** 소용돌이치다 **visibility** 시야, 눈에 보이는 정도 [선택지 어휘] **affectionate** 애정 어린 **sympathetic** 동정적인; 공감[동조]하는 **mournful** 슬픔에 잠긴

20 필자 주장 ④

소재 시류에 휩쓸리지 않는 삶의 자세

해설 우리는 수많은 외부적 요인에 의해 정체성이 규정될 수 있는 위험 속에서 살고 있기 때문에, 진정한 자신의 모습을 점검하고 자신의 삶을 주체적으로 결정할 수 있어야 한다는 내용이므로 필자의 주장으로 가장 적절한 것은 ④이다.

해석 우리는 거품 속에서 살지 않는다. 우리는 다양한 측면을 가진, 역동적인 환경에서 산다. 즉, 매일 우리에게 무엇을 믿고 말하고 행하고 입어야 할지 말해주는 천 개의 목소리가 있는 것 같다. 그것들은 우리에게 삶은 어떠해야 하는지, 우리의 시간을 무엇을 하며 써야 하는지 말해준다. 이러한 목소리에 귀 기울이고 그것들이 우리 머릿속에 뿌리내리게 하며 그것에 굴복하는 것은 쉽다. 오늘날 인기 있는 것이면 무엇이든지 (우리 머릿속이) 그것에 의해 '쥐어짜져서 형성되기'가 쉽다. 그러나 우리는 '아니오'라고 말할 힘을 가지고 있다. 우리는 '이건 내가 아니야. 이건 내가 되고 싶은 모습이 아니야.'라고 말할 힘이 있다. 우리가 생각하는 것과 우리가 하는 선택들을 관찰하고 감시함으로써, 우리는 '현 시대'에 아니라고 말할 수 있다. 주제문 우리에게는 우리 삶의 방향을 결정할 힘이 있다.

구문 [5행~7행] It(가주어) is easy to give in to these voices(진주어), / **listening** to them [and] **allowing** them to take root inside our heads.
It은 가주어이고 to부정사구가 진주어이다. 분사구문 listening ~ them과 allowing ~ heads는 and로 연결되어 병렬구조를 이루며 '~하면서'의 의미를 가진다. 「allow+O+C(to-v) (O가 v하는 것을 허용하다)」 구문이 쓰였다.

[11행~13행] By observing and monitoring what we think about [and] *the choices* [(which[that]) we make], / we can say no to "the present age."
밑줄 친 부분은 observing and monitoring의 공통 목적어로, and로 연결되어 병렬구조를 이룬다.

어휘 **dynamic** 역동적인 **give in to** ~에 굴복하다 **take root** 뿌리를 내리다 **squeeze** 짜내다, 압착하다 **whatever** ~한 것이면 무엇이든지 **observe** 관찰하다; 준수하다 **monitor** 감시하다 **determine** 결정하다 **direction** 방향; (주로 복수형) 지시, 명령

21 밑줄 함의 ⑤

소재 인간의 학습 능력과 지식 전수

해설 인간 두뇌의 강점은 학습할 수 있는 능력이며, 인간은 조상 대대로 물려받은 지식을 축적할 수 있다. 이러한 의미에서 신생아가 '거인의 어깨 위에 서있다'는 것은 ⑤ '조상들이 획득한 지식을 사용한다'는 것을 의미한다.

해석 대략 25만 년 전에 수천 명의 호모사피엔스가 새로운 환경에 적응할 정도로 충분히 수준 높은 두뇌뿐만 아니라 한 세대에서 다음 세대로의 지식 전달 능력도 진화시켜온 두뇌의 도움을 받아 아프리카 밖으로 이주했다. 우리는 학습하도록 태어났다. 글쓰기와 인터넷이 발명되기 한참 전에도 인간은 어떤 다른 동물도 할 수 없었던 방식으로 서로 소통하는 능력을 가지고 있었다. 의사소통과 함께 테크놀로지와 기술의 폭발이 도래했다. 이것은 우리 유전자에 있는 정보가 아니라 오히려 다른 사람들에게서 배운 지식이었다. 주제문 우리의 부모와 그들(= 우리 부모)의 부모와 그들 이전의 그들의 부모의 부모는 각 세대로부터 물려받은 수천 년의 지식을 갖고 있었다. 그것이 모든 신생아들은 거인의 어깨 위에 서있다고 과학자들이 말하는 이유이다.

① 기꺼이 지적 진보를 이룬다
② 생존하는 법을 배우는 데 매우 많은 시간을 쓴다
③ 도움이 필요할 때 다른 사람들로부터 도움을 받는다
④ 배우기 위해 다른 사람들에게 주의를 기울인다

구문 [1행~6행] ~ a few thousand Homo sapiens migrated out of Africa, / **aided** by *a brain* [that was sophisticated **enough to** adapt to new environments] but also *one* [that had evolved *the capacity* (for the transmission of knowledge ~ to the next)].

aided 이하는 수동 의미의 분사구문이다. a brain과 one은 각각 관계대명사절의 수식을 받으며, one은 a brain을 지칭한다. 「형용사 enough to-v」는 'v할 정도로 충분히 …한'의 뜻이다.

[9행~10행] With communication *came*(V) *an explosion*(S) (in technology and skills).

부사구가 문두로 오면서 주어와 동사의 위치가 바뀐 도치구문이다.

[10행~12행] This was [not] *information*(A) (in our genes) [but] rather *knowledge*(B) (learned from others).

「not A but B」는 'A가 아니라 B'의 뜻이다. A와 B에 해당하는 각각의 명사는 전명구와 과거분사구의 수식을 받고 있다.

어휘 **approximately** 대략 **migrate** 이주하다, 이동하다 **aid** 돕다; 도움 **sophisticated** 수준 높은; 정교한, 복잡한; 세련된 **adapt** 적응하다; 맞추다, 조정하다 **evolve** 발달[진화]시키다 **capacity** 능력; 수용력 **transmission** 전달, 전파 **explosion** 폭발적인 증가 **gene** 유전자 **pass down** ~을 물려주다 **newborn** 갓 태어난, 신생의 [선택지 어휘] **intellectual** 지적인 **progress** 진보, 발달 **intelligence** 지능; 정보 **ancestor** 조상

22 글의 요지 ②

소재 예술의 사회 반영

해설 예술은 예술 자체로서만 감상해야 한다는 견해도 있지만, 예술은 예술가가 당대의 사회를 자신의 눈을 통해 표현한 것이므로 사회를 배제한 예술 감상은 불완전할 수밖에 없다는 내용의 글이므로 요지로 가장 적절한 것은 ②이다.

해석 예술은 외부와 단절된 상태에서 존재해야 하며, 그것의 아름다움과 그것이 관람자에게서 이끌어내는 감정을 위해 감상되어야 한다고 주장할 수 있을 것이다. 그러나 어떤 예술은 그것이 어디에서 나왔는지를 이해하지 않고서는 적절히 이해될 수 없다. 사회적으로 용인되는 것, 사회적으로 금지된 것, 그리고 사회적으로 웃기는 것은 예술가가 당대의 사회를 묘사하는 방식으로 예술가의 눈을 통해 보일 수 있다. 어떤 사회에서 웃기는 것이 다른 사회에서는 반대가 될 수도 있다. 우리가 과거 시대의 방식 혹은 현재 시대의 방식을 볼 수 있게 하는 것은 예술을 통해서이다. 주제문 예술은 많은 상황에서 예술가를 위한 뮤즈로서의 역할을 했던 사회의 반영이다. 사회에 관한 인식이 없으면, 그것의 메시지는 옮기는 과정에서 손실될 수 있다.

구문 [1행~3행] It(가주어) could be argued that art should exist in a vacuum(진주어) [and] be appreciated for its beauty and *the emotions* [that it induces ● from its viewer].

It은 가주어이고 that절이 진주어이다. that절에서 should 다음의 동사원형 exist와 be appreciated가 병렬구조를 이룬다. 목적격 관계대명사 that이 이끄는 관계사절은 the emotions를 수식한다.

[9행~10행] **It is** *through the art* **that** we can see *the way* [times were] or *the way* [times are].

「It is ~ that ...」 강조구문은 It is와 that 사이의 표현을 강조하며 '~한 것은 바로 …이다'의 뜻이다. 두 개의 [ ] 부분은 각각 앞의 the way를 수식하는 관계부사절로 선행사가 the way이므로 관계부사 how를 생략했다. the way how의 형태로는 쓰지 않는 것에 유의하자.

어휘 **vacuum** 공백; 진공 (상태) **appreciate** 감상하다; 진가를 인정하다; 감사하다 **induce** 유도[유발]하다 **properly** 적절히 **acceptable** 받아들일 수 있는 **forbidden** 금지된 **comical** 웃기는, 재미있는 **portray** 묘사하다, 그리다 **opposite** 반대(되는 것); (정)반대의 **reflection** 반영; 반사; 심사숙고 **serve as** ~로서의 역할을 하다 **circumstances** 상황 **societal** 사회의, 사회에 관한 **recognition** 인식 **translation** (다른 형태로) 옮김, 변형; 번역

23 글의 주제 ③

소재 토양의 상태 판단에 도움을 주는 잡초

해설 정원의 잡초는 토양의 비옥도와 산성도, 배수 상태 및 기를 수 있는 식물의 범위를 알려주는 지표로 활용될 수 있다는 내용의 글이므로 주제로 가장 적절한 것은 ③ '토양 상태의 지표로서의 잡초'이다.

해석 주제문 잡초는 당신에게 당신의 정원에 관한 많은 것을 얘기해줄 수 있다. 잡초가 빠르게 증식하면 토양이 극히 비옥하여 비료가 필요치 않을 것이다. 잡초의 양이 다양하면 정원에 광범위한 식물을 기를 수 있을 것이다. 그렇지 않다면, 토양 종류를 판단하는 것이 가치 있을 것이다. 잡초는 낮은 pH(산성 토양), 높은 pH(알칼리성 토양), 그리고 형편없는 배수와 같은 토양의 품질에 관한 중요한 단서들을 제공할 수 있다. 예를 들어 대단히 산성인 토양은 민들레를 산출할 것이며, 반면에 공작국화는 약산성 토양에서 발견된다. 잡초와 그것이 선호하는 토양의 종류에 관해 배우는 것은 당신의 정원으로 더 나은 장소를 선택하거나 토양의 상태를 판단하려고 애쓸 때 지침으로서 그 지식을 사용하는 데 도움이 될 수 있다.

① 잡초의 생태적 적응력
② 정원에서 자라는 잡초의 종류들
④ 정원의 잡초를 관리하는 방법들
⑤ 잡초 경합이 작물 생장에 미치는 영향들

구문 [1행~3행] If your weeds multiply rapidly, it(가주어) is likely that your soil is extremely fertile(진주어) [and] that you do not need fertilizer(진주어).

it은 가주어이고 접속사 that으로 시작되는 두 개의 that절이 진주어이다.

[11행~14행] Learning about weeds and *the types of soil* [(which[that]) they prefer ●](S) can help(V) you(O) **choose** a better spot for your garden(C1) [or] **use** the knowledge as guides / when trying to determine the state of your soil(C2).

Learning ~ prefer는 동명사구 주어이며 동사는 can help이다. they prefer는 앞에 목적격 관계대명사가 생략되어 the types of soil을 수식하며, they는 weeds를 지칭한다. 「help+O+(to)-v」은 'O가 v하는 것을 돕다'의 뜻인데, choose와 use로 시작되는 두 개의 원형부정사구가 목적격보어로 병렬구조를 이룬다.

어휘 **weed** 잡초 **multiply** 증대하다 **rapidly** 빠르게 **likely** ~할 것 같은 **fertile** 비옥한; 생식력 있는 **fertilizer** 비료 **diverse** 다양한 **a wide range of** 광범위한 **worthwhile** 가치 있는 **clue** 단서, 실마리 **acid** 산성의; 산성

cf. **acidic** 산성의; 매우 신 **alkaline** 알칼리성의 **drainage** 배수 **spot** 곳, 장소 **state** 상태 [선택지 어휘] **ecological** 생태계의 **adaptability** 적응성, 순응성 **indicator** 지표, 척도 **condition** 상태 **crop** (농)작물

24 글의 제목 ①

소재 사멸한 언어 구하기

해설 사멸한 언어도 그것을 학습하려는 사람이 생기고, 그들을 가르칠 충분한 자원과 지역사회의 관심이 있다면 되살릴 수 있다는 내용의 글이므로 제목으로 가장 적절한 것은 ① '사멸 언어를 어떻게 구할 수 있을까?'이다.

해석 언어가 사멸해도 그 언어에 관한 문서화가 충분히 되어 있다면 그것을 구할 기회는 있다. 심지어 과거 수십 년간 죽은 언어들도 그 언어를 극적으로 소생시킨 회생 노력을 목도한 바 있다. 히브리어와 콘월어는 그러한 두 가지 예다. 이 언어들은 회생 노력으로 인해 주류적으로 쓰일 수 있도록 재소환되기까지는 사멸 상태였다. 그것들을 회생시킨 비결은 두 경우 모두에서 그 언어를 열성적인 학습자에게 가르칠 충분한 자원과 그 언어를 구하는 것에 대한 강한 지역사회의 관심이 있었다는 데 있다. 어떤 언어를 배울 때에도 동기부여는 중요하다. 언어가 사람과 문화 양측에 의미하는 바를 이해하는 것이 사람들이 들어와서 언어를 구하고 싶어 하도록 독려하는 비결이다. 주제문 **동기부여가 존재하고 언어 학습자들에게 안정적이고 지원해주는 환경이 있다면, 그 언어를 구할 가능성은 증가한다.**

② 사멸 언어: 원인과 결과
③ 사멸 언어가 중요한 이유
④ 언어는 언제 사멸 위기에 처하게 되는가?
⑤ 곧 사라질 사멸 위기의 언어들

구문 [3행~5행] Even *languages* [that have died in the past several decades] have seen *revitalization efforts* [that brought the language back to life dramatically].
(S: Even languages ~ decades / V: have seen / O: revitalization efforts ~ dramatically)
주어와 목적어를 수식하는 관계사절이 이어져 주어와 목적어가 길어진 형태이다.

[13행~15행] Understanding (O)what language means to both a person and a culture / is key to **inspiring** *people* **to want** to step in and save the language.
(S: Understanding ~ culture / V: is)
Understanding ~ culture가 동명사 주어이며 is가 동사이다. 주어에서 what ~ a culture는 동사 understand의 목적어 역할을 하는 명사절이다. 「both A and B」는 'A와 B 둘 다'의 뜻이다. 「inspire+O+C(to-v) (O가 v하도록 격려하다)」 구문이 쓰였다. want to 다음의 동사원형 step in과 save는 병렬구조를 이룬다.

어휘 **go extinct** 사멸[멸종]되다 *cf.* **extinct** 사멸한, 멸종된 **provided** (만약) ~라면 **documentation** 기록, 문서화 **decade** 십 년 **revitalization** 회생 **effort** 노력 **bring A back to life** A를 되살리다 **dramatically** 극적으로 **Hebrew** 히브리어 **Cornish** 콘월어(잉글랜드 콘월 지방에서 사용했던 켈트어) **reintroduce** 재도입하다 **mainstream** 주류의 **resource** 자원 **eager** 열망하는, 열성적인 **inspire** (감정 등을) 불어넣다; 영감을 주다; 격려하다 **supportive** 지원하는, 도와주는 **chances** 가능성, 확률 [선택지 어휘] **endangered** 사멸[멸종] 위기에 처한 **disappear** 사라지다

25 도표 이해 ③

소재 외국인들에 대한 미국 주택 판매율 통계

해설 멕시코가 2007년 가장 많은 구매자에서 2012년에 세 번째로 많은 구매자로 떨어진 것은 맞지만, 여섯 나라 중 가장 큰 구매율 하락을 보인 나라는 영국이다. 따라서 ③이 도표의 내용과 일치하지 않는다.

해석 〈외국인들에 대한 미국 주택 판매〉

주제문 **위 도표는 2007년과 2012년의 외국인들에 대한 미국 주택 판매를 캐나다, 중국, 멕시코, 영국, 인도, 프랑스를 포함한 여섯 개의 선별된 국가들의 구매자 비율로 보여준다.** ① 캐나다와 중국 두 나라 모두 구매자 비율이 2007년과 비교하여 2012년에 더 높았으며, 캐나다에서 가장 큰 증가를 보였다. ② 2012년의 가장 많은 구매자인 캐나다는 중국의 구매의 두 배보다 많이 차지했고, 그 관계는 2007년에서도 보였다. ③ 반면, 멕시코는 2007년에 가장 많은 구매자에서 2012년에 세 번째로 많은 구매자로 떨어졌는데, 그것은 여섯 나라 중 가장 큰 하락을 보인 것이다. ④ 영국과 인도는 2012년에 각각 6%의 구매율로 같았는데, 그 구매율은 프랑스의 구매율의 두 배였다. ⑤ 인도와 프랑스는 전자(인도)는 6%, 후자(프랑스)는 3%에 변함없이 머무르면서 구매 비율의 변화를 보이지 않았다.

구문 [14행~16행] India and France showed no change / in their proportion of purchases, / **with** *the former* **remaining** steady at 6% and *the latter* (remaining steady) at 3%.
with ~ 3%는 and로 병렬 연결된 「with+O+v-ing」의 구조로서 'O가 v한 채로[v하면서]'를 의미한다. the latter 뒤의 remaining steady는 중복되어 생략되었다.

어휘 **selected** 선별된, 선택된 *cf.* **select** 선발하다 **relative to** ~에 비교[비례]하여 **account for** (부분·비율을) 차지하다; 설명하다 **purchase** 구매(하다) **drop** 줄어들다 **proportion** 비율; 부분 **the former** (둘 중) 전자(의) (↔ **the latter** 후자(의)) **steady** 변함[변동]없는; 꾸준한

26 내용 불일치 ②

소재 Herbert Spencer의 활동

해설 두 번째 문장에서 Herbert Spencer는 1841년부터가 아니라 1841년까지 수년 간 철도 회사에서 일했다고 했으므로 ②가 글의 내용과 일치하지 않는다.

해석 Herbert Spencer는 1820년 잉글랜드에서 태어났다. ① Spencer는 처음에는 아버지가 북돋아준 과학적 흥미를 따라 공학을 공부했다. ② 1841년까지 수년 동안, 그는 런던과 버밍엄 철도 회사에서 일하는 토목기사로 고용됐다. ③ 철도를 건설하는 동안 발견된 화석을 조사하다가 진화에 대한 그의 관심이 생겼다고 한다. Spencer는 나중에 문필가로서의 경력을 시작하고 자신의 과학적 흥미의 일부를 추구하기 위하여 철도 업계를 떠났다. ④ 그는 〈The Non-Conformist〉에 기고하는 것부터 시작했는데, 〈정부의 적정 영역〉이라는 일련의 편지를 썼다. 이것은 그의 첫 번째 주요 저작이었으며 개인주의와 자유방임주의에 대한 그의 기본 개념을 포함했는데, 이는 나중에 그의 〈사회정역학〉(1850년)과 다른 저작물들에서 좀 더 완전히 발전되었다. ⑤ 개인의 권리와 국가 측의 불간섭이라는 이상이 특히 강조되었다.

구문 [6행~8행] His interest in evolution / is said **to have arisen** from the examination of *fossils* (discovered during the construction of railroads).
「to have p.p.」는 술어동사(is said)보다 먼저 일어난 일을 서술할 때 쓰는 표현이다. ( ) 부분은 수동의 뜻으로 fossils를 수식하는 과거분사구이다.

[16행~18행] Especially stressed were the right of the individual and the ideal of noninterference on the part of the state.
(C: Especially stressed / V: were / S: the right ~ state)
보어가 주어에 비해 매우 짧을 경우, 이해를 쉽게 하기 위해 문두로 보내고 주어와 동사를 도치하는 경우가 종종 있다.

어휘 **initially** 처음에 **pursue** 따르다; 추구하다 **engineering** 공학 **civil engineer** 토목기사 **evolution** 진화 **arise** 생기다 **examination** 조사, 검토; 시험 **fossil** 화석 **construction** 건설, 공사 **industry** 산업 **take up** (직장 등을) 시작하다; ~을 계속하다; 자리를 잡다 **a literary career** 문필가로서의 경력 **contribute to** ~에 기고하다; ~에 기부하다 **Non-conformist** 비국교도; 일반적 관행을 따르지 않는 사람 **sphere** (활동·영향·관심의) 영역; 구(球) **ideal** 이상; 이상적인 **noninterference** 불간섭 **on the part of** ~측의, ~쪽에서 **state** 국가; 주(州); 상태

27 안내문 불일치 ③

소재 신입생 오리엔테이션 자원봉사 기회

해설 자격 요건에서 9월 3~4일에 의무 교육에 참가해야 한다고 했으므로 의무 교육 기간은 2일임을 알 수 있다. 따라서 ③이 안내문의 내용과 일치하지 않는다.

해석

신입생 오리엔테이션
자원봉사 기회

신입생 오리엔테이션 자원봉사팀에 합류하여 신입생들과 편입생들이 새로운 Standford 대학생으로서 맞이하는 첫날을 환영해 주세요.

일자: ① 2020년 9월 8일 월요일~9월 12일 금요일 (입학식은 오리엔테이션의 마지막 날 오전 10시에 시작합니다.)

신입생들을 환영하는 데 대단히 중요한 역할을 맡습니다.
- 신입생들 맞이하기
- 학생들을 기숙사로 데려다주기
- ② 행사를 위한 탁자와 의자 준비하기
- ② 학생들에게 워크숍으로 가는 길을 안내하고 일반적인 질문에 답변하기

자격 요건:
- ③ 9월 3~4일에는 의무 교육에 참가해야 합니다
- ④ 9월 8~12일에 참가할 시간이 있어야 합니다 (일정 충돌 안 됨)

⑤ 모든 자원봉사자들은 2주 일찍 기숙사로 입사할 수 있습니다.

어휘 **entrance ceremony** 입학식 **play a role** 역할을 맡다 **critical** 대단히 중요한; 비판적인 **residence** 거주(지) **set up** 준비하다; 설치하다 **direct** (길을) 안내하다; ~로 향하다; 지휘[감독]하다 **general** 일반[보편]적인 **requirements** 자격 요건 **mandatory** 의무적인 **available** 시간이 있는; 이용할 수 있는 **conflict** 충돌, 갈등

28 안내문 일치 ⑤

소재 장애를 가진 성인과 십 대를 위한 행사

해설 장애가 있는 성인과 십 대를 위해 마련된 활동을 소개하는 안내문이다. 십 대 수강료는 30달러이고 성인 수강료는 35달러이므로 ⑤가 안내문과 일치한다.

해석

모험의 날들
장애를 가진 성인과 십 대를 위한 활동

재미난 공예, 운동, 기타 활동들, 그리고 이어지는 즐겁고 친목을 도모하는 바비큐에 함께 하세요!
① 우리는 격주 토요일에 만납니다. 활동은 오전 10시에 시작되고 바비큐는 오후 12시 30분에 시작될 것입니다.

- ② 참가를 위해서는 사전 등록과 납부를 하셔야 합니다.
- 모든 활동은 휠체어 접근이 가능합니다.
- 도움이 필요한 참가자들은 도우미를 데려와야 합니다. ③ 어떤 활동이나 바비큐도 도우미에게는 요금이 청구되지 않습니다.
- ④ 바비큐 손님이 '곁들여 먹을 음식'을 가져오는 것을 환영하지만 의무적인 것은 아닙니다.
- ⑤ 월 요금: 성인 1인당 35달러, 십 대는 1인당 30달러

모든 활동은 Rosemont의 Bennett Road 704번지에 있는 Bennett Senior 센터에서 열립니다.

더 많은 정보를 알려면 774-9345-6285로 Robin Sykes에게 연락하시거나 sykestobeyou@angelmail.com로 이메일을 주십시오.

구문 [3행~4행] Join us for fun crafts, exercise, and other activities, / (being) **followed** by a fun and social barbecue!
followed는 앞에 나온 내용에 덧붙여서 설명하는 분사구문을 이끌며 앞에 being이 생략되어 있다. (being) followed by는 '뒤이어, 잇달아'로 해석하면 자연스럽다.

어휘 **disability** (신체적 · 정신적) 장애 **craft** 공예 **social** 친목의, 사교적인 **pre-registration** 사전 등록 **payment** 지불, 납입 **require** ~을 필요로 하다

accessible 접근하기 쉬운 **charge** (요금 · 값을) 청구하다; 요금; 책임 **side dish** 곁들임 요리, 반찬

29 밑줄 어법 ④

소재 전염병을 피해 교회로 간 시민들과 그들이 들어오지 못하게 막은 사제들

해설 ④ permitting이 되려면 gave up의 목적어가 돼서 '재물이 남아있는 것을 허락하는 것을 포기했다'의 의미가 되는데 이는 문맥상 맞지 않다. gave up과 병렬구조를 이루도록 permitted로 고치면 '수도사들은 되던지기를 포기하고 재물이 남아있는 것을 허락했다'의 의미가 되어 문맥상 자연스럽다.

오답 분석 ① '~하기 위하여'라는 '목적'의 의미를 나타내는 to부정사를 사용했다. 문장의 주어는 the citizens이고 동사는 descended이다. ② the monks and priests를 지칭하는 소유격이므로 their를 썼다. ③ 수도사들이 겁먹게 하는 상황이 아니라 자신들이 겁먹은 상황이므로 수동 의미의 과거분사가 적절히 쓰였다. ⑤ the money가 주어이고 remained가 동사이며 untouched는 the money의 상태를 설명하는 보어이다. 돈이 '손대지지 않은' 상태이므로 과거분사 형태를 썼다.

해석 1347년에 흑사병이 유럽 전역에서 창궐했을 때, 독일 뤼베크의 시민들은 신의 분노를 피하기 위하여 막대한 양의 돈과 재물을 가지고 교회로 내려갔다. 이 교회 안의 수도사들과 사제들은 오염이 두려워서 그들의 문을 걸어 잠갔고 시민들이 들어오는 것을 허락하지 않으려 했다. 군중들은 벽 너머로 귀중품, 동전, 금과 보석을 던졌다. 겁에 질린 수도사들은 그것들을 전부 되던졌다. 앞뒤로 던지기가 몇 시간 계속되었고, 마침내 수도사들은 되던지기를 포기하고 재물이 남아있는 것을 허락했다. 몇 시간 안에 무더기가 3, 4피트 높이로 생겼고, 이 사건 이후로 몇 달 동안 돈은 손대지 않은 상태로 남아 있었다.

어휘 **the Black Plague** 흑사병, 페스트 **rage** 창궐하다, 맹위를 떨치다; 격렬한 분노 **descend** 내려가다 **enormous** 거대한 **riches** 재물, 부 **monk** 수도사 **priest** 사제 **contamination** 오염 **valuables** 귀중품 **jewel** 보석 **frightened** 겁먹은 **back-and-forth** 앞뒤의 **toss** 던지다 **incident** 사건

30 밑줄 어휘 ⑤

소재 농장 문화에 익숙한 스웨덴 사람들

해설 스웨덴이 농업 기반 사회였으며, 도시화된 후에도 스웨덴 사람들의 마음속에는 여전히 농장과 자연으로 돌아가려고 하는 생각이 남아 있다는 내용이 글 중반부까지 이어지고 있다. 후반부의 This is also true of younger Swedes(이것은 또한 젊은 스웨덴 사람들에게도 마찬가지이다)를 통해 스웨덴의 젊은이들도 부모들처럼 시골 생활을 동경한다는 것을 알 수 있으므로, ⑤ opposite는 similar와 같이 유사성을 의미하는 단어로 바꾸어야 한다.

해석 최근까지 스웨덴은 농업 기반 사회였다. 1900년대 초 산업혁명이 노동자들을 도시로 유입시킬 때까지 대략 90%의 가정이 농장에서 살았다. 스웨덴은 ① 급격하게 산업화된 도시 기반의 나라로 바뀌었다. 따라서 많은 스웨덴 사람들은 농장에서의 삶을 기억한다. 농장에 대한 ② 유대감은 여전히 매우 강하게 남아있다. 비록 대부분의 스웨덴 사람들은 일상적인 도시 생활을 즐기긴 하지만, 그 과거가 그렇게 ③ 멀지 않기 때문에, 스웨덴 사람들은 마음속으로는 여전히 조상들의 방식으로 쉽게 돌아갈 수 있는 농부들이다. 주제문 농장으로 돌아가고 자연으로 돌아가자는 낭만주의가 스웨덴 문화의 큰 부분을 구성한다. 스웨덴 사람들은 자신들에게 더 소박했던 시절을 생각나게 할 수 있는 시골로 ④ 탈출하기를 갈망한다. 이것은 또한 스마트폰에 상당히 많은 양의 시간을 바치는 것처럼 보이는 젊은 스웨덴 사람들에게도 마찬가지이다. 하지만(많은 시간을 스마트폰을 사용하며 보내기는 하지만), 시골에서 이 젊은 스웨덴 사람들은 자신들의 부모와 ⑤ 반대되는(→ 유사한) 방식으로 행동한다.

구문 [7행~10행] Although they enjoy everyday city life, // most Swedes are still *peasants* at heart [**who** could easily return to the ways of their ancestors], // because the past is not too distant.
관계대명사 who가 가리키는 선행사는 바로 앞에 있는 heart가 아니라 peasants이다.

어휘 **agriculturally** 농업적으로, 농사와 관련하여 *cf.* **agriculture** 농업 **the Industrial Revolution** 산업혁명 *cf.* **industrialized** 산업화한 **Swede** 스웨덴 사람 **tie** 유대감, 유대 관계 **remain** 여전히 ~이다; 남다 **peasant** 농부, 소작농 **ancestor** 선조, 조상 **distant** 먼; 거리를 두는 **romanticism** 낭만주의 **constitute** 구성하다; 설립[제정]하다 **long for** ~을 갈망하다 **remind A of B** A에게 B를 생각나게 하다 **devote A to B** B에 A를 바치다[쏟다] **significant** 상당한 **still** 하지만; 여전히 **fashion** 방식; 유행

31 빈칸 추론 ③

소재 구두시험에서 겸손의 미덕

해설 대학원의 구두시험에서 대학원생은 시험관인 교수와의 권력 관계에서 하부에 있고, 교수는 원하는 무엇이든, 언제든 질문할 수 있는 데 반해 대학원생은 불손하거나 자신감만 내비쳐도 불리해질 수 있으므로 ③ '겸손(humility)'을 갖추는 것이 필요할 것이다.

해석 대학원 시절에 나는 내 분야에 충분한 배경지식을 갖추고 있는지를 시험하는, 흔히 있는 구두시험에 직면했다. 어떤 교수님들이 위원회에 계시는지를 아는 것은 내가 어떤 질문이 제시될지 예측하게 해 주었다. 그렇기는 하지만 구두시험은 대학원에서 그들이 당신을 통제하거나 지배하거나 (당신에 대한) 권력을 쥘 수 있는 경우 중 하나이다. 시험관들은 그럴 마음만 있으면 그들 맘대로 그저 어떤 것에 관해서도 질문할 수 있었다. 당신은 과속 때문에 당신을 세운 경찰관에게 할 것처럼 그것들(= 질문들)에 답하여 최선을 다한다. 당신이 무례한 경향이 있다면, 긴장한 체 하는 편이 낫다. 심지어 온건한 자신감조차 몇몇 시험관들로 하여금 당신이 당신 생각보다 재능이 떨어진다는 것을 깨닫게 할 마음이 생기게 할 수 있다. 당신이 하는 몸짓, 자세, 혹은 어조가 당신이 몇 달 뒤에 시험의 일부를 다시 치르게 할 수 있다. 주제문 따라서 구두시험 동안에는 겸손이 성공한다.

① 긍정성 ② 정직 ④ 인내 ⑤ 열정

구문 [3행~5행] Knowing O′which professors were on the committee (S) allowed (V) me (O) to predict (C) O′which questions might be asked.

Knowing~committee는 동명사 주어이고 동사는 allowed이다. which~committee는 간접의문문으로 Knowing의 목적어이다. 「allow+O+to-v (O가 v하는 것을 허락하다)」 구문이 쓰였다. which ~ asked 역시 간접의문문이며 predict의 목적어이다.

어휘 **graduate school** 대학원 **usual** 흔히 하는[있는] **oral** 구두의, 말의 **sufficient** 충분한 **committee** 위원회 **even so** 그렇기는 하지만 **occasion** 경우, 때 **dominate** 지배하다 **inclined** (~할) 생각이 있는 **pull ~ over** (~가 길 한쪽으로) 차를 대게 하다 **be prone to** ~하는 경향이 있다 **discourtesy** 무례 **pretend to-v** v인 체하다 **inspire** 마음이 생기게 하다, 고무시키다 **talented** 재능 있는 **posture** 자세 **pay off** 성공하다, 성과가 있다

32 빈칸 추론 ①

소재 의사 결정이 자아 상태에 미치는 영향

해설 선택지가 많으면 선택이 지연되며 선택을 한 후에는 잘한 선택이었는지 의구심이 남는다. 반면에 선택권이 없으면 선택의 책임은 면제받지만 이는 우울한 상황이다. 결국 이 모든 경우들은 ① '승자가 없는 상황'이라고 정리할 수 있다.

해석 잉글랜드 시인 Edward Young이 말했듯이, "미루는 버릇은 시간 도둑이다." 이용할 수 있는 온갖 선택들과 제시되는 다른 유혹들이 있는 상황에서, 우리는 지금 해야 하는 일을 너무 늦을 때까지 미룬다. 주제문 의사 결정에 관한 이 모든 일은 우리 자아가 우리가 제시 받는 선택들의 처분에 놓여 있음을 여러분에게 명확히 말해줄 것이다. 우리의 의사 결정 능력은 상황에 달려있다. 선택이 너무 많으면, 대안이 서로를 상쇄하고, 우리에게는 망설임만 남는다. 우리가 정말 결정을 할 때조차도, 올바른 선택을 했는지를 숙고하느라 만족감이 낮아진다. 우리에게 선택이 없다면, 아무 문제도 없고 탓할 것은 세상이다. 그러나 그때 우리는 우울해진다. 그러나 우리가 이상적인 것으로 판명되지 않는 것을 선택할 때, 그러면 현명하게 선택하지 않았기에 그것은 우리 잘못이다. 많은 경우 승자가 없는 상황이 된다.

② 오엑스 문제
③ 투쟁 – 도피 접근법 (= 갑작스런 자극에 투쟁할 것인가 도주할 것인가에 대한 본능적 반응)
④ 무가치 판단
⑤ 근심 걱정 없는 과정

어휘 **observe** (의견을) 말하다; 관찰하다; 준수하다 **temptation** 유혹 **put off** 미루다 **at the mercy of** ~의 처분대로 **capacity** 능력, 수용력 **dependent** 달려 있는, 의존하는 **alternative** 대안 **cancel ~ out** ~을 상쇄하다 **hesitation** 주저, 망설임 **dwell on** ~을 깊이 생각하다, 숙고하다 *cf.* **dwell** 살다, 거주하다 **be to blame** ~의 탓이다 **depressed** 우울한 **turn out** 드러나다, 입증되다 **ideal** 이상적인; 이상

33 빈칸 추론 ⑤

소재 Hemingway의 글쓰기 비법

해설 Hemingway가 꾸준히 글을 쓸 수 있었던 비법은 앞으로의 전개를 알고 있는 상태에서 작업을 중단한 것이었다. 그러면 다음 날 아침에 이어서 글을 빨리 쓰고 싶을 것이고 작업을 수월하게 시작할 수 있기 때문이다. 여기서 그가 사용한 전략은 글쓰기를 ⑤ '진행하고자 하는 갈망을 이용한' 것이다.

해석 Ernest Hemingway(어니스트 헤밍웨이)는 인간 본성의 열렬한 학생이었고, 자신의 수행을 증진시키기 위해 목표를 정했다. 많은 작가들처럼 Hemingway는 글쓰기의 가장 힘든 부분은 매일 시작하는 것이라는 점을 발견했다. 주제문 그래서 그는 자신만의 글쓰기 관행을 개발했다. 인터뷰를 하는 동안 "하루에 얼마나 쓰셔야 합니까?"라는 질문을 받았을 때, Hemingway는 "최고의 방법은 잘 진행되고 있을 때, 그리고 다음에 무슨 일이 생길지 알 때 항상 멈추는 것입니다. 소설을 쓸 때 그렇게 매일 하면 결코 막히지 않을 겁니다."라고 충고했다. 그는 매일 한 장(章)을 거의 완성하지만, 완전히는 완성하지 않은 채로 멈추는 관행을 개발했다. 다음 날 아침에 그는 진행하고자 하는 갈망을 이용할 수 있었고 그 장을 완성하기 위해 열심히 앉아있을 수 있었다. 일단 일에 몰두하고 기분이 좋아지면, 그는 다음 장이 거의 완성될 때까지 글쓰기를 계속할 수 있었다.

① 단시간에 많은 일을 할
② 밤에 취한 휴식으로 활력을 얻을
③ 분할 정복 기법을 사용할
④ 밤사이에 갑자기 영감이 떠오르기를 기다릴

구문 [11행~12행] He developed a practice of stopping each day **with** *a chapter* **almost, but not quite, complete.**

「with+O+형용사」는 'O가 ~한 채로'의 뜻이다.

[14행~15행] Once (he was) immersed in work [and] feeling good, ~.

접속사 Once는 '일단 ~하면'의 뜻이며, 뒤에 he was가 생략되어 있다. 분사 immersed와 feeling이 병렬구조를 이룬다.

어휘 **keen** 열정적인, 열렬한 **performance** 수행 **tough** 힘든 **stuck** 막힌; 꼼짝도 못 하는 **chapter** 장(章) **not quite** 완전히 ~하지는 않은 **eagerly** 열심히 **immersed in** ~에 몰두한 [선택지 어휘] **vitality** 활력, 생명력 **inspiration** 영감 **strike** (생각이) 갑자기 떠오르다; 때리다, 치다 **take advantage of** ~을 이용하다

34 빈칸 추론 ③

소재 과학과 미술사의 차이점

해설 빈칸 문장에 표현된 '과거'나 '문화적 관행'은 본문에서 '과학'과 대비되는 것이다. 추구하는 목표가 있어 문제 해결을 완료할 수 있는 과학과는 달리, 문화적 관행을 해석하는 것은 광범위한 인간의 생각을 재해석하여 새로운 의미를 찾아내는 과정이므로, 이를 다른 말로 표현하여 빈칸을 완성하면 ③ '그것은 옳고 그름의 문제가 아니라 통찰을 찾는 것의 문제이다'가 된다.

해석 주제문 과학과 미술사 사이에는 한 가지 중요한 차이점이 있다. 과학자는 결국에는 효과적인 암 치료제인 약을 발견할 수도 있고, 그러면 그녀의 일은 완료되거나, 적어도 그

12

것의 한 단계가 종료 지점에 달한다. 그러나 역사, 미술, 그리고 문화의 해석은 다르다. 그것들은 매우 광범위한 인간의 생각과 경험을 표현해서 미술사가가 추구할 한 가지 결과만 있는 것은 아니다. 각 개인, 각 세대, 각 문화는 미술 작품을 재해석하면서 그 안에서 새로운 의미를 찾아낸다. 분명히, 어떤 주장은 다른 주장보다 더 설득력이 있고, 어떤 주장은 더 광범위한 증거를 더 잘 설명한다. 그러나 우리가 과거를 해석하거나 문화적 관행을 해석하는 것에 관해 이야기할 때, 그것은 옳고 그름의 문제가 아니라 통찰을 찾는 것의 문제이다.

① 그것은 미래를 향한 우리의 목표와 항상 연결되어야 한다
② 우리는 과학 또한 복잡한 역사가 있음을 인정할 필요가 있다
④ 중요한 것은 과거의 사실이 아니라 현재의 사건이다
⑤ 우리는 모든 증거를 모아서 가장 설득력 있는 부분을 받아들여야 한다

구문 [6행~8행] ~ they express such a wide range of human ideas and experiences that there is *no one result* for the art historian **to seek**.

「such ~ that ...」은 '너무 ~해서 …하다'의 뜻이다. such 다음에는 「such a(n)+형용사+명사」의 어순을 따른다. for the art historian은 to seek의 의미상 주어이며, to seek은 no one result를 수식한다.

어휘 **in the end** 결국 **treatment** 치료(법); 취급 **phase** 단계, 국면 **closure** 종료[종결] **interpretation** 해석 *cf.* **reinterpret** 재해석하다 **a wide range of** 광범위한 **generation** 세대; (전기 · 열 등의) 발생 **significance** 의미; 중요성 **argument** 주장; 논쟁 **persuasive** 설득력 있는 **account for** ~을 설명하다 **evidence** 증거 [선택지 어휘] **accept** 인정하다, 받아들이다 **complicated** 복잡한 **insight** 통찰(력) **matter** 중요하다, 문제가 되다; 물질; 문제 **gather** 모으다 **evidence** 증거

35 무관한 문장 ④

소재 직장생활에 대한 조언

해설 직장에서 모든 일을 혼자서 처리하려 하지 말고, 항상 자신이 모든 일의 중심이 될 필요도 없다고 조언하는 내용의 글이다. 반면에 ④는 동료가 도움을 요청하면 기꺼이 도와야 한다는 내용으로 글의 흐름과 맞지 않는다.

해석 만약 당신이 직장에서 점점 더 많은 시간을 계속해서 보내고 있다면 당신은 너무 많이 (일을) 하고 있거나 아니면 그것을 제대로 하지 않고 있는 것 둘 중의 하나이다. 그리고 잠깐만, 애초부터 그것이 정말로 당신의 일이었는가? 주제문 당신이 스스로 그 일을 하기로 선택했건 또는 상사에게서 일을 받았건 간에 당신의 직장 생활에서 한도를 설정하라. 이는 (직장에) 도착하는 시간과 귀가하는 시간을 설정하고 당신의 몸이 필요로 하는 모든 휴식을 틈틈이 취하는 것을 의미한다. 그리고 그것은 또한 인간관계를 형성하고 해야 할 다른 중요한 일들을 할 시간을 계획하는 것을 의미하기도 한다. 동료가 당신에게 도움을 요청하면 기꺼이 그리고 정중하게 그 요청에 응답해야 한다. 마지막으로, 모든 것을 처리하는 것이 당신의 일이 아니란 점과 당신이 모든 경기에서 가장 중요한 선수가 될 수는 없다는 것을 기억하라.

어휘 **continually** 계속해서 **either A or B** A 아니면 B 둘 중 하나 **whether A or B** A이든 아니면 B이든 **limit** 한도, 한계; 제한하다 **take a break** 휴식을 취하다 **in between** 틈틈이, 중간에 **colleague** 동료 **willingly** 기꺼이 **request** 요청(하다) **handle** 처리하다, 다루다

36 글의 순서 ①

소재 속임수를 탐지하는 데 능하다는 믿음의 함정

해설 주어진 글의 많은 사람들이 자신은 속임수를 잘 탐지한다며 내놓는 개인적인 일화적 증거가 (A) 첫 부분의 '그런 입증되지 않은 증거(such unproved evidence)'와 연결된다. (A)의 후반부에서는 거짓말에 대한 판단 실수를 범하게 되면 이를 어떻게 인식할 수 있는지에 대한 의문을 제시하고, 이에 대한 답변(거짓말을 탐지하고 파악할 방도는 없다)이 제시된 (C)가 (A) 다음에 위치해야 한다. (C) 후반부에서는 거짓말 탐지 정확성은 우연보다 조금 더 나은 것에 불과하다고 진술하며, '구체적으로(Specifically)'라고 연결되는 (B)에서는 그 확률을 55퍼센트라는 구체적인 수치로 제시하고 있으므로 (A)가 마지막에 와야 한다. 따라서 정답은 ① '(A)-(C)-(B)'이다.

해석 많은 사람들은 자신들이 속임수를 탐지하는 데 매우 능하다고 믿는다. 그들은 자신들 주변의 다른 사람들은 그렇게 예민하지 않을 때 자신들이 거짓말을 정확히 탐지해냈던 사례들을 끌어대기까지 할지도 모른다.

(A) 주제문 그런 입증되지 않은 증거가 갖는 문제는 언제 거짓말을 믿는 우를 범하는지 알기가 어렵다는 것이다. 누군가가 거짓말을 하고 있다는 독립적인 증거가 이후에 있지 않다면, 여러분은 자신의 부정확한 판단을 어떻게 발견할 것인가?

(C) 당연히, 성공적인 거짓말은 탐지되지 않고 그것에 대해 계속 파악할 방법은 없다. 사실, 많은 실험 전체에서 평균적인 탐지 정확성은 우연보다 단지 조금 더 나을 뿐이다.

(B) 구체적으로 말해, 50퍼센트라는 우연의 정확성의 기준점을 가지고 볼 때 평균적인 탐지 정확성은 대략 55퍼센트이다. 게다가 판단에 있어서의 확신과 정확성 사이에는 관계가 거의 없거나 전무하다.

구문 [15행~16행] By definition, successful lies(S) go(V) undetected(C) / and **there is no way of keeping** track of them.

undetected는 주어의 상태를 설명하는 보어로, 거짓말이 '탐지되지 않는' 상태이므로 과거분사를 사용했다. 「there is no way of v-ing」는 'v할 방법이 없다'의 뜻이다. them은 (successful) lies를 지칭한다.

어휘 **detect** 탐지하다, 찾다 *cf.* **detection** 탐지 **deception** 속임수 **cite** (이유 · 예를) 끌어대다, 인용하다 **spot** 찾다 **sensitive** 예민한, 민감한 **unproved** 증명되지 않은 **evidence** 증거 **independent** 독립적인 **incorrect** 부정확한 **judgment** 판단 **specifically** 구체적으로 말하면 **baseline** 기준치 **chance** 우연; 기회 **accuracy** 정확성 **average** 평균의 **approximately** 대략 **confidence** 확신, 자신(감) **by definition** 당연히, 분명히 **keep track of** ~에 대해 계속 파악하고[알고] 있다 **scores of** 많은; 수십의 **slightly** 약간

37 글의 순서 ⑤

소재 우주의 화학적 구성 변화

해설 우주의 화학적 구성이 변화했다는 주어진 글 다음에는, 우주가 처음에는 수소와 헬륨 100퍼센트였는데 이 비율이 98퍼센트로 감소되었다는 (C)가 나온다. 이러한 변화가 어떻게 생겼는지에 대한 (C)의 마지막 문장의 질문을 받아서 (B)에서 별의 중심부에서 생성됐던 무거운 원소가 별의 폭발과 함께 우주 공간으로 나오게 된다는 답변이 제시된다. (A)의 In this way는 (B)에서 언급된 '별의 폭발로 무거운 원소가 우주 공간으로 나오는 방식'을 지칭하며, 이렇게 해서 우주의 구성이 바뀌고, 별은 핵융합으로 무거운 원소를 생성한다는 내용으로 글이 마무리된다. 따라서 적절한 글의 순서는 ⑤ '(C)-(B)-(A)'이다.

해석 주제문 우주가 팽창과 냉각을 계속하면서 별과 은하가 생성되기 시작했고, 우주의 화학적 구성은 변화했다.

(C) 처음에 우주는 100% 수소와 헬륨이었던 반면, 오늘날 그것은 무게로 봤을 때 98%의 수소와 헬륨, 그리고 2%의 다른 모든 원소들이다. 우주 구성의 그러한 변화는 어떻게 발생했는가?

(B) 별이 죽을 때, 많은 경우 폭발적으로 죽는데, 별의 중심부에서 생성됐던 더 무거운 원소들이 행성 사이의 공간으로 돌아가서 새로운 별에 포함되는 데 쓰일 수 있다.

(A) 이러한 방식으로 우주의 구성은 더 무거운 원소들에 의해 점차 향상된다. 별의 일생 주기 전체에 걸쳐 별은 핵융합에 의해 더 가벼운 원소들이 더 무거운 원소들로 변환되는 많은 핵반응을 겪는다.

어휘 **expand** 팽창[확장]하다 **chemical** 화학적인; 화학 물질 **makeup** 구성 **composition** 구성 (요소); 작곡 **gradually** 점차 **enhance** 향상시키다 **element** (화학) 원소; 요소, 성분 **undergo** 겪다 **be converted into** ~로 변환[전환]되다 **nuclear fusion** 핵융합 **explosively** 폭발적으로 **core** 중심부, 핵심 **interstellar** 행성 간의 **inclusion** 포함 **initially** 처음에 **hydrogen** 수소 **helium** 헬륨

38 문장 넣기 ④

소재 상품의 생산 집단과 수익 집단의 괴리

해설 ④의 앞 문장에서는 자동차는 노동자들이 함께 노동하여 생산한다는 내용이 나온다. But으로 시작되는 주어진 문장은 수익이 노동자들에게 가지 않는다는 내용이다. ④의 다음 문장은 '그것'이 공장 소유자에게 간다고 했는데, '그것'은 주어진 문장에서 언급된 '노동자에게 돌아가지 않는 수익'임을 알 수 있다. 따라서 주어진 문장이 ④에 들어가야 글의 흐름이 자연스럽다.

해석 상품은 식품, 의류, 치약 같이 당신이 구매하는 물품인 반면 서비스는 이발, 의료 검진, 자동차 수리와 같은 행동을 의미한다. 주제문 자본주의에서 상품과 서비스는 사회적으로 생산되지만, 그것들과 그것들이 생성하는 부는 사적으로 소유된다. 예를 들어 당신이 자동차 공장에 방문한다면, 당신은 각각의 노동자가 오직 한 대의 차를 엔진부터 나사까지, 처음부터 만들면서 구성하는 것을 보지는 않을 것이다. 오히려 당신은 노동자 각자가 최종 제품인 차를 만드는 것을 돕기 위해 다른 업무 혹은 일련의 업무들을 수행하며 노동자들이 함께 노동하는 것을 볼 것이다. 그러나 차가 대리점으로 가서 판매될 때, 실현된 수익은 노동자들 간에 분배되도록 공장으로 돌려보내지지 않는다. 그것은 누구든 공장을 소유한 사람에게 간다. 이 경우에는 주주들인데, 회사의 주식을 구매한 사람들 말이다. 최대 주주들이 가장 많은 수익을 실현시킨다.

구문 [9행~12행] For example, **if** you **were to** visit a car factory, // you **wouldn't see** each worker **constructing** only one car, **building** it from scratch, from engine to nuts.
(V: wouldn't see, O: each worker, C: constructing ~)

「If+S´+were to-v, S+would+동사원형 (~한다면 …할 것이다)」의 가정법 과거 문장이다. 「see+O+C(v-ing) (O가 v하고 있는 것을 보다)」 구문이 쓰였다. 목적어와 목적격보어의 관계가 능동이므로 현재분사 constructing과 building이 쓰였다.

어휘 **make one's way to** ~로 나아가다 **dealership** 대리점 **clothing** 의류 **toothpaste** 치약 **check-up** 검진 **capitalism** 자본주의 **wealth** 부, 재산 **privately** 사적으로 **construct** 건설하다, 구성하다 **from scratch** 맨 처음부터 **nut** 너트, 나사 **a series of** 일련의 **shareholder** 주주 **stock** 주식

39 문장 넣기 ④

소재 미국의 공공재 증가의 필요성

해설 주어진 문장의 these라는 지시어를 통해 '사회적 혜택'에 대한 내용이 앞서 언급되었을 것임을 알 수 있다. ④의 앞에는 공공재에 의한 여러 가지 사회적 혜택이 언급되었고, 뒤에는 무료 공공재에 대한 구체적인 예시가 나오고 있으므로 주어진 문장은 ④에 들어가는 것이 가장 적절하다.

해석 주제문 미국에는 대중교통, 공원, 공공 박물관과 도서관 같은 공공재가 상당히 증가해야 한다. 그리고 그것들은 이용자들에게 무료여야 한다. 그러한 공공재는 그것들에 상응하는 사유재, 예를 들어 자가용이나 깔끔하게 정돈된 정원, 미술 소장품, 책과 같은 것들을 누릴 형편이 안 되는 사람들의 삶의 질을 향상시킨다. 이런 식으로, 공공재는 정체되어 있거나 감소하는 임금의 영향을 어느 정도 상쇄한다. 공공재는 일반적으로, 부족한 자원과 환경에 사적인 재화보다 영향을 덜 끼치고, 일자리를 창출하며, 경제에 전반적인 수요를 증가시킨다. 그것들(= 공공재)을 무료로 만드는 것은 이러한 사회적 혜택을 극대화한다. 예를 들어, 고속철도를 포함하여, 확대된 무료 대중교통 시스템은 미국인들이 낭비되는 시간과 기름에 일 년에 850억 달러가 넘는 비용을 들이게 하는 것으로 추정되는 교통 체증을 상당히 감소시킬 것이고, 탄소 배출도 줄일 것이다. 그 혜택은 비용보다 훨씬 더 크다.

어휘 **maximize** 극대화하다(↔ **minimize** 최소화하다) **societal** 사회의 **benefit** 혜택, 이득 **sizable** 상당한 크기의 **public goods** 공공재(↔ **private goods** 사유재) **free of charge** 무료의 **afford** (~을 할 금전적·시간적) 여유가 되다 **equivalent** (~에) 상당하는 것, 등가물; 동등한 **neatly** 깔끔하게; 솜씨 있게 **offset** 상쇄[벌충]하다 **scarce** 부족한, 희귀한 **overall** 전반적인, 전체의 **expanded** 확대된, 확장된 *cf.* **expansion** 확대, 확장 **significantly** 상당히, 크게; 의미 있게 **traffic congestion** 교통 체증(= **traffic jam**) *cf.* **congestion** (인구의) 밀집, 과잉; (교통의) 혼잡 **estimate** 추정[추산]하다; 추정(치); 견적서 **emission** (빛·열·가스 등의) 배출 **outweigh** ~보다 더 크다[대단하다]

40 요약문 완성 ④

소재 상황에 따른 결과의 해석 차이

해설 실험 참가자들은 '평소와 같은 시간/장소를 택했다면 좋았을 것이다'라는 가정을 했고, 또한 평소와 다른 경로를 택해서 사고를 당한 사람은 평소와 같은 경로에서 사고를 당한 사람보다 부정적인 감정이 더 심했을 거라고 생각했다. 즉, '일상적인(routine)' 상황보다 '예외적인(exceptional)' 상황에서 발생한 부정적인 결과를 더욱 좋지 못한 것으로 받아들인다는 내용으로 요약할 수 있으므로 정답은 ④이다.

해석 심리학자 Kahneman과 Tversky는 Jones 씨가 직장에서 집으로 가던 길에 다치게 된 교통사고로 이어진 사건들을 기술하는 시나리오를 만들었다. 한 가지 버전에서 Jones 씨는 보통 때 직장을 나섰지만 물가를 따라 나 있는 경치를 즐기려고 집에 가는 색다른 길을 택했다. 다른 버전에서 그는 몇 가지 잡무를 보려고 직장에서 특별히 일찍 나섰지만 집에 가는 보통의 경로를 택했다. 참가자들은 Jones 씨의 가족이 "~하기만 했다면" 문장을 어떻게 완성할 거라고 생각하는지에 대해 질문을 받았다. 참가자들은 "그가 그 날 더 일찍 나서기만 했다면"이라고 말하는 것보다 "그가 보통 때에 나서기만 했다면" 혹은 "그가 보통 때의 경로를 택하기만 했다면"이라고 말할 가능성이 더 높았다. 다른 시나리오 연구에 따르면 사람들은 또한 집으로 가는 색다른 경로로 가는 동안 사고에 연루된 사람이 집으로 가는 보통의 경로로 가는 동안 비슷한 사고에 연루된 사람보다 기분이 더 안 좋을 거라고 느꼈다.

⬇

사람들은 (부정적인) 동일한 결과가 (B) 일상적인 행동에서 나올 때보다 이러한(= 부정적인) 결과가 (A) 예외적인 행동에서 나올 때, 부정적인 결과에 의해 기분이 더 안 좋아지는 경향이 있다.

구문 [1행~4행] Psychologists Kahneman and Tversky created *a scenario* (describing *the events* (leading to *a car accident*) [in which Mr. Jones was injured on his way home from work]).

describing ~ from work 전체는 a scenario를 수식한다. 그 안에서 leading ~ accident는 the events를 수식하고, in which ~ work는 a car accident를 수식한다.

[8행~10행] Participants were asked / how (they thought) Mr. Jones's family would complete "If only ..." sentences.
(S: Participants, V: were asked, O: how ~ sentences)

how ~ sentences는 능동태 문장(They asked participants how ~ sentences.)에서 asked의 직접목적어였으며, 간접목적어를 주어로 하는 수동태 문장이 되면서 동사 뒤에 목적어로 남았다. how절에서 they thought는 삽입절이며 they는 participants를 지칭한다.

[14행~18행] Another scenario study showed // that people also felt // that *someone* (involved in a car accident / while taking an unusual route home) would be more upset / than *someone* (involved in a similar accident / while taking the normal route home).

( ) 부분은 각각 앞의 someone을 수식하는 과거분사구이다.

어휘 **describe** 묘사하다, 기술하다 **lead to A** A를 초래하다, A로 이어지다 **injure** 다치게 하다 **on one's way home** ~가 집으로 가는 길에 **version** 판형 **regular** 보통의; 정기적인, 규칙적인 **unusual** 색다른, 특이한 **shore** 물가 **chore** 잡일, 허드렛일 **normal** 보통의, 정상적인 **involved in** ~에 연루된[관련된] **result from** ~로부터 발생하다 [선택지 어휘] **routine** 일상적인; 판에 박힌 **self-directed** 자발적인, 스스로 방향을 정하는 **prospective** 장래의; 곧 있을

41~42 장문 41 ⑤ 42 ⑤

소재 불안 증상의 원인

해설 41. 불안 증상의 원인에는 환경, 뇌의 화학적, 구조적 이상, 유전, 유년기의 학습 등 내적 요인과 외적 요인이 모두 포함된다는 내용의 글이다. 따라서 글의 제목으로 가장 적절한 것은 ⑤ '불안: 우리 안에서 촉발되는가, 밖에서 촉발되는가?'이다.

① 언제 불안은 만성이 되는가? ② 불안 장애 치료하고 예방하기
③ 불안 장애의 징후와 증상 ④ 불안: 인식, 평가, 치료

42. (e)의 다음 문장에서 한 의학 연구팀이 만성적 걱정과 관련된 유전자 변이를 발견했다고 했으므로, 그들은 만성적 걱정이 학습되는 것이 아니라 유전적인 것일지도 모른다고 믿을 것이다. 따라서 (e)의 learned를 genetic으로 바꿔 써야 한다.

해석 우리 모두는 결국 서로 다른 시기에 어느 정도 불안을 경험한다. 그것이 두뇌가 우리로 하여금 위험에 맞서거나 달아나도록, 혹은 스트레스를 많이 받는 상황을 처리하도록 준비하게 하는 방식이다. 중요한 사업상의 회의나 기말고사 전에, 혹은 의료 검진의 결과를 기다리고 있을 때 불안을 느끼는 것은 (a) 정상이다. 그러나 때때로 불안은 실제 상황과 비교해서 꽤 (b) 심하거나 과장될 수 있다. 이것은 개인의 삶에 영향을 미치는 강렬한 신체적 감각, 불안한 생각, 걱정과 회피하는 행동으로 이어질 수 있다. 불행히도 많은 사람들은 우울증이나 불안과 같은 정서적 장애를 개인의 약함의 징후로 보는 경향이 있다. 그러나 의학 연구가 밝혀낸 바에 따르면 이러한 평가는 완전히 (c) 잘못된 것이라고 한다. 주제문 불안과 다른 정서적 장애의 정확한 원인들이 아직 완전히 이해되지는 않았지만, (d) 환경적 스트레스 요인이 막대한 역할을 한다는 점은 분명하다. 우리는 극단적인 혹은 오랫동안 지속되는 스트레스가 기분과 행동을 조절하는 뇌의 화학 작용에 변화를 일으킬 수 있다는 것을 안다. 게다가 두뇌의 특정 구조는 불안 장애를 가진 사람들에게 이상이 있음을 보여주는 경향이 있다. 주제문 반면에 몇몇 과학자들은 지금 만성적 걱정이 (e) 학습되는(→ 유전적인) 것일지도 모른다고 믿는다. 예를 들어 작년에 매사추세츠 종합병원의 한 팀이 만성적 불안 및 과도한 생각과 관련된 유전자 변이를 발견했다. 주제문 몇몇 전문가들은 불안 발작, 만성적 불안 및 다른 증상들이 생물학적 질병을 암시한다고 믿는 반면 다양한 학습 이론들은 불안이 유년기에 학습된 행동이라고 주장한다.

구문 [11행~13행] ~, many people tend to **view** emotional disorders such as depression or anxiety **as** a sign of personal weakness;
「view A as B」는 'A를 B로 보다'의 뜻이다.

어휘 **anxiety** 불안 **escape** 달아나다, 탈출하다 **deal with** ~을 다루다 **at times** 때때로 **severe** 심한 **exaggerate** 과장하다 **in relation to** ~와 비교해서; ~에 관하여 **intense** 강렬한 **sensation** 감각, 느낌 **avoidant** 회피성의 **disorder** 장애 **sign** 징후, 표시 **assessment** 평가 **precise** 정확한 **stressor** 스트레스 요인 **tremendous** 거대한 **long-lasting** 오랫동안 지속되는 **mood** 기분 **abnormality** 이상, 변칙 **chronic** 만성적인 **gene variation** 유전자 변이 **associated with** ~와 관련된 **anxiety attack** 불안 발작 **symptom** 증상 **indicate** 가리키다, 암시하다 [선택지 어휘] **trigger** 일으키다, 촉발하다

43~45 장문 43 ④ 44 ④ 45 ②

소재 각자의 의무를 소홀히 하면 다 같이 멸망하게 된다는 배(腹)에 관한 우화

해설 43. (A)는 로마제국에서 일어난 세금 납부 거부 시위를 제지하려고 관리가 파견되어 연설을 했다는 내용으로, 그 연설의 첫 부분이 나오는 (C)가 가장 먼저 이어져야 한다. 연설의 주요 내용은 배에 대한 우화인데, 신체 부위들이 아무것도 하지 않고 받아먹기만 하는 배를 벌주려고 하다가 모두 굶어죽고 말았다는 ④ '(C)-(D)-(B)'의 순서로 이어져야 알맞다.

44. (d)는 손과 발을 칭찬하고 배는 비난한 혀(the Tongue)이다. 나머지는 모두 배(the Belly)를 가리킨다.

45. (B)에서 신체 부위들은 실수를 깨닫고 몸을 정상적으로 되돌리기 위해 필사적으로 노력했다고 했으므로 ②가 글의 내용과 일치하지 않는다.

해석 (A) 옛날 옛적에 로마제국의 어느 지역에서 대규모 시민연합이 세금 납부를 거부하기 시작했다. 그들은 거리에서 시위를 했고 지나가려는 모든 세금 징수원들에게 공격을 가했다. 국가를 운영하는 데 필요한 돈을 징수할 수 없었고, 불안 상태가 확산될 것을 두려워한 원로원은 위기를 막기 위해 Menenius Agrippa라는 이름의 관리를 파견했다. Menenius Agrippa가 마을에 도착했을 때 그는 성난 군중에게 다음과 같이 연설했다.
(C) 로마 시민 여러분! 여러분은 '배(腹) 이야기'를 들어보았습니까? 한때 사람의 ③ 신체 몇몇 부위가 배의 행동 때문에 기분이 상하는 일이 일어났고, 그에 따라 (c) 그(= 배)에게 필수적인 공급물을 제공하지 않기로 결의했습니다. 우선 ④ 혀는 신체 다른 부위들의 (마음속) 깊은 분개를 자극하는, 배에 대항하는 연설을 했습니다. (d) 그(= 혀)는 부지런한 손과 발은 매우 칭찬했으나 '뚱뚱하고 게으르며 쓸모없는 배'는 비난했습니다. 혀는 자신들 노동의 산물이 '아무것도 하지 않고 받아만 먹는' 배에게 돌아가는 것이 얼마나 불공평한지를 주장했습니다.
(D) 이 연설은 우레와 같은 박수를 받았고 곧바로 손은 더 이상 일을 하지 않겠다고, 발은 이제 배를 여기저기 데리고 다니는 일은 끝났다고, 그리고 치아는 이제 다시 (e) 그(= 배)가 소화를 시킬 수 있게 빵을 그렇게 많이 조각조각 씹어주지 않겠다고 선언했습니다. 이렇게 그들이 소리를 지르고 불평을 하는 와중에 ⑤ 배는 그들에게 진정하고 그런 말도 안 되고 무의미한 짓을 중단해줄 것을 간청했습니다.
(B) "여러분 각자는 분명히 이해해야 합니다. 나는 여러분이 나에게 보내는 모든 것을 바로 즉시 당신들이 필요로 하는 것으로 전환하고, ① 우리 모두에게 도움이 되도록 우리 몸 구석구석에 분배합니다."라고 (a) 그(= 배)는 말했습니다. 그러나 배는 그들의 마음을 바꿀 수 없었습니다. 그때부터 신체 각 부위는 배에게 도움을 주는 것을 멈췄고 그로 인해 (b) 그(= 배)는 곧 굶주렸으며 몸은 점점 더 야위어 뼈만 남게 되었습니다. ② 마침내 치아와 혀, 손과 발은 자신들이 엄청난 실수를 저질렀다는 것을 깨닫고는 다시 (몸이) 정상적으로 활동하도록 필사적으로 노력했습니다. 그러나 때는 이미 너무 늦어서 그들 모두는 함께 죽어버리고 말았습니다.

구문 [(A) 5행~7행] (Being) **Unable** to collect *the money* (necessary for running the state), and **fearing** the unrest would spread, / the Senate sent an official ~.
주절의 주어인 the Senate를 의미상 주어로 하는 두 개의 분사구문이 and로 연결되어 있다. 문맥상 동시에 일어난 일을 나타내므로 '~하면서'라고 해석하면 된다.

[(B) 1행~4행] "Each of you," said he, "must surely understand // that *everything* [you send to me] I immediately convert ● to your needs, and distribute ● / throughout our Body / **for the good of** us all."
(S: Each of you / V: must surely understand / O: that절 / O': everything / S': I / V'1: convert / V'2: distribute)
문장 전체의 목적어 역할을 하는 that절 내의 어순은 「O+S+V」이며 원래 목적어 everything의 자리는 ●이다. 목적어 everything you send to me를 강조하려고 앞에 두었다. for the good of는 '~의 이익을 위하여'란 뜻이다.

[(C) 9행~11행] He claimed // how unfair **it** was **that** the products of their labor went to *the Belly* "[who never does a thing to help himself]."
(O: how unfair ~ himself)
claim의 목적어로 how가 이끄는 절이 왔다. 이 절은 「it(가주어) ~ that(진주어)」의 구조로 that 이하를 주어로 해석하도록 한다.

[(D) 2행~6행] ~ the Hands declared that they would work no more, // the Feet (declared) that they were finished carrying the Belly everywhere, // and the Teeth (declared) that they would never again chew ~.
(S1: the Hands / V1: declared / O1: that they would work no more / S2: the Feet / O2: that they were finished carrying the Belly everywhere / S3: the Teeth / O3: that they would never again chew ~)
세 개의 절이 접속사 and로 연결된 형태로, 두 번째와 세 번째 절에서는 반복되는 동사 declared가 생략되어 있는 형태이다.

어휘 (A) **region** 지역, 지방 **empire** 제국 **association** 연합(체); 연관; 협회 **demonstrate** 시위에 참가하다; 입증하다; (행동으로) 보여주다, 설명하다 **attempt to-v** v하려고 시도하다 **pass through** 지나가다, 거쳐 가다 **unrest** (사회적) 불안, 불만 **crisis** 위기 **address** 연설하다; 연설; 주소 *cf.* **make[give, deliver] a speech** 연설을 하다 (B) **surely** 분명히, 확실히 **convert to** ~로 전환하다 **distribute** 분배하다; 배포하다 **throughout** 도처에; ~ 동안 죽 **assistance** 도움, 원조 **desperately** 필사적으로; 절망적으로 **perish** 죽다; 소멸되다 (C) **belly** 《신체》 배(腹), 복부 **offend** 기분을 상하게 하다 **resolve to-v** (공식적으로) v하기로 결의[결정]하다 **refuse A B** A에게 B를 주지 않기로 하다 **supply** 생필품, 보급품 **stir up** 감정을 불러일으키다; (휘저어) 고무시키다 **resentment** 분개, 분노 **highly** 매우 **condemn** 비난하다 **claim** 주장하다 **product** (어떤 과정에 의한) 산물, 결과물; 제품 **labor** 노동 **help oneself** 마음껏 먹다[하다] (D) **applause** 박수 **declare** 선언하다 **digest** (음식을) 소화하다 **amid** ~하는 와중에[중간에] **beg A to-v** A가 v하도록 간청하다 **senseless** 무의미한; 분별없는

쎄듀 초·중등 커리큘럼

예비초 | 초1 | 초2 | 초3 | 초4 | 초5 | 초6

구문	신간 천일문 365 일력 | 초1-3 |	교육부 지정 초등 필수 영어 문장
구문	초등코치 천일문 SENTENCE	1001개 통문장 암기로 완성하는 초등 영어의 기초
문법	초등코치 천일문 GRAMMAR	1001개 예문으로 배우는 초등 영문법
문법	왓츠 Grammar	Start (초등 기초 영문법) / Plus (초등 영문법 마무리)
독해	왓츠 리딩 70 / 80 / 90 / 100 A / B	쉽고 재미있게 완성되는 영어 독해력
어휘	초등코치 천일문 VOCA&STORY	1001개의 초등 필수 어휘와 짧은 스토리
어휘	패턴으로 말하는 초등 필수 영단어 1 / 2	문장 패턴으로 완성하는 초등 필수 영단어
ELT	Oh! My PHONICS 1 / 2 / 3 / 4	유·초등학생을 위한 첫 영어 파닉스
ELT	Oh! My SPEAKING 1 / 2 / 3 / 4 / 5 / 6	핵심 문장 패턴으로 더욱 쉬운 영어 말하기
ELT	Oh! My GRAMMAR 1 / 2 / 3	쓰기로 완성하는 첫 초등 영문법

예비중 | 중1 | 중2 | 중3

구문	천일문 STARTER 1 / 2	중등 필수 구문 & 문법 총정리
문법	천일문 GRAMMAR LEVEL 1 / 2 / 3	예문 중심 문법 기본서
문법	GRAMMAR Q Starter 1, 2 / Intermediate 1, 2 / Advanced 1, 2	학기별 문법 기본서
문법	잘 풀리는 영문법 1 / 2 / 3	문제 중심 문법 적용서
문법	GRAMMAR PIC 1 / 2 / 3 / 4	이해가 쉬운 도식화된 문법서
문법	1센치 영문법	1권으로 핵심 문법 정리
문법+어법	첫단추 BASIC 문법·어법편 1 / 2	문법·어법의 기초
문법+쓰기	EGU 영단어&품사 / 문장 형식 / 동사 써먹기 / 문법 써먹기 / 구문 써먹기	서술형 기초 세우기와 문법 다지기
문법+쓰기	올씀 1 기본 문장 PATTERN	내신 서술형 기본 문장 학습
쓰기	거침없이 Writing LEVEL 1 / 2 / 3	중등 교과서 내신 기출 서술형
쓰기	중학 영어 쓰작 1 / 2 / 3	중등 교과서 패턴 드릴 서술형
어휘	신간 천일문 VOCA 중등 스타트/필수/마스터	2800개 중등 3개년 필수 어휘
어휘	어휘끝 중학 필수편	중학 필수어휘 1000개
어휘	어휘끝 중학 마스터편	고난도 중학어휘 +고등기초 어휘 1000개
독해	신간 ReadingGraphy LEVEL 1 / 2 / 3 / 4	중등 필수 구문까지 잡는 흥미로운 소재 독해
독해	Reading Relay Starter 1, 2 / Challenger 1, 2 / Master 1, 2	타교과 연계 배경 지식 독해
독해	READING Q Starter 1, 2 / Intermediate 1, 2 / Advanced 1, 2	예측/추론/요약 사고력 독해
독해전략	리딩 플랫폼 1 / 2 / 3	논픽션 지문 독해
독해유형	Reading 16 LEVEL 1 / 2 / 3	수능 유형 맛보기 + 내신 대비
독해유형	첫단추 BASIC 독해편 1 / 2	수능 유형 독해 입문
듣기	Listening Q 유형편 / 1 / 2 / 3	유형별 듣기 전략 및 실전 대비
듣기	쎄듀 빠르게 중학영어듣기 모의고사 1 / 2 / 3	교육청 듣기평가 대비